THE EMC
Write-In
READER

Reading Strategies and Test Practice

BIRCH LEVEL

EMCParadigm Publishing Company

Staff Credits

Editorial

Laurie Skiba
Managing Editor

Brenda Owens
Editor

Becky Palmer
Reading Specialist

Nichola Torbett
Associate Editor

Jennifer Joline Anderson
Associate Editor

Diana Moen
Associate Editor

Mary Curfman
Editorial Consultant

Paul Spencer
Art and Photo Researcher

Design and Production

Shelley Clubb
Production Manager

Matthias Frasch
*Cover Designer and
Production Specialist*

Jennifer Wreisner
Text Designer

Erica Tava
Production Specialist

Lisa Beller
Production Specialist

Sharon O'Donnell
Proofreader

ISBN 0-8219-2914-3
© 2004 EMC Corporation

Published by EMC/Paradigm Publishing
875 Montreal Way
St. Paul, Minnesota 55102
www.emcp.com
E-mail: educate@emcp.com

Printed in the United States of America
10 9 8 7 6 5 4 3 2 1   XXX   10 09 08 07 06 05 04

Consultants and Contributors

Maria Callis
Reading Specialist/Department Chair
Trafalgar Middle School
Cape Coral, Florida

Shari Carlson
English/Reading Instructor
Fridley Middle School
Fridley, Minnesota

T. Carolyn Coleman
Language Arts/Reading Instructor
Gwinnett County Schools
Lawrenceville, Georgia

Dr. Edmund J. Farrell
Emeritus Professor of English Education
University of Texas at Austin
Austin, Texas

Sharon Kremer
Language Arts Instructor
Denton High School
Denton, Texas

Lisa Larnerd
English Department Chairperson
Basic High School
Henderson, Nevada

Beth Lee
Language Arts Instructor
Heritage Middle School
Longmont, Colorado

Cecilia Lewis
Language Arts Instructor
Mariner High School
Cape Coral, Florida

John Oricchio
Educational Consultant
Port Washington, New York

John Owens
Literacy Specialist
Heritage Middle School
Longmont, Colorado

Mary Spychalla
English/Reading Instructor
Valley Middle School
Apple Valley, Minnesota

Contents

UNIT 8 READING INFORMATIONAL AND VISUAL MEDIA

UNIT 9 DEVELOPING VOCABULARY SKILLS

UNIT 10 TEST-TAKING STRATEGIES

Overview of Skills

VOCABULARY SKILLS

Overview of Features

The EMC Write-In Reader helps you to interact with reading selections as never before! This portable anthology guides you in using reading strategies—reading tools that help you get more meaning from what you read. Questions and tips in the margins prompt you to record your thoughts and notes as you read. Using selections from the *Literature and the Language Arts* textbook, *The EMC Write-In Reader* gives you an opportunity to complete rich reading tasks, expand your reading skills, and increase your test-taking abilities.

The EMC Write-In Reader shows you how to use reading strategies before, during, and after reading and includes activities that develop your comprehension, fluency, and vocabulary skills.

The EMC Write-In Reader helps you learn how reading strategies work, how to combine them, and how to apply them to any reading task. These eight active reading strategies help you interact with a text to create meaning.

1. Read with a Purpose
2. Connect to Prior Knowledge
3. Write Things Down
4. Make Predictions
5. Visualize
6. Use Text Organization
7. Tackle Difficult Vocabulary
8. Monitor Your Reading Progress

Detailed instruction on one reading strategy is carried through the before, during, and after stages of the reading process for each selection.

The EMC Write-In Reader offers a unique text organization, including

- an **introduction to reading** unit that defines and explains the reading process, the eight reading strategies, and fix-up strategies to use when you have trouble
- a unit focusing on **essential reading skills** and tasks evaluated on standardized tests
- a unit for each **genre,** or kind of text, with an introduction on how to apply reading strategies to that genre
- a unit on **vocabulary development** to help you unlock word meaning
- a unit on **standardized test practice** to help you prepare for state and national tests
- an appendix of **fluency activities** to build word recognition skills, silent reading fluency, and oral reading fluency
- an appendix containing a multitude of **reading strategy graphic organizers**

Become a successful, active reader with *The EMC Write-In Reader!*

BEFORE READING

1 **Reader's Resource** provides background information to help you **set a purpose** for reading.

2 The **Active Reading Strategy** gives you step-by-step instruction on how to use the reading strategy **before reading**.

3 A **Graphic Organizer** for each selection helps you to **visualize** and **understand text organization** as you read.

CONNECT

1 **Reader's resource**

"Catch the Moon" appears in Judith Ortiz Cofer's collection of short stories, *An Island Like You* (1996). The Puerto Rican boys and girls depicted in these stories are all struggling in different ways to determine their futures as they advance from adolescence to adulthood. They live in the *barrio*, a Spanish-speaking neighborhood. Luis Cintrón, the main character of "Catch the Moon," searches for a way to find meaning in his life. After six months in juvenile hall, he is working off the rest of his time in his father's junkyard.

4 **Word watch**

PREVIEW VOCABULARY

decapitate	makeshift
dismantle	mint
ebony	mock
escort	relic
harass	vintage
mahogany	vulgar

5 **Reader's journal**

What would you be willing to do to fit in with a gang or group?

_____
_____
_____
_____
_____

"CATCH THE MOON"
by Judith Ortiz Cofer

2 *Active* READING STRATEGY

MAKE PREDICTIONS

Before Reading ▶ PREVIEW THE SELECTION

❑ Read the Reader's Resource and discuss the information in class.
❑ Skim the selection, looking at the pictures and getting familiar with the Words for Everyday Use.
❑ In the first column of the Predictions Chart below, jot down the clues about the story you found from previewing.
❑ Work with the class to form predictions about the content of the story based on these clues.

Graphic Organizer **3**

Clues	Predictions	What Really Happens

---

4 **WordWatch** gives you the opportunity to **preview** the vocabulary Words for Everyday Use for the selection.

5 **Reader's Journal** helps you to **connect** with what you know and to your own life.

Catch the Moon

Judith Ortiz Cofer

L uis Cintrón sits on top of a six-foot pile of hubcaps and
watches his father walk away into the steel jungle of his
car junkyard. Released into his old man's custody after six
months in juvenile hall—for breaking and entering—and he
didn't even take anything. He did it on a dare. But the old
lady with the million cats was a light sleeper, and good with
her aluminum cane. He has a scar on his head to prove it.

Now Luis is wondering whether he should have stayed in
and done his full time. Jorge Cintrón of Jorge Cintrón &
10 Son, Auto Parts and Salvage, has decided that Luis should
wash and polish every hubcap in the yard. The hill he is sitting on is only the latest couple of hundred wheel covers
that have come in. Luis grunts and stands up on top of his
silver mountain. He yells at no one, "Someday, son, all this
will be yours," and sweeps his arms like the Pope blessing a
crowd over the piles of car sandwiches and mounds of
metal parts that cover this acre of land outside the city. He
is the "Son" of Jorge Cintrón & Son, and so far his father
has had more than one reason to wish it was plain Jorge
20 Cintrón on the sign.

Luis has been getting in trouble since he started high school
two years ago, mainly because of the "social group" he

During Reading ▶ 6

MAKE PREDICTIONS
☐ Follow along in the text as
you or your teacher read
aloud the first page.
☐ Next, work with the class
to identify clues from this
passage.
☐ Record the clues in the
first column of your chart.
From these clues, make a
prediction about
characters and events to
come. Record your
prediction in your chart.
☐ Read the remainder of the
story on your own. Stop at
the end of each page to
record clues, make
predictions, and adjust
and check the accuracy of
previous predictions.

7

READ ALOUD

Read the following
Spanish words from the
selection aloud, using the
pronunciations given
below.

Luis	lü-ēs'
Jorge	hôr'-hā
Cintrón	sēn-trōn'
Tiburones	tē-bü-rō'-nās'
tiburón	tē-bü-rōn
barrio	bä'-rē-ō
cementerio	sā-mən-tā'-rē-ō
señorita	sān-yə-rē'-tä
sí	sē
hijo	ē'-hō

**6 During
Reading** instruc-
tion in the margin
tells you how to
apply the reading
strategy as you
read.

7 Read Aloud
activities in the
margins help you
to **build fluency**
by giving you the
chance to speak
and listen to ideas
you are trying to
understand.

DURING READING

8 Mark the Text activities ask you to **underline or highlight** information in the text to help you read actively and organize your thoughts (see example).

9 Literary Tools explain **literary techniques and concepts** and help you recognize these elements as you read.

10 Note the Facts questions give you the space to **make notes** about factual information as you read (see example).

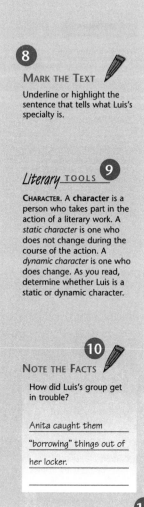

8

MARK THE TEXT

Underline or highlight the sentence that tells what Luis's specialty is.

Literary TOOLS **9**

CHARACTER. A **character** is a person who takes part in the action of a literary work. A *static character* is one who does not change during the course of the action. A *dynamic character* is one who does change. As you read, determine whether Luis is a static or dynamic character.

NOTE THE FACTS **10**

How did Luis's group get in trouble?

Anita caught them "borrowing" things out of her locker.

organized—a bunch of guys who were into harassing the local authorities. Their thing was taking something to the limit on a dare or, better still, doing something dangerous, like breaking into a house, not to steal, just to prove that they could do it. That was Luis's specialty, coming up with very complicated plans, like military strategies, and assigning the "jobs" to guys who wanted to join the Tiburones.

30 *Tiburón* means "shark," and Luis had gotten the name from watching an old movie about a Puerto Rican gang called the Sharks[1] with his father. Luis thought it was one of the dumbest films he had ever seen. Everybody sang their lines, and the guys all pointed their toes and leaped in the air when they were supposed to be slaughtering each other. But he liked their name, the Sharks, so he made it Spanish and had it air-painted on his black T-shirt with a killer shark under it, jaws opened wide and dripping with blood. It didn't take long for the other guys in the barrio[2]
40 to ask about it.

Man, had they had a good time. The girls were interested too. Luis outsmarted everybody by calling his organization a social club and registering it at Central High. That meant they were legal, even let out of last-period class on Fridays for their "club" meetings. It was just this year, after a couple of botched jobs, that the teachers had started getting suspicious. The first one to go wrong was when he sent Kenny Matoa to *borrow* some "souvenirs" out of Anita Robles's locker. He got caught. It seems that Matoa had
50 been reading Anita's diary and didn't hear her coming down the hall. Anita was supposed to be in the gym at that time but had copped out with the usual female excuse of cramps. You could hear her screams all the way to Market Street.

She told the principal all she knew about the Tiburones, and Luis had to talk fast to convince old Mr. Williams that the club did put on cultural activities such as the Save the Animals talent show. What Mr. Williams didn't know was

---

11 1. **Sharks**. Fictional Puerto Rican gang from the movie *West Side Story*
2. **barrio**. Spanish-speaking neighborhood in the United States

words for everyday use   ha • rass (ha ras') vt., annoy persistently. *The boy harassed the girl by pulling her ponytail repeatedly.* **12**

11 Footnotes explain references, unusual usage, and uncommon terms or words.

12 Words for Everyday Use includes the definition and pronunciation for new vocabulary. A sample sentence demonstrates the use of the word in context.

that the animal that was being "saved" with the ticket sales was Luis's pet boa, which needed quite a few live mice to stay
60 healthy and happy. They kept E.S. (which stood for "Endangered Species") in Luis's room, but she belonged to the club and it was the members' responsibility to raise the money to feed their mascot. So last year they had sponsored their first annual Save the Animals talent show, and it had been a great success. The Tiburones had come dressed as Latino Elvises and did a grand finale to "All Shook Up" that made the audience go wild. Mr. Williams had smiled when Luis talked, maybe remembering how the math teacher, Mrs. Laguna, had dragged him out in the aisle to rock-and-roll
70 with her. Luis had gotten out of that one, but barely.

His father was a problem too. He objected to the T-shirt logo, calling it disgusting and <u>vulgar</u>. Mr. Cintrón prided himself on his own neat, elegant style of dressing after work, and on his manners and large vocabulary, which he picked up by taking correspondence courses in just about everything. Luis thought that it was just his way of staying busy since Luis's mother had died, almost three years ago, of cancer. He had never gotten over it.

All this was going through Luis's head as he slid down the
80 hill of hubcaps. The tub full of soapy water, the can of polish, and the bag of rags had been neatly placed in front of a <u>makeshift</u> table made from two car seats and a piece of plywood. Luis heard a car drive up and someone honk their horn. His father emerged from inside a new red Mustang that had been totaled. He usually <u>dismantled</u> every small feature by hand before sending the vehicle into the *cementerio*,[3] as he called the lot. Luis watched as the most beautiful girl he had ever seen climbed out of a <u>vintage</u> white Volkswagen Bug. She stood in the sunlight in her white sundress waiting for
90 his father, while Luis stared. She was like a smooth wood

---

3. *cementerio.* Cemetery (Spanish)

words for everyday use	**vul • gar** (vəl'gər) *adj.*, lacking in cultivation, perception, or taste. *Emily thought the fake flowers on Jessica's dress were <u>vulgar</u>, or lacking in taste.*
	make • shift (māk' shift) *adj.*, crude and temporary substitute. *A <u>makeshift</u> clinic was set up by the accident site with a table made of plywood and sawhorses.*
	dis • man • tle (dis man' təl) *vt.*, take apart. *Jed <u>dismantled</u> the bookcase and placed the disassembled boards in the moving truck.*
	vin • tage (vin' tij) *adj.*, dating from the past. *The <u>vintage</u> ice cream maker was made in the 1930s.*

13

FIX-UP IDEA

Read in Shorter Chunks
If you have difficulty applying the reading strategy, read in shorter chunks. You might stop and record clues as you come to them. You might also stop as soon as you have enough information to adjust or check a previous prediction. Continue applying the fix-up idea as needed.

THINK AND REFLECT **14**

Does Luis's explanation for why his father takes correspondence courses seem believable? Why, or why not? **(Evaluate)**

_____

_____

_____

15 *Use* THE STRATEGY

MAKE PREDICTIONS. Make sure to stop at the end of each page to record clues, make predictions, and adjust and check the accuracy of previous predictions.

13 Fix-Up Ideas help you get back on track if you encounter problems or lose focus.

14 Think and Reflect questions deepen your understanding of what you are reading.

15 Use the Strategy reminds you to use the strategy to read actively.

AFTER READING

16 After Reading activities follow up on the reading strategy and help you to summarize, synthesize, and reflect on the material you have read.

17 Reading Skills and Test Practice develops essential reading skills assessed on standardized tests.

Reflect ON YOUR READING

After Reading ▶ IDENTIFY THE SEQUENCE OF EVENTS

After you finish reading, review the predictions in your chart and verify or adjust them as necessary now that you have all of the information. Using your chart as a guide, make a flow chart to show the sequence of events. When you finish your chart, share it with a partner.

17 Reading Skills and Test Practice

SEQUENCE OF EVENTS
Discuss with your partner how best to answer the following questions about sequence of events.

1. Read the following list of events.

   Luis is working for his father.
   Luis meets Naomi.
   Luis borrows his father's car.

   Which of the following events comes next in the sequence?

   a. Luis's mother dies.
   b. Luis is sent to juvenile hall.
   c. Luis gets caught breaking and entering.
   d. Luis drives to Naomi's house.

What is the correct answer to the question above? How were you able to eliminate the other answers? How did your use of the reading strategy help you answer the question?

_____
_____
_____

2. Which of the events comes last in the story?
   a. Luis's mother dies.
   b. Luis realizes he misses his mother.
   c. Luis finds the hubcap for Naomi.
   d. Luis visits his mother's grave in the middle of the night.

What is the correct answer to the question above? How were you able to eliminate the other answers? How did your use of the reading strategy help you answer the question?

_____
_____

UNIT 3 / READING FICTION **131**

Investigate, Inquire, and Imagine

RECALL: GATHER FACTS
1a. Why does Luis spend six months in juvenile hall?

INTERPRET: FIND MEANING
1b. What is the underlying reason for Luis's disruptive behavior? Is he a typical gang member? Explain.

ANALYZE: TAKE THINGS APART
4a. What behaviors does Luis exhibit to indicate he is a good son?

SYNTHESIZE: BRING THINGS TOGETHER
4b. Why does Luis want to create a new relationship with his father?

EVALUATE: MAKE JUDGMENTS
5a. Is Luis justified in putting down his father because he owns a junkyard?

EXTEND: CONNECT IDEAS
5b. Luis thinks that the hubcap he gives Naomi is "the first good thing he had given anyone in a long time." This act represents a turning point in Luis's life. Make predictions about how his life will be different six months later.

WordWorkshop

IDENTIFYING IDIOMS. An **idiom** is an expression that cannot be understood from the meaning of its separate words, but must be learned as a whole. For example, the expression "give way," meaning "retreat," is an idiom. Determine which of the following expressions from the selection are idioms by trying to substitute new words for the words in the expression. Write an *I* in the blank next to each expression you believe to be an idiom. Write *E* next to expressions that are not idioms. Then write, in your own words, the meaning of each of the idioms and expressions.

_____ 1. old man (as in *his old man's custody*)

_____

_____ 2. breaking and entering

_____

_____ 3. copped out

_____

_____ 4. walk down memory lane

_____

_____ 5. house arrest

_____

18 Investigate, Inquire, and Imagine questions further your under-standing of the reading, from basic recall and interpret questions to those that ask you to analyze, synthesize, evaluate, and extend your ideas. Some questions also ask you to look at a specific point of view or a different perspective.

19 WordWorkshop activities apply vocabulary development concepts to the words from the selection.

How to use this book

20 Literary Tools follows up on the literary techniques and concepts introduced during reading and asks you to apply your understanding.

21 Read-Write Connection gives you the opportunity to write about your responses to the selection.

22 Beyond the Reading activities extend the ideas, topics, and themes from the selection.

Literary Tools 20

CHARACTER. A **character** is a person who takes part in the action of a literary work. A *static character* is one who does not change during the course of the action. A *dynamic character* is one who does change. Is Luis a static or dynamic character? Explain your answer using evidence from the selection.

_____

_____

_____

_____

Read-Write Connection 21

How do you think Luis's life will change now that he has accepted his mother's death?

_____

_____

_____

_____

_____

_____

_____

Beyond the Reading 22

COMPARE AND CONTRAST. If you like this story, you might enjoy reading Judith Ortiz Cofer's collection of short stories, *An Island Like You*. Choose your two favorite stories and write a compare-contrast essay about them.

GO ONLINE. Visit the EMC Internet Resource Center at **emcp.com** to find links and additional activities for this selection.

Unit ONE

Introduction *to* READING

PURPOSES OF READING

As a reader, you read for different purposes. You might **read for experience**—for insights into ideas, other people, and the world around you. You can also **read to learn**. This is the kind of reading done most often in school. When you read to learn, you may read textbooks, newspapers and newsmagazines, and visual "texts" such as art and photographs. The purpose of this type of reading is to gain knowledge. Third, you can **read for information**. When you read in this way, you are looking for specific data in sources such as reference materials, tables, databases, and diagrams.

Reading for Experience

READING LITERATURE

The most important reason to read literature is to educate your imagination. Reading literary works, which include fiction, nonfiction, poetry, and drama, will train you to think and feel in new ways. In the process of reading literary works and thinking about your own and others' responses to them, you will exercise your imagination and grow in ways that might otherwise have been impossible.

Reading to Learn

READING TEXTBOOKS AND NONFICTION

When you are reading to learn, you have two main goals: to expand your knowledge on a particular topic and to remember the information later. When you read to learn, you will often work with textbooks; reference books; periodicals such as newspapers, journals, and newsmagazines; and related art and photographs.

Textbooks provide a broad overview of a course of study in an objective, factual way. Other types of nonfiction works provide

NOTE THE FACTS

What are three purposes for reading?

_____

_____

_____

information about people, places, things, events, and ideas. Types of nonfiction include histories, biographies, autobiographies, and memoirs. Periodicals such as newspapers, journals, and newsmagazines contain an enormous amount of information about current events around the world. While few people have time to read everything that appears in news periodicals, it is important to stay aware of what is going on in the world around you.

Reading for Information

READING INTERNET, REFERENCE, AND VISUAL MATERIALS

When you are reading for information, you are looking for information that answers a specific, immediate question; that helps you learn how to do something; or that will help you make a decision or draw a conclusion about something. One of the most important things for you to learn in school is how to find, process, and think about the vast amount of information available to you in online and printed reference works, graphic aids, and other visual materials.

THE READING PROCESS

The reading process begins before you actually start to read. Before reading, you are developing your own purpose and expectations for what you are about to read. These are related to what you already know and what you have experienced. During reading, you use your natural habits and responses to help you understand what you are reading. After reading, you think about and reflect on what you have read. All readers use a reading process, even if they don't think about it. By becoming aware of this process, you can become a more effective reader. The reading process can be broken down into three stages: before reading, during reading, and after reading.

Before Reading

Have a plan for reading actively. Before you begin to read, establish a plan for reading actively by setting a purpose, previewing the material, and connecting with what you already know.

- ❑ **Set a purpose** for reading. Know why you are reading and what information you seek. Are you reading for experience or enjoyment, reading to learn, or reading for specific information?
- ❑ **Preview** the organization of the material. Glance at any visuals and think about how they add to the meaning of the text. Skim headings and introductory paragraphs.
- ❑ **Connect** with what you know. Thinking about how what you are reading connects to your own life and to prior experience.

Before Reading

ASK YOURSELF

- What's my purpose for reading this?
- What is this going to be about?
- How is this information organized?
- What do I already know about the topic?
- How can I apply this information to my life?

During Reading

Use reading strategies to read actively. **Reading strategies** are actions you can take on paper, in your head, or aloud that help you understand what you are reading. During reading, you will use reading strategies to read actively. Keep in mind that you will often use a combination of these strategies to read a single text.

❏ **Read aloud** to build reading fluency and give oral emphasis to ideas you are trying to understand. Hearing words aloud helps you untangle difficult ideas. Listen to your teacher read passages aloud or read aloud by yourself or with a partner.

❏ **Write things down** to note your responses to what you are reading. Methods such as highlighting and marking a text, taking or making notes, and creating graphic organizers help you read actively and organize your thoughts. Underline or copy to your notebook the main points. Note unusual or interesting ideas or things you don't understand. Jot down words you need to define. Write your reactions to what you read.

❏ **Think and reflect** by asking questions to further your understanding of what you are reading. Asking questions helps you to pinpoint parts of the text that are confusing. You can ask questions in your head, or you may write them down.

Check your reading and use fix-up ideas. Monitor your reading comprehension by paying attention to how well you understand what you are reading. If you find yourself just reading the words but not actually understanding or getting the meaning of what you are reading, try a **fix-up idea** such as rereading, reading in shorter chunks, changing your reading rate, or trying a new reading strategy to get back on track. A fix-up idea will be presented with each reading strategy accompanying the selections in this text. For more information on fix-up ideas, see pages 14–15.

After Reading

Reflect on your reading. After you finish reading, summarize, synthesize, and reflect on the material you have read.

■ **Summarize** what you have read to help identify, understand, and remember the main and sub-points in the text.

■ **Synthesize** the different ideas presented in the material by pulling them together to make sense out of what you have read and to draw conclusions. Reread any sections you don't remember clearly. Answer any questions you had.

■ **Extend** your reading by examining how your knowledge has grown and identifying the questions you still have about the material.

ASK YOURSELF

■ What is the best way to accomplish my purpose for reading?
■ What do I want or need to find out while I'm reading?
■ What is the essential information presented here?
■ What is the importance of what I am reading?

CHECK YOUR READING

■ Do I understand what I just read?
■ What can I do to make the meaning more clear?

After Reading

ASK YOURSELF

■ What did I learn from what I have read?
■ What is still confusing?
■ What do I need to remember from my reading?
■ What effect did this text have on me?
■ What else do I want to know about this topic?

USING ACTIVE READING STRATEGIES

Reading actively means thinking about what you are reading as you read it. A reading strategy, or plan, helps you read actively and get more from your reading. As a reader, you may choose how to unlock the meaning of each text you read. This book will introduce you to eight of the many strategies that develop active reading. The following strategies can be applied at each stage of the reading process: before, during, and after reading.

Active Reading Strategies

1. Read with a Purpose
2. Connect to Prior Knowledge
3. Write Things Down
4. Make Predictions
5. Visualize
6. Use Text Organization
7. Tackle Difficult Vocabulary
8. Monitor Your Reading Progress

As you become experienced with each of the reading strategies, you will be able to use two or three strategies at a time, instead of just one. In doing this, you will become a thoughtful, active, and successful reader—not only in your English language arts classes but also in other content areas, during testing situations, and beyond the classroom. You will learn which strategies work best for you and use these strategies in every reading task you encounter.

1 Read with a Purpose

Before you begin reading, think about your reason for reading the material. You might be reading from a textbook to complete a homework assignment, skimming a magazine for information about one of your hobbies, or reading a novel for your own personal enjoyment. Know why you are reading and what information you seek. Decide on your purpose for reading as clearly as you can. Be aware that the purpose of your reading may change as you read.

Read with a Purpose

Before Reading	Establish a purpose for reading
During Reading	Read with this purpose in mind
After Reading	Reflect on how the purpose affected the reading experience

---

THE READING PROCESS

BEFORE READING

Have a plan for reading
- ❑ Set a purpose
- ❑ Preview
- ❑ Connect

DURING READING

Use reading strategies
- ❑ Read aloud
- ❑ Write things down
- ❑ Think and reflect
- ❑ Check your reading and use fix-up ideas

AFTER READING

Reflect on your reading
- ❑ Summarize
- ❑ Synthesize
- ❑ Extend

After you determine your purpose for reading, you can choose a method of reading that fits that purpose. Scanning, skimming, and close reading are three different ways of reading.

SCANNING. When you **scan**, you look through written material quickly to locate particular information. Scanning is useful when, for example, you want to find an entry in an index or a definition in a textbook chapter. To scan, simply run your eye down the page, looking for a key word. When you find the key word, slow down and read carefully.

SKIMMING. When you **skim,** you glance through material quickly to get a general idea of what it is about. Skimming is an excellent way to get a quick overview of material. It is useful for previewing a chapter in a textbook, for surveying material to see if it contains information that will be useful to you, and for reviewing material for a test or essay. When skimming, look at titles, headings, and words that appear in boldface or colored type. Also read topic sentences of paragraphs, first and last paragraphs of sections, and any summaries or conclusions. In addition, glance at illustrations, photographs, charts, maps, or other graphics.

READING CLOSELY. When you **read closely**, you read slowly and carefully, looking at each sentence and taking the time to absorb its meaning before going on. Close reading is appropriate when you are reading for pleasure or studying a textbook chapter for the first time. If you encounter words that you do not understand, try to figure them out from context or look them up in a dictionary. You may want to record such words in a word study notebook. The act of writing a word will help you to remember it later. When reading for school, take notes using a rough outline form or other note-taking format. Writing the material will help you to remember it.

Setting a purpose gives you something to focus on as you read. For example, you might read the user's manual for your new phone to find out how to program speed-dial numbers. Or, you might read a mystery novel to find out which character committed the crime.

A few of the purposes you might have for reading Gish Jen's personal essay "An Ethnic Trump," Unit 7, page 398, might be to learn something about the author's life, to learn about some challenges faced by multiethnic people, or to learn how children perceive race and ethnicity. You may also read to identify certain elements, such as anecdotes the author uses to illustrate her ideas. From the following background information given in the Reader's Resource for this selection, decide on a purpose for reading "An Ethnic Trump."

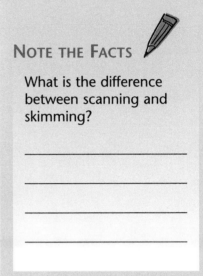

NOTE THE FACTS

What is the difference between scanning and skimming?

_____

_____

_____

_____

MARK THE TEXT

Go back over the pages in this unit and highlight or underline a colored head. Then underline a head in boldface.

Write a purpose you could have for reading "An Ethnic Trump" on the lines below. (Connect)

_____

_____

_____

"An Ethnic Trump" is a personal essay about Gish Jen's experiences as the mother of a biracial child. Jen is Chinese American and her husband is of Irish descent. Yet somehow, people think of their son, Luke, as mainly Chinese. Jen ponders what it means to be multiracial in American society, and she wonders how important it really is to hold on to one's ethnic heritage.

② Connect to Prior Knowledge

Prior knowledge is what you already know or have already experienced before reading something. Before and during reading, think about what you already know about the topic or subject matter. By connecting to your prior knowledge, you will increase your interest in and understanding of what you read. The Reader's Journal activities that come before each selection in this book provide an opportunity to connect to experiences in your own life. Information in the Reader's Resource expands your knowledge of what you are about to read.

Connect to Prior Knowledge	
Before Reading	Think about what you already know about the topic
During Reading	Use what you already know about the topic to make inferences and predictions
After Reading	Describe how the reading experience expanded your knowledge of the topic

Read the Reader's Resource background information for the article "Where Stars Are Born," Unit 8, page 468. Think about what you already know about the game of baseball, the players, and the Dominican Republic.

Based on what you know about baseball, the players, and the Dominican Republic, what do you think you might learn from this article? (Connect)

_____

_____

_____

The Dominican Republic, where Sammy Sosa was born, is a country in the Caribbean that occupies the eastern two-thirds of the island Hispaniola. The country of Haiti takes up the other, western third of the island. The Dominican Republic's main industries are tourism and sugar production. San Pedro de Macorís, the city where Sammy Sosa was born, is famous for its baseball players.

3 Write Things Down

Writing things down helps you pay attention to the words on a page. It is an excellent way to remember important ideas. Methods such as highlighting and marking or coding a text, taking or making notes, and creating graphic organizers help you read actively and organize your thoughts.

Write Things Down	
Before Reading	Have a plan for writing things down: sticky notes, handwritten notes, highlighting, or charts to fill in
During Reading	Use a method for writing things down; ask questions; respond
After Reading	Summarize things written down

Highlighting and marking a text helps you locate key ideas. Mark important ideas, things you would like to come back to, things that are confusing, things you like or dislike, and things with which you agree or disagree. You may highlight the text itself or use sticky notes and bookmarks to keep track of your thoughts.

As you read, find a way to connect to what you are reading by **coding** your reactions. Use the following system to keep track of your reactions in the margins or on sticky notes. Create additional notations for reactions you have that are not listed.

YES	I agree with this
NO	I disagree with this
?	I do not understand this
W	I wonder …
+	I like this part
–	I do not like this part
!	This is like something else I know
√	This seems important
∞	I need to come back and look at this
___	_____
___	_____

If you do not have sticky notes, keep track of your reactions in a chart like the one on the next page.

NOTE THE FACTS

What are some methods of writing things down?

_____

_____

_____

_____

MARK THE TEXT

Circle the things you can mark or highlight as you read.

Reading TIP

Additional ways to take notes:
- outline
- make lists
- create a cluster or a chart
- write down main ideas and your responses
- use a tape recorder

Reactions Chart

Page, Column, or Line Number:	Short note about my reactions
Ex: p. 6, col. 1	The kid in this story reminds me of my friend Brad.

After reading, summarize your reactions and compare them to those of your classmates.

Here is a summary of my reactions: _I liked the story because it reminded me of my friend and I could identify with it._

Here is how my reactions were the same as those of my classmates: _Some of my classmates thought the story was unrealistic._

Here is how my reactions were different from those of my classmates: _The story seemed realistic to me because I know a person like the main character in real life_

Taking or making notes helps you select ideas you consider important. _Paraphrase,_ or write in your own words, what you have read and put it into notes you can read later. Taking or making notes is also a quick way for you to retell what you have just read. Since you cannot write in, mark up, or highlight in a textbook or library book, make a response bookmark like the one on the next page and use it to record your thoughts and reactions. As you read, ask yourself questions, make predictions, react to ideas, identify key points, and/or write down unfamiliar words.

Response Bookmark

Page #	Questions, Predictions, Reactions, Key Points, and Unfamiliar Words
46	What does the sergeant-major mean when he says the third wish was for death?
	I think something bad will happen to Herbert.
	New words for me: condoling, proferred

Graphic organizers help you organize ideas as you read. For instance, if you are reading an essay that compares two authors, you might use a Venn diagram or a cluster chart to collect information about each author. If you are reading about an author's life, you may construct a time line. As you read a selection, create your own method for gathering and organizing information. You might use your own version of a common graphic organizer (see Appendix B) or invent a new way to show what the selection describes. Signal words in the text can help you construct an organizer.

NOTE THE FACTS

How can using a graphic organizer help you as you read?

_____

_____

_____

Signal Words	Common Graphic Organizer
descriptive words: *also, for instance, for example, in the beginning, in addition, the main reason, one point*	Character Chart, page B-8 Sensory Details Chart, page B-9 Summary Chart, page B-12
sequence words: *after, as before, next, now, on, first, second, finally*	Time Line, page B-10 Story Strip, page B-10 Plot Diagram, page B-11
comparison-and-contrast words: *as well as, but, either/or, likewise, on the other hand, similarly*	Pro and Con Chart, page B-6 Cluster Chart, page B-7 Venn Diagram, page B-7
cause-and-effect words: *as a result, because, if/then, since, therefore, this led to*	Note-Taking Chart, page B-6 Cause-and-Effect Chart, page B-12 Drawing Conclusions Log, page B-13

After reading the following paragraph from the Greek myth "Echo and Narcissus," as retold by Walker Brents in Unit 5, page 239, write down the answers to the questions in the margin. Highlight or underline the sentences that provide the answer to the second question.

What is an echo? How does this myth explain the origins of an echo?

_____

_____

_____

_____

_____

There was one nymph, Echo by name, who saw Narcissus chasing deer into nets in the hills. Echo was instantly seized by love and could not overcome it. Secretly, she followed him through the wilderness, waiting for her chance to make herself known to him—but one thing held her back: she could not initiate speech on her own. She could only repeat what was said to her. This was her condition, and it had come about because one day the goddess Hera was questioning the nymphs about her husband Zeus. She asked them where Zeus was, suspecting that the unfaithful god had been chasing the lovely nymphs and dwelling among them. Indeed he had, and while he was making his escape Echo distracted Hera with a flow of entertaining conversation. When Hera learned she had been fooled, she cursed Echo, saying, "From now on your words will not be your own. You will only be able to repeat what is said to you. That way your powers to beguile and distract will be curtailed."

4 Make Predictions

When you **make predictions** during reading, you are making guesses about what the reading is going to be about or what might happen next. Before you read, make predictions based on clues from the page and from what you already know about the topic. Continue to make guesses as you read. The guesses do not have to be correct. When you pause during reading, gather information that helps you make more predictions and check predictions you have already made.

Reading TIP

By learning to make predictions while you read, you become more engaged in what you're reading and you remember more information.

Make Predictions	
Before Reading	Gather information and make preliminary predictions
During Reading	Continue making predictions
After Reading	Analyze and verify predictions

Read the first two paragraphs from Judith Ortiz Cofer's short story "Catch the Moon," Unit 3, page 121. Look for clues that might give you an idea about what will happen in this story.

Luis Cintrón sits on top of a six-foot pile of hubcaps and watches his father walk away into the steel jungle of his car junkyard. Released into his old man's custody after six months in juvenile hall—for breaking and entering—and he didn't even take anything. He did it on a dare. But the old lady with the million cats was a light sleeper, and good with her aluminum cane. He has a scar on his head to prove it.

Now Luis is wondering whether he should have stayed in and done his full time. Jorge Cintrón of Jorge Cintrón & Son, Auto Parts and Salvage, has decided that Luis should wash and polish every hubcap in the yard. The hill he is sitting on is only the latest couple of hundred wheel covers that have come in. Luis grunts and stands up on top of his silver mountain. He yells at no one, "Someday, son, all this will be yours," and sweeps his arms like the Pope blessing a crowd over the piles of car sandwiches and mounds of metal parts that cover this acre of land outside the city. He is the "Son" of Jorge Cintrón & Son, and so far his father has had more than one reason to wish it was plain Jorge Cintrón on the sign.

Prediction Chart

Predictions	Clues	What Really Happens
Luis and his father will have a conflict	Luis wonders if he should have stayed in juvenile hall	

5 Visualize

Reading is more than simply sounding out words. It is an active process that requires you to use your imagination. When you **visualize,** you form a picture or an image in your mind of the action and descriptions in a text. Each reader's images will be different based on his or her prior knowledge and experience. Keep in mind that there are no "right" or "wrong" visualizations.

Visualize

Before Reading	Begin to picture what may happen
During Reading	Create mind pictures as you read
After Reading	Draw or summarize what you saw in your mind pictures

THINK AND REFLECT

Now, based on the clues in the excerpt, make a **prediction** about what might happen later in the story. Record your prediction in the first column of the chart. In the second column, tell what clues led you to make this prediction. After you read the rest of the story, you would be able to record what really happens in the story and compare that to your original predictions. **(Predict)**

Read the following excerpt from Maya Angelou's *I Know Why the Caged Bird Sings*, Unit 7, page 371. Pay attention to how Angelou creates the setting. Keep in mind that *setting* includes time, place, and also the details used to create that time and place. As you read, try to visualize the characters and their actions.

When I was three and Bailey four, we had arrived in the musty little town, wearing tags on our wrists which instructed—"To Whom It May Concern"—that we were Marguerite and Bailey Johnson Jr., from Long Beach, California, en route to Stamps, Arkansas, c/o Mrs. Annie Henderson.

Our parents had decided to put an end to their calamitous marriage, and Father shipped us home to his mother. A porter had been charged with our welfare—he got off the train the next day in Arizona—and our tickets were pinned to my brother's inside coat pocket.

I don't remember much of the trip, but after we reached the segregated southern part of the journey, things must have looked up. Negro passengers, who always traveled with loaded lunch boxes, felt sorry for "the poor little motherless darlings" and plied us with cold fried chicken and potato salad.

6 Use Text Organization

Text organization refers to the different ways a text may be presented or organized. If you are aware of the ways different texts are organized, you will find it easier to understand what you read. For example, familiarity with typical plot elements—the exposition, rising action, climax, falling action, and resolution—is important for understanding the events in a short story or novel. Focusing on signal words and text patterns is important for understanding nonfiction and informational text. For instance, transition words, such as *first*, *second*, *next*, *then*, and *finally*, might indicate that an essay is written in chronological, or time, order.

Use Text Organization	
Before Reading	Preview organizational features (look over headings, pictures, format)
During Reading	Be aware of organizational features as you read
After Reading	Discuss how the text organization affected your reading experience

In this excerpt from *The Learning Highway: Smart Students and the Net* in Unit 8, page 457, by Trevor Owen and Ron Owston, look for signal words that help to identify the organization of the text.

THINK AND REFLECT

How do the headings help organize the information and help you predict what is coming next? What transition words indicate that this text will be organized in chronological order? **(Analyze)**

_____

_____

_____

_____

> **Four Steps to Finding Facts**
>
> Often you'll want to find specific facts, statistics, definitions, and other data. For instance, we might want to know the answer to questions such as:
> - How high is Mount Everest?
> - What is the GNP of France?
> - What countries belong to the British Commonwealth?
> - Who wrote the novel *The Sun Also Rises?*
>
> Here are the steps we suggest you take to find answers to questions such as these.
>
> **Step 1**
>
> Think of the most obvious search words, paying particular attention to key nouns: for example, *height, elevation, Mount Everest* would be good for the first question above. Enter these words into a comprehensive search index, such as Altavista, and connect the keywords with appropriate search operators. For Altavista these might be +*(height or elevation)* + *"Mount Everest."* Then do the search. If you don't find what you want, go to the next step.

7 Tackle Difficult Vocabulary

How do you deal with new or unfamiliar words as you read? Learning how to tackle difficult vocabulary leads to improved reading comprehension. In some cases, you may want to identify and define new vocabulary before reading. Use context clues to guess meanings, find definitions in the dictionary, and decode words by recognizing common word parts to find meanings on your own.

Tackle Difficult Vocabulary	
Before Reading	Have a plan for tackling difficult words
During Reading	Use context, word structure, footnotes, or a dictionary; ask for help
After Reading	Describe how vocabulary affected your reading experience

Reading TIP

You increase your ability to understand what you read in class and on standardized tests if you take the time to learn new words. One of the best ways to learn new words is to **associate an image** with the meaning of a new word. For instance, you might associate the word *affirm* with an image of two people firmly shaking hands. What image might you associate with the word *nomadic?* Draw that image here.

Read the following excerpt from "The Most Dangerous Game" by Richard Connell, Unit 3, page 82. Note any unfamiliar vocabulary you encounter. Record the word or words in your notebook. Then, go back to the word in the text and use context clues, words nearby that provide hints about the meaning, and word parts to unlock the meaning. If necessary, consult a dictionary.

THINK AND REFLECT

Based on the context clues, what might the definition of *palpable* be?

_____

_____

> Off there to the right—somewhere—is a large island," said Whitney. "It's rather a mystery—"
>
> "What island is it?" Rainsford asked.
>
> "The old charts call it 'Ship-Trap Island,' " Whitney replied. "A suggestive name, isn't it? Sailors have a curious dread of the place. I don't know why. Some superstition—"
>
> "Can't see it," remarked Rainsford, trying to peer through the dank tropical night that was palpable as it pressed its thick warm blackness in upon the yacht.

READ ALOUD

Reading fluency is your ability to read something quickly and easily. Increase your reading fluency by rereading a 100–150-word passage aloud several times. Reread the passage until you are able to read through it in less than a minute without making any mistakes. Read the passage to a partner and have your partner track your errors, or read the passage into a tape recorder, play back your recording, and keep track of your own errors. For additional fluency practice, see Appendix A.

8 Monitor Your Reading Progress

All readers occasionally have difficulty as they read. As you read, you should always **monitor**, or pay attention to, your progress, stopping frequently to check how well you are understanding what you are reading. If you encounter problems or lose focus, use a **fix-up idea** to get back on track. Readers who know how to apply fix-up ideas are well on the way to reading independence. They know when they are having a problem and are able to adjust and get back on track.

USING FIX-UP IDEAS

The following **fix-up ideas** can help you "fix up" any confusion or lack of attention you experience as you read. You probably use many of these already.

- **Reread.** If you don't understand a sentence, paragraph, or section the first time through, go back and reread it. Each time you reread a text, you understand and remember more.

- **Read in shorter chunks.** Break a long text into shorter chunks. Read through each "chunk." Then go back and make sure you understand that section before moving on.

- **Read aloud.** If you are having trouble keeping your focus, try reading aloud to yourself. Go somewhere private and read aloud, putting emphasis and expression in your voice. Reading aloud also allows you to untangle difficult text by talking your way through it.

- **Ask questions.** As you read, stop and ask yourself questions about the text. These questions may help you pinpoint things that are confusing you or things that you want to come back to later. You can ask questions in your head, or jot them down in the margins or on a piece of paper.

- **Change your reading rate.** Your reading rate is how fast or slow you read. Good readers adjust their rate to fit the situation. In some cases, when you just need to get the general idea or main points of a reading, or if the reading is simple, you will want to read through it quickly and not get bogged down. Other times, such as when a text is difficult or contains a lot of description, you will need to slow down and read carefully.

- **Create a mnemonic device.** A mnemonic (ni mä′ nik) device is a memory trick. If you need to remember specific information from a text, think of a trick to help you do it. One way is to make up an acronym, or abbreviation, to help you remember a list of items. For example, the acronym *HOMES* can help you remember the names of the five great lakes, Huron, Ontario, Michigan, Erie, and Superior. Another method is to create a short memory aid. If you need to remember that in the eardrum, the anvil comes before the stirrup, remember "the letter *a* comes before the letter *s*."

Reading TIP

As you read, use your classmates as resources to help you uncover the meaning in a selection. Working with a partner or a small group can increase your understanding of what you read.

THINK ALOUD. When you **think aloud**, you communicate your thoughts aloud to your classmates about what you are reading. Thinking aloud helps you share ideas about the text and ways in which to read it.

SHARE FIX-UP IDEAS. When you **share fix-up ideas**, you and your classmates can figure out ways to deal with difficult sections of a text.

Monitor Your Reading Progress

Before Reading	Be aware of fix-up ideas that ease reading problems
During Reading	Use fix-up ideas
After Reading	Evaluate the fix-up ideas used

Choose and Use Reading Strategies

Before reading the excerpt below, review with a partner how to use each of these reading strategies. (see pages 4–15).

1. Read with a Purpose
2. Connect to Prior Knowledge
3. Write Things Down
4. Make Predictions
5. Visualize
6. Use Text Organization
7. Tackle Difficult Vocabulary
8. Monitor Your Reading Progress

Now apply at least two of these reading strategies as you read this excerpt from Stephen Vincent Benét's short story "The Devil and Daniel Webster." Use the margins and mark up the text to show how you are using the reading strategies to read actively.

> It's a story they tell in the border country, where Massachusetts joins Vermont and New Hampshire. Yes, Dan'l Webster's dead—or, at least, they buried him. But every time there's a thunderstorm around Marshfield, they say you can hear his rolling voice in the hollows of the sky. And they say that if you go to his grave and speak loud and clear, "Dan'l Webster —Dan'l Webster!" the ground'll begin to shiver and the trees begin to shake. And after a while you'll hear a deep voice saying, "Neighbor, how stands the Union?" Then you better answer the Union stands as she stood, rock-bottomed and copper-sheathed, one and indivisible, or he's liable to rear right out of the ground. At least, that's what I was told when I was a youngster.

On Your Own

Apply the reading strategies you have learned in this unit to your own reading. Select a passage from your favorite book, magazine, or newspaper, and try one of the following activities.

FLUENTLY SPEAKING. Reread a 100–150-word passage aloud several times. Reread the passage until you are able to read through it in less than a minute without making any mistakes. Read the passage to a partner and have your partner track your errors, or read the passage into a tape recorder, play back your recording, and keep track of your own errors.

PICTURE THIS. As you read, create a drawing, painting, sculpture, or other visual representation of the images that come into your mind.

PUT IT IN WRITING. Write an informal essay about the piece you have selected. Explain why you like to read this type of material. Discuss what you like about it and why you find it interesting. How does this writing relate to your own life?

Unit TWO

ESSENTIAL READING SKILLS

Each of the reading strategies we've discussed in Unit 1 helps you learn to think, question, and respond while you read. By using the eight reading strategies, you will be able to demonstrate your mastery of the following reading skills:

- Identify the Author's Purpose
- Find the Main Idea
- Make Inferences
- Use Context Clues
- Analyze Text Organization
- Identify Sequence of Events
- Compare and Contrast
- Evaluate Cause and Effect
- Classify and Reorganize Information
- Distinguish Fact from Opinion
- Interpret Visual Aids
- Understand Literary Elements
- Draw Conclusions

Using these skills as you read helps you to become an independent, thoughtful, and active reader who can accomplish tasks evaluated on tests, particularly standardized tests. Standardized test practice connected to these skills follows each selection in this book.

Reading TIP

For more practice on test-taking skills, see Unit 10, Test-Taking Strategies, pages 499–512.

Reading TIP

To **identify the author's purpose**, ask yourself

- Why did the author create this piece of writing?
- Is the author simply sharing information or trying to convince me of something?
- Is he or she writing to entertain or trying to make a point?

A writer's **purpose** is his or her aim or goal. Being able to figure out an author's purpose, or purposes, is an important reading skill. An author may write with one or more of the purposes listed in the following chart. A writer's purpose corresponds to a specific mode of writing and will work well with various forms of writing.

Purposes of Writing

Purpose	Mode	Writing Forms
to reflect	personal/ expressive writing	diary entry, personal letter, autobiography, personal essay
to entertain, to describe, to enrich, and to enlighten	imaginative/ descriptive writing	poem, character sketch, play
to tell a story, to narrate a series of events	narrative writing	short story, biography, legend, myth, history
to inform, to explain	informative/ expository writing	news article, research report, expository essay, book review
to persuade	persuasive/ argumentative writing	editorial, petition, political speech, persuasive essay

Once you identify what the author is trying to do, you can evaluate, or judge, whether the author did a good job of achieving that purpose. For example, you may judge that the author of a persuasive essay made a good and convincing argument. Or, you may decide that the novel you are reading has a boring plot. In other words, the author has done a bad job of entertaining readers!

Read the following paragraph from Annie Dillard's essay "It's Not Talent; It's Just Work," Unit 7, page 405, and try to determine what the essay is about. Is the author trying to entertain, persuade, inform, or reflect? What information leads you to this answer?

It's hard work, doing something with your life. The very thought of hard work makes me queasy. I'd rather die in peace. Here we are, all equal and alike and none of us much to write home about— and some people choose to make themselves into physicists or thinkers or major-league pitchers, knowing perfectly well that it will be nothing but hard work. But I want to tell you that it's not as bad as it sounds. Doing something does not require discipline; it creates its own discipline—with a little help from caffeine.

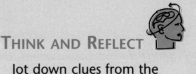

THINK AND REFLECT

Jot down clues from the paragraph that help you determine the author's purpose. (Infer)

_____

_____

_____

_____

Find the Main Idea

The **main idea** is a brief statement of what the author wants you to know, think, or feel after reading the text. In some cases, the main idea will actually be stated. Check the first and last paragraphs for a sentence that sums up the entire passage. Usually, the author will not tell you what the main idea is, and you will have to infer it.

In general, nonfiction texts have main ideas; literary texts (poems, novels, plays, and personal essays) have themes. Sometimes, however, the term *main idea* is used to refer to the theme of a literary work, especially an essay or poem. Both deal with the central idea in a written work.

A good way to find the main or overall idea of a whole selection (or part of a selection) is to gather important details into a Main Idea Map like the one below. Use the details to determine the main or overall message. This will help you to draw conclusions about the main idea when you finish reading.

Reading TIP

To **infer the main idea,** ask yourself

- Who or what is this passage about?
- What does the author want me to know, think, or feel about this "who" or "what"?
- If I had to tell someone in one sentence what this passage is about, what would I say?

Main Idea Map

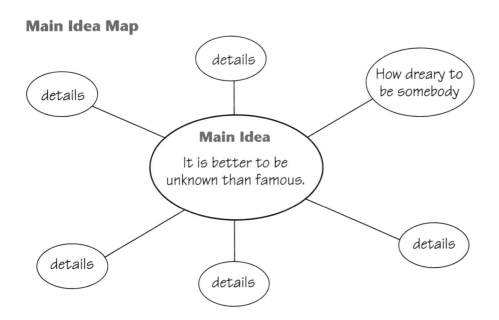

Reading TIP

As you make inferences, remember that each reference needs to fit with all of the clues in the text and with your prior knowledge.

Make Inferences

By paying close attention to what you read, it is possible to make inferences about what the writer is trying to communicate. **Making an inference** means putting together the clues given in the text with your own prior knowledge.

Inference Chart

Text	What I Infer
"Follow my lead!"	Dædalus did not take time to teach his son about flying.
Detail from text That was the extent of of the flying lesson.	**Conclusions I draw about the meaning** Dædalus was a careless father.

Reading TIP

Sometimes you can determine the meaning of a word by using the context as a clue. For example, the word choice or feel of a passage in general may give you an idea of the meaning of a word.

Use Context Clues

You can often figure out the meaning of an unfamiliar word by using context clues. **Context clues** are words and phrases near a difficult word that provide hints about the meaning of the word. The context in which a word is used may help you guess what a word means without having to look it up in the dictionary.

The following table explains the different kinds of context clues and shows words that signal each type of clue. Look for these words in the sentences around an unfamiliar word to see if they signal a context clue.

Context Clues

comparison clue	shows a comparison, or how the unfamiliar word is like something that might be familiar to you
signal words EXAMPLE	*and, like, as, just as, as if, as though*

Like a mouse darting away from the cat, I *bolted* from the room. (If the speaker acted like the mouse, he or she must have run away fast, so *bolted* must mean "ran away.")

contrast clue	shows that something contrasts, or differs in meaning, from something else
signal words	*but, nevertheless, on the other hand, however, although, though, in spite of*

EXAMPLE

My sister remains *aloof* from everyone; I, on the other hand, tend to get too involved in people's lives. (The words *on the other* hand signal a contrast between the speaker and her sister. If the speaker gets too involved, her sister must stay uninvolved. *Aloof* must mean "uninvolved or indifferent.")

restatement clue	uses different words to express the same idea
signal words	*that is, in other words, or*

EXAMPLE

Curtiss loves to exaggerate. He makes everything seem bigger and better than it really is. (As the second sentence suggests, *exaggerate* means "make something seem greater than it is.")

examples clue	gives examples of other items to illustrate the meaning of something
signal words	*including, such as, for example, for instance, especially, particularly*

EXAMPLE

Many *invertebrates*, such as sponges, jellyfish, starfish, and squid, live in the ocean, but others, like spiders and many worms, live on land. (If you know enough about the animals listed, you can guess that *invertebrates* are animals that don't have backbones.)

cause-and-effect clue	tells you that something happened as a result of something else
signal words	*if/then, when/then, thus, therefore, because, so, as a result of, consequently*

EXAMPLE

Kelly's *immunity* to chicken pox prevented her from getting the disease even after being exposed multiple times. (If having immunity caused Kelly not to get sick, *immunity*, must mean "resistance to disease or illness.")

NOTE THE FACTS

What does a restatement clue do? Write an example of a restatement clue.

_____

_____

_____

_____

Analyze Text Organization

Writing can be organized in different ways. To be an effective reader you need to know how to analyze how the text is organized. When you analyze something, you break it down into parts and then think about how the parts are related to each other and to the whole.

Reading TIP

Transition words connect ideas. They indicate how a text is organized. Look for words that
- describe main points (descriptive words)
- show sequence (sequence words)
- show comparison and contrast (comparison-and-contrast words)
- show cause and effect (cause-and-effect words)

Chronological or Time Order

Events are given in the order in which they happen or should be done. Events are connected by transition words such as *first, second, next, then,* and *finally.* Chronological order is often used to relate a narrative, as in a short story; to write a how-to article on a topic like building a bird feeder; or to describe a process, such as what happens when a volcano erupts.

Spatial or Location Order

Parts are described in order of their location in space, for example, from back to front, left to right, or top to bottom. Descriptions are connected by transition words or phrases such as *next to, beside, above, below, beyond,* and *around.* Spatial order could be used for an article that discusses a project's physical aspects, such as describing the remodeling of a kitchen, or for a descriptive passage in literature, as in establishing the setting of a science fiction story set in a space station.

Order of Importance

Details are listed from least important to most important or from most important to least important; transition phrases are used such as *more important, less important, most important,* and *least important.* For example, a speech telling voters why they should elect you class president could build from the least important reason to the most important reason.

Comparison-and-Contrast Order

Details of two subjects are presented in one of two ways. In the first method, the characteristics of one subject are presented, followed by the characteristics of the second subject. This method could be used to organize an essay that compares and contrasts two fast-food chains, and to tell why one is superior to the other.

In the second method, both subjects are compared and contrasted with regard to one quality, then with regard to a second quality, and so on. An essay organized according to this method could compare the platforms of two political parties issue by issue: the environment, the economy, and so forth. Ideas are connected by transition words and phrases that indicate similarities or differences, such as *likewise, similarly, in contrast, a different kind,* and *another difference.*

Cause-and-Effect Order

One or more causes are followed by one or more effects, or one or more effects are followed by one or more causes. Transition words and phrases that indicate cause and effect include *one cause, another effect, as a result, consequently,* and *therefore.* Cause-and-effect organization might be used for a public health announcement warning about the dangers of playing with fire or an essay discussing the outbreak of World War I and the events that led up to it.

Classification or Sorting Order

Items are classified, or grouped, in categories to show how one group is similar to or different from another. Items in the same category should share one or more characteristics. For example, Edgar Allan Poe, Agatha Christie, and Stephen King can be classified together as mystery writers. Transition words that indicate classification order are the same words that indicate comparison-and-contrast order, words such as *likewise, similarly, in contrast, a different kind,* and *another difference.*

Identify Sequence of Events

Sequence refers to the order in which things happen. When you read certain types of writing, such as a short story, a novel, a biography of a person's life, or a history book, keep track of the sequence of events. You might do this by making a time line or a sequence map.

Time Line

To make a time line, draw a line and divide it into equal parts like the one on the next page. Label each part with a date or a time. Then add key events at the right places along the time line.

METHODS OF TEXT ORGANIZATION

- Chronological order
- Spatial order
- Order of importance
- Comparison-and-contrast order
- Cause-and-effect order
- Classification order

NOTE THE FACTS

How can you keep track of sequence of events?

_____

_____

_____

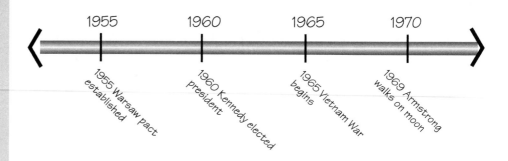

Sequence Map

In each box, draw pictures that represent key events in a selection. Then write a caption under each box that explains each event. Draw the events in the order in which they occur.

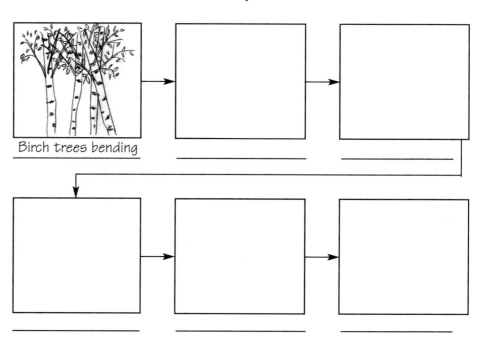

Birch trees bending

Compare and Contrast

Comparing and contrasting are closely related processes. When you **compare** one thing to another you describe similarities between the two things; when you **contrast** two things you describe their differences. To compare and contrast, begin by listing the features of each subject. Then go down both lists and check whether each feature is shared or not. You can also show similarities and differences in a Venn diagram. A Venn diagram uses two slightly overlapping circles. The outer part of each circle shows what aspects of two things are different from each other. The inner, or shared, part of each circle shows what aspects the two things share.

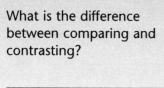

Venn Diagram

Write down ideas about Topic 1 in the first circle and ideas about Topic 2 in the second circle. The area in which the circles overlap should contain ideas common to both topics.

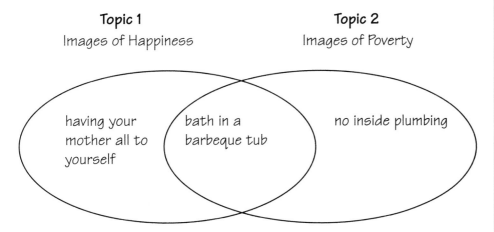

Topic 1
Images of Happiness

Topic 2
Images of Poverty

having your mother all to yourself

bath in a barbeque tub

no inside plumbing

Evaluate Cause and Effect

When you evaluate **cause and effect**, you are looking for a logical relationship between a cause or causes and one or more effects. A writer may present one or more causes followed by one or more effects, or one or more effects followed by one or more causes. Transitional, or signal, words and phrases that indicate cause and effect include *one cause*, *another effect*, *as a result*, *consequently*, and *therefore*. As a reader, you determine whether the causes and effects in a text are reasonable. A graphic organizer like the one below will help you to recognize relationships between causes and effects.

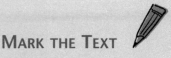

MARK THE TEXT

Highlight or underline what you do when you evaluate cause and effect.

Cause-and-Effect Chart

Keep track of what happens in a story and why in a chart like the one below. Use cause-and-effect signal words to help you identify causes and their effects.

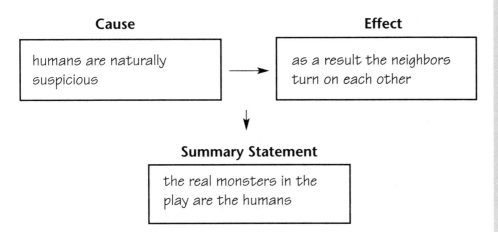

Cause

humans are naturally suspicious

Effect

as a result the neighbors turn on each other

Summary Statement

the real monsters in the play are the humans

Classify and Reorganize Information

To **classify** is to put into classes or categories. Items in the same category should share one or more characteristics. A writer may group things to show similarities and name the categories to clarify how one group is similar or different from another. For example, whales can be classified by their method of eating as *baleen* or *toothed*. Classifying or reorganizing the information into categories as you read increases your understanding.

The key step in classifying is choosing categories that fit your purpose. Take classification notes in a chart like the one below to help you organize separate types or groups and sort their characteristics.

Classification Chart

Category 1	Category 2	Category 3
Total Solar Eclipses	Great Comets	Planetary Conjunctions
Items in Category	**Items in Category**	**Items in Category**
August 21, 2017 April 8, 2024	Halley's Hale-Bopp	
Details and Characteristics	**Details and Characteristics**	**Details and Characteristics**
happens once every 360 years	have uncharted orbits of thousands of years	

Distinguish Fact from Opinion

A **fact** is a statement that could be proven by direct observation. Every statement of fact is either true or false. The following statement is an example of fact:

> Many Greek myths deal with human emotion. (This statement is a fact that can be proven by examining the content of Greek myths.)

An **opinion** is a statement that expresses an attitude or desire, not a fact about the world. One common type of opinion statement is a *value statement*. A value statement expresses an attitude toward something.

> Ancient Greece produced some **beautiful** and **inspiring** myths. (The adjectives used to describe myths express an attitude or opinion toward something that cannot be proven.)

MARK THE TEXT

Underline or highlight the definition of a fact and the definition of an opinion.

Value statements often include judgment words such as the following:

attractive	honest	ugly
awesome	junk	unattractive
beautiful	kind	valuable
cheap	mean	wonderful
dishonest	nice	worthless
excellent	petty	
good	treasure	

NOTE THE FACTS

What are value statements? What are three words you could add to the chart at left?

_____

_____

_____

_____

A **policy statement** is an opinion that tells not what is but what someone believes should be. Such statements usually include words like *should, should not, ought, ought not, must,* or *must not.*

> The president **should** be reelected.
> You **must not** play your radio during study hall.

A **prediction** makes a statement about the future. Because the future is unpredictable, most predictions can be considered opinions.

> People will live longer in the future.
> Tomorrow will be partly cloudy.

When evaluating a fact, ask yourself whether it can be proven through direct observation or by checking a reliable source such as a reference book or an unbiased expert. An opinion is as good as the facts that support it. When reading or listening, be critical about the statements that you encounter. It may be helpful to make a chart like the one below to help distinguish fact from opinion as you read.

Reading TIP

To **distinguish fact from opinion** ask yourself: Is this a fact or is this an opinion? If it is a statement of fact, can it be proven or does it seems likely? If it is an opinion, can it be supported by facts?

Fact or Opinion Chart

Fact: The language with the greatest number of speakers is Mandarin Chinese.	**Opinion:** Mandarin Chinese is the greatest language in the world.
Proof: Over nine hundred million people speak Mandarin Chinese.	**Support:** More people speak Mandarin Chinese than any other language, but English is spoken more widely around the globe.
Fact:	**Opinion:**
Proof:	**Support:**

Interpret Visual Aids

Visual aids are charts, graphs, pictures, illustrations, photos, maps, diagrams, spreadsheets, and other materials that present information. Many writers use visual aids to present data in understandable ways. Information visually presented in tables, charts, and graphs can help you find information, see trends, discover facts, and uncover patterns.

Reading Graphics	
Before Reading	■ Determine the subject of the graphic by reading the title, headings, and other textual clues.
	■ Determine how the data are organized, classified, or divided by reading the labels along rows or columns.
During Reading	■ Survey the data and look for trends by comparing columns and rows, noting changes among information fields, looking for patterns, or navigating map sections.
	■ Use legends, keys, and other helpful sections in the graphic.
After Reading	■ Check footnotes or references for additional information about the data and their sources.
	■ List conclusions or summarize the data

Pie Chart

A **pie chart** is a circle that stands for a whole group or set. The circle is divided into parts to show the divisions of the whole. When you look at a pie chart, you can see the relationships of the parts to one another and to the whole.

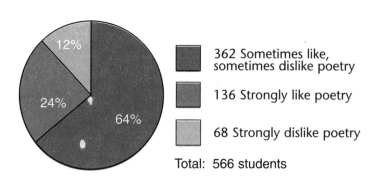

362 Sometimes like, sometimes dislike poetry

136 Strongly like poetry

68 Strongly dislike poetry

Total: 566 students

NOTE THE FACTS

What are two things you can do with graphics at the during-reading stage?

_____

_____

_____

_____

NOTE THE FACTS

Do more students strongly like or strongly dislike poetry?

_____

_____

Bar Graph

A **bar graph** compares amounts of something by representing the amounts as bars of different lengths. In the bar graph below, each bar represents the value in dollars of canned goods donated by several communities to a food drive. To read the graph, simply imagine a line drawn from the edge of the bar to the bottom of the graph. Then read the number. For example, the bar graph below shows that the community of Russell Springs donated $600 worth of goods during the food drive.

DOLLAR VALUE OF DONATED GOODS TO CANNED FOOD DRIVE

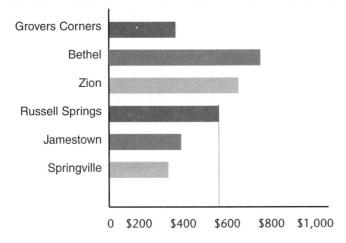

Map

A **map** is a representation, usually on a surface such as paper or a sheet of plastic, of a geographic area showing various significant features of that area.

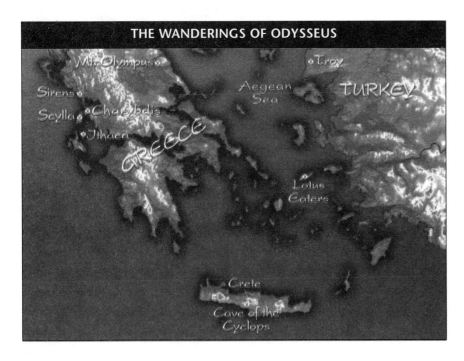

THE WANDERINGS OF ODYSSEUS

Mt. Olympus · Troy
Sirens · Aegean Sea · TURKEY
Scylla · Charybdis
Ithaca GREECE
Lotus Eaters
Crete
Cave of the Cyclops

NOTE THE FACTS

Which community donated the largest amount of goods during the food drive? What was the dollar value?

_____

_____

Understand Literary Elements

Literary elements are the terms and techniques that are used in literature. When you read literature, you need to be familiar with the literary terms and reading skills listed below. These literary elements are explained in more detail in Unit 3, Reading Fiction, pages 36–38. Other literary elements are described in Units 4–7. Here are descriptions of the reading skills needed for some of the most common literary elements.

- **RECOGNIZE MOOD AND TONE. Mood** is the atmosphere or emotion conveyed by a literary work. A writer creates mood by using concrete details to describe the setting, characters, or events. The writer can evoke in the reader an emotional response—such as fear, discomfort, longing, or anticipation—by working carefully with descriptive language and sensory details. The mood of a work might be dark, mysterious, gloomy, cheerful, inspiring, or peaceful. **Tone** is the writer's attitude toward the subject or toward the reader of a work. Examples of different tones that a work may have include familiar, ironic, playful, sarcastic, serious, and sincere.

- **UNDERSTAND POINT OF VIEW. Point of view** is the vantage point, or perspective, from which a story or narrative is told. Stories are typically written from the following points of view:

first-person point of view	narrator uses words such as *I* and *we*
second-person point of view	narrator uses *you*
third-person point of view	narrator uses words such as *he, she, it,* and *they*

- **ANALYZE CHARACTER AND CHARACTERIZATION.** A **character** is a person (or sometimes an animal) who takes part in the action of a story. **Characterization** is the literary techniques writers use to create characters and make them come alive. Writers use the following techniques to create characters:

direct description	describing the physical features, dress, and personality of the character
behavior	showing what characters say, do, or think
interaction with others	showing what other characters say or think about them
internal state	revealing the character's private thoughts and emotions

Reading TIP

A **character chart** can be used as a graphic organizer to keep track of character development as you read. See the example in Appendix B, page B-8.

- **EXAMINE PLOT DEVELOPMENT.** The plot is basically what happens in a story. A **plot** is a series of events related to a *central conflict*, or struggle. A typical plot involves the introduction of a conflict, its development, and its eventual resolution. The elements of plot include the following:

exposition	sets the tone or mood, introduces the characters and setting, and provides necessary background information
inciting incident	introduces a central conflict with or within one or more characters
rising action	develops a central conflict with or within one or more characters and develops toward a high point of intensity
climax	the high point of interest or suspense in the plot where something decisive happens
falling action	the events that follow the climax
resolution	the point at which the central conflict is ended or resolved
dénouement	any material that follows the resolution and that ties up loose ends

Reading TIP

A graphic organizer called a **plot diagram** can be used to chart the plot of a literature selection. Refer to the example in Appendix B, page B-11.

Draw Conclusions

When you **draw conclusions,** you are gathering pieces of information and then deciding what that information means.

This passage from a *Newsweek* magazine article, "Ghost of Everest," Unit 8, page 439, describes weather conditions considered "moderate" on Mount Everest.

> As expedition leader Eric Simonson told *Newsweek* from base camp "there was very little winter snow, and the temperatures have been moderate by Everest standards," exposing areas usually covered. By Everest standards, "moderate" meant temperatures well below zero with winds of 30 miles an hour or more.

The key idea in this passage is that the weather conditions on Mount Everest are moderate. However, the supporting points, "temperatures well below zero" and "winds of 30 miles an hour or more," lead to the overall conclusion that the weather conditions are brutal and might be dangerous.

What kind of graphic organizer can help you draw conclusions? What can it help you with?

_____

_____

_____

Drawing conclusions is an essential part of reading. It may be helpful to use a graphic organizer such as a chart or log to keep track of the information you find while you are reading and the conclusions you draw.

Drawing Conclusions Log

Key Idea	Key Idea	Key Idea
weather conditions on Mount Everest are considered moderate		
Supporting Points	**Supporting Points**	**Supporting Points**
temperatures well below zero winds of 30 miles an hour or more		
Overall Conclusion		
weather conditions are actually brutal and dangerous		

Unit 2 READING
Review

Choose and Use Reading Skills

Before reading the excerpt below, review with a partner how to use each of these essential reading skills.

- Identify the Author's Purpose
- Find the Main Idea
- Make Inferences
- Use Context Clues
- Analyze Text Organization
- Identify Sequence of Events
- Compare and Contrast
- Evaluate Cause and Effect
- Classify and Reorganize Information
- Distinguish Fact from Opinion
- Interpret Visual Aids
- Understand Literary Elements
- Draw Conclusions

Read this excerpt from *Mississippi Solo* by Eddy L. Harris using some of the reading skills from this unit. After you finish the passage, answer the questions that follow.

We were up before the sun. The air was soft and fine, but cold. The morning seemed brittle. When the sun finally rose it looked like it would have taken any excuse at all and gone back to bed. The same for me, so it was quickly tea and soup, break camp and head on down to the lake.

Without much ado we unloosed the canoe from its perch atop the car and set it in the water. I tied an extra paddle to one of the cross struts in the canoe, slipped a line through the stern, and I was ready.

Nothing else needed to be stowed in the canoe because Robinovich had agreed to stay on for the day and meet me periodically along this early portion of the river. Just to make sure I got the hang of it and to put both our minds at ease.

I took a long hug and a kiss, donned my yellow life jacket, and I was away.

The lake invites me with its stillness. Any turbulence might have discouraged me, but the water is so calm and pretty and the morning so quiet and finally beginning to take on some color that I shove off easily and paddle straight out to where the water is deep and cold and scariest. I suddenly have no fear of falling in and if not for the river calling me I could easily stay here and paddle up and down this lake all day.

But the river does call. I turn my canoe north and glide toward it.

What do you think is the author's purpose? What type of writing does he use? What ideas does the author want to communicate?

_____

_____

_____

Who is Robinovich? How can you infer what kind of relationship the narrator has with this person?

_____

_____

How can you guess the meaning of the word _turbulence_ by the context clues?

_____

_____

Make a prediction about what might happen to the narrator on the first day of his trip. What obstacles might he face? What makes you think so?

_____

_____

On Your Own

FLUENTLY SPEAKING. Select a 100–150-word passage from a book, magazine, or newspaper that you are currently reading. Working with a partner, take turns reading the passage aloud several times. Break it down into shorter sections and alternate reading paragraphs or sentences.

PICTURE THIS. Find an article that contains data of some sort. Think about how can this data be presented using a visual aid, such as a table, chart, or graph. Do you notice any trends or patterns in the information? Draw a visual aid, such a pie chart or bar graph, to present the information in a more understandable way.

PUT IT IN WRITING. Read a short article from a magazine or newspaper. Now go back and reread the first and last paragraphs. Write a summary of the main idea. What is it that the author wants you to know, think or feel after reading this text? Is the main idea stated, or did you have to infer it?

Unit THREE

Reading Fiction

Fiction is prose writing that tells an invented or imaginary story. *Prose* is writing that uses straightforward language and differs from poetry because it doesn't have a rhythmic pattern. Some fiction, such as the historical novel, is based on fact, while other forms, such as the fantasy tale, are highly unrealistic. Fictional works may vary in structure and length.

Forms of Fiction

The oldest form of fiction is the stories told in the oral, or folk, tradition, which include myths, legends, and fables. The most common forms of fiction are short stories, novels, and novellas.

THE SHORT STORY. A **short story** is a brief work of fiction that tells a story. It usually focuses on a single episode or scene and involves a limited number of characters. Although a short story contains all the main elements of fiction—character, setting, plot, and theme—it may not fully develop each element. The selections in this unit are examples of short stories.

THE NOVEL. A **novel** is a long work of fiction that usually has more complex elements than a short story. Its longer format allows the elements of fiction to be more fully developed. A **novella** is a work of fiction that is longer than a typical short story but shorter than a typical novel.

Types of fiction include **romances**, tales that feature the adventures of legendary figures such as Alexander the Great and King Arthur; **historical fiction,** which is partly based on actual historical events and is partly invented; and **science fiction,** imaginative literature based on scientific principles, discoveries, or laws that often deals with the future, the distant past, or worlds other than our own.

Reading TIP

The term fiction comes from the Latin *fictio,* meaning something invented.

NOTE THE FACTS

Is a novella longer or shorter than a typical novel?

_____

_____

Elements of Fiction

CHARACTER. A character is a person (or sometimes an animal) who takes part in the action of a story. The following are some useful terms for describing characters.

protagonist (main character)	central figure in a story
antagonist	character who struggles against the protagonist
major character	character with a significant role in the action of the story
minor character	character who plays a lesser role
one-dimentional character (flat character)	character who exhibits a single dominant quality (character trait)
three dimensional character (full or rounded character)	character who exhibits the complexity of traits of a human being
static character	character who does not change during the course of the story
dynamic character	character who does change during the course of the story
stock character	character found again and again in different literary works

CHARACTERIZATION. Characterization is the use of literary techniques to create a character and make them come alive. Writers use the following techniques to create characters:

direct description	describing the physical features, dress, and personality of the character
behavior	showing what the characters says or does
interaction with others	showing what other characters say or think about the character
internal state	revealing the character's private thoughts and emotions

SETTING. The **setting** of a work of fiction is the time and place in which the events take place. In fiction, setting is most often revealed by description of landscape, scenery, buildings, weather, and season. Setting reveals important information about the time period, geographical location, cultural environment, and physical conditions in which the characters live.

MOOD AND TONE. Mood is the atmosphere or emotion created by a literary work. A writer creates mood by using concrete details to describe the setting, characters, or events. The mood of a work might be dark, mysterious, gloomy, cheerful, inspiring, or peaceful.

Tone is the writer's attitude toward the subject or toward the reader of a work. The tone of a work might be familiar, ironic, playful, sarcastic, serious, or sincere.

POINT OF VIEW. Point of view is the vantage point from which a story is told. You need to consider point of view to understand the perspective from which the events in the story are being told. Stories are typically written from the following points of view:

first-person point of view	narrator uses words such as *I* and *we*
second-person point of view	narrator uses *you*
third-person point of view	narrator uses words such as *he, she, it,* and *they*

Most of the literature you read will be told from either the first-person or third-person point of view. In stories written from a first-person point of view, the narrator may be a participant or a witness of the action. In stories told from a third-person point of view, the narrator generally stands outside the action. In some stories, the narrator's point of view is *limited*. In this case the narrator can reveal only his or her private, internal thoughts or those of a single character. In other stories, the narrator's point of view is *omniscient*. In such stories the narrator can reveal the private, internal thoughts of any character.

CONFLICT. A **conflict** is a struggle between two forces in a literary work. A plot involves the introduction, development, and eventual resolution of a conflict. A struggle that takes place between a character and an outside force is called an *external conflict*. A struggle that takes place within a character is called an *internal conflict*.

PLOT. When you read short stories or novels, it helps to know the parts of a plot. The plot is basically what happens in a story. A **plot** is a series of events related to a central conflict, or struggle. A typical plot involves the introduction of a conflict, its development, and its eventual resolution. The elements of plot include the following:

Reading TIP

The writer can create mood, or cause in the reader an emotional response—such as fear, discomfort, or longing—by working carefully with descriptive language and sensory details.

NOTE THE FACTS

In what point of view can the narrator reveal the private, internal thoughts of any character?

_____

_____

Reading TIP

One side of the central conflict in a work of fiction is usually taken by the main character. That character may struggle against another character, against the forces of nature, against society or social norms, against fate, or against some elements within himself or herself.

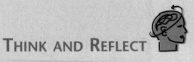
exposition	sets the tone or mood, introduces the characters and setting, and provides necessary background information
inciting incident	event that introduces a central conflict
rising action	develops a central conflict and rises toward a high point of intensity
climax	the high point of interest or suspense in the plot where something decisive happens
falling action	the events that follow the climax
resolution	the point at which the central conflict is ended or resolved
dénouement	any material that follows the resolution and that ties up loose ends

Use a **plot diagram** like the one that follows to chart the plot of a literature selection.

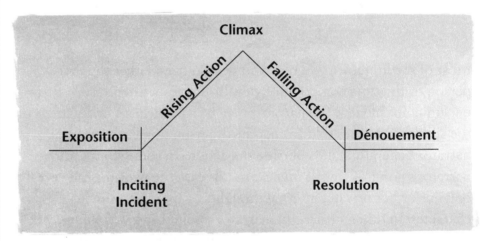

Become an Active Reader

The instruction in this unit gives you an in-depth look at how to use one active reading strategy for each story. Questions and tips in the margins keep your attention focused on reading actively. White space in the margins allows you to add your own comments and strategy ideas. Brief margin notes guide your use of additional strategies. Learning how to use several strategies in combination will ensure your complete understanding of what you are reading. When you have difficulty, use fix-up ideas to correct the problem. For further information about the active reading strategies, see Unit 1, pages 4–15.

Active Reading Strategy Checklists

When reading fiction, you need to be aware of the plot (or what happens), the characters, and the setting. The following checklists offer things to consider as you read fiction.

1 READ WITH A PURPOSE. Before reading about imagined events and characters, gives yourself a purpose, or something to look for, as you read. Say to yourself

- ❏ I want to look for . . .
- ❏ I need to learn what happens to . . .
- ❏ I want to experience what it is like in . . .
- ❏ I want to understand . . .

2 CONNECT TO PRIOR KNOWLEDGE. Being aware of what you already know and thinking about it as you read can help you keep track of what's happening and will increase your knowledge. As you read, say to yourself

- ❏ I already know this about the story . . .
- ❏ This part of the story reminds me of . . .
- ❏ I think this part of the story is like . . .
- ❏ My experience tells me that . . .
- ❏ I like this description because . . .

3 WRITE THINGS DOWN. As you read short stories or novels, writing things down is very important. Possible ways to write things down include:

- ❏ Underline character's names.
- ❏ Write messages on sticky notes.
- ❏ Highlight the setting.
- ❏ Create a graphic organizer to keep track of plot elements.
- ❏ Use a code in the margin that shows how you respond to the characters, setting, or events. For instance, you can mark a description you like with a "+."

4 MAKE PREDICTIONS. Because fiction includes information about characters, settings, and events, make predictions about these story elements. Your predictions will help you think about what lies ahead. Make predictions like the following:

- ❏ I predict that this character will . . .
- ❏ The setting of this story makes me think that . . .
- ❏ I bet there will be a conflict between . . .
- ❏ This event in the story makes me guess that . . .

Reading TIP

Sometimes a purpose will be a directive from a teacher: "Look for foreshadowing." Other times you can set your own purpose by previewing the title, the opening paragraphs, and instructional information that are part of the story.

Reading TIP

Instead of writing down a short response, use a symbol or a short word to indicate your response. Use codes like the ones listed below.

+	I like this.
–	I don't like this.
√	This is important.
Yes	I agree with this.
No	I disagree with this.
?	I don't understand this.
!	This is like something I know.
↩	I need to come back to this later.

5 VISUALIZE. Visualizing, or allowing the words on the page to create images in your mind, is one of the most important things to do while reading fiction. Become part of the action. "See" what the author describes. Make statements like

- ❑ I imagine the setting to look like . . .
- ❑ This description of the main character makes me . . .
- ❑ I picture that this is what happens in this section . . .
- ❑ I envision myself in the action by . . .

6 USE TEXT ORGANIZATION. Fiction writing has a plot that you can follow. Use the plot, or the series of events, to keep track of what is happening. Say to yourself

- ❑ The exposition, or introduction, tells me . . .
- ❑ The central conflict centers on . . .
- ❑ The climax, or high point of interest, occurs when . . .
- ❑ The resolution, or the outcome, of this story lets me know . . .
- ❑ Signal words like *first*, *then*, and *finally* explain . . .

7 TACKLE DIFFICULT VOCABULARY. Difficult words in a story can get in the way of your ability to follow the events in a work of fiction. Use aids that a text provides, consult a dictionary, or ask someone about words you do not understand. When you come across a word you do not know, say to yourself

- ❑ The context tells me that this word means . . .
- ❑ A dictionary definition provided in the story shows that the word means . . .
- ❑ My work with the word before class helps me know that the word means . . .
- ❑ A classmate said that the word means . . .
- ❑ I can skip knowing the exact meaning of this word because . . .

8 MONITOR YOUR READING PROGRESS. All readers encounter difficulty when they read, especially if the reading material is not self-selected. When you have to read something, note problems you are having and fix them. The key to reading success is knowing when you are having difficulty. To fix problems, say to yourself

- ❑ Because I do not understand this part, I will . . .
- ❑ Because I am having trouble staying interested in the story, I will . . .
- ❑ Because the words are too hard, I will . . .
- ❑ Because the story is very long, I will . . .
- ❑ Because I cannot remember what I have just read, I will . . .

Fix-Up Ideas

- ■ Reread
- ■ Ask a question
- ■ Read in shorter chunks
- ■ Read aloud
- ■ Retell
- ■ Work with a partner
- ■ Unlock difficult words
- ■ Vary your reading rate
- ■ Choose a new reading strategy
- ■ Create a mnemonic device

How to Use Reading Strategies with Fiction

Read the following excerpts to discover how you might use reading strategies as you read fiction.

Excerpt 1. Note how a reader uses active reading strategies while reading this excerpt from "Thank You, M'am," page 146.

READ WITH A PURPOSE

After reading this paragraph, I want to know what happens to the boy.

VISUALIZE

I picture a tall, angry woman with huge hands and a big black purse. The boy she is shaking looks scared.

CONNECT TO PRIOR KNOWLEDGE

This makes me think of the purse that my grandmother carries.

MAKE PREDICTIONS

I bet she turns the boy in to the police.

She was a large woman with a large purse that had everything in it but hammer and nails. It had a long strap, and she carried it slung across her shoulder. It was about eleven o'clock at night, dark, and she was walking alone, when a boy ran up behind her and tried to snatch her purse. The snap broke with the single tug the boy gave it from behind. But the boy's weight and the weight of the purse combined caused him to lose his balance. Instead of taking off full blast as he had hoped, the boy fell on his back on the sidewalk and his legs flew up. The large woman simply turned around and kicked him right square in his blue-jeaned sitter. Then she reached down, picked the boy up by his shirtfront, and shook him until his teeth rattled.

Excerpt 2. Note how a reader uses active reading strategies while reading this excerpt from "The Gift of the Magi," page 110.

WRITE THINGS DOWN

I can keep track of what happens in a sequence chart.

USE TEXT ORGANIZATION

Words like *now, one was,* and *the other was* signal important ideas.

TACKLE DIFFICULT VOCABULARY

The definitions of *imputation* and *parsimony* at the bottom of the page help me know that "bulldozing the grocer and the vegetable man and the butcher" means that Della got these stores to lower their prices.

MONITOR YOUR READING PROGRESS

I will use this break in the story to retell what has happened so far.

One dollar and eighty-seven cents. That was all. And sixty cents of it was in pennies. Pennies saved one and two at a time by bulldozing the grocer and the vegetable man and the butcher until one's cheeks burned with the silent <u>imputation</u> of <u>parsimony</u> that such close dealing implied. Three times Della counted it. One dollar and eighty-seven cents. And the next day would be Christmas…

Now, there were two possessions of the James Dillingham Youngs in which they both took a mighty pride. One was Jim's gold watch that had been his father's and his grandfather's. The other was Della's hair. Had the Queen of Sheba[3] lived in the flat across the air shaft, Della would have let her hair hang out the window some day to dry just to depreciate Her Majesty's jewels and gifts. Had King Solomon been the janitor, with all his treasures piled up in the basement, Jim would have pulled out his watch every time he passed, just to see him pluck at his beard from envy.

Reader's resource

"The Monkey's Paw" was published in 1902. It is for this story that W. W. Jacobs (1863–1943) is most well known. A classic horror story, it creates in the reader a sense of foreboding dread. Jacobs achieves this suspenseful effect by introducing into the ordinary everyday life of the White family the odd artifact of the monkey's paw. As you read, note the details that help to create its suspenseful mood.

Word watch

PREVIEW VOCABULARY

amiably	keenly
apathy	liability
attribute	maligned
avaricious	oppressive
averted	persist
burly	poised
compensation	presumptuous
condole	proffered
credulity	prosaic
dubiously	provoke
enthralled	reverberate
frivolous	simian
furtively	subdued
inaudible	torrent
intercept	

Reader's journal

If you were granted three wishes, what would they be?

_____

_____

_____

"The Monkey's Paw"
by W. W. Jacobs

Active READING STRATEGY

MAKE PREDICTIONS

Before Reading ▶ PREVIEW THE SELECTION

❑ Read the Reader's Resource and discuss how other horror stories you know create a sense of foreboding, or dread.

❑ **Foreshadowing**, the act of presenting materials that hint at events to occur later in a story, can help you make predictions about what will happen as you read.

❑ Prepare to use a graphic organizer during reading to record examples of foreshadowing and make predictions by previewing the Predictions Chart below.

Graphic Organizer

Foreshadowing	Predictions	Adjustments to My Predictions

The Monkey's Paw

W. W. Jacobs

During Reading

MAKE PREDICTIONS

❑ Follow along in the text as you or your teacher reads the beginning of the story aloud.

❑ Work with the class to record foreshadowing from the text and form predictions about events to come.

❑ Record examples of foreshadowing in the first column of your chart. From the foreshadowing, make predictions about what will happen later.

❑ Read the remainder of the story on your own. Stop at the end of each page to record foreshadowing, make predictions, and adjust and verify previous predictions in your chart.

Without, the night was cold and wet, but in the small parlor of Laburnum Villa the blinds were drawn, and the fire burned brightly.

Father and son were at chess, the former, who possessed ideas about the game involving radical changes, putting his king into such sharp and unnecessary perils that it even <u>provoked</u> comment from the white-haired old lady knitting placidly by the fire.

"Hark at the wind," said Mr. White, who, having seen a fatal mistake after it was too late, was <u>amiably</u> desirous of preventing his son from seeing it.

"I'm listening," said the latter, grimly surveying the board as he stretched out his hand. "Check."

"I should hardly think that he'd come tonight," said his father, with his hand <u>poised</u> over the board.

10

READ ALOUD

Find descriptive passages that create a suspenseful mood and read them aloud. Use your voice to underscore the mood.

MARK THE TEXT

Underline or highlight the words and phrases in lines 17–22 that create a suspenseful, ominous mood.

Literary TOOLS

SETTING. The **setting** of a literary work is the time and place in which it occurs, together with all the details used to create a sense of a particular time and place. As you read, pay attention to how the setting in this story helps to create the mood.

"Mate,"[1] replied the son.

"That's the worst living so far out," bawled Mr. White, with sudden and unlooked-for violence. "Of all the beastly, slushy, out-of-the-way places to live in, this is the worst.

20 Pathway's a bog, and the road's a <u>torrent</u>. I don't know what people are thinking about. I suppose because only two houses in the road are let; they think it doesn't matter."

"Never mind, dear," said his wife soothingly. "Perhaps you'll win the next one."

Mr. White looked up sharply, just in time to <u>intercept</u> a knowing glance between mother and son. The words died away on his lips, and he hid a guilty grin in his thin gray beard.

"There he is," said Herbert White, as the gate banged
30 loudly and heavy footsteps came toward the door.

The old man rose with hospitable haste, and opening the door, was heard <u>condoling</u> with the new arrival. The new arrival also condoled with himself, so that Mrs. White said, "Tut, tut!" and coughed gently as her husband entered the room, followed by a tall, <u>burly</u> man, beady of eye and rubicund of visage.[2]

"Sergeant-Major Morris," he said, introducing him.

The sergeant-major shook hands, and taking the <u>proffered</u> seat by the fire, watched contentedly while his
40 host got out whisky and tumblers and stood a small copper kettle on the fire.

At the third glass, his eyes got brighter, and he began to talk; the little family circle regarding with eager interest this visitor from distant parts, as he squared his broad shoulders in the chair and spoke of wild scenes and doughty[3] deeds; of wars and plagues and strange peoples.

"Twenty-one years of it," said Mr. White, nodding at his

---

1. **Mate.** The winning move in chess, capturing your opponent's king, is announced with "Checkmate."
2. **rubicund of visage.** Pink-faced
3. **doughty.** Brave

words for everyday use	tor • rent (tôr´ənt) n., swift, violent stream. *The gentle stream becomes a raging <u>torrent</u> when the snow melts.*
	in • ter • cept (in´tər sept´) vt., seize or stop on the way. *In class Reggie <u>intercepted</u> the note Sandy was sending to Brian.*
	con • dole (kən dōl´) vi., sympathize. *I <u>condoled</u> with Yolanda about her failing grade.*
	bur • ly (bʉr´lē) adj., big and strong. *Although not <u>burly</u> like many football players, John has speed and agility that make him a good running back.*
	prof • fered (präf´ərd) part., offered courteously. *The cookie <u>proffered</u> to me by the hostess was dry and tasteless.*

wife and son. "When he went away he was a slip of a youth in the warehouse. Now look at him."

"He don't look to have taken much harm," said Mrs. White politely.

"I'd like to go to India myself," said the old man, "just to look round a bit, you know."

"Better where you are," said the sergeant-major, shaking his head. He put down the empty glass, and sighing softly, shook it again.

"I should like to see those old temples and fakirs[4] and jugglers," said the old man. "What was that you started telling me the other day about a monkey's paw or something, Morris?"

"Nothing," said the soldier hastily. "Leastways, nothing worth hearing."

"Monkey's paw?" said Mrs. White curiously.

"Well, it's just a bit of what you might call magic, perhaps," said the sergeant-major offhandedly.

His three listeners leaned forward eagerly. The visitor absentmindedly put his empty glass to his lips and then set it down again. His host filled it for him.

"To look at," said the sergeant-major, fumbling in his pocket, "it's just an ordinary little paw, dried to a mummy."

He took something out of his pocket and proffered it. Mrs. White drew back with a grimace, but her son, taking it, examined it curiously.

"And what is there special about it?" inquired Mr. White as he took it from his son, and having examined it, placed it upon the table.

"It had a spell put on it by an old fakir," said the sergeant-major, "a very holy man. He wanted to show that fate ruled people's lives, and that those who interfered with it did so to their sorrow. He put a spell on it so that three separate men could each have three wishes from it."

His manner was so impressive that his hearers were conscious that their light laughter jarred somewhat.

"Well, why don't you have three, sir?" said Herbert White cleverly.

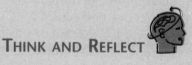

THINK AND REFLECT

Reread lines 77–81. Do you find the sergeant-major's story believable? Why, or why not? **(Evaluate)**

_____

_____

_____

The soldier regarded him in the way that middle age is wont to regard <u>presumptuous</u> youth. "I have," he said quietly, and his blotchy face whitened.

90 "And did you really have the three wishes granted?" asked Mrs. White.

"I did," said the sergeant-major, and his glass tapped against his strong teeth.

"And has anybody else wished?" <u>persisted</u> the old lady.

"The first man had his three wishes. Yes," was the reply. "I don't know what the first two were, but the third was for death. That's how I got the paw."

His tones were so grave that a hush fell upon the group.

"If you've had your three wishes, it's no good to you now, then, Morris," said the old man at last. "What do you keep

100 it for?"

The soldier shook his head. "Fancy, I suppose," he said slowly. "I did have some idea of selling it, but I don't think I will. It has caused enough mischief already. Besides, people won't buy. They think it's a fairy tale; some of them, and those who do think anything of it, want to try it first and pay me afterward."

"If you could have another three wishes," said the old man, eyeing him <u>keenly</u>, "would you have them?"

"I don't know," said the other. "I don't know."

110 He took the paw, and dangling it between his forefinger and thumb, suddenly threw it upon the fire. White, with a slight cry, stooped down and snatched it off.

"Better let it burn," said the soldier solemnly.

"If you don't want it, Morris," said the other, "give it to me."

"I won't," said his friend doggedly. "I threw it on the fire. If you keep it, don't blame me for what happens. Pitch it on the fire again like a sensible man."

The other shook his head and examined his new

120 possession closely. "How do you do it?" he inquired.

USE THE STRATEGY

MAKE PREDICTIONS. What might the sergeant-major's reply be foreshadowing?

_____

_____

_____

FIX-UP IDEA

Read Short Sections
If you have difficulty applying the reading strategy, read in shorter sections. Instead of stopping at the end of each page, you might stop as you encounter foreshadowing to record it and form predictions. You might also stop as soon as you have enough information to adjust or verify a previous prediction. Continue applying the fix-up idea as you read.

4. **fakirs.** Person who, for religious purposes, lives a thoughtful life of poverty and self-denial

words for everyday use

pre • sump • tu • ous (prē zump´choo əs) *adj.*, arrogant. *Allan was presumptuous to tell everyone he was the new class president before the votes were counted.*

per • sist (pər sist´) *vi.*, continue insistently. *Alicia persisted in talking to a classmate, even after the teacher asked for silence.*

keen • ly (kēn´lē) *adv.*, sharply. *Jerome listened keenly to Jim's play-by-play account because he didn't want to miss a detail about the game he hadn't been able to attend.*

"Hold it up in your right hand and wish aloud," said the sergeant-major, "but I warn you of the consequences."

"Sounds like the *Arabian Nights*," said Mrs. White, as she rose and began to set the supper. "Don't you think you might wish for four pairs of hands for me?"

Her husband drew the talisman[5] from his pocket, and then all three burst into laughter as the sergeant-major, with a look of alarm on his face, caught him by the arm.

"If you must wish," he said gruffly, "wish for something 130 sensible."

Mr. White dropped it back into his pocket, and placing chairs, motioned his friend to the table. In the business of supper, the talisman was partly forgotten, and afterward the three sat listening in an <u>enthralled</u> fashion to a second installment of the soldier's adventures in India.

"If the tale about the monkey's paw is not more truthful than those he has been telling us," said Herbert, as the door closed behind their guest, just in time for him to catch the last train, "we shan't make much out of it."

140 "Did you give him anything for it, Father?" inquired Mrs. White, regarding her husband closely.

"A trifle," said he, coloring slightly. "He didn't want it, but I made him take it. And he pressed me again to throw it away."

"Likely," said Herbert, with pretended horror. "Why, we're going to be rich, and famous and happy. Wish to be an emperor, Father, to begin with; then you can't be henpecked."

He darted round the table, pursued by the <u>maligned</u> Mrs. 150 White armed with an antimacassar.[6]

Mr. White took the paw from his pocket and eyed it <u>dubiously</u>. "I don't know what to wish for, and that's a fact," he said slowly. "It seems to me I've got all I want."

---

5. **talisman.** Magic charm
6. **antimacassar.** Cover on a chair or sofa, which prevents soiling

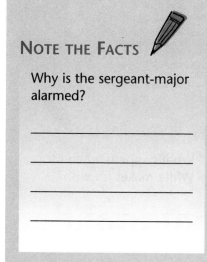

NOTE THE FACTS

Why is the sergeant-major alarmed?

_____

_____

_____

_____

MARK THE TEXT

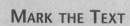

Underline the sentence that tells why Mr. White doesn't know what to wish for.

"If you only cleared the house, you'd be quite happy, wouldn't you?" said Herbert, with his hand on his shoulder. "Well, wish for two hundred pounds, then; that'll just do it."

His father, smiling shamefacedly at his own <u>credulity</u>, held up the talisman, as his son, with a solemn face, somewhat marred by a wink at his mother, sat down at the piano and struck a few impressive chords.

"I wish for two hundred pounds," said the old man distinctly.

A fine crash from the piano greeted the words, interrupted by a shuddering cry from the old man. His wife and son ran toward him.

"It moved," he cried, with a glance of disgust at the object as it lay on the floor. "As I wished, it twisted in my hand like a snake."

"Well, I don't see the money," said his son as he picked it up and placed it on the table, "and I bet I never shall."

"It must have been your fancy, Father," said his wife, regarding him anxiously.

He shook his head. "Never mind, though; there's no harm done, but it gave me a shock all the same."

They sat down by the fire again while the two men finished their pipes. Outside, the wind was higher than ever, and the old man started nervously at the sound of a door banging upstairs. A silence unusual and depressing settled upon all three, which lasted until the old couple rose to retire for the night.

"I expect you'll find the cash tied up in a big bag in the middle of your bed," said Herbert, as he bade them good night, "and something horrible squatting up on top of the wardrobe watching you as you pocket your ill-gotten gains."

He sat alone in the darkness, gazing at the dying fire, and seeing faces in it. The last face was so horrible and so <u>simian</u> that he gazed at it in amazement. It got so vivid that, with a little uneasy laugh, he felt on the table for a glass containing a little water to throw over it. His hand grasped the monkey's paw, and with a little shiver, he wiped his hand on his coat and went up to bed.

words for everyday use	**cre • du • li • ty** (krə dōō´lə tē) *n.*, tendency to believe too readily. *Brian took advantage of his little sister's <u>credulity</u> and told her eating more than three pieces of Halloween candy would make her sick.* **sim • i • an** (sim´ē ən) *adj.*, like an ape or a monkey. *Jake's <u>simian</u> antics made his friends laugh.*

NOTE THE FACTS

What happens when Mr. White makes his wish?

_____

_____

Use **THE STRATEGY**

MAKE PREDICTIONS. Make sure to stop at the end of each page to record foreshadowing, make predictions, and adjust previous predictions.

In the brightness of the wintry sun next morning as it streamed over the breakfast table, he laughed at his fears. There was an air of prosaic wholesomeness about the room that it had lacked on the previous night, and the dirty, shrivelled little paw was pitched on the sideboard with a carelessness which betokened[7] no great belief in its virtues.

"I suppose all old soldiers are the same," said Mrs. White. "The idea of our listening to such nonsense! How could wishes be granted in these days? And if they could, how could two hundred pounds hurt you, Father?"

200

"Might drop on his head from the sky," said the frivolous Herbert.

"Morris said the things happened so naturally," said his father, "that you might if you so wished attribute it to coincidence."

"Well, don't break into the money before I come back," said Herbert as he rose from the table. "I'm afraid it'll turn you into a mean, avaricious man, and we shall have to disown you."

His mother laughed, and following him to the door, watched him down the road; and returning to the breakfast table, was very happy at the expense of her husband's credulity. All of which did not prevent her from scurrying to the door at the postman's knock, nor prevent her from referring somewhat shortly to retired sergeant-majors of bibulous[8] habits when she found that the post brought a tailor's bill.

210

"Herbert will have some more of his funny remarks, I expect, when he comes home," she said, as they sat at dinner.

"I dare say," said Mr. White, pouring himself out some beer. "But for all that, the thing moved in my hand; that I'll swear to."

220

"You thought it did," said the old lady soothingly.

"I say it did," replied the other. "There was no thought

---

7. **betokened.** Indicated
8. **bibulous.** Tending to drink too much

words for everyday use	pro • sa • ic (prō zā´ik) *adj.*, commonplace; dull. *Prosaic objects, such as vases and bowls, are the focus of many still-life paintings.*
	friv • o • lous (friv´ə ləs) *adj.*, not properly serious. *"If you don't change this frivolous attitude toward practicing," warned Mr. Linnehan, "you'll never become a good flute player."*
	at • trib • ute (ə trib´yoot) *vt.*, think of as resulting from. *Chandra attributes her sculpting ability to natural talent and hard work.*
	av • a • ri • cious (av´ə rish´əs) *adj.*, greedy. *Scrooge's avaricious habits left him without friends.*

THINK AND REFLECT

What are the family's feelings about the wish in the morning? **(Infer)**

_____

_____

_____

about it; I had just—What's the matter?"

His wife made no reply. She was watching the mysterious movements of a man outside, who, peering in an undecided fashion at the house, appeared to be trying to make up his mind to enter. In mental connection with the two hundredpounds, she noticed that the stranger was well

230 dressed, and wore a silk hat of glossy newness. Three times he paused at the gate, and then walked on again. The fourth time he stood with his hands upon it, and then with sudden resolution flung it open and walked up the path. Mrs. White at the same moment placed her hands behind her, and hurriedly unfastening the strings of her apron, put that useful article of apparel beneath the cushion of her chair.

She brought the stranger, who seemed ill at ease, into the room. He gazed at her <u>furtively</u>, and listened in a preoccupied fashion as the old lady apologized for the

240 appearance of the room, and her husband's coat, a garment that he usually reserved for the garden. She then waited, as patiently as her sex would permit, for him to broach his business; but he was at first strangely silent.

"I—was asked to call," he said at last, and stooped and picked a piece of cotton from his trousers. "I come from Maw and Meggins."

The old lady started. "Is anything the matter?" she asked breathlessly. "Has anything happened to Herbert? What is it? What is it?"

250 Her husband interposed. "There, there, Mother," he said hastily. "Sit down, and don't jump to conclusions. You've not brought bad news, I'm sure, sir," and he eyed the other wistfully.

"I'm sorry—" began the visitor.

"Is he hurt?" demanded the mother wildly.

The visitor bowed in assent. "Badly hurt," he said quietly, "but he is not in any pain."

"Oh, thank God!" said the old woman, clasping her hands. "Thank God for that! Thank—"

260 She broke off suddenly as the sinister meaning of the

> **words for everyday use**
> **fur • tive • ly** (fur´tiv lē) _adv._, stealthily; not openly. _Kim looked around <u>furtively</u> before dropping her suggestion in the suggestion box._

assurance dawned upon her, and she saw the awful confirmation of her fears in the other's <u>averted</u> face. She caught her breath, and turning to her slower-witted husband, laid her trembling old hand upon his. There was a long silence.

"He was caught in the machinery," said the visitor at length in a low voice.

"Caught in the machinery," repeated Mr. White, in a dazed fashion, "yes."

270 He sat staring blankly out at the window, and taking his wife's hand between his own, pressed it as he had been wont to do in their old courting days nearly forty years before.

"He was the only one left to us," he said, turning gently to the visitor. "It is hard."

The other coughed, and rising, walked slowly to the window. "The firm wished me to convey their sincere sympathy with you in your great loss," he said, without looking round. "I beg that you will understand I am only their servant and merely obeying orders."

280 There was no reply. The old woman's face was white, her eyes staring, and her breath <u>inaudible</u>. On the husband's face was a look such as his friend the sergeant-major might have carried into his first action.

"I was to say that Maw and Meggins disclaim all responsibility," continued the other. "They admit no <u>liability</u> at all, but in consideration of your son's services, they wish to present you with a certain sum as <u>compensation</u>."

Mr. White dropped his wife's hand, and rising to his feet, gazed with a look of horror at his visitor. His dry lips shaped

290 the words, "How much?"

"Two hundred pounds," was the answer.

Unconscious of his wife's shriek, the old man smiled faintly, put out his hands like a sightless man, and dropped, a senseless heap, to the floor.

In the huge new cemetery, some two miles distant, the old

NOTE THE FACTS

How does the first wish come true?

_____

_____

_____

_____

people buried their dead, and came back to a house steeped in shadow and silence. It was all over so quickly that at first they could hardly realize it, and remained in a state of expectation as though of something else to happen—

300 something else that was to lighten this load, too heavy for old hearts to bear.

But the days passed, and expectation gave place to resignation—the hopeless resignation of the old, sometimes miscalled <u>apathy</u>. Sometimes they hardly exchanged a word, for now they had nothing to talk about, and their days were long to weariness.

It was about a week after, that the old man, waking suddenly in the night, stretched out his hand and found himself alone. The room was in darkness, and the sound of <u>subdued</u> weeping

310 came from the window. He raised himself in bed and listened.

"Come back," he said tenderly. "You will be cold."

"It is colder for my son," said the old woman, and wept afresh.

The sound of her sobs died away on his ears. The bed was warm, and his eyes heavy with sleep. He dozed fitfully, and then slept, until a sudden wild cry from his wife awoke him with a start.

"The paw!" she cried wildly. "The monkey's paw!"

He started up in alarm. "Where? Where is it? What's the

320 matter?"

She came stumbling across the room toward him. "I want it," she said quietly. "You've not destroyed it?"

"It's in the parlor, on the bracket," he replied, marvelling. "Why?"

She cried and laughed together, and bending over, kissed his cheek.

"I only just thought of it," she said hysterically. "Why didn't I think of it before? Why didn't *you* think of it?"

"Think of what?" he questioned.

330 "The other two wishes," she replied rapidly. "We've only had one."

"Was not that enough?" he demanded fiercely.

| words for everyday use | **ap • a • thy** (ap´ə thē) *n.,* indifference; lack of emotion. *The media blamed low voter turnout on citizens' <u>apathy</u> over the mayoral candidates.*

sub • dued (səb dōō´d) *part.,* diminished; lessened in intensity. *The art exhibit balanced the intense colors of Monica's oil paintings with the more <u>subdued</u> tones of Vanessa's watercolors.* |

"No," she cried triumphantly. "We'll have one more. Go down and get it quickly, and wish our boy alive again."

The man sat up in bed and flung the bedclothes from his quaking limbs. "Good God, you are mad!" he cried, aghast.

"Get it," she panted. "Get it quickly, and wish—Oh, my boy, my boy!"

340   Her husband struck a match and lit the candle. "Get back to bed," he said unsteadily. "You don't know what you are saying."

"We had the first wish granted," said the old woman feverishly. "Why not the second?"

"A coincidence," stammered the old man.

"Go and get it and wish," cried his wife, quivering with excitement.

The old man turned and regarded her, and his voice shook. "He has been dead ten days, and besides he—I would
350   not tell you else, but—I could only recognize him by his clothing. If he was too terrible for you to see then, how now?"

"Bring him back," cried the old woman, and dragged him toward the door. "Do you think I fear the child I have nursed?"

He went down in the darkness, and felt his way to the parlor, and then to the mantelpiece. The talisman was in its place, and a horrible fear that the unspoken wish might bring his mutilated son before him ere he could escape
360   from the room seized upon him, and he caught his breath as he found that he had lost the direction of the door. His brow cold with sweat, he felt his way round the table, and groped along the wall until he found himself in the small passage with the unwholesome thing in his hand.

Even his wife's face seemed changed as he entered the room. It was white and expectant, and to his fears, seemed to have an unnatural look upon it. He was afraid of her.

"*Wish!*" she cried, in a strong voice.

"It is foolish and wicked," he faltered.

370   "*Wish!*" repeated his wife.

He raised his hand. "I wish my son alive again."

The talisman fell to the floor, and he regarded it fearfully. Then he sank trembling into a chair as the old woman, with burning eyes, walked to the window and raised the blind.

He sat until he was chilled with the cold, glancing

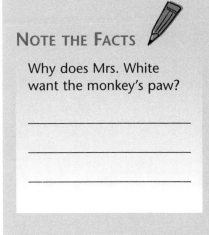

NOTE THE FACTS

Why does Mrs. White want the monkey's paw?

_____

_____

_____

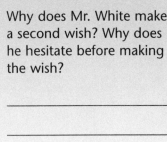

READ ALOUD

Read aloud the highlighted text on this page. What fear does Mr. White have?

_____

_____

NOTE THE FACTS

Why does Mr. White make a second wish? Why does he hesitate before making the wish?

_____

_____

_____

_____

occasionally at the figure of the old woman peering through the window. The candle-end, which had burned below the rim of the china candlestick, was throwing pulsating shadows on the ceiling and walls, until, with a flicker larger than the rest, it expired. The old man, with an unspeakable sense of relief at the failure of the talisman, crept back to his bed, and a minute or two afterward the old woman came silently and apathetically beside him.

Neither spoke, but lay silently listening to the ticking of the clock. A stair creaked, and a squeaky mouse scurried noisily through the wall. The darkness was <u>oppressive</u>, and after lying for some time screwing up his courage, he took the box of matches, and striking one, went downstairs for a candle.

At the foot of the stairs the match went out, and he paused to strike another; and at the same moment a knock, so quiet and stealthy as to be scarcely audible, sounded on the front door.

The matches fell from his hand and spilled in the passage. He stood motionless, his breath suspended until the knock was repeated. Then he turned and fled swiftly back to his room, and closed the door behind him. A third knock sounded through the house.

"*What's that?*" cried the old woman, starting up.

"A rat," said the old man in shaking tones—"a rat. It passed me on the stairs."

His wife sat up in bed listening. A loud knock resounded through the house.

"It's Herbert!" she screamed. "It's Herbert!"

She ran to the door, but her husband was before her, and catching her by the arm, held her tightly.

"What are you going to do?" he whispered hoarsely.

"It's my boy; it's Herbert!" she cried, struggling mechanically. "I forgot it was two miles away. What are you holding me for? Let go. I must open the door."

"For God's sake, don't let it in," cried the old man, trembling.

"You're afraid of your own son," she cried, struggling.

DRAW A PICTURE

380

390

400

410

"Let me go. I'm coming, Herbert; I'm coming."

There was another knock, and another. The old woman, with a sudden wrench, broke free and ran from the room. Her husband followed to the landing, and called after her appealingly as she hurried downstairs. He heard the chain rattle back and the bottom bolt drawn slowly and stiffly from the socket. Then the old woman's voice, strained and 420 panting.

"The bolt," she cried loudly. "Come down. I can't reach it."

But her husband was on his hands and knees, groping wildly on the floor in search of the paw. If he could only find it before the thing outside got in. A perfect fusillade[9] of knocks <u>reverberated</u> through the house, and he heard the scraping of a chair as his wife put it down in the passage against the door. He heard the creaking of the bolt as it came slowly back, and at the same moment he found the monkey's paw, and frantically breathed his third and 430 last wish.

The knocking ceased suddenly, although the echoes of it were still in the house. He heard the chair drawn back, and the door opened. A cold wind rushed up the staircase, and a long, loud wail of disappointment and misery from his wife gave him courage to run down to her side, and then to the gate beyond. The street lamp flickering opposite shone on a quiet and deserted road. ∎

---

9. **fusillade.** Simultaneous discharge of many firearms

words for everyday use

re • ver • ber • ate (ri vʉr´bə rāt´) *vi.*, resound; echo. *Must you play your music so loudly that it <u>reverberates</u> throughout the whole house?*

THINK AND REFLECT

Why is the man afraid to open the door? **(Interpret)**

_____

_____

_____

_____

THINK AND REFLECT

What was Mr. White's third wish? **(Infer)**

_____

_____

_____

Reflect ON YOUR READING

When you finish your Predictions Chart, review the foreshadowing you recorded. Then, write a paragraph discussing how foreshadowing helped create the suspenseful, foreboding mood in the story. Share your paragraph with a partner, and discuss how the foreshadowing and atmosphere affected your reading experience.

THINK-ALOUD NOTES

_____

_____

_____

_____

_____

_____

_____

_____

_____

Reading Skills and Test Practice

ANALYZE LITERARY ELEMENTS

READ, THINK, AND EXPLAIN. How do the setting and the foreshadowing work together to create a suspenseful, foreboding mood? Support your answer with evidence from the text. Use your own paper as needed.

_____

_____

REFLECT ON YOUR RESPONSE. Compare your response with that of your partner and talk about how the information you wrote down while reading helped form your response.

_____

_____

Investigate, Inquire, and Imagine

RECALL: GATHER FACTS
1a. What spell was put on the monkey's paw by a fakir? Why did the fakir put the spell on the paw?

➤ **INTERPRET: FIND MEANING**
1b. What relationship between human life and fate is described in this story? How are the fakir's ideas about fate proved true?

ANALYZE: TAKE THINGS APART
2a. What human weaknesses are revealed by members of the White family in this story?

➤ **SYNTHESIZE: BRING THINGS TOGETHER**
2b. Why does Mr. White make a third wish?

EVALUATE: MAKE JUDGMENTS
3a. Who believes most strongly in the power of the monkey's paw—Sergeant-Major Morris, Mr. White, or Mrs. White? Explain your answer.

➤ **EXTEND: CONNECT IDEAS**
3b. Do you believe fate, coincidence, or humans will determine your future? Explain your answer.

Literary Tools

SETTING. The **setting** of a literary work is the time and place in which it occurs, together with all the details used to create a sense of a particular time and place. Complete the cluster chart below to describe the setting. One example has been done for you.

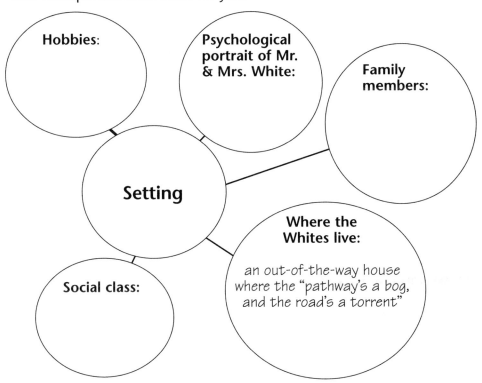

WordWorkshop

WORD ROOTS. **Word roots** are word parts that cannot stand alone but that have meaning that can aid you in deciphering the meanings of words that you don't know. A helpful clue about word roots: when you strip away the prefix and/or suffix from a word, you are left with a word root.

EXAMPLE
apathy   (word root: *path,* meaning feeling or suffering)

prefix: *a,* meaning not or without
suffix: *y,* meaning characterized by
word meaning: characterized by not feeling or by not suffering

Several of the Words for Everyday Use for this selection contain commonly used Greek and Latin word roots. For each of the words below, define the prefix and/or suffix that joins with the word root. Then, define the complete word as a sum of its parts. The meaning of the word root for each word has been given. Compare your derived definitions with those given in the Words for Everyday Use boxes in your textbook. For a list of prefixes and suffixes and their definitions, see Unit 9, pages 482–484.

1. amiably (word root: *am/ami*, meaning love or friend)

   _____

2. compensation (word root: *pen/pend*, meaning weigh; estimate; pay; hang)

   _____

3. credulity (word root: *cred*, meaning believe or trust)

   _____

4. inaudible (word root: *aud*, meaning hear)

   _____

5. provoke (word root: *voc/vok*, meaning voice; call)

   _____

Read-Write Connection

Imagine that you are Mr. White. Reflect on the night of Sergeant-Major Morris's visit, when he brought the monkey's paw to your home. Explain how your view of the monkey's paw changed after that.

_____

_____

_____

_____

_____

_____

_____

_____

Beyond the Reading

RESEARCH FATE. Research the concept of fate as it is expressed in the literature, religions, and philosophy of various cultures. What does fate mean to you? Do you believe in fate? Why, or why not?

GO ONLINE. Visit the EMC Internet Resource Center at **emcp.com** to find links and additional activities for this selection.

"To Build a Fire"

by Jack London

Active READING STRATEGY

WRITE THINGS DOWN

Before Reading ▶ PREVIEW THE SELECTION

- ❏ Read the Reader's Resource. Then, discuss with a few of your classmates the kind of person who likely would have traveled to the Yukon for the gold rush.
- ❏ In the first column of the Character Chart below list physical traits and personality traits you would expect such a person to have.
- ❏ As you read the selection, you will check any traits that apply to the main character.
- ❏ In the third column, you will add traits the man has that are not helpful to a gold prospector in the Yukon.

Graphic Organizer

Physical and Personality Traits	Traits of Main Character	Traits That Are Not Helpful

CONNECT

Reader's *resource*

One of hundreds of thousands of people who joined the Klondike Gold Rush in the late 1890s, Jack London (1876–1916) had firsthand experience surviving a winter in the Yukon, a region in northwest Canada and the setting of **"To Build a Fire,"** published in 1908. These daring adventurers stormed north to Alaska, carrying heavy loads over steep snow-covered trails, building boats and trying not to drown in life-threatening rapids, surviving scurvy and frigid temperatures, all on the hopes of becoming rich. London was a master storyteller and published many stories, plays, and novels during his short but spirited life.

Word watch

PREVIEW VOCABULARY

agitation	nucleus
apathetically	pall
apprehension	peremptorily
conflagration	poignant
conjectural	reiterate
ebb	thresh
imperative	undulation

Reader's *journal*

How do you know when to listen to someone's advice and when to follow your own ideas instead?

_____

_____

Write Things Down

- ❏ Follow along in the text as your teacher reads the first three paragraphs aloud.
- ❏ Discuss with your classmates what kind of person the man is.
- ❏ Make notes in your chart about the man's traits.
- ❏ Read the remainder of the selection on your own. Continue recording information about the main character as you read.

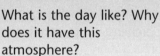

Note the Facts

What is the day like? Why does it have this atmosphere?

_____

_____

_____

_____

To Build a Fire

Jack London

Day had broken cold and grey, exceedingly cold and grey, when the man turned aside frm the main Yukon[1] and climbed the high earth-bank, where a dim and little-traveled trail led eastward through the fat spruce timber-land. It was a steep bank, and he paused for breath at the top, excusing the act to himself by looking at his watch. It was nine o'clock. There was no sun nor hint of sun, though there was not a cloud in the sky. It was a clear day, and yet there seemed an intangible <u>pall</u> over the face of things, a

10   subtle gloom that made the day dark, and that was due to the absence of sun. This fact did not worry the man. He was used to the lack of sun. It had been days since he had seen the sun, and he knew that a few more days must pass before that cheerful orb, due south, would just peep above the sky-line and dip immediately from view.

---

1. **Yukon.** Territory and river in northwestern Canada

words for everyday use   **pall** (pôl) *n.,* covering that obscures or cloaks gloomily. *A heavy <u>pall</u> of disappointment hung over the crowd after they heard the announcement that the band would not play.*

The man flung a look back along the way he had come. The Yukon lay a mile wide and hidden under three feet of ice. On top of this ice were as many feet of snow. It was all pure white, rolling in gentle <u>undulations</u> where the ice jams of the freeze-up had formed. North and south, as far as his eye could see, it was unbroken white, save for a dark hairline that curved and twisted from around the spruce-covered island to the south, and that curved and twisted away into the north, where it disappeared behind another spruce-covered island. This dark hairline was the trail—the main trail—that led south five hundred miles to the Chilcoot Pass, Dyea,[2] and salt water; and that led north seventy miles to Dawson, and still on to the north a thousand miles to Nulato,[3] and finally to St. Michael on Bering Sea, a thousand miles and half a thousand more.

But all this—the mysterious, far-reaching hairline trail, the absence of sun from the sky, the tremendous cold, and the strangeness and weirdness of it all—made no impression on the man. It was not because he was long used to it. He was a newcomer in the land, a *chechaquo*,[4] and this was his first winter. The trouble with him was that he was without imagination. He was quick and alert in the things of life, but only in the things, and not in the significances. Fifty degrees below zero meant eighty-odd degrees of frost. Such fact impressed him as being cold and uncomfortable, and that was all. It did not lead him to meditate upon his frailty as a creature of temperature, and upon man's frailty in general, able only to live within certain narrow limits of heat and cold; and from there on it did not lead him to the <u>conjectural</u> field of immortality and man's place in the universe. Fifty degrees below zero stood for a bite of frost that hurt and that must be guarded against by the use of mittens, earflaps, warm moccasins, and thick socks. Fifty degrees below zero was to him just precisely fifty degrees

---

2. **Chilcoot Pass, Dyea.** *Chilcoot Pass*—mountain pass leading to the Klondike; *Dyea*—once a town in Alaska that marked the beginning of the Yukon trail
3. **Dawson . . . Nulato.** Gold-mining towns in the Yukon
4. *chechaquo.* Newcomer

MARK THE TEXT

Underline or highlight the sentences that tell what the man's limitations are.

words for everyday use	**un • du • la • tion** (un´dyo͞o lā´shən) *n.,* wave; curve. *The <u>undulations</u> of the water reached our dangling feet.* **con • jec • tur • al** (kən jek´chər əl) *adj.,* based on guesses. *The study of the universe is highly <u>conjectural</u>, based as it is on theories.*

below zero. That there should be anything more to it than that was a thought that never entered his head.

As he turned to go on, he spat speculatively. There was a sharp, explosive crackle that startled him. He spat again. And again, in the air, before it could fall to the snow, the spittle crackled. He knew that at fifty below spittle crackled on the snow, but this spittle had crackled in the air. Undoubtedly it was colder than fifty below—how much colder he did not know. But the temperature did not matter. He was bound for the old claim on the left fork of Henderson Creek, where the boys were already. They had come over across the divide from the Indian Creek country, while he had come the roundabout way to take a look at the possibilities of getting out logs in the spring from the islands in the Yukon. He would be in to camp by six o'clock: a bit after dark, it was true, but the boys would be there, a fire would be going, and a hot supper would be ready. As for lunch, he pressed his hand against the protruding bundle under his jacket. It was also under his shirt, wrapped up in a handkerchief and lying against the naked skin. It was the only way to keep the biscuits from freezing. He smiled agreeably to himself as he thought of those biscuits, each cut open and sopped in bacon grease, and each enclosing a generous slice of fried bacon.

He plunged in among the big spruce trees. The trail was faint. A foot of snow had fallen since the last sled had passed over, and he was glad he was without a sled, traveling light. In fact, he carried nothing but the lunch wrapped in the handkerchief. He was surprised, however, at the cold. It certainly was cold, he concluded, as he rubbed his numb nose and cheekbones with his mittened hand. He was a warm-whiskered man, but the hair on his face did not protect the high cheekbones and the eager nose that thrust itself aggressively into the frosty air.

At the man's heels trotted a dog, a big native husky, the proper wolf dog, gray-coated and without any visible or temperamental difference from its brother, the wild wolf. The animal was depressed by the tremendous cold. It knew that it was no time for traveling. Its instinct told it a truer tale than was told to the man by the man's judgment. In reality, it was not merely colder than fifty below zero: it

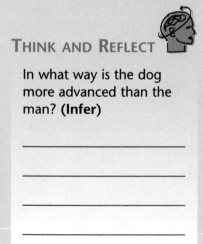

NOTE THE FACTS

What is the man's errand?

_____

_____

_____

THINK AND REFLECT

In what way is the dog more advanced than the man? **(Infer)**

_____

_____

_____

_____

was colder than sixty below, than seventy below. It was seventy-five below zero. Since the freezing point is thirty-two above zero, it meant that one hundred and seven degrees of frost obtained. The dog did not know anything about thermometers. Possibly in its brain there was no sharp consciousness of a condition of very cold such as was in the man's brain. But the brute had its instinct. It experienced a vague but menacing <u>apprehension</u> that subdued it and made it slink along at the man's heels, and that made it

100 question eagerly every unwonted movement of the man as if expecting him to go into camp or to seek shelter somewhere and build a fire. The dog had learned fire, and it wanted fire, or else to burrow under the snow and cuddle its warmth away from the air.

The frozen moisture of its breathing had settled on its fur in a fine powder of frost, and especially were its jowls, muzzle, and eyelashes whitened by its crystalled breath. The man's red beard and mustache were likewise frosted, but more solidly, the deposit taking the form of ice and

110 increasing with every warm, moist breath he exhaled. Also, the man was chewing tobacco, and the muzzle of ice held his lips so rigidly that he was unable to clear his chin when he expelled the juice. The result was that a crystal beard of the color and solidity of amber was increasing its length on his chin. If he fell down it would shatter itself, like glass, into brittle fragments. But he did not mind the appendage. It was the penalty all tobacco chewers paid in that country, and he had been out before in two cold snaps. They had not been so cold as this, he knew, but by the spirit thermometer[5]

120 at Sixty Mile he knew they had been registered at fifty below and at fifty-five.

He held on through the level stretch of woods for several miles, crossed a wide flat, and dropped down a bank to the frozen bed of a small stream. This was Henderson Creek, and he knew he was ten miles from the forks. He looked at his

5. **spirit thermometer.** Thermometer that uses alcohol instead of mercury because of the lower freezing point of alcohol

words for everyday use

ap • pre • hen • sion (ap´rē hen´shən) n., anxiety, dread. *Brett's <u>apprehension</u> mounted as the ski lift reached one thousand feet.*

NOTE THE FACTS

What signals to the man that it is much colder than he estimated?

_____

_____

_____

_____

CONFLICT. A **conflict** is a struggle between two forces in a literary work. One side of the central conflict in a work of fiction is usually taken by the main character. That character may struggle against another character, against the forces of nature, against society or social norms, against fate, or against some elements within himself or herself. A struggle that takes place between a character and some outside force is called an *external conflict*. A struggle that takes place within a character is called an *internal conflict*. As you read, think about what kind of conflict takes place in this story.

THINK AND REFLECT

What responses does the man have toward the cold? What does he think about to motivate himself to continue? **(Interpret)**

_____

_____

_____

_____

watch. It was ten o'clock. He was making four miles an hour, and he calculated that he would arrive at the forks at half past twelve. He decided to celebrate that event by eating his lunch there.

130   The dog dropped in again at his heels, with a tail drooping discouragement, as the man swung along the creek bed. The furrow of the old sled trail was plainly visible, but a dozen inches of snow covered the marks of the last runners. In a month no man had come up or down that silent creek. The man held steadily on. He was not much given to thinking, and just then particularly he had nothing to think about save that he would eat lunch at the forks and that at six o'clock he would be in camp with the boys. There was nobody to talk to; and, had there been, speech would have been impossible

140   because of the ice-muzzle on his mouth. So he continued monotonously to chew tobacco and to increase the length of his amber beard.

Once in a while the thought <u>reiterated</u> itself that it was very cold and that he had never experienced such cold. As he walked along he rubbed his cheekbones and nose with the back of his mittened hand. He did this automatically, now and again changing hands. But rub as he would, the instant he stopped his cheekbones went numb, and the following instant the end of his nose went numb. He was sure to frost his

150   cheeks; he knew that, and experienced a pang of regret that he had not devised a nose strap of the sort Bud wore in cold snaps. Such a strap passed across the cheeks, as well, and saved them. But it didn't matter much, after all. What were frosted cheeks? A bit painful, that was all: they were never serious.

Empty as the man's mind was of thoughts, he was keenly observant, and he noticed the changes in the creek, the curves and bends and timber jams, and always he sharply noted where he placed his feet. Once, coming around a bend, he shied abruptly, like a startled horse, curved away from the

160   place where he had been walking, and retreated several paces back along the trail. The creek he knew was frozen clear to the bottom—no creek could contain water in that arctic

words for everyday use   re • it • er • ate (rē it′ ə rāt′) *vt.*, repeat. *The teachers <u>reiterated</u> to the principal their argument for smaller class sizes.*

winter—but he knew also that there were springs that bubbled out from the hillsides and ran along under the snow and on top the ice of the creek. He knew that the coldest snaps never froze these springs, and he knew likewise their danger. They were traps. They hid pools of water under the snow that might be three inches deep, or three feet. Sometimes a skin of ice half an inch thick covered them, and in turn was covered by the snow. Sometimes there were alternate layers of water and ice skin, so that when one broke through he kept on breaking through for a while, sometimes wetting himself to the waist.

That was why he had shied in such panic. He had felt the give under his feet and heard the crackle of a snow-hidden ice skin. And to get his feet wet in such a temperature meant trouble and danger. At the very least it meant delay, for he would be forced to stop and build a fire, and under its protection to bare his feet while he dried his socks and moccasins. He stood and studied the creek bed and its banks, and decided that the flow of water came from the right. He reflected awhile, rubbing his nose and cheeks, then skirted to the left, stepping gingerly and testing the footing for each step. Once clear of the danger, he took a fresh chew of tobacco and swung along at his four-mile gait.

In the course of the next two hours he came upon several similar traps. Usually the snow above the hidden pools had a sunken, candied appearance that advertised the danger. Once again, however, he had a close call; and once, suspecting danger, he compelled the dog to go on in front. The dog did not want to go. It hung back until the man shoved it forward, and then it went quickly across the white, unbroken surface. Suddenly it broke through, floundered to one side, and got away to firmer footing. It had wet its forefeet and legs, and almost immediately the water that clung to it turned to ice. It made quick efforts to lick the ice off its legs, then dropped down in the snow and began to bite out the ice that had formed between the toes. This was a matter of instinct. To permit the ice to remain would mean sore feet. It did not know this. It merely obeyed the mysterious prompting that arose from the deep crypts of its being. But the man knew, having achieved a judgment on the subject, and he removed the mitten from his right hand and helped tear out the ice particles. He did not expose his fingers more than a minute,

NOTE THE FACTS

What danger does the man know?

_____

_____

_____

_____

Use THE STRATEGY

WRITE THINGS DOWN. As you read, make sure to stop at the end of each page to record information about the main character in your chart.

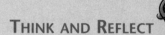

Think and Reflect

How does the man feel about what he has been told now? **(Interpret)**

_____

_____

_____

_____

and was astonished at the swift numbness that smote them. It certainly was cold. He pulled on the mitten hastily, and beat the hand savagely across his chest.

At twelve o'clock the day was at its brightest. Yet the sun was too far south on its winter journey to clear the horizon. 210 The bulge of the earth intervened between it and Henderson Creek, where the man walked under a clear sky at noon and cast no shadow. At half-past twelve, to the minute, he arrived at the forks of the creek. He was pleased at the speed he had made. If he kept it up, he would certainly be with the boys by six. He unbuttoned his jacket and shirt and drew forth his lunch. The action consumed no more than a quarter of a minute, yet in that brief moment the numbness laid hold of the exposed fingers. He did not put the mitten on, but, instead, struck the fingers a dozen sharp smashes against his 220 leg. Then he sat down on a snowcovered log to eat. The sting that followed upon the striking of his fingers against his leg ceased so quickly that he was startled. He had had no chance to take a bite of biscuit. He struck the fingers repeatedly and returned them to the mitten, baring the other hand for the purpose of eating. He tried to take a mouthful. but the ice muzzle prevented. He had forgotten to build a fire and thaw out. He chuckled at his foolishness, and as he chuckled he noted the numbness creeping into the exposed fingers. Also, he noted that the stinging which had first come 230 to his toes when he sat down was already passing away. He wondered whether the toes were warm or numb. He moved them inside the moccasins and decided that they were numb.

He pulled the mitten on hurriedly and stood up. He was a bit frightened. He stamped up and down until the stinging returned into the feet. It certainly was cold, was his thought. That man from Sulphur Creek had spoken the truth when telling how cold it sometimes got in the country. And he had laughed at him at the time! That showed one must not be too sure of things. There was no mistake about it, it was cold. 240 He strode up and down, stamping his feet and <u>threshing</u> his arms, until reassured by the returning warmth. Then he got out matches and proceeded to make a fire. From the under-growth, where high water of the previous spring had lodged a supply of seasoned twigs, he got his firewood. Working carefully from a small beginning, he soon had a roaring fire, over which he thawed the ice from his face and in the protection of which he ate his biscuits. For the moment the cold of space was outwitted. The dog took satisfaction in the fire, stretching out close enough for warmth and far enough away to escape being singed.

When the man had finished, he filled his pipe and took his comfortable time over a smoke. Then he pulled on his mittens, settled the earflaps of his cap firmly about his ears, and took the creek trail up the left fork. The dog was disappointed and yearned back toward the fire. This man did not know cold. Possibly all the generations of his ancestry had been ignorant of cold, of real cold, of cold one hundred and seven degrees below freezing point. But the dog knew; all its ancestry knew, and it had inherited the knowledge. And it knew that it was not good to walk abroad in such fearful cold. It was the time to lie snug in a hole in the snow and wait for a curtain of cloud to be drawn across the face of outer space whence this cold came. On the other hand, there was no keen intimacy between the dog and the man. The one was the toil slave of the other, and the only caresses it had ever received were the caresses of the whiplash and of harsh and menacing throat sounds that threatened the whiplash. So the dog made no effort to communicate its apprehension to the man. It was not concerned in the welfare of the man; it was for its own sake that it yearned back toward the fire. But the man whistled, and spoke to it with the sound of whiplashes, and the dog swung in at the man's heels and followed after.

The man took a chew of tobacco and proceeded to start a new amber beard. Also, his moist breath quickly powdered with white his mustache, eyebrows, and lashes. There did not seem to be so many springs on the left fork of the Henderson, and for half an hour the man saw no signs of any. And then it happened. At a place where there were no signs, where the soft, unbroken snow seemed to advertise solidity beneath, the man broke through. It was not deep. He wet himself halfway to the knees before he floundered out to the firm crust.

250

260

270

280

READ ALOUD

Reread the highlighted passage aloud. What does the dog think should happen?

_____

_____

_____

_____

NOTE THE FACTS

What happens unexpectedly?

_____

_____

_____

_____

NOTE THE FACTS

What does the man see as the negative consequences of his accident?

_____

_____

_____

_____

ASK A QUESTION

_____

_____

He was angry, and cursed his luck aloud. He had hoped to get into camp with the boys at six o'clock, and this would delay him an hour, for he would have to build a fire and dry out his footgear. This was <u>imperative</u> at that low temperature —he knew that much; and he turned aside to the bank, which he climbed. On top, tangled in the underbrush about the trunks of several small spruce trees, was a high-water deposit of dry firewood—sticks and twigs, principally, but also larger portions of seasoned branches and fine, dry, last year's grasses. He threw down several large pieces on top of the snow. This served for a foundation and prevented the young flame from drowning itself in the snow it otherwise would melt. The flame he got by touching a match to a small shred of birch bark that he took from his pocket. This burned even more readily than paper. Placing it on the foundation, he fed the young flame with wisps of dry grass and with the tiniest dry twigs.

He worked slowly and carefully, keenly aware of his danger. Gradually, as the flame grew stronger, he increased the size of the twigs with which he fed it. He squatted in the snow, pulling the twigs out from their entanglement in the brush and feeding directly to the flame. He knew there must be no failure. When it is seventy-five below zero, a man must not fail in his first attempt to build a fire—that is, if his feet are wet. If his feet are dry, and he fails, he can run along the trail for half a mile and restore his circulation. But the circulation of wet and freezing feet cannot be restored by running when it is seventy-five below. No matter how fast one runs, the wet feet will freeze the harder.

All this the man knew. The old-timer on Sulphur Creek had told him about it the previous fall, and now he was appreciating the advice. Already all sensation had gone out of his feet. To build the fire he had been forced to remove his mittens, and the fingers had quickly gone numb. His pace of four miles an hour had kept his heart pumping blood to the surface of his body and to all the extremities. But the instant he stopped, the action of the pump eased down. The cold of

290

300

310

320

words
for
everyday
use

im • per • a • tive (im per´ə tiv) *adj.*, absolutely necessary. *"It is <u>imperative</u> that you be at work when the shift starts,"* the supervisor explained.

space smote the unprotected tip of the planet, and he, being on that unprotected tip, received the full force of the blow. The blood of his body recoiled before it. The blood was alive, like the dog, and like the dog it wanted to hide away and cover itself up from the fearful cold. So long as he walked four miles an hour, he pumped that blood, willy-nilly, to the surface; but now it ebbed away and sank down into the recesses of his body. The extremities were the first to feel its absence. His wet feet froze the faster, and his exposed fingers

330 numbed the faster, though they had not yet begun to freeze. Nose and cheeks were already freezing, while the skin of all his body chilled as it lost its blood.

But he was safe. Toes and nose and cheeks would be only touched by the frost, for the fire was beginning to burn with strength. He was feeding it with twigs the size of his finger. In another minute he would be able to feed it with branches the size of his wrist, and then he could remove his wet foot-gear, and, while it dried, he could keep his naked feet

340 warm by the fire, rubbing them at first, of course, with snow. The fire was a success. He was safe. He remembered the advice of the old-timer on Sulphur Creek, and smiled. The old-timer had been very serious in laying down the law that no man must travel alone in the Klondike after fifty below. Well, here he was; he had had the accident; he was alone; and he had saved himself. Those old-timers were rather woman-ish, some of them, he thought. All a man had to do was to keep his head, and he was all right. Any man who was a man could travel alone. But it was surprising, the rapidity with

350 which his cheeks and nose were freezing. And he had not thought his fingers could go lifeless in so short a time. Lifeless they were, for he could scarcely make them move together to grip a twig, and they seemed remote from his body and from him. When he touched a twig, he had to look and see whether or not he had hold of it. The wires were pretty well down between him and his finger ends.

All of which counted for little. There was the fire, snapping and crackling and promising life with every dancing flame.

words for everyday use

ebb (eb) *vi.*, flow back; recede. *The tide ebbed, taking a bottle out to sea.*

MARK THE TEXT

Underline or highlight the sentences that compare the man's blood to something else.

THINK AND REFLECT

What does the fire symbolize in such cold? (Interpret)

_____

_____

He started to untie his moccasins. They were coated with ice; the thick German socks were like sheaths of iron halfway to the knees; and the moccasin strings were like rods of steel all twisted and knotted as by some <u>conflagration</u>. For a moment he tugged with his numb fingers, then, realizing the folly of it, he drew his sheath-knife.

But before he could cut the strings, it happened. It was his own fault or, rather, his mistake. He should not have built the fire under the spruce tree. He should have built it in the open. But it had been easier to pull the twigs from the brush and drop them directly on the fire. Now the tree under which he had done this carried a weight of snow on its boughs. No wind had blown for weeks, and each bough was fully freighted. Each time he had pulled a twig he had communicated a slight <u>agitation</u> to the tree—an imperceptible agitation, so far as he was concerned, but an agitation sufficient to bring about the disaster. High up in the tree one bough capsized its load of snow. This fell on the boughs beneath, capsizing them. This process continued, spreading out and involving the whole tree. It grew like an avalanche, and it descended without warning upon the man and the fire, and the fire was blotted out! Where it had burned was a mantle of fresh and disordered snow.

The man was shocked. It was as though he had just heard his own sentence of death. For a moment he sat and stared at the spot where the fire had been. Then he grew very calm. Perhaps the old-timer on Sulphur Creek was right. If he had only had a trail mate he would have been in no danger now. The trail mate could have built the fire. Well, it was up to him to build the fire over again, and this second time there must be no failure. Even if he succeeded, he would most likely lose some toes. His feet must be badly frozen by now, and there would be some time before the second fire was ready.

Such were his thoughts, but he did not sit and think them. He was busy all the time they were passing through

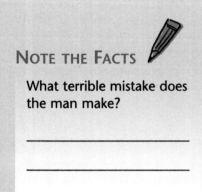

What terrible mistake does the man make?

_____

_____

words for everyday use	con • fla • gra • tion (kän´flə grā´shən) n., destructive fire. *Fire stations from ten towns were called out to fight the <u>conflagration</u> in Ashton.*
	ag • i • ta • tion (aj´ə tā´shən) n., appreciable motion or disturbance. *The <u>agitation</u> of the washing machine made the box of detergent fall on the floor.*

his mind. He made a new foundation for a fire, this time in the open, where no treacherous tree could blot it out. Next, he gathered dry grasses and tiny twigs from the high-water flotsam.[6] He could not bring his fingers together to pull them out, but he was able to gather them by the handful. In this way he got many rotten twigs and bits of green moss that were undesirable, but it was the best he could do. He worked methodically, even collecting an armful of the larger branches to be used later when the fire gathered strength. And all the while the dog sat and watched him, a certain yearning wistfulness in its eyes, for it looked upon him as the fire provider, and the fire was slow in coming.

When all was ready, the man reached in his pocket for a second piece of birch bark. He knew the bark was there, and, though he could not feel it with his fingers, he could hear its crisp rustling as he fumbled for it. Try as he would, he could not clutch hold of it. And all the time, in his consciousness, was the knowledge that each instant his feet were freezing. This thought tended to put him in a panic, but he fought against it and kept calm. He pulled on his mittens with his teeth, and threshed his arms back and forth, beating his hands with all his might against his sides. He did this sitting down, and he stood up to do it; and all the while the dog sat in the snow, its wolf brush of a tail curled around warmly over its forefeet, its sharp wolf ears pricked forward intently as it watched the man. And the man, as he beat and threshed with his arms and hands, felt a great surge of envy as he regarded the creature that was warm and secure in its natural covering.

After a time he was aware of the first faraway signals of sensation in his beaten fingers. The faint tingling grew stronger till it evolved into a stinging ache that was excruciating, but which the man hailed with satisfaction. He stripped the mitten from his right hand and fetched forth the birch bark. The exposed fingers were quickly going numb again. Next he brought out his bunch of sulphur matches. But the tremendous cold had already driven the life out of his fingers. In his effort to separate one match from the others, the whole bunch fell in the snow. He tried to pick it out of the snow, but failed. The dead fingers could neither touch

NOTE THE FACTS

What does the man feel is happening? What is his reaction?

_____

_____

_____

_____

6. **flotsam.** Odds and ends washed up by the water

nor clutch. He was very careful. He drove the thought of his freezing feet, and nose, and cheeks, out of his mind, devoting his whole soul to the matches. He watched, using the sense of vision in place of that of touch, and when he saw his fingers on each side the bunch, he closed them—that is, he willed to close them, for the wires were down, and the fingers did not obey. He pulled the mitten on the right hand, and beat it fiercely against his knee. Then, with both mittened hands, he scooped the bunch of matches, along with much snow, into his lap. Yet he was no better off.

After some manipulation he managed to get the bunch between the heels of his mittened hands. In this fashion he carried it to his mouth. The ice crackled and snapped when by a violent effort he opened his mouth. He drew the lower jaw in, curled the upper lip out of the way, and scraped the bunch with his upper teeth in order to separate a match. He succeeded in getting one, which he dropped on his lap. He was no better off. He could not pick it up. Then he devised a way. He picked it up in his teeth and scratched it on his leg. Twenty times he scratched before he succeeded in lighting it. As it flamed he held it with his teeth to the birch bark. But the burning brimstone went up his nostrils and into his lungs, causing him to cough spasmodically. The match fell into the snow and went out.

The old-timer on Sulphur Creek was right, he thought in the moment of controlled despair that ensued: after fifty below, a man should travel with a partner. He beat his hands, but failed in exciting any sensation. Suddenly he bared both hands, removing the mittens with his teeth. He caught the whole bunch between the heels of his hands. His arm muscles not being frozen enabled him to press the hand heels tightly against the matches. Then he scratched the bunch along his leg. It flared into flame, seventy sulphur matches at once! There was no wind to blow them out. He kept his head to one side to escape the strangling fumes, and held the blazing bunch to the birch bark. As he so held it, he became aware of sensation in his hand. His flesh was burning. He could smell it. Deep down below the surface he could feel it. The sensation developed into pain that grew acute. And still he endured it, holding the flame of the matches clumsily to the bark that would not light readily because his own burning hands were in the way, absorbing most of the flame.

Mark the Text

Underline or highlight the text that tells what advice the man failed to follow.

At last, when he could endure no more, he jerked his hands apart. The blazing matches fell sizzling into the snow, but the birch bark was alight. He began laying dry grasses and the tiniest twigs on the flame. He could not pick and choose, for he had to lift the fuel between the heels of his hands. Small pieces of rotten wood and green moss clung to the twigs, and he bit them off as well as he could with his teeth. He cherished the flame carefully and awkwardly. It meant life, and it must not perish. The withdrawal of blood from the surface of his body now made him begin to shiver, and he grew more awkward. A large piece of green moss fell squarely on the little fire. He tried to poke it out with his fingers, but his shivering frame made him poke too far, and he disrupted the <u>nucleus</u> of the little fire, the burning grasses and tiny twigs separating and scattering. He tried to poke them together again, but in spite of the tenseness of the effort, his shivering got away with him, and the twigs were hopelessly scattered. Each twig gushed a puff of smoke and went out. The fire provider had failed. As he looked <u>apathetically</u> about him, his eyes chanced on the dog, sitting across the ruins of the fire from him, in the snow, making restless, hunching movements, slightly lifting one forefoot and then the other, shifting its weight back and forth on them with wistful eagerness.

The sight of the dog put a wild idea into his head. He remembered the tale of the man, caught in a blizzard, who killed a steer and crawled inside the carcass, and so was saved. He would kill the dog and bury his hands in the warm body until the numbness went out of them. Then he could build another fire. He spoke to the dog, calling it to him; but in his voice was a strange note of fear that frightened the animal, who had never known the man to speak in such way before. Something was the matter, and its suspicious nature sensed danger—it knew not what danger, but somewhere, somehow, in its brain arose an apprehension of the man. It flattened its ears down at the sound of

480

490

500

510

NOTE THE FACTS

What plan does the man devise?

_____

_____

_____

_____

words for everyday use	**nu • cle • us** (noo′klē əs) *n.*, core; central part. *The two aircraft carriers formed the <u>nucleus</u> of the fleet.*
	ap • a • thet • i • cal • ly (ap′ə thet′ə kə lē) *adv.*, without emotion. *The crowd listened <u>apathetically</u> to the speaker.*

THINK AND REFLECT

Why does the author portray the man in the posture of a dog at this point in the story? What similarities exist between the man and the dog at this moment? (Synthesize)

_____

_____

_____

_____

NOTE THE FACTS

How does the plan proceed?

_____

_____

_____

_____

the man's voice, and its restless, hunching movements and the liftings and shiftings of its forefeet became more pronounced; but it would not come to the man. He got on his hand and knees and crawled toward the dog. This unusual posture again excited suspicion, and the animal sidled mincingly away.

520   The man sat up in the snow for a moment and struggled for calmness. Then he pulled on his mittens, by means of his teeth, and got upon his feet. He glanced down at first in order to assure himself that he was really standing up, for the absence of sensation in his feet left him unrelated to the earth. His erect position in itself started to drive the webs of suspicion from the dog's mind; and when he spoke <u>peremptorily</u>, with the sound of whiplashes in his voice, the dog rendered its customary allegiance and came to him. As it came within reaching distance, the man lost his control. His arms flashed out to the dog, and he experi-

530 enced genuine surprise when he discovered that his hands could not clutch, that there was neither bend nor feeling in the fingers. He had forgotten for the moment that they were frozen and that they were freezing more and more. All this happened quickly, and before the animal could get away, he encircled its body with his arms. He sat down in the snow, and in this fashion held the dog, while it snarled and whined and struggled.

    But it was all he could do, hold its body encircled in his arms and sit there. He realized that he could not kill the

540 dog. There was no way to do it. With his helpless hands he could neither draw nor hold his sheath-knife nor throttle the animal. He released it, and it plunged wildly away, with tail between its legs, and still snarling. It halted forty feet away and surveyed him curiously, with ears sharply pricked forward. The man looked down at his hands in order to locate them, and found them hanging on the ends of his arms. It struck him as curious that one should have to use his eyes in order to find out where his hands were. He began threshing his arms back and forth, beating the

words for everyday use

per • emp • to • ri • ly (pər emp′tə ri lē) adv., commandingly. The admiral spoke <u>peremptorily</u> to his crew.

550 mittened hands against his sides. He did this for five minutes, violently, and his heart pumped enough blood up to
the surface to put a stop to his shivering. But no sensation
was aroused in the hands. He had an impression that they
hung like weights on the ends of his arms, but when he
tried to run the impression down, he could not find it.

A certain fear of death, dull and oppressive, came to him.
This fear quickly became <u>poignant</u> as he realized that it was
no longer a mere matter of freezing his fingers and toes, or
of losing his hands and feet, but that it was a matter of life
560 and death with the chances against him. This threw him
into a panic, and he turned and ran up the creekbed along
the old, dim trail. The dog joined in behind and kept up
with him. He ran blindly, without intention, in fear such as
he had never known in his life. Slowly, as he plowed and
floundered through the snow, he began to see things
again—the banks of the creek, the old timber jams, the
leafless aspens, and the sky. The running made him feel
better. He did not shiver. Maybe, if he ran on, his feet
would thaw out: and, anyway, if he ran far enough, he
570 would reach camp and the boys. Without doubt he would
lose some fingers and toes and some of his face; but the
boys would take care of him, and save the rest of him when
he got there. And at the same time there was another
thought in his mind that said he would never get to the
camp and the boys; that it was too many miles away, that
the freezing had too great a start on him, and that he would
soon be stiff and dead. This thought he kept in the background and refused to consider. Sometimes it pushed itself
forward and demanded to be heard, but he thrust it back
580 and strove to think of other things.

It struck him as curious that he could run at all on feet so
frozen that he could not feel them when they struck the
earth and took the weight of his body. He seemed to himself
to skim along above the surface, and to have no connection
with the earth. Somewhere he had once seen a winged

words for everyday use

poign • ant (poin´yənt) *adj.,* sharp; painful. *Poignant* memories of his months in a refugee camp washed over Li.

MAKE PREDICTIONS. What do you think will happen to the man?

_____

_____

_____

Mercury,[7] and he wondered if Mercury felt as he felt when skimming over the earth.

His theory of running until he reached camp and the boys had one flaw in it: he lacked the endurance. Several times he stumbled, and finally he tottered, crumpled up, and fell. When he tried to rise, he failed. He must sit and rest, he decided, and next time he would merely walk and keep on going. As he sat and regained his breath, he noted that he was feeling quite warm and comfortable. He was not shivering, and it even seemed that a warm glow had come to his chest and trunk. And yet, when he touched his nose or cheeks, there was no sensation. Running would not thaw them out. Nor would it thaw out his hands and feet. Then the thought came to him that the frozen portions of his body must be extending. He tried to keep this thought down, to forget it, to think of something else; he was aware of the panicky feeling that it caused, and he was afraid of the panic. But the thought asserted itself, and persisted, until it produced a vision of his body totally frozen. This was too much, and he made another wild run along the trail. Once he slowed down to a walk, but the thought of the freezing extending itself made him run again.

And all the time the dog ran with him, at his heels. When he fell down a second time, it curled its tail over its forefeet and sat in front of him, facing him, curiously eager and intent. The warmth and security of the animal angered him, and he cursed it till it flattened down its ears appeasingly. This time the shivering came more quickly upon the man. He was losing in his battle with the frost. It was creeping into his body from all sides. The thought of it drove him on, but he ran no more than a hundred feet, when he staggered and pitched headlong. It was his last panic. When he had recovered his breath and control, he sat up and entertained in his mind the conception of meeting death with dignity. However, the conception did not come to him in such terms. His idea of it was that he had been making a fool of himself, running around like a chicken with its head cut off—such was the simile that occurred to him. Well, he was bound to freeze anyway, and

NOTE THE FACTS

A **simile** is a comparison using *like* or *as*. In lines 621–624, to what does the man compare his behavior?

_____

_____

---

7. **Mercury.** In Roman mythology, Mercury, the messenger of the gods, is depicted with winged feet.

he might as well take it decently. With this new-found peace of mind came the first glimmerings of drowsiness. A good idea, he thought, to sleep off to death. It was like taking an anaesthetic. Freezing was not so bad as people thought. There were lots worse ways to die.

630   He pictured the boys finding his body next day. Suddenly he found himself with them, coming along the trail and looking for himself. And, still with them, he came around a turn in the trail and found himself lying in the snow. He did not belong with himself any more, for even then he was out of himself; standing with the boys and looking at himself in the snow. It certainly was cold, was his thought. When he got back to the States he could tell the folks what real cold was. He drifted on from this to a vision of the old-timer on

640 Sulphur Creek. He could see him quite clearly, warm and comfortable, and smoking a pipe.

    "You were right, old hoss; you were right," the man mumbled to the old-timer of Sulphur Creek.

    Then the man drowsed off into what seemed to him the most comfortable and satisfying sleep he had ever known. The dog sat facing him and waiting. The brief day drew to a close in a long, slow twilight. There were no signs of a fire to be made, and, besides, never in the dog's experience

650 had it known a man to sit like that in the snow and make no fire. As the twilight drew on, its eager yearning for the fire mastered it, and with a great lifting and shifting of forefeet, it whined softly, then flattened its ears down in anticipation of being chidden[8] by the man. But the man remained silent. Later, the dog whined loudly. And still later it crept close to the man and caught the scent of death. This made the animal bristle and back away. A little longer it delayed, howling under the stars that leaped and danced and shone brightly in the cold sky. Then it turned

660 and trotted up the trail in the direction of the camp it knew, where were the other food providers and fire providers. ■

---

8. **chidden.** Scolded

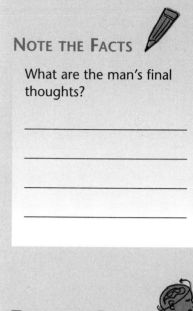

NOTE THE FACTS

What are the man's final thoughts?

_____

_____

_____

_____

THINK AND REFLECT

The author never mentions the man's name in the story. What does the man symbolize? (Synthesize)

_____

_____

_____

Reflect ON YOUR READING

When you finish the story, review the notes you made in your chart. Then, write a character sketch of the main character. Use your own paper as necessary. Be sure to use evidence from the text to support your opinions. When you finish, share your character sketch with your before-reading group. Discuss how the man in the story is similar to or different from the person you described in the before-reading activity.

_____

_____

_____

_____

THINK-ALOUD NOTES

_____

_____

_____

_____

_____

_____

_____

_____

_____

_____

Reading Skills and Test Practice

IDENTIFY THE AUTHOR'S PURPOSE

Discuss with your group how best to answer the following questions about the author's purpose.

1. The author wants the reader to think that the man is
   a. kind.
   b. sarcastic.
   c. detached.
   d. good-natured.

What is the correct answer to the question above? How were you able to eliminate the other answers? How did your use of the reading strategy help you answer the question?

_____

_____

2. Which statement best describes what the author probably thinks about the Yukon?
   a. He thinks that it is challenging but easily conquerable.
   b. He thinks that it is dangerous and should be taken seriously.
   c. He thinks that it is hospitable and a place to make an easy life.
   d. He thinks that it should be avoided at all costs.

What is the correct answer to the question above? How were you able to eliminate the other answers? How did your use of the reading strategy help you answer the question?

_____

_____

Investigate, Inquire, and Imagine

RECALL: GATHER FACTS
1a. Against what does the man lose his battle?

INTERPRET: FIND MEANING
1b. How will the boys at camp learn of the man's death?

ANALYZE: TAKE THINGS APART
2a. Identify the mistakes the man makes.

SYNTHESIZE: BRING THINGS TOGETHER
2b. Why does the author state that the man's limitation is that he is without imagination?

EVALUATE: MAKE JUDGMENTS
3a. Evaluate the advice of the old-timer of Sulphur Creek.

EXTEND: CONNECT IDEAS
3b. How do think the author's personal experiences in the Klondike might have inspired him to write this story?

Literary Tools

CONFLICT. A **conflict** is a struggle between two forces in a literary work. What is the external conflict, or outside force, against which the main character struggles? What events cause the main character's downfall? Could his death have been prevented?

_____

_____

_____

_____

WordWorkshop

BASE WORDS AND SUFFIXES. A **base word** is a basic word part that can stand alone. Many words are formed by adding prefixes and suffixes to base words. If you are unfamiliar with a word that is formed with a prefix or a suffix, check to see if you know the meaning of the base word and meaning of the prefix or suffix. Underline the base word once and the suffix twice in each of the following words from "To Build a Fire." Next, look up each suffix in a dictionary and write two additional words that end with the same suffix.

1. uncomfortable _____   _____

2. solidity _____   _____

3. eastward _____   _____

4. numbness _____   _____

5. sensation _____   _____

Read-Write Connection

Imagine that you are one of the men waiting at the camp for the return of the solitary traveler. Why do you think he is late in returning to camp? What concerns do you have for his safety?

_____

_____

_____

_____

_____

_____

_____

_____

_____

Beyond the Reading

NATURALISM. "To Build a Fire" is an example of Naturalism. **Naturalism** was a literary movement of the late nineteenth and early twentieth centuries that saw actions and events as resulting unavoidably from biological or environmental forces. Often these forces were beyond the understanding or control of the characters subjected to them. Research Naturalism online or at the library and find other famous writers from this movement. Read another story by an author who was influenced by this movement and compare it to "To Build a Fire." What similarities or differences do you find?

GO ONLINE. Visit the EMC Internet Resource Center at **emcp.com** to find links and additional activities for this selection.

"The Most DANGEROUS Game"
by Richard Connell

Active READING STRATEGY

TACKLE DIFFICULT VOCABULARY

Before Reading ▶ **PREVIEW SELECTION VOCABULARY**

- ❑ Copy the list of vocabulary words your teacher has written on the board. Leave space after each word to record its definition.
- ❑ Preview the list of words, and copy the list of words in the first column of the graphic organizer below.
- ❑ In the second column, write what you think the word might mean.
- ❑ As you read the story, you will uncover the definitions of the words, as well as any other unfamiliar words, using context clues, word parts, and any other techniques you find useful.

Graphic Organizer

Word	My Definition	Actual Definition

CONNECT

Reader's resource

In **"The Most Dangerous Game,"** two highly skilled and experienced hunters, the famous Rainsford and cultured Zaroff, share an enthusiasm for the sport of big-game hunting. Through various techniques of characterization, such as dialogue and direct description, the author, Richard Connell (1893–1949), creates the different physical traits and beliefs of each character.

Word watch

PREVIEW VOCABULARY

acknowledge	imperative
amenity	indolently
analytical	inevitable
animate	intricate
appraise	lacerated
barbarous	medieval
condone	palpable
conduct	precariously
cower	preserve
cunning	prospect
dank	protruding
deplorable	realist
depreciate	receding
diverting	recoil
disarming	scruple
extremity	solicitous
forge	taint
futile	tangible
glaring	uncanny
grisly	wan

Reader's journal

Describe what you think it would be like to be shipwrecked on a desert island. How would you find shelter and food?

TACKLE DIFFICULT VOCABULARY

❑ Follow along in the selection as your teacher reads the first page aloud.

❑ Locate the following words in the text: *dank, palpable,* and *realist.* (Do not read the definitions provided in the Words for Everyday Use box.)

❑ Try to determine the meanings of the words by using context clues, word parts, and so on. Then, record the definition in your graphic organizer.

❑ Check your work by reading the Words for Everyday Use definitions. Adjust your definitions as necessary.

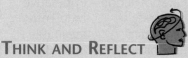

THINK AND REFLECT

What is ominous about the name of the island? **(Infer)**

_____

_____

_____

_____

NOTE THE FACTS

What sport does Rainsford consider to be the best in the world?

_____

The Most DANGEROUS Game

Richard Connell

"Off there to the right—somewhere—is a large island," said Whitney. "It's rather a mystery—"

"What island is it?" Rainsford asked.

"The old charts call it 'Ship-Trap Island,'" Whitney replied. "A suggestive name, isn't it? Sailors have a curious dread of the place. I don't know why. Some superstition—"

"Can't see it," remarked Rainsford, trying to peer through the <u>dank</u> tropical night that was <u>palpable</u> as it pressed its thick warm blackness in upon the yacht.

10   "You've good eyes," said Whitney, with a laugh, "and I've seen you pick off a moose moving in the brown fall bush at four hundred yards, but even you can't see four miles or so through a moonless Caribbean night."

"Nor four yards," admitted Rainsford. "Ugh! It's like moist black velvet."

"It will be light enough in Rio,"[1] promised Whitney. "We should make it in a few days. I hope the jaguar guns have come from Purdey's. We should have some good hunting up the Amazon. Great sport, hunting."

20   "The best sport in the world," agreed Rainsford.

"For the hunter," amended Whitney. "Not for the jaguar."

"Don't talk rot, Whitney," said Rainsford. "You're a big-game hunter, not a philosopher. Who cares how a jaguar feels?"

---

1. **Rio.** Rio de Janeiro, then the capital of Brazil

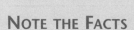

words for everyday use

dank (daŋk) *adj.,* disagreeably damp. *The <u>dank</u> air of the cellar rotted the potatoes.*

pal • pa • ble (pal′pə bəl) *adj.,* perceptible; noticeable. *The anger between Cara and Diane was <u>palpable</u>, even though neither said a word.*

"Perhaps the jaguar does," observed Whitney.

"Bah! They've no understanding."

"Even so, I rather think they understand one thing—fear. The fear of pain and the fear of death."

"Nonsense," laughed Rainsford. "This hot weather is making you soft, Whitney. Be a <u>realist</u>. The world is made up of two classes—the hunters and the hunted. Luckily, you and I are the hunters. Do you think we've passed that island yet?"

"I can't tell in the dark. I hope so."

"Why?" asked Rainsford.

"The place has a reputation—a bad one."

"Cannibals?" suggested Rainsford.

"Hardly. Even cannibals wouldn't live in such a God-forsaken place. But it's gotten into sailor lore, somehow. Didn't you notice that the crew's nerves seemed a bit jumpy today?"

"They were a bit strange, now you mention it. Even Captain Nielsen—"

"Yes, even that tough-minded old Swede, who'd go up to the devil himself and ask him for a light. Those fishy blue eyes held a look I never saw there before. All I could get out of him was: 'This place has an evil name among sea-faring men, sir.' Then he said to me, very gravely: 'Don't you feel anything?'— as if the air about us was actually poisonous. Now, you mustn't laugh when I tell you this—I did feel something like a sudden chill.

"There was no breeze. The sea was as flat as a plate-glass window. We were drawing near the island then. What I felt was a—a mental chill; a sort of sudden dread."

"Pure imagination," said Rainsford. "One superstitious sailor can <u>taint</u> the whole ship's company with his fear."

"Maybe. But sometimes I think sailors have an extra sense that tells them when they are in danger. Sometimes I think evil is a <u>tangible</u> thing—with wave lengths, just as sound and light have. An evil place can, so to speak, broadcast vibrations of evil. Anyhow, I'm glad we're getting out of this zone. Well, I think I'll turn in now, Rainsford."

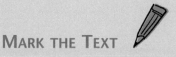

MARK THE TEXT

Highlight the statement that supports Rainsford's allegiance to the hunter, not the hunted.

Literary TOOLS

IRONY. Irony is a difference between appearance and reality. *Verbal irony* occurs when a statement is made that implies its opposite. *Irony of situation* occurs when an event violates the expectations of the characters. Look for an example of each type of irony as you read.

words for everyday use

re • al • ist (rē′ə list) *n.*, person concerned with real things. *There are times when one must be a <u>realist</u> and put dreams aside.*

taint (tānt) *vt.*, infect. *Many old houses have been <u>tainted</u> by lead in paint.*

tan • gi • ble (tan′jə bəl) *adj.*, having actual form. *Although I had no <u>tangible</u> evidence, I felt certain that someone had gone through my locker.*

"I'm not sleepy," said Rainsford. "I'm going to smoke another pipe on the afterdeck."[2]

"Good night, then, Rainsford. See you at breakfast."

"Right. Good night, Whitney."

There was no sound in the night as Rainsford sat there, but the muffled throb of the engine that drove the yacht swiftly through the darkness, and the swish and ripple of the wash of the propeller.

70 Rainsford, reclining in a steamer chair, <u>indolently</u> puffed on his favorite brier. The sensuous drowsiness of the night was on him. "It's so dark," he thought, "that I could sleep without closing my eyes; the night would be my eyelids—"

An abrupt sound startled him. Off to the right he heard it, and his ears, expert in such matters, could not be mistaken. Again he heard the sound, and again. Somewhere, off in the blackness, someone had fired a gun three times.

Rainsford sprang up and moved quickly to the rail, mystified. He strained his eyes in the direction from which the

80 reports had come, but it was like trying to see through a blanket. He leaped upon the rail and balanced himself there, to get greater elevation; his pipe, striking a rope, was knocked from his mouth. He lunged for it; a short, hoarse cry came from his lips as he realized he had reached too far and had lost his balance. The cry was pinched off short as the blood-warm waters of the Caribbean Sea[3] closed over his head.

He struggled up to the surface and tried to cry out, but the wash from the speeding yacht slapped him in the face

90 and the salt water in his open mouth made him gag and strangle. Desperately he struck out with strong strokes after the <u>receding</u> lights of the yacht, but he stopped before he had swum fifty feet. A certain coolheadedness had come to him; it was not the first time he had been in

Use THE STRATEGY

TACKLE DIFFICULT VOCABULARY.
As you read, make sure to use context clues, word parts, and any other techniques you find useful to understand the meaning of words you do not know.

---

2. **afterdeck.** Part of a ship's deck between the middle and the rear
3. **Caribbean Sea.** Tropical and subtropical body of water near the eastern coast of the Americas in the western Atlantic

words for everyday use	in • do • lent • ly (in′də lənt lē) *adv.,* idly; lazily. *The cat lay <u>indolently</u> in her favorite sunny spot on the couch.* re • ced • ing (ri sēd′iŋ) *part.,* moving away from; becoming more distant. *We kidded Dad about his <u>receding</u> hairline.*

a tight place. There was a chance that his cries could be heard by someone aboard the yacht, but that chance was slender, and grew more slender as the yacht raced on. He wrestled himself out of his clothes, and shouted with all his power. The lights of the yacht became faint and ever-vanishing fireflies; then they were blotted out entirely by the night.

Rainsford remembered the shots. They had come from the right, and doggedly he swam in that direction, swimming with slow, deliberate strokes, conserving his strength. For a seemingly endless time he fought the sea. He began to count his strokes; he could do possibly a hundred more and then—

Rainsford heard a sound. It came out of the darkness, a high screaming sound, the sound of an animal in an extremity of anguish and terror.

He did not recognize the animal that made the sound; he did not try to; with fresh vitality he swam toward the sound. He heard it again; then it was cut short by another noise, crisp, staccato.

"Pistol shot," muttered Rainsford, swimming on.

Ten minutes of determined effort brought another sound to his ears—the most welcome he had ever heard—the muttering and growling of the sea breaking on a rocky shore. He was almost on the rocks before he saw them; on a night less calm he would have been shattered against them. With his remaining strength he dragged himself from the swirling waters. Jagged crags appeared to jut into the opaqueness, he forced himself upward, hand over hand. Gasping, his hands raw, he reached a flat place at the top. Dense jungle came down to the very edge of the cliffs. What perils that tangle of trees and underbrush might hold for him did not concern Rainsford just then. All he knew was that he was safe from his enemy, the sea, and that utter weariness was on him. He flung himself down at the jungle edge and tumbled headlong into the deepest sleep of his life.

When he opened his eyes he knew from the position of

THINK AND REFLECT

Why does Rainsford swim in the direction of the shots? **(Interpret)**

_____

_____

_____

NOTE THE FACTS

What is unusual about the sound that Rainsford hears?

_____

_____

_____

_____

words
for
everyday
use

ex • trem • i • ty (ek strem´ə tē) n., greatest degree. *The marathon runner reached the extremity of her endurance at the twenty-sixth mile.*

the sun that it was late in the afternoon. Sleep had given him new vigor; a sharp hunger was picking at him. He looked about him, almost cheerfully.

"Where there are pistol shots, there are men. Where there are men, there is food," he thought. But what kind of men, he wondered, in so forbidding a place? An unbroken front of snarled and jagged jungle fringed the shore.

He saw no sign of a trail through the closely knit web of weeds and trees; it was easier to go along the shore, and Rainsford floundered along by the water. Not far from where he had landed, he stopped.

Some wounded thing, by the evidence a large animal, had thrashed about in the underbrush; the jungle weeds were crushed down and the moss was <u>lacerated</u>; one patch of weeds was stained crimson. A small, glittering object not far away caught Rainsford's eye and he picked it up. It was an empty cartridge.

"A twenty-two," he remarked. "That's odd. It must have been a fairly large animal too. The hunter had his nerve with him to tackle it with a light gun. It's clear that the brute put up a fight. I suppose the first three shots I heard was when the hunter flushed his quarry[4] and wounded it. The last shot was when he trailed it here and finished it."

He examined the ground closely and found what he had hoped to find—the print of hunting boots. They pointed along the cliff in the direction he had been going. Eagerly he hurried along, now slipping on a rotten log or a loose stone, but making headway; night was beginning to settle down on the island.

Bleak darkness was blacking out the sea and jungle when Rainsford sighted the lights. He came upon them as he turned a crook in the coast line and his first thought was that he had come upon a village, for there were many lights. But as he <u>forged</u> along he saw to his great astonishment that all the lights were in one enormous building—a lofty structure with pointed towers plunging upward into

THINK AND REFLECT

What sign does Rainsford find? Why is he glad to see this sign? **(Infer)**

_____

_____

_____

4. **flushed his quarry.** Forced the animal out of its hiding place

words for everyday use	lac • er • at • ed (las´ər āt´əd) *part.*, torn; mangled. *Someone's feet could be <u>lacerated</u> by this broken glass on the sidewalk.*
	forge (fôrj) *vi.*, move forward. *Mrs. Keillor <u>forged</u> through the story problems, leaving many of the students behind.*

the gloom. His eyes made out the shadowy outlines of a palatial château; it was set on a high bluff, and on three sides

170   of it cliffs dived down to where the sea licked greedy lips in the shadows.

"Mirage," thought Rainsford. But it was no mirage, he found, when he opened the tall spiked iron gate. The stone steps were real enough; the massive door with a leering gargoyle[5] for a knocker was real enough; yet about it all hung an air of unreality.

He lifted the knocker, and it creaked up stiffly, as if it had never before been used. He let it fall, and it startled him with its booming loudness. He thought he heard steps within; the

180   door remained closed. Again Rainsford lifted the heavy knocker, and let it fall. The door opened then, opened as suddenly as if it were on a spring, and Rainsford stood blinking in the river of <u>glaring</u> gold light that poured out. The first thing Rainsford's eyes discerned was the largest man Rainsford had ever seen—a gigantic creature, solidly made and blackbearded to the waist. In his hand the man held a long-barreled revolver, and he was pointing it straight at Rainsford's heart.

Out of the snarl of beard two small eyes regarded

190   Rainsford.

"Don't be alarmed," said Rainsford, with a smile which he hoped was <u>disarming</u>. "I'm no robber. I fell off a yacht. My name is Sanger Rainsford of New York City."

The menacing look in the eyes did not change. The revolver pointed as rigidly as if the giant were a statue. He gave no sign that he understood Rainsford's words, or that he had even heard them. He was dressed in uniform, a black uniform trimmed with gray astrakhan.[6]

"I'm Sanger Rainsford of New York," Rainsford began again.

200   "I fell off a yacht. I am hungry."

The man's only answer was to raise with his thumb the hammer of his revolver. Then Rainsford saw the man's free

---

5. **gargoyle.** Grotesquely carved figure
6. **astrakhan.** Fur made from the pelt of young lambs

---

words for everyday use

glar • ing (gler´iŋ) adj., shining too brightly. *The <u>glaring</u> headlights stunned the deer.*

dis • arm • ing (dis ärm´iŋ) adj., removing fear or hostility. *Even the grumpiest customer found the server's friendly personality <u>disarming</u>.*

FIX-UP IDEA

Choose a New Strategy
If you have difficulty applying the reading strategy, try using a different strategy, such as visualizing, to help you understand the story and unfamiliar words. Use your visualizations to help you determine the meaning of the words you don't know.

Mark the Text

Underline the phrase that tells what Rainsford is known for.

hand go to his forehead in a military salute, and he saw him click his heels together and stand at attention. Another man was coming down the broad marble steps, an erect, slender man in evening clothes. He advanced to Rainsford and held out his hand.

In a cultivated voice marked by a slight accent that gave it added precision and deliberateness, he said: "It is a very

210 great pleasure and honor to welcome Mr. Sanger Rainsford, the celebrated hunter, to my home."

Automatically Rainsford shook the man's hand.

"I've read your book about hunting snow leopards in Tibet, you see," explained the man. "I am General Zaroff."

Rainsford's first impression was that the man was singularly handsome; his second was that there was an original, almost bizarre quality about the general's face. He was a tall man past middle age, for his hair was a vivid white; but his thick eyebrows and pointed military mustache were as black

220 as the night from which Rainsford had come. His eyes, too, were black and very bright. He had high cheek bones, a sharp-cut nose, a spare, dark face, the face of a man used to giving orders, the face of an aristocrat. Turning to the giant in uniform, the general made a sign. The giant put away his pistol, saluted, withdrew.

"Ivan is an incredibly strong fellow," remarked the general, "but he has the misfortune to be deaf and dumb. A simple fellow, but I'm afraid, like all his race, a bit of a savage."

"Is he Russian?"

230 "He is a Cossack,"[7] said the general, and his smile showed red lips and pointed teeth. "So am I."

"Come," he said, "we shouldn't be chatting here. We can talk later. Now you want clothes, food, rest. You shall have them. This is a most restful spot."

Ivan had reappeared, and the general spoke to him with lips that moved but gave forth no sound.

"Follow Ivan, if you please, Mr. Rainsford," said the general. "I was about to have my dinner when you came. I'll wait for you. You'll find that my clothes will fit you, I

240 think."

It was to a huge, beam-ceilinged bedroom with a

---

7. **Cossack.** Member of a group of people from southern Russia known for equestrian skill and fighting ability

canopied bed big enough for six men that Rainsford followed the silent giant. Ivan laid out an evening suit, and Rainsford, as he put it on, noticed that it came from a London tailor who ordinarily cut and sewed for none below the rank of duke.

The dining room to which Ivan <u>conducted</u> him was in many ways remarkable. There was a <u>medieval</u> magnificence about it; it suggested a baronial hall of feudal times[8] with

250 its oaken panels, its high ceiling, its vast refectory table[9] where twoscore[10] men could sit down to eat. About the hall were the mounted heads of many animals—lions, tigers, elephants, moose, bears; larger or more perfect specimens Rainsford had never seen. At the great table the general was sitting, alone.

"You'll have a cocktail, Mr. Rainsford," he suggested. The cocktail was surpassingly good; and, Rainsford noted, the table appointments were of the finest—the linen, the crystal, the silver, the china.

260 They were eating *borsch*,[11] the rich, red soup with whipped cream so dear to Russian palates. Half apologetically General Zaroff said: "We do our best to preserve the <u>amenities</u> of civilization here. Please forgive any lapses. We are well off the beaten track, you know. Do you think the champagne has suffered from its long ocean trip?"

"Not in the least," declared Rainsford. He was finding the general a most thoughtful and affable host, a true cosmopolite.[12] But there was one small trait of the general's that made Rainsford uncomfortable. Whenever he looked up

270 from his plate he found the general studying him, <u>appraising</u> him narrowly.

---

8. **baronial hall of feudal times.** Dining room in a medieval mansion
9. **refectory table.** Large table in the dining room
10. **twoscore.** Forty
11. ***borsch*.** Russian soup made of beets
12. **cosmopolite.** Person having a worldwide rather than a provincial scope

words for everyday use	**con • duct** (kən dukt´) *vt.*, lead. *The hostess <u>conducted</u> us to a quiet table by the window.* **me • di • e • val** (mə dē´vəl) *adj.*, suggestive of the Middle Ages. *<u>Medieval</u> European castles were built as fortresses.* **a • men • i • ty** (ə men´ə tē) *n.*, desirable feature. *What <u>amenities</u> does the Carlton Hotel offer?* **ap • praise** (ə prāz´) *vt.*, judge the worth of. *The jeweler <u>appraised</u> the diamond ring.*

NOTE THE FACTS

What about General Zaroff makes Rainsford uncomfortable?

_____

_____

_____

_____

"Perhaps," said General Zaroff, "you were surprised that I recognized your name. You see, I read all books on hunting published in English, French, and Russian. I have but one passion in my life, Mr. Rainsford, and it is the hunt."

"You have some wonderful heads here," said Rainsford as he ate a particularly well cooked filet mignon. "That Cape buffalo is the largest I ever saw."

"Oh, that fellow. Yes, he was a monster."

280 "Did he charge you?"

"Hurled me against a tree," said the general. "Fractured my skull. But I got the brute."

"I've always thought," said Rainsford, "that the Cape buffalo is the most dangerous of all big game."

For a moment the general did not reply; he was smiling his curious redlipped smile. Then he said slowly: "No. You are wrong, sir. The Cape buffalo is not the most dangerous big game." He sipped his wine. "Here in my <u>preserve</u> on this island," he said in the same slow tone, "I hunt more danger-

290 ous game."

Rainsford expressed his surprise. "Is there big game on this island?"

The general nodded. "The biggest."

"Really?"

"Oh, it isn't here naturally, of course. I have to stock the island."

"What have you imported, General?" Rainsford asked. "Tigers?"

The general smiled. "No," he said. "Hunting tigers

300 ceased to interest me some years ago. I exhausted their possibilities, you see. No thrill left in tigers, no real danger. I live for danger, Mr. Rainsford."

The general took from his pocket a gold cigarette case and offered his guest a long black cigarette with a silver tip; it was perfumed and gave off a smell like incense.

"We will have some capital hunting, you and I," said the general. "I shall be most glad to have your society."

"But what game—" began Rainsford.

words
for
everyday
use

pre • serve (prē zurv´) *n.*, place maintained for regulated hunting. *The animals on the big-game <u>preserve</u> became endangered species.*

"I'll tell you," said the general. "You will be amused, I
310 know. I think I may say, in all modesty, that I have done a
rare thing. I have invented a new sensation. May I pour you
another glass of port, Mr. Rainsford?"

"Thank you, General."

The general filled both glasses and said: "God makes
some men poets. Some He makes kings, some beggars. Me
He made a hunter. My hand was made for the trigger, my
father said. He was a very rich man with a quarter of a million acres in the Crimea,[13] and he was an ardent sportsman.
When I was only five years old he gave me a little gun, spe-
320 cially made in Moscow for me, to shoot sparrows with.
When I shot some of his prize turkeys with it, he did not
punish me; he complimented me on my marksmanship. I
killed my first bear in the Caucasus when I was ten. My
whole life has been one prolonged hunt. I went into the
army—it was expected of noblemen's sons—and for a time
commanded a division of Cossack cavalry, but my real interest was always the hunt. I have hunted every kind of game
in every land. It would be impossible for me to tell you how
many animals I have killed."

330 The general puffed at his cigarette.

"After the debacle in Russia[14] I left the country, for it was
imprudent for an officer of the Czar to stay there. Many
noble Russians lost everything. I, luckily, had invested heavily in American securities, so I shall never have to open a
tea room in Monte Carlo or drive a taxi in Paris. Naturally,
I continued to hunt—grizzlies in your Rockies, crocodiles
in the Ganges,[15] rhinoceroses in East Africa. It was in
Africa that the Cape buffalo hit me and laid me up for six
340 months. As soon as I recovered I started for the Amazon to
hunt jaguars, for I had heard they were unusually <u>cunning</u>.
They weren't." The Cossack sighed. "They were no match
at all for a hunter with his wits about him and a high-

---

13. **Crimea.** Peninsula on the Black Sea in southwestern Russia
14. **debacle in Russia.** Russian Revolution of 1917 during which the czar was
overthrown and wealthy landowners lost their property
15. **Ganges.** River in India, viewed by the Hindus as sacred

**words
for
everyday
use**

cun • ning (kun´in) *adj.*, crafty, skillful. *The child's <u>cunning</u> moves at chess amazed
her adult opponent.*

powered rifle. I was bitterly disappointed. I was lying in my tent with a splitting headache one night when a terrible thought pushed its way into my mind. Hunting was beginning to bore me! And hunting, remember, had been my life. I have heard that in America business men often go to pieces when they give up the business that has been their life."

350 "Yes, that's so," said Rainsford.

The general smiled. "I had no wish to go to pieces," he said. "I must do something. Now, mine is an <u>analytical</u> mind, Mr. Rainsford. Doubtless that is why I enjoy the problems of the chase."

"No doubt, General Zaroff."

"So," continued the general, "I asked myself why the hunt no longer fascinated me. You are much younger than I am, Mr. Rainsford, and have not hunted as much, but you perhaps can guess the answer."

360 "What was it?"

"Simply this: hunting had ceased to be what you call 'a sporting proposition.' It had become too easy. I always got my quarry. Always. There is no greater bore than perfection."

The general lit a fresh cigarette.

"No animal had a chance with me any more. That is no boast; it is a mathematical certainty. The animal had nothing but his legs and his instinct. Instinct is no match for reason. When I thought of this it was a tragic moment for me, I can tell you."

370 Rainsford leaned across the table, absorbed in what his host was saying.

"It came to me as an inspiration what I must do," the general went on.

"And that was?"

The general smiled the quiet smile of one who has faced an obstacle and surmounted it with success. "I had to invent a new animal to hunt," he said.

"A new animal? You're joking."

"Not at all," said the general. "I never joke about hunting.

380 I needed a new animal. I found one. So I bought this island,

words for everyday use

an • a • lyt • ic • al (an´ə lit´i kəl) *adj.*, skilled in breaking a whole into its parts and examining relationships. *Brad's <u>analytical</u> skills helped him score well on his College Boards.*

built this house, and here I do my hunting. The island is perfect for my purposes—there are jungles with a maze of trails in them, hills, swamps—"

"But the animal, General Zaroff?"

"Oh," said the general, "it supplies me with the most exciting hunting in the world. No other hunting compares with it for an instant. Every day I hunt, and I never grow bored now, for I have a quarry with which I can match my wits."

Rainsford's bewilderment showed in his face.

390   "I wanted the ideal animal to hunt," explained the general. "So I said: 'What are the attributes of an ideal quarry?' And the answer was, of course: 'It must have courage, cunning, and, above all, it must be able to reason.' "

"But no animal can reason," objected Rainsford.

"My dear fellow," said the general, "there is one that can."

"But you can't mean—" gasped Rainsford.

"And why not?"

"I can't believe you are serious, General Zaroff. This is a <u>grisly</u> joke."

400   "Why should I not be serious? I am speaking of hunting."

"Hunting? General Zaroff, what you speak of is murder."

The general laughed with entire good nature. He regarded Rainsford quizzically. "I refuse to believe that so modern and civilized a young man as you seem to be harbors romantic ideas about the value of human life. Surely your experiences in the war—"

"Did not make me <u>condone</u> coldblooded murder," finished Rainsford stiffly.

410   Laughter shook the general. "How extraordinarily droll you are!" he said. "One does not expect nowadays to find a young man of the educated class, even in America, with such a naive, and, if I may say so, mid-Victorian point of view.[16] It's like finding a snuff-box in a limousine. Ah, well, doubtless you had Puritan ancestors. So many Americans

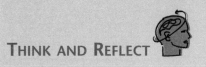

THINK AND REFLECT

What actions has General Zaroff taken to regain his interest in hunting? **(Interpret)**

_____

_____

_____

_____

THINK AND REFLECT

What animal does Zaroff hunt? **(Infer)**

_____

_____

_____

_____

_____

16. **mid-Victorian point of view.** During the reign of Queen Victoria, in the late nineteenth century, the English had a very strict code of moral behavior.

words for everyday use	**gris • ly** (griz´lē) *adj.*, terrifying; horrifying. *The jurors had to examine* <u>grisly</u> *photographs of the murder scene.* **con • done** (kən dōn´) *vt.*, forgive or overlook an offense. *"Let it be known that I never* <u>condone</u> *cheating," exclaimed the teacher.*

appear to have had. I'll wager you'll forget your notions when you go hunting with me. You've a genuine new thrill in store for you, Mr. Rainsford."

"Thank you, I'm a hunter, not a murderer."

420 "Dear me," said the general, quite unruffled, "again that unpleasant word. But I think I can show you that your <u>scruples</u> are quite ill founded."

"Yes?"

"Life is for the strong, to be lived by the strong, and, if need be, taken by the strong. The weak of the world were put here to give the strong pleasure. I am strong. Why should I not use my gift? If I wish to hunt, why should I not? I hunt the scum of the earth—a thoroughbred horse or hound is worth more than a score of them."

430 "But they are men," said Rainsford hotly.

"Precisely," said the general. "That is why I use them. It gives me pleasure. They can reason, after a fashion. So they are dangerous."

"But where do you get them?"

The general's left eyelid fluttered down in a wink. "This island is called Ship-Trap," he answered. "Sometimes an angry god of the high seas sends them to me. Sometimes, when Providence is not so kind, I help Providence a bit. Come to the window with me."

440 Rainsford went to the window and looked out toward the sea.

"Watch! Out there!" exclaimed the general, pointing into the night. Rainsford's eyes saw only blackness, and then, as the general pressed a button, far out to sea Rainsford saw the flash of lights.

The general chuckled. "They indicate a channel," he said, "where there's none; giant rocks with razor edges crouch like a sea monster with wide-open jaws. They can crush a ship as easily as I crush this nut." He dropped a walnut on the hardwood floor and brought his heel grinding down on

450 it. "Oh, yes," he said casually, as if in answer to a question, "I have electricity. We try to be civilized here."

"Civilized? And you shoot down men?"

words for everyday use

scru • ple (skroo ´pəl) *n.*, qualm; uneasiness about something one thinks is wrong. *Breanna's <u>scruples</u> prevented her from keeping the fifty-dollar bill she found.*

A trace of anger was in the general's black eyes; but it was there for but a second, and he said, in his most pleasant manner: "Dear me, what a righteous young man you are! I assure you I do not do the thing you suggest. That would be <u>barbarous</u>. I treat these visitors with every consideration. They get plenty of good food and exercise. They get into splendid physical condition. You shall see for yourself

460   tomorrow."

"What do you mean?"

"We'll visit my training school," smiled the general. "It's in the cellar. I have about a dozen pupils down there now. They're from the Spanish bark San Lucar that had the bad luck to go on the rocks out there. A very inferior lot, I regret to say. Poor specimens and more accustomed to the deck than to the jungle."

He raised his hand, and Ivan, who served as waiter, brought thick Turkish coffee. Rainsford, with an effort,

470   held his tongue in check.

"It's a game, you see," pursued the general blandly. "I suggest to one of them that we go hunting. I give him a supply of food and an excellent hunting knife. I give him three hours' start. I am to follow, armed only with a pistol of the smallest caliber and range. If my quarry eludes me for three whole days, he wins the game. If I find him"—the general smiled—"he loses."

"Suppose he refuses to be hunted?"

"Oh," said the general, "I give him his option, of course. He

480   need not play the game if he doesn't wish to. If he does not wish to hunt, I turn him over to Ivan. Ivan once had the honor of serving as official knouter to the Great White Czar,[17] and he has his own ideas of sport. Invariably, Mr. Rainsford, invariably they choose the hunt."

"And if they win?"

The smile on the general's face widened. "To date I have not lost," he said.

DRAW A PICTURE

---

17. **Ivan . . . Czar.** During the reign of Alexander III (1881–1894) of Russia, Ivan was the official flogger, who whipped prisoners severely.

words for everyday use

bar • ba • rous (bär´bə rəs) *adj.*, cruel; brutal; uncultured. *The practice of applying leeches to purify the blood seems <u>barbarous</u> to us now.*

Then he added, hastily: "I don't wish you to think me a braggart, Mr. Rainsford. Many of them afford only the most elementary sort of problem. Occasionally I strike a tartar.[18] One almost did win. I eventually had to use the dogs."

"The dogs?"

"This way, please. I'll show you."

The general steered Rainsford to a window. The lights from the windows sent a flickering illumination that made grotesque patterns on the courtyard below, and Rainsford could see moving about there a dozen or so huge black shapes; as they turned toward him, their eyes glittered greenly.

"A rather good lot, I think," observed the general. "They are let out at seven every night. If anyone should try to get into my house—or out of it—something extremely regrettable would occur to him." He hummed a snatch of song from the Folies Bergère.

"And now," said the general, "I want to show you my new collection of heads. Will you come with me to the library?"

"I hope," said Rainsford, "that you will excuse me tonight, General Zaroff. I'm really not feeling at all well."

"Ah, indeed?" the general inquired <u>solicitously</u>. "Well, I suppose that's only natural, after your long swim. You need a good, restful night's sleep. Tomorrow you'll feel like a new man, I'll wager. Then we'll hunt, eh? I've one rather promising <u>prospect</u>—"

Rainsford was hurrying from the room.

"Sorry you can't go with me tonight," called the general. "I expect rather fair sport—a big, strong sailor. He looks resourceful—Well, good night, Mr. Rainsford; I hope you have a good night's rest."

The bed was good and the pajamas of the softest silk, and he was tired in every fiber of his being, but nevertheless Rainsford could not quiet his brain with the opiate of sleep. He lay, eyes wide open. Once he thought he heard stealthy steps in the corridor outside his room. He sought to throw open the door; it would not open. He went to the window

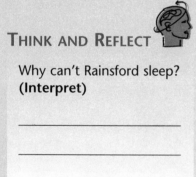

THINK AND REFLECT

What is the real reason Rainsford feels ill? (Infer)

_____

_____

_____

_____

THINK AND REFLECT

Why can't Rainsford sleep? (Interpret)

_____

_____

_____

---

18. **strike a tartar.** Meet one who is difficult to control

words for everyday use	so • lic • i • tous • ly (sə lis´ə təs lē) *adv.*, showing concern. *The nurse <u>solicitously</u> asked questions about the patient's injuries.*
	pros • pect (prä´spekt´) *n.*, likely candidate. *With her experience in middle-school government, Angela is an excellent <u>prospect</u> for class office in high school.*

and looked out. His room was high up in one of the towers. The lights of the château were out now, and it was dark and silent; but there was a fragment of sallow moon, and by its <u>wan</u> light he could see, dimly, the courtyard; there, weaving in and out in the pattern of shadow, were black, noiseless forms; the hounds heard him at the window and looked up,

530   expectantly, with their green eyes. Rainsford went back to the bed and lay down. By many methods he tried to put himself to sleep. He had achieved a doze when, just as morning began to come, he heard, far off in the jungle, the faint report of a pistol.

General Zaroff did not appear until luncheon. He was dressed faultlessly in the tweeds of a country squire. He was solicitous about the state of Rainsford's health.

"As for me," sighed the general, "I do not feel so well. I am worried, Mr. Rainsford. Last night I detected traces of

540   my old complaint."

To Rainsford's questioning glance the general said: "Ennui. Boredom."

Then, taking a second helping of crêpes suzette,[19] the general explained: "The hunting was not good last night. The fellow lost his head. He made a straight trail that offered no problems at all. That's the trouble with these sailors. They have dull brains to begin with, and they do not know how to get about in the woods. They do excessively stupid and obvious things. It's becoming most annoy-

550   ing. Will you have another glass of Chablis, Mr. Rainsford?"

"General," said Rainsford firmly, "I wish to leave this island at once."

The general raised his thickets of eyebrows; he seemed hurt. "But, my dear fellow," the general protested, "you've only just come. You've had no hunting—"

"I wish to go today," said Rainsford. He saw the dead black eyes of the general on him, studying him. General Zaroff's face suddenly brightened.

---

19. **crêpes suzette.** Thin pancakes eaten as a dessert

words for everyday use

wan (wän) *adj.,* pale; faint. *The <u>wan</u> glow of the flashlight indicated it needed new batteries.*

560　He filled Rainsford's glass with venerable Chablis from a dusty bottle.

"Tonight," said the general, "we will hunt—you and I."

Rainsford shook his head. "No, General," he said, "I will not hunt."

The general shrugged his shoulders and delicately ate a hot-house grape. "As you wish, my friend," he said. "The choice rests entirely with you. But may I not venture to suggest that you will find my idea of sport more <u>diverting</u> than Ivan's?"

He nodded toward the corner to where the giant stood,
570　scowling, his thick arms crossed on his huge chest.

"You don't mean—" cried Rainsford.

"My dear fellow," said the general, "have I not told you I always mean what I say about hunting? This is really an inspiration. I drink to a foe worthy of me at last."

The general raised his glass, but Rainsford sat staring at him.

"You'll find this game worth playing," the general said enthusiastically. "Your brain against mine. Your woodcraft against mine. Your strength and stamina against mine. Outdoor chess! And the stake is not without value, eh?"

580　"And if I should win—" began Rainsford huskily.

"I'll cheerfully <u>acknowledge</u> myself defeated if I do not find you by midnight of the third day," said General Zaroff. "My sloop will place you on the mainland near a town."

The general read what Rainsford was thinking.

"Oh, you can trust me," said the Cossack. "I will give you my word as a gentleman and a sportsman. Of course you, in turn, must agree to say nothing of your visit here."

"I'll agree to nothing of the kind," said Rainsford.

"Oh," said the general, "in that case—But why discuss that
590　now? Three days hence we can discuss it over a bottle of Veuve Cliquot, unless—"

The general sipped his wine.

Then a businesslike air <u>animated</u> him. "Ivan," he said to Rainsford, "will supply you with hunting clothes, food, a

words for everyday use

di • vert • ing (də vurt´iŋ) *adj.,* amusing. *Do you find weight training <u>diverting</u> or hard work?*

ac • knowl • edge (ak näl´ij) *vt.,* admit to be true. *Juanita <u>acknowledged</u> that the dent in her parents' car wasn't there when she had left home.*

an • i • mate (an´i māt´) *vt.,* put into motion. *Excitement <u>animated</u> Oliver's face as he discussed his plans for the summer.*

knife. I suggest you wear moccasins; they leave a poorer trail. I suggest too that you avoid the big swamp in the southeast corner of the island. We call it Death Swamp. There's quicksand there. One foolish fellow tried it. The <u>deplorable</u> part of it was that Lazarus followed him. You can imagine my feelings, Mr. Rainsford. I loved Lazarus; he was the finest hound in my pack. Well, I must beg you to excuse me now. I always take a siesta after lunch. You'll hardly have time for a nap, I fear. You'll want to start, no doubt. I shall not follow till dusk. Hunting at night is so much more exciting than by day, don't you think? *Au revoir,*[20] Mr. Rainsford, *au revoir.*"

General Zaroff, with a deep, courtly bow, strolled from the room.

From another door came Ivan. Under one arm he carried khaki hunting clothes, a haversack of food, a leather sheath containing a long-bladed hunting knife; his right hand rested on a cocked revolver thrust in the crimson sash about his waist. . . .

Rainsford had fought his way through the bush for two hours. "I must keep my nerve. I must keep my nerve," he said through tight teeth.

He had not been entirely clearheaded when the château gates snapped shut behind him. His whole idea at first was to put distance between himself and General Zaroff, and, to this end, he had plunged along, spurred on by the sharp rowels of something very like panic. Now he had got a grip on himself, had stopped, and was taking stock of himself and the situation.

He saw that straight flight was <u>futile</u>; inevitably it would bring him face to face with the sea. He was in a picture with a frame of water, and his operations, clearly, must take place within that frame.

"I'll give him a trail to follow," muttered Rainsford, and he struck off from the rude paths he had been following into the trackless wilderness. He executed a series of <u>intricate</u> loops;

---

20. *Au revoir.* Until we meet again (French)

WHAT DO YOU WONDER?

_____

_____

_____

_____

words for everyday use	**de • plor • a • ble** (dē plôr´ə bəl) *adj.,* unfortunate; wretched. *Conditions in tenement houses were* <u>deplorable</u> *in the early 1900s.*
	fu • tile (fyoot´'l) *adj.,* hopeless. *Nancy realized that her headache made it* <u>futile</u> *to keep studying.*
	in • tri • cate (in´tri kit) *adj.,* complex. *The* <u>intricate</u> *design on the turquoise earrings reminded Melanie of a Navajo painting she had seen.*

READ ALOUD

Read aloud the highlighted passage beginning on line 628 through line 647. What is Rainsford's plan? How does he plan to outwit General Zaroff?

_____

_____

_____

_____

he doubled on his trail again and again, recalling all the lore of the fox hunt, and all the dodges of the fox. Night found him leg-weary, with hands and face lashed by the branches, on a thickly wooded ridge. He knew it would be insane to blunder on through the dark, even if he had the strength. His need for rest was imperative and he thought: "I have played the fox, now I must play the cat of the fable."[21] A

640 big tree with a thick trunk and outspread branches was nearby, and, taking care to leave not the slightest mark, he climbed up into the crotch, and stretching out on one of the broad limbs, after a fashion, rested. Rest brought him new confidence and almost a feeling of security. Even so zealous a hunter as General Zaroff could not trace him there, he told himself; only the devil himself could follow that complicated trail through the jungle after dark. But, perhaps, the general was a devil—

An apprehensive night crawled slowly by like a wounded

650 snake, and sleep did not visit Rainsford, although the silence of a dead world was on the jungle. Toward morning when a dingy gray was varnishing the sky, the cry of some startled bird focused Rainsford's attention in that direction. Something was coming through the bush, coming slowly, carefully, coming by the same winding way Rainsford had come. He flattened himself down on the limb, and through a screen of leaves almost as thick as tapestry, he watched. The thing that was approaching was a man.

It was General Zaroff. He made his way along with his eyes

660 fixed in utmost concentration on the ground before him. He paused, almost beneath the tree, dropped to his knees and studied the ground. Rainsford's impulse was to hurl himself down like a panther, but he saw the general's right hand held something metallic—a small automatic pistol.

The hunter shook his head several times, as if he were puzzled. Then he straightened up and took from his case one of his black cigarettes; its pungent incense-like smoke floated up to Rainsford's nostrils.

Rainsford held his breath. The general's eyes had left the

670 ground and were traveling inch by inch up the tree.

---

21. **"I have played . . . fable."** He has used the trickery of the fox to escape his pursuer; now he must use the cunning of a cat to further escape.

Rainsford froze there, every muscle tensed for a spring. But the sharp eyes of the hunter stopped before they reached the limb where Rainsford lay; a smile spread over his brown face. Very deliberately he blew a smoke ring into the air; then he turned his back on the tree and walked carelessly away, back along the trail he had come. The swish of the underbrush against his hunting boots grew fainter and fainter.

680   The pent-up air burst hotly from Rainsford's lungs. His first thought made him feel sick and numb. The general could follow a trail through the woods at night; he could follow an extremely difficult trail; he must have <u>uncanny</u> powers; only by the merest chance had the Cossack failed to see his quarry.

Rainsford's second thought was even more terrible. It sent a shudder of cold horror through his whole being. Why had the general smiled? Why had he turned back?

Rainsford did not want to believe what his reason told him was true, but the truth was as evident as the sun that had by
690   now pushed through the morning mists. The general was playing with him! The general was saving him for another day's sport! The Cossack was the cat; he was the mouse. Then it was that Rainsford knew the full meaning of terror.

"I will not lose my nerve. I will not."

He slid down from the tree, and struck off again into the woods. His face was set and he forced the machinery of his mind to function. Three hundred yards from his hiding place he stopped where a huge dead tree leaned <u>precariously</u> on a smaller, living one. Throwing off his sack of food,
700   Rainsford took his knife from its sheath and began to work with all his energy.

The job was finished at last, and he threw himself down behind a fallen log a hundred feet away. He did not have to wait long. The cat was coming again to play with the mouse.

Following the trail with the sureness of a bloodhound, came General Zaroff. Nothing escaped those searching black eyes, no crushed blade of grass, no bent twig, no

THINK AND REFLECT

Why does Zaroff blow the smoke ring? What does he want to communicate? (Infer)

_____

_____

_____

_____

NOTE THE FACTS

What second thoughts does Rainsford have?

_____

_____

_____

words for everyday use	un • can • ny (un kan´ē) *adj.*, beyond normal. *Joe has an <u>uncanny</u> sense of direction and never seems to get lost.*
	pre • car • i • ous • ly (prē ker´ē əs lē) *adv.*, insecurely. *The bus in the film rested <u>precariously</u> at the edge of a cliff.*

mark, no matter how faint, in the moss. So intent was the Cossack on his stalking that he was upon the thing
710   Rainsford had made before he saw it. His foot touched the <u>protruding</u> bough that was the trigger. Even as he touched it, the general sensed his danger and leaped back with the agility of an ape. But he was not quite quick enough; the dead tree, delicately adjusted to rest on the cut living one, crashed down and struck the general a glancing blow on the shoulder as it fell; but for his alertness, he must have been smashed beneath it. He staggered, but he did not fall; nor did he drop his revolver. He stood there, rubbing his injured shoulder, and Rainsford, with fear again gripping
720   his heart, heard the general's mocking laugh ring through the jungle.

    "Rainsford," called the general, "if you are within the sound of my voice, as I suppose you are, let me congratulate you. Not many men know how to make a Malay man-catcher. Luckily, for me, I too have hunted in Malacca.[22] You are proving interesting, Mr. Rainsford. I am going now to have my wound dressed; it's only a slight one. But I shall be back. I shall be back."

    When the general, nursing his bruised shoulder, had gone,
730   Rainsford took up his flight again. It was flight now, a desperate, hopeless flight, that carried him on for some hours. Dusk came, then darkness, and still he pressed on. The ground grew softer under his moccasins; the vegetation grew ranker, denser; insects bit him savagely. Then, as he stepped forward, his foot sank into the ooze. He tried to wrench it back, but the muck sucked viciously at his foot as if it were a giant leech. With a violent effort, he tore his foot loose. He knew where he was now. Death Swamp and its quicksand.

    His hands were tight closed as if his nerve were something
740   tangible that someone in the darkness was trying to tear from his grip. The softness of the earth had given him an idea. He stepped back from the quicksand a dozen feet or so, and, like some huge prehistoric beaver, he began to dig.

---

22. **Malacca.** Region in the southwestern Malay Peninsula in Asia

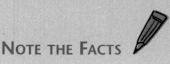

NOTE THE FACTS

In what place does Rainsford find himself?

_____

words for everyday use

pro • trud • ing (prō trōōd´iŋ) *adj.*, jutting out. *The babysitter knew where Ryan was hiding when she saw a small <u>protruding</u> foot.*

Rainsford had dug himself in in France, when a second's delay meant death. That had been a placid pastime compared to his digging now. The pit grew deeper; when it was above his shoulders, he climbed out and from some hard saplings cut stakes and sharpened them to a fine point. These stakes he planted in the bottom of the pit with the points sticking up. With flying fingers he wove a rough carpet of weeds and branches and with it he covered the mouth of the pit. Then, wet with sweat and aching with tiredness, he crouched behind the stump of a lightning-charred tree.

He knew his pursuer was coming; he heard the padding sound of feet on the soft earth, and the night breeze brought him the perfume of the general's cigarette. It seemed to Rainsford that the general was coming with unusual swiftness; he was not feeling his way along, foot by foot. Rainsford, crouching there, could not see the general, nor could he see the pit. He lived a year in a minute. Then he felt an impulse to cry aloud with joy, for he heard the sharp crackle of the breaking branches as the cover of the pit gave way; he heard the sharp scream of pain as the pointed stakes found their mark. He leaped up from his place of concealment. Then he <u>cowered</u> back. Three feet from the pit a man was standing, with an electric torch[23] in his hand.

"You've done well, Rainsford," the voice of the general called. "Your Burmese tiger pit[24] has claimed one of my best dogs. Again you score. I think, Mr. Rainsford, I'll see what you can do against my whole pack. I'm going home for a rest now. Thank you for a most amusing evening."

At daybreak Rainsford, lying near the swamp, was awakened by a sound that made him know that he had new things to learn about fear. It was a distant sound, faint and wavering, but he knew it. It was the baying of a pack of hounds.

Rainsford knew he could do one of two things. He could stay where he was and wait. That was suicide. He could flee.

750

760

770

---

23. **torch.** Flashlight (British)
24. **Burmese tiger pit.** Deep pit used to trap tigers in Burma, a country located in Southeast Asia that is today known as Myanmar

words for everyday use

cow • er (kau´ər) *vi.,* crouch in fear. *The little boy was afraid of the trick-or-treaters and <u>cowered</u> behind his mother.*

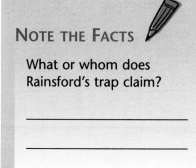

That was postponing the <u>inevitable</u>. For a moment he stood
780   there, thinking. An idea that held a wild chance came to him,
and, tightening his belt, he headed away from the swamp.

    The baying of the hounds drew nearer, then still nearer,
nearer, ever nearer. On a ridge Rainsford climbed a tree.
Down a watercourse, not a quarter of a mile away, he could
see the bush moving. Straining his eyes, he saw the lean
figure of General Zaroff; just ahead of him Rainsford made
out another figure whose wide shoulders surged through
the tall jungle weeds; it was the giant Ivan, and he seemed
pulled forward by some unseen force; Rainsford knew that
790   Ivan must be holding the pack in leash.

    They would be on him any minute now. His mind
worked frantically. He thought of a native trick he had
learned in Uganda. He slid down the tree. He caught hold
of a springy young sapling and to it he fastened his hunting
knife, with the blade pointing down the trail; with a bit of
wild grapevine he tied back the sapling. Then he ran for his
life. The hounds raised their voices as they hit the fresh
scent. Rainsford knew now how an animal at bay feels.

    He had to stop to get his breath. The baying of the hounds
800   stopped abruptly, and Rainsford's heart stopped too. They
must have reached the knife.

    He shinned excitedly up a tree and looked back. His
pursuers had stopped. But the hope that was in Rainsford's
brain when he climbed died; for he saw in the shallow
valley that General Zaroff was still on his feet. But Ivan was
not. The knife, driven by the <u>recoil</u> of the springing tree,
had not wholly failed.

    Rainsford had hardly tumbled to the ground when the
pack took up the cry again.

810   "Nerve, nerve, nerve!" he panted, as he dashed along. A
blue gap showed between the trees dead ahead. Ever nearer
drew the hounds. Rainsford forced himself on toward that
gap. He reached it. It was the shore of the sea. Across a
cove he could see the gloomy gray stone of the château.
Twenty feet below him the sea rumbled and hissed.

NOTE THE FACTS

What happens to Ivan? How?

_____

_____

_____

_____

words for everyday use	**in • ev • i • ta • ble** (in ev´i tə bəl) _n._, that which cannot be avoided. _Although the students tried everything in the book to postpone it, the <u>inevitable</u> was that there would be a test tomorrow._ **re • coil** (rē´koil´) _n._, state of flying back when released. _Hiroshi smacked himself in the face with the <u>recoil</u> of the rubber band he meant to shoot at Tom._

Rainsford hesitated. He heard the hounds. Then he leaped far out into the sea. . . .

When the general and his pack reached the place by the sea, the Cossack stopped. For some minutes he stood

820 regarding the blue-green expanse of water. He shrugged his shoulders. Then he sat down, took a drink of brandy from a silver flask, lit a perfumed cigarette, and hummed a bit from *Madame Butterfly.*[25]

General Zaroff had an exceedingly good dinner in his great paneled dining hall that evening. With it he had a bottle of Pol Roger and half a bottle of Chambertin. Two slight annoyances kept him from perfect enjoyment. One was the thought that it would be difficult to replace Ivan; the other was that his quarry had escaped him; of course the American

830 hadn't played the game—so thought the general as he tasted his after-dinner liqueur. In his library he read, to soothe himself, from the works of Marcus Aurelius.[26] At ten he went up to his bedroom. He was deliciously tired, he said to himself, as he locked himself in. There was a little moonlight, so, before turning on his light, he went to the window and looked down at the courtyard. He could see the great hounds, and he called: "Better luck another time," to them. Then he switched on the light.

A man, who had been hiding in the curtains of the bed,

840 was standing there.

"Rainsford!" screamed the general. "How in God's name did you get here?"

"Swam," said Rainsford. "I found it quicker than walking through the jungle."

The general sucked in his breath and smiled. "I congratulate you," he said. "You have won the game."

Rainsford did not smile. "I am still a beast at bay," he said, in a low, hoarse voice. "Get ready, General Zaroff."

The general made one of his deepest bows. "I see," he

850 said. "Splendid! One of us is to furnish a repast for the hounds. The other will sleep in this very excellent bed. En garde, Rainsford. . . ."

He had never slept in a better bed, Rainsford decided. ■

25. ***Madame Butterfly.*** Opera by Puccini
26. **Marcus Aurelius.** Roman emperor and philosopher who ruled from AD 160 to 180

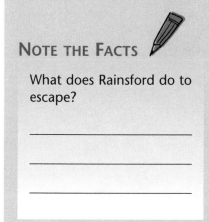

NOTE THE FACTS

What does Rainsford do to escape?

_____

_____

_____

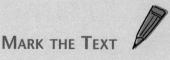

MARK THE TEXT

Highlight the two things that bother General Zaroff.

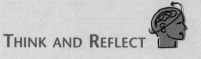

THINK AND REFLECT

Why does Rainsford return and confront General Zaroff? What other options does he have? **(Evaluate)**

_____

_____

_____

_____

Reflect ON YOUR READING

After you finish the story, review your list of vocabulary. Then, work with a reading partner to list synonyms (words with the same meaning) and antonyms (words with the opposite meaning) of ten of your words. Use a thesaurus if necessary. When you finish your list, write ten synonyms and ten antonyms on a sheet of paper. Exchange your list with another pair of students, and work to identify the vocabulary words that match the synonyms and antonyms. When finished, evaluate and discuss your quizzes.

Word	Synonyms	Antonyms

THINK-ALOUD NOTES

Reading Skills and Test Practice

USE CONTEXT CLUES
Discuss with your partner how best to answer the following question about words in context.

1. Read the following lines from the story.

> They were eating borsch, the rich, red soup with whipped cream so dear to Russian palates. Half apologetically General Zaroff said: "We do our best to preserve the amenities of civilization here. Please forgive any lapses. We are well off the beaten track, you know. Do you think the champagne has suffered from its long ocean trip?"

Based on the context clues, which of the following is the best definition for *amenities?*
a. good food
b. hard-to-purchase items
c. something conducive to comfort or pleasure
d. something detestable

What is the correct answer to the question above? How were you able to eliminate the other answers? How did your use of the reading strategy help you answer the question?

Investigate, Inquire, and Imagine

RECALL: GATHER FACTS → INTERPRET: FIND MEANING

1a. Why does Rainsford agree to become "the hunted" in General Zaroff's game?

1b. What actions on the part of Rainsford show his extraordinary skill as a hunter?

ANALYZE: TAKE THINGS APART → SYNTHESIZE: BRING THINGS TOGETHER

2a. What different meanings does the word *game* have in the story?

2b. How do you think Rainsford will change after having been "the hunted"?

PERSPECTIVE: LOOK AT OTHER VIEWS → EMPATHY: SEE FROM INSIDE

3a. If you were Rainsford, would you consider Zaroff's rules of the game fair? Why, or why not?

3b. If you were Rainsford at the end of the story, how would you regard the captive men in the cellar? What would you do for them?

WordWorkshop

PREFIXES, SUFFIXES, AND WORD ROOTS. A **prefix** is a letter or a group of letters add to the beginning of a word to change its meaning. A **suffix** is a group of letters added to the end of a word to change its meaning. Identify the prefixes and suffixes in the following words. Then, identify the part of the word that is left if you separate the prefix and the suffix. This is the **word root**. For lists of prefixes, suffixes, and word roots, see Unit 9, pages 482–486.

1. **disarming**

   prefix: _____ suffix: _____ word root: _____

2. **imperative**

   prefix: _____ suffix: _____ word root: _____

3. **indolently**

   prefix: _____ suffix: _____ word root: _____

4. **inevitable**

   prefix: _____ suffix: _____ word root: _____

5. **intricate**

   prefix: _____ suffix: _____ word root: _____

Literary Tools

IRONY. **Irony** is a difference between appearance and reality. *Verbal irony* occurs when a statement is made that implies its opposite. *Irony of situation* occurs when an event violates the expectations of the characters. What examples of verbal irony and irony of situation did you find as you read the story?

_____

_____

_____

_____

_____

Read-Write Connection

Imagine that you are the famous hunter Rainsford in this story. Think about an early comment you made to Whitney, "Who cares how a jaguar feels?" Explain how you feel about this statement after your experience with General Zaroff.

_____

_____

_____

_____

_____

_____

Beyond the Reading

RESEARCH RUSSIAN HISTORY. When Zaroff mentions "the debacle in Russia," he is referring to the Russian Revolution of 1917 during which the Czar was overthrown and wealthy landowners lost their property. Do some research in the library or on the Internet to learn more about the Russian Revolution of 1917. What did the revolutionaries hope to accomplish? What happened to members of the nobility afterward? What does Zaroff mean when he says, "I shall never have to open a tea room in Monte Carlo or drive a taxi in Paris"?

GO ONLINE. Visit the EMC Internet Resource Center at **emcp.com** to find links and additional activities for this selection.

"The Gift of the Magi"

by O. Henry

Active READING STRATEGY

WRITE THINGS DOWN

Before Reading ➤ PREVIEW VOCABULARY

❑ With a partner, review the Words for Everyday Use and the footnotes at the bottom of the selection's pages. Read each word, its definition, and the sentence in which it is used.

❑ Copy the words and their definitions into the Word Map below.

❑ Choose a word, and have your partner use it in a new sentence. Write the sentence in the graphic organizer.

❑ Then, have your partner choose a word for you to use in a new sentence. Continue taking turns until you have covered all of the words.

Graphic Organizer

Unfamiliar word:
Definition:
Word parts I recognize:
Context clues:
New sentence using word:

CONNECT

Reader's resource

O. Henry (1862–1910) was the pseudonym of William Sydney Porter. O. Henry's stories are famous for their distinctive surprise endings in which an ironic event occurs that violates expectations of the characters or the reader. **"The Gift of the Magi"** contains, perhaps, the most surprise ending of all. The story, first published in 1906, appeared in the short story collection *The Four Million*, twenty-five stories set in the author's favorite locale, New York City.

Word watch

PREVIEW VOCABULARY

adornment	meretricious
agile	nimble
appertain	parsimony
duplication	predominate
falter	prudence
imputation	scrutiny
inconsequential	subside
laboriously	

Reader's journal

What have you done to give a special gift to someone?

_____

_____

_____

TACKLE DIFFICULT VOCABULARY

❑ Follow along in the text as your teacher reads aloud the first paragraph.

❑ Identify any difficult words and work as a class to unlock their meanings, using context clues and word parts.

❑ Record the words and their meanings in your graphic organizer or notebook.

❑ Read the remainder of the selection on your own. Stop when you encounter a difficult word and try to use context clues or word parts to unlock meaning. Continue to record difficult words and their meanings in your graphic organizer or notebook.

NOTE THE FACTS

How much money does Della have? How does she manage to save it?

_____

_____

_____

THINK AND REFLECT

What is bothering Della? (Interpret)

_____

_____

_____

The Gift of the Magi

O. Henry

One dollar and eighty-seven cents. That was all. And sixty cents of it was in pennies. Pennies saved one and two at a time by bulldozing the grocer and the vegetable man and the butcher until one's cheeks burned with the silent <u>imputation</u> of <u>parsimony</u> that such close dealing implied. Three times Della counted it. One dollar and eighty-seven cents. And the next day would be Christmas.

There was clearly nothing to do but flop down on the shabby little couch and howl. So Della did it. Which insti-
10 gates the moral reflection that life is made up of sobs, sniffles, and smiles, with sniffles <u>predominating</u>.

While the mistress of the home is gradually <u>subsiding</u> from the first stage to the second, take a look at the home. A furnished flat at $8 per week. It did not exactly beggar

---

words for everyday use

im • pu • ta • tion (im pyoo tā´shən) *n.*, charge; claim. *The defense attorney's imputation was that the plaintiff was not telling the whole truth.*

par • si • mo • ny (pär´ sə mō´nē) *n.*, stinginess. *Bronwen's parsimony extended to leaving inadequate tips.*

pre • dom • i • nate (prē däm´ ə nāt´) *vi.*, prevail. *Of the many types of birds that come to our backyard, finches seem to predominate.*

sub • side (səb sīd´) *vi.*, settle; lessen in intensity. *After his father's anger subsided, Luis asked to borrow the car.*

description, but it certainly had that word on the lookout for the mendicancy[1] squad.

In the vestibule below was a letter box into which no letter would go, and an electric button from which no mortal finger could coax a ring. Also <u>appertaining</u> thereunto was a card bearing the name "Mr. James Dillingham Young."

The "Dillingham" had been flung to the breeze during a former period of prosperity when its possessor was being paid $30 per week. Now, when the income was shrunk to $20, the letters of "Dillingham" looked blurred, as though they were thinking seriously of contracting to a modest and unassuming D. But whenever Mr. James Dillingham Young came home and reached his flat above he was called "Jim" and greatly hugged by Mrs. James Dillingham Young, already introduced to you as Della. Which is all very good.

Della finished her cry and attended to her cheeks with the powder rag. She stood by the window and looked out dully at a gray cat walking a gray fence in a gray backyard. Tomorrow would be Christmas Day, and she had only $1.87 with which to buy Jim a present. She had been saving every penny she could for months, with this result. Twenty dollars a week doesn't go far. Expenses had been greater than she had calculated. They always are. Only $1.87 to buy a present for Jim. Her Jim. Many a happy hour she had spent planning for something nice for him. Something fine and rare and sterling—something just a little bit near to being worthy of the honor of being owned by Jim.

There was a pier glass[2] between the windows of the room. Perhaps you have seen a pier glass in an $8 flat. A very thin and very <u>agile</u> person may, by observing his reflection in a rapid sequence of longitudinal strips, obtain a fairly accurate conception of his looks. Della, being slender, had mastered the art.

Suddenly she whirled from the window and stood before the glass. Her eyes were shining brilliantly, but her face had

---

1. **mendicancy.** Begging
2. **pier glass.** Narrow mirror set between two windows

PLOT AND THEME. A **plot** is a series of events related to a central conflict, or struggle. A **theme** is a central idea in a literary work. In "The Gift of the Magi," the plot focuses on a married couple who make personal sacrifices to buy Christmas gifts for each other. As you read, notice how the plot helps to develop the theme of the story.

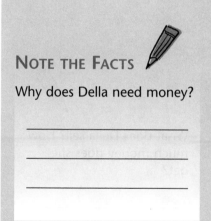

NOTE THE FACTS

Why does Della need money?

_____

_____

_____

MARK THE TEXT

Circle the text that tells what two possessions the Youngs are most proud of.

50   lost its color within twenty seconds. Rapidly she pulled down her hair and let it fall to its full length.

Now, there were two possessions of the James Dillingham Youngs in which they both took a mighty pride. One was Jim's gold watch that had been his father's and his grandfather's. The other was Della's hair. Had the Queen of Sheba[3] lived in the flat across the air shaft, Della would have let her hair hang out the window some day to dry just to depreciate Her Majesty's jewels and gifts. Had King

60   Solomon[4] been the janitor, with all his treasures piled up in the basement, Jim would have pulled out his watch every time he passed, just to see him pluck at his beard from envy.

So now Della's beautiful hair fell about her rippling and shining like a cascade of brown waters. It reached below her knee and made itself almost a garment for her. And then she did it up again nervously and quickly. Once she faltered for a minute and stood still while a tear or two splashed on the worn red carpet.

70   On went her old brown jacket; on went her old brown hat. With a whirl of skirts and with the brilliant sparkle still in her eyes, she fluttered out the door and down the stairs to the street.

Where she stopped the sign read: "Mme. Sofronie. Hair Goods of All Kinds." One flight up Della ran, and collected herself, panting. Madame, large, too white, chilly, hardly looked the "Sofronie."

"Will you buy my hair?" asked Della.

"I buy hair," said Madame. "Take yer hat off and let's have

80   a sight at the looks of it."

Down rippled the brown cascade.

"Twenty dollars," said Madame, lifting the mass with a practiced hand.

"Give it to me quick," said Della.

NOTE THE FACTS

What does Della sell? How much money does she get?

_____

_____

3. **Queen of Sheba.** Biblical queen
4. **King Solomon.** Biblical king

words for everyday use	de • pre • ci • ate (di prē´shē āt) *vt.*, lower in value. *Although the stock depreciated, Mr. Talbot hung onto it hoping that its value would rise again.*
	fal • ter (fôl´tər) *vi.*, hesitate. *I expected Kate to stumble over her words when giving the speech, but she never faltered.*

Oh, and the next two hours tripped by on rosy wings.
Forget the hashed metaphor. She was ransacking the stores
for Jim's present.

She found it at last. It surely had been made for Jim and
no one else. There was no other like it in any of the stores,
and she had turned all of them inside out. It was a platinum
fob chain[5] simple and chaste in design, properly proclaiming
its value by substance alone and not by <u>meretricious</u>
ornamentation—as all good things should do. It was even
worthy of The Watch. As soon as she saw it she knew that
it must be Jim's. It was like him. Quietness and value—the
description applied to both. Twenty-one dollars they took
from her for it, and she hurried home with the eighty-seven
cents. With that chain on his watch Jim might be properly
anxious about the time in any company. Grand as the watch
was, he sometimes looked at it on the sly on account of the
old leather strap that he used in place of a chain.

When Della reached home her intoxication gave way a
little to <u>prudence</u> and reason. She got out her curling irons
and lighted the gas and went to work repairing the ravages
made by generosity added to love. Which is always a
tremendous task, dear friends—a mammoth task.

Within forty minutes her head was covered with tiny,
close-lying curls that made her look wonderfully like a
truant schoolboy. She looked at her reflection in the mirror
long, carefully, and critically.

"If Jim doesn't kill me," she said to herself, "before he
takes a second look at me, he'll say I look like a Coney
Island[6] chorus girl. But what could I do—oh! what could I
do with a dollar and eighty-seven cents?"

At seven o'clock the coffee was made and the frying
pan was on the back of the stove hot and ready to cook
the chops.

90

100

110

Use THE STRATEGY

TACKLE DIFFICULT VOCABULARY.
Stop when you encounter a
difficult word and review the
text to locate context clues.
You might also try to identify
word parts to help you unlock
meaning. Be sure to record
the difficult words and their
meanings in your graphic
organizer or notebook.

NOTE THE FACTS

What does Della do when
she gets home?

_____
_____
_____
_____

WHAT DO YOU
WONDER?

_____
_____

---

5. **fob chain.** Chain for a pocket watch
6. **Coney Island.** Section of Brooklyn, New York, known for its amusement park

words for everyday use

mer • e • tri • cious (mer′ə trish′əs) *adj.,* alluring in a false, showy way. *Sonia cast aside the <u>meretricious</u> scarves and selected a modest one.*

pru • dence (prōōd′ns) *n.,* sound judgment. *Jack showed <u>prudence</u> when he started a money market account with the money he received for Christmas.*

Jim was never late. Della doubled the fob chain in her hand and sat on the corner of the table near the door that he always entered. Then she heard his step on the stair away down on the first flight, and she turned white for just a moment. She had a habit of saying little silent prayers about the simplest everyday things, and now she whispered: "Please God, make him think I am still pretty."

The door opened and Jim stepped in and closed it. He looked thin and very serious. Poor fellow, he was only twenty-two—and to be burdened with a family! He needed a new overcoat and he was without gloves.

Jim stopped inside the door, as immovable as a setter at the scent of quail. His eyes were fixed upon Della, and there was an expression in them that she could not read, and it terrified her. It was not anger, nor surprise, nor disapproval, nor horror, nor any of the sentiments that she had been prepared for. He simply stared at her fixedly with that peculiar expression on his face.

Della wriggled off the table and went for him.

"Jim, darling," she cried, "don't look at me that way. I had my hair cut off and sold it because I couldn't have lived through Christmas without giving you a present. It'll grow out again—you won't mind, will you? I just had to do it. My hair grows awfully fast. Say 'Merry Christmas,' Jim, and let's be happy. You don't know what a nice—what a beautiful, nice gift I've got for you."

"You've cut off your hair?" asked Jim, <u>laboriously</u>, as if he had not arrived at that patent fact yet even after the hardest mental labor.

"Cut it off and sold it," said Della. "Don't you like me just as well, anyhow? I'm me without my hair, ain't I?"

Jim looked about the room curiously.

"You say your hair is gone?" he said, with an air almost of idiocy.

"You needn't look for it," said Della. "It's sold, I tell you—sold and gone, too. It's Christmas Eve, boy. Be good to me, for it went for you. Maybe the hairs of my head were numbered,"

words for everyday use

la • bo • ri • ous • ly (lə bôr´ē əs lē) adv., with difficulty. At the dreaded sound of her alarm clock, Lisa <u>laboriously</u> dragged herself out of bed.

NOTE THE FACTS

How does Jim react to Della's appearance at first?

_____

_____

_____

_____

FIX-UP IDEA

Ask Questions

If you are having trouble following the selection, stop and ask yourself questions about the text. These questions will help you pinpoint things that are confusing you or things that you want to come back to later. You can ask questions in your head, or jot them down in the margins.

she went on with a sudden serious sweetness, "but nobody could ever count my love for you. Shall I put the chops on, Jim?"

Out of his trance Jim seemed quickly to wake. He enfolded his Della. For ten seconds let us regard with discreet scrutiny some inconsequential object in the other direction. Eight dollars a week or a million a year—what is the difference? A mathematician or a wit would give you the wrong answer. The magi[7] brought valuable gifts, but that was not among them. This dark assertion will be illuminated later on.

Jim drew a package from his overcoat pocket and threw it upon the table.

"Don't make any mistake, Dell," he said, "about me. I don't think there's anything in the way of a haircut or a shave or a shampoo that could make me like my girl any less. But if you'll unwrap that package you may see why you had me going awhile at first."

White fingers and nimble tore at the string and paper. And then an ecstatic scream of joy; and then, alas! a quick feminine change to hysterical tears and wails, necessitating the immediate employment of all the comforting powers of the lord of the flat.

For there lay The Combs—the set of combs, side and back, that Della had worshiped for long in a Broadway window. Beautiful combs, pure tortoise shell, with jeweled rims just the shade to wear in the beautiful vanished hair. They were expensive combs, she knew, and her heart had simply craved and yearned over them without the least hope of possession. And now, they were hers, but the tresses that should have adorned the coveted adornments were gone.

But she hugged them to her bosom, and at length she was able to look up with dim eyes and a smile and say: "My hair grows so fast, Jim!"

160

170

180

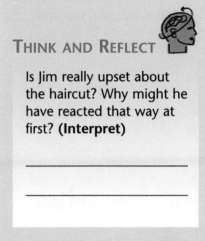

THINK AND REFLECT

Is Jim really upset about the haircut? Why might he have reacted that way at first? **(Interpret)**

_____

_____

MARK THE TEXT

Highlight or underline the sentence that tells what Jim has purchased for Della.

---

7. **magi.** Wise men from the East who brought gifts to the infant Jesus

words for everyday use

scru • ti • ny (skrŌŌt´'n ē) n., careful, searching look. *The house looked nice from afar, but closer scrutiny revealed peeling paint and rotting woodwork.*

in • con • se • quen • tial (in kän´si kwen´shəl) adj., unimportant. *The problem that seemed so important last week now seems inconsequential.*

nim • ble (nim´bəl) adj., agile. *Karen was the nimble teammate who seemed to dance on the balance beam.*

a • dorn • ment (ə dôrn´mənt) n., ornament, decoration. *The adornment of the Christmas tree was a family tradition.*

And then Della leaped up like a little singed cat and cried, "Oh, oh!"

Jim had not yet seen his beautiful present. She held it out to him eagerly upon her open palm. The dull precious metal seemed to flash with a reflection of her bright and ardent spirit.

"Isn't it a dandy, Jim? I hunted all over town to find it. You'll have to look at the time a hundred times a day now. Give me your watch. I want to see how it looks on it."

Instead of obeying, Jim tumbled down on the couch and 200 put his hands under the back of his head and smiled.

"Dell," said he, "let's put our Christmas presents away and keep 'em awhile. They're too nice to use just at present. I sold the watch to get the money to buy your combs. And now suppose you put the chops on."

The magi, as you know, were wise men—wonderfully wise men—who brought gifts to the Babe in the manger. They invented the art of giving Christmas presents. Being wise, their gifts were no doubt wise ones, possibly bearing the privilege of exchange in case of <u>duplication</u>. And here I 210 have lamely related to you the uneventful chronicle of two foolish children in a flat who most unwisely sacrificed for each other the greatest treasures of their house. But in a last word to the wise of these days let it be said that of all who give gifts these two were the wisest. Of all who give and receive gifts, such as they are wisest. Everywhere they are wisest. They are the magi. ■

NOTE THE FACTS

What possession does Jim sell for money to buy Della's gift?

_____

_____

READ ALOUD

Read the highlighted text aloud. What similarity exists between the magi and the characters in this story? Why does the narrator call Della and Jim not foolish but wise?

_____

_____

_____

_____

_____

_____

words for everyday use

du • pli • ca • tion (doo′ pli kā′shən) *n.*, copy, double. *This letter is a <u>duplication</u> of the one I sent you last week that was lost in the mail.*

Reflect ON YOUR READING

After reading, review your list of difficult words and their definitions. Then, work with a partner to create a crossword puzzle with at least ten of the words. You might provide definitions, synonyms, antonyms, or other hints as crossword clues. When you and your partner finish the puzzle, exchange puzzles with another pair of students and work with your partner to complete the new crossword. When finished, evaluate the puzzles with the other pair of students. Evaluate each puzzle on its neatness, completeness, understandability, ease of use, and difficulty level.

Reading Skills and Test Practice

USE CONTEXT CLUES

Discuss with your partner how best to answer the following question about words in context.

Read the following sentence from the story.

> It was a platinum fob chain simple and chaste in design, properly proclaiming its value by substance alone and not by <u>meretricious</u> ornamentation—as all good things should do.

Based on the context clues, which is the best synonym for *meretricious?*

a. simple
b. platinum
c. gaudy
d. ugly

What is the correct answer to the question above? How were you able to eliminate the other answers? How did your use of the reading strategy help you answer the question?

_____

_____

_____

_____

THINK-ALOUD
NOTES

_____
_____
_____
_____
_____
_____
_____
_____
_____
_____
_____

Investigate, Inquire, and Imagine

RECALL: GATHER FACTS ➤ **INTERPRET: FIND MEANING**

1a. What reaction does Della fear Jim may have upon seeing her bobbed hair?

1b. How does Jim reassure Della?

ANALYZE: TAKE THINGS APART ➤ **SYNTHESIZE: BRING THINGS TOGETHER**

2a. How does the narrator interact with the reader in this story? Provide several examples that illustrate this interaction. Then discuss (analyze) whether or not you find the narrator's commentary helpful or intrusive.

2b. Why does the narrator say about Della and Jim, "Of all who give and receive gifts these two were the wisest"? How does this passage relate to the title of the story?

PERSPECTIVE: LOOK AT OTHER VIEWS ➤ **EMPATHY: SEE FROM INSIDE**

3a. What in Della or Jim's character causes them to give the gifts they do? What do you think leads to such a capacity?

3b. Taking the perspective of Della or Jim, write a paragraph telling whether or not it was a mistake to buy the gift you did. For example, if you were Jim, would you take the combs back and try to buy back your watch? Why, or why not?

Literary Tools

PLOT AND THEME. A **plot** is a series of events related to a central conflict, or struggle. A **theme** is a central idea in a literary work. Complete the sequence chart below to map out each event as it happens in the story. Try to determine what the plot reveals about the theme. What do you consider to be the main theme of the story?

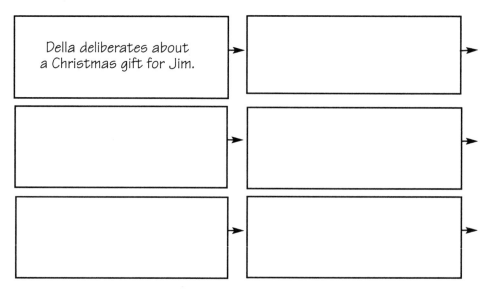

Della deliberates about a Christmas gift for Jim.

WordWorkshop

Complete the exercise below. You may use a dictionary and a thesaurus.

1. Look up *appertain* in a sentence. Note its definition. Then use *appertain* in a sentence.

   _____

   _____

2. List two synonyms for *agile.*

   _____   _____

3. Provide two antonyms for *nimble.*

   _____   _____

4. Use the dictionary to look up *predominate.* Does the word derive from the joining of a prefix and base word or one longer Latin word?

   _____

5. Which of the following actions would most clearly be an act of *prudence?*

   _____

   a. calling in sick to work to go to the beach
   b. saving money toward college
   c. helping out at a nursing home in the morning before school

Read-Write Connection

Imagine that you are either Della or Jim in this story. Using your own paper, write about why you wanted to give your spouse an expensive gift that you could not really afford.

Beyond the Reading

LITERARY CRITIQUE. Locate a copy of O. Henry's short story collection *The Four Million,* or another of his collections of short stories from the library. Select and read a short story from the collection. Then write a short review about the story. Compare the story to "The Gift of the Magi." Does it have a similar theme? Discuss the similarities and differences between the main characters. Does it use examples of irony? What do you like or not like about the story? Would you recommend it to your friends? Why, or why not?

GO ONLINE. Visit the EMC Internet Resource Center at **emcp.com** to find links and additional activities for this selection.

"Catch the Moon"

by Judith Ortiz Cofer

Reader's resource

"**Catch the Moon**" appears in Judith Ortiz Cofer's collection of short stories, *An Island Like You* (1996). The Puerto Rican boys and girls depicted in these stories are all struggling in different ways to determine their futures as they advance from adolescence to adulthood. They live in the *barrio*, a Spanish-speaking neighborhood. Luis Cintrón, the main character of "Catch the Moon," searches for a way to find meaning in his life. After six months in juvenile hall, he is working off the rest of his time in his father's junkyard.

Word watch

PREVIEW VOCABULARY

decapitate	makeshift
dismantle	mint
ebony	mock
escort	relic
harass	vintage
mahogany	vulgar

Reader's journal

What would you be willing to do to fit in with a gang or group?

_____

_____

_____

_____

_____

Active READING STRATEGY

MAKE PREDICTIONS

Before Reading ➤ PREVIEW THE SELECTION

❑ Read the Reader's Resource and discuss the information in class.
❑ Skim the selection, looking at the pictures and getting familiar with the Words for Everyday Use.
❑ In the first column of the Predictions Chart below, jot down the clues about the story you found from previewing.
❑ Work with the class to form predictions about the content of the story based on these clues.

Graphic Organizer

Clues	Predictions	What Really Happens

Catch the Moon

Judith Ortiz Cofer

During Reading

MAKE PREDICTIONS

❑ Follow along in the text as you or your teacher read aloud the first page.

❑ Next, work with the class to identify clues from this passage.

❑ Record the clues in the first column of your chart. From these clues, make a prediction about characters and events to come. Record your prediction in your chart.

❑ Read the remainder of the story on your own. Stop at the end of each page to record clues, make predictions, and adjust and check the accuracy of previous predictions.

READ ALOUD

Read the following Spanish words from the selection aloud, using the pronunciations given below.

Luis	lü-ēs′
Jorge	hôr′-hā
Cintrón	sēn-trōn′
Tiburones	tē-bü-rō′-nās′
tiburón	tē-bü-rōn
barrio	bä′-rē-ō
cementerio	sā-mən-tā′-rē-ō
señorita	sān-yə-rē′-tä
sí	sē
hijo	ē′-hō

uis Cintrón sits on top of a six-foot pile of hubcaps and watches his father walk away into the steel jungle of his car junkyard. Released into his old man's custody after six months in juvenile hall—for breaking and entering—and he didn't even take anything. He did it on a dare. But the old lady with the million cats was a light sleeper, and good with her aluminum cane. He has a scar on his head to prove it.

Now Luis is wondering whether he should have stayed in and done his full time. Jorge Cintrón of Jorge Cintrón & Son, Auto Parts and Salvage, has decided that Luis should wash and polish every hubcap in the yard. The hill he is sitting on is only the latest couple of hundred wheel covers that have come in. Luis grunts and stands up on top of his silver mountain. He yells at no one, "Someday, son, all this will be yours," and sweeps his arms like the Pope blessing a crowd over the piles of car sandwiches and mounds of metal parts that cover this acre of land outside the city. He is the "Son" of Jorge Cintrón & Son, and so far his father has had more than one reason to wish it was plain Jorge Cintrón on the sign.

Luis has been getting in trouble since he started high school two years ago, mainly because of the "social group" he

MARK THE TEXT

Underline or highlight the sentence that tells what Luis's specialty is.

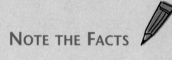

Literary TOOLS

CHARACTER. A **character** is a person who takes part in the action of a literary work. A *static character* is one who does not change during the course of the action. A *dynamic character* is one who does change. As you read, determine whether Luis is a static or dynamic character.

organized—a bunch of guys who were into <u>harassing</u> the local authorities. Their thing was taking something to the limit on a dare or, better still, doing something dangerous, like breaking into a house, not to steal, just to prove that they could do it. That was Luis's specialty, coming up with very complicated plans, like military strategies, and assigning the "jobs" to guys who wanted to join the Tiburones.

30   *Tiburón* means "shark," and Luis had gotten the name from watching an old movie about a Puerto Rican gang called the Sharks[1] with his father. Luis thought it was one of the dumbest films he had ever seen. Everybody sang their lines, and the guys all pointed their toes and leaped in the air when they were supposed to be slaughtering each other. But he liked their name, the Sharks, so he made it Spanish and had it air-painted on his black T-shirt with a killer shark under it, jaws opened wide and dripping with blood. It didn't take long for the other guys in the barrio[2]

40   to ask about it.

    Man, had they had a good time. The girls were interested too. Luis outsmarted everybody by calling his organization a social club and registering it at Central High. That meant they were legal, even let out of last-period class on Fridays for their "club" meetings. It was just this year, after a couple of botched jobs, that the teachers had started getting suspicious. The first one to go wrong was when he sent Kenny Matoa to *borrow* some "souvenirs" out of Anita Robles's locker. He got caught. It seems that Matoa had

50   been reading Anita's diary and didn't hear her coming down the hall. Anita was supposed to be in the gym at that time but had copped out with the usual female excuse of cramps. You could hear her screams all the way to Market Street.

    She told the principal all she knew about the Tiburones, and Luis had to talk fast to convince old Mr. Williams that the club did put on cultural activities such as the Save the Animals talent show. What Mr. Williams didn't know was

---

1. **Sharks.** Fictional Puerto Rican gang from the movie *West Side Story*
2. **barrio.** Spanish-speaking neighborhood in the United States

words for everyday use	**ha • rass** (hə ras') *vt.,* annoy persistently. *The boy <u>harassed</u> the girl by pulling her ponytail repeatedly.*

that the animal that was being "saved" with the ticket sales
was Luis's pet boa, which needed quite a few live mice to stay
60   healthy and happy. They kept E.S. (which stood for
"Endangered Species") in Luis's room, but she belonged to
the club and it was the members' responsibility to raise the
money to feed their mascot. So last year they had sponsored
their first annual Save the Animals talent show, and it had
been a great success. The Tiburones had come dressed as
Latino Elvises and did a grand finale to "All Shook Up" that
made the audience go wild. Mr. Williams had smiled when
Luis talked, maybe remembering how the math teacher, Mrs.
Laguna, had dragged him out in the aisle to rock-and-roll
70   with her. Luis had gotten out of that one, but barely.

His father was a problem too. He objected to the T-shirt
logo, calling it disgusting and <u>vulgar</u>. Mr. Cintrón prided
himself on his own neat, elegant style of dressing after work,
and on his manners and large vocabulary, which he picked up
by taking correspondence courses in just about everything.
Luis thought that it was just his way of staying busy since
Luis's mother had died, almost three years ago, of cancer. He
had never gotten over it.

All this was going through Luis's head as he slid down the
80   hill of hubcaps. The tub full of soapy water, the can of polish,
and the bag of rags had been neatly placed in front of a
<u>makeshift</u> table made from two car seats and a piece of ply-
wood. Luis heard a car drive up and someone honk their
horn. His father emerged from inside a new red Mustang that
had been totaled. He usually <u>dismantled</u> every small feature
by hand before sending the vehicle into the *cementerio,*[3] as he
called the lot. Luis watched as the most beautiful girl he had
ever seen climbed out of a <u>vintage</u> white Volkswagen Bug.
She stood in the sunlight in her white sundress waiting for
90   his father, while Luis stared. She was like a smooth wood

---

3. *cementerio.* Cemetery (Spanish)

words for everyday use	vul • gar (vəl′gər) *adj.*, lacking in cultivation, perception, or taste. *Emily thought the fake flowers on Jessica's dress were <u>vulgar</u>, or lacking in taste.*
	make • shift (māk′ shift) *adj.*, crude and temporary substitute. *A <u>makeshift</u> clinic was set up by the accident site with a table made of plywood and sawhorses.*
	dis • man • tle (dis man′ təl) *vt.*, take apart. *Jed <u>dismantled</u> the bookcase and placed the disassembled boards in the moving truck.*
	vin • tage (vin′ tij) *adj.*, dating from the past. *The <u>vintage</u> ice cream maker was made in the 1930s.*

FIX-UP IDEA

Read in Shorter Chunks
If you have difficulty applying the reading strategy, read in shorter chunks. You might stop and record clues as you come to them. You might also stop as soon as you have enough information to adjust or check a previous prediction. Continue applying the fix-up idea as needed.

THINK AND REFLECT

Does Luis's explanation for why his father takes correspondence courses seem believable? Why, or why not? **(Evaluate)**

_____

_____

_____

Use THE STRATEGY

MAKE PREDICTIONS. Make sure to stop at the end of each page to record clues, make predictions, and adjust and check the accuracy of previous predictions.

carving. Her skin was <u>mahogany</u>, almost black, and her arms and legs were long and thin, but curved in places so that she did not look bony and hard—more like a ballerina. And her <u>ebony</u> hair was braided close to her head. Luis let his breath out, feeling a little dizzy. He had forgotten to breathe. Both the girl and his father heard him. Mr. Cintrón waved him over.

"Luis, the señorita here has lost a wheel cover. Her car is twenty-five years old, so it will not be an easy match. 100 Come look on this side."

Luis tossed a wrench he'd been holding into a toolbox like he was annoyed, just to make a point about slave labor. Then he followed his father, who knelt on the gravel and began to point out every detail of the hubcap. Luis was hardly listening. He watched the girl take a piece of paper from her handbag.

"Señor Cintrón, I have drawn the hubcap for you, since I will have to leave soon. My home address and telephone number are here, and also my parents' office number." She 110 handed the paper to Mr. Cintrón, who nodded.

"Sí, señorita, very good. This will help my son look for it. Perhaps there is one in that stack there." He pointed to the pile of caps that Luis was supposed to wash and polish. "Yes, I'm almost certain that there is a match there. Of course, I do not know if it's near the top or the bottom. You will give us a few days, yes?"

Luis just stared at his father like he was crazy. But he didn't say anything because the girl was smiling at him with a funny expression on her face. Maybe she thought he had 120 X-ray eyes like Superman, or maybe she was <u>mocking</u> him.

"Please call me Naomi, Señor Cintrón. You know my mother. She is the director of the funeral home. . . ." Mr. Cintrón seemed surprised at first; he prided himself on having a great memory. Then his friendly expression changed to one of sadness as he recalled the day of his wife's burial. Naomi did not finish her sentence. She reached over and placed her hand on Mr. Cintrón's arm for a moment.

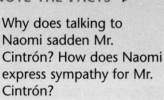

NOTE THE FACTS

Why does Naomi Ramirez come to the junkyard?

_____

_____

_____

_____

NOTE THE FACTS

Why does talking to Naomi sadden Mr. Cintrón? How does Naomi express sympathy for Mr. Cintrón?

_____

_____

_____

_____

_____

words for everyday use

ma • hog • a • ny (mə hä′ gə nē) *adj.*, colored deep brown like mahogany wood. *The <u>mahogany</u> cushions matched the wood in the room.*
eb • o • ny (e′ bə nē) *adj.*, black. *The keys on a piano are <u>ebony</u> and ivory.*
mock (mäk) *vt.*, treat with contempt or ridicule. *The boys <u>mocked</u> their new classmate by imitating his gestures and walk.*

Then she said "Adiós" softly, and got in her shiny white car.
She waved to them as she left, and her gold bracelets flash-
130 ing in the sun nearly blinded Luis.

Mr. Cintrón shook his head. "How about that," he said as
if to himself. "They are the Dominican owners of Ramirez
Funeral Home." And, with a sigh, "She seems like such a
nice young woman. Reminds me of your mother when she
was her age."

Hearing the funeral parlor's name, Luis remembered
too. The day his mother died, he had been in her room at
the hospital while his father had gone for coffee. The
alarm had gone off on her monitor and nurses had come
140 running in, pushing him outside. After that, all he recalled
was the anger that had made him punch a hole in his bedroom wall. And afterward he had refused to talk to anyone
at the funeral. Strange, he did see a black girl there who
didn't try like the others to talk to him, but actually
ignored him as she <u>escorted</u> family members to the viewing room and brought flowers in. Could it be that the
skinny girl in a frilly white dress had been Naomi? She
didn't act like she had recognized him today, though. Or
maybe she thought that he was a jerk.

150 Luis grabbed the drawing from his father. The old man
looked like he wanted to walk down memory lane. But Luis
was in no mood to listen to the old stories about his falling
in love on a tropical island. The world they'd lived in
before he was born wasn't his world. No beaches and palm
trees here. Only junk as far as he could see. He climbed
back up his hill and studied Naomi's sketch. It had obviously been done very carefully. It was signed "Naomi Ramirez"
in the lower right-hand corner. He memorized the telephone number.

160 Luis washed hubcaps all day until his hands were red and
raw, but he did not come across the small silver bowl that
would fit the VW. After work he took a few practice
Frisbee shots across the yard before showing his father
what he had accomplished: rows and rows of shiny rings

READ ALOUD

Read aloud the
highlighted text on this
page. Where has Luis seen
Naomi before?

_____

_____

_____

_____

_____

MAKE A NOTE

_____

_____

_____

_____

words for everyday use

es • cort (es′ kärt) vt., accompany as an escort. *The director <u>escorted</u> his leading lady to the premiere.*

drying in the sun. His father nodded and showed him the bump on his temple where one of Luis's flying saucers had gotten him.

"Practice makes perfect, you know. Next time you'll probably <u>decapitate</u> me." Luis heard him struggle with the
170 word *decapitate*, which Mr. Cintrón pronounced in syllables. Showing off his big vocabulary again, Luis thought. He looked closely at the bump, though. He felt bad about it.

"They look good, hijo." Mr. Cintrón made a sweeping gesture with his arms over the yard. "You know, all this will have to be classified. My dream is to have all the parts divided by year, make of car, and condition. Maybe now that you are here to help me, this will happen."

"Pop . . ." Luis put his hand on his father's shoulder. They were the same height and build, about five foot six
180 and muscular. "The judge said six months of free labor for you, not life, okay?" Mr. Cintrón nodded, looking distracted. It was then that Luis suddenly noticed how gray his hair had turned—it used to be shiny black like his own—and that there were deep lines in his face. His father had turned into an old man and he hadn't even noticed.

"Son, you must follow the judge's instructions. Like she said, next time you get in trouble, she's going to treat you like an adult, and I think you know what that means. Hard time, no breaks."

190 "Yeah, yeah. That's what I'm doing, right? Working my hands to the bone instead of enjoying my summer. But listen, she didn't put me under house arrest, right? I'm going out tonight."

"Home by ten. She did say something about a curfew, Luis." Mr. Cintrón had stopped smiling and was looking upset. It had always been hard for them to talk more than a minute or two before his father got offended at something Luis said, or at his sarcastic tone. He was always doing something wrong.

200 Luis threw the rag down on the table and went to sit in his

NOTE THE FACTS

What is Mr. Cintrón's plan for the junkyard? What does Luis think of this idea?

_____

_____

_____

_____

words for everyday use   **de • cap • i • tate** (di ka′ pə tāt) *vt.*, behead. *Marie-Antoinette and Louis XVI were* <u>decapitated</u> *by the guillotine.*

father's ancient Buick, which was in <u>mint</u> condition. They drove home in silence.

After sitting down at the kitchen table with his father to eat a pizza they had picked up on the way home, Luis asked to borrow the car. He didn't get an answer then, just a look that meant "Don't bother me right now."

Before bringing up the subject again, Luis put some ice cubes in a Baggie and handed it to Mr. Cintrón, who had made the little bump on his head worse by rubbing it. It
210   had GUILTY written on it, Luis thought.

"Gracias, hijo." His father placed the bag on the bump and made a face as the ice touched his skin.

They ate in silence for a few minutes more; then Luis decided to ask about the car again.

"I really need some fresh air, Pop. Can I borrow the car for a couple of hours?"

"You don't get enough fresh air at the yard? We're lucky that we don't have to sit in a smelly old factory all day. You know that?"

220   "Yeah, Pop. We're real lucky." Luis always felt irritated that his father was so grateful to own a junkyard, but he held his anger back and just waited to see if he'd get the keys without having to get in an argument.

"Where are you going?"

"For a ride. Not going anywhere. Just out for a while. Is that okay?"

His father didn't answer, just handed him a set of keys, as shiny as the day they were manufactured. His father polished everything that could be polished: doorknobs,
230   coins, keys, spoons, knives, and forks, like he was King Midas[4] counting his silver and gold. Luis thought his father must be really lonely to polish utensils only he used anymore. They had been picked out by his wife, though, so they were like <u>relics</u>. Nothing she had ever owned

---

4. **King Midas**. Legendary Phrygian king who is given the power of turning everything he touches to gold

| words for everyday use | **mint** (mint) *adj.*, unmarred as if fresh from a mint. *Looking for a silver dollar that did not have any flaws, the coin collector noticed one that was in <u>mint</u> condition.* |
| | **rel • ic** (re′ lik) *n.*, memento from a past time. *The nineteenth-century communion goblet was a <u>relic</u> that the congregation cherished.* |

could be thrown away. Only now the dishes, forks, and spoons were not used to eat the yellow rice and red beans, the fried chicken, or the mouth-watering sweet plantains[5] that his mother had cooked for them. They were just kept in the cabinets that his father had turned into a museum
240 for her. Mr. Cintrón could cook as well as his wife, but he didn't have the heart to do it anymore. Luis thought that maybe if they ate together once in a while things might get better between them, but he always had something to do around dinnertime and ended up at a hamburger joint. Tonight was the first time in months they had sat down at the table together.

Luis took the keys. "Thanks," he said, walking out to take his shower. His father kept looking at him with those sad, patient eyes. "Okay. I'll be back by ten, and keep the ice on
250 that egg," Luis said without looking back.

He had just meant to ride around his old barrio, see if any of the Tiburones were hanging out at El Building, where most of them lived. It wasn't far from the single-family home his father had bought when the business started paying off: a house that his mother lived in for three months before she took up residence at St. Joseph's Hospital. She never came home again. These days Luis wished he still lived in that tiny apartment where there was always something to do, somebody to talk to.

260 Instead Luis found himself parked in front of the last place his mother had gone to: Ramirez Funeral Home. In the front yard was a huge oak tree that Luis remembered having climbed during the funeral to get away from people. The tree looked different now, not like a skeleton, as it had then, but green with leaves. The branches reached to the second floor of the house, where the family lived.

For a while Luis sat in the car allowing the memories to flood back into his brain. He remembered his mother before the illness changed her. She had not been beautiful,
270 as his father told everyone; she had been a sweet lady, not pretty but not ugly. To him, she had been the person who always told him that she was proud of him and loved him. She did that every night when she came to his bedroom door to say good-night. As a joke he would sometimes ask her,

---

5. **plantain**. Banana-like fruit

"Proud of what? I haven't done anything." And she'd always say, "I'm just proud that you are my son." She wasn't perfect or anything. She had bad days when nothing he did could make her smile, especially after she got sick. But he never heard her say anything negative about anyone. She always blamed *el destino*, fate, for what went wrong. He missed her. He missed her so much. Suddenly a flood of tears that had been building up for almost three years started pouring from his eyes. Luis sat in his father's car, with his head on the steering wheel, and cried, "Mami,[6] I miss you."

When he finally looked up, he saw that he was being watched. Sitting at a large window with a pad and a pencil on her lap was Naomi. At first Luis felt angry and embarrassed, but she wasn't laughing at him. Then she told him with her dark eyes that it was okay to come closer. He walked to the window, and she held up the sketch pad on which she had drawn him, not crying like a baby, but sitting on top of a mountain of silver disks, holding one up over his head. He had to smile.

The plate-glass window was locked. It had a security bolt on it. An alarm system, he figured, so nobody would steal the princess. He asked her if he could come in. It was soundproof too. He mouthed the words slowly for her to read his lips. She wrote on the pad, "I can't let you in. My mother is not home tonight." So they looked at each other and talked through the window for a little while. Then Luis got an idea. He signed to her that he'd be back, and drove to the junkyard.

Luis climbed up on his mountain of hubcaps. For hours he sorted the wheel covers by make, size, and condition, stopping only to call his father and tell him where he was and what he was doing. The old man did not ask him for explanations, and Luis was grateful for that. By lamppost light, Luis worked and worked, beginning to understand a little why his father kept busy all the time. Doing something that had a beginning, a middle, and an end did something to your head. It was like the satisfaction Luis got out of planning "adventures" for his Tiburones, but there was another element involved here that had nothing to do with

6. **Mami**. Mom (Spanish)

THINK AND REFLECT

What does crying for his mother do for Louis? (Interpret)

_____

_____

_____

DRAW A PICTURE

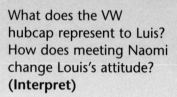

THINK AND REFLECT

How does Luis's treasure hunt help him understand both his father and himself? (Interpret)

_____

_____

_____

_____

THINK AND REFLECT

What does the VW hubcap represent to Luis? How does meeting Naomi change Louis's attitude? (Interpret)

_____

_____

_____

_____

showing off for others. This was a treasure hunt. And he knew what he was looking for.

Finally, when it seemed that it was a hopeless search, when it was almost midnight and Luis's hands were cut and bruised from his work, he found it. It was the perfect match for Naomi's drawing, the moon-shaped wheel cover for her car, Cinderella's shoe. Luis jumped off the small mound of disks left under him and shouted, "Yes!" He looked around and saw neat stacks of hubcaps that he would wash the next day. He would build a display wall for his father. People would be able to come into the yard and point to whatever they wanted.

Luis washed the VW hubcap and polished it until he could see himself in it. He used it as a mirror as he washed his face and combed his hair. Then he drove to the Ramirez Funeral Home. It was almost pitch-black, since it was a moonless night. As quietly as possible, Luis put some gravel in his pocket and climbed the oak tree to the second floor. He knew he was in front of Naomi's window—he could see her shadow through the curtains. She was at a table, apparently writing or drawing, maybe waiting for him. Luis hung the silver disk carefully on a branch near the window, then threw the gravel at the glass. Naomi ran to the window and drew the curtains aside while Luis held on to the thick branch and waited to give her the first good thing he had given anyone in a long time. ∎

Reflect ON YOUR READING

After you finish reading, review the predictions in your chart and verify or adjust them as necessary now that you have all of the information. Using your chart as a guide, make a flow chart to show the sequence of events. When you finish your chart, share it with a partner.

Reading Skills and Test Practice

SEQUENCE OF EVENTS

Discuss with your partner how best to answer the following questions about sequence of events.

1. Read the following list of events.

> Luis is working for his father.
> Luis meets Naomi.
> Luis borrows his father's car.

Which of the following events comes next in the sequence?

a. Luis's mother dies.
b. Luis is sent to juvenile hall.
c. Luis gets caught breaking and entering.
d. Luis drives to Naomi's house.

What is the correct answer to the question above? How were you able to eliminate the other answers? How did your use of the reading strategy help you answer the question?

_____

_____

_____

2. Which of the events comes last in the story?
a. Luis's mother dies.
b. Luis realizes he misses his mother.
c. Luis finds the hubcap for Naomi.
d. Luis visits his mother's grave in the middle of the night.

What is the correct answer to the question above? How were you able to eliminate the other answers? How did your use of the reading strategy help you answer the question?

_____

_____

_____

Investigate, Inquire, and Imagine

RECALL: GATHER FACTS →
1a. Why does Luis spend six months in juvenile hall?

INTERPRET: FIND MEANING
1b. What is the underlying reason for Luis's disruptive behavior? Is he a typical gang member? Explain.

ANALYZE: TAKE THINGS APART →
2a. What behaviors does Luis exhibit to indicate he is a good son?

SYNTHESIZE: BRING THINGS TOGETHER
2b. Why does Luis want to create a new relationship with his father?

EVALUATE: MAKE JUDGMENTS →
3a. Is Luis justified in putting down his father because he owns a junkyard?

EXTEND: CONNECT IDEAS
3b. Luis thinks that the hubcap he gives Naomi is "the first good thing he had given anyone in a long time." This act represents a turning point in Luis's life. Make predictions about how his life will be different six months later.

WordWorkshop

IDENTIFYING IDIOMS. An **idiom** is an expression that cannot be understood from the meaning of its separate words, but must be learned as a whole. For example, the expression "give way," meaning "retreat," is an idiom. Determine which of the following expressions from the selection are idioms by trying to substitute new words for the words in the expression. Write an *I* in the blank next to each expression you believe to be an idiom. Write *E* next to expressions that are not idioms. Then write, in your own words, the meaning of each of the idioms and expressions.

_____ 1. old man (as in *his old man's custody*)

_____

_____ 2. breaking and entering

_____

_____ 3. copped out

_____

_____ 4. walk down memory lane

_____

_____ 5. house arrest

_____

Literary Tools

CHARACTER. A **character** is a person who takes part in the action of a literary work. A *static character* is one who does not change during the course of the action. A *dynamic character* is one who does change. Is Luis a static or dynamic character? Explain your answer using evidence from the selection.

_____

_____

_____

_____

Read-Write Connection

How do you think Luis's life will change now that he has accepted his mother's death?

_____

_____

_____

_____

_____

_____

_____

_____

Beyond the Reading

COMPARE AND CONTRAST. If you like this story, you might enjoy reading Judith Ortiz Cofer's collection of short stories, *An Island Like You*. Choose your two favorite stories and write a compare-contrast essay about them.

GO ONLINE. Visit the EMC Internet Resource Center at **emcp.com** to find links and additional activities for this selection.

Reader's resource

"The Interlopers" revolves on a conflict between the characters Ulrich von Gradwitz and Georg Znaeym. Their conflict over the border between their lands has been burning between their families for three generations. By the end of the story each man realizes that he has more to fear than his neighbor's hatred. Saki (1870–1916) is the pen name of Hector Hugh Munro, who also wrote two novels, three plays, and one history.

Word watch

PREVIEW VOCABULARY

compromise	pinion
embitter	plight
endeavor	precipitous
languor	reconciliation
marauder	restraining

Reader's journal

How have you resolved conflict in a relationship or put an end to a grudge?

_____

_____

_____

_____

"The Interlopers"
by Saki

Active READING STRATEGY

USE TEXT ORGANIZATION

Before Reading ➜ MAKE A PLOT CHART

❑ Review the definitions of *conflict* and *plot* in the introduction to this unit on pages 37–38.
❑ Preview the Plot Chart below.
❑ As you read, fill in the plot elements as they happen in the story.

Graphic Organizer

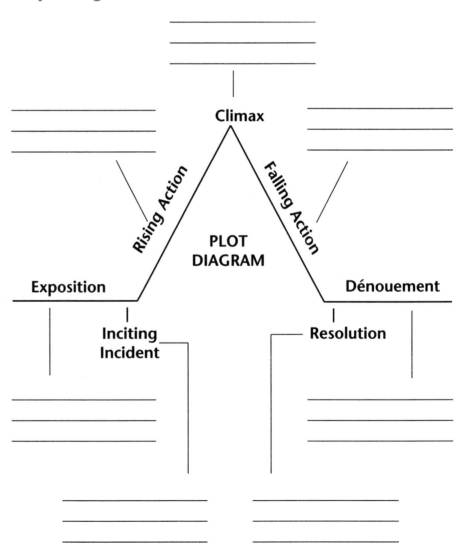

The Interlopers[1]

SAKI

During Reading

COMPLETE THE PLOT CHART

- ❏ Listen as your teacher reads the first three paragraphs of the story. What do you learn in these paragraphs? What part of the plot does this correspond to?
- ❏ Continue reading the selection on your own.
- ❏ Make notes about the plot on your Plot Chart. Remember, that your ideas may change as you read further in the story.

I n a forest of mixed growth somewhere on the eastern spurs of the Carpathians,[2] a man stood one winter night watching and listening, as though he waited for some beast of the woods to come within the range of his vision, and, later, of his rifle. But the game for whose presence he kept so keen an outlook was none that figured in the sportsman's calendar as lawful and proper for the chase; Ulrich von Gradwitz patrolled the dark forest in quest of a human enemy.

10 The forest lands of Gradwitz were of wide extent and well stocked with game; the narrow strip of <u>precipitous</u> woodland that lay on its outskirt was not remarkable for the game it harbored or the shooting it afforded, but it was the most jealously guarded of all its owner's territorial possessions. A famous lawsuit, in the days of his grandfather, had wrested it from the illegal possession of a neighboring family of petty landowners;[3] the dispossessed party had never acquiesced in the judgment of the Courts, and a long series of poaching affrays[4] and similar scandals had <u>embittered</u> the relationships between the families for three generations. The neighbor
20 feud had grown into a personal one since Ulrich had come to be head of his family; if there was a man in the world whom

NOTE THE FACTS

With whom has the family of Ulrich von Gradwitz been in dispute? About what?

_____

_____

_____

_____

---

1. **Interlopers.** People who meddle, or intrude, in other people's concerns
2. **eastern spurs . . . Carpathians.** Ridges projecting from a mountain chain; the Carpathian Mountains extend from southern Poland to northeastern Romania
3. **petty landowners.** Owners of small pieces of land
4. **poaching affrays.** Attacks for the purpose of stealing game from someone else's property

words for everyday use

pre • cip • i • tous (prë sip´ə təs) *adj.,* steep. *The <u>precipitous</u> trail up the steep mountain was difficult even for the most seasoned climbers.*

em • bit • ter (em bit´ər) *vt.,* make resentful. *Lucy didn't let her friend's betrayal <u>embitter</u> her; she was not resentful of her friend.*

MARK THE TEXT

Underline the sentence that tells why Ulrich watches the forest.

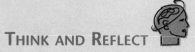

THINK AND REFLECT

What emotion does Ulrich feel toward Georg Znaeym? (Infer)

_____

_____

he detested and wished ill to it was Georg Znaeym, the inheritor of the quarrel and the tireless game-snatcher and raider of the disputed border-forest. The feud might, perhaps, have died down or been <u>compromised</u> if the personal ill-will of the two men had not stood in the way; as boys they had thirsted for one another's blood, as men each prayed that misfortune might fall on the other, and this wind-scourged winter night Ulrich had banded together his

30 foresters to watch the dark forest, not in quest of four-footed quarry, but to keep a look-out for the prowling thieves whom he suspected of being afoot from across the land boundary. The roebuck,[5] which usually kept in the sheltered hollows during a storm-wind, were running like driven things tonight, and there was movement and unrest among the creatures that were wont to sleep through the dark hours. Assuredly there was a disturbing element in the forest, and Ulrich could guess the quarter from whence it came.

He strayed away by himself from the watchers whom he

40 had placed in ambush on the crest of the hill, and wandered far down the steep slopes amid the wild tangle of undergrowth, peering through the tree-trunks and listening through the whistling and skirling of the wind and the restless beating of the branches for sight or sound of the <u>marauders</u>. If only on this wild night, in this dark, lone spot, he might come across Georg Znaeym, man to man, with none to witness—that was the wish that was uppermost in his thoughts. And as he stepped round the trunk of a huge beech he came face to face with the man he sought.

50 The two enemies stood glaring at one another for a long silent moment. Each had a rifle in his hand, each had hate in his heart and murder uppermost in his mind. The chance had come to give full play to the passions of a lifetime. But a man who has been brought up under the code of a <u>restraining</u> civilization cannot easily nerve himself to shoot down his

---

5. **roebuck.** Male of the roe deer

words for everyday use

com • pro • mise (käm´prə mīz) _vi._, settle by having both sides make concessions. _Bill wanted a heated dessert and I wanted something cold, so we <u>compromised</u> on a hot fudge sundae._

ma • raud • er (mə rôd ər) _n._, one who raids and plunders. _The <u>marauders</u> raided the villagers' stored crops, took their livestock, and set their fields ablaze._

re • strain • ing (ri strān´ in) _adj._, controlling or disciplining. _Under the <u>restraining</u> hand of their mother, the children's freedom was reined in when they became too unruly._

neighbor in cold blood and without word spoken, except for an offense against his hearth and honor.[6] And before the moment of hesitation had given way to action a deed of Nature's own violence overwhelmed them both. A fierce shriek of the storm had been answered by a splitting crash over their heads, and ere they could leap aside a mass of falling beech tree had thundered down on them. Ulrich von Gradwitz found himself stretched on the ground, one arm numb beneath him and the other held almost as helplessly in a tight tangle of forked branches, while both legs were pinned beneath the fallen mass. His heavy shooting-boots had saved his feet from being crushed to pieces, but if his fractures were not as serious as they might have been, at least it was evident that he could not move from his present position till some one came to release him. The descending twigs had slashed the skin of his face, and he had to wink away some drops of blood from his eyelashes before he could take in a general view of the disaster. At his side, so near that under ordinary circumstances he could almost have touched him, lay Georg Znaeym, alive and struggling, but obviously as helplessly pinioned down as himself. All round them lay a thick-strewn wreckage of splintered branches and broken twigs.

Relief at being alive and exasperation at his captive plight brought a strange medley of pious thank-offerings and sharp curses to Ulrich's lips. Georg, who was nearly blinded with the blood which trickled across his eyes, stopped his struggling for a moment to listen, and then gave a short, snarling laugh.

"So you're not killed, as you ought to be, but you're caught, anyway," he cried; "caught fast. Ho, what a jest, Ulrich von Gradwitz snared in his stolen forest. There's real justice for you!"

And he laughed again, mockingly and savagely.

"I'm caught in my own forest-land," retorted Ulrich. "When my men come to release us you will wish, perhaps, that you were in a better plight than caught poaching on a neighbor's land, shame on you."

Georg was silent for a moment; then he answered quietly:

---

6. **hearth and honor.** Home and reputation

> **words for everyday use**
>
> **pin • ion** (pin´ yən) vt., bind. *The cowboy pinioned the calf so he could brand it.*
> **plight** (plīt) n., dangerous situation. *The plight of the heroine, cornered on the top of a skyscraper, filled the audience with fear.*

NOTE THE FACTS

What happens before either man has a chance to speak or shoot?

_____

_____

_____

_____

Literary TOOLS

AIM. A writer's **aim** is his or her purpose, or goal. An author may write with one or more purpose. (Review the Purposes of Writing chart in Unit 2, page 18.) As you read, try to determine Saki's principal aim in writing this story.

Use THE STRATEGY

USE TEXT ORGANIZATION. As you read, make notes about the plot on your plot chart. Look for the main conflict and its resolution as the story unfolds. Remember, your ideas may change as you read further in the story.

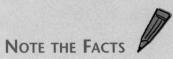

Whom do the men believe will save them? What do they plan to do when they are saved?

_____

_____

_____

_____

DRAW A PICTURE

"Are you sure that your men will find much to release? I have men, too, in the forest tonight, close behind me, and *they* will be here first and do the releasing. When they drag me out from under these damned branches it won't need much clumsiness on their part to roll this mass of trunk right over on the top of you. Your men will find you dead under a fallen beech tree. For form's sake I shall send my condolences to your family."

"It is a useful hint," said Ulrich fiercely. "My men had orders to follow in ten minutes' time, seven of which must have gone by already, and when they get me out—I will remember the hint. Only as you will have met your death poaching on my lands I don't think I can decently send any message of condolence to your family."

"Good," snarled Georg, "good. We fight this quarrel out to the death, you and I and our foresters, with no cursed interlopers to come between us. Death and damnation to you, Ulrich von Gradwitz."

"The same to you, Georg Znaeym, forest-thief, game-snatcher."

Both men spoke with the bitterness of possible defeat before them, for each knew that it might be long before his men would seek him out or find him; it was a bare matter of chance which party would arrive first on the scene.

Both had now given up the useless struggle to free themselves from the mass of wood that held them down; Ulrich limited his <u>endeavours</u> to an effort to bring his one partially free arm near enough to his outer coat-pocket to draw out his wine-flask. Even when he had accomplished that operation it was long before he could manage the unscrewing of the stopper or get any of the liquid down his throat. But what a Heaven-sent draught it seemed! It was an open winter, and little snow had fallen as yet, hence the captives suffered less from the cold than might have been the case at that season of the year; nevertheless, the wine was warming and reviving to the wounded man, and he looked across with something like a throb of pity to where his enemy lay, just keeping the groans of pain and weariness from crossing his lips.

words for everyday use	en • deav • or or en • deav • our (en dev´ər) n., attempt, effort. *Hillary's first endeavor to dock the boat failed; her second attempt succeeded.*

"Could you reach this flask if I threw it over to you?" asked
Ulrich suddenly; "there is good wine in it, and one may as well
be as comfortable as one can. Let us drink, even if tonight one of
us dies."

"No, I can scarcely see anything; there is so much blood
caked round my eyes," said Georg, "and in any case I don't drink
wine with an enemy."

Ulrich was silent for a few minutes, and lay listening to the
weary screeching of the wind. An idea was slowly forming and
growing in his brain, an idea that gained strength every time
that he looked across at the man who was fighting so grimly
against pain and exhaustion. In the pain and <u>languor</u> that
Ulrich himself was feeling the old fierce hatred seemed to be
dying down.

"Neighbor," he said presently, "do as you please if your men
come first. It was a fair compact.[7] But as for me, I've changed
my mind. If my men are the first to come you shall be the first
to be helped, as though you were my guest. We have
quarrelled like devils all our lives over this stupid strip of forest,
where the trees can't even stand upright in a breath of wind.
Lying here tonight, thinking, I've come to think we've been
rather fools; there are better things in life than getting the
better of a boundary dispute. Neighbor, if you will help me to
bury the old quarrel I—I will ask you to be my friend."

Georg Znaeym was silent for so long that Ulrich thought,
perhaps, he had fainted with the pain of his injuries. Then he
spoke slowly and in jerks.

"How the whole region would stare and gabble[8] if we rode
into the market-square together. No one living can
remember seeing a Znaeym and a von Gradwitz talking to
one another in friendship. And what peace there would be
among the forester folk if we ended our feud tonight. And if
we choose to make peace among our people there is none
other to interfere, no interlopers from outside. . . . You would
come and keep the Sylvester night[9] beneath my roof, and I

---

7. **compact.** Agreement
8. **gabble.** Chatter; talk
9. **Sylvester night.** New Year's Eve, December 31; named after Saint Sylvester

words for everyday use

lan • guor (laŋ´gər) *n.,* lack of interest, listlessness. *The speaker's dullness and the stifling room filled us with <u>languor</u>.*

Reading STRATEGY REVIEW

MAKE PREDICTIONS. Make predictions as you read and record them in a graphic organizer or write notes in the margins. What do you think Ulrich's statement in lines 130–132 might foreshadow? Do you think both men will survive this accident?

READ ALOUD

Read the highlighted passage aloud. What does Ulrich begin to think as he looks at Georg? What does he decide?

_____

_____

_____

_____

FIX-UP IDEA

Unlock Difficult Words
As you read, jot unfamiliar words in your notebook. Use context clues or word parts to determine the meanings of words. If you cannot determine the meanings using one of these methods, consult a dictionary.

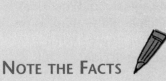

THINK AND REFLECT

What effect would their reconciliation have on the villagers? (Interpret)

_____

_____

_____

_____

NOTE THE FACTS

What do the men decide to do?

_____

_____

would come and feast on some high day at your castle. . . . I would never fire a shot on your land, save when you invited me as a guest; and you should come and shoot with me down in the marshes where the wildfowl are. In all the countryside there are none that could hinder if we willed to make peace. I never thought to have wanted to do other than hate you all my life, but I think I have changed my mind about things too, this last half-hour. And you offered me your wine-flask. . . . Ulrich von Gradwitz, I will be your friend."

For a space both men were silent, turning over in their minds the wonderful changes that this dramatic <u>reconciliation</u> would bring about. In the cold, gloomy forest, with the wind tearing in fitful gusts through the naked branches and whistling round the tree-trunks, they lay and waited for the help that would now bring release and succor to both parties. And each prayed a private prayer that his men might be the first to arrive, so that he might be the first to show honorable attention to the enemy that had become a friend.

Presently, as the wind dropped for a moment, Ulrich broke silence.

"Let's shout for help," he said; "in this lull our voices may carry a little way."

"They won't carry far through the trees and undergrowth," said Georg, "but we can try. Together, then."

The two raised their voices in a prolonged hunting call.

"Together again," said Ulrich a few minutes later, after listening in vain for an answering halloo.

"I heard something that time, I think," said Ulrich.

"I heard nothing but the pestilential[10] wind," said Georg hoarsely.

There was silence again for some minutes, and then Ulrich gave a joyful cry.

"I can see figures coming through the wood. They are following in the way I came down the hillside."

---

10. **pestilential.** Of or related to a pestilence, regarded as dangerous or harmful

words for everyday use	**rec • on • cil • i • a • tion** (rek´ən sil´ē ā´shən) _n._, settling of problems or disputes. _Jeff and Hetty put their long grudge aside and reached a <u>reconciliation</u>._

Both men raised their voices in as loud a shout as they could muster.

"They hear us! They've stopped. Now they see us. They're
200 running down the hill towards us," cried Ulrich.

"How many of them are there?" asked Georg.

"I can't see distinctly," said Ulrich; "nine or ten."

"Then they are yours," said Georg; "I had only seven out
with me."

"They are making all the speed they can, brave lads," said
Ulrich gladly.

"Are they your men?" asked Georg. "Are they your men?" he
repeated impatiently as Ulrich did not answer.

"No," said Ulrich with a laugh, the idiotic chattering laugh of
210 a man unstrung with hideous fear.

"Who are they?" asked Georg quickly, straining his eyes to
see what the other would gladly not have seen.

"*Wolves.*" ■

NOTE THE FACTS

What do the men think
they see in the distance?
What do they actually see?

_____

_____

_____

Reflect ON YOUR READING

With a partner, compare the ideas you wrote on your Plot Chart. Identify the central conflict in the story. Then work together to identify each part of the story.

_____

_____

_____

_____

Reading Skills and Test Practice

ANALYZE PLOT DEVELOPMENT

READ, THINK, AND EXPLAIN. Analyze the plot of "The Interlopers." Identify the central conflict of the story. Explain how this conflict is developed and resolved. How is the event that follows the conflict resolution an example of irony?

_____

_____

_____

_____

_____

_____

_____

_____

_____

_____

REFLECT ON YOUR RESPONSE. Compare your response with that of your partner and talk about how the information you gathered helped you form your response.

THINK-ALOUD NOTES

Investigate, Inquire, and Imagine

RECALL: GATHER FACTS
1a. What do the two men do when they meet face to face?

INTERPRET: FIND MEANING
1b. What event shows "Nature's own violence" to be stronger than the violence of either man?

ANALYZE: TAKE THINGS APART
2a. Identify the changes that take place in Ulrich and Georg while they are trapped together underneath the beech tree.

SYNTHESIZE: BRING THINGS TOGETHER
2b. Why do you think the changes occur in the two men?

EVALUATE: MAKE JUDGMENTS
3a. How strong is the new bond of friendship between Ulrich and Georg? Would it endure if they were to live? Explain your reasoning.

EXTEND: CONNECT IDEAS
3b. The beech tree is a classical symbol for a loving couple in much of literature. Why is it significant that it is a beech tree that strikes Ulrich and Georg? Is Saki using the symbol ironically? What might he be foreshadowing?

WordWorkshop

ADJECTIVE SUFFIXES. An **adjective suffix** is a word part that attaches to the end of a word root and changes the word to an adjective—a word that modifies a noun or pronoun. The following commonly used suffixes are adjective suffixes. Note that there are other suffixes that signal adjectives in one case, but nouns in another, and verbs in yet another. This chart includes suffixes that function strictly as adjective suffixes.

Adjective suffixes		
Suffix	**Meaning(s)**	**Examples of use**
–ous –eous –ious	possessing the qualities of	joyous gaseous insidious
–able	capable of	comfortable
–ible	tending toward	responsible

Speed Round. Pair up with a classmate. Set 30 seconds on the clock. Write down as many words ending in *–ous, –eous,* and *–ious* as you can. While you are working, your partner should list words ending in *–able* and *–ible.* List your words below. Who wrote down more words?

_____   _____   _____

_____   _____   _____

_____   _____   _____

_____   _____   _____

Literary Tools

AIM. A writer's **aim** is his or her purpose, or goal. What do you think is Saki's principal aim in writing the short story "The Interlopers"? Is he writing to reflect, to entertain, to tell a story, to inform, or to persuade? What do you think he is trying to communicate? Does he accomplish his aim? Explain.

_____

_____

_____

_____

Read-Write Connection

Imagine you are one of the men, Ulrich or Georg, trapped underneath the beech tree in the forest. Describe your present feelings about all of the years you have spent quarreling with your neighbor.

_____

_____

_____

_____

_____

_____

_____

_____

_____

_____

Beyond the Reading

SHORT STORY. Write your own short story that revolves around the plot element of conflict between two characters. Use a long-standing grudge between the characters as the conflict in the story. Resolve the conflict between the two characters, having each character learn something in the process.

GO ONLINE. Visit the EMC Internet Resource Center at **emcp.com** to find links and additional activities for this selection.

"Thank You, M'am"

by Langston Hughes

Active READING STRATEGY

READ WITH A PURPOSE

Before Reading ▶ **SET A PURPOSE FOR READING**

- ❑ Read the information in the Reader's Resource.
- ❑ Skim the selection, familiarizing yourself with the footnoted words and phrases.
- ❑ Discuss the information you gather. Then share with the class the purposes a reader might have for reading this selection, keeping in mind that it is fiction.
- ❑ Next, set your own purpose for reading. Record this purpose in the before-reading section of the Reader's Purpose Chart below.
- ❑ As you read, you will identify information in the text that helps you achieve your purpose.

Graphic Organizer

Before Reading Set a purpose for reading.
During Reading Take notes on what you learn.
After Reading Reflect on your purpose and what you learned.

CONNECT

Reader's resource

"**Thank You, M'am**" tells the story of a boy who tries to steal and is reformed by his victim. These are the only two characters in the story. "Thank You, M'am" was published in 1958 in Langston Hughes's collection of short stories *Something in Common.* Hughes's stories and poetry portray the joys and miseries of ordinary African Americans. He typically wrote about African Americans living in Harlem, a section of New York City.

Reader's journal

Think about the following situations: a neighbor picks flowers from your garden; your sibling borrows your favorite sweatshirt without asking; a classmate looks at your test answers. How would you respond to each of these situations?

_____

_____

_____

_____

_____

_____

READ WITH A PURPOSE

❑ Follow along in the text as
your teacher reads aloud
the first paragraph.

❑ Then, discuss the events
and characters presented
in these first pages of the
selection.

❑ Jot down any information
that helps you attain your
purpose for reading in the
during-reading section of
the graphic organizer.

❑ Read the remainder of the
selection on your own.
Stop as you encounter
clues that help you
achieve your purpose and
jot down these clues in
your graphic organizer.

NOTE THE FACTS

What does the boy try to
steal? What does his
intended victim do to him?

_____

_____

_____

THINK AND REFLECT

What does Mrs. Jones's
reaction to the attempted
robbery say about the
kind of person she is?
(Interpret)

_____

_____

_____

Langston Hughes

She was a large woman with a large purse that had everything in it but hammer and nails. It had a long strap, and
she carried it slung across her shoulder. It was about eleven
o'clock at night, dark, and she was walking alone, when a boy
ran up behind her and tried to snatch her purse.

The strap broke with the single tug the boy gave it from
behind. But the boy's weight and the weight of the purse
combined caused him to lose his balance. Instead of taking
off full blast as he had hoped, the boy fell on his back on
10   the sidewalk and his legs flew up. The large woman simply
turned around and kicked him right square in his blue-
jeaned sitter. Then she reached down, picked the boy up by
his shirt front, and shook him until his teeth rattled.

After that the woman said, "Pick up my pocketbook, boy,
and give it here."

She still held him tightly. But she bent down enough to
permit him to stoop and pick up her purse. Then she said,
"Now ain't you ashamed of yourself?"

Firmly gripped by his shirt front, the boy said, "Yes'm."

20   The woman said, "What did you want to do it for?"

The boy said, "I didn't aim to."

She said, "You a lie!"

By that time two or three people passed, stopped, turned
to look, and some stood watching.

"If I turn you loose, will you run?" asked the woman.

"Yes'm," said the boy.

"Then I won't turn you loose," said the woman. She did
not release him.

"Lady, I'm sorry," whispered the boy.

30 "Um-hum! And your face is dirty. I got a great mind to wash your face for you. Ain't you got nobody home to tell you to wash your face?"

"No'm," said the boy.

"Then it will get washed this evening," said the large woman starting up the street, dragging the frightened boy behind her.

He looked as if he were fourteen or fifteen, frail and willow-wild,[1] in tennis shoes and blue jeans.

The woman said, "You ought to be my son. I would teach 40 you right from wrong. Least I can do right now is to wash your face. Are you hungry?"

"No'm," said the being-dragged boy. "I just want you to turn me loose."

"Was I bothering *you* when I turned that corner?" asked the woman.

"No'm."

"But you put yourself in contact with *me*," said the woman. "If you think that that contact is not going to last awhile, you got another thought coming. When I get through with you, 50 sir, you are going to remember Mrs. Luella Bates Washington Jones."

Sweat popped out on the boy's face and he began to struggle. Mrs. Jones stopped, jerked him around in front of her, put a half nelson[2] about his neck, and continued to drag him up the street. When she got to her door, she dragged the boy inside, down a hall, and into a large kitchenette-furnished room[3] at the rear of the house. She switched on the light and left the door open. The boy could hear other roomers laughing and talking in the large house. Some of their doors were 60 open, too, so he knew he and the woman were not alone. The woman still had him by the neck in the middle of her room.

She said, "What is your name?"

"Roger," answered the boy.

"Then, Roger, you go to that sink and wash your face," said the woman, whereupon she turned him loose—at last.

---

1. **willow-wild.** Thin, graceful, and flexible like a willow tree
2. **half nelson.** Wrestling hold in which one arm is pressed under the opponent's arm and one hand pressed to the back of the neck (as opposed to the full nelson in which both arms are pressed under the opponent's arms and both hands pressed to the back of the neck)
3. **kitchenette-furnished room.** *kitchenette*—very small kitchen typical of urban apartment buildings; *furnished room*—room rented with furniture

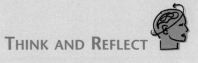
Why do you think Mrs. Jones wants to know about Roger's home life? **(Infer)**

_____

_____

_____

_____

Literary TOOLS

CHARACTERIZATION.
Characterization is the use of literary techniques to create a character. Review the methods of characterization in the introduction to this unit on page 36. As you read, pay attention to the techniques the author uses to portray the two main characters in this story.

READ ALOUD

Read aloud the dialogue between Mrs. Jones and Roger in lines 62–83. What surprising thing does Roger do when Mrs. Jones turns him loose?

_____

_____

_____

What reason does Roger
give for trying to steal
money from Mrs. Jones?
How does she respond to
this?

_____

_____

_____

_____

FIX-UP IDEA

Choose a New Strategy
If you have difficulty
applying the reading
strategy, try a different
strategy, such as
responding to the text.
Read a few paragraphs.
Then stop and respond to
what you have read. Write
the page number in your
notebook. Then write
your comments. For
example, write down
what you would do if you
were in a character's
situation, ask a question,
or connect to an
experience of your own.
Keep responding to the
text throughout the
selection.

Roger looked at the door—looked at the woman—looked at the door—*and went to the sink.*

"Let the water run until it gets warm," she said. "Here's a clean towel."

70 "You gonna take me to jail?" asked the boy, bending over the sink.

"Not with that face, I would not take you nowhere," said the woman. "Here I am trying to get home to cook me a bite to eat and you snatch my pocketbook! Maybe you ain't been to your supper either, late as it be. Have you?"

"There's nobody home at my house," said the boy.

"Then we'll eat," said the woman. "I believe you're hungry—or been hungry—to try to snatch my pocketbook!"

"I want a pair of blue suede shoes," said the boy.

80 "Well, you didn't have to snatch *my* pocketbook to get some suede shoes," said Mrs. Luella Bates Washington Jones. "You could of asked me."

"M'am?"

The water dripping from his face, the boy looked at her. There was a long pause. A very long pause. After he had dried his face and not knowing what else to do, dried it again, the boy turned around, wondering what next. The door was open. He could make a dash for it down the hall. He could run, run, run, *run!*

90 The woman was sitting on the daybed.[4] After a while she said, "I were young once and I wanted things I could not get."

There was another long pause. The boy's mouth opened. Then he frowned, not knowing he frowned.

The woman said, "Um-hum! You thought I was going to say *but,* didn't you? You thought I was going to say, *but I didn't snatch people's pocketbooks.* Well, I wasn't going to say that." Pause. Silence. "I have done things, too, which I would not tell you, son—neither tell God, if He didn't already know.

100 Everybody's got something in common. So you set down while I fix us something to eat. You might run that comb through your hair so you will look presentable."

In another corner of the room behind a screen was a gas plate and an icebox.[5] Mrs. Jones got up and went behind the

---

4. **daybed.** Bed that can be a sofa during the day
5. **gas plate and an icebox.** *gas plate*—small cooking surface fueled by gas; *icebox*—cabinet containing ice for keeping food cold

screen. The woman did not watch the boy to see if he was going to run now, nor did she watch her purse, which she left behind her on the daybed. But the boy took care to sit on the far side of the room, away from the purse, where he thought she could easily see him out of the corner of her eye if she wanted to. He did not trust the woman *not* to trust him.[6] And he did not want to be mistrusted now.

"Do you need somebody to go to the store," asked the boy, "maybe to get some milk or something?"

"Don't believe I do," said the woman, "unless you just want sweet milk yourself. I was going to make cocoa out of this canned milk I got here."

"That will be fine," said the boy.

She heated some lima beans and ham she had in the ice-box, made the cocoa, and set the table. The woman did not ask the boy anything about where he lived, or his folks, or anything else that would embarrass him. Instead, as they ate, she told him about her job in a hotel beauty shop that stayed open late, what the work was like, and how all kinds of women came in and out, blondes, redheads, and Spanish. Then she cut him a half of her ten-cent cake.

"Eat some more, son," she said.

When they were finished eating, she got up and said, "Now here, take this ten dollars and buy yourself some blue suede shoes. And next time, do not make the mistake of latching onto *my* pocketbook *nor nobody else's*—because shoes got by devilish ways will burn your feet. I got to get my rest now. But from here on in, son, I hope you will behave yourself."

She led him down the hall to the front door and opened it. "Good night! Behave yourself, boy!" she said, looking out into the street as he went down the steps.

The boy wanted to say something other than, "Thank you, m'am," to Mrs. Luella Bates Washington Jones, but although his lips moved, he couldn't even say that as he turned at the foot of the barren stoop and looked up at the large woman in the door. Then she shut the door. ∎

---

6. **He did not . . . trust him.** He did not believe that she would mistrust him (but he wasn't sure)

MARK THE TEXT

Underline or highlight the text that tells where Roger sat as Mrs. Jones prepared the meal.

THINK AND REFLECT

Why doesn't Roger want to be mistrusted now? (Interpret)

_____

_____

_____

_____

NOTE THE FACTS

What does Mrs. Jones give to Roger? About what does she warn him? What does she wish?

_____

_____

_____

_____

Reflect ON YOUR READING

After reading, review your notes and complete the last section of the Reader's Purpose Chart. Write a paragraph that describes your purpose for reading and the results of reading with that purpose. For example, if your purpose was to identify theme, write a paragraph that identifies the theme and that discusses the clues you used to determine the theme. When you finish, share and discuss your writing with a small group.

THINK-ALOUD
NOTES

_____

_____

_____

_____

_____

_____

_____

_____

_____

_____

_____

Reading Skills and Test Practice

DETERMINE THE AUTHOR'S PURPOSE
READ, THINK, AND EXPLAIN. Author Langston Hughes included the story "Thank You, M'am" in a collection of short stories called *Something in Common*. Why might Hughes have included this story in a collection with that title?

_____

_____

_____

_____

_____

_____

_____

REFLECT ON YOUR RESPONSE. Compare your response with that of your partner and talk about how the information you wrote down while reading helped form your response.

Investigate, Inquire, and Imagine

RECALL: GATHER FACTS
1a. What personal information does Mrs. Jones share with Roger?

→ INTERPRET: FIND MEANING
1b. How does Mrs. Jones get Roger to trust her?

ANALYZE: TAKE THINGS APART
2a. Why doesn't Mrs. Jones call the police and have Roger arrested? Why does she help him?

→ SYNTHESIZE: BRING THINGS TOGETHER
2b. Why do you think Roger goes to the sink instead of the door when he has a chance to run away? What about Mrs. Jones causes him to stay?

EVALUATE: MAKE JUDGMENTS
3a. At the conclusion of the story, Roger is incapable of uttering an expression of thanks to Mrs. Jones. Is this ending realistic? Why, or why not?

→ EXTEND: CONNECT IDEAS
3b. Predict how Roger's encounter with Mrs. Jones will change his life. What life lessons do you think he has learned?

Literary Tools

CHARACTERIZATION. **Characterization** is the use of literary techniques to create a character. Complete the Venn diagram below, listing what you know about Mrs. Jones and Roger. What do they have in common? Which techniques of characterization does the author use to bring these two characters to life?

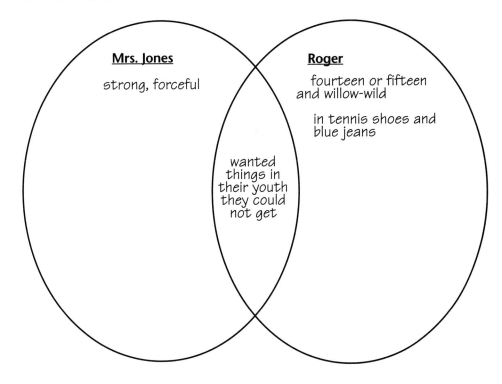

Mrs. Jones

strong, forceful

wanted things in their youth they could not get

Roger

fourteen or fifteen and willow-wild

in tennis shoes and blue jeans

WordWorkshop

DIALECT. A **dialect** is a version of a language spoken by the people of a particular place, time, or social group. The dialogue between Mrs. Jones and Roger is written in the spoken dialect of African Americans living in Harlem at the time the story was written. Using the chart below, add examples of dialect used in "Thank You, M'am" to the Dialect column. Add a standard English equivalent for each word to the Standard English column. One example has been done for you.

Dialect	Standard English
yes'm	yes, m'am

Read-Write Connection

What do you think Roger will do the next time he wants something he cannot afford?

_____

_____

_____

_____

_____

Beyond the Reading

SOCIAL STUDIES. Hughes's stories and poetry portray the joys and miseries of the ordinary African-American individual during the first half of the twentieth century. Explore the political and cultural African-American movements that were popular during his lifetime. Who were the leaders? What did they advocate? How might these movements have influenced Hughes's writing?

GO ONLINE. Visit the EMC Internet Resource Center at **emcp.com** to find links and additional activities for this selection.

Unit 3 READING Review

Choose and Use Reading Strategies

Before reading the excerpt below, review with a partner how to use each of these reading strategies with fiction.

1. Read with a Purpose
2. Connect to Prior Knowledge
3. Write Things Down
4. Make Predictions
5. Visualize
6. Use Text Organization
7. Tackle Difficult Vocabulary
8. Monitor Your Reading Progress

Now apply at least two of these reading strategies as you read this excerpt from the opening of the story "The Scarlet Ibis" by James Hurst. Use the margins and mark up the text to show how you are using the reading strategies to read actively.

It was in the clove of seasons, summer was dead but autumn had not yet been born, that the ibis lit in the bleeding tree. The flower garden was stained with rotting brown magnolia petals and ironweeds grew rank amid the purple phlox. The five o'clocks by the chimney still marked time, but the oriole nest in the elm was untenanted and rocked back and forth like an empty cradle. The last graveyard flowers were blooming, and their smell drifted across the cotton field and through every room of our house, speaking softly the names of our dead.

It's strange that all this is still so clear to me, now that that summer has long since fled and time has had its way. A grindstone stands where the bleeding tree stood, just outside the kitchen door, and now if an oriole sings in the elm, its song seems to die up in the leaves, a silvery dust. The flower garden is prim, the house a gleaming white, and the pale fence across the yard stands straight and spruce. But sometimes (like right now), as I sit in the cool, green-draped parlor, the grindstone begins to turn, and time with all its changes is ground away—and I remember Doodle.

WordWorkshop

WORD SORT. Choose some of the Words for Everyday Use from Unit 3 that are unfamiliar to you and write a word in each of the boxes below. Then write its definition and part of speech. You may refer to the page number listed to review the definition and part of speech. Then sort the words using one of the following methods.

- ■ Same parts of speech
- ■ Words with similar or opposite meanings
- ■ Words with prefixes and suffixes
- ■ Words that relate to each other or that can be used together
- ■ Other sorting method: _____

Word: Definition: Part of Speech:	Word: Definition: Part of Speech:	Word: Definition: Part of Speech:
Word: Definition: Part of Speech:	Word: Definition: Part of Speech:	Word: Definition: Part of Speech:
Word: Definition: Part of Speech:	Word: Definition: Part of Speech:	Word: Definition: Part of Speech:
Word: Definition: Part of Speech:	Word: Definition: Part of Speech:	Word: Definition: Part of Speech:
Word: Definition: Part of Speech:	Word: Definition: Part of Speech:	Word: Definition: Part of Speech:

Literary Tools

Select the best literary element on the right to complete each sentence on the left. Write the correct letter in the blank.

_____1. The isolation of the Whites' house in "The Monkey's Paw" is an example of how _____ can help to create the mood of the story.

_____2. In "To Build a Fire," the main _____ is a struggle of human versus the environment.

_____3. The surprise ending in "The Most Dangerous Game" is an example of _____.

_____4. The main _____ of "The Gift of the Magi" is that sacrifice is the greatest gift of love.

_____5. In "Catch the Moon," Luis is an example of a dynamic _____.

_____6. The _____ is what happens in a story.

_____7. In "The Interlopers," the author's _____ is to make a point by sharing a story.

_____8. Dialogue is one of the _____ techniques used to help the reader get to know Mrs. Jones and Roger in "Thank You, M'am."

a. aim, 137

b. character, 122

c. characterization, 147

d. conflict, 64

e. irony, 83

f. plot, 111

g. setting, 44

h. theme, 111

On Your Own

FLUENTLY SPEAKING. Retell one of the stories from this unit to a classmate or family member. Give detailed descriptions of the setting and characters, and try not to leave out any of the events that take place in the story.

PICTURE THIS. Draw a story strip to represent key events in one of the stories from this unit. Then write a caption under each box that explains each event. Draw the events in the order in which they occurred.

PUT IT IN WRITING. Choose another short story by one of the authors from this unit or by one of your favorite authors. Write a literary review of the story for your school newspaper. Include a brief summary of the plot— but not enough to spoil the suspense. Do you consider the story to be well written? Was the story believable? Why, or why not? Did you enjoy it? On a scale of one to ten, how would you rate it and why? To what kind of reader would you recommend this story?

Unit FOUR

READING Poetry

Defining the word *poetry* is difficult because poems take so many different forms. They do not have to be written down; some are chanted or sung. Some poems rhyme and have a consistent rhythm, but others do not.

Poetry differs from prose in that it packs more meaning into fewer words and often uses meter, rhyme, and rhythm more obviously. One thing that all poems have in common is that they use imaginative language carefully chosen and arranged to communicate experiences, thoughts, or emotions.

There are many different kinds of poetry. Some common kinds are listed below. The most common techniques of poetry involve imagery, shape, rhythm, and sound. Each of these techniques is also discussed below.

Forms of Poetry

NARRATIVE POETRY. A **narrative poem** is a poem that tells a story. The excerpt from the *Odyssey* in this unit is an example of a narrative poem.

DRAMATIC POETRY. A **dramatic poem** is a poem that relies heavily on dramatic elements such as monologue (speech by a single character) or dialogue (conversation involving two or more characters). Audre Lorde's "Hanging Fire" could be considered a dramatic poem.

LYRIC POETRY. A **lyric poem** is a highly musical verse that expresses the emotions of a speaker. Many of the poems in this unit are lyric poems, including Emily Dickinson's "I'm Nobody! Who are you?" and Edna St. Vincent Millay's "The Courage That My Mother Had." **Sonnets, odes, free verse, elegies, haiku**, and **imagist poems** are all forms of lyric poetry.

NOTE THE FACTS

How is poetry different from other kinds of writing?

_____

_____

_____

Techniques of Poetry: Imagery

An **image** is language that creates a concrete representation of an object or experience. An image is also the vivid mental picture created in the reader's mind by that language. For example, in Jane Kenyon's poem "Otherwise" she writes "I ate / cereal, sweet / milk, ripe, flawless / peach." The pictures created in your mind of the bowl of cereal, the white milk, and the perfect peach are images. When considered in a group, images are called **imagery**. Poets use colorful, vivid language and figures of speech to create imagery. A **figure of speech** is language meant to be understood imaginatively instead of literally. The following are common figures of speech:

Figures of Speech	Definitions	Examples
metaphor	figure of speech in which one thing is written about as if it were another	"morning is a new sheet of paper"
simile	comparison using *like* or *as*	"courage like a rock"
personification	figure of speech in which an idea, animal, or thing is described as if it were a person	"Dawn spread out her fingertips of rose"

THINK AND REFLECT

Write an example of personification. **(Apply)**

_____

_____

_____

Techniques of Poetry: Shape

The shape of a poem is how it looks on the page. Poems are often divided into stanzas, or groups of lines. The following are some common types of stanzas:

Stanza Name	Number of Lines
couplet	two
triplet or tercet	three
quatrain	four
quintain	five
sestet	six
heptastich	seven
octave	eight

A **concrete poem**, or **shape poem**, is one with a shape that suggests its subject. Some critics consider Robert Frost's "Birches" to be a shape poem. It has a single long stanza of lines that are all nearly the same length and looks something like a thin, tall birch tree.

Techniques of Poetry: Rhythm

RHYTHM. The **rhythm** is the pattern of beats or stresses in a line. A regular rhythmic pattern is called a **meter**. Units of rhythm are called **feet**. A **foot** consists of some combination of weakly stressed (˘) and strongly stressed (/) syllables, as follows.

Type of Foot	Pattern	Example
iamb, or **iambic foot**	˘ /	˘ / afraid
trochee, or **trochaic foot**	/ ˘	/ ˘ freedom
anapest, or **anapestic foot**	˘ ˘ /	˘ ˘ / in a flash
dactyl, or **dactylic foot**	/ ˘ ˘	/ ˘ ˘ feverish
spondee, or **spondaic foot**	/ /	/ / baseball

The following terms are used to describe the number of feet in a line of poetry.

Term	# of Feet	Example
monometer	one foot	˘ / Today ˘ / We play
dimeter	two feet	/ ˘ ˘ / ˘ Following | closely
trimeter	three feet	˘ / ˘ / ˘ / God shed | His light | on thee
tetrameter	four feet	/ ˘ / ˘ / ˘ / ˘ In the | greenest | of our | valleys
pentameter	five feet	˘ / ˘ / ˘ / A vast | re pub | lic famed| ˘ / ˘ / through ev | ry clime
hexameter or Alexandrine	six feet	˘ / ˘ / ˘ / In o | ther's eyes | we see | ˘ / ˘ / ˘ / ourselves | the truth | to tell

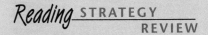
VISUALIZE. Draw a picture of what a shape poem about clouds might look like.

THINK AND REFLECT

List two words that would be an example of sight rhyme. (Apply)

_____

_____

_____

NOTE THE FACTS

What is the difference between assonance and consonance?

_____

_____

_____

Techniques of Poetry: Sound

RHYME. **Rhyme** is the repetition of sounds at the ends of words. **End rhyme** is rhyme that occurs at the ends of lines. **Internal rhyme** occurs within lines. **Sight rhyme** occurs when two words are spelled similarly but pronounced differently. **Rhyme scheme** is a pattern of end rhymes.

ALLITERATION. **Alliteration** is the repetition of initial consonant sounds. The following line from Robert Frost's "Birches" contains two examples of alliteration: "Soon the sun's warmth makes them shed crystal shells."

ASSONANCE. **Assonance** is the repetition of vowel sounds in stressed syllables that end with different consonant sounds as in "*dragged* to the withered *bracken*" in "Birches."

CONSONANCE. **Consonance** is a kind of slant rhyme in which the ending consonant sounds match, but the preceding vowel sound does not, as in *wind* and *sound*.

ONOMATOPOEIA. **Onomatopoeia** is the use of words or phrases that sound like the things to which they refer, like *caw*, *clink*, and *murmur*.

USING READING STRATEGIES WITH POETRY

Active Reading Strategy Checklists

The following checklists offer strategies for reading poetry.

1 READ WITH A PURPOSE. Before reading a poem, give yourself a purpose, or something to look for, as you read. Sometimes a purpose will be a directive from a teacher: "Pay attention to repeated words and phrases." Other times you can set your own purpose by previewing the title, the opening lines, and other information that is presented with the poem. Say to yourself

❏ I want to look for . . .
❏ I want to experience . . .
❏ I want to enjoy . . .
❏ I wonder . . .
❏ I want to see if . . .

2 CONNECT TO PRIOR KNOWLEDGE. Being aware of what you already know and thinking about it as you read can help you keep track of what's happening and will increase your knowledge. As you read, say to yourself

❏ I already know this about the poem's subject matter . . .
❏ This part of the poem reminds me of . . .
❏ I think this part of the poem is like . . .

❏ My experience tells me that . . .

❏ If I were the speaker, I would feel . . .

❏ I associate this image with . . .

3 **WRITE THINGS DOWN.** As you read poetry, write down how the poem helps you "see" what is described. Possible ways to write things down include

❏ Underline words and phrases that appeal to your five senses.

❏ Write down your questions and comments.

❏ Highlight figures of speech and phrases you enjoy.

❏ Create a graphic organizer to keep track of your responses.

❏ Use a code in the margin that shows how you respond to the poem. For instance, you can use

! for "This is like something I have experienced"

? for "I don't understand this"

√ for "This seems important"

4 **MAKE PREDICTIONS.** Before you read a poem, use information about the author, the subject matter, and the title to make a guess about what a poem may describe. As you read, confirm or deny your predictions, and make new ones based on how the poem develops. Make predictions like the following.

❏ The title tells me that . . .

❏ I predict that this poem will be about . . .

❏ This poet usually writes about . . .

❏ I think the poet will repeat . . .

❏ These lines in the poem make me guess that . . .

5 **VISUALIZE.** Visualizing, or allowing the words on the page to create images in your mind, is extremely important while reading poetry. In order to visualize the words, change your reading pace and savor the words. Allow the words to affect all of your senses. Make statements such as

❏ The words help me see . . .

❏ The words help me hear . . .

❏ The words help me feel . . .

❏ The words help me taste . . .

❏ The words help me smell . . .

6 **USE TEXT ORGANIZATION.** When you read a poem, pay attention to punctuation and line breaks. Learn to chunk the lines in a poem so they make sense. Try reading all the way to the end of the sentence rather than stopping at each line break. Punctuation, rhythm, repetition, and line length offer clues that help you vary your reading rate and word emphasis. Say to yourself

Reading TIP

Increase your enjoyment of poetry by reading it aloud. Read the lines as though you were the speaker of the poem.

❑ The punctuation in these lines helps me . . .

❑ The writer started a new stanza here because . . .

❑ The writer repeats this line because . . .

❑ The rhythm of this poem makes me think of . . .

❑ These short lines affect my reading speed by . . .

Reading TIP

If a poem has difficult vocabulary, read the poem, tackle the vocabulary you don't understand, and reread the poem.

7 **TACKLE DIFFICULT VOCABULARY.** Difficult words in a poem can get in the way of your ability to respond to the poet's words and ideas. Use context clues that the lines provide, consult a dictionary, or ask someone about words you do not understand. When you come across a difficult word in a poem, say to yourself

❑ The lines near this word tell me that this word means . . .

❑ A definition provided with the poem shows that the word means . . .

❑ My work with the word before reading helps me know that the word means . . .

❑ A classmate said that the word means . . .

8 **MONITOR YOUR READING PROGRESS.** All readers encounter difficulty when they read, especially if the reading material is not self-selected. When you have to read something, take note of problems you are having and fix them. The key to reading success is knowing when you are having difficulty. To fix problems, say to yourself

❑ Because I don't understand this part, I will . . .

❑ Because I'm having trouble staying connected to the ideas in the poem, I will . . .

❑ Because the words in the poem are too hard, I will . . .

❑ Because the poem is long, I will . . .

❑ Because I can't retell what the poem is about, I will . . .

Reading TIP

Find a partner and take turns reading the poems aloud.

Become an Active Reader

The instruction with the poems in this unit gives you an in-depth look at how to use one reading strategy for each poem. Brief margin notes guide your use of additional strategies. Working with one active reading strategy for each poem will greatly increase your reading success and enjoyment. Use the space in the margins to add your own comments and strategy ideas. Learn how to use several strategies in combination to ensure your complete understanding of what you are reading. When you have difficulty, use fix-up ideas to fix a problem. For further information about the active reading strategies, see Unit 1, pages 4–15.

FIX-UP IDEAS

- Reread
- Read in shorter chunks
- Read aloud
- Ask questions
- Change your reading rate

How to Use Reading Strategies with Poetry

Read the following excerpts to discover how you might use reading strategies as you read poetry.

Excerpt 1. Note how a reader uses active reading strategies while reading this excerpt from "Casey at the Bat" by Ernest Lawrence Thayer.

READ WITH A PURPOSE

After reading the first stanza, I want to know what will happen to the Mudville team.

VISUALIZE

I am imagining a baseball field with lots of fans in the stands. The words "sickly silence" make me imagine them as still and anxious.

CONNECT TO PRIOR KNOWLEDGE

I know that "the Mudville nine" refers to the nine players on a baseball team.

MAKE PREDICTIONS

I think Casey will get to bat because the title is "Casey at the Bat."

The outlook wasn't brilliant for the Mudville nine that day;
The score stood four to two with but one inning more to play.
And then when Cooney died at first, and Barrows did the same,
A sickly silence fell upon the patrons of the game.

A straggling few got up to go in deep despair. The rest
Clung to that hope which spring eternal in the human breast;
They thought if only Casey could but get a whack at that—
We'd put up even money now with Casey at the bat.

But Flynn preceded Casey, as did also Jimmy Blake,
And the former was a lulu and the latter was a cake;
So upon that stricken multitude grim melancholy sat,
For there seemed to be little chance of Casey's getting to the bat.

Excerpt 2. Note how a reader uses active reading strategies while reading this excerpt from "The Bells" by Edgar Allan Poe.

WRITE THINGS DOWN

I can keep track of what the "alarum bells" are like in a cluster chart.

USE TEXT ORGANIZATION

Exclamation points help me to know that the speaker is excited or alarmed by the sound of these bells.

TACKLE DIFFICULT VOCABULARY

Footnotes at the bottom of the page explain these words. I'll read them and then reread the lines.

TACKLE DIFFICULT VOCABULARY

The context lets me know that *clamorous* must mean "loud."

Hear the loud alarum bells[5]—
Brazen bells!
What a tale of terror, now, their turbulency[6] tells!
In the startled ear of night
How they scream out their affright![7]
Too much horrified to speak,
They can only shriek, shriek,
Out of tune,
In a clamorous appealing to the mercy of the fire,
In a mad expostulation[8] with the deaf and frantic fire,
Leaping higher, higher, higher,
With a desperate desire,
And a resolute endeavor
Now—now to sit, or never,
By the side of the pale-faced moon.

Reader's resource

"Birches," published in 1915, is set in rural New England where author Robert Frost (1864–1963) grew up. Sometimes, in that part of the country, winter rain falls on trees and then freezes, so that the branches and twigs appear to be made of crystal. Young birches, carrying that heavy load of ice, are often bent to the ground. As you read, notice how these bent trees remind the speaker of something he did as a child.

Word watch

PREVIEW VOCABULARY

bracken
lash
subdue

Reader's journal

What activities help you forget your worries?

_____

_____

_____

_____

_____

_____

_____

_____

"BIRCHES"

by Robert Frost

Active READING STRATEGY

VISUALIZE

Before Reading ▶ **PREVIEW THE SELECTION**

❏ Look over the Words for Everyday Use and footnotes to the poem.
❏ Read the Reader's Resource. Close your eyes and imagine the tree branches weighed down with ice.
❏ Preview the Visualization Chart below. You will use this chart to keep track of your visualizations by doing a quick sketch of each. Under each sketch, note the line numbers of the lines you are sketching.

Graphic Organizer

Lines _____	Lines _____	Lines _____
Lines _____	Lines _____	Lines _____

BIRCHES

Robert Frost

During Reading

VISUALIZE THE POEM

❑ As your teacher or a group member reads lines 1–9 aloud, close your eyes and visualize the scene.

❑ Sketch your visualization in the first box of the graphic organizer. Discuss your visualizations with your class or group. Use as many sensory details as you can in your discussion.

❑ Take turns reading the rest of the poem aloud with your group members. Visualize the images from the text. Every time you change readers, sketch what you are visualizing in one of the boxes.

MARK THE TEXT

Underline or highlight the words that tell you what the speaker would like to think bends the birches. Then underline or highlight what actually bends them.

Literary TOOLS

METAPHOR AND SIMILE. In a **metaphor**, one thing is spoken or written about as if it were another. A **simile** is a comparison using *like* or *as*. As you read, look for comparisons that help you visualize.

W hen I see birches bend to left and right
Across the lines of straighter darker trees,
I like to think some boy's been swinging them.
But swinging doesn't bend them down to stay
5   As ice storms do. Often you must have seen them
Loaded with ice a sunny winter morning
After a rain. They click upon themselves
As the breeze rises, and turn many-colored
As the stir cracks and crazes their enamel.[1]
10 Soon the sun's warmth makes them shed crystal shells
Shattering and avalanching on the snow crust—
Such heaps of broken glass to sweep away
You'd think the inner dome of heaven had fallen.
They are dragged to the withered <u>bracken</u> by the load,
15 And they seem not to break; though once they are bowed

---

1. **crazes their enamel.** Scratches the shiny white surface of the birch trunk

words for everyday use

brack • en (brak´ən) *n.*, large, coarse, weedy ferns occurring in meadows and woods. *The deer heard the hunter step on the <u>bracken</u> and vanished.*

FIX-UP IDEA

Take a Break
If you have trouble visualizing, stop and work with your group to identify images—word pictures—and metaphors in the text that can help you form a picture in your mind.

Use THE STRATEGY

VISUALIZE. Visualize the images in lines 28–40. Then describe how the boy who lives far from town entertains himself.

_____

_____

_____

Reading STRATEGY REVIEW

CONNECT TO PRIOR KNOWLEDGE. Have you ever done anything like what the boy is doing? How did it feel?

_____

_____

_____

So low for long, they never right themselves:
You may see their trunks arching in the woods
Years afterwards, trailing their leaves on the ground
Like girls on hands and knees that throw their hair
20 Before them over their heads to dry in the sun.
But I was going to say when Truth broke in
With all her matter of fact about the ice storm,
I should prefer to have some boy bend them
As he went out and in to fetch the cows—
25 Some boy too far from town to learn baseball,
Whose only play was what he found himself,
Summer or winter, and could play alone.
One by one he <u>subdued</u> his father's trees
By riding them down over and over again
30 Until he took the stiffness out of them,
And not one but hung limp, not one was left
For him to conquer. He learned all there was
To learn about not launching out too soon
And so not carrying the tree away
35 Clear to the ground. He always kept his poise
To the top branches, climbing carefully
With the same pains you use to fill a cup
Up to the brim, and even above the brim.
Then he flung outward, feet first, with a swish,
40 Kicking his way down through the air to the ground.
So was I once myself a swinger of birches.
And so I dream of going back to be.
It's when I'm weary of considerations,
And life is too much like a pathless wood
45 Where your face burns and tickles with the cobwebs[2]
Broken across it, and one eye is weeping
From a twig's having <u>lashed</u> across it open.
I'd like to get away from earth awhile
And then come back to it and begin over.

---

2. **cobwebs.** The speaker refers to the weblike pattern of lines across the face, perhaps brought on by his grief as well as his age.

words for everyday use	
sub • due (sub dōō′) *vt.*, overcome; control; reduce. *With their powerful longbows, the English soldiers quickly <u>subdued</u> the Scottish rebels.*
lash (lash) *vt.*, strike hard with great force. *The driver <u>lashed</u> the horse so it would gallop.*

50 May no fate willfully misunderstand me
And half grant what I wish and snatch me away
Not to return. Earth's the right place for love:
I don't know where it's likely to go better.
I'd like to go by climbing a birch tree,
55 And climb black branches up a snow-white trunk
Toward heaven, till the tree could bear no more,
But dipped its top and set me down again.
That would be good both going and coming back.
One could do worse than be a swinger of birches. ∎

THINK AND REFLECT

What misunderstanding does the speaker want to avoid? What does he mean instead? **(Synthesize)**

_____

_____

_____

Reflect ON YOUR READING

After you finish reading, review the sketches you made of images from the poem, and choose your favorite. What do you like about the image? Discuss your choice with your group.

_____

_____

_____

_____

_____

THINK-ALOUD NOTES

_____

_____

_____

_____

_____

_____

_____

_____

_____

_____

Reading Skills and Test Practice

IDENTIFY CAUSE AND EFFECT

Discuss with your group the best way to answer the following questions on cause and effect.

1. What two possible causes for the birches' bowing branches are explored in the poem?
   a. a snowstorm and a thunderstorm
   b. boys swinging on the branches and lightning
   c. a hurricane and a windstorm
   d. boys swinging on the branches and an ice storm

What is the correct answer to the question above? How were you able to eliminate the other answers? How did your use of the reading strategy help you answer the question?

_____

_____

2. What makes the trees "shed crystal shells"?
   a. the breeze
   b. the boys swinging on the branches
   c. the snow
   d. the warmth of the sun

What is the correct answer to the question above? How were you able to eliminate the other answers? How did your use of the reading strategy help you answer the question?

_____

_____

Investigate, Inquire, and Imagine

RECALL: GATHER FACTS

1a. How does the speaker describe the birch trees when they lose their ice? What makes the speaker talk about the reality of ice storms and their effect on birches?

INTERPRET: FIND MEANING

1b. What might it say about human frailty and the power of nature if an ice storm and not some boy bent the trees?

ANALYZE: TAKE THINGS APART

2a. In the last line, the speaker says, "One could do worse than be a swinger of birches." What does it mean to be a swinger of birches?

SYNTHESIZE: BRING THINGS TOGETHER

2b. Why does the speaker want to be a swinger of birches?

PERSPECTIVE: LOOK AT OTHER VIEWS

3a. Why is the speaker content to "dream" about swinging from birches?

EMPATHY: SEE FROM INSIDE

3b. Imagine yourself in the speaker's place. How could you make the experience come alive again?

Literary Tools

METAPHOR AND SIMILE. In a **metaphor**, one thing is spoken or written about as if it were another: her eyes were stars. A **simile** is a comparison using *like* or *as:* her eyes were like stars. The two things being compared in a metaphor or simile are the writer's actual subject, called the *tenor*, and the thing to which the subject is compared, called the *vehicle*. In the chart below, list as many metaphors and similes from the poem as you can, and identify the tenor and vehicle for each. One example has been done for you.

Tenor	Vehicle
ice on branches	crystal shells

What characteristic of life is represented by a pathless wood?

_____

_____

_____

WordWorkshop

METAPHORS AND SIMILES. In this selection, you learned about two kinds of figures of speech: metaphors and similes. One way to remember new vocabulary words is to link them in your mind to something you already know. If you make up a metaphor or simile using the new word in a comparison to something familiar, you will more easily remember the meaning of the new word. Use each word below in a metaphor or simile. Use your own paper as needed.

1. bracken _____

2. subdue _____

3. enamel _____

4. wither _____

5. lash _____

Read-Write Connection

Do you understand the speaker's feelings as he dreams of swinging on birches? What childhood activities do you miss, and why?

_____

_____

_____

_____

_____

_____

Beyond the Reading

EXPLORE NATURAL EVENTS. Which natural events interest you the most? Choose one of these phenomena, and invent a creative explanation for it. Use Robert Frost's creative explanation of the bent birches as a model. Then research the scientific explanation for the event you have chosen. You might start by looking in an encyclopedia or on the Internet. Once you have found the real explanation for the phenomena, write a few paragraphs identifying which explanation you prefer, and why.

GO ONLINE. Visit the EMC Internet Resource Center at **emcp.com** to find links and additional activities for this selection.

"I'm Nobody! Who are you?"

by Emily Dickinson

Active READING STRATEGY

WRITE THINGS DOWN

Before Reading ➤ PREVIEW THE SELECTION

❑ What does it mean to be a nobody? What does it mean to be somebody? In the chart below, jot down your associations with each word. For example, under Nobody, you might write "lonely" or "not popular." Brainstorm as many ideas as you can.

❑ Read the Reader's Resource at the right. Write down in your chart the associations you think Emily Dickinson might have had with the words *nobody* and *somebody*. Leave the Speaker's Associations section blank for now.

Graphic Organizer

	Nobody	Somebody
My Associations		
Emily Dickinson's Likely Associations		
Speaker's Associations		

CONNECT

Reader's resource

"I'm Nobody! Who are you?" was written by Emily Dickinson (1830–1886). Many of Dickinson's more than one thousand poems deal with themes of privacy and solitude. Dickinson herself is known for being solitary and living a very quiet, private life. As you read this poem, notice how she subtly criticizes those who seek out a very different kind of life than hers.

Word watch

PREVIEW VOCABULARY

bog

Reader's journal

Do you consider yourself a private, introverted person who needs a lot of time alone? Or are you an extroverted person who is more outgoing and loves to socialize with others? Explain.

_____

_____

_____

_____

_____

_____

_____

WRITE THINGS DOWN

- ❑ Follow along as your teacher reads the poem aloud. Watch for the speaker's attitude toward being a "nobody."
- ❑ Write down in the chart the words and phrases the speaker would associate with being a "nobody."
- ❑ Reread the poem on your own. Watch for the speaker's attitude toward being a "somebody."
- ❑ Write down in the chart the words and phrases the speaker would associate with being a "somebody."

FIX-UP IDEA

Connect to Prior Knowledge
If you have trouble understanding what the speaker feels about being a "nobody," review what you learned about Emily Dickinson in the Reader's Resource. What might her lifestyle and themes tell you about how she views "nobodies"?

Use THE STRATEGY

WRITE THINGS DOWN. What does the speaker feel it's like to be "somebody"? Write the answer in your chart.

I'm Nobody! Who are you?

Emily Dickinson

I'm Nobody! Who are you?
Are you—Nobody—Too?
Then there's a pair of us?
Don't tell! they'd advertise—you know!

5　How dreary—to be—Somebody!
How public—like a Frog—
To tell one's name—the livelong June—
To an admiring <u>Bog</u>! ■

---

words for everyday use　　bog (bäg) *n.*, wet, spongy ground; small marsh or swamp. *The field guide listed the birds living in the bog.*

Reflect ON YOUR READING

After Reading ▶ COMPARE AND CONTRAST

After finishing your chart, write a paragraph comparing and contrasting your attitudes toward being a "nobody" or a "somebody" to those presented in the poem. Were your feelings different, or do you feel the same way the speaker does about fame and privacy? Did reading the poem give you a new perspective?

_____

_____

_____

_____

Reading Skills and Test Practice

IDENTIFY MAIN IDEAS

Discuss with your partner how best to answer the following questions about main ideas.

1. What is the main idea of this poem?
   a. It is better to be "somebody" than to be "nobody."
   b. It is better to be unknown than to be famous.
   c. Don't advertise the fact that you are a "nobody."
   d. Admiring fans make a life in the public eye worth the hassle.

What is the correct answer to the question above? How were you able to eliminate the other answers? How did your use of the reading strategy help you answer the question?

_____

_____

2. The title of this poem was taken from the first line. If you were to choose a new title for the poem, which would be best?
   a. "I Want to Be Somebody"
   b. "The Glory of Fame"
   c. "Fame—Who Needs It?"
   d. "Looking for Somebody"

What is the correct answer to the question above? How were you able to eliminate the other answers? How did your use of the reading strategy help you answer the question?

_____

_____

THINK-ALOUD
NOTES

_____

_____

_____

_____

_____

_____

_____

_____

_____

_____

_____

Investigate, Inquire, and Imagine

RECALL: GATHER FACTS
1a. Who does the speaker say she is?

INTERPRET: FIND MEANING
1b. How does the speaker feel about her identity?

ANALYZE: TAKE THINGS APART
2a. Analyze the speaker's feelings about fame and about people who admire the famous.

SYNTHESIZE: BRING THINGS TOGETHER
2b. What seems to be the theme of "I'm Nobody! Who are you?"?

PERSPECTIVE: LOOK AT OTHER VIEWS
3a. From what you have learned about her, why do you think Emily Dickinson published so few poems during her life?

EMPATHY: SEE FROM INSIDE
3b. If you were Emily Dickinson, how would you react to each of the following?
- a request for a public poetry reading of your poems
- a quiet picnic with a friend
- a newspaper article about your literary contributions and personal life
- a secret you are asked to keep for a friend

Literary Tools

SIMILE. A **simile** is a comparison using *like* or *as*. Look for the simile in stanza 2. The two things being compared in a simile are the writer's actual subject, called the *tenor*, and the thing to which the subject is compared, called the *vehicle*. What are the tenor and the vehicle of the simile in this poem?

_____

_____

What feelings does Dickinson convey about the tenor by using this vehicle?

_____

_____

What is one simile that would express the opposite feeling about the tenor?

_____

_____

WordWorkshop

CONNOTATION. Words have both denotations and connotations. A **denotation** is the basic meaning of a word. A **connotation** is an emotional association attached to a word or expression. Describe the connotation of each of the following words from Dickinson's poem.

1. nobody _____

2. dreary _____

3. public _____

4. frog _____

5. bog _____

Read-Write Connection

Imagine that reporters have located the speaker of this poem. How might such a person feel about being discovered?

_____

_____

_____

_____

_____

_____

_____

Beyond the Reading

COMPARE VIEWS OF FAME. Choose a celebrity or another well-known person who interests you. Find out how this person feels about issues of fame and privacy. You might read interviews, a biography, or an autobiography. How does this person's view of fame compare to the view of the speaker in the poem? Report your findings to the class.

GO ONLINE. Visit the EMC Internet Resource Center at **emcp.com** to find links and additional activities for this selection.

Reader's resource

"Mirror" first appeared in *The New Yorker* in 1963. The poem was later included as part of the collection *Crossing the Water*, which was published eight years after Sylvia Plath's suicide at the age of 31. As you read, consider what the poem has to say about the power of mirrors.

Word watch

PREVIEW VOCABULARY

agitation
preconception

Reader's journal

What do you see when you look in the mirror?

_____

_____

_____

_____

_____

_____

_____

_____

_____

_____

"MIRROR"

by Sylvia Plath

Active READING STRATEGY

CONNECT TO PRIOR KNOWLEDGE

Before Reading ➤ **ACTIVATE PRIOR KNOWLEDGE**

❑ Respond to the Reader's Journal question on this page. Consider these questions as you write: Does the person in the mirror look like the real you? Are you ever unhappy with your reflection? Are you ever surprised to see how much your appearance has changed as you've grown older?

❑ Have you ever thought about reflection from the perspective of the mirror? What does the mirror "see" all day long? In the cluster chart below, you will record qualities of the two kinds of "mirrors" in the poem. One example has been done for you. Draw additional circles as needed.

Graphic Organizer

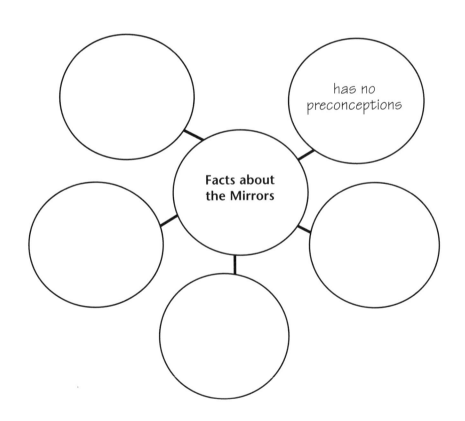

Sylvia Plath

I am silver and exact. I have no <u>preconceptions</u>.
Whatever I see I swallow immediately
Just as it is, unmisted by love or dislike.
I am not cruel, only truthful—
5   The eye of a little god, four-cornered.
Most of the time I meditate on the opposite wall.
It is pink, with speckles. I have looked at it so long
I think it is a part of my heart. But it flickers.
Faces and darkness separate us over and over.

10   Now I am a lake. A woman bends over me,
Searching my reaches for what she really is.
Then she turns to those liars, the candles or the moon.
I see her back, and reflect it faithfully.
She rewards me with tears and an <u>agitation</u> of hands.
15   I am important to her. She comes and goes.
Each morning it is her face that replaces the darkness.
In me she has drowned a young girl, and in me an old woman
Rises toward her day after day, like a terrible fish. ■

During Reading

CONNECT TO PRIOR
KNOWLEDGE

❑ Follow along as your
teacher reads stanza 1
aloud. Record facts about
the mirror in your cluster
chart. Why does the
mirror say it is truthful?
Why might some people
say that the mirror is
cruel?

❑ Read the second stanza
on your own. How is the
lake related to a mirror?
Why does the woman
shed tears and move her
hands around violently?

Literary TOOLS

SPEAKER. The **speaker** is the
character who speaks in or
narrates a poem—the voice
assumed by the writer. What
does the speaker tell the
reader about itself in line 4?
Record the answer in your
cluster chart.

FIX-UP IDEA

Visualize
If you have difficulty
understanding the poem,
try visualizing what the
mirror sees. Picture the
scene at the lake. Read
each line and pause to
form an image.

words for everyday use	**pre • con • cep • tion** (prē kən sep′ shən) *n.*, idea formed beforehand. *Lakeisha had a <u>preconception</u> that summer school would be more relaxed.*
	a • gi • ta • tion (a jə tā′ shən) *n.*, movement with an irregular, rapid, or violent action. *The <u>agitation</u> of the water ceased when the wind lessened.*

Reflect ON YOUR READING

After Reading ➤ EXAMINE YOUR CONNECTIONS

On your own paper, write a brief essay discussing the power of mirrors. Include the ideas in the poem, and connect them to your own experience. To help you gather ideas for your essay, answer the questions that follow.

- Why is looking in the mirror so important to the woman in the poem, even though seeing her reflection makes her cry?

- How important are mirrors to you?

- How important are they to most teenagers?

- What relationship do you think most people have to their mirrors?

- Do you think a mirror has the power to reflect who people really are?

THINK-ALOUD
NOTES

_____

_____

_____

_____

_____

_____

_____

_____

_____

_____

Reading Skills and Test Practice

COMPARE AND CONTRAST
Discuss with your partner how best to answer the following compare and contrast questions.

1. Which of the following do the mirror and the lake have in common?
   a. They are both silver.
   b. They both cause despair.
   c. They both reflect what is in front of them.
   d. They both lie.

What is the correct answer to the question above? How were you able to eliminate the other answers? How did your use of the reading strategy help you answer the question?

_____

_____

2. How do candles or the moon differ from the lake?
   a. They are important to the woman, while the lake is not.
   b. They lie, while the lake tells the truth.
   c. They make the woman look ugly, while the lake makes her beautiful.
   d. Like the lake, they are personified.

What is the correct answer to the question above? How were you able to eliminate the other answers? How did your use of the reading strategy help you answer the question?

_____

Investigate, Inquire, and Imagine

RECALL: GATHER FACTS
1a. Whom has the woman drowned? Who rises toward her "day after day"?

INTERPRET: FIND MEANING
1b. Who are the young girl and the old woman? Why is the old woman "like a terrible fish"?

ANALYZE: TAKE THINGS APART
2a. What qualities do the mirror and the lake share?

SYNTHESIZE: BRING THINGS TOGETHER
2b. How does the lake make the woman feel? How can you tell? Why do you think the lake is so important to her?

EVALUATE: MAKE JUDGMENTS
3a. Why do you think the speaker calls the moon and candles "liars"?

EXTEND: CONNECT IDEAS
3b. Both Narcissus in "The Story of Echo and Narcissus" in Unit 5, pages 238–241, and the woman in "Mirror" bend over the water. How are their perceptions about their reflections different?

Literary Tools

SPEAKER. The **speaker** is the character who speaks in or narrates a poem—the voice assumed by the writer. Review your cluster chart. What can be inferred about the speaker from what it says about its reflections?

_____

_____

What pronoun does the speaker use?

_____

_____

What does the speaker mean when it says that the wall has become a part of its heart? How is this ironic?

_____

_____

WordWorkshop

SYNONYMS AND ANTONYMS. Synonym or antonym questions give you a word and ask you to select the word that has the same meaning (for a **synonym**) or the opposite meaning (for an **antonym**). You must select the best answer even if none is exactly correct. For this type of question, you should consider all the choices to see which is best. Read the following underlined words from the poem. From the choices listed after each one, circle the one most similar to the meaning of the underlined word as it is used in the poem.

1. <u>exact</u>—fine, precise, correct, punctual

2. <u>preconception</u>—prejudice, idea, birth, construction

3. <u>unmisted</u>—clear, rainy, teary, opaque

4. <u>agitation</u>—disturbance, shaking, commotion, excitement

5. <u>terrible</u>—fearful, awesome, great, difficult

Read-Write Connection

What do you think the woman is thinking as she peers at herself in the lake?

_____

_____

_____

_____

_____

_____

_____

Beyond the Reading

DRAW A MIRROR IMAGE. Read a short story or novel that has a teenager as one of the main characters. When you have finished the reading, draw a large mirror. Imagine the character from your story or novel looking into the mirror. What does he or she see? Inside the mirror, draw items and images that represent the character's self-image. Be prepared to explain your choices to the class.

GO ONLINE. Visit the EMC Internet Resource Center at **emcp.com** to find links and additional activities for this selection.

"Nikki-Rosa"

by Nikki Giovanni

Active READING STRATEGY

VISUALIZE

Before Reading ➤ PREVIEW THE SELECTION

❑ Read the information in the Reader's Resource.
❑ Respond to the Reader's Journal question.
❑ Look over the Venn diagram below. As you read, record images of poverty in one circle and images of happiness in the other. If an image suggests both happiness and poverty, write it in the overlapping part of the circles.
❑ Based on these clues, what do you think this selection will be about? What images do you expect to find in the poem? Discuss your predictions with the class.

Graphic Organizer

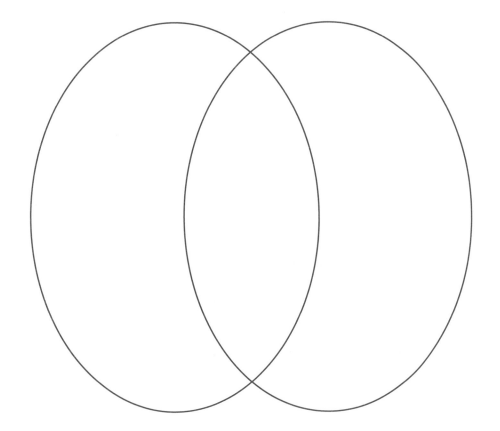

Images of Happiness   Images of Poverty

Reader's resource

The title **"Nikki-Rosa"** refers to the author's nickname as a child. In this poem, well-known writer and educator Nikki Giovanni (1943–) writes about memories of a childhood just prior to the beginning of the Civil Rights movement. This movement was dedicated to achieving equality for all Americans, regardless of racial or ethnic background. A number of anti-discrimination laws were passed because of this movement, but prejudices and economic inequalities continued. During this time, many well-meaning white writers wrote about the problems of African Americans. These books often overlooked the strengths in the African-American community.

Reader's journal

What would you want a biographer to say about your childhood?

_____
_____
_____
_____
_____
_____
_____
_____
_____

VISUALIZE

- ❏ Visualize as your teacher reads aloud the first four lines of "Nikki-Rosa."
- ❏ Discuss the images in these lines and record them in the Venn diagram.
- ❏ Read the rest of the poem on your own. As you read, visualize the images. Record the most striking details in your Venn diagram.

NOTE THE FACTS

What broad generalization does the speaker make in lines 1 and 2?

_____

_____

_____

THINK AND REFLECT

Is the generalization the speaker makes in lines 1 and 2 really true for her? Why, or why not? **(Evaluate)**

_____

_____

FIX-UP IDEA

Ask a Question
If you are having trouble, write down a question in the margin about something you don't understand. Reread to answer the question.

Nikki-Rosa

Nikki Giovanni

childhood remembrances are always a drag
if you're Black
you always remember things like living in Woodlawn[1]
with no inside toilet
5 and if you become famous or something
they never talk about how happy you were to have your
      mother
all to yourself and
how good the water felt when you got your bath from one
      of those
big tubs that folk in chicago barbecue in
10 and somehow when you talk about home
it never gets across how much you
understood their feelings
as the whole family attended meetings about Hollydale
and even though you remember
15 your biographers never understand
your father's pain as he sells his stock[2]
and another dream goes
and though you're poor it isn't poverty that
concerns you
20 and though they fought a lot
it isn't your father's drinking that makes any difference
but only that everybody is together and you
and your sister have happy birthdays and very good
      Christmasses
and I really hope no white person ever has cause to write
      about me
25 because they never understand Black love is Black wealth
      and they'll
probably talk about my hard childhood and never
      understand that
all the while I was quite happy   ■

---

1. **Woodlawn.** Neighborhood in Chicago
2. **stock.** Share of ownership in a business that can be bought, sold, or traded

Reflect ON YOUR READING

After Reading IDENTIFY THE MOOD

When you finish reading the poem, review your Venn diagram. What feelings are associated with each image in the poem? Discuss your answers with a partner.

_____

_____

_____

_____

_____

_____

Reading Skills and Test Practice

IDENTIFY THE MAIN IDEA

Write an essay in response to the following prompts. Use your own paper as needed.

READ, THINK, AND EXPLAIN. What is the speaker's main idea in this poem? Use evidence from the text to explain your answer.

_____

_____

_____

_____

REFLECT ON YOUR RESPONSE. Compare your response with that of your partner and talk about how your visualizations and the details you recorded in your graphic organizer helped you form your response.

_____

_____

_____

_____

THINK-ALOUD
NOTES

_____

_____

_____

_____

_____

_____

_____

_____

_____

_____

_____

Investigate, Inquire, and Imagine

RECALL: GATHER FACTS
1a. What, according to the speaker, do people not say about the childhoods of famous African Americans?

→ INTERPRET: FIND MEANING
1b. Why does the speaker hope that "no white person ever has cause to write about" her?

ANALYZE: TAKE THINGS APART
2a. Identify aspects of a darker side to the speaker's childhood.

→ SYNTHESIZE: BRING THINGS TOGETHER
2b. Summarize what "Black love is Black wealth" means to the speaker.

PERSPECTIVE: LOOK AT OTHER VIEWS
3a. The speaker in this poem doesn't think a biographer would understand what her childhood was all about because she was poor. What could the speaker tell the biographer about her childhood so that he or she would truly understand it?

→ EMPATHY: SEE FROM INSIDE
3b. If you were the speaker and a biographer wrote a distorted biography about your childhood, what could you do to set the record straight?

Literary Tools

PARADOX. A **paradox** is a seemingly contradictory statement, idea, or event. Often a writer will express a paradox in order to make a point in an arresting or memorable way. What paradox does the speaker of this poem express about poverty?

_____

_____

How does the speaker's use of paradox make her point more memorable?

_____

_____

WordWorkshop

WORDSTORMING. Wordstorming is the brainstorming of words. When you wordstorm, your goal is to think of as many words as you can related to a particular topic. This selection deals with a situation that looks one way from the outside but feels a different way from the inside. Wordstorm as many words as you can that have to do with something not being what it seems. Share your wordstorming with the class, and see how many more words you can think of together.

Words about something not being what it seems:

_____

_____

_____

_____

Read-Write Connection

Of what from her childhood is the speaker proud?

_____

_____

_____

_____

Beyond the Reading

READ ABOUT DIVERSITY. Read a book about a person whose background is different from yours. You could read a biography, an autobiography, a memoir, or a novel, and the person could be from a different racial or ethnic background, a different socioeconomic class, or a different country. Write an essay in which you discuss aspects of the person's life that are difficult for you to understand and aspects that seem similar to your own life.

GO ONLINE. Visit the EMC Internet Resource Center at **emcp.com** to find links and additional activities for this selection.

Reader's *resource*

Audre Lorde (1934–1992) began writing poetry when she was growing up in Harlem. She has said, "When I couldn't find the poems to express the things I was feeling, that's what started me writing poetry, and that was when I was twelve or thirteen." In **"Hanging Fire,"** a fourteen-year-old girl discusses her situation in life. The phrase in the title means "a delay filled with dread." It was originally used to refer to the pause between the lighting of gunpowder and the actual firing of a gun.

Reader's *journal*

What worries or concerns do you have?

_____

_____

_____

_____

_____

_____

_____

_____

_____

_____

_____

_____

"Hanging Fire"

by Audre Lorde

Active READING STRATEGY

WRITE THINGS DOWN

Before Reading ▶ PREVIEW THE SELECTION

❑ Respond to the Reader's Journal prompt. You may write on the lines to the left, on your own paper, or in a private journal.
❑ Read the Reader's Resource, look over the cluster chart below, and preview the picture on the next page.
❑ Discuss with the class what you think this poem will be about.

Graphic Organizer

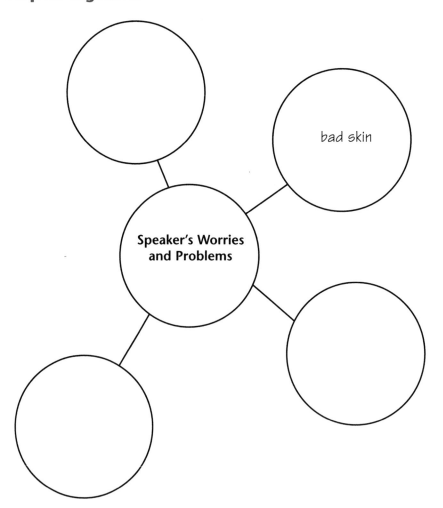

Hanging Fire

I am fourteen
and my skin has betrayed me
the boy I cannot live without
still sucks his thumb
5   in secret
how come my knees are
always so ashy
what if I die
before morning
10   and momma's in the bedroom
with the door closed.

I have to learn how to dance
in time for the next party
my room is too small for me
15   suppose I die before graduation
they will sing sad melodies
but finally
tell the truth about me
There is nothing I want to do
20   and too much
that has to be done
and momma's in the bedroom
with the door closed.

Nobody even stops to think
25   about my side of it
I should have been on Math Team
my marks were better than his
why do I have to be
the one
30   wearing braces
I have nothing to wear tomorrow
will I live long enough
to grow up
and momma's in the bedroom
35   with the door closed. ■

Audre Lorde

Reflect ON YOUR READING

After Reading → SYNTHESIZE WHAT YOU HAVE WRITTEN

Imagine that you are a counselor, and the speaker has just read you this poem as a way of explaining her feelings to you. Write a paragraph for the speaker's file. In the paragraph, summarize how the speaker is feeling. When you are finished, compare your paragraph with those of your group members.

_____

_____

_____

_____

THINK-ALOUD
NOTES

_____

_____

_____

_____

_____

_____

_____

_____

_____

_____

_____

Reading Skills and Test Practice

IDENTIFY THE MOOD
Discuss with your partner how best to answer the following questions about mood.

1. Which of the following words best describes the mood of this poem?
   a. depressed
   b. anxious
   c. angry
   d. sad

What is the correct answer to the question above? How were you able to eliminate the other answers?

_____

_____

2. The speaker's primary worry seems to be
   a. her own death.
   b. her boyfriend.
   c. her knees.
   d. her mother's illness.

What is the correct answer to the question above? How were you able to eliminate the other answers? How did your use of the reading strategy help you answer the question?

_____

_____

Investigate, Inquire, and Imagine

RECALL: GATHER FACTS → INTERPRET: FIND MEANING

1a. In stanza 2, what problems and worries does the speaker have?

1b. In what ways is the speaker "hanging fire"—waiting for something to happen?

2a. What does the speaker say will happen if she dies before graduation?

2b. What is the "truth" about the speaker?

ANALYZE: TAKE THINGS APART → SYNTHESIZE: BRING THINGS TOGETHER

3a. What evidence can you find that the speaker is troubled?

3b. Prescribe ways in which the speaker might resolve some of her problems.

EVALUATE: MAKE JUDGMENTS → EXTEND: CONNECT IDEAS

4a. To what degree does the speaker's mother contribute to her problems?

4b. How do the speaker's problems in "Nikki-Rosa" (page 182) compare with the speaker's problems in "Hanging Fire"?

Literary Tools

REPETITION. **Repetition** is the conscious reuse of a sound, word, phrase, sentence, or other element. What element is repeated in this poem?

_____

_____

What feeling do you associate with the repetition of this element? How does the repetition contribute to the mood of the poem?

_____

_____

Do you think the meaning of the repeated element changes at all each time it occurs? If so, in what way does it change?

_____

_____

WordWorkshop

SEMANTIC FAMILIES. A **semantic family** is a group of words related by topic. For example, all of the words related to architecture form one semantic family. Working with semantic families helps you broaden your vocabulary. It also helps you learn the fine gradations in meaning that allow you to pick the perfect word for what you want to express. The words below belong to the semantic family of human emotions. Learn the meanings of any words that are unfamiliar to you.

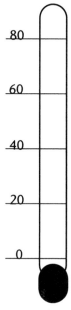

ire	depression	loneliness
joy	pleasure	dismay
boredom	fear	contentment
despair	ecstasy	anxiety

List at least three more emotion words on the lines below. Try to choose words that won't occur to your classmates.

_____ _____ _____

Get into groups of four. As a group, place all of the emotion words, including those you listed above, on a thermometer like this one. Put the most positive emotions on top and the least positive on the bottom. Your group's listing will probably differ from those of the other groups. (For example, which is more positive, *ire* or *fear?*) Be prepared to defend your group's choices.

Read-Write Connection

What do you think the speaker would tell her mother if her mother were available?

_____

_____

_____

Beyond the Reading

CREATE A POETRY COLLECTION. Read other poems by Nikki Giovanni and Audre Lorde. Then pair Giovanni poems with Lorde poems based on theme, subject, point of view, metaphor, or any other characteristic you discover. Finally, make a booklet of the paired poems and write an introduction to explain each pairing.

GO ONLINE. Visit the EMC Internet Resource Center at **emcp.com** to find links and additional activities for this selection.

"miss rosie"

by Lucille Clifton

Active READING STRATEGY

VISUALIZE

Before Reading ➤ **PREVIEW THE SELECTION**

❑ Read the information in the Reader's Resource.

❑ Review the definitions of *simile* and *metaphor* on page 165. Write three similes or metaphors that convey striking images about people. Discuss with the class how similes and metaphors can help readers visualize.

_____

_____

_____

_____

❑ Preview the graphic organizer below. As you read, you will use this chart to record the tenors and vehicles of the similes and metaphors you find.

Graphic Organizer

Tenor	Vehicle

CONNECT

Reader's resource

The poem **"miss rosie"** shows poet Lucille Clifton's interest in human toughness and survival in the face of hardships. In her poems, Clifton (1936–) often employs African-American ways of speaking in her examinations of family relationships and life in the urban ghetto: "I am a Black woman poet, and I sound like one," Clifton has said. As you read, notice how Clifton uses figurative language—writing or speech meant to be understood imaginatively rather than literally—to paint a clear portrait of the woman named in the title.

Reader's journal

When have you needed to adjust to or recover from a bad experience or difficult change in your life?

_____

_____

_____

_____

_____

_____

_____

_____

_____

_____

VISUALIZE

❑ As your teacher reads the poem aloud, picture Miss Rosie. On your own paper, write a brief description of her. Share your description with a few of your classmates.

❑ Reread the poem on your own. Identify the similes and metaphors the poet uses. Write the tenor and vehicle of each in your graphic organizer.

MARK THE TEXT

Underline the startling comparison that begins the poem.

NOTE THE FACTS

What was Miss Rosie's nickname?

_____

_____

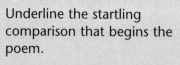

FIX-UP IDEA

Read Short Sections
If you have trouble with the lack of punctuation in this poem, try reading it in three short sections, starting each with "when I watch you . . ."

Lucille Clifton

when i watch you
wrapped up like garbage
sitting, surrounded by the smell
of too old potato peels
5   or
when i watch you
in your old man's shoes
with the little toe cut out
sitting, waiting for your mind
10 like next week's grocery
i say
when i watch you
you wet brown bag of a woman
who used to be the best looking gal in georgia
15 used to be called the Georgia Rose
i stand up
through your destruction
i stand up ■

Reflect ON YOUR READING

After Reading **DESCRIBE MISS ROSIE**

When you finish reading, sketch a picture of Miss Rosie in the box below. Then write a description of her in your own words. Share your sketch with your group from the during-reading activity.

_____

_____

_____

Reading Skills and Test Practice

COMPARE AND CONTRAST

READ, THINK, AND EXPLAIN. Compare and contrast Miss Rosie now to what she used to be. Use evidence from the text to support your answer.

_____

_____

_____

REFLECT ON YOUR RESPONSE. Compare your response with that of your partner and talk about how the information you wrote down while reading helped form your response.

_____

_____

_____

THINK-ALOUD NOTES

_____

_____

_____

_____

_____

_____

_____

_____

_____

Investigate, Inquire, and Imagine

RECALL: GATHER FACTS
1a. What does the speaker say she does when she watches Miss Rosie?

→ INTERPRET: FIND MEANING
1b. What does it mean to do this?

ANALYZE: TAKE THINGS APART
2a. What conditions afflict Miss Rosie?

→ SYNTHESIZE: BRING THINGS TOGETHER
2b. How does Miss Rosie live her life?

EVALUATE: MAKE JUDGMENTS
3a. Why might Miss Rosie have such an effect on the speaker?

→ EXTEND: CONNECT IDEAS
3b. If you were the speaker, what two things could you do for Miss Rosie?

Literary Tools

SPEAKER. The **speaker** is the character who speaks in, or narrates, a poem. How does the speaker feel about Miss Rosie?

_____

_____

_____

How would you describe the speaker's manner of speaking? (You might want to read the poem aloud again as you consider this question.)

_____

_____

_____

What emotions are expressed by the way in which the speaker speaks?

_____

_____

_____

WordWorkshop

WORD ROOTS. A **word root** is a word part that is not a complete word by itself. Word roots need suffixes and prefixes to make complete words. Many word roots come from Greek and Latin. Using your knowledge of words containing the roots in the left column, draw a line matching each one with its correct meaning in the right column.

1. struc   watch; see; observe
2. spec/spect/spic   mind; soul
3. aud   say; declare
4. dic/dict   hear
5. anim   build

Read-Write Connection

What things have you seen people stand up through?

_____

_____

_____

_____

_____

_____

_____

_____

Beyond the Reading

ILLUSTRATE A POETRY COLLECTION. Read at least ten more poems by Lucille Clifton. Then, for each of these poems, create or find an image that shows what the poem is about. For example, for "miss rosie," you might include the drawing you created of the title character. You can draw or paint the images, take photographs, or find images in magazines or other sources. Create a booklet in which you pair each poem with the illustration you have found for it.

GO ONLINE. Visit the EMC Internet Resource Center at **emcp.com** to find links and additional activities for this selection.

Reader's resource

The author of **"The Courage That My Mother Had,"** Edna St. Vincent Millay, was not only a successful poet and playwright but also a political activist in the late 1920s and early 1930s. As such, she might have been particularly interested in courage, the subject of this poem. Raised in New England, Millay (1892–1950) was also familiar with the granite mined there. Granite is a hard, durable rock that may be pink, dark gray, or light gray. It is commonly thought to be formed from molten rock called magma. Granite is often used in building and in the creation of gravestones. As you read, notice how Millay uses the reference to granite in this poem.

Word watch

PREVIEW VOCABULARY

brooch
quarry

Reader's journal

What quality do you most admire in another person that you would like to possess yourself?

_____

_____

_____

_____

"The Courage That My Mother Had"

by Edna St. Vincent Millay

Active READING STRATEGY

WRITE THINGS DOWN

Before Reading ➤ **PREVIEW THE SELECTION**

❑ Review the definitions of *metaphor* and *simile* on page 169.
❑ With a partner, write an example of each.

_____

_____

_____

_____

Graphic Organizer

Tenor	Vehicle

The Courage That My Mother Had

Edna St. Vincent Millay

WRITE THINGS DOWN

❑ Follow along as your teacher reads stanza 1 aloud. Identify the metaphor. What is the tenor? What is the vehicle? Record these in your graphic organizer. What do the two things have in common?

❑ Read the rest of the poem independently. Identify any other metaphors or similes.

MARK THE TEXT

Underline the thing the speaker's mother took with her to the grave.

NOTE THE FACTS

What did the speaker's mother leave her? How does she feel about this item (lines 5–8)?

_____

_____

_____

The courage that my mother had
Went with her, and is with her still:
Rock from New England quarried;
Now granite in a granite hill.

5   The golden brooch my mother wore
She left behind for me to wear;
I have no thing I treasure more:
Yet, it is something I could spare.

    Oh, if instead she'd left to me
10   The thing she took into the grave!—
That courage like a rock, which she
Has no more need of, and I have. ■

FIX-UP IDEA

Find a Purpose for Reading
Use your imagination to complete the sentence "Courage is like _____." Now read the poem to find out what the speaker says courage is like.

---

words for everyday use

quar • ry (kwôr´ē) *vt.*, remove stone from ground. *The miners quarried the granite by blasting into the hillside.*

brooch (brōch) *n.*, decorative pin. *Nathalie fastened the brooch on her blazer.*

Reflect ON YOUR READING

After you finish reading, write a paragraph about the figures of speech Millay uses to describe courage. Explain whether you think her comparison is memorable, original, or effective, and why.

_____

_____

_____

_____

Reading Skills and Test Practice

COMPARE AND CONTRAST

Discuss with your partner how best to answer the following comparison-and-contrast questions.

1. The description of Millay in the Reader's Resource shows that Millay
   a. is more courageous than the speaker in the poem.
   b. is more fearful than the speaker in the poem.
   c. received a larger inheritance than the speaker in the poem.
   d. had a worse relationship with her mother than the speaker in the poem.

What is the correct answer to the question above? How were you able to eliminate the other answers?

_____

_____

2. What best describes the contrast between the speaker in the poem and her mother?
   a. The daughter is wild and the mother is down to earth.
   b. The daughter is sad and the mother is happy.
   c. The daughter is fearful and the mother is daring.
   d. The daughter is sentimental and the mother is sensible.

What is the correct answer to the question above? How were you able to eliminate the other answers? How did your use of the reading strategy help you answer the question?

_____

_____

_____

_____

_____

_____

_____

_____

_____

_____

_____

_____

Investigate, Inquire, and Imagine

RECALL: GATHER FACTS → INTERPRET: FIND MEANING
1a. What went to the grave with the speaker's mother?
1b. What does the speaker wish her mother had left her?

ANALYZE: TAKE THINGS APART → SYNTHESIZE: BRING THINGS TOGETHER
2a. Why might the speaker need her mother's courage right now?
2b. How does the speaker feel about her mother? How can you tell?

EVALUATE: MAKE JUDGMENTS → EXTEND: CONNECT IDEAS
3a. In your opinion, what would be the best way for the speaker to honor the memory of her mother? Explain.
3b. Compare the speaker's view of her mother to the view the speaker of "Hanging Fire" (page 187) has of her mother. Compare and contrast the two mothers.

Literary Tools

RHYME, SIGHT RHYME, AND RHYME SCHEME. **Rhyme** is the repetition of sounds at the end of words. **Sight rhyme** occurs when two words are spelled similarly but pronounced differently *(cave, have)*. **Rhyme scheme** is a pattern of end rhymes, or rhymes at the ends of lines. Which pairs of words rhyme in the poem?

_____

_____

Which words are examples of sight rhyme?

_____

_____

Use the graphic organizer below to identify the rhyme scheme of this poem.

line 1	a
line 2	b

WordWorkshop

VOCABULARY CLUSTERS. Think of a person you admire. Then brainstorm in the margin a list of at least ten words that capture your feelings for the person. Try to select precise words that express exactly what you mean. Use a dictionary or thesaurus as necessary.

Then make a cluster chart to group your words into categories. Add additional circles as needed.

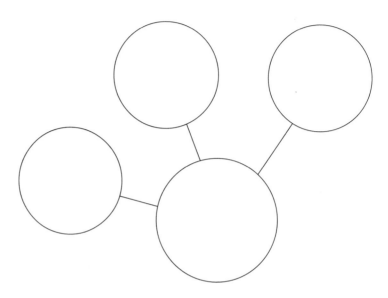

Read-Write Connection

What personal qualities would you most like to "inherit" from your parents or from other adults in your life? What can you do to begin developing those qualities in yourself? Use your own paper or a journal to explore these questions.

Beyond the Reading

EXPLORE POETRY AND ACTIVISM. Find out more about Edna St. Vincent Millay's political activism and about Fascism. You might start by using an encyclopedia or doing an Internet search. Then examine a few of Edna St. Vincent Millay's political poems. Write brief interpretations of at least two poems, explaining how they relate to Millay's activism.

GO ONLINE. Visit the EMC Internet Resource Center at **emcp.com** to find links and additional activities for this selection.

"Otherwise"

by Jane Kenyon

and

"The Old Life"

by Donald Hall

Active READING STRATEGY

CONNECT TO PRIOR KNOWLEDGE

Before Reading ➤ **ACTIVATE PRIOR KNOWLEDGE**

❑ Respond in writing to the Reader's Journal questions. Then discuss your responses with a few of your classmates. Think about a typical day in your life or about your day today. Make a list of sensory details—details that appeal to the senses of sight, hearing, smell, taste, and touch—that describe the day.

_____

_____

_____

❑ Read the Reader's Resource, noting the circumstances under which these poems were written.
❑ Preview the Sensory Details Chart below. In this chart, you will record the sensory details you encounter in the two poems.

Graphic Organizer

Sight	Sound	Touch	Taste	Smell

CONNECT

Reader's resource

Jane Kenyon and Donald Hall were husband and wife. Both of them were poets, and both fought battles with cancer. Kenyon wrote **"Otherwise"** before she was diagnosed with the leukemia that would take her life in 1995. After the diagnosis, she remembered this poem and wondered if it had been prophetic, or had foretold the future. She used it as the centerpiece of what she knew would be her last poetry collection. Hall recovered from his cancer to publish **"The Old Life"** as part of a collection that examines the fascination and love he holds for his work.

Word watch

PREVIEW VOCABULARY

aquamarine
engagement

Reader's journal

How would you describe your morning routine?

_____

_____

_____

What could have happened today to change your day?

_____

_____

_____

❏ As your teacher reads
"Otherwise" aloud, notice
how the speaker's day
compares to yours. How
does the biographical
information about Kenyon
affect your reading of the
poem?

❏ Read "The Old Life" on
your own. Consider the
same questions as they
pertain to this poem.
Make notes about your
ideas.

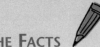

NOTE THE FACTS

How does the speaker
describe her legs in lines 1
and 2?

_____

_____

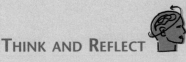

THINK AND REFLECT

What does this description
say about the speaker's
health? **(Interpret)**

_____

_____

_____

_____

MARK THE TEXT

Underline the kind of day the
speaker plans.

Jane Kenyon

I got out of bed
on two strong legs.
It might have been
otherwise. I ate
5   cereal, sweet
milk, ripe, flawless
peach. It might
have been otherwise.
I took the dog uphill
10   to the birch wood.
All morning I did
the work I love.

At noon I lay down
with my mate. It might
15   have been otherwise.
We ate dinner together
at a table with silver
candlesticks. It might
have been otherwise.
20   I slept in a bed
in a room with paintings
on the walls, and
planned another day
just like this day.
25   But one day, I know,
it will be otherwise. ■

The Old Life

Donald Hall

Snow fell in the night.
At five-fifteen I woke to a bluish
    mounded softness where
the Honda was. Cat fed and coffee made,
5   I broomed snow off the car
and drove to the Kearsarge Mini-Mart
    before Amy opened
to yank my Globe[1] out of the bundle.
    Back, I set my cup of coffee
10 beside Jane, still half-asleep,
    murmuring stuporous[2]
thanks in the <u>aquamarine</u> morning.
    Then I sat in my blue chair
with blueberry bagels and strong
15   black coffee reading news,
the obits, the comics, and the sports.
    Carrying my cup twenty feet,
I sat myself at the desk
    for this day's lifelong
20 <u>engagement</u> with the one task and desire. ■

---

1. **Globe**. *The Boston Globe*, a daily newspaper published in Boston, Massachusetts
2. **stuporous**. Dazed or semiconscious; not fully alert

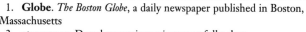

NOTE THE FACTS

What happened overnight (line 17)?

_____

NOTE THE FACTS

What does the speaker do after reading the paper (lines 17–20)?

_____

_____

FIX-UP IDEA

Visualize
If you have difficulty applying the reading strategy, try visualizing the images of the speakers' days. Put yourself in the speakers' place. How would you feel?

words for everyday use

a • qua • ma • rine (ä kwə mə rēn´) *adj.*, pale blue to light greenish blue. *The water of the Mediterranean was <u>aquamarine</u> near the shore.*

en • gage • ment (in gāj´ mənt) *n.*, act of being involved. *Brett's <u>engagement</u> in so many extracurricular activities after school worried his parents.*

Reflect ON YOUR READING

After Reading ➤ EXAMINE THE PROCESS

With your group from the before-reading activity, compare the connections you made during reading. How did prior knowledge affect your reading experience? Why do you think Kenyon considered "Otherwise" to be prophetic?

_____

_____

_____

_____

_____

THINK-ALOUD NOTES

_____

_____

_____

_____

_____

_____

_____

_____

_____

_____

Reading Skills and Test Practice

SYNTHESIZE INFORMATION FROM MULTIPLE TEXTS
READ, THINK, AND EXPLAIN. How are the speakers' lives described in the poems similar? Use evidence from the poems to support your answer.

_____

_____

_____

_____

_____

REFLECT ON YOUR RESPONSE. Compare your response with that of your partner and talk about how the information you wrote down while reading helped form your response.

_____

_____

_____

_____

Investigate, Inquire, and Imagine

RECALL: GATHER FACTS
1a. In "Otherwise," what does the speaker say will happen one day?

→ INTERPRET: FIND MEANING
1b. What alternate realities do you think the speaker is referring to?

2a. In "The Old Life," why does the speaker sit at his desk?

2b. What is the "one task and desire"? How can a day's work be lifelong?

ANALYZE: TAKE THINGS APART
3a. Compare and contrast the speakers' mornings in "Otherwise" and "The Old Life."

→ SYNTHESIZE: BRING THINGS TOGETHER
3b. How do the speakers of both poems interact with each other? Sometimes the speaker of a poem is the poet, but sometimes it is not. Which is the case for these two poems? How can you tell?

EVALUATE: MAKE JUDGMENTS
4a. Hall calls American poetry after 1950 "a poetry of experiences more than of ideas. The experience is presented often without comment, and the words of the description must supply the emotion which the experience generates. . . ." How do "Otherwise" and "The Old Life" support this assessment of contemporary poetry?

→ EXTEND: CONNECT IDEAS
4b. What do you think Jane Kenyon and Donald Hall value most in life? What leads you to this conclusion?

WordWorkshop

USING SPECIFIC, DESCRIPTIVE LANGUAGE. Both "Otherwise" and "The Old Life" contain very specific descriptive language. We know, for example, that the candlesticks in the first poem are silver and that the birch wood lies uphill. We also know that the speaker of the second poem drives a Honda, gets his paper at the Kearsarge Mini-Mart, and takes his coffee black. It is these details that render the speakers' ordinary days into poetry.

Fill in the chart below with specific sensory details about your everyday life. What are the sights, smells, textures, tastes, and sounds of your daily life? Take time to pick the precise words that describe your day. Use a thesaurus, if you like, to find the word with just the right connotations and nuances of meaning.

Sight	Smell	Taste	Hearing	Touch

Literary Tools

DESCRIPTION. **Description** is a type of writing that presents images of a character, an object, or a scene. Descriptions use *sensory details*—words or phrases that describe how things look, sound, smell, taste, or feel. Review your graphic organizer listing the sensory details in these poems. How would the poems be different without the use of sensory details?

_____

_____

Which sensory detail in each poem do you find most striking? Why?

_____

_____

Read-Write Connection

How do both speakers feel about the day they have described? What emotion do the poems generate?

_____

_____

_____

_____

_____

_____

_____

Beyond the Reading

EAVESDROP ON SOMEONE'S DAILY LIFE. Read another passage that records a writer's day-to-day life. You might read the published journals, diaries, or letters of a well-known person from literature, pop culture, or history, or seek out other poems that portray the poets' everyday lives. Then create a project that reflects the life of the writer as it is represented in the work you have read. Your project could be a scrapbook, a poster for a movie about the person's life, a calendar from a representative year in the person's life, a diagram of the person's home or workspace, or anything else that will give your class a sense of that person's life.

GO ONLINE. Visit the EMC Internet Resource Center at **emcp.com** to find links and additional activities for this selection.

The ODYSSEY

from BOOK NINE and BOOK TWELVE
by Homer, translated by Robert Fitzgerald

Active READING STRATEGY

USE TEXT ORGANIZATION

Before Reading ➤ PREVIEW THE POEM'S ORGANIZATION

❑ Read the Reader's Resource. What kind of person do you expect Odysseus to be, based on what you now know about him and about heroic epics?

❑ Preview the map on page 208. Remember to refer back to this map to help you understand the settings of the poem.

❑ Page through the poem to see how it is organized. How are the section breaks indicated?

❑ Preview the Summarize Sections Chart below. Begin a chart like this on your own paper. In this chart, you will record summaries of each section of the poem.

Graphic Organizer

Summarize Sections Chart
Summary of Section 1:
Summary of Section 2:

Reader's *journal*

What qualities do you think make a person a hero?

_____

_____

_____

_____

_____

CONNECT

Reader's *resource*

The *Odyssey* is a **heroic epic**, or a long verse story that tells the life story of a great hero. Composed by Homer, the most famous poet of ancient Greece, this epic focuses on the hero Odysseus, whose name means "wanderer" in ancient Greek. King of the Greek city of Ithaca, the clever Odysseus leads his soldiers to a victory over the Trojans by means of a trick that gets them inside the walled city of Troy. Most of the *Odyssey* tells the story of his ten-year voyage home from Troy, over the course of which Odysseus and his men narrowly escape capture by various monsters and nearly give in to temptations that would lead them to their deaths. In this excerpt, you will read about two of their adventures. First, they venture into the land of the Cyclopes, the giant, one-eyed sons of the sea god Poseidon. In the second, the sailors are nearly tempted off-course by the singing of the enchanting Sirens.

Word *watch*

PREVIEW VOCABULARY

annex	pectoral
ardor	plunder
avenge	ponderous
carrion	prodigious
chafe	rogue
civility	sage
cordial	stow
din	titanic
fume	

USE ORGANIZATIONAL FEATURES

❑ Listen as your teacher reads the first section aloud. On your graphic organizer, write down a summary of the first section.

❑ Read the rest of the poem section by section. Whenever there is a break in the text, stop to summarize what has taken place in the section you have just read.

NOTE THE FACTS

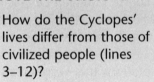

How do the Cyclopes' lives differ from those of civilized people (lines 3–12)?

_____

_____

_____

_____

_____

DRAW A PICTURE

Homer

... In the next land we found were Cyclopes,[1]
giants, louts, without a law to bless them.
In ignorance leaving the fruitage of the earth in mystery
to the immortal gods, they neither plow
5   nor sow by hand, nor till the ground, though grain—
wild wheat and barley—grows untended, and
wine-grapes, in clusters, ripen in heaven's rain.
Cyclopes have no muster and no meeting,
no consultation or old tribal ways,
10   but each one dwells in his own mountain cave
dealing out rough justice to wife and child,
indifferent to what the others do.

                        Well, then:
across the wide bay from the mainland
there lies a desert island, not far out
15   but still not close inshore. Wild goats in hundreds
breed there; and no human being comes
upon the isle to startle them—no hunter
of all who ever tracked with hounds through forests
or had rough going over mountain trails.

---

1. **Cyclopes**. One-eyed giants

20 The isle, unplanted and untilled, a wilderness,
    pastures goats alone. And this is why:
    good ships like ours with cheekpaint at the bows
    are far beyond the Cyclopes. No shipwright
    toils among them, shaping and building up
25 symmetrical trim hulls to cross the sea
    and visit all the seaboard towns, as men do
    who go and come in commerce over water.
    This isle—seagoing folk would have <u>annexed</u> it
    and built their homesteads on it: all good land,
30 fertile for every crop in season: lush
    well-watered meads[2] along the shore, vines in profusion,
    prairie, clear for the plow, where grain would grow
    chin high by harvest time, and rich sub-soil.
    The island cove is landlocked, so you need
35 no hawsers[3] out astern, bow-stones or mooring:
    run in and ride there till the day your crews
    <u>chafe</u> to be under sail, and a fair wind blows.
    You'll find good water flowing from a cavern
    through dusky poplars into the upper bay.

40 Here we made harbor. Some god guided us
    that night, for we could barely see our bows
    in the dense fog around us, and no moonlight
    filtered through the overcast. No look-out,
    nobody saw the island dead ahead,
45 nor even the great landward rolling billow
    that took us in: we found ourselves in shallows,
    keels grazing shore: so furled our sails
    and disembarked where the low ripples broke.
    There on the beach we lay, and slept till morning.

50 When Dawn[4] spread out her finger tips of rose
    we turned out marvelling, to tour the isle,
    while Zeus's shy nymph daughters flushed wild goats

---

2. **meads**. Meadows
3. **hawsers**. Large ropes for mooring or towing a ship
4. **Dawn.** The Greek goddess of dawn is called Eos; in Roman mythology her name is Aurora.

| words for everyday use | **an • nex** (ə neks´) *vt.*, add on or attach. *Hitler <u>annexed</u> Poland in 1939, adding it to the countries he claimed for Germany.*
chafe (chāf) *vi.*, be impatient or vexed. *Sitting in bumper-to-bumper traffic, Bernice <u>chafed</u> at the delay.* |

READ ALOUD

Read lines 40–49 aloud. Then, in your graphic organizer, summarize the section that ends with these lines. Be sure to explain where the Greeks spend the night. **(Synthesize)**

Literary **TOOLS**

PERSONIFICATION.
Personification is a figure of speech in which an idea, animal, or thing is described as if it were a person. Notice how dawn is personified in this section and also in the story of the Sirens.

REPETITION. Repetition is the writer's conscious reuse of a sound, word, phrase, sentence, or other element. Notice that line 68 is similar to line 50. Why might a poet who composed his work orally use stock phrases, or formulas, again and again?

_____

_____

_____

_____

_____

Reading STRATEGY REVIEW

VISUALIZE. Form a picture in your mind of the scene described in lines 80–86. Sketch your picture here.

down from the heights—a breakfast for my men.
We ran to fetch our hunting bows and long-shanked

55   lances from the ships, and in three companies
we took our shots. Heaven gave us game a-plenty:
for every one of twelve ships in my squadron
nine goats fell to be shared; my lot was ten.
So there all day, until the sun went down,

60   we made our feast on meat galore, and wine—
wine from the ship, for our supply held out,
so many jars were filled at Ismaros
from stores of the Cicones[5] that we <u>plundered</u>.
We gazed, too, at Cyclopes Land, so near;

65   we saw their smoke, heard bleating from their flocks.
But after sundown, in the gathering dusk,
we slept again above the wash of ripples.

When the young Dawn with finger tips of rose
came in the east, I called my men together
and made a speech to them:

70   "Old shipmates, friends,
the rest of you stand by; I'll make the crossing
in my own ship, with my own company,
and find out what the mainland natives are—
for they may be wild savages, and lawless,

75   or hospitable and god fearing men."

At this I went aboard, and gave the word
to cast off by the stern. My oarsmen followed,
filing in to their benches by the rowlocks,
and all in line dipped oars in the grey sea.

80   As we rowed on, and nearer to the mainland,
at one end of the bay, we saw a cavern
yawning above the water, screened with laurel,

---

5. **Cicones.** Allies of the Trojans and Odysseus's enemies. Odysseus and his men had attacked the Cicones and taken jars of supplies from them.

words for everyday use	**plun • der** (plun´dər) *vt.*, steal or take by trickery or by force. *In 1204 European crusaders burned and <u>plundered</u> Constantinople, the jewel of the Byzantine Empire.*

and many rams and goats about the place
inside a sheepfold—made from slabs of stone
85   earthfast between tall trunks of pine and rugged
towering oak trees.

                    A prodigious man
slept in this cave alone, and took his flocks
to graze afield—remote from all companions,
knowing none but savage ways, a brute
90   so huge, he seemed no man at all of those
who eat good wheaten bread; but he seemed rather
a shaggy mountain reared in solitude.
We beached there, and I told the crew
to stand by and keep watch over the ship;
95   as for myself I took my twelve best fighters
and went ahead. I had a goatskin full
of that sweet liquor that Euanthês' son,
Maron, had given me. He kept Apollo's
holy grove at Ismaros; for kindness
100   we showed him there, and showed his wife and child,
he gave me seven shining golden talents[6]
perfectly formed, a solid silver winebowl,
and then this liquor—twelve two-handled jars
of brandy, pure and fiery. Not a slave
105   in Maron's household knew this drink; only
he, his wife and the storeroom mistress knew;
and they would put one cupful—ruby-colored,
honey-smooth—in twenty more of water,
but still the sweet scent hovered like a fume
110   over the winebowl. No man turned away
when cups of this came round.
                    A wineskin full
I brought along, and victuals[7] in a bag,
for in my bones I knew some towering brute

---

6. **talents.** Coins
7. **victuals.** Food

| words for everyday use | pro • di • gious (prō dij´əs) *adj.*, exceptional; of great size or power. *The young violinist had* <u>prodigious</u> *talent and tremendous energy.* |
| | fume (fyo͞om) *n.*, smoke, gas, or vapor. *As Vaughn filled the tank, he turned his head away to avoid breathing the gasoline* <u>fumes</u>. |

MARK THE TEXT

Underline the metaphor used to describe the appearance of the man in the cave.

THINK AND REFLECT

What does this metaphor suggest about the man? **(Interpret)**

_____

_____

_____

Use THE STRATEGY

WRITE THINGS DOWN. Don't forget to summarize lines 86–115 in your graphic organizer.

115   a wild man, ignorant of <u>civility</u>.

We climbed, then, briskly to the cave. But Cyclops
had gone afield, to pasture his fat sheep,
so we looked round at everything inside:
a drying rack that sagged with cheeses, pens
120   crowded with lambs and kids, each in its class:
firstlings apart from middlings, and the "dewdrops,"
or newborn lambkins, penned apart from both.
And vessels full of whey[8] were brimming there—
bowls of earthenware and pails for milking.
My men came pressing round me, pleading:

125   "Why not
take these cheeses, get them <u>stowed</u>, come back,
throw open all the pens, and make a run for it?
We'll drive the kids and lambs aboard. We say
put out[9] again on good salt water!"
                          Ah,
130   how sound that was! Yet I refused. I wished
to see the caveman, what he had to offer—
no pretty sight, it turned out, for my friends.

We lit a fire, burnt an offering,
and took some cheese to eat; then sat in silence
135   around the embers, waiting. When he came
he had a load of dry boughs on his shoulder
to stoke his fire at suppertime. He dumped it
with a great crash into that hollow cave,
and we all scattered fast to the far wall.
140   Then over the broad cavern floor he ushered
the ewes he meant to milk. He left his rams
and he-goats in the yard outside, and swung
high overhead a slab of solid rock

---

8. **whey.** Milky liquid left over from the making of cheese
9. **put out.** Set sail

words for everyday use	civ • il • i • ty (sə vil′ə tē) n., manners; civilized ways. *The pet store owner always treats us with <u>civility</u>, even when we make a complaint.*
	stow (stō) vt., put away, especially aboard a ship. *The flight attendant <u>stowed</u> my heavy bag in the overhead compartment.*

NOTE THE FACTS

What do Odysseus's advisors suggest in lines 125–129?

_____

_____

_____

THINK AND REFLECT

Was Odysseus's decision a good one? How can you tell? **(Evaluate)**

_____

_____

_____

to close the cave. Two dozen four-wheeled wagons,
145 with heaving wagon teams, could not have stirred
the tonnage of that rock from where he wedged it
over the doorsill. Next he took his seat
and milked his bleating ewes. A practiced job
he made of it, giving each ewe her suckling;
150 thickened his milk, then, into curds and whey,
sieved out the curds to drip in withy[10] baskets,
and poured the whey to stand in bowls
cooling until he drank it for his supper.
When all these chores were done, he poked the fire,
155 heaping on brushwood. In the glare he saw us.

"Strangers," he said, "who are you? And where from?
What brings you here by sea ways—a fair traffic?[11]
Or are you wandering rogues, who cast your lives
like dice, and ravage other folk by sea?"
160 We felt a pressure on our hearts, in dread
of that deep rumble and that mighty man.
But all the same I spoke up in reply:

"We are from Troy, Achaeans, blown off course
by shifting gales on the Great South Sea;
165 homeward bound, but taking routes and ways
uncommon; so the will of Zeus would have it.
We served under Agamemnon, son of Atreus—
the whole world knows what city
he laid waste, what armies he destroyed.
170 It was our luck to come here; here we stand,
beholden for your help, or any gifts
you give—as custom is to honor strangers.[12]
We would entreat you, great Sir, have a care
for the gods' courtesy; Zeus will avenge
the unoffending guest."

---

10. **withy.** Made of willow twigs
11. **fair traffic.** Honest trade
12. **as custom . . . strangers.** Among the ancient Greeks, treating visitors
well was considered a sacred obligation.

| words for everyday use | rogue (rōg) n., wicked or rascally person. "Stop, rogue," cried the soldier, brandishing his sword. |
| | a • venge (ə venj´) vt., get revenge for a wrongdoing. War broke out between the two countries when one side sought to avenge an attack on a small village. |

THINK AND REFLECT

How strong is the Cyclops? How do you know? **(Interpret)**

_____

_____

_____

NOTE THE FACTS

What does Odysseus ask of the Cyclops in lines 170–172? On what does he base this request?

_____

_____

_____

_____

He answered this
from his brute chest, unmoved:

"You are a ninny,
or else you come from the other end of nowhere,
telling me, mind the gods! We Cyclopes
180   care not a whistle for your thundering Zeus
or all the gods in bliss; we have more force by far.
I would not let you go for fear of Zeus—
you or your friends—unless I had a whim to.
Tell me, where was it, now, you left your ship—
around the point, or down the shore, I wonder?"

He thought he'd find out, but I saw through this,
185   and answered with a ready lie:

"My ship?
Poseidon Lord,[13] who sets the earth a-tremble,
broke it up on the rocks at your land's end.
A wind from seaward served him, drove us there.
190   We are survivors, these good men and I."

Neither reply nor pity came from him,
but in one stride he clutched at my companions
and caught two in his hands like squirming puppies
to beat their brains out, spattering the floor.
195   Then he dismembered them and made his meal,
gaping and crunching like a mountain lion—
everything: innards, flesh, and marrow bones.
We cried aloud, lifting our hands to Zeus,
powerless, looking on at this, appalled;
200   but Cyclops went on filling up his belly
with manflesh and great gulps of whey,
then lay down like a mast among his sheep.
My heart beat high now at the chance of action,
and drawing the sharp sword from my hip I went
205   along his flank to stab him where the midriff
holds the liver. I had touched the spot
when sudden fear stayed me: if I killed him
we perished there as well, for we could never

---

13. **Poseidon Lord.** Greek god of the sea

NOTE THE FACTS

What does Odysseus tell the Cyclops about the ship in lines 186–190?

_____

_____

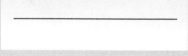

THINK AND REFLECT

Why does Odysseus lie about the ship? **(Interpret)**

_____

_____

READ ALOUD

Read lines 191–210 aloud. What does the Cyclops eat for dinner?

_____

_____

210   move his ponderous doorway slab aside.
So we were left to groan and wait for morning.

When the young Dawn with finger tips of rose
lit up the world, the Cyclops built a fire
and milked his handsome ewes, all in due order,
putting the sucklings to the mothers. Then,
215   his chores being all dispatched, he caught
another brace of men to make his breakfast,
and whisked away his great door slab
to let his sheep go through—but he, behind,
reset the stone as one would cap a quiver.[14]
220   There was a din of whistling as the Cyclops
rounded his flock to higher ground, then stillness.
And now I pondered how to hurt him worst
if but Athena[15] granted what I prayed for.
Here are the means I thought would serve my turn:

225   a club, or staff, lay there along the fold—
an olive tree, felled green and left to season
for Cyclops' hand. And it was like a mast
a lugger of twenty oars, broad in the beam—
a deep-sea-going craft—might carry:
230   so long, so big around, it seemed. Now I
chopped out a six-foot section of this pole
and set it down before my men, who scraped it;
and when they had it smooth, I hewed again
to make a stake with pointed end. I held this
235   in the fire's heart and turned it, toughening it,
then hid it, well back in the cavern, under
one of the dung piles in profusion there.
Now came the time to toss for it: who ventured
along with me? whose hand could bear to thrust
240   and grind that spike in Cyclops' eye, when mild
sleep had mastered him? As luck would have it,

---

14. **cap a quiver.** Put the top on a container for arrows
15. **Athena.** Greek goddess of wisdom to whom Odysseus, known for his
intelligence, often turns for guidance

FIX-UP IDEA

Tackle Difficult Vocabulary
If you have trouble summarizing, find a partner who is also having trouble, and follow these steps. Read a section once to get the overall sense. Then use definitions, footnotes, and context clues to find meanings for words you don't know. Use a dictionary if necessary. Finally, go back and reread the section, and then summarize it.

NOTE THE FACTS

What is Odysseus's plan (lines 239–241)?

_____

_____

_____

the men I would have chosen won the toss—
four strong men, and I made five as captain.

At evening came the shepherd with his flock,
245   his woolly flock. The rams as well, this time,
entered the cave: by some sheep-herding whim—
or a god's bidding—none were left outside.
He hefted[16] his great boulder into place
and sat him down to milk the bleating ewes
250   in proper order, put the lambs to suck,
and swiftly ran through all his evening chores.
Then he caught two more men and feasted on them.
My moment was at hand, and I went forward
holding an ivy bowl of my dark drink,
looking up, saying:

255   "Cyclops, try some wine.
Here's liquor to wash down your scraps of men.
Taste it, and see the kind of drink we carried
under our planks. I meant it for an offering
if you would help us home. But you are mad,
260   unbearable, a bloody monster! After this,
will any other traveler come to see you?"

He seized and drained the bowl, and it went down
so fiery and smooth he called for more:

"Give me another, thank you kindly. Tell me,
265   how are you called? I'll make a gift will please you.
Even Cyclopes know the wine-grapes grow
out of grassland and loam in heaven's rain,
but here's a bit of nectar and ambrosia!"[17]

Three bowls I brought him, and he poured them down.
270   I saw the fuddle and flush come over him,
then I sang out in cordial tones:

THINK AND REFLECT

Why do you think
Odysseus gives the
Cyclops so much wine?
(Interpret)

_____

_____

---

16. **hefted.** Lifted
17. **ambrosia.** Food of the gods

words for everyday use   **cor • dial** (kôr´jəl) *adj.,* friendly. *The Red Cross nurses were <u>cordial</u>, greeting Brent warmly when he went to give blood.*

> "Cyclops,
> you ask my honorable name? Remember
> the gift you promised me, and I shall tell you.
> My name is Nohbdy: mother, father, and friends,
> everyone calls me Nohbdy."

275   And he said:

"Nohbdy's my meat, then, after I eat his friends.
Others come first. There's a noble gift, now."
Even as he spoke, he reeled and tumbled backward,
his great head lolling to one side; and sleep
280 took him like any creature. Drunk, hiccuping,
he dribbled streams of liquor and bits of men.

Now, by the gods, I drove my big hand spike
deep in the embers, charring it again,
and cheered my men along with battle talk
285 to keep their courage up: no quitting now.
The pike of olive, green though it had been,
reddened and glowed as if about to catch.
I drew it from the coals and my four fellows
gave me a hand, lugging it near the Cyclops
290 as more than natural force nerved them; straight
forward they sprinted, lifted it, and rammed it
deep in his crater eye, and I leaned on it
turning it as a shipwright turns a drill
in planking, having men below to swing
295 the two-handled strap that spins it in the groove.
So with our brand we bored that great eye socket
while blood ran out around the red hot bar.
Eyelid and lash were seared; the pierced ball
hissed broiling, and the roots popped.

                         In a smithy
300 one sees a white-hot axehead or an adze[18]
plunged and wrung in a cold tub, screeching steam—
the way they make soft iron hale and hard—:
just so that eyeball hissed around the spike.
The Cyclops bellowed and the rock roared round him,

---

18. **adze.** Axe-like tool with a curved blade

READ ALOUD

Read lines 272–274 aloud. What does Odysseus say his name is? What English word does this name sound like?

_____

_____

NOTE THE FACTS

What do the Greeks do to the Cyclops in lines 290–299?

_____

_____

_____

Reading STRATEGY REVIEW

MAKE PREDICTIONS. Given what you know about the Greeks and the Cyclops, what do you think will happen now?

_____

_____

_____

305　and we fell back in fear. Clawing his face
　　　he tugged the bloody spike out of his eye,
　　　threw it away, and his wild hands went groping;
　　　then he set up a howl for Cyclopes
　　　who lived in caves on windy peaks nearby.
310　Some heard him; and they came by divers[19] ways
　　　to clump around outside and call:

　　　　　　　　　　　　　　　"What ails you,
　　　Polyphemos? Why do you cry so sore
　　　in the starry night? You will not let us sleep.
　　　Sure no man's driving off your flock? No man
　　　has tricked you, ruined you?"

315　　　　　　　　　　　　　　　Out of the cave
　　　the mammoth Polyphemos roared in answer:

　　　"Nohbdy, Nohbdy's tricked me, Nohbdy's ruined me!"

　　　To this rough shout they made a sage reply:

　　　"Ah well, if nobody has played you foul
320　there in your lonely bed, we are no use in pain
　　　given by great Zeus. Let it be your father,
　　　Poseidon Lord, to whom you pray."

　　　　　　　　　　　　　　　So saying
　　　they trailed away. And I was filled with laughter
　　　to see how like a charm the name deceived them.
325　Now Cyclops, wheezing as the pain came on him,
　　　fumbled to wrench away the great doorstone
　　　and squatted in the breach with arms thrown wide
　　　for any silly beast or man who bolted—
　　　hoping somehow I might be such a fool.
330　But I kept thinking how to win the game:

words for everyday use

sage (sāj) adj., wise. Shakespeare offers sage advice, as in Hamlet when he says, "To thine own self be true."

THINK AND REFLECT

In what way do the Cyclopes misunderstand Polyphemos's cries? (Infer)
What do you think will be the effect of this misunderstanding? (Extend)

_____

_____

_____

_____

_____

death sat there huge; how could we slip away?
I drew on all my wits, and ran through tactics,
reasoning as a man will for dear life,
until a trick came—and it pleased me well.
335　The Cyclops' rams were handsome, fat, with heavy
fleeces, a dark violet.

　　　　　　　　　　Three abreast
I tied them silently together, twining
cords of willow from the ogre's bed;
then slung a man under each middle one
340　to ride there safely, shielded left and right.
So three sheep could convey each man. I took
the woolliest ram, the choicest of the flock,
and hung myself under his kinky belly,
pulled up tight, with fingers twisted deep
345　in sheepskin ringlets for an iron grip.
So, breathing hard, we waited until morning.

When Dawn spread out her finger tips of rose
the rams began to stir, moving for pasture,
and peals of bleating echoed round the pens
350　where dams[20] with udders full called for a milking.
Blinded, and sick with pain from his head wound,
the master stroked each ram, then let it pass,
but my men riding on the <u>pectoral</u> fleece
the giant's blind hands blundering never found.
355　Last of them all my ram, the leader, came,
weighted by wool and me with my meditations.
The Cyclops patted him, and then he said:

"Sweet cousin ram, why lag behind the rest
in the night cave? You never linger so
360　but graze before them all, and go afar
to crop sweet grass, and take your stately way
leading along the streams, until at evening

---

20. **dams.** Female sheep

Literary TOOLS

PERSONIFICATION. Review the definition of personification on page 209. What is personified in line 331?

_____

_____

NOTE THE FACTS

What does Odysseus do with the rams in lines 336–340?

_____

_____

THINK AND REFLECT

What is Odysseus's plan involving the rams? **(Infer)**

_____

_____

_____

_____

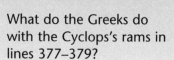

THINK AND REFLECT

In what way is the Cyclops's wish that the ram could tell him where Odysseus is ironic? (Analyze)

_____

_____

_____

NOTE THE FACTS

What do the Greeks do with the Cyclops's rams in lines 377–379?

_____

_____

NOTE THE FACTS

What does the Cyclops do in lines 395–399 in response to Odysseus's taunts?

_____

_____

_____

you run to be the first one in the fold.
Why, now, so far behind? Can you be grieving
365   over your Master's eye? That <u>carrion</u> rogue
and his accurst companions burnt it out
when he had conquered all my wits with wine.
Nohbdy will not get out alive, I swear.
Oh, had you brain and voice to tell
370   where he may be now, dodging all my fury!
Bashed by this hand and bashed on this rock wall
his brains would strew the floor, and I should have
rest from the outrage Nohbdy worked upon me."

He sent us into the open, then. Close by,
375   I dropped and rolled clear of the ram's belly,
going this way and that to untie the men.
With many glances back, we rounded up
his fat, stiff-legged sheep to take aboard,
and drove them down to where the good ship lay.
380   We saw, as we came near, our fellows' faces
shining; then we saw them turn to grief
tallying those who had not fled from death.
I hushed them, jerking head and eyebrows up,
and in a low voice told them: "Load this herd;
385   move fast, and put the ship's head toward the breakers."
They all pitched in at loading, then embarked
and struck their oars into the sea. Far out,
as far off shore as shouted words would carry,
I sent a few back to the adversary:

390   "O Cyclops! Would you feast on my companions?
Puny, am I, in a Caveman's hands?
How do you like the beating that we gave you,
you damned cannibal? Eater of guests
under your roof! Zeus and the gods have paid you!"
395   The blind thing in his doubled fury broke
a hilltop in his hands and heaved it after us.
Ahead of our black prow it struck and sank

words for everyday use	**car • ri • on** (kar´ē ən) *adj.,* literally, like a piece of dead meat; figuratively, something disgusting or repulsive. *The vultures gathered for a <u>carrion</u> feast in the middle of the road.*

whelmed in a spuming geyser, a giant wave
that washed the ship stern foremost back to shore.
400 I got the longest boathook out and stood
fending us off, with furious nods to all
to put their backs into a racing stroke—
row, row, or perish. So the long oars bent
kicking the foam sternward,[21] making head
405 until we drew away, and twice as far.
Now when I cupped my hands I heard the crew
in low voices protesting:
                              "Godsake, Captain!
Why bait the beast again? Let him alone."

"That tidal wave he made on the first throw
all but beached us."

410   "All but stove us in!"
"Give him our bearing with your trumpeting,
he'll get the range and lob a boulder."

                              "Aye.
He'll smash our timbers and our heads together!"

I would not heed them in my glorying spirit,
but let my anger flare and yelled:

415   "Cyclops,
if ever mortal man inquire
how you were put to shame and blinded, tell him
Odysseus, raider of cities, took your eye:
Laërtês' son, whose home's on Ithaca!"

420 At this he gave a mighty sob and rumbled:

"Now comes the weird[22] upon me, spoken of old.
A wizard, grand and wondrous, lived here—Télemos,
a son of Eurymos; great length of days
he had in wizardry among the Cyclopes,
425 and these things he foretold for time to come:

---

21. **sternward.** Toward the rear of a ship or boat
22. **weird.** Fate or destiny

THINK AND REFLECT

Why does the crew
protest when Odysseus
starts to taunt the Cyclops
again? (Interpret)

_____

_____

ASK A QUESTION

_____

_____

_____

_____

THINK AND REFLECT

It takes Odysseus ten years to get home. Why might that be? **(Extend)**

_____

_____

_____

my great eye lost, and at Odysseus's hands.
Always I had in mind some giant, armed
in giant force, would come against me here.
But this, but you—small, pitiful and twiggy—
430   you put me down with wine, you blinded me.
Come back, Odysseus, and I'll treat you well,
praying the god of earthquake[23] to befriend you—
his son I am, for he by his avowal
fathered me, and, if he will, he may
435   heal me of this black wound—he and no other
of all the happy gods or mortal men."

Few words I shouted in reply to him:

"If I could take your life I would and take
your time away, and hurl you down to hell!
440   The god of earthquake could not heal you there!"

At this he stretched his hands out in his darkness
toward the sky of stars, and prayed Poseidon:

"O hear me, lord, blue girdler of the islands,
if I am thine indeed, and thou art father:
445   grant that Odysseus, raider of cities, never
see his home: Laërtês' son, I mean,
who kept his hall on Ithaca. Should destiny
intend that he shall see his roof again
among his family in his father land,
450   far be that day, and dark the years between.
Let him lose all companions, and return
under strange sail to bitter days at home."

In these words he prayed, and the god heard him.
Now he laid hands upon a bigger stone
455   and wheeled around, <u>titanic</u> for the cast,

---

23. **the god of earthquake.** Poseidon, god of the seas, who could cause earthquakes and tidal waves with his three-pronged spear, or trident

words for everyday use

ti • tan • ic (tī tan´ik) *adj.*, of great size, strength, or power. *The <u>titanic</u> blue whale is larger than many of the largest dinosaurs.*

to let it fly in the black-prowed vessel's track.
But it fell short, just aft the steering oar,
and whelming seas rose giant above the stone
to bear us onward toward the island.

                                      There
460   as we ran in we saw the squadron waiting,
the trim ships drawn up side by side, and all
our troubled friends who waited, looking seaward.
We beached her, grinding keel[24] in the soft sand,
and waded in, ourselves, on the sandy beach.
465   Then we unloaded all the Cyclops' flock
to make division, share and share alike,
only my fighters voted that my ram,
the prize of all, should go to me. I slew him
by the sea side and burnt his long thighbones
470   to Zeus beyond the stormcloud, Kronos' son,[25]
who rules the world. But Zeus disdained my offering;
destruction for my ships he had in store
and death for those who sailed them, my companions.
Now all day long until the sun went down
475   we made our feast on mutton and sweet wine,
till after sunset in the gathering dark
we went to sleep above the wash of ripples.

When the young Dawn with finger tips of rose
touched the world, I roused the men, gave orders
480   to man the ships, cast off the mooring lines;
and filing in to sit beside the rowlocks
oarsmen in line dipped oars in the gray sea.
So we moved out, sad in the vast offing,[26]
having our precious lives, but not our friends.

from BOOK TWELVE

. . . As Circe[27] spoke, Dawn mounted her golden throne,
and on the first rays Circe left me, taking

NOTE THE FACTS

What does Odysseus do with the prize ram in lines 468–471?

_____

_____

Literary TOOLS

Foreshadowing is the act of presenting material that hints at events to occur later. Look for the two events foreshadowed in lines 471–473.

NOTE THE FACTS

How do the Greeks feel as they leave the island (lines 483–484)? Why?

_____

_____

_____

---

24. **keel.** Bottom ridge of a ship
25. **Kronos' son.** Kronos, or Chronos, the god of time, was the father of Zeus, the chief of the Greek gods.
26. **offing.** Leaving
27. **Circe.** Sorceress who, by means of drugs and incantations, was able to change humans into animals. She was the daughter of Helios and the ocean nymph Perse.

her way like a great goddess up the island.
I made straight for the ship, roused up the men
5   to get aboard and cast off at the stern;
They scrambled to their places by the rowlocks
and all in line dipped oars in the gray sea.
But soon an off-shore breeze blew to our liking—
a canvas-bellying breeze, a lusty shipmate
10 sent by the singing nymph with sunbright hair.
So we made fast the braces,[28] and we rested,
letting the wind and steersman work the ship.
The crew being now silent before me, I
addressed them, sore at heart:

                              "Dear friends,
15 more than one man, or two, should know those things
Circe foresaw for us and shared with me,
so let me tell her forecast: then we die
with our eyes open, if we are going to die,
or know what death we baffle if we can. Sirens
20 weaving a haunting song over the sea
we are to shun, she, and their green shore
all sweet with clover; yet she urged that I
alone should listen to their song. Therefore
you are to tie me up, tight as a splint,
25 erect along the mast, lashed to the mast,
and if I shout and beg to be untied,
take more turns of the rope to muffle me."

I rather dwelt on this part of the forecast,
while our good ship made time, bound outward down
30 the wind for the strange island of Sirens.
Then all at once the wind fell, and a calm
came over all the sea, as though some power
lulled the swell.

                              The crew were on their feet
briskly, to furl the sail, and stow it; then,
35 each in place, they poised the smooth oar blades
and sent the white foam scudding by. I carved
a massive cake of beeswax into bits

28. **made fast the braces.** Tied down the ropes that control the movement
of the sails

and rolled them in my hands until they softened—
no long task, for a burning heat came down
40   from Helios,[29] lord of high noon. Going forward
I carried wax along the line, and laid it
thick on their ears. They tied me up, then, plumb
amidships, back to the mast, lashed to the mast,
and took themselves again to rowing. Soon,
45   as we came smartly within hailing distance,
the two Sirens, noting our fast ship
off their point, made ready, and they sang:

> *This way, oh turn your bows,*
> *Achaea's glory,*
> 50   *As all the world allows—*
> *Moor and be merry.*
>
> *Sweet coupled airs we sing.*
> *No lonely seafarer*
> *Holds clear of entering*
> 55   *Our green mirror.*
>
> *Pleased by each purling[30] note*
> *Like honey twining*
> *From her throat and my throat,*
> *Who lies a-pining?*
>
> 60   *Sea rovers here take joy*
> *Voyaging onward,*
> *As from our song of Troy*
> *Graybeard and rower-boy*
> *Goeth more learnèd.[31]*
>
> 65   *All feats on that great field*
> *In the long warfare,*
> *Dark days the bright gods willed,*
> *Wounds you bore there,*

---

29. **Helios.** Sun god
30. ***purling.*** Swirling; rippling
31. ***learnèd.*** The accent over the *e* shows that it is to be pronounced
as a separate syllable.

NOTE THE FACTS

What does Odysseus do
with the wax in lines
36–42?

_____

_____

_____

MARK THE TEXT

Underline what the Sirens
command the Greeks to do.

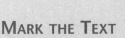

THINK AND REFLECT

What details do the Sirens
include in their song to
target it specifically to
Odysseus and his crew?
(Analyze)

_____

_____

_____

_____

_____

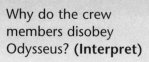

NOTE THE FACTS

How does Odysseus try to communicate with the crew? What does he want (lines 75–79)?

_____

_____

_____

70   *Argos'*[32] *old soldiery*
           On Troy beach teeming,
       Charmed out of time we see.
       No life on earth can be
           Hid from our dreaming.

       The lovely voices in <u>ardor</u> appealing over the water
75   made me crave to listen, and I tried to say,
       "Untie me!" to the crew, jerking my brows;
       but they bent steady to the oars. Then Perimêdês
       got to his feet, he and Eur'ylokhos,
       and passed more line about, to hold me still.
80   So all rowed on, until the Sirens
       dropped under the sea rim, and their singing
       dwindled away.
                              My faithful company
       rested on their oars now, peeling off
       the wax that I had laid thick on their ears;
85   then set me free. . . . ■

---

32. *Argos.* Belonging to Argos, an ancient Greek city-state

---

words for everyday use

ar • dor (är′dər) *n.*, eagerness; passion; enthusiasm. *Daniel Webster spoke with such <u>ardor</u> that even his opponents listened with awe.*

Reflect ON YOUR READING

SHARE YOUR SUMMARIES

Compare your summaries with those of a partner. Discuss the events in the poem, and create a list of the most important events below. Share this list with the class.

_____

_____

_____

_____

Reading Skills and Test Practice

USE CONTEXT CLUES

Discuss with your group how best to answer the following questions about words in context.

1. Read the following passage.

> When the young Dawn with finger tips of rose
> came in the east, I called my men together. . . .

To which time of day does the passage refer? How did you infer this meaning? Support your answer with evidence from the passage.

_____

_____

2. Read the following passage.

> Three abreast
> I tied them [sheep] silently together . . .
> then slung a man under each middle one
> to ride there safely, shielded left and right . . .
> the master stroked each ram, then let it pass,
> but my men riding on the pectoral fleece
> the giant's blind hands blundering never found.

What is the meaning of the word *pectoral*? Which clues from the text did you use to determine the meaning? Support your answer with details from the text.

_____

_____

THINK-ALOUD NOTES

_____

_____

_____

_____

_____

_____

_____

_____

_____

_____

_____

_____

Investigate, Inquire, and Imagine

RECALL: GATHER FACTS
1a. In what way does Odysseus ignore the wishes of his companions when they first enter the Cyclops's cave? How do the Greeks escape from Polyphemos? What does Odysseus do when he and his sailors have left Cyclopes Land?

INTERPRET: FIND MEANING
1b. What aspects of Odysseus's personality are revealed by the plan he creates to escape from Polyphemos? What aspects are revealed by his disregard for his crewmembers' advice?

ANALYZE: TAKE THINGS APART
2a. Identify the mythological characters that help or hinder Odysseus on his journey.

SYNTHESIZE: BRING THINGS TOGETHER
2b. Explain how Odysseus's beliefs in these mythological characters affect his behavior.

EVALUATE: MAKE JUDGMENTS
3a. On a scale of one to ten, rate the effectiveness of Odysseus as a leader. Explain your answer.

EXTEND: CONNECT IDEAS
3b. Compare Odysseus to other legendary heroes and discuss how they are similar and different.

WordWorkshop

USING CONTEXT CLUES. The *Odyssey* is one of the most studied works of literature in the world. Reading it can be a challenge, but it is also rewarding. To understand it, use all the context clues you can, consider the parts of difficult words, ask for help when you need it, and have a dictionary nearby. Use your own paper to answer the following questions.

1. One type of context clue is **restatement**. The author may tell you the meaning of a word or phrase you do not know by using different words to express the same idea in surrounding sentences. Using context clues, explain what *In ignorance leaving the fruitage of the earth in mystery to the immortal gods* (Book Nine, lines 3–4) means.
2. Another kind of context clue involves **comparison** or **contrast**. Reread Book Nine, lines 8–12. Explain how lines 10–12 help to clarify the meaning of lines 8 and 9.
3. Another type of context clue is **apposition**. Apposition is renaming something in different words. Identify an example of apposition in Book Nine, line 20.
4. Reread lines 163–176. Predict the meanings of the following words: *gales, beholden, entreat, unoffending.*
5. Verify your predictions above by looking up the words in a dictionary. Write the definition for each below.

Literary Tools

PERSONIFICATION. **Personification** is a figure of speech in which an idea, animal, or thing is described as if it were a person. In what ways is dawn personified in Book Nine, line 50, and Book Twelve, line 1?

_____

_____

_____

Why is it logical for Homer to personify dawn?

_____

_____

_____

Read-Write Connection

Which qualities do you admire in Odysseus, and why?

_____

_____

_____

_____

_____

_____

_____

_____

_____

Beyond the Reading

RESEARCH GREEK GODS AND GODDESSES. Find out more about one of the Greek gods or goddesses mentioned in this excerpt of the *Odyssey*. You might start by looking through Edith Hamilton's book called *Mythology* or a copy of *Bulfinch's Mythology*. For what is your god or goddess known? What interesting stories are associated with him or her? Act out a story about your god or goddess for the class.

GO ONLINE. Visit the EMC Internet Resource Center at **emcp.com** to find links and additional activities for this selection.

Choose and Use Reading Strategies

Before reading the poem below, review with a partner how to use each of these reading strategies.

1. Read with a Purpose
2. Connect to Prior Knowledge
3. Write Things Down
4. Make Predictions
5. Visualize
6. Use Text Organization
7. Tackle Difficult Vocabulary
8. Monitor Your Reading Progress

Now apply at least two of these reading strategies as you read "A Poison Tree" by William Blake. Use the margins and mark up the text to show how you are using the reading strategies to read actively.

I was angry with my friend:
I told my wrath, my wrath did end.
I was angry with my foe:
I told it not, my wrath did grow.

And I water'd it in fears,
Night and morning with my tears;
And I sunnéd it with smiles,
And with soft deceitful wiles.

And it grew both day and night,
Till it bore an apple bright;
And my foe beheld it shine,
And he knew that it was mine,

And into my garden stole,
When the night had veil'd the pole:
In the morning glad I see
My foe outstretch'd beneath the tree.

WordWorkshop

agitation, 177
annex, 209
aquamarine, 203
ardor, 226
avenge, 213
bog, 172
bracken, 165
brooch, 197
carrion, 220
chafe, 209
civility, 212
cordial, 216
din, 215
engagement, 203

fume, 211
lash, 166
pectoral, 219
plunder, 210
ponderous, 215
preconception, 177
prodigious, 211
quarry, 197
rogue, 213
sage, 218
stow, 212
subdue, 166
titanic, 222

SEMANTIC MAP. Work with a partner or small group to fill in the Vocabulary Cluster with words from the list. The categories have been labeled for you, and you may add circles wherever you like. You don't need to use every word, but you should try to place as many as possible. Be prepared to explain why you have placed the words in the category you have.

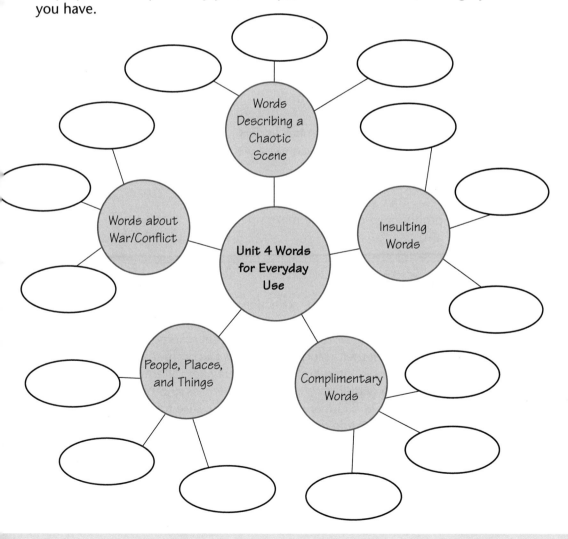

Literary Tools

Select the best literary element on the right to complete each sentence on the left. Write the correct letter in the blank.

_____ 1. In "Hanging Fire," Audre Lorde uses the lines "and momma's in the bedroom / with the door closed" to end each stanza. This is an example of _____.

_____ 2. The individual whose wrath grows an apple in "A Poison Tree" is the poem's_____.

_____ 3. Saying that "life is too much like a pathless wood" involves using a(n)_____.

_____ 4. Applied to "The Poison Tree" above, the letters *aabb* refer to the poem's_____.

_____ 5. When the speaker of "Nikki-Rosa" claims to be both wealthy and poor, she is establishing a(n)_____.

_____ 6. In "The Poison Tree," *foe* and *grow* have the same ending sounds. This means that they_____.

_____ 7. When the speaker of "miss rosie" calls Rosie a "wet brown bag of a woman," she is using a(n)_____.

_____ 8. The use of sensory details to portray the bent birch trees is_____.

_____ 9. Suggesting that Dawn has fingers that she can spread is an example of_____.

____ 10. A pair of words—such as *low* and *cow*—that are spelled similarly but pronounced differently make up a(n)_____.

a. description, 206

b. metaphor, 169

c. paradox, 184

d. personification, 228

e. repetition, 189

f. rhyme, 199

g. rhyme scheme, 199

h. sight rhyme, 199

i. speaker, 179, 194

j. simile, 169, 174

On Your Own

FLUENTLY SPEAKING. Search poetry collections and the Internet until you find a poem that you like. Form a small group of people who like the same poem. Prepare a choral reading of the poem. In a choral reading, several people read a text aloud together, using vocal effects to communicate the meaning of the poem. You could alternate slow and fast lines; alternate loud and soft or high and low pitched lines; emphasize key words and phrases by reading them all together or in a louder or softer voice; pause for a certain number of silent beats before continuing; or even read the poem in a round with overlapping voices. Rehearse the choral reading until the whole group is ready to perform it smoothly for the class.

Unit FIVE

READING Folk Literature

Human beings are storytelling creatures. Long before people invented writing, they were telling stories about the lives of their gods and heroes. The best of their stories were passed by word of mouth from generation to generation, from folk to folk. These early stories were told in the form of poems, songs, and what we would now call prose tales.

Stories, poems, and songs passed by word of mouth from person to person are important elements of a group's culture. Eventually, many of these verbally transmitted stories, poems, and songs were written down. **Folk literature** is the written versions of these stories, poems, and songs. Folk literature is full of literary devices that helped storytellers remember the stories. These devices include the use of repetition, common phrases such as "once upon a time" and "they lived happily ever after," and familiar characters and events. Some common forms of folk literature are defined below.

Types of Folk Literature

MYTHS. **Myths** are stories that explain objects or events in the natural world as resulting from the action of some supernatural force or entity, most often a god. Every early culture around the globe has produced its own myths. Two Greek myths appear in this unit: "Echo and Narcissus," retold by Walker Brents, and "The Story of Dædalus and Icarus," translated by Rolfe Humphries.

FOLK TALES. **Folk tales** are brief stories passed by word of mouth from generation to generation in a particular culture. "Goha and the Pot," found in this unit, is a North African folk tale. **Fairy tales** are folk tales that contain supernatural beings, such as fairies, dragons, ogres, and animals that have human qualities. "The White Snake," found in this unit, is a famous fairy tale from the European

NOTE THE FACTS

What is folk literature?

_____

_____

_____

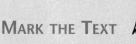

MARK THE TEXT

Highlight or underline six types of folk literature. Start here and and continue on the next page.

THINK AND REFLECT

Cinderella and Snow White are well-known fairy tale characters. Can you think of others?

_____

_____

_____

folk tradition. **Tall tales** are colorful stories that depict the exaggerated wild adventures of North American folk heroes. Many of these heroes and stories revolve around the American frontier and the Wild West.

PARABLES. **Parables** are very brief stories told to teach a moral lesson. Some of the most famous parables are those told by Jesus in the Bible. "The Prodigal Son," found in this unit, is one such parable.

FABLES. **Fables** are brief stories, often with animal characters, told to express a moral. Famous fables include those of Æsop and Jean de La Fontaine. In this unit you will find the fable "The Fox and the Crow" by Æsop.

FOLK SONGS. **Folk songs** are traditional or composed songs typically made up of stanzas, a refrain, and a simple melody. They express commonly shared ideas or feelings and may be narrative (telling a story) or lyrical (expressing an emotion). Traditional folk songs are anonymous songs that have been transmitted orally. Examples include the ballad "John Henry," found in this unit.

LEGENDS. **Legends** are stories that have been passed down through time. These stories are popularly thought of as historical but without evidence that the events occurred.

USING READING STRATEGIES WITH FOLK LITERATURE

Active Reading Strategy Checklists

In the stories, poems, and songs that are a part of folk literature, storytellers want to entertain their audience and to pass along cultural ideas and beliefs. The following checklists offer strategies for reading folk literature.

1 READ WITH A PURPOSE. Give yourself a purpose, or something to look for, as you read. Often, you can set a purpose for reading by previewing the title, the opening lines, and instructional information. Other times, a teacher may set your purpose: "Write down tricks that one character plays on another." To read with a purpose say to yourself

❑ I want to look for . . .

❑ I will keep track of . . .

❑ I want to find out what happens to . . .

❑ I want to understand how . . .

❑ The message of this selection is . . .

2 CONNECT TO PRIOR KNOWLEDGE. Connect to what you already know about a particular culture and its storytelling traditions. To connect to prior knowledge, say to yourself

❑ I know that this type of folk literature has . . .

❑ The events in this selection remind me of . . .

❑ Something similar I've read is . . .

❑ I like this part of the selection because . . .

3 WRITE THINGS DOWN. Create a written record of the cultural ideas and beliefs that a storyteller passes along. To keep a written record

❑ Underline characters' names.

❑ Write down your thoughts about the storyteller's ideas and beliefs.

❑ Highlight what the characters do.

❑ Create a graphic organizer to keep track of the sequence of events.

❑ Use a code to respond to what happens.

4 MAKE PREDICTIONS. Use information about the title and subject matter to guess what a folk literature selection will be about. Confirm or deny your predictions, and make new ones based on what you learn. To make predictions, say to yourself

❑ The title tells me that the selection will be about . . .

❑ I predict that this character will . . .

❑ Tales from this cultural tradition usually . . .

❑ The conflict between the characters will be resolved by . . .

❑ I think the selection will end with. . .

5 VISUALIZE. Visualizing, or allowing the words on the page to create images in your mind, helps you understand a storyteller's account. In order to visualize what happens in a folk literature selection, imagine that you are the storyteller. Read the words in your head with the type of expression and feeling that the storyteller might use with an audience. Make statements such as

Reading TIP

Instead of writing down a short response, use a symbol or a short word to indicate your response. Use codes like the ones listed below.

+	I like this.
–	I don't like this.
√	This is important.
Yes	I agree with this.
No	I disagree with this.
?	I don't understand this.
!	This is like something I know.
ᕬ	I need to come back to this later.

Reading TIP

Sketching story events helps you remember and understand them.

- ❏ I imagine the characters sound like . . .
- ❏ My sketch of what happens includes . . .
- ❏ I picture this sequence of events . . .
- ❏ I envision the characters as . . .

6 USE TEXT ORGANIZATION. When you read folk literature, pay attention to signal words such as "first," "a few days later," and "the main thing." These words identify important ideas and the sequence of events. Find places to stop occasionally, and retell what has happened so far. Say to yourself

- ❏ The introductory paragraphs tell me this selection will be about . . .
- ❏ The main conflict centers on . . .
- ❏ The high point of interest is . . .
- ❏ I can summarize this section by . . .
- ❏ The message of this selection is that . . .

7 TACKLE DIFFICULT VOCABULARY. Difficult words can hinder your ability to understand folk literature. Use context, consult a dictionary, or ask someone about words you do not understand. When you come across a difficult word, say to yourself

- ❏ The words around the difficult word tell me it must mean . . .
- ❏ A dictionary definition shows that the word means . . .
- ❏ My work with the word before reading helps me know that the word means . . .
- ❏ A classmate said that the word means . . .

8 MONITOR YOUR READING PROGRESS. All readers encounter difficulty when they read, especially if they are reading assigned material and not something they have chosen on their own. When you are assigned to read folk literature, note the problems you are having and fix them. The key to reading success is knowing when you are having difficulty. To fix problems, say to yourself

- ❏ Because I don't understand this part, I will . . .
- ❏ Because I'm having trouble staying connected, I will . . .
- ❏ Because the words are hard, I will . . .
- ❏ Because this selection is long, I will . . .
- ❏ Because I can't retell what this section was about, I will . . .

Reading **TIP**

If the words in a selection are difficult to pronounce, practice saying them aloud before you read.

FIX-UP IDEAS

- ■ Reread
- ■ Ask a question
- ■ Read in shorter chunks
- ■ Read aloud
- ■ Retell
- ■ Work with a partner
- ■ Unlock difficult words
- ■ Vary your reading rate
- ■ Choose a new reading strategy
- ■ Create a mnemonic device

How to Use Reading Strategies with Folk Literature

Use the following excerpts to discover how you might use reading strategies as you read folk literature.

Excerpt 1. Note how a reader uses active reading strategies while reading this excerpt from "The White Snake" by Jacob and Wilhelm Grimm, page 255.

READ WITH A PURPOSE

I want to find out what task the servant must perform.

VISUALIZE

I picture the King's daughter smiling and wearing a long, flowing dress.

CONNECT TO PRIOR KNOWLEDGE

This reminds me of other fairy tales where a beautiful princess must choose a worthy husband.

So now he had to use his own legs, and when he had gone a long way he came to a great town. There was much noise and thronging in the streets, and there came a man on a horse, who proclaimed,

"That the King's daughter seeks a husband, but he who wishes to marry her must perform a difficult task, and if he cannot carry it through successfully, he must lose his life."

Many had already tried, but had lost their lives, in vain. The young man, when he saw the King's daughter, was so dazzled by her great beauty, that he forgot all danger, went to the King and offered himself as a wooer.

MAKE PREDICTIONS

Stories like this usually end happily, so I predict that the servant will perform the tasks and marry the Princess.

Excerpt 2. Note how a reader uses active reading strategies while reading this excerpt from "The Story of Dædalus and Icarus" by Ovid, page 246.

USE TEXT ORGANIZATION

Reading to the end of thoughts, not to the end of lines, helps me follow events.

WRITE THINGS DOWN

I can write down events that foreshadow what will happen to Dædalus and Icarus.

Homesick for homeland, Dædalus hated Crete
And his long exile there, but the sea held him.
"Though Minos[1] blocks escape by land or water,"
Dædalus said, "surely the sky is open,
And that's the way we'll go. Minos' <u>dominion</u>
Does not include the air." He turned his thinking
Toward unknown arts, changing the laws of nature.
He laid out feathers in order, first the smallest,
A little larger next it, and so continued,
The way that pan-pipes[2] rise in gradual sequence.

MONITOR YOUR READING PROGRESS

Rereading the opening lines helps me understand them.

TACKLE DIFFICULT VOCABULARY

The footnotes help me understand Dædalus's plan.

---

1. **Minos.** King of Crete who would not allow Dædalus to leave Crete
2. **pan-pipes.** Instruments made of reeds of various lengths

"Echo and Narcissus"

retold by Walker Brents

People in ancient Greece and Rome believed supernatural gods and goddesses directed events in their world. These supernatural beings were more powerful than humans, but they experienced human emotions such as jealousy and passion. The myth of **"Echo and Narcissus"** shows the human qualities of the gods and explains the origin of two things in nature, a *narcissus* flower and an *echo*. A narcissus is a lilylike flower with a showy yellow or white bloom. An *echo* is a sound repetition that occurs when sound waves bounce off a hard surface.

Word watch

PREVIEW VOCABULARY

beguile	ebb
curtail	enigmatic
disintegrate	oblivious

Reader's journal

What qualities do you find attractive in another person? Is physical appearance as important as other aspects such as personality or intellectual qualities? Why, or why not?

_____

_____

_____

_____

Active READING STRATEGY

WRITE THINGS DOWN

Before Reading ➤ PREVIEW

❑ Brainstorm ideas about mythology. List what you know about Greek and Roman gods and goddesses.
❑ Read the Reader's Resource.
❑ Prepare to fill in the chart below as you read.

Graphic Organizer

Stopping Point	Question 1	Answer 1	Question 2	Answer 2
After line 43	What is an *echo?*		How does Greek mythology explain an *echo?*	
After line 49	Who is the character named Echo?		What happened to Echo?	
After line 82	Who is the character named Narcissus?		What happened to Narcissus?	
At the end of the story	What is a *narcissus flower?*		How does Greek mythology explain a *narcissus flower?*	

Echo & Narcissus

retold by Walker Brents

During Reading

FILL IN A CHART

- ❑ Follow along in the text as your teacher reads through line 43 aloud.
- ❑ Discuss the Greeks' explanation for an echo.
- ❑ Go back to your graphic organizer and fill in the Answer 1 and Answer 2 columns of the first row.
- ❑ Read the remainder of the myth aloud with a partner. Alternate reading and listening tasks.
- ❑ Answer the rest of the questions in the graphic organizer as you read.

READ ALOUD

To make reading the myth easier, practice saying the Greek names found in the myth.

Liriope (lə rī′ ō pē)
Tiresias (tī rē′ sē əs)
Narcissus (när si′ səs)
Hera (hir′ ə, or her′ ə)
Zeus (züs)
Nemesis (ne′ mə sis)

MARK THE TEXT

Underline or highlight words or phrases in this passage that show how others react to Narcissus and how he treats them.

Liriope the river nymph gave birth to a beautiful child. She brought him to the blind seer Tiresias to ask his destiny. Tiresias predicted that the boy would live a long life, but only if he never "came to know himself."

The child was named Narcissus. As he grew, his beauty increased. His dazzling looks had a strange effect upon the woodland spirits, the naiads and the dryads,[1] around whom he spent his days. They all fell in love with him, but he was <u>oblivious</u>, interested only in hunting in the hills with his companions. His pride in his beauty grew so great that he had nothing but scorn for the feelings of others.

There was one nymph, Echo by name, who saw Narcissus chasing deer into nets in the hills. Echo was instantly seized by love and could not overcome it. Secretly, she followed him through the wilderness, waiting for her chance to make herself known to him—but one thing held her back: she could not initiate speech on her own. She could only repeat

10

---

1. **the naiads and the dryads.** Nymphs of the water and of trees

words for everyday use

o • bliv • i • ous (ə bliv′vē əs) *adj.*, unaware; lacking attention. *Pete cranked up the volume of the television, <u>oblivious</u> to the fact that he was disturbing everyone's sleep.*

NOTE THE FACTS

Who punished Echo and how was she punished?

_____

_____

_____

Use THE STRATEGY

WRITE THINGS DOWN. After line 49, stop reading to fill in your graphic organizer. Who is the character named Echo? What happened to Echo?

what was said to her. This was her condition, and it had come about because one day the goddess Hera was

20 questioning the nymphs about her husband Zeus. She asked them where Zeus was, suspecting that the unfaithful god had been chasing the lovely nymphs and dwelling among them. Indeed he had, and while he was making his escape Echo distracted Hera with a flow of entertaining conversation. When Hera learned she had been fooled, she cursed Echo, saying, "From now on your words will not be your own. You will only be able to repeat what is said to you. That way your powers to <u>beguile</u> and distract will be <u>curtailed</u>."

Thereafter Echo could only repeat the words she heard.
30 She could not announce herself to Narcissus. She trailed him silently, hoping for the right circumstance to meet him and declare her love. One day Narcissus had wandered away from his companions, and was in the forest looking for them. Echo was nearby, but Narcissus did not see her. "Is anyone here?" he cried. "Here," she answered. "Come to me," he called out. "Come to me," she replied. "Do not avoid me," he pleaded. She said the same to him. "Let us meet," he announced. This was her chance. She stepped out of hiding and stood before him smiling, saying, "Let us
40 meet." He fell back from her scornfully. "You are not the one I seek. I would die before I would be near you." Echo advanced toward him, pleading, "I would be near you." But he ran from her.

Haunted by his rejection and crushed by shame, Echo hid herself in caves and covered herself with leaves. She began to waste away and disappear. In the end only her bones were left, and these became rocks. But her voice remained. Travelers and wanderers heard it sometimes, answering them with their own words. Still Echo did not forget Narcissus.

50 Meanwhile, Narcissus too fell victim to a curse. Another nymph had fallen in love with him, but was also spurned. This one cried to the heavens for vengeance: "May Narcissus fall into a love that is not returned!" The goddess of righteous anger, Nemesis, heard these words. And so it

words
for
everyday
use

be • guile (bi gīal´) *vt.*, lead by deception; distract. *When my little brother screamed for a toy he wanted, I <u>beguiled</u> him with the promise of an ice cream cone.*
cur • tail (kər tāl´) *vt.*, make less as if by cutting away a part. *The dictator's power was <u>curtailed</u> when his army was defeated.*

happened that on a sunny and hot day Narcissus found himself at a pond to which no shepherd's flocks had been, from which no goats had drunk. It was a wild place. A green meadow surrounded it, and tall trees shaded it from the sun and sheltered it from winds. Putting his face to the waters in order to quench his thirst, Narcissus caught sight for the first time of his own reflection. He was astonished by the beautiful face that met his eye.

"What star-like eyes are these; what smooth skin! That forehead, that jaw, that gorgeous flowing hair! Who are you? Draw near to me!" He reached his hands to the water, but the reflected image <u>disintegrated</u>. He waited for it to reappear. "Only the surface of these waters parts us. No fortress gates nor city walls; no long rocky highway, no impenetrable forest nor unclimbable mountain stands between us. Yet I cannot reach you! How can this be?" He cried to the endless skies, "How is it that when I find my love his very nearness keeps us far apart?" But there was no answer.

Narcissus could not leave this place. Entranced by his own reflection, he began to waste away from hunger and thirst. His strength and his life <u>ebbed</u> away and did not return. Echo hovered around him, invisible and unforgetting. Her disembodied voice repeated his final word, which was "Alas." He died, and his spirit left his body. Even on the boat of souls, crossing the river between this world and the other one, Narcissus leaned over the edge, looking into those waters, trying to catch a glimpse of the image that so captivated him.

The nymphs heard of his death and went to the pond to retrieve his body for the funeral ceremony. But when they got there, they found no corpse, only a new blossom with snowy petals and a yellow corona.[2] The flower came to be called "Narcissus," in honor of one who, in the <u>enigmatic</u> words of Tiresias, "came to know himself," and fell in love. ■

---

2. **corona.** Trumpet-shaped part of the inner cup of a flower such as the daffodil

words for everyday use

dis • in • te • grate (di sin′ tə grāt′) vt., break apart. *The note <u>disintegrated</u> into tiny pieces after it had accidentally gone through the wash.*

ebb (eb′) vi., decline; fall to a lower or worse state. *My determination <u>ebbed</u>, and I became depressed as I realized how difficult it would be to reach my goal.*

en • ig • ma • tic (e′ nig ma′ tik) adj., mysterious; hard to decipher. *Julia is so <u>enigmatic</u>; I can never seem to understand where she is coming from.*

FIX-UP IDEA

Reread
If you have difficulty understanding a paragraph in the myth, reread it aloud to a partner. Help each other unlock difficult words and ideas. You may need to reread some sentences several times. Rereading makes it easier to fill in your chart.

Use THE STRATEGY

WRITE THINGS DOWN. At the end of the story, write down what happened to Narcissus in your graphic organizer.

Reflect ON YOUR READING

Share the information in your chart with the class, and discuss the origins of the words *echo* and *narcissus*. How does writing things down help you?

_____

_____

_____

_____

_____

THINK-ALOUD NOTES

_____

_____

_____

_____

_____

_____

_____

_____

_____

_____

Reading Skills and Test Practice

IDENTIFY CAUSE AND EFFECT

Discuss with your group how best to answer the following cause-and-effect questions.

1. What causes Echo to lose her ability to speak her own thoughts?
   a. her love of Narcissus
   b. her love of herself
   c. her trickery of Hera
   d. her hatred of Zeus

What is the correct answer to the question above? How were you able to eliminate other answers? How did your use of the reading strategy help you?

_____

_____

2. Which of the following did NOT cause Narcissus to die young?
   a. He came to know himself.
   b. He spurned Echo and the other nymphs who loved him.
   c. He was excessively proud of his beauty.
   d. He realized how cruel he had been to Echo.

What is the correct answer to the question above? How were you able to eliminate other answers? How did your use of the reading strategy help you?

_____

_____

Investigate, Inquire, and Imagine

RECALL: GATHER FACTS

1a. With whom does Narcissus fall in love? Who caused this to happen?

→ INTERPRET: FIND MEANING

1b. Why does Nemesis punish Narcissus?

ANALYZE: TAKE THINGS APART

2a. What metamorphoses, or transformations, occur in "Echo and Narcissus"?

→ SYNTHESIZE: BRING THINGS TOGETHER

2b. This story explains two phenomena in nature. What are these phenomena, and how are they explained?

PERSPECTIVE: LOOK AT OTHER VIEWS →

3a. From the nymphs' perspective, what is Narcissus's crime? Explain whether you think Narcissus's punishment is appropriate to the crime.

EMPATHY: SEE FROM INSIDE

3b. Imagine you were Narcissus and everyone was instantly captivated by your exceptional good looks. Would you find this annoying? How would you react?

Literary Tools

SUSPENSION OF DISBELIEF. **Suspension of disbelief** is the act by which the reader willingly sets aside his or her skepticism to participate imaginatively in the work being read. The willingness to suspend disbelief, to participate imaginatively in a story being read, is the most important attribute, beyond literacy, that a person can bring to the act of reading literature. Which elements of the story require you to suspend your disbelief? Why?

Supernatural Events That Require Suspension of Disbelief	Why These Elements Are Unbelievable
Hera is able to put a curse on Echo.	People can't put a curse on someone else.

WordWorkshop

MNEMONIC DEVICES

REMEMBERING MEANINGS AND SPELLINGS. Look through "Echo and Narcissus." Find five words whose meanings or spellings are unfamiliar or difficult. Write them on the lines below. Add mnemonic devices, or memory aids, behind each word that help you remember the meanings or spellings. Example: *Malodorous* means having a bad odor because *mal* means bad and the word *odor* is in the word.

_____

_____

_____

_____

_____

Read-Write Connection

Do you feel sympathy toward Narcissus, or do you think he deserves his fate? Explain your answer.

_____

_____

_____

_____

_____

_____

_____

_____

_____

Beyond the Reading

THE GREEK PANTHEON. Read about the Greek pantheon, or the temple where all of the Greek gods lived. Learn more about the major gods and their roles, or find information about some of the minor gods and earthly heroes. Create a booklet that describes ten of these figures and what they did.

GO ONLINE. Visit the EMC Internet Resource Center at **emcp.com** to find links and additional activities for this selection.

"The Story of Dædalus and Icarus"

from the *Metamorphoses*
by Ovid, translated by Rolfe Humphries

Active READING STRATEGY

MAKE PREDICTIONS

Before Reading ➤ **GATHER INFORMATION AND MAKE PRELIMINARY PREDICTIONS**

- ❑ Read the Reader's Resource.
- ❑ Make predictions about what will happen to Dædalus and Icarus.
- ❑ Fill in the Predictions Chart below as you read.

Graphic Organizer

Stop	Predict What Will Happen to	Clues That Led to This Prediction
After reading the Reader's Resource	Dædalus and Icarus:	
After line 20	Dædalus and Icarus:	
After line 49	Icarus:	
After line 70	The sister's son:	

CONNECT

Reader's resource

"The Story of Dædalus and Icarus" is about the brilliant mythical inventor Dædalus and his son and their escape from captivity in Crete, an island ruled by King Minos. This version of the tale was written by Ovid and translated by Rolfe Humphries. Ovid is the pen name of Publius Ovidius Naso (43 BC–AD 18), one of the greatest of the Latin poets. Ovid lived at the time of the emperor Augustus, when the Roman Empire was in its golden age.

Word watch

PREVIEW VOCABULARY

dominion
plumage
traverse

Reader's journal

Humans fantasized about flying long before airplanes were invented. Write about an improbable adventure you would like to experience.

_____

_____

_____

_____

_____

MAKE PREDICTIONS

❏ As your teacher reads aloud, listen for clues that predict what will happen to Dædalus and Icarus. When your teacher reaches line 20, make a prediction in your chart.

❏ Continue reading the poem silently with a partner. Make more predictions when you reach lines 49 and 70.

READ ALOUD

Read these Greek names aloud before you begin reading.

Ovid (ö′ vid)
Dædalus (ded′ ə ləs or de dã′ ləs)
Crete (crēt)
Minos (mē′ nos)
Icarus (i′ kə rəs)
Samos (sa′ mos)
Juno (joo′ nō)
Delos (de′ los)
Paros (pä′ ros)
Lebinthus (le bin′ thəs)
Calymne (cä lim′ nā)
Minerva (mi nər′ va)
Perdix (pər′ dix)

Literary TOOLS

FORESHADOWING.
Foreshadowing is the act of presenting materials that hint at events to occur later in a story. Reread lines 14–20. What might they foreshadow?

_____

_____

_____

The Story of Dædalus and Icarus

FROM THE Metamorphoses

Ovid, translated by Rolfe Humphries

Homesick for homeland, Dædalus hated Crete
And his long exile there, but the sea held him.
"Though Minos blocks escape by land or water,"
Dædalus said, "surely the sky is open,
5   And that's the way we'll go. Minos' <u>dominion</u>
Does not include the air." He turned his thinking
Toward unknown arts, changing the laws of nature.
He laid out feathers in order, first the smallest,
A little larger next it, and so continued,
10   The way that pan-pipes[1] rise in gradual sequence.
He fastened them with twine and wax, at middle,
At bottom, so, and bent them, gently curving,
So that they looked like wings of birds, most surely.
And Icarus, his son, stood by and watched him,
15   Not knowing he was dealing with his downfall,
Stood by and watched, and raised his shiny face
To let a feather, light as down, fall on it,
Or stuck his thumb into the yellow wax,
Fooling around, the way a boy will, always,
20   Whenever a father tries to get some work done.
Still, it was done at last, and the father hovered,
Poised, in the moving air, and taught his son:
"I warn you, Icarus, fly a middle course:
Don't go too low, or water will weigh the wings down;
25   Don't go too high, or the sun's fire will burn them.
Keep to the middle way. And one more thing,
No fancy steering by star or constellation,

_____

1. **pan-pipes.** Instruments made of reeds of various lengths

words for everyday use

do • min • ion (də min′yən) *n.*, governed territory. *Until 1973 the Bahama Islands in the Caribbean were within the <u>dominion</u> of Great Britain.*

Follow my lead!" That was the flying lesson,
And now to fit the wings to the boy's shoulders.
30   Between the work and warning the father found
His cheeks were wet with tears, and his hands trembled.
He kissed his son (*Good-bye*, if he had known it),
Rose on his wings, flew on ahead, as fearful
As any bird launching the little nestlings[2]
35   Out of high nest into thin air. *Keep on,*
Keep on, he signals, *follow me!* He guides him
In flight—O fatal art!—and the wings move
And the father looks back to see the son's wings moving.
Far off, far down, some fisherman is watching
40   As the rod dips and trembles over the water,
Some shepherd rests his weight upon his crook,
Some ploughman on the handles of the ploughshare,
And all look up, in absolute amazement,
At those air-borne above. They must be gods!
45   They were over Samos, Juno's sacred island,
Delos and Paros toward the left, Lebinthus
Visible to the right, and another island,
Calymne, rich in honey. And the boy
Thought *This is wonderful!* and left his father,
50   Soared higher, higher, drawn to the vast heaven,
Nearer the sun, and the wax that held the wings
Melted in that fierce heat, and the bare arms
Beat up and down in air, and lacking oarage[3]
Took hold of nothing. *Father!* he cried, and *Father!*
55   Until the blue sea hushed him, the dark water
Men call the Icarian now. And Dædalus,
Father no more, called "Icarus, where are you!
Where are you, Icarus? Tell me where to find you!"
And saw the wings on the waves, and cursed his talents,
60   Buried the body in a tomb, and the land
Was named for Icarus.
                              During the burial
A noisy partridge, from a muddy ditch,
Looked out, drummed with her wings in loud approval.
No other bird, those days, was like the partridge,
65   Newcomer to the ranks of birds; the story

---

2. **nestlings.** Young birds that have not left the nest yet
3. **oarage.** Ability to propel

FIX-UP IDEA

Use Text Organization
Read complete sentences.
Stop at the end of
thoughts, not at the end
of lines.

Use THE STRATEGY

MAKE PREDICTIONS. At line 49,
add a prediction to your
chart: What will happen to
Icarus?

NOTE THE FACTS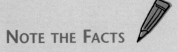

Underline or highlight the
words or phrases that tell you
what does happen to Icarus.

Reflects no credit on Dædalus. His sister,
Ignorant of the fates, had sent her son
To Dædalus as apprentice, only a youngster,
Hardly much more than twelve years old, but clever,
70   With an inventive turn of mind. For instance,
Studying a fish's backbone for a model,
He had notched a row of teeth in a strip of iron,
Thus making the first saw, and he had bound
Two arms of iron together with a joint
75   To keep them both together and apart,
One standing still, the other <u>traversing</u>
In a circle, so men came to have the compass.
And Dædalus, in envy, hurled the boy
Headlong from the high temple of Minerva,
80   And lied about it, saying he had fallen
Through accident, but Minerva, kind protectress
Of all inventive wits, stayed him in air,
Clothed him with <u>plumage</u>; he still retained his aptness
In feet and wings, and kept his old name, Perdix,
85   But in the new bird-form, Perdix, the partridge,
Never flies high, nor nests in trees, but flutters
Close to the ground, and the eggs are laid in hedgerows.
The bird, it seems, remembers, and is fearful
Of all high places. ■

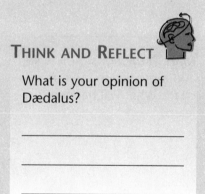

Use THE STRATEGY

MAKE PREDICTIONS. At line 70, add a prediction to your chart: What will happen to the sister's son?

THINK AND REFLECT

What is your opinion of Dædalus?

_____

_____

_____

words for everyday use	**tra • verse** (trə vʉrs´) vi., turn; swivel. *The point guard snatched the ball and quickly <u>traversed</u> to the other side of the court.* **plum • age** (ploom´ij) n., bird's feathers. *The parrot is easy to see because of its bright blue <u>plumage</u>.*

Reflect ON YOUR READING

After Reading ▶ ANALYZE AND VERIFY PREDICTIONS

Finish reading the mythic poem. What happened to people who were close to Dædalus? How did using the reading strategy help you read the poem?

_____

_____

_____

Reading Skills and Test Practice

MAKE INFERENCES

Discuss with your partner how best to answer the following questions about making inferences.

1. Which line from the poem best shows that Dædalus was a careless father?
   a. Homesick for homeland, Dædalus hated Crete.
   b. He kissed his son (Good-bye, if he had known it).
   c. Follow my lead! That was the flying lesson.
   d. He laid out feathers in order, first the smallest.

What is the correct answer to the question above? How were you able to eliminate other answers?

_____

_____

2. Read these lines from the poem.

   During the burial
   A noisy partridge, from a muddy ditch,
   Looked out, drummed with her wings in loud approval.

   These lines let readers know that
   a. the sister's son died before Icarus died.
   b. Icarus was turned into a partridge.
   c. the partridge was named after Icarus.
   d. the partridge was happy about Icarus's death.

What is the correct answer to the question above? How were you able to eliminate other answers?

_____

_____

THINK-ALOUD NOTES

_____

_____

_____

_____

_____

_____

_____

_____

_____

_____

_____

_____

UNIT 5 / READING FOLK LITERATURE   249

Investigate, Inquire, and Imagine

RECALL: GATHER FACTS
1a. What is the problem Dædalus has at the beginning of the story? How does he try to solve it?

→ INTERPRET: FIND MEANING
1b. What special gift does Dædalus have?

ANALYZE: TAKE THINGS APART
2a. How does the role of the supernatural differ in the stories of Echo and Narcissus and Dædalus and Icarus?

→ SYNTHESIZE: BRING THINGS TOGETHER
2b. What do you think is the moral of each of the two selections?

EVALUATE: MAKE JUDGMENTS
3a. Dædalus was considered the greatest inventor in ancient times. What did you learn about Dædalus from Ovid's story? Do you think he was justly punished? Explain.

→ EXTEND: CONNECT IDEAS
3b. What did the people of the ancient world believe about their gods?

Literary Tools

FORESHADOWING. **Foreshadowing** is the act of presenting materials that hint at events to occur later in a story. Use the chart below to list examples of foreshadowing in "The Story of Dædalus and Icarus."

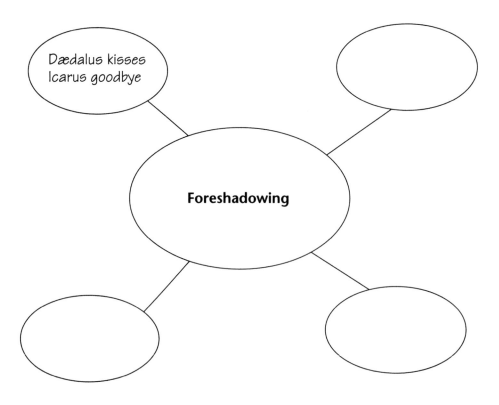

Dædalus kisses Icarus goodbye

Foreshadowing

WordWorkshop

USE CONTEXT CLUES. Look back to "The Story of Dædalus and Icarus." For each of the words from the selection, note surrounding language that conveys the meaning of the word. Then estimate the meaning of the word using those context clues. If you can't estimate the meaning of a word using context clues, circle the word, look it up in the dictionary, and copy the most appropriate definition for it according to the way it is used in the selection. For more information on using context clues, see pages 19–22 in Unit 2.

1. gradual sequence (line 10)

   Context clues: _____

   Estimated definition: _____

2. hovered (line 21)

   Context clues: _____

   Estimated definition: _____

3. ploughman (line 42)

   Context clues: _____

   Estimated definition: _____

4. protectress (line 81)

   Context clues: _____

   Estimated definition: _____

5. hedgerows (line 87)

   Context clues: _____

   Estimated definition: _____

Read-Write Connection

"The Story of "Dædalus and Icarus" is one of the most familiar stories in Western literature. Why do you think it has remained so popular over the centuries? Use your own paper to discuss the myth's popularity.

Beyond the Reading

STORIES WITH STAYING POWER. Reread a myth you remember reading in the past—one that is not included in this unit. Draw a sequence of events chart that lists what happens in the myth. Then write a short analysis of why this myth has stood the test of time. What aspects of the myth appealed to you? What aspects of the myth might have appealed to people in generations throughout time?

GO ONLINE. Visit the EMC Internet Resource Center at **emcp.com** to find links and additional activities for this selection.

Reader's resource

Many of the fairy tales you may be familiar with began as folk songs and stories from the European oral tradition and were later transcribed on paper. Similar tales are told in many different countries and cultures. The Chinese and Native Americans, for example, have versions of the Cinderella tale. In **"The White Snake,"** a story collected by Jacob (1785–1863) and Wilhelm (1786–1859) Grimm, a servant's kindness to animals enables him to win the hand of a princess.

Word watch

PREVIEW VOCABULARY
abroad   plume
anxiety   superintendence
contrive

Reader's journal

In this story, the king grants the hero one favor. If a powerful person promised you one favor, what would you choose? Explain.

_____

_____

_____

_____

_____

"The White Snake"

by Jacob and Wilhelm Grimm,
translated by Lucy Crane

Active READING STRATEGY

WRITE THINGS DOWN

Before Reading ▶ **PREVIEW THE SELECTION**

❑ Read the definition for *fairy tale* in the Literary Tools section on page 258.
❑ Discuss what kinds of people and events usually appear in fairy tales.
❑ As you read, summarize sections of "The White Snake" in a Summary Chart like the one below.

Graphic Organizer

Summary of section 1 (line 1–line 22):
Summary of section 2 (line 23–line 73):
Summary of section 3 (line 74–line 120):
Summary of section 4 (line 120–end):

THE WHITE

 SNAKE

Jacob and Wilhelm Grimm, translated by Lucy Crane

During Reading

WRITE THINGS DOWN

❑ Follow along in the text as your teacher reads aloud the first page of the story, stopping at line 22.
❑ Work together as a class to summarize what has happened in the story so far.
❑ Write a summary in the graphic organizer.
❑ Read the remainder of the story on your own.
❑ Summarize events in your graphic organizer as you read.

 long time ago there lived a King whose wisdom was noised <u>abroad</u> in all the country. Nothing remained long unknown to him, and it was as if the knowledge of hidden things was brought to him in the air. However, he had one curious custom. Every day at dinner, after the table had been cleared and every one gone away, a trusty servant had to bring in one other dish. But it was covered up, and the servant himself did not know what was in it, and no one else knew, for the King waited until he was quite alone

10 before he uncovered it. This had gone on a long time, but at last there came a day when the servant could restrain his curiosity no longer, but as he was carrying the dish away he took it into his own room. As soon as he had fastened the door securely, he lifted the cover, and there he saw a white snake lying on the dish. After seeing it he could not resist the desire to taste it, and so he cut off a small piece and put it in his mouth. As soon as it touched his tongue he heard outside his window a strange chorus of delicate voices. He went and listened, and found that it was the sparrows

20 talking together, and telling each other all they had seen in the fields and woods. The virtue of the snake had given him power to understand the speech of animals.

Now it happened one day that the Queen lost her most splendid ring, and suspicion fell upon the trusty servant, who had the general <u>superintendence</u>, and he was accused of stealing it. The King summoned him to his presence, and

MARK THE TEXT

Mark words or phrases in this passage that describe how the servant acquires a special ability.

NOTE THE FACTS

What almost gets the servant in trouble?

_____

_____

_____

words for everyday use

a • broad (ə brôd´) *adv.,* far and wide. *News of President Lincoln's assassination quickly spread <u>abroad</u> in the land.*
su • per • in • ten • dence (soo´pər in tend´ens) *n.,* supervision; management. *City officials have given <u>superintendence</u> of the arts festival to Ms. Irene Pizzuti.*

FIX-UP IDEA

Ask a Question
If you have difficulty using the reading strategy, ask questions as you read. Asking and answering questions increases your ability to understand and remember what you read. Ask and answer a *who, what, where, when, why,* or *how* question whenever you have trouble. For instance, to get ready for reading on your own after your teacher reads aloud, you might ask, "What does the servant do next?"

NOTE THE FACTS

Why does the servant refuse the King's offer?

_____

_____

_____

after many reproaches told him that if by the next day he was not able to name the thief he should be considered guilty, and punished. It was in vain that he protested his innocence;

30 he could get no better sentence. In his uneasiness and <u>anxiety</u> he went out into the courtyard, and began to consider what he could do in so great a necessity. There sat the ducks by the running water and rested themselves, and <u>plumed</u> themselves with their flat bills, and held a comfortable chat. The servant stayed where he was and listened to them. They told how they had waddled about all yesterday morning and found good food; and then one of them said pitifully, "Something lies very heavy in my craw,[1]—it is the ring that was lying under the Queen's

40 window; I swallowed it down in too great a hurry."

Then the servant seized her by the neck, took her into the kitchen, and said to the cook,

"Kill this one, she is quite ready for cooking."

"Yes," said the cook, weighing it in her hand; "there will be no trouble of fattening this one—it has been ready ever so long."

She then slit up its neck, and when it was opened the Queen's ring was found in its craw. The servant could now clearly prove his innocence, and in order to make up for

50 the injustice he had suffered the King permitted him to ask some favour for himself, and also promised him the place of greatest honour in the royal household.

But the servant refused it, and only asked for a horse and money for travelling, for he had a fancy to see the world, and look about him a little. So his request was granted, and he set out on his way; and one day he came to a pool of water, by which he saw three fishes who had got entangled in the rushes, and were panting for water. Although fishes are usually considered dumb creatures, he understood very

60 well their lament that they were to perish so miserably; and as he had a compassionate heart he dismounted from his

---

1. **craw.** Stomach of an animal

words for everyday use	**anx • i • e • ty** (aŋ zī´ə tē) *n.,* worry; apprehension. *Feeling a certain amount of* <u>anxiety</u> *before giving a speech is perfectly normal.*
	plume (ploom) *vt.,* preen, or clean and arrange one's feathers. *After splashing in the birdbath, the cardinal sat on the edge and* <u>plumed</u> *itself.*

horse, and put the three fishes back again into the water.
They quivered all over with joy, stretched out their heads,
and called out to him,

"We will remember and reward thee, because thou hast
delivered us." He rode on, and after a while he heard a small
voice come up from the sand underneath his horse's feet. He
listened, and understood how an ant-king was complaining,

"If only these men would keep off, with their great
70 awkward beasts! Here comes this stupid horse treading
down my people with his hard hoofs!"

The man then turned his horse to the side-path, and the
ant-king called out to him,

"We will remember and reward thee!"

The path led him through a wood, and there he saw a
father-raven and mother-raven standing by their nest and
throwing their young ones out.

"Off with you! young gallows-birds!"[2] cried they; "we
cannot stuff you any more; you are big enough to fend for
80 yourselves!" The poor young ravens lay on the ground,
fluttering, and beating the air with their pinions, and crying,

"We are poor helpless things, we cannot fend for ourselves,
we cannot even fly! we can only die of hunger!"

Then the kind young man dismounted, killed his horse
with his dagger, and left it to the young ravens for
food. They came hopping up, feasted away at it, and cried,

"We will remember and reward thee!"

So now he had to use his own legs, and when he had gone
a long way he came to a great town. There was much noise
90 and thronging in the streets, and there came a man on a
horse, who proclaimed,

"That the King's daughter seeks a husband, but he who
wishes to marry her must perform a difficult task, and if he
cannot carry it through successfully, he must lose his life."

Many had already tried, but had lost their lives, in vain.
The young man, when he saw the King's daughter, was so
dazzled by her great beauty, that he forgot all danger, went
to the King and offered himself as a wooer.

Then he was led to the sea-side, and a gold ring was
100 thrown into the water before his eyes. Then the King told

---

2. **gallows-birds.** Creatures who deserve to be hanged

Reading TIP

A **motif** is any element that
recurs in a literary work. Note
the fairy tale motif of items
occurring in sets of three as
you read.

Use THE STRATEGY

WRITE THINGS DOWN. Stop at
line 74 to add a summary to
your chart.

DRAW A PICTURE

Draw a picture of the
creatures the servant
helps.

Use THE STRATEGY

WRITE THINGS DOWN. Add a
summary of lines 75–120 to
your chart.

him that he must fetch the ring up again from the bottom of
the sea, saying,

"If you come back without it, you shall be put under the
waves again and again until you are drowned."

Every one pitied the handsome young man, but they went,
and left him alone by the sea. As he was standing on the
shore and thinking of what he should do, there came three
fishes swimming by, none other than those he had set free.
The middle one had a mussel in his mouth, and he laid it on
110 the strand at the young man's feet; and when he took it up
and opened it there was the gold ring inside! Full of joy he
carried it to the King, and expected the promised reward;
but the King's daughter, proud of her high birth,[3] despised
him, and set him another task to perform. She went out into
the garden, and strewed about over the grass ten sacks full
of millet seed.[4]

"By the time the sun rises in the morning you must have
picked up all these," she said, "and not a grain must be
wanting."

120 The young man sat down in the garden and considered
how it was possible to do this task, but he could
<u>contrive</u> nothing, and stayed there, feeling very sorrowful,
and expecting to be led to death at break of day. But when
the first beams of the sun fell on the garden he saw that the
ten sacks were all filled, standing one by the other, and not
even a grain was missing. The ant-king had arrived in the
night with his thousands of ants, and the grateful creatures
had picked up all the millet seed, and filled the sacks with
great industry. The King's daughter came herself into the
130 garden and saw with astonishment that the young man had
performed all that had been given him to do. But she could
not let her proud heart melt, but said,

"Although he has completed the two tasks, he shall not be
my bridegroom unless he brings me an apple from the tree
of life."

---

3. **high birth.** Being born into a noble family
4. **millet seed.** Seed of a grain grown for food

---

words for everyday use

con • trive (kən trīv´) vt., devise, plan; bring about by strategy or difficulty. *After
several days, Kaila finally <u>contrived</u> a way to finish the science experiment.*

The young man did not know where the tree of life was to be found, but he set out and went on and on, as long as his legs could carry him, but he had no hope of finding it. When he had gone through three kingdoms he came one
140 evening to a wood, and seated himself under a tree to go to sleep; but he heard a rustling in the boughs, and a golden apple fell into his hand. Immediately three ravens flew towards him, perched on his knee, and said,

"We are the three young ravens that you delivered from starving; when we grew big, and heard that you were seeking the golden apple, we flew over the sea to the end of the earth, where the tree of life stands, and we fetched the apple."

Full of joy the young man set off on his way home, and
150 brought the golden apple to the King's beautiful daughter, who was without any further excuse.

So they divided the apple of life, and ate it together; and their hearts were filled with love, and they lived in undisturbed happiness to a great age. ■

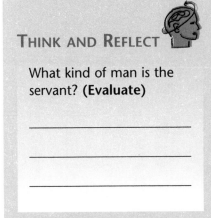

THINK AND REFLECT

What kind of man is the servant? (Evaluate)

_____

_____

_____

Use THE STRATEGY

WRITE THINGS DOWN. Add a summary to your chart of what happens at the end of the story.

Reflect ON YOUR READING

After Reading ▶ WRITE A SUMMARY

After reading, use your summaries of each section to write a summary of the entire story. Include only the most important events and ideas. Then join a classmate, and compare summaries. Make any changes necessary to your summary.

_____

_____

_____

_____

Reading Skills and Test Practice

IDENTIFY CAUSE AND EFFECT

Discuss with your group how best to answer the following questions about cause and effect.

1. What immediate effect did eating the white snake have on the servant?
   a. He was able to leave the kingdom.
   b. He was able to understand the animals' speech.
   c. He was able to marry the princess.
   d. He won the favor of the king.

What is the correct answer to the question above? How were you able to eliminate other answers? How did your use of the reading strategy help you?

_____

_____

2. Which of the following traits led to the servant's ability to marry the princess?
   a. courage
   b. persistence
   c. curiosity
   d. kindness

What is the correct answer to the question above? How were you able to eliminate other answers? How did your use of the reading strategy help you?

_____

_____

Investigate, Inquire, and Imagine

RECALL: GATHER FACTS
1a. Why does the servant choose to perform the tasks set for him? How do the animals he previously met help him?

→ ### INTERPRET: FIND MEANING
1b. What is the nature of the tasks that the servant has to perform to marry the princess? Why does the servant need supernatural helpers to perform these tasks?

ANALYZE: TAKE THINGS APART
2a. How is this fairy tale similar to the first two myths in this unit? How is it different?

→ ### SYNTHESIZE: BRING THINGS TOGETHER
2b. How is this tale similar to other fairy tales you know? List the similar elements. For example, this tale, like many others, has a happy ending. Why might this sort of ending be common in fairy tales?

EVALUATE: MAKE JUDGMENTS
3a. Do you think the tasks are fair? Why does the princess continue to ask more tasks of the young man? What motivates the young man to continue despite the tremendous odds? Do you think he is foolish, or should he be admired for his determination?

→ ### EXTEND: CONNECT IDEAS
3b. What qualities were admired in young men at the time this fairy tale was first being told? What qualities were admired in young women? What idea of love is presented in this tale?

Literary Tools

FAIRY TALE. A **fairy tale** is a story that deals with mischievous spirits and other supernatural occurrences, often in medieval settings. What elements occur frequently in fairy tales that you know? List these elements. Here are some ideas to prompt your thinking: tests, curses, and good versus evil. Why do you think that fairy tales are traditionally told or read to children?

_____

_____

_____

_____

_____

WordWorkshop

Lexical Phrases. **Lexical phrases** are ready-made nuggets of languages. They are groups of words that people are so accustomed to hearing and saying that we say them and respond to them almost automatically. Phrases such as *in a nutshell, in order to, all in all, by the way, as far as I know, as far as I can tell, it would seem to me, on one hand, on the other hand.* These phrases make it easy to string sentences together in writing and conversation.

As you read "The White Snake," you probably noticed phrases that are quite familiar to you—not phrases that you use every day, but phrases that let you know that you are reading a fairy tale. These, too, are lexical phrases. "The White Snake's" opening line, "A long time ago," is a common lexical phrase.

1. Look back at the selection and identify two more examples of lexical phrases.

   _____

   _____

2. Does the use of these lexical phrases add or take away from the selection? Why?

   _____

   _____

3. When might it be important to avoid using lexical phrases?

   _____

   _____

Read-Write Connection

Which fairy tales were your favorites when you were younger, and why? Use your own paper to write your response.

Beyond the Reading

Read Aloud. With a small group, choose a culture and find out what kind of fairy tales that culture has transmitted from generation to generation. Find a tale from that culture that you would like to read aloud. When your group finds a tale, practice reading it aloud several times. Then read it aloud to the class.

Go Online. Visit the EMC Internet Resource Center at **emcp.com** to find links and additional activities for this selection.

"THE PRODIGAL SON"

from the King James Bible

Active READING STRATEGY

TACKLE DIFFICULT VOCABULARY

Before Reading ➤ PREVIEW THE SELECTION AND THE VOCABULARY

❑ Read the Reader's Resource.
❑ Skim the selection and make a Word Map like the one below for each of the Words for Everyday Use.
❑ With a partner, complete a word map for each word.

Graphic Organizer

A challenging word or phrase:	Definition:

Word parts I recognize:	Synonyms:

Sentence that contains the word or phrase:

A picture that illustrates the word or phrase:

CONNECT

Reader's resource

"**The Prodigal Son**" is one of several parables found in the New Testament of the Bible told by Jesus to serve as a guide to moral behavior.

The Bible has had a profound effect on Western culture. For two thousand years, the stories in the Bible have influenced the literature, art, music, and ways of life of people in the Middle East, Europe, and Latin America. In addition, for much of the history of the United States, the one book found in most homes was a copy of the Bible.

The **King James Bible** was published in England in 1611 during the reign of King James I. This version was a translation into English done by forty-seven scholars who used both previous translations and texts written in original ancient languages.

Word watch

PREVIEW VOCABULARY

compassion	famine
diligently	riotous
entreat	transgress

Reader's journal

If you suddenly had a lot of money to spend, how would you spend it, and why?

_____

_____

_____

TACKLE DIFFICULT VOCABULARY

- ❑ Follow along in the text as your teacher reads the first ten verses aloud. Keep the definition of *diligently* in mind as your teacher reads, and remember that the *–eth* ending is treated as an *s* today.
- ❑ When your teacher finishes reading, rephrase lines that contain new words or footnotes. Discuss verses that you find confusing.
- ❑ Read the remainder of the parable on your own.
- ❑ Mark verses that you find confusing with a "?" next to them.

Reading STRATEGY REVIEW

WRITE THINGS DOWN. Look for words and phrases in the parable that describe wasteful and extravagant actions. Underline these words and phrases in one color of ink. Use another color of ink to underline words and phrases that describe actions that are not wasteful and extravagant.

THE PRODIGAL [1] SON

from the King James Bible

Then drew near unto him all the publicans[2] and sinners for to hear him.

2   And the Pharisees[3] and scribes murmured, saying, This man receiveth sinners, and eateth with them.

3   And he spake this parable unto them, saying,

4   What man of you, having an hundred sheep, if he lose one of them, doth not leave the ninety and nine in the wilderness, and go after that which is lost, until he find it?

5   And when he hath found it, he layeth it on his shoulders, rejoicing.

6   And when he cometh home, he calleth together his friends and neighbors, saying unto them, Rejoice with me; for I have found my sheep which was lost.

7   I say unto you, that likewise joy shall be in heaven over one sinner that repenteth,[4] more than over ninety and nine just persons, which need no repentance.

8   Either what woman having ten pieces of silver, if she lose one piece, doth not light a candle and sweep the house, and seek diligently till she find it?

9   And when she hath found it, she calleth her friends and her neighbors together, saying, Rejoice with me for I have found the piece which I had lost.

---

1. **Prodigal.** Extravagant; characterized by wasteful expenditure
2. **publicans.** Money collectors in ancient Judea
3. **Pharisees.** Members of an ancient Jewish party or fellowship
4. **repenteth.** Repents, feels sorry for sins

> **words for everyday use**
>
> **dil • i • gent • ly** (dil´ə jənt lē) *adv.*, carefully and steadily. *Because Mrs. Chang diligently weeds and waters her vegetable garden, it produces abundantly.*

10   Likewise, I say unto you, there is joy in the presence of the angels of God over one sinner that repenteth.

11   And he said, A certain man had two sons:

12   And the younger of them said to his father, Father, give me the portion of goods that falleth to me. And he divided unto them his living.

13   And not many days after the younger son gathered all together, and took his journey into a far country, and there wasted his substance with <u>riotous</u> living.

14   And when he had spent all, there arose a mighty <u>famine</u> in that land; and he began to be in want.

15   And he went and joined himself to a citizen of that country; and he sent him into his fields to feed swine.

16   And he would fain[5] have filled his belly with the husks that the swine did eat: and no man gave unto him.

17   And when he came to himself, he said, How many hired servants of my father's have bread enough and to spare, and I perish with hunger!

18   I will arise and go to my father, and will say unto him, Father, I have sinned against heaven, and before thee,

19   And am no more worthy to be called thy son: make me as one of the hired servants.

20   And he arose, and came to his father. But when he was yet a great way off, his father saw him, and had <u>compassion</u> and ran, and fell on his neck and kissed him.

21   And the son said unto him Father, I have sinned against heaven, and in thy sight and am no more worthy to be called thy son.

22   But the father said to his servants, Bring forth the best robe, and put it on him; and put a ring on his hand, and shoes on his feet:

23   And bring hither the fatted calf, and kill it, and let us eat, and be merry:

---

5. **fain.** Gladly

words for everyday use

ri • ot • ous (rī´ət əs) *adj.,* without restraint; dissolute. *Concerned about her <u>riotous</u> ways at college, Karla's parents advised her to go to fewer parties.*

fam • ine (fam´in) *n.,* widespread shortage of food. *The <u>famine</u> in Ireland was caused by potato blight.*

com • pas • sion (kəm pash´ən) *n.,* sympathy; pity. *The volunteers at the animal shelter show great <u>compassion</u> for lost and injured animals.*

Literary TOOLS

SYMBOL. A **symbol** is a thing that stands for or represents itself and something else. What might the shepherd and his lost sheep symbolize?

_____

_____

_____

FIX-UP IDEA

Choose a New Strategy If rephrasing lines with difficult vocabulary is not helping you understand the parable, try rereading it aloud a verse at a time and substitute definitions for difficult words as you reread. Remember to change *–eth* endings to an *s* sound. For instance, reread the title as "The Wasteful Son," and reread verse 2 aloud as "And the *tax collectors* and scribes murmured, saying, This man *receives* sinners and *eats* with them."

THINK AND REFLECT

Why does the father treat the young son so kindly? **(Analyze)**

_____

_____

_____

READ ALOUD

After you finish reading, find a partner. Reread verses you found confusing, and help each other rephrase them.

24   For this my son was dead, and is alive again; he was lost, and is found. And they began to be merry.

25   Now his elder son was in the field: and as he came and drew nigh to the house, he heard music and dancing.

26   And he called one of the servants, and asked what these things meant.

27   And he said unto him, Thy brother is come; and thy father hath killed the fatted calf, because he hath received him safe and sound.

28   And he was angry, and would not go in: therefore came his father out, and <u>entreated</u> him.

29   And he answering said to his father, Lo, these many years do I serve thee, neither <u>transgressed</u> I at any time thy commandment: and yet thou never gavest me a kid,[6] that I might make merry with my friends:

30   But as soon as this thy son was come, which hath devoured thy living with harlots, thou hast killed for him the fatted calf.

31   And he said unto him, Son, thou art ever with me, and all that I have is thine.

32   It was meet[7] that we should make merry, and be glad: for this thy brother was dead, and is alive again; and was lost, and is found. ■

---

6. **kid.** Baby goat
7. **meet**. Fitting

words for everyday use	
	en • treat (en trēt´) vt., implore; beg. _Freddie_ <u>entreated</u> _his mother to let him have a puppy._
	trans • gress (trans gres´) vt., break a commandment; sin. _Marie, a highly moral person, would never_ <u>transgress</u> _the commandment "Thou shalt not steal."_

Reflect ON YOUR READING

Write a parable about what might happen next to the younger or older son. Use all of the new WordWatch words in your parable. If you would like, you can make your story sound like an old parable by using the *–eth* ending. Share your story with the class.

Reading Skills and Test Practice

USE CONTEXT CLUES
Discuss with your group how best to answer the following questions about definitions of words used in the parable.

1. Read the following sentence from the parable.

> I say unto you, that likewise joy shall be in heaven over one sinner that <u>repenteth</u>, more than over ninety and nine just persons, which need no repentance.

Based on the context clues, which is the best definition of the word *repen*t?
a. repeat a wrongdoing
b. ask forgiveness for sins
c. gain a reward
d. seek revenge

What is the correct answer to the question above? How were you able to eliminate other answers? How did your use of the reading strategy help you?

2. Read the following passage from the parable.

> And the younger of them said to his father, Father, give me the portion of goods that falleth to me. And he divided unto them his living.
>
> And not many days after the younger son gathered all together and took his journey into a far country, and there wasted all his substance with <u>riotous</u> living.

Based on the context clues, which is the best definition of the word *riotous*?
a. wild and unrestrained
b. religious
c. destructive
d. careful and thrifty

What is the correct answer to the question above? How were you able to eliminate other answers? How did your use of the reading strategy help you?

THINK-ALOUD
NOTES

Investigate, Inquire, and Imagine

RECALL: GATHER FACTS
1a. How does the younger son spend his money? Why does he decide to return home?

INTERPRET: FIND MEANING
1b. Why is "The Prodigal Son" an appropriate name for the parable? Do you think it takes courage for the younger son to return home? Explain.

ANALYZE: TAKE THINGS APART
2a. Identify the characteristics of the prodigal son, the father, and the elder son, and identify the relationship of the father to each of his sons. What role does the elder son play in the parable?

SYNTHESIZE: BRING THINGS TOGETHER
2b. What lesson does the parable teach? How do the characters and their roles make this an effective vehicle for this lesson?

EVALUATE: MAKE JUDGMENTS
3a. Describe, then evaluate, the father's relationship to each of his sons. Do you think he treats them fairly? Explain.

EXTEND: CONNECT IDEAS
3b. Put yourself in the younger son's place. How will you live your life now that you have returned home and have been forgiven by your father?

Literary Tools

SYMBOL. A **symbol** is a thing that stands for or represents itself and something else. In the chart below, identify what the lost sheep, the lost silver coin, and the prodigal son symbolize .

Symbol	What It Represents
shepherd	God
The lost sheep	
the lost silver coin	
the prodigal son	

Why does the writer of this parable provide so many examples of lost things?

_____

_____

WordWorkshop

Archaic Words. **Archaic words** are words that used to be common in a language but that have, over the years, fallen out of use. *Serf* is an archaic word for servant and *truncheon* is an archaic word for a long, rectangular serving plate made of wood. The King James Bible contains many archaic words, mostly from Middle English. Determine the modern equivalent of each archaic word below, and then use it in a sentence.

EXAMPLE   smote
Modern equivalent: past tense of "smite," to strike or hit forcefully
Sentence: The angry batter <u>smote</u> the ground with her bat.

1. publican (verse 1)
   Modern equivalent: _____

   Sentence: _____

2. scribe (verse 2)
   Modern equivalent: _____

   Sentence: _____

3. spake (verse 3)
   Modern equivalent: _____

   Sentence: _____

4. doth (verse 4)
   Modern equivalent: _____

   Sentence: _____

5. fain (verse 5)
   Modern equivalent: _____

   Sentence: _____

Read-Write Connection

Use your own paper to write about a time in which you forgave someone for a wrong that he or she committed. How did forgiving the person make you feel?

Beyond the Reading

Read an Advice Column. Find an advice column for teens that discusses how teens can solve family problems. Read the column by using the Write Things Down reading strategy. Take notes on important facts and respond to the article's ideas. Decide how you want to take notes: use a graphic organizer, underline important ideas, or highlight important parts of the text. To make responses, use the coding method described in the Reading Tip on page 238, or create your own method. After you finish reading, summarize your notes and your coded responses. Share your summary with the class.

Go Online. Visit the EMC Internet Resource Center at **emcp.com** to find links and additional activities for this selection.

"GOHA AND THE POT"

North African Folk Tale, retold by
Mahmoud Ibrahim Mostafa

Reader's resource

"Goha and the Pot" is a trickster tale. Trickster tales are traditional stories that are passed on by word of mouth. The tales usually involve deceit, or a trick of some kind. The trickster figure, usually a clever underdog, typically outwits a slower-witted character. Trickster tales have been told around the world, especially in native North and South American cultures and in Africa. In Africa, common trickster animals include the hare, the spider, and the tortoise. Many African tales also feature human tricksters. The author of this version of the tale, Mahmoud Ibrahim Mostafa, was born in 1943 in Cairo, Egypt, and practiced medicine in Columbia, South Carolina, for many years.

Reader's journal

When have you seen or heard of people behaving foolishly because of greed?

_____

_____

_____

Active READING STRATEGY

READ WITH A PURPOSE

Before Reading ➤ SET A PURPOSE FOR READING

❑ Read the Reader's Resource.
❑ Read "Goha and the Pot" aloud with a partner.
❑ Set a purpose: Look for tricks that one character plays on another.
❑ In the Story Strip below, sketch Goha's actions in the order that they happen.

Graphic Organizer

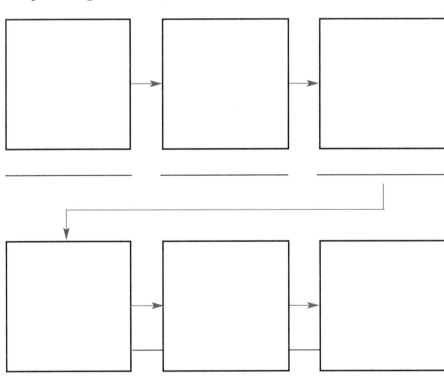

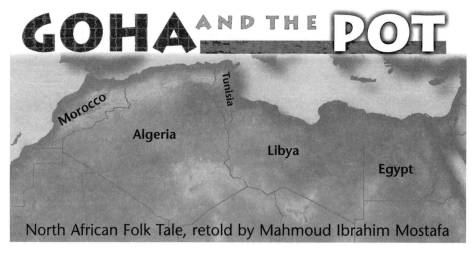

GOHA AND THE POT

North African Folk Tale, retold by Mahmoud Ibrahim Mostafa

During Reading

READ WITH A PURPOSE

- ☐ Highlight or underline tricks that one character plays on another.
- ☐ Draw pictures of the tricks in a Story Strip.

One day, many, many years ago, Goha wanted to fix a meal for his family. He found that he needed a big pot, so he went to his next door neighbor to ask if he might borrow a big brass pot. The neighbor was reluctant to lend him the pot, but Goha promised that he would return it to his neighbor the following day.

To the surprise of his neighbor, Goha returned the next day with the big brass pot that he had borrowed and another one, smaller than the first. The neighbor felt that Goha must
10   have made a mistake since he had lent Goha one pot, but Goha said that there was no mistake at all. He explained that overnight the pot he had borrowed went into labor and gave birth to this nice, shiny, little pot, and Goha insisted that the small pot also belonged to his neighbor!

A few days later, Goha returned to the same neighbor and asked if he could borrow another pot. This time the neighbor did not have any trouble giving him two big pots, thinking that Goha would return with more pots anyway. And indeed, when Goha returned the two big pots, he also
20   brought two smaller, shining pots, much to the delight of his neighbor.

The next time Goha knocked on his neighbor's door, before he could even say a word, the neighbor gave him a basket full of big pots. In fact he gave Goha all the pots he had in his possession. His neighbor did not stop there, however; he even helped to carry the pots to Goha's house.

Days passed, then weeks, and the neighbor began to worry, but he did not mention his concern to Goha, hoping that Goha would come by some day soon with a whole room full
30   of pots. After three whole months had gone by, the neighbor decided to go to Goha to inquire about his pots. Upon his

Literary TOOLS

PERSONIFICATION.
Personification is a figure of speech in which something not human is described as if it were human. As you read, identify what is personified in this tale.

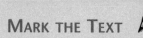

MARK THE TEXT

Underline or highlight why the neighbor is not reluctant to lend Goha a pot the second time.

VISUALIZE. Draw a picture of Goha and the neighbor that shows how they each feel at the end of the folk tale.

inquiry, Goha with a very sad face said to his neighbor, "My dear neighbor, I'm saddened to tell you that your pots are all dead!"

The neighbor was furious, and he shouted, "Are you a madman? Pots don't die!"

Then Goha quietly said, "My dear neighbor, you were very willing to accept the fact that pots can have babies, weren't you? Why for goodness' sake don't you accept that they can also die?" ■

40

Reflect ON YOUR READING

After Reading ➤ CREATE A MORALITY TALE

After you finish reading, discuss the tricks that Goha played on his neighbor. What lesson did the neighbor learn? Write that lesson on the lines below.

_____

_____

On another sheet of paper, create a short trickster tale that teaches this same lesson. Share your tale with your classmates.

THINK-ALOUD
NOTES

Reading Skills and Test Practice

IDENTIFY MAIN IDEAS
Discuss with your partner how best to answer the following questions about main ideas.

1. Which of the following adjectives best describes Goha's neighbor?
   a. unfriendly
   b. clever
   c. honest
   d. greedy

What is the correct answer to the question above? How were you able to eliminate other answers? How did your use of the reading strategy help you?

_____

_____

_____

2. Which of the following best states the moral of the story?
   a. Watch out for tricky neighbors.
   b. You reap what you sow.
   c. Greed does not pay.
   d. Honesty is the best policy.

What is the correct answer to the question above? How were you able to eliminate other answers? How did your use of the reading strategy help you?

_____

_____

_____

Investigate, Inquire, and Imagine

RECALL: GATHER FACTS
1a. What happens when Goha asks to borrow a pot the second time? the third time?

INTERPRET: FIND MEANING
1b. Why does the neighbor give Goha so many pots? Why do you think Goha returns with more pots the first two times he borrows a pot?

ANALYZE: TAKE THINGS APART
2a. Analyze the character of the neighbor based on his actions throughout the story. What kind of a person is he? Why do you think Goha tricks his neighbor?

SYNTHESIZE: BRING THINGS TOGETHER
2b. What do you think is the moral, or lesson, of "Goha and the Pot"?

EVALUATE: MAKE JUDGMENTS
3a. What do you think of Goha's behavior toward his neighbor? Is he clever or cruel? Does his neighbor deserve to be tricked? Why, or why not?

EXTEND: CONNECT IDEAS
3b. What would happen today in your community if someone like Goha performed a trick on his neighbor like the one in "Goha and the Pot"?

Literary Tools

PERSONIFICATION. **Personification** is a figure of speech in which something not human is described as if it were human. What is personified in this story? What human qualities are given to this object or objects? What events does personification explain in this story? What does the story's outcome suggest about personification?

_____

_____

_____

_____

_____

_____

_____

_____

_____

_____

WordWorkshop

SYNONYMS. The word *synonym* is from the Greek for "same + name."
Synonyms are words or expressions of the same language that have the
same or nearly the same meaning in some or all senses.
Match each of the following words from "Goha and the Pot" with the
word that has the most similar meaning. Look up any words that you do
not know in the dictionary.

_____1.	meal	a. pledge
_____2.	promise	b. gleaming
_____3.	surprise	c. ownership
_____4.	neighbor	d. enraged
_____5.	borrowed	e. question
_____6.	shining	f. breakfast
_____7.	possession	g. disquiet
_____8.	concern	h. friend
_____9.	inquiry	i. mooched
_____10.	furious	j. astonishment

When you have finished the matching exercise, reread "Goha and the
Pot" aloud with a partner. Replace words from the selection with their
matched synonyms.

Read-Write Connection

If you were Goha's neighbor, how would you feel about being tricked?
Would the trick cause you to reevaluate your own behavior? Explain.

_____

_____

_____

_____

Beyond the Reading

FALSE ADVERTISING. Collect ads in magazines or the newspaper that are
"too good to be true." Highlight or underline the claims you think are
untrue. Make a list of the claims you think are false, and write down your
reasons for why the claims are false.

GO ONLINE. Visit the EMC Internet Resource Center at **emcp.com** to find
links and additional activities for this selection.

"The Fox and the Crow"
by Æsop

Reader's resource

Many fables from ancient times involved foxes, crows, mice, and lions. Æsop, the author attributed to **"The Fox and the Crow"** may or may not have been a real person. His name has traditionally been associated with a collection of Greek fables, but since no reliable historical record of Æsop exists, it might be that the fables simply originated in the oral tradition of Greece. Some ancient writers, however, say that Æsop was a real person born around 620 BC in Samos, Greece.

Word watch

PREVIEW VOCABULARY

surpass

Reader's journal

In your opinion, is there a difference between flattery and praise? Explain.

_____

_____

_____

Active READING STRATEGY

CONNECT TO PRIOR KNOWLEDGE

Before Reading ➤ **ACTIVATE PRIOR KNOWLEDGE**

❑ Read the Reader's Resource.
❑ Create a Venn diagram like the one below.
❑ Add the names "Goha" and "Goha's neighbor" to the "Goha and the Pot" circle.
❑ Write down words or phrases that describe these characters. Go back and review "Goha and the Pot" on pages 269–270, if necessary.

Graphic Organizer

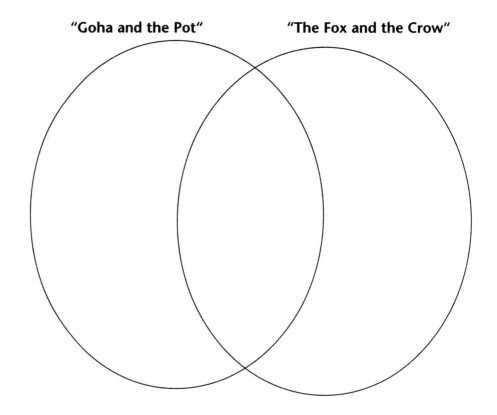

"Goha and the Pot"   "The Fox and the Crow"

The Fox and the Crow

Æsop

CONNECT TO PRIOR KNOWLEDGE

❏ In the "The Fox and the Crow" circle of your Venn diagram, write down the names "Fox" and "Crow." As you read, write down words that describe these characters.

❏ As you read, think about whether the characters exhibit a single dominant quality or a number of complex qualities.

Reading STRATEGY
REVIEW

PROGRESS. You will find it easier to compare "The Fox and the Crow" and "Goha and the Pot" if you reread the two selections aloud.

A Fox once saw a Crow fly off with a piece of cheese in its beak and settle on a branch of a tree. "That's for me, as I am a Fox," said Master Reynard,[1] and he walked up to the foot of the tree.

"Good day, Mistress Crow," he cried. "How well you are looking today: how glossy your feathers; how bright your eye. I feel sure your voice must <u>surpass</u> that of other birds, just as your figure does; let me hear but one song from you that I may greet you as the Queen of Birds."

10 The Crow lifted up her head and began to caw her best, but the moment she opened her mouth the piece of cheese fell to the ground, only to be snapped up by Master Fox. "That will do," said he. "That was all I wanted. In exchange for your cheese I will give you a piece of advice for the future—

"Do not trust flatterers." ■

---

1. **Master Reynard.** Fox in the medieval beast epic *Reynard the Fox*

words for everyday use	**sur • pass** (sər pas´) *vt.*, go beyond. *Because Matt grew like a weed, he soon* <u>*surpassed*</u> *the other boys in height.*

Reflect ON YOUR READING

With a partner, look over your descriptions of the characters in "Goha and the Pot" and "The Fox and Crow." Summarize how the characters are alike and different. Share your summaries with the class. Are these characters like other characters you know?

_____

_____

_____

_____

_____

_____

_____

_____

_____

_____

_____

_____

_____

_____

_____

Reading Skills and Test Practice

IDENTIFY CHARACTER DEVELOPMENT
Discuss with your group how best to answer the following questions about character development.

1. What motivation does Fox have for flattering Crow?
   a. Fox likes Crow.
   b. Fox wants something from Crow.
   c. Fox hopes to become friends with Crow.
   d. Fox wants to eat Crow.

What is the correct answer to the question above? How were you able to eliminate other answers? How did your use of the reading strategy help you?

_____

_____

2. What characteristic does the crow possess?
   a. kindness
   b. cleverness
   c. anger
   d. vanity

What is the correct answer to the question above? How were you able to eliminate other answers? How did your use of the reading strategy help you?

_____

_____

Investigate, Inquire, and Imagine

RECALL: GATHER FACTS
1a. How does Crow lose the cheese?

→ INTERPRET: FIND MEANING
1b. Why doesn't Crow realize that she is going to lose the cheese?

ANALYZE: TAKE THINGS APART
2a. What character traits does Crow have that make her accept Fox's flattery so readily?

→ SYNTHESIZE: BRING THINGS TOGETHER
2b. How would you state the moral, or lesson, of the fable?

EVALUATE: MAKE JUDGMENTS
3a. How do you think Crow feels about Fox's flattery? How might she feel after realizing she has been tricked? Do you think Crow deserved to be tricked in this way? Do you feel sympathy for her?

→ EXTEND: CONNECT IDEAS
3b. How are the characters in "The Fox and the Crow" similar to the characters in the North African folk tale "Goha and the Pot"? Use words and phrases from the selections to explain your response.

Literary Tools

CHARACTER. A **character** is a person (or sometimes an animal) who figures in the action of a literary work. A *one-dimensional character* is one who exhibits a single dominant quality, or character trait. A *three-dimensional character* is one who exhibits the complexity of traits associated with actual human beings. A *stock character* is one who is found again and again in different literary works.

What kind of character is Fox? _____

What kind of character is Crow? _____

List traits that each exhibits in the chart below._____

Fox	Crow

WordWorkshop

SUPERLATIVES. **Superlatives** are words that describe something as being the first among many. Probably the most well-known superlative is *best*. *Most* is a superlative, as well. Often, people will use superlatives in praising or flattering someone. Many adjectives can be turned into superlatives by adding the prefix *–est*, or by using *most* as a modifying adverb. Take the adjectives below and turn them into superlatives. Decide whether the words require you to add *–est*, to add *most*, or to use another, similar word. Then use them in a sentence in the space provided. Use a dictionary to look up a word if you do not know its definition.

EXAMPLE   clever
Superlative form: cleverest
Sentence: She was the <u>cleverest</u> chess player in the school.

1. good
   Superlative form: _____

   Sentence: _____
2. crazy
   Superlative form: _____

   Sentence: _____
3. ingenious
   Superlative form: _____

   Sentence: _____
4. fit
   Superlative form: _____

   Sentence: _____
5. bright
   Superlative form: _____

   Sentence: _____

Read-Write Connection

Explain why a person might offer insincere praise to someone else. Use your own paper as necessary.

_____

_____

Beyond the Reading

FABLES AROUND THE WORLD. Examine fables, or lesson tales, from other cultures that feature talking animals. Make a map of the world that includes countries and cultures that have produced tales in which animals are given the ability to think and speak as humans do. Label each country or culture and list the characteristics of some of its tales.

GO ONLINE. Visit the EMC Internet Resource Center at **emcp.com** to find links and additional activities for this selection.

"John Henry"

from *Mules and Men*
retold by Zora Neale Hurston

Active READING STRATEGY

USE TEXT ORGANIZATION

Before Reading ▶ **PREVIEW BACKGROUND INFORMATION AND TEXT ORGANIZATION**

❑ Read the Reader's Resource. Highlight or underline what you learn about John Henry.

❑ Scan "John Henry." How is the text organized? Notice the repetition in the last two lines of each stanza. This repetition helps you identify the main idea in each stanza.

❑ As you read, write a summary of each verse in "John Henry."

Graphic Organizer

Verse 1:	Verse 2:
Verse 3:	Verse 4:
Verse 5:	Verse 6:
Verse 7:	Verse 8:
Verse 9:	Summary:

CONNECT

Reader's resource

"John Henry," an African-American folk song, tells the story of a steel driver, a railroad worker whose grueling job it was to drill holes in rock for explosives used to blast railroad tunnels. They hammered a steel bit into solid rock with a sledge hammer. According to one version of the legend, John Henry was working on the Big Bend Tunnel in West Virginia when he bet his foreman he could drive steel faster than a new steam drill. The effort killed mighty John Henry, but he is remembered as a symbol of the unconquerable spirit of the American worker. This selection, retold by Zora Neale Hurston (1891–1960), is just one of 100 or more versions of the famous folk song, which originated in the oral tradition and has no single known author.

Reader's journal

In what kinds of contests have you participated? Which have been the most difficult?

_____

_____

_____

_____

_____

_____

_____

_____

USE TEXT ORGANIZATION TO IDENTIFY MAIN IDEAS

❑ Follow along in the text as your teacher reads aloud the first two stanzas. Discuss each verse, and write a summary of each in your graphic organizer.

❑ Read the rest of the song on your own. Write a brief summary of each verse in your graphic organizer.

WHAT DO YOU WONDER?

After you read the first verse of the folk song, what do you wonder about John Henry?

_____

_____

_____

FIX-UP IDEA

Visualize
If you have trouble summarizing the ideas in each verse, visualize what happens in each. Pay attention to words and phrases that help you create a mind picture. As you finish each verse, draw a quick picture that shows what the verse describes.

from *Mules and Men*
retold by Zora Neale Hurston

John Henry driving[1] on the right hand side,
Steam drill driving on the left,
Says, 'fore I'll let your steam drill beat me down
I'll hammer my fool self to death,
5   Hammer my fool self to death.

John Henry told his Captain,
When you go to town
Please bring me back a nine pound hammer
And I'll drive your steel on down,
10   And I'll drive your steel on down.

John Henry told his Captain,
Man ain't nothing but a man,
And 'fore I'll let that steam drill beat me down
I'll die with this hammer in my hand,
15   Die with this hammer in my hand.

Captain ast John Henry,
What is that storm I hear?
He says Cap'n that ain't no storm,
'Tain't nothing but my hammer in the air,
20   Nothing but my hammer in the air.

John Henry told his Captain,
Bury me under the sills of the floor,
So when they get to playing good old Georgy skin,[2]
Bet 'em fifty to a dollar more,
25   Fifty to a dollar more.

_____

1. **driving.** Using a hammer to drive metal stakes into railroad ties
2. **Georgy skin.** Gambling game played by railroad workers

John Henry had a little woman,
The dress she wore was red,
Says I'm going down the track,
And she never looked back.
30   I'm going where John Henry fell dead,
Going where John Henry fell dead.

Who's going to shoe your pretty lil feet?
And who's going to glove your hand?
Who's going to kiss your dimpled cheek?
35   And who's going to be your man?
Who's going to be your man?

My father's going to shoe my pretty lil feet;
My brother's going to glove my hand;
My sister's going to kiss my dimpled cheek;
40   John Henry's going to be my man,
John Henry's going to be my man.

Where did you get your pretty lil dress?
The shoes you wear so fine?
I got my shoes from a railroad man,
45   My dress from a man in the mine,
My dress from a man in the mine. ■

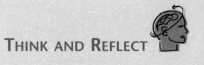

THINK AND REFLECT

What do lines 32–46 tell you about the woman in the folk song? **(Infer)**

_____

_____

_____

READ ALOUD

Practice singing or saying the song aloud. If you have access to an audio version of the folk song, imitate the way the song is sung or read.

Reflect ON YOUR READING

> **After Reading** ➤ WRITE A CHARACTER SKETCH

When you have finished reading, review your sentences. Write a short character sketch of John Henry based on the information from your main idea sentences. When you finish, share your character sketch and sentences with a partner. Compare and contrast your sentences and your character sketch with your partner's, and discuss how you came to your conclusions about John Henry's character.

Reading Skills and Test Practice

IDENTIFY CHARACTER DEVELOPMENT

Discuss with your partner how best to answer the following questions about character development.

1. Read the following lines from the folk song.

   John Henry driving on the right hand side,
   Steam drill driving on the left,
   Says,'fore I'll let your steam drill beat me down
   I'll hammer my fool self to death,
   Hammer my fool self to death.

Which of the following character traits is John Henry implied to have in this verse?
   a. ignorance
   b. hatred
   c. greed
   d. pride

What is the correct answer to the question above? How were you able to eliminate other answers? How did your use of the reading strategy help you?

_____

_____

2. Read the following lines from the folk song.

   John Henry had a little woman,
   The dress she wore was red,
   Says I'm going down the track,
   And she never looked back.
   I'm going where John Henry fell dead,
   Going where John Henry fell dead.

Which of the following character traits is John Henry's girlfriend implied to have in the lines from the folk song in question 2?

    a. greed
    b. anger
    c. loyalty
    d. indignation

What is the correct answer to the question above? How were you able to eliminate other answers? How did your use of the reading strategy help you?

_____

_____

Investigate, Inquire, and Imagine

RECALL: GATHER FACTS
1a. What does John Henry decide in verse 1 of the song?

→ **INTERPRET: FIND MEANING**
1b. What tone and mood are set in verse 1?

ANALYZE: TAKE THINGS APART
2a. Identify John Henry's characteristics, as revealed in his dialogue with the Captain.

→ **SYNTHESIZE: BRING THINGS TOGETHER**
2b. What makes John Henry a hero?

EVALUATE: MAKE JUDGMENTS
3a. Why do you think John Henry put himself against the power and speed of the steam drill? What did it mean to him? What did he value more than technological innovations?

→ **EXTEND: CONNECT IDEAS**
3b. Make a list of modern situations in which people oppose technology. Can people against "progress" win? Why, or why not?

Literary Tools

FOLK SONG. A **folk song** is a traditional or composed song typically made up of stanzas, a refrain, and a simple melody. A form of folk literature, folk songs are expressions of commonly shared ideas or feelings and may be narrative or lyrical in style. Traditional folk songs are anonymous songs that have been transmitted orally. What elements make "John Henry" a folk song?

_____

_____

_____

_____

WordWorkshop

DIALECT. A **dialect** is a version of a language spoken by the people of a particular place, time, or social group. Some of the language of "John Henry" is from a dialect spoken in the past in the rural South. Using the chart below, add examples of dialect used in "John Henry" to the Dialect column. Add a standard English equivalent for each word to the Standard English column. One example has been done for you.

Dialect	Standard English
'fore	before

Read-Write Connection

What can machines do better than you, and what can you do better than machines?

_____

_____

_____

_____

_____

Beyond the Reading

CONTEMPORARY FOLK SONGS. Read and analyze the lyrics of contemporary folk artists such as Joan Baez, Janis Ian, Judy Collins, James Taylor, and the Indigo Girls. What are common themes of modern folk songs?

GO ONLINE. Visit the EMC Internet Resource Center at **emcp.com** to find links and additional activities for this selection.

Unit 5 READING Review

Choose and Use Reading Strategies

Before reading the excerpt below, review with a partner how to use reading strategies with Folk Literature, pages 237–239.

① Read with a Purpose
② Connect to Prior Knowledge
③ Write Things Down
④ Make Predictions
⑤ Visualize
⑥ Use Text Organization
⑦ Tackle Difficult Vocabulary
⑧ Monitor Your Reading Progress

Next, apply at least two of these reading strategies as you read the excerpt from "Aladdin and the Wonderful Lamp," a story from *The Arabian Nights,* retold by Andrew Lang. Use the margins and mark up the text to show how you are using the reading strategies to read actively.

There once lived a poor tailor, who had a son called Aladdin, a careless, idle boy who would do nothing but play all day long in the streets with little idle boys like himself. This so grieved the father that he died; yet, in spite of his mother's tears and prayers, Aladdin did not mend his ways. One day, when he was playing in the streets as usual, a stranger asked him his age, and if he were not the son of Mustapha the tailor.

"I am, sir," replied Aladdin, "but he died a long while ago." On this the stranger, who was a famous African magician, fell on his neck and kissed him, saying: "I am your uncle, and knew you from your likeness to my brother. Go to your mother and tell her I am coming."

Aladdin ran home, and told his mother of his newly found uncle. "Indeed, child," she said, "your father had a brother, but I always thought he was dead."

However, she prepared supper, and bade Aladdin seek his uncle, who came laden with wine and fruit. He presently fell down and kissed the place where Mustapha used to sit, bidding Aladdin's mother not to be surprised at not having seen him before, as he had been forty years out of the country. He then turned to Aladdin, and asked him his trade, at which the boy hung his head, while his mother burst into tears. On learning that Aladdin was idle and would learn no trade, he offered to take a shop for him and stock it with merchandise. Next day he bought Aladdin a fine suit of clothes, and took him all over the city, showing him the sights, and brought him home at nightfall to his mother, who was overjoyed to see her son so fine. Next day the magician led Aladdin into some beautiful gardens a long way outside the city gates. They sat down by a fountain, and the magician pulled a cake from his girdle, which he divided between them. They then journeyed onwards till they almost reached the mountains. Aladdin was so tired that he begged to go back, but the magician beguiled him with pleasant stories, and led him on in spite of himself.

At last they came to two mountains divided by a narrow valley. "We will go no farther," said the false uncle. "I will show you something wonderful; only do you gather up sticks while I kindle a fire."

WordWorkshop

UNIT 5 WORDS FOR EVERYDAY USE

abroad, 253
anxiety, 254
beguile, 240
compassion, 263
contrive, 256
curtail, 240
diligently, 262
disintegrate, 241
dominion, 246
ebb, 241
enigmatic, 241

entreat, 264
famine, 263
oblivious, 239
plumage, 248
plume, 254
riotous, 263
surpass, 275
superintendence, 253
transgress, 264
traverse, 248

WORD SORT

1. Make boxes like the ones below on another sheet of paper.

EXAMPLE	Word:	Word:
Word: abroad	**Part of speech:**	**Part of speech:**
Part of speech: adverb	**Definition:**	**Definition:**
Definition: far and wide		

2. Cut the boxes apart. Write one of the Words for Everyday Use on each box, along with its part of speech and a definition.

3. When you have completed all of your cards, sort them using one of the following methods.
   - Same parts of speech
   - Words with similar or opposite meanings
   - Words with prefixes and suffixes
   - Words that relate to each other or that can be used together
   - My own sorting method:_____

   Show how you sorted the words in the chart below.

4. Resort the words using one of the other methods, or create a new sorting method of your own. Show your second sorting method in the chart below.

Sorting Method 1

Sorting Method 2

Literary Tools

Select a literary element from the column on the right that best completes each sentence on the left. Write the correct letter in the blank.

_____1. In "The Prodigal Son," the lost flock of sheep are a(n) ___ of God's lost followers.

_____2. Repetition in a(n) ___ allows people to join in at regular points.

_____3. When one of the crows in "The White Snake" says, "Something lies very heavy in my craw," the storyteller is using ___.

_____4. To think that pumpkins can turn into stagecoaches and mice can turn into footmen requires a(n) ___.

_____5. In "Goha and the Pot," Goha takes part in most of the action and is a main ___.

_____6. "That the King's daughter seeks a husband" is a common element in a(n) ___.

_____7. The line "He kissed his son (*Good-bye*, if he had know it)," is an example of ___.

_____8. In "The White Snake," the three fishes and the three ravens are examples of a recurring element known as a(n) ___.

a. suspension of disbelief, 243

b. foreshadowing, 250

c. fairy tale, 259

d. character, 277

e. symbol, 266

f personification, 272

g. folk song, 283

h. motif, 255

On Your Own

FLUENTLY SPEAKING. Find a children's picture book that retells a song or story from the folk tradition. Make an audiotape of the book for younger children to hear. Record the story and listen to your reading. Note corrections you would like to make to your reading, and rerecord the story. Do this rereading and rerecording two or three times. When you record your final reading, make sure that you use lots of expression in your voice. The expression in your voice will help younger readers understand what happens.

PICTURE THIS. Make quick sketches of the main characters in each of the selections in this unit. Use descriptions in the selections to make your sketches. Choose three or four of your sketches and include them in a picture that tells a new story.

PUT IT IN WRITING. Choose one of the selections in this unit and rewrite it as a short drama. You may add scenes to your drama that show what might have happened after the selection you read ended. Act out your drama for the class.

Unit SIX

READING Drama

A **drama,** or *play*, is a story told through characters played by actors. Early groups of people around the world enacted ritual scenes related to hunting, warfare, or religion. From these, drama arose. Western drama as we know it began in ancient Greece.

Types of Drama

Most dramas can be classified as either comedies or tragedies. A **comedy** originally was any work with a happy ending. The term is widely used today to refer to any humorous work, especially one prepared for the stage or screen. A **tragedy** initially was a drama that told the story of the fall of a person of high status. In recent years, the word *tragedy* has been used to describe any play about the downfall of a central character, or *protagonist*, who wins the audience's sympathies.

Elements of Drama

THE PLAYWRIGHT AND THE SCRIPT. The author of a play is the **playwright.** A playwright has limited control in deciding how his or her work is presented. Producers, directors, set designers, and actors all interpret a playwright's work and present their interpretations to the audience.

SCRIPT. A **script** is the written text from which a drama is produced. It contains dialogue and stage directions and may be divided into acts and scenes. Scripts for television screenplays, such as Rod Serling's "The Monsters Are Due on Maple Street" in this unit, include instructions for how the play should be filmed.

DIALOGUE. The speech of the actors in a play is called **dialogue.** In a play, dialogue appears after the names of characters. A speech given by one character is called a **monologue.** A speech given by a character alone on stage is called a **soliloquy.** A statement intended to be heard by the audience but not by other characters on the stage is called an **aside.**

NOTE THE FACTS

What is the difference between a comedy and a tragedy?

_____

_____

_____

THINK AND REFLECT

When might a playwright want a character to speak in an aside?

_____

_____

_____

_____

ACTS AND SCENES. An **act** is a major part of the play. One-act, three-act, and five-act plays are all common. The plays of ancient Rome and of Elizabethan England were typically divided into **five acts**, including Shakespeare's *The Tragedy of Romeo and Juliet* in this unit. A **scene** is a short section of a drama, and typically begins with the entrance of one or more characters. The number of scenes in each act may vary.

STAGE DIRECTIONS. **Stage directions** are notes included in a script to describe how the playwright wants something to be presented or performed onstage. Stage directions can describe lighting, costumes, music, sound effects, or other elements of a play. They can also describe entrances and exits, gestures, tone of voice, or other elements related to the acting of a play. Stage directions sometimes provide background information. In stage directions, the parts of the stage are described from the actor's point of view, as shown in the diagram below. Paying attention to the stage directions can help you understand the action in a play even when you cannot see it performed.

Reading STRATEGY
REVIEW

VISUALIZE. Using the Parts of a Stage diagram, mark where characters would go if stage directions told them to *exit left*.

THE PARTS OF A STAGE

Up Right	Up Center	Up Left
Right Center	Center	Left Center
Down Right	Down Center	Down Left

SPECTACLE. The spectacle includes all the elements of the drama that are presented to the audience's senses. The set, props, special effects, lighting, and costumes are all part of the spectacle.

Active Reading Strategy Checklists

When reading drama, be aware of the plot (what happens), the setting, the characters, the dialogue (what the characters say), and the stage directions (how the characters say their lines and the actions they take onstage). The following checklists offer things to consider as you read drama.

1 READ WITH A PURPOSE. Before reading drama, give yourself a purpose, or something to look for, as you read. Sometimes a purpose will be a directive from a teacher: "Chart the references to stars in the prologue and in act 2, scene 2." Other times you can set your own purpose by previewing the opening lines and instructional information. Say to yourself

- ❏ I want to look for . . .
- ❏ I need to learn what happens to . . .
- ❏ I want to experience how . . .
- ❏ I want to understand why . . .
- ❏ I want to figure out what causes . . .

2 CONNECT TO PRIOR KNOWLEDGE. Being aware of what you already know and thinking about it as you read can help you understand the characters and events. As you read, say to yourself

- ❏ The setting is a lot like . . .
- ❏ What happens here is similar to what happens in . . .
- ❏ This character is like . . .
- ❏ The ending reminds me of . . .
- ❏ I like this description because . . .

3 WRITE THINGS DOWN. As you read drama, write down important ideas that the author is sharing with readers. Possible ways to write things down include

- ❏ Underline important information in the stage directions.
- ❏ Write down things you want to remember about how the characters might say their lines.
- ❏ Highlight lines you want to read aloud.
- ❏ Create a graphic organizer to keep track of people and events.
- ❏ Use a code in the margin that shows how you respond to the action. For instance, you can use
    ! for "This is like something I have experienced"
    ? for "I don't understand this"
    √ for "This seems important"

Reading TIP

Become an actor! Practice reading parts of the play aloud using a voice that expresses what the characters feel.

USE A CODE

Here's a way to code the text.
- \+   I like this
- –   I don't like this
- √   This is important
- Yes   I agree with this
- No   I disagree with this
- ?   I don't understand this
- W   I wonder…
- !   This is like something I know
- ↶   I need to come back to this later

Create additional code marks to note other reactions you have.

4 MAKE PREDICTIONS. As you read drama, use information in the stage directions and the dialogue to make guesses about what will happen next. Make predictions like the following.

- ❏ The title makes me predict that . . .
- ❏ The stage directions make me think that . . .
- ❏ I think the selection will end with . . .
- ❏ I think there will be a conflict between . . .
- ❏ The dialogue makes me guess that . . .

Reading **TIP**

Sketch what the setting and the characters look like. The sketch will help you envision the action.

5 VISUALIZE. Visualizing, or allowing the words on the page to create images in your mind, helps you understand the action and how the characters may say their lines. In order to visualize the setting, the characters, and the action, make statements such as

- ❏ The setting and props . . .
- ❏ This character speaks . . .
- ❏ This character's movements are . . .
- ❏ This character wears . . .
- ❏ Over the course of the play, this character's behavior . . .
- ❏ The words help me see, hear, feel, smell, taste . . .

6 USE TEXT ORGANIZATION. When you read drama, pay attention to the dialogue, the characters, and the action. Learn to stop occasionally and retell what you have read. Say to yourself

- ❏ The stage directions help me pay attention to . . .
- ❏ The exposition, or introduction, is about . . .
- ❏ The central conflict centers on . . .
- ❏ The climax, or high point of interest, occurs when . . .
- ❏ The resolution, or the outcome, of the play is that . . .
- ❏ My summary of this scene is . . .

Reading **TIP**

Insert synonyms for difficult words into the dialogue as you read. If you are unsure about a synonym that will work, ask a classmate about the synonym he or she would use.

7 TACKLE DIFFICULT VOCABULARY. Difficult words in drama can get in the way of your ability to understand the characters and events. Use context, consult a dictionary, or ask someone about words you do not understand. When you come across a difficult word in a drama, say to yourself

- ❏ The lines near this word tell me that this word means . . .
- ❏ A dictionary definition shows that the word means . . .
- ❏ My work with the word before reading helps me know that the word means . . .
- ❏ A classmate said that the word means . . .
- ❏ This word is pronounced . . .

8 **MONITOR YOUR READING PROGRESS.** All readers encounter difficulty when they read, especially if the reading material is not self-selected. When you have to read something, note problems you are having and fix them. The key to reading success is knowing when you are having difficulty. To fix problems, say to yourself

- ❑ Because I don't understand this part, I will . . .
- ❑ Because I'm having trouble staying connected to what I'm reading, I will . . .
- ❑ Because the words in the play are too hard, I will . . .
- ❑ Because the play is long, I will . . .
- ❑ Because I can't retell what happened here, I will . . .

Become an Active Reader

The instruction with the drama selections in this unit gives you an in-depth look at how to use one strategy for each selection. Brief margin notes guide your use of additional strategies. Using one active reading strategy will greatly increase your reading success and enjoyment. Use the white space in the margins to add your own comments and strategy ideas. Learn how to use several strategies in combination to ensure your complete understanding of what you are reading. When you have difficulty, try a fix-up idea. For further information about the active reading strategies, see Unit 1, pages 4–15.

FIX-UP IDEAS

- ■ Reread
- ■ Ask a question
- ■ Read in shorter chunks
- ■ Read aloud
- ■ Retell
- ■ Work with a partner
- ■ Unlock difficult words
- ■ Vary your reading rate
- ■ Choose a new reading strategy
- ■ Create a mnemonic device

How to Use Reading Strategies with Drama

Note how a reader uses active reading strategies while reading this excerpt from *The Tragedy of Romeo and Juliet* by William Shakespeare, page 327.

READ WITH A PURPOSE

I want to find out if their love is going to last.

CONNECT TO PRIOR KNOWLEDGE

This sounds like the dialogue in the movie *Roxane*.

TACKLE DIFFICULT VOCABULARY

By reading the definition at the bottom of the page, I can see that "Her eye discourses" means that Juliet's eyes express her feelings.

ROMEO. But soft, what light through yonder window breaks?
It is the east, and Juliet is the sun.
Arise, fair sun, and kill the envious moon,
Who is already sick and pale with grief
That thou, her maid, art far more fair than she.
Be not her maid, since she is envious;
Her vestal livery is but sick and green,
And none but fools do wear it; cast it off.
It is my lady, O, it is my love!
O that she knew she were!
She speaks, yet she says nothing; what of that?
Her eye <u>discourses</u>, I will answer it.
I am too bold, 'tis not to me she speaks.
Two of the fairest stars in all the heaven,
Having some business, do entreat her eyes
To twinkle in their spheres till they return.
What if her eyes were there, they in her head?
The brightness of her cheek would shame those stars,
As daylight doth a lamp; her eyes in heaven
Would through the airy region stream so bright
That birds would sing and think it were not night.
See how she leans her cheek upon her hand!
O that I were a glove upon that hand,
That I might touch that cheek!

MONITOR YOUR READING PROGRESS

Rereading the first five lines makes them easier to understand.

USE TEXT ORGANIZATION

This speech is long, but I can summarize it—Romeo is standing under Juliet's window thinking about her beauty and wishing she knew he loved her.

VISUALIZE

I can picture Romeo standing below Juliet's balcony.

MAKE PREDICTIONS

I predict that Juliet will fall in love with a guy like this.

WRITE THINGS DOWN

I can keep track of examples of the star motif in a graphic organizer.

THE TRAGEDY OF ROMEO AND JULIET

by William Shakespeare

Active READING STRATEGY

WRITE THINGS DOWN

Before Reading ➤ **PREVIEW THE SELECTION**

❑ Read the Reader's Resource information on pages 296.
❑ Preview the cast of characters on page 297. Pay attention to which characters side with the Montagues, which characters side with the Capulets, and which are neutral.
❑ Note that the play is divided into five acts and multiple scenes, although the selection you are reading includes only act 1 and the first two scenes of act 2.
❑ As you read, you will be recording summaries of each scene. Work with the Summarize Sections Chart below.

Graphic Organizer

On your own paper, create a chart like the one below. Label each act and scene and summarize each section. You will need a section for each of the five scenes in act 1 and for the first two scenes in act 2.

Summary of act 1, scene 1: The Montague and Capulet servants get into a fight. Romeo's cousin, Benvolio, promises Romeo's parents he will see what is bothering Romeo.
Summary of act 1, scene 2:
Summary of act 1, scene 3:
Summary of act 1, scene 4:

Word watch

PREVIEW VOCABULARY

Act 1	Act 2
adversary	adjacent
augment	bounty
brow	discourse
courtier	enmity
devout	idolatry
flourish	impute
forefeit	inconstant
fray	invocation
grievance	procure
lineament	repose
mutiny	substantial
nuptial	
pernicious	
posterity	
propagate	
purge	
siege	
transgression	
vex	
visage	

Reader's journal

What causes people to fall in love?

_____

_____

_____

_____

Reader's resource

Reading STRATEGY REVIEW

SET A PURPOSE FOR READING.
What is a tragic flaw?
What should you look for
to help identify the tragic
flaws of Romeo and Juliet?

_____

_____

_____

THE TRAGEDY OF ROMEO AND JULIET. A **tragedy** traditionally presents a sad tale of the fall of a noble character or characters. This fall usually happens because of a personal failing called a **tragic flaw.** As you read _The Tragedy of Romeo and Juliet,_ think about what actions of Romeo and Juliet lead them into trouble. Doing so will help you to identify their tragic flaws.

When Romeo, a Montague, and Juliet, a Capulet, fall in love, they know that their warring families will not approve. This creates a **conflict,** or _struggle,_ that can only lead to disaster.

This play, like others written during the time of Queen Elizabeth I, is divided into five acts. An **act** is a major section of a play. Each act is divided into several **scenes,** short parts that begin and end with characters entering or exiting the stage.

WILLIAM SHAKESPEARE AND HIS WORLD. William Shakespeare (1564–1616) is often called the greatest playwright who ever lived. Even now, nearly 400 years after his death, his plays are still popular. Even though it is sometimes hard to understand the Elizabethan English his characters speak, modern audiences enjoy Shakespeare's plays because of the way they depict human nature and the emotions and struggles all people face. In Shakespeare's time, people from all levels of society attended the theater, from the nobility to the poorest workers. Shakespeare wrote his plays to provide something for everyone: lyrical poetry, philosophical ideas, physical comedy, and swashbuckling sword fights.

William Shakespeare was born to Mary Arden and John Shakespeare in Stratford-upon-Avon, a small English village on the banks of the river Avon. Stratford-upon-Avon was a rural town, and Shakespeare's plays have many references to plants and animals of the nearby woods and fields. Shakespeare married Anne Hathaway, who was also from the same town, and had three children.

By 1592, he was living and working in London, England's largest city. There he became a successful actor, playwright, and theater owner. He also wrote magnificent poetry. His theater company, the Lord Chamberlain's Men, became the most popular acting troupe in London. They performed at the Globe Theater and in a small indoor theater called Blackfriars. In 1594, Shakespeare's company performed two plays in front of Queen Elizabeth I. The acting troupe became servants of King James I in 1603 after Elizabeth's death, and changed their name to the King's Men.

Dividing his time between Stratford-upon-Avon and London, he devoted himself to writing plays instead of acting in them. He wrote at least 36 plays, including _Hamlet, Macbeth, Julius Cæsar, King Lear, Othello, A Midsummer Night's Dream, The Tempest,_ and _Romeo and Juliet._ During a performance of _Henry VIII_ in 1613, a cannon fired as a sound effect accidentally burned down the Globe Theater. Afterward, Shakespeare retired to Stratford-upon-Avon. He died at age 52, but his plays have lived on to delight audiences through the ages and around the world.

NOTE THE FACTS

What makes Shakespeare's
plays still enjoyable today?

_____

_____

_____

THE TRAGEDY OF ROMEO AND JULIET

WILLIAM SHAKESPEARE

CHARACTERS IN THE PLAY

CHORUS
ESCALUS, *Prince of Verona*
PARIS, *a young nobleman, kinsman to the Prince*
MONTAGUE ⎤ *heads of two houses at*
CAPULET ⎦ *variance with each other*
An OLD MAN, *of the Capulet family*
ROMEO, *son to Montague*
MERCUTIO, *kinsman to the Prince, and friend to Romeo*
BENVOLIO, *nephew to Montague, and friend to Romeo*
TYBALT, *nephew to Lady Capulet*
PETRUCHIO, *a (mute) follower of Tybalt*
FRIAR LAWRENCE ⎤ *Franciscans*
FRIAR JOHN ⎦
BALTHASAR, *servant to Romeo*
ABRAM, *servant to Montague*
SAMPSON ⎤
GREGORY ⎬ *servants to Capulet*
CLOWN ⎦
PETER, *servant to Juliet's nurse*
PAGE *to Paris*
APOTHECARY
Three MUSICIANS

LADY MONTAGUE, *wife to Montague*
LADY CAPULET, *wife to Capulet*
JULIET, *daughter to Capulet*
NURSE *to Juliet*
CITIZENS *of Verona; several* GENTLEMEN *and* GENTLEWOMEN *of both houses;* MASKERS, TORCH-BEARERS, PAGES, GUARDS, WATCHMEN, SERVANTS, *and* ATTENDANTS

During Reading ➤

WRITE THINGS DOWN

❑ Assign characters and read your parts aloud. Someone should also read the stage directions. You can change characters at the change of scenes.
❑ When you are not reading out loud, follow along in the text.
❑ As you read, record summaries of each scene. Work with the Summarize Sections chart on page 299. At the end of each page and scene, stop reading and write a summary of what has happened so far. Record important information about the setting and the characters.
❑ Label your summaries by act and scene.
❑ Work with a small group to compare your summaries and to discuss your thoughts about the play.

READ ALOUD

Read aloud the names of characters in the play until you are comfortable with them.

Literary _TOOLS_

PROLOGUE AND SONNET. A **prologue** is an introduction to a literary work. This play begins with a prologue spoken by the Chorus, usually played by a group of actors who chant the lines together.

The prologue in this play takes the form of a **sonnet,** a fourteen-line poem with a beat pattern called iambic pentameter. A Shakespearean sonnet is divided into four parts: the first four lines (quatrain 1), the second four lines (quatrain 2), the third four lines (quatrain 3), and the last two lines (the final couplet). Mark the text, labeling each quatrain and the final couplet.

Reading _STRATEGY_
REVIEW

TACKLE DIFFICULT VOCABULARY. Many words are used differently today than they were in Shakespeare's time. As you read, consult the vocabulary definitions and footnotes at the bottom of the page. What does it mean to be "star-cross'd" (line 6)? What does the word "traffic" mean in line 12?

_____

_____

THE PROLOGUE

Enter CHORUS.

Two households, both alike in dignity,[1]
In fair Verona, where we lay our scene,
From ancient grudge break to new <u>mutiny</u>,
Where civil blood makes civil hands unclean.[2]

5 From forth the fatal loins of these two foes
A pair of star-cross'd[3] lovers take their life;
Whose misadventur'd piteous overthrows
Doth with their death bury their parents' strife.
The fearful passage of their death-mark'd love,

10 And the continuance of their parents' rage,
Which, but their children's end, nought could remove,
Is now the two hours' traffic[4] of our stage;
The which if you with patient ears attend,
What here shall miss, our toil shall strive to mend.[5]

Exit.

ACT 1
SCENE 1: A PUBLIC PLACE IN VERONA

Enter SAMPSON *and* GREGORY, *with swords and bucklers, of the house of Capulet.*

SAMPSON. Gregory, on my word, we'll not carry coals.[6]
GREGORY. No, for then we should be colliers.[7]
SAMPSON. I mean, and we be in choler,[8] we'll draw.
GREGORY. Ay, while you live, draw your neck out of
5 collar.[9]

PROLOGUE / ACT 1, SCENE 1
  1. **alike in dignity.** Of the same rank (both noble)
  2. **civil blood . . . civil hands unclean.** Citizens are guilty of shedding one another's blood
  3. **star-cross'd.** Opposed by the stars, which were believed to control fate
  4. **traffic.** Business; action
  5. **What here . . . to mend.** What we do not do well in tonight's performance, we shall correct in the future, based on your reactions.
  6. **carry coals.** Perform menial work; figuratively, put up with insults
  7. **colliers.** Coal miners
  8. **be in choler.** Be angry
  9. **draw your neck . . . collar.** Keep from being hanged; note the play on words in "colliers," "choler," and "collar"

words for everyday use mu • ti • ny (myo͞ot´´n ē) *n.,* revolt against constituted authority. *The crew's* <u>mutiny</u> *against Captain Bligh is recounted in* Mutiny on the Bounty.

SAMPSON.   I strike quickly, being mov'd.

GREGORY.   But thou art not quickly mov'd to strike.

SAMPSON.   A dog of the house of Montague moves me.

GREGORY.   To move is to stir, and to be valiant is to stand;
10   therefore, if thou art mov'd, thou run'st away.

SAMPSON.   A dog of that house shall move me to stand! I
will take the wall[10] of any man or maid of Montague's.

GREGORY.   That shows thee a weak slave, for the weakest
goes to the wall.[11]

15 **SAMPSON.**   'Tis true, and therefore women, being the
weaker vessels, are ever thrust to the wall; therefore I will
push Montague's men from the wall, and thrust his maids to
the wall.

GREGORY.   The quarrel is between our masters, and us
20   their men.

SAMPSON.   'Tis all one; I will show myself a tyrant: when I
have fought with the men, I will be civil with the maids; I will
cut off their heads.

GREGORY.   The heads of the maids?

25 **SAMPSON.**   Ay, the heads of the maids, or their maiden-
heads, take it in what sense thou wilt.

GREGORY.   They must take it in sense that feel it.

SAMPSON.   Me they shall feel while I am able to stand, and
'tis known I am a pretty piece of flesh.

30 **GREGORY.**   'Tis well thou art not fish; if thou hadst, thou
hadst been poor-John.[12] Draw thy tool, here comes two of
the house of Montagues.

Enter two other servingmen ABRAM *and* BALTHASAR.

SAMPSON.   My naked weapon is out. Quarrel, I will back
thee.[13]

35 **GREGORY.**   How, turn thy back and run?

SAMPSON.   Fear me not.

GREGORY.   No, marry, I fear thee!

SAMPSON.   Let us take the law of our sides,[14] let them begin.

GREGORY.   I will frown as I pass by, and let them take it as
40   they list.[15]

---

10. **take the wall.** Inner part of a sidewalk, near the wall, was cleaner, so
people allowed their superiors to walk there as a matter of courtesy.
11. **weakest . . . wall.** The weakest gives way.
12. **poor-John.** Inexpensive fish
13. **back thee.** Assist you
14. **take the law of our sides.** Have the law on our side
15. **list.** Wish

Reading TIP

Read aloud quatrain 1 of the Prologue. Then paraphrase it, or repeat what it says in your own words. Paraphrase quatrains 2 and 3 and the final couplet. The prologue introduces the **exposition**, background information about the characters, setting, or conflict. What do you learn from the prologue? What characters will this play involve? Where does the story take place? What conflict is established?

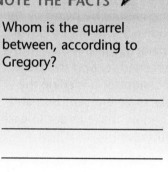

NOTE THE FACTS

Whom is the quarrel between, according to Gregory?

_____

_____

_____

FIX-UP IDEA

Ask a Question
If you have difficulty using the reading strategy of writing things down, ask questions to help you focus on important events and characters. Before reading a page, review the questions in the margins, like the one above. Then, as the play is read aloud, jot down your answers to the questions. Use these answers to help you fill in your chart.

READ ALOUD

Read aloud the highlighted text on this page. What act leads to the fight between the servants of the Capulets and Montagues?

_____

_____

_____

Literary TOOLS

ASIDE. An **aside** is a statement made by a character in a play, intended to be heard by the audience but not by other characters in the play. In the screened text on this page, highlight or underline the places where Sampson and Gregory make asides to each other.

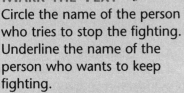

MARK THE TEXT

Circle the name of the person who tries to stop the fighting. Underline the name of the person who wants to keep fighting.

NOTE THE FACTS

What does Tybalt say about peace?

_____

_____

_____

SAMPSON. Nay, as they dare. I will bite my thumb[16] at them, which is disgrace to them if they bear it.

ABRAM. Do you bite your thumb at us, sir?

SAMPSON. I do bite my thumb, sir.

45 **ABRAM.** Do you bite your thumb at us, sir?

SAMPSON. [*Aside to* GREGORY.] Is the law of our side if I say ay?

GREGORY. [*Aside to* SAMPSON.] No.

SAMPSON. No, sir, I do not bite my thumb at you, sir, but

50 I bite my thumb, sir.

GREGORY. Do you quarrel, sir?

ABRAM. Quarrel, sir? No, sir.

SAMPSON. But if you do, sir, I am for you. I serve as good a man as you.

55 **ABRAM.** No better?

SAMPSON. Well, sir.

Enter BENVOLIO.

GREGORY. Say "better," here comes one of my master's kinsmen.

SAMPSON. Yes, better, sir.

60 **ABRAM.** You lie.

SAMPSON. Draw, if you be men. Gregory, remember thy washing[17] blow.

They fight.

BENVOLIO. Part, fools!
Put up your swords, you know not what you do. *Beats down their swords.*
Enter TYBALT.

65 **TYBALT.** What, art thou drawn among these heartless hinds?[18]
Turn thee, Benvolio, look upon thy death.

BENVOLIO. I do but keep the peace. Put up thy sword,
Or manage it to part these men with me.

70 **TYBALT.** What, drawn and talk of peace? I hate the word
As I hate hell, all Montagues, and thee.
Have at thee, coward!

They fight.

Enter three or four CITIZENS *with clubs or partisans.*[19]

---

16. **bite my thumb.** Gesture of contempt or insult
17. **washing.** Slashing
18. **heartless hinds.** Cowardly creatures
19. ***partisans.*** Broad-bladed spears

Citizens. Clubs, bills,[20] and partisans! Strike! Beat them down! Down with the Capulets! Down with the Montagues!

Enter old Capulet *in his gown, and his wife* Lady Capulet.

Capulet. What noise is this? Give me my long sword ho!

Lady Capulet. A crutch, a crutch! why call you for a sword?

Capulet. My sword, I say! Old Montague is come,
And flourishes his blade in spite of me.

Enter old Montague *and his wife* Lady Montague.

Montague. Thou villain Capulet!—Hold me not, let me go.

Lady Montague. Thou shalt not stir one foot to seek a foe.

Enter Prince Escalus *with his* Train.

Prince. Rebellious subjects, enemies to peace,
Profaners of this neighbor-stained steel[21]—
Will they not hear?—What ho, you men, you beasts!
That quench the fire of your pernicious rage
With purple fountains issuing from your veins—
On pain of torture, from those bloody hands
Throw your mistempered[22] weapons to the ground,
And hear the sentence of your moved prince.
Three civil brawls, bred of an airy word,
By thee, old Capulet, and Montague,
Have thrice[23] disturb'd the quiet of our streets,
And made Verona's ancient citizens
Cast by their grave beseeming ornaments[24]
To wield old partisans, in hands as old,

20. **bills.** Hooked blades attached to long shafts
21. **Profaners . . . steel.** People who profane, or make contemptible, their weapons by staining them with their neighbors' blood
22. **mistempered.** Hardened for an improper use
23. **thrice.** Three times
24. **Cast . . . ornaments.** Throw aside those objects, like canes, appropriate for old age

words for everyday use

flour • ish (flʉr´ish) *vt.,* wave in the air. *The veteran flourished the American flag during the Memorial Day parade.*

per • ni • cious (pər nish´əs) *adj.,* fatal; deadly. *The pernicious bullet, lodged in Dylan's lung, caused his death.*

Reading Strategy Review

Find a Purpose for Reading. As you read the play, set your own purpose to keep yourself interested. What do you want to look for? What do you want to understand?

Note the Facts

Why does the fighting between the Capulets and Montagues disturb Prince Escalus?

MARK THE TEXT

Circle the lines that tell what punishment the Montagues and Capulets will face if they do not stop fighting.

Reading STRATEGY REVIEW

CONNECT TO PRIOR KNOWLEDGE. Think about the relationship you have with an aunt or uncle. How much information does Benvolio, Romeo's cousin, give to Romeo's parents, Lady and Lord Montague?

Reading STRATEGY REVIEW

USE TEXT ORGANIZATION. A sentence doesn't always stop at the end of a line. Instead, it ends only when you see a period, question mark, or exclamation point. A comma or semi-colon signals that you should slow down in your reading. Read lines 110–116. After the sentence, "I drew to part them," underline Benvolio's next full sentence. Then take the sentence one phrase at a time and summarize it.

_____

_____

_____

_____

Cank'red[25] with peace, to part your cank'red hate;

100 If ever you disturb our streets again
Your lives shall pay the <u>forfeit</u> of the peace.
For this time all the rest depart away.
You, Capulet, shall go along with me,
And, Montague, come you this afternoon,

105 To know our farther pleasure in this case,
To old Free-town, our common judgment-place.
Once more, on pain of death, all men depart.

Exeunt all but MONTAGUE, LADY MONTAGUE, *and* BENVOLIO.

MONTAGUE. Who set this ancient quarrel new abroach?[26]
Speak, nephew, were you by when it began?

110 **BENVOLIO.** Here were the servants of your <u>adversary</u>,
And yours, close fighting ere[27] I did approach.
I drew to part them. In the instant came
The fiery Tybalt, with his sword prepar'd,
Which, as he breath'd defiance to my ears,

115 He swung about his head and cut the winds,
Who, nothing hurt withal,[28] hiss'd him in scorn.
While we were interchanging thrusts and blows,
Came more and more, and fought on part and part,
Till the Prince came, who parted either part.

120 **LADY MONTAGUE.** O, where is Romeo? Saw you him today?
Right glad I am he was not at this <u>fray</u>.

BENVOLIO. Madam, an hour before the worshipp'd sun
Peer'd forth the golden window of the east,

125 A troubled mind drive[29] me to walk abroad,
Where, underneath the grove of sycamore

---

25. **Cank'red.** Malignant
26. **abroach.** Open and flowing freely
27. **ere.** Before
28. **nothing hurt withal.** Not harmed as a result
29. **drive.** Drove

words for everyday use

for • feit (fôr´fit) *n.*, penalty or fine one pays because of a crime or infraction. *Because we did not have enough players on our team, we had to accept a <u>forfeit</u> and go home without playing.*

ad • ver • sar • y (ad´vər ser´ē) *n.*, opponent; enemy. *In court the defendant's <u>adversary</u> is the prosecuting attorney.*

fray (frā) *n.*, noisy quarrel or fight. *The <u>fray</u> at the Martins' apartment woke the neighbors.*

That westward rooteth from this city side,
So early walking did I see your son.
Towards him I made, but he was ware[30] of me,
130 And stole into the covert[31] of the wood.
I, measuring his affections by my own,
Which then most sought where most might not be found,
Being one too many by my weary self,
Pursued my humor not pursuing his,[32]
135 And gladly shunn'd who gladly fled from me.

MONTAGUE. Many a morning hath he there been seen,
With tears <u>augmenting</u> the fresh morning's dew,
Adding to clouds more clouds with his deep sighs,
But all so soon as the all-cheering sun
140 Should in the farthest east begin to draw
The shady curtains from Aurora's[33] bed,
Away from light steals home my heavy son,
And private in his chamber pens himself,
Shuts up his windows, locks fair daylight out,
145 And makes himself an artificial night.
Black and portendous[34] must this humor[35] prove,
Unless good counsel may the cause remove.

BENVOLIO. My noble uncle, do you know the cause?

MONTAGUE. I neither know it, nor can learn of him.

150 **BENVOLIO.** Have you importun'd[36] him by any means?

MONTAGUE. Both by myself and many other friends,
But he, his own affections' counsellor,
Is to himself (I will not say how true)
But to himself so secret and so close,
155 So far from sounding[37] and discovery,

NOTE THE FACTS

What happened when Benvolio saw Romeo?

_____

_____

_____

READ ALOUD

Read aloud the highlighted text on this page. According to Romeo's father, Lord Montague, how does Romeo spend his nights and days?

_____

_____

_____

---

30. **ware.** Wary
31. **covert.** Cover; hiding place
32. **Pursued . . . his.** Followed my own mood by not following him
33. **Aurora's.** Of the Roman goddess of dawn
34. **portendous.** Ominous; portentous
35. **humor.** Moody behavior
36. **importun'd.** Questioned
37. **sounding.** Being understood

words for everyday use aug • ment (ôg ment´) vt., make greater in size, strength, or quantity. Julian wanted his boss to <u>augment</u> his salary so he could earn more money.

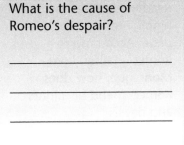
NOTE THE FACTS

What is the cause of Romeo's despair?

_____

_____

_____

Literary TOOLS

BLANK VERSE. Blank verse is unrhymed poetry written in iambic pentameter. An *iambic pentameter* line consists of five *feet,* each containing two syllables. The first syllable has a weak beat or stress and the second has a strong stress:

˘ / ˘ / ˘
A las | that love, | whose
/ ˘ / ˘ /
view | is muf | fled still,

Follow the example above to separate each line in the bracketed section (lines 181–184) into iambic pentameter. Mark where the syllables should be divided. Check to make sure you have five groupings of two syllables each. Then mark the weak and strong stresses in each line.

As is the bud bit with an envious[38] worm,
Ere he can spread his sweet leaves to the air
Or dedicate his beauty to the sun.
Could we but learn from whence[39] his sorrows grow,
160   We would as willingly give cure as know.
      Enter ROMEO.
      BENVOLIO.   See where he comes. So please you step aside,
      I'll know his grievance, or be much denied.
      MONTAGUE.   I would thou wert[40] so happy by thy stay
      To hear true shrift.[41] Come, madam, let's away.
      Exeunt MONTAGUE *and* LADY.
165   **BENVOLIO.**   Good morrow, cousin.
      ROMEO.   Is the day so young?
      BENVOLIO.   But new strook[42] nine.
      ROMEO.   Ay me, sad hours seem long.
      Was that my father that went hence[43] so fast?
170   **BENVOLIO.**   It was. What sadness lengthens Romeo's
         hours?
      ROMEO.   Not having that which, having, makes them
         short.
      BENVOLIO.   In love?
175   **ROMEO.**   Out—
      BENVOLIO.   Of love?
      ROMEO.   Out of her favor where I am in love.
      BENVOLIO.   Alas that love, so gentle in his view,
      Should be so tyrannous and rough in proof!
180   **ROMEO.**   Alas that love, whose view is muffled still,[44]
      Should, without eyes, see pathways to his will!
      Where shall we dine? O me! what fray was here?
      Yet tell me not, for I have heard it all:
      Here's much to do with hate, but more with love.

38. **envious.** Vicious
39. **whence.** What place
40. **wert.** Were
41. **shrift.** Confession
42. **strook.** Struck
43. **hence.** From here
44. **whose view . . . still.** Love is conventionally pictured as blind.

words for everyday use   **griev • ance** (grēv´əns) *n.,* complaint or resentment. *The teacher's grievance over reassignment to social studies classes was heard by a mediator.*

185   Why then, O brawling love! O loving hate!

O any thing, of nothing first create!⁴⁵

O heavy lightness, serious vanity,

Misshapen chaos of well-seeming forms,

Feather of lead, bright smoke, cold fire, sick health,

190   Still-waking sleep, that is not what it is!

This love feel I, that feel no love in this.⁴⁶

Dost thou not laugh?

BENVOLIO.   No, coz,⁴⁷ I rather weep.

ROMEO.   Good heart, at what?

195   **BENVOLIO.**   At thy good heart's oppression.

ROMEO.   Why, such is love's <u>transgression</u>.

Griefs of mine own lie heavy in my breast,

Which thou wilt <u>propagate</u> to have it press'd

With more of thine.⁴⁸ This love that thou hast shown

200   Doth add more grief to too much of mine own.

Love is a smoke made with the fume of sighs,

Being <u>purg'd</u>, a fire sparkling in lovers' eyes,

Being <u>vex'd</u>, a sea nourish'd with loving tears.

What is it else? a madness most discreet,

205   A choking gall, and a preserving sweet.

Farewell, my coz.

BENVOLIO.   Soft,⁴⁹ I will go along;

And if you leave me so, you do me wrong.

ROMEO.   Tut, I have lost myself, I am not here:

210   This is not Romeo, he's some other where.

BENVOLIO.   Tell me in sadness,⁵⁰ who is that you love?

ROMEO.   What, shall I groan and tell thee?

---

45. **O any thing . . . create!** All things created (by God) out of nothing

46. **O brawling love . . . no love in this.** Romeo's string of contradictions shows the confused state he is in. He feels good because he is in love and also feels bad because his love is not returned. His language suggests that he is in love with love.

47. **coz.** Cousin (said of any relative)

48. **Griefs of mine own . . . of thine.** The grief in my heart will multiply if it feels the further weight of your grief.

49. **Soft.** One moment; used as an interjection

50. **in sadness.** With gravity or seriousness

words for everyday use	**trans • gres • sion** (trans gresh´ən) *n.*, offense. *Jolene felt sorry for her <u>transgression</u> and put the money back in Kim's jacket.*
	prop • a • gate (präp´ə gāt) *vt.*, reproduce; multiply. *Because the minks had <u>propagated</u>, the farmer had to build an additional pen.*
	purge (pʉrj) *vt.*, cleanse of impurities. *Stalin wanted to <u>purge</u> the Soviet Union of dissenters.*
	vex (veks) *vt.*, disturb; annoy; irritate. *Jim <u>vexed</u> his sister with repeated demands to borrow ten dollars.*

Literary **TOOLS**

OXYMORON. An **oxymoron** is a statement that contradicts itself. Words and phrases like *brawling love* and *loving hate* in line 185 are oxymorons that develop a complex meaning from two seemingly contradictory elements. Romeo uses more oxymorons in lines 187–190. List at least five on the lines below.

_____

_____

_____

_____

_____

NOTE THE FACTS

What makes Benvolio sad? How does this affect Romeo?

_____

_____

_____

THINK AND REFLECT

What does Romeo's attitude reveal about his character? **(Infer)**

_____

_____

_____

READ ALOUD

Read aloud the screened text on this page. How is Romeo's love, Rosaline, like the Roman goddess Diana?

_____

_____

_____

THINK AND REFLECT

How likely is it that Rosaline will love Romeo as he loves her? **(Infer)**

_____

_____

_____

NOTE THE FACTS

What advice does Benvolio give to Romeo, who loves someone who does not love him?

_____

_____

_____

BENVOLIO.   Groan? why, no;
But sadly tell me, who?

215 **ROMEO.**   Bid a sick man in sadness make his will—
A word ill urg'd to one that is so ill!
In sadness, cousin, I do love a woman.

BENVOLIO.   I aim'd so near when I suppos'd you lov'd.

ROMEO.   A right good mark-man![51] And she's fair I love.

220 **BENVOLIO.**   A right fair mark,[52] fair coz, is soonest hit.

ROMEO.   Well, in that hit you miss: she'll not be hit
With Cupid's arrow, she hath Dian's wit;[53]
And in strong proof[54] of chastity well arm'd,
From Love's weak childish bow she lives uncharm'd.[55]

225 She will not stay[56] the <u>siege</u> of loving terms,
Nor bide th' encounter of assailing eyes,
Nor ope her lap to saint-seducing gold.[57]
O, she is rich in beauty, only poor
That, when she dies, with beauty dies her store.[58]

230 **BENVOLIO.**   Then she hath sworn that she will still[59] live
     chaste?

ROMEO.   She hath, and in that sparing[60] makes huge
     waste;
For beauty starv'd with her severity

235 Cuts beauty off from all <u>posterity</u>.
She is too fair, too wise, wisely too fair,
To merit bliss by making me despair.
She hath forsworn to love, and in that vow
Do I live dead that live to tell it now.

240 **BENVOLIO.**   Be rul'd by me, forget to think of her.

ROMEO.   O, teach me how I should forget to think.

---

51. **mark-man.** Marksman, one who shoots well
52. **mark.** Target
53. **Dian's wit.** Beliefs of Diana, the Roman goddess of chastity and of the hunt. Romeo's beloved is like Diana in not wanting to marry.
54. **proof.** Armor
55. **uncharm'd.** Not under the spell of
56. **stay.** Abide
57. **Nor ope . . . gold.** The reference is to Danaë, in Roman mythology, whom Jupiter visited in the form of a shower of gold.
58. **dies her store.** Her beauty will die with her, for she left no children.
59. **still.** Always
60. **sparing.** Thriftiness

words for everyday use

siege (sēj) _n._, persistent attempt to gain control. _During the <u>siege</u> of the castle, the baron's men spilled tar on the invaders._

pos • ter • i • ty (päs ter´ə tē) _n._, all succeeding generations. _The founding fathers wanted the Bill of Rights to be enjoyed by <u>posterity</u>._

BENVOLIO.   By giving liberty unto thine eyes:
Examine other beauties.
ROMEO.   'Tis the way
245 To call hers, exquisite, in question more.[61]
These happy masks that kiss fair ladies' brows,
Being black, puts us in mind they hide the fair.
He that is strooken[62] blind cannot forget
The precious treasure of his eyesight lost.
250 Show me a mistress that is passing[63] fair,
What doth her beauty serve but as a note
Where I may read who pass'd that passing fair?
Farewell, thou canst not teach me to forget.
BENVOLIO.   I'll pay that doctrine, or else die in debt.[64]

Exeunt.

SCENE 2: A STREET IN VERONA

Enter CAPULET, COUNTY PARIS, *and the Clown, Capulet's*
SERVANT.

CAPULET.   But Montague is bound as well as I,
In penalty alike, and 'tis not hard, I think,
For men so old as we to keep the peace.
PARIS.   Of honorable reckoning[1] are you both,
5 And pity 'tis you liv'd at odds so long.
But now, my lord, what say you to my suit?[2]
CAPULET.   But saying o'er what I have said before:
My child is yet a stranger in the world,
She hath not seen the change of fourteen years;
10 Let two more summers wither in their pride,
Ere we may think her ripe to be a bride.
PARIS.   Younger than she are happy mothers made.
CAPULET.   And too soon marr'd are those so early made.
Earth hath swallowed all my hopes but she;
15 She's the hopeful lady of my earth.[3]

---

61. **'Tis the way . . . more.** That's the way to make her great beauty even more evident.
62. **strooken.** Struck
63. **passing.** Extremely; surpassing others
64. **pay that . . . debt.** Teach you that lesson or die still under obligation to you

ACT 1, SCENE 2
1. **Of honorable reckoning.** With a favorable reputation
2. **suit.** Pleading
3. **hopeful . . . earth.** The one who will inherit my land, and the one who makes my world seem hopeful

WRITE THINGS DOWN. Don't forget to summarize the events in each scene as soon as you have read it.

MARK THE TEXT

Read lines 7–11 and underline the lines of text that tell you how old Juliet is. Then circle the text that tells what age her father thinks is appropriate for her to marry.

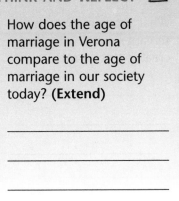

THINK AND REFLECT

How does the age of marriage in Verona compare to the age of marriage in our society today? **(Extend)**

_____

_____

_____

NOTE THE FACTS

Who wishes to marry
Juliet? What does her
father say this person
should do?

_____

_____

_____

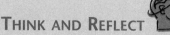

THINK AND REFLECT

What problem does the
servant's inability to read
create? (**Interpret**)

_____

_____

_____

But woo her, gentle Paris, get her heart,
My will to her consent is but a part;
And she agreed, within her scope of choice
Lies my consent and fair according voice.
20 This night I hold an old accustom'd feast,
Whereto I have invited many a guest,
Such as I love, and you, among the store
One more, most welcome, makes my number more.
At my poor house look to behold this night
25 Earth-treading stars that make dark heaven light.
Such comfort as do lusty young men feel
When well-apparell'd April on the heel
Of limping winter treads, even such delight
Among fresh fennel[4] buds shall you this night
30 Inherit[5] at my house; hear all, all see;
And like her most whose merit most shall be;
Which on more view of many, mine, being one,
May stand in number, though in reck'ning none.[6]
Come go with me. [_To_ SERVANT.] Go, sirrah,[7] trudge about
35 Through fair Verona, find those persons out
Whose names are written there, and to them say,
My house and welcome on their pleasure stay.[8]

Exit with PARIS.

SERVANT. Find them out whose names are written here! It
is written that the shoemaker should meddle with his yard
40 and the tailor with his last, the fisher with his pencil and
the painter with his nets; but I am sent to find those persons whose names are here writ, and can never find what
names the writing person hath here writ. I must to the
learned. In good time!

Enter BENVOLIO _and_ ROMEO.

45 **BENVOLIO.** Tut, man, one fire burns out another's burning,
One pain is less'ned by another's anguish;
Turn giddy, and be holp[9] by backward turning;

---

4. **fennel.** Plant with yellow flowers and a sweet aroma
5. **Inherit.** Experience
6. **May stand . . . none.** She may be one of a number of women, but when
you reckon, or make calculations, about which is the best, you will find that
none compares to her.
7. **sirrah.** Form of address used by a person of higher rank when speaking to
a person of a lesser social rank
8. **on their pleasure stay.** Wait to see what will be their pleasure
9. **holp.** Helped; cured

One desperate grief cures with another's languish:[10]
Take thou some new infection to thy eye,
50 And the rank poison of the old will die.
    ROMEO.   Your plantan leaf[11] is excellent for that.
    BENVOLIO.   For what, I pray thee?
    ROMEO.   For your broken shin.
    BENVOLIO.   Why, Romeo, art thou mad?
55 ROMEO.   Not mad, but bound more than a madman is;
    Shut up in prison, kept without my food,
    Whipt and tormented and—God-den,[12] good fellow.
    SERVANT.   God gi' god-den. I pray, sir, can you read?
    ROMEO.   Ay, mine own fortune in my misery.
60 SERVANT.   Perhaps you have learn'd it without book.
    But I pray, can you read any thing you see?
    ROMEO.   Ay, if I know the letters and the language.
    SERVANT.   Ye say honestly, rest you merry!
    ROMEO.   Stay, fellow, I can read.
65 (He reads the letter.) "Signior Martino and his wife and
    daughters; County Anselme and his beauteous sisters; the
    lady widow of Vitruvio; Signior Placentio and his lovely
    nieces; Mercutio and his brother Valentine; mine uncle
    Capulet, his wife, and daughters; my fair niece Rosaline,
70 and Livia; Signior Valentio and his cousin Tybalt; Lucio
    and the lively Helena." A fair assembly. Whither should
    they come?
    SERVANT.   Up.
    ROMEO.   Whither? to supper?
75 SERVANT.   To our house.
    ROMEO.   Whose house?
    SERVANT.   My master's.
    ROMEO.   Indeed I should have ask'd thee that before.
    SERVANT.   Now I'll tell you without asking. My master is
80 the great rich Capulet, and if you be not of the house of
    Montagues, I pray come and crush[13] a cup of wine. Rest
    you merry!

                                                    Exit.

READ ALOUD

Working in pairs, have one person read the part of the Servant and the other read the part of Romeo in the highlighted box. How does Romeo find out about the party at the Capulet house?

_____

_____

_____

---

10. **languish.** State of depression
11. **plantan leaf.** Leaf of the plantain, applied to soothe minor wounds
12. **God-den.** Good evening
13. **crush.** Drink

NOTE THE FACTS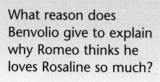

Who will be at Capulet's feast? What advice does Benvolio give to Romeo?

_____

_____

BENVOLIO. At this same ancient feast of Capulet's
Sups the fair Rosaline whom thou so loves,
With all the admired beauties of Verona.
85 Go thither,[14] and with unattainted[15] eye
Compare her face with some that I shall show,
And I will make thee think thy swan a crow.
ROMEO. When the <u>devout</u> religion of mine eye
Maintains such falsehood, then turn tears to fires;
90 And these,[16] who, often drown'd, could never die,
Transparent heretics, be burnt for liars!
One fairer than my love! The all-seeing sun
Ne'er saw her match since first the world begun.
BENVOLIO. Tut, you saw her fair, none else being by,
95 Herself pois'd with herself in either eye;
But in that crystal scales let there be weigh'd
Your lady's love against some other maid
That I will show you shining at this feast,
And she shall scant show well that now seems best.
100 **ROMEO.** I'll go along no such sight to be shown,
But to rejoice in splendor of mine own. _Exeunt._

NOTE THE FACTS

What reason does Benvolio give to explain why Romeo thinks he loves Rosaline so much?

_____

_____

THINK AND REFLECT

How wise do you find Benvolio's advice to Romeo? Why? (Evaluate)

_____

_____

SCENE 3: CAPULET'S HOUSE

Enter CAPULET'S WIFE, _and_ NURSE.

LADY CAPULET. Nurse, where's my daughter? Call her forth to me.
NURSE. Now by my maidenhead at twelve year old,
I bade her come. What, lamb! What, ladybird!
5 God forbid! Where's this girl? What, Juliet!

Enter JULIET.

JULIET. How now, who calls?
NURSE. Your mother.
JULIET. Madam, I am here,
What is your will?

NOTE THE FACTS

What is Juliet's immediate response to her mother? What does this reflect about her relationship to Lady Capulet?

_____

_____

14. **thither.** There
15. **unattainted.** Untainted; not with preconceived ideas
16. **these.** These eyes

> **words for everyday use**
> de • vout (di vout´) _adj.,_ religious; pious. _A_ <u>devout</u> _woman, Mrs. Bacholl went to Mass every weekend._

10   **LADY CAPULET.**   This is the matter. Nurse, give leave[1] a
            while,
        We must talk in secret. Nurse, come back again,
        I have rememb'red me, thou s'[2] hear our counsel.
        Thou knowest my daughter's of a pretty age.
15   **NURSE.**   Faith, I can tell her age unto an hour.
        LADY CAPULET.   She's not fourteen.
        NURSE.   I'll lay fourteen of my teeth—
        And yet, to my teen[3] be it spoken, I have but four—
        She's not fourteen. How long is it now
20   To Lammas-tide?[4]
        LADY CAPULET.   A fortnight[5] and odd days.
        NURSE.   Even or odd, of all days in the year,
        Come Lammas-eve at night shall she be fourteen,
        Susan and she—God rest all Christian souls!—
25   Were of an age. Well, Susan is with God,
        She was too good for me. But as I said,
        On Lammas-eve at night shall she be fourteen,
        That shall she, marry, I remember it well.
        'Tis since the earthquake now aleven[6] years,
30   And[7] she was wean'd—I never shall forget it—
        Of all the days of the year, upon that day;
        For I had then laid wormwood to my dug,[8]
        Sitting in the sun under the dove-house wall.
        My lord and you were then at Mantua—
35   Nay, I do bear a brain—but as I said,
        When it did taste the wormwood on the nipple
        Of my dug and felt it bitter, pretty fool,
        To see it teachy[9] and fall out wi' th' dug!
        Shake, quoth the dove-house;[10] 'twas no need, I trow,[11]
40   To bid me trudge.
        And since that time it is aleven years,

NOTE THE FACTS

What does Lady Capulet tell the Nurse to do?

_____

_____

_____

THINK AND REFLECT

Why do you think Lady Capulet changes her mind? **(Infer)**

_____

_____

_____

Reading STRATEGY
                    REVIEW

VISUALIZE. Draw a picture showing the relationship between Juliet and her mother. Especially pay attention to drawing their facial expressions.

ACT 1, SCENE 3
  1. **give leave.** Leave us
  2. **thou s'.** You shall or you should
  3. **teen.** Sorrow
  4. **Lammas-tide.** First of August
  5. **fortnight.** Fourteen nights
  6. **aleven.** Eleven
  7. **And.** Since
  8. **laid wormwood to my dug.** Applied the bitter herb called wormwood
to her breast to wean the child
  9. **teachy.** Touchy
10. **Shake . . . dove-house.** The dove house shook because of the earthquake.
11. **trow.** Believe

For then she could stand high-lone;[12] nay, by th' rood,[13]
She could have run and waddled all about;
For even the day before, she broke her <u>brow</u>,
45 And then my husband—God be with his soul!
'A[14] was a merry man—took up the child.
"Yea," quoth he, "dost thou fall upon thy face?
Thou wilt fall backward when thou hast more wit,
Wilt thou not, Jule?" and by my holidam,[15]
50 The pretty wretch left crying and said, "Ay."[16]
To see now how a jest shall come about![17]
I warrant,[18] and I should live a thousand years,
I never should forget it: "Wilt thou not, Jule?" quoth he;
And, pretty fool, it stinted[19] and said, "Ay."

55 **LADY CAPULET.** Enough of this, I pray thee hold thy
peace.
NURSE. Yes, madam, yet I cannot choose but laugh
To think it should leave crying and say, "Ay."
And yet I warrant it had upon it[20] brow
60 A bump as big as a young cock'rel's stone[21]—
A perilous knock—and it cried bitterly.
"Yea," quoth my husband, "fall'st upon thy face?
Thou wilt fall backward when thou comest to age,
Wilt thou not, Jule?" It stinted and said, "Ay."
65 **JULIET.** And stint thou too, I pray thee, nurse, say I.
NURSE. Peace, I have done. God mark thee to his grace![22]
Thou wast the prettiest babe that e'er I nurs'd.
And I might live to see thee married once,
I have my wish.

READ ALOUD

Read aloud the highlighted text on this page, assigning the parts of Lady Capulet, the Nurse, and Juliet to different people if possible. How do Juliet and her mother act toward the Nurse? How does the Nurse respond?

_____

_____

_____

_____

_____

12. **stand high-lone.** Stand upright
13. **rood.** Cross
14. **'A.** He
15. **holidam.** Holiness, sometimes referring to the Virgin Mary
16. **Ay.** Aye, or yes
17. **To see . . . about!** The nurse is expressing pleasure at seeing her husband's joke come true.
18. **warrant.** Swear or guarantee
19. **stinted.** Stopped (crying)
20. **it.** Its
21. **cock'rel's stone.** Part of a young male chicken
22. **God mark . . . grace!** God grant grace to you!

words for everyday use

brow (brou) *n.,* forehead. *Jed wiped the sweat from his <u>brow</u>.*

70   **LADY CAPULET.**   Marry, that "marry" is the very theme
    I came to talk of. Tell me, daughter Juliet,
    How stands your dispositions to be married?
    JULIET.   It is an honor that I dream not of.
    NURSE.   An honor! were not I thine only nurse,
75   I would say thou hadst suck'd wisdom from thy teat.
    LADY CAPULET.   Well, think of marriage now; younger
      than you,
    Here in Verona, ladies of esteem,
    Are made already mothers. By my count,
80   I was your mother much upon these years
    That you are now a maid. Thus then in brief:
    The valiant Paris seeks you for his love.
    NURSE.   A man, young lady! Lady, such a man
    As all the world—why, he's a man of wax.[23]
85   **LADY CAPULET.**   Verona's summer hath not such a flower.
    NURSE.   Nay, he's a flower, in faith, a very flower.
    LADY CAPULET.   What say you? can you love the gentle-
      man?
    This night you shall behold him at our feast;
90   Read o'er the volume of young Paris' face,
    And find delight writ there with beauty's pen;
    Examine every married[24] <u>lineament</u>,
    And see how one another lends content;
    And what obscur'd in this fair volume lies
95   Find written in the margent[25] of his eyes.
    This precious book of love, this unbound[26] lover,
    To beautify him, only lacks a cover.
    The fish lives in the sea, and 'tis much pride
    For fair without the fair within to hide.[27]
100   That book in many's eyes doth share the glory,

---

23. **he's a man of wax.** He is as handsome as a wax figure of a man. The
nurse means this as a compliment, but a wax figure is less than a real person,
so the compliment is unintentionally an insult.
24. **married.** Well matched or put together; also a pun on the usual sense of the word
25. **margent.** Margin, as in a book
26. **unbound.** Like a book unbound, he is unbound by marriage.
27. **The fish . . . hide.** It is as appropriate for a good man to be handsome
as it is for a fish to live in the sea.

words for everyday use

lin • e • a • ment (lin´ē ə mənt) *n.,* definite shape, contour, or line, especially of
the face. *Her fine <u>lineaments</u> made her the very image of her mother.*

MARK THE TEXT

Circle the line that reflects
how Juliet feels about getting
married.

NOTE THE FACTS

What do Lady Capulet and
the Nurse think of Paris
and his wish to marry
Juliet?

_____

_____

_____

READ ALOUD

Blank verse is unrhymed
poetry written in iambic
pentameter. It is
frequently used in drama
because its rhythms are
closest to those of natural
speech. **Iambic
pentameter** is a line of
poetry that has five feet.
Each *foot,* or group of two
syllables, has a weak beat
followed by a strong beat
(de light´). Read aloud the
text in the screened box.
Pay attention to the
rhythm of the lines. Circle
the ends of the lines that
rhyme. What qualities
does Lady Capulet seem
to have? How do her lines
reflect this?

_____

_____

_____

That in gold clasps locks in the golden story;
So shall you share all that he doth possess,
By having him, making yourself no less.

NURSE. No less! nay, bigger: women grow by men.

105   **LADY CAPULET.** Speak briefly, can you like of Paris' love?[28]

JULIET. I'll look to like, if looking liking move;
But no more deep will I endart[29] mine eye
Than your consent gives strength to make it fly.
Enter SERVINGMAN.

110   **SERVINGMAN.** Madam, the guests are come, supper serv'd up, you call'd, my young lady ask'd for, the nurse curs'd in the pantry,[30] and every thing in extremity. I must hence to wait; I beseech you follow straight.   *Exit.*

LADY CAPULET. We follow thee. Juliet, the County

115   stays.[31]

NURSE. Go, girl, seek happy nights to happy days.

                               Exeunt.

SCENE 4: IN FRONT OF CAPULET'S HOUSE

Enter ROMEO, MERCUTIO, BENVOLIO, *with five or six other* MASKERS;[1] TORCH-BEARERS.

ROMEO. What, shall this speech be spoke for our excuse?
Or shall we on without apology?

BENVOLIO. The date is out of such prolixity:[2]
We'll have no Cupid hoodwink'd with a scarf,[3]

5   Bearing a Tartar's painted bow of lath,[4]
Scaring the ladies like a crow-keeper,[5]
Nor no without-book prologue,[6] faintly spoke

---

28. **like of Paris' love.** Love someone like Paris
29. **endart.** Shoot like a dart
30. **the nurse . . . pantry.** The kitchen help are cursing because the nurse is not there to help.
31. **the County stays.** The Count (Paris) waits.

ACT 1, SCENE 4
1. **Maskers.** People wearing masks, dressed in costumes for the party
2. **The date . . . prolixity.** Such a speech, given by maskers arriving at a party, is out of fashion.
3. **Cupid hoodwink'd with a scarf.** Cupid was the Roman god of love, said to pierce lovers with his arrows. To be hoodwinked meant, literally, to be blindfolded with a scarf tied around the head.
4. **Bearing . . . lath.** Carrying, like Cupid or like a Tartar, a small bow of painted strips of wood
5. **crow-keeper.** Scarecrow
6. **without-book prologue.** Memorized introduction

After the prompter,[7] for our entrance;
But let them measure us by what they will,
10   We'll measure them a measure[8] and be gone.
      ROMEO.   Give me a torch, I am not for this ambling;[9]
Being but heavy, I will bear the light.
      MERCUTIO.   Nay, gentle Romeo, we must have you dance.
      ROMEO.   Not I, believe me. You have dancing shoes
15   With nimble soles, I have a soul of lead
So stakes me to the ground I cannot move.
      MERCUTIO.   You are a lover, borrow Cupid's wings,
And soar with them above a common bound.[10]
      ROMEO.   I am too sore enpierced with his shaft
20   To soar with his light feathers, and so bound
I cannot bound a pitch above dull woe;
Under love's heavy burthen[11] do I sink.
      MERCUTIO.   And, to sink in it, should you burthen love—
Too great oppression for a tender thing.
25   **ROMEO.**   Is love a tender thing? It is too rough,
Too rude, too boist'rous, and it pricks like thorn.
      MERCUTIO.   If love be rough with you, be rough with
          love;
Prick love for pricking, and you beat love down.
30   Give me a case to put my <u>visage</u> in, [*Puts on a mask.*]
A visor for a visor![12] what care I
What curious eye doth cote[13] deformities?
Here are the beetle brows[14] shall blush for me.
      BENVOLIO.   Come knock and enter, and no sooner in,
35   But every man betake him to his legs.[15]

---

7. **After the prompter.** Repeating lines given by a prompter, a person whose job it is to help an actor who has forgotten the lines
8. **measure them a measure.** Give them a dance
9. **Give me . . . ambling.** Romeo wishes to carry a torch because he wants to avoid ambling, or dancing, being too heavy-hearted for such frivolity.
10. **a common bound.** Ordinary leap as might be made by an ordinary, untalented dancer
11. **burthen.** Burden
12. **visor for a visor!** A visor is a mask. Mercutio is suggesting that his face is also a mask because he is a jester, one who hides his feelings behind his wit.
13. **cote.** See; notice
14. **beetle brows.** Bushy eyebrows
15. **betake him to his legs.** Begin dancing

words for everyday use

vis • age (viz´ij) *n.*, face. *Emily could tell from John's <u>visage</u> that he did not love her anymore.*

NOTE THE FACTS

What is Mercutio's attitude about Romeo's heavy heart?

_____

_____

_____

ASK A QUESTION

_____

_____

_____

_____

ROMEO. A torch for me. Let wantons light of heart
Tickle the senseless rushes[16] with their heels.
For I am proverb'd with a grandsire phrase,[17]
I'll be a candle-holder and look on:[18]

40   The game was ne'er so fair, and I am done.
MERCUTIO. Tut, dun's the mouse, the constable's own word.[19]
If thou art Dun, we'll draw thee from the mire
Of this sir-reverence love, wherein thou stickest

45   Up to the ears. Come, we burn daylight,[20] ho!
ROMEO. Nay, that's not so.
MERCUTIO.   I mean, sir, in delay
We waste our lights in vain, like lights by day!
Take our good meaning, for our judgment sits

50   Five times in that ere once in our five wits.
ROMEO. And we mean well in going to this mask,
But 'tis no wit to go.
MERCUTIO.   Why, may one ask?
ROMEO. I dreamt a dream tonight.

55   **MERCUTIO.**   And so did I.
ROMEO. Well, what was yours?
MERCUTIO.   That dreamers often lie.[21]
ROMEO. In bed asleep, while they do dream things true.
MERCUTIO. O then I see Queen Mab[22] hath been with

60   you.
She is the fairies' midwife, and she comes
In shape no bigger than an agot-stone[23]
On the forefinger of an alderman,
Drawn with a team of little atomi[24]

65   Over men's noses as they lie asleep.
Her chariot is an empty hazel-nut,
Made by the joiner squirrel or old grub,
Time out a' mind the fairies' coachmakers.

---

16. **rushes.** Plants used as a floor covering
17. **grandsire phrase.** Proverb, or phrase known to our grandfathers
18. **I'll be . . . look on.** Romeo recalls the proverb, "A good candle-holder or spectator makes a good gamester."
19. **dun's . . . word.** A mouse is dun—a dull, grayish brown. Romeo has just suggested that he will be an onlooker, which makes Mercutio think of a hidden, quiet mouse. A constable, or police officer, might describe a stealthy criminal in that way.
20. **burn daylight.** Waste time
21. **lie.** Mercutio puns on the word *lie*, implying both "rest" and "tell falsehoods."
22. **Queen Mab.** Fairy creature
23. **agot-stone.** Agate used as a stone in a ring
24. **atomi.** Tiny beings

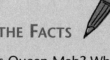

NOTE THE FACTS

Who is Queen Mab? What is she like? Read Mercutio's speech in lines 59–102. As you read, underline qualities of Queen Mab. Then summarize what you learn about her on the lines below.

_____

_____

_____

_____

_____

Her waggon-spokes made of long spinners' legs,
70   The cover of the wings of grasshoppers,
      Her traces of the smallest spider web,
      Her collars of the moonshine's wat'ry beams,
      Her whip of cricket's bone, the lash of film,
      Her waggoner a small grey-coated gnat,
75   Not half so big as a round little worm
      Prick'd from the lazy finger of a maid.[25]
      And in this state she gallops night by night
      Through lovers' brains, and then they dream of love;
      O'er <u>courtiers'</u> knees, that dream on cur'sies[26] straight;
80   O'er lawyers' fingers, who straight dream on fees;
      O'er ladies' lips, who straight on kisses dream,
      Which oft the angry Mab with blisters plagues,
      Because their breath with sweetmeats tainted are.
      Sometime she gallops o'er a courtier's nose,
85   And then dreams he of smelling out a suit;[27]
      And sometime comes she with a tithe-pig's[28] tail
      Tickling a parson's nose as 'a lies asleep,
      Then he dreams of another benefice.[29]
      Sometime she driveth o'er a soldier's neck,
90   And then dreams he of cutting foreign throats,
      Of breaches, ambuscadoes,[30] Spanish blades,
      Of healths five fadom deep;[31] and then anon[32]
      Drums in his ear, at which he starts and wakes,
      And being thus frighted, swears a prayer or two,
95   And sleeps again. This is that very Mab
      That plats the manes of horses in the night,
      And bakes the elf-locks in foul sluttish hairs,

---

25. **Not half . . . maid.** According to a folk belief, worms grew in the fingers
of lazy girls.
26. **on cur'sies.** Of curtsies, or bows
27. **smelling out a suit.** Thinking of something to request for oneself of a
high-born or noble person
28. **tithe-pig.** Pig given as payment of tithes, dues owed to a parish
29. **benefice.** Church office that provides a living for its holder
30. **breaches, ambuscadoes.** Breaching, or breaking
through fortifications; ambushes
31. **healths five fadom deep.** Drinks five fathoms deep. A fathom is a unit
of measure of water equal to six feet in depth.
32. **anon.** At once

words for everyday use

cour • ti • er (kôrt´ē ər) *n.,* attendant at a royal court. *The <u>courtier</u> lived at court and attended the king's entertainments.*

READ ALOUD

Read the lines in the highlighted box. What does Queen Mab do to lovers?

_____

_____

_____

Reading STRATEGY REVIEW

VISUALIZE. As you read, draw pictures in the margins that illustrate the details of Queen Mab and what she does to people as they dream.

Which, once untangled, much misfortune bodes.[33]
This is the hag, when maids lie on their backs,
100   That presses them and learns them first to bear,
Making them women of good carriage.[34]
This is she—
ROMEO.   Peace, peace, Mercutio, peace!
Thou talk'st of nothing.
105   **MERCUTIO.**   True, I talk of dreams,
Which are the children of an idle brain,
Begot of nothing but vain fantasy,
Which is as thin of substance as the air,
And more inconstant than the wind, who woos
110   Even now the frozen bosom of the north,
And, being anger'd, puffs away from thence,
Turning his side to the dew-dropping south.
BENVOLIO.   This wind you talk of blows us from
   ourselves:
115   Supper is done, and we shall come too late.
ROMEO.   I fear, too early, for my mind misgives
Some consequence yet hanging in the stars
Shall bitterly begin his fearful date
With this night's revels, and expire the term
120   Of a despised life clos'd in my breast
By some vile forfeit of untimely death.
But He that hath the steerage of my course
Direct my sail! On, lusty gentlemen!
BENVOLIO.   Strike, drum.

They march about the stage and stand to one side.

SCENE 5: A HALL IN CAPULET'S HOUSE

And SERVINGMEN *come forth with napkins.*

1. SERVINGMAN.   Where's Potpan, that he helps not to
take away? He shift a trencher?[1] he scrape a trencher?
2. SERVINGMAN.   When good manners shall lie all in one
or two men's hands, and they unwash'd too, 'tis a foul thing.

33. **bakes . . . bodes.** A folk belief was that elves matted the hair of lazy or
slovenly people and that to unmat this hair was to bring bad luck.
34. **good carriage.** Pun, one sense of which is "women who are carrying (babies)"

ACT 1, SCENE 5
1. **trencher.** Platter

FORESHADOWING.
Foreshadowing is the act of presenting materials that hint at events to occur later in a story. What is "hanging in the stars" in line 117? What does Romeo think is fated to happen? How does he respond to his fear about this?

MAKE PREDICTIONS. Based on the foreshadowing in lines 116–123, what do you predict will happen?

_____

_____

_____

_____

1. SERVINGMAN. Away with the join-stools,[2] remove the court-cupboard, look to the plate. Good thou, save me a piece of marchpane,[3] and, as thou loves me, let the porter let in Susan Grindstone and Nell. [*Exit Second Servant.*] Anthony and Potpan!

Enter ANTHONY *and* POTPAN.

ANTHONY. Ay, boy, ready.

1. SERVINGMAN. You are look'd for and call'd for, ask'd for and sought for, in the great chamber.

POTPAN. We cannot be here and there too. Cheerly, boys, be brisk a while, and the longer liver take all.

Exeunt.

Enter CAPULET, LADY CAPULET, JULIET, TYBALT, NURSE, SERVINGMEN, *and all the* GUESTS *and* GENTLEWOMEN *to the Maskers.*

CAPULET. Welcome, gentlemen! Ladies that have their toes
Unplagu'd with corns will walk a bout with you.
Ah, my mistresses, which of you all
Will now deny to dance? She that makes dainty,[4]
She I'll swear hath corns. Am I come near ye now?
Welcome, gentlemen! I have seen the day
That I have worn a visor and could tell
A whispering tale in a fair lady's ear,
Such as would please; 'tis gone, 'tis gone, 'tis gone.
You are welcome, gentlemen! Come, musicians, play.

Music plays, and they dance.

A hall, a hall! give room! and foot it, girls.
More light, you knaves, and turn the tables up;
And quench the fire, the room is grown too hot.
Ah, sirrah, this unlook'd-for sport comes well.
Nay, sit, nay, sit, good cousin Capulet,
For you and I are past our dancing days.
How long is't now since last yourself and I
Were in a mask?

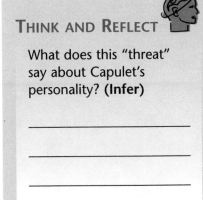

2. **join-stools.** Wooden stools, made by carpenters called joiners
3. **marchpane.** Marzipan, a type of candy
4. **makes dainty.** Behaves shyly by refusing to dance

Is Romeo speaking of
Rosaline here? How do
you know this?

_____

_____

_____

2. CAPULET.   By'r lady, thirty years.

35   **CAPULET.**   What, man? 'tis not so much, 'tis not so much:
'Tis since the <u>nuptial</u> of Lucentio,
Come Pentecost[5] as quickly as it will,
Some five and twenty years, and then we mask'd.

2. CAPULET.   'Tis more, 'tis more. His son is elder,[6] sir;

40   His son is thirty.

CAPULET.   Will you tell me that?
His son was but a ward two years ago.

ROMEO.   [*To a Servingman.*] What lady's that which doth
enrich the hand

45   Of yonder knight?

SERVINGMAN.   I know not, sir.

ROMEO.   O, she doth teach the torches to burn bright!
It seems she hangs upon the cheek of night
As a rich jewel in an Ethiop's[7] ear—

50   Beauty too rich for use, for earth too dear!
So shows a snowy dove trooping with crows,
As yonder lady o'er her fellows shows.
The measure done, I'll watch her place of stand,
And touching hers, make blessed my rude hand.

55   Did my heart love till now? Forswear it, sight!
For I ne'er saw true beauty till this night.

TYBALT.   This, by his voice, should be a Montague.
Fetch me my rapier, boy. What dares the slave
Come hither, cover'd with an antic face,

60   To fleer[8] and scorn at our solemnity?
Now, by the stock and honor of my kin,
To strike him dead I hold it not a sin.

CAPULET.   Why, how now, kinsman, wherefore storm you
so?

---

5. **Pentecost.** Christian festival on the seventh Sunday after Easter, marking
the descent of the Holy Spirit on the disciples after the resurrection of Jesus
  6. **elder.** Older
  7. **Ethiop's.** Of a person from Ethiopia, a country in Africa
  8. **fleer.** Mock

**words
for
everyday
use**   nup • tial (nup´shəl) *n.,* wedding; marriage (usu. used in plural). *The couple's
nuptials were to be held in the bride's hometown.*

65 **TYBALT.** Uncle, this is a Montague, our foe;
A villain that is hither come in spite
To scorn at our solemnity this night.
CAPULET. Young Romeo is it?
TYBALT. 'Tis he, that villain Romeo.
70 **CAPULET.** Content thee, gentle coz, let him alone,
'A bears him like a portly gentleman;[9]
And to say truth, Verona brags of him
To be a virtuous and well-govern'd youth.
I would not for the wealth of all this town
75 Here in my house do him disparagement;
Therefore be patient, take no note of him;
It is my will, the which if thou respect,
Show a fair presence and put off these frowns,
An ill-beseeming semblance for a feast.
80 **TYBALT.** It fits when such a villain is a guest.
I'll not endure him.
CAPULET. He shall be endured.
What, goodman boy?[10] I say he shall, go to!
Am I the master here, or you? go to!
85 You'll not endure him! God shall mend my soul,
You'll make a mutiny among my guests!
You will set cock-a-hoop![11] you'll be the man!
TYBALT. Why, uncle, 'tis a shame.
CAPULET. Go to, go to,
90 You are a saucy boy. Is't so indeed?
This trick may chance to scath you,[12] I know what.
You must contrary me![13] Marry, 'tis time.—
Well said, my hearts!—You are a princox,[14] go,
Be quiet, or—More light, more light!—For shame,
95 I'll make you quiet, what!—Cheerly, my hearts!

TYBALT. Patience perforce with willful choler meeting
Makes my flesh tremble in their different greeting.
I will withdraw, but this intrusion shall,
Now seeming sweet, convert to bitt'rest gall.[15]

Exit.

---

9. **portly gentleman.** Well-mannered nobleman
10. **goodman boy.** The term *goodman* was used to address non-nobles.
Goodman boy is an insult because Tybalt is being called both common and a boy.
11. **set cock-a-hoop.** Act wildly
12. **trick . . . you.** Behavior will hurt you
13. **contrary me.** Go contrary to me, or contradict me
14. **princox.** Sassy boy
15. **gall.** Something bitter to endure

NOTE THE FACTS

How does Capulet feel about Romeo's presence at the feast?

_____

_____

_____

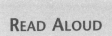

READ ALOUD

Read aloud Tybalt's lines in the highlighted box. What does Tybalt plan to do?

_____

_____

_____

100   **ROMEO.**   [_To Juliet._] If I profane with my unworthiest hand

This holy shrine, the gentle sin[16] is this,

My lips, two blushing pilgrims, ready stand

To smooth that rough touch with a tender kiss.

105   **JULIET.**   Good pilgrim, you do wrong your hand too much,

Which mannerly devotion shows in this:

For saints have hands that pilgrims' hands do touch,

And palm to palm is holy palmers'[17] kiss.

110   **ROMEO.**   Have not saints lips, and holy palmers too?

JULIET.   Ay, pilgrim, lips that they must use in pray'r.

ROMEO.   O then, dear saint, let lips do what hands do,

They pray—grant thou, lest faith turn to despair.

JULIET.   Saints do not move, though grant for prayers'

115   sake.

ROMEO.   Then move not while my prayer's effect I take.

Thus from my lips, by thine, my sin is purg'd.

Kissing her.

JULIET.   Then have my lips the sin that they have took.

ROMEO.   Sin from my lips? O trespass sweetly urg'd!

120   Give me my sin again.

Kissing her again.

JULIET.   You kiss by th' book.

NURSE.   Madam, your mother craves a word with you.

ROMEO.   What is her mother?

NURSE.   Marry, bachelor,

125   Her mother is the lady of the house,

And a good lady, and a wise and virtuous.

I nurs'd her daughter that you talk'd withal;[18]

I tell you, he that can lay hold of her

Shall have the chinks.[19]

130   **ROMEO.**   Is she a Capulet?

O dear account! my life is my foe's debt.[20]

BENVOLIO.   Away, be gone, the sport is at the best.[21]

ROMEO.   Ay, so I fear, the more is my unrest.

NOTE THE FACTS

How does Romeo find out Juliet's identity? What does he think when he learns she is a Capulet?

_____

_____

_____

_____

_____

---

16. **sin.** Fine or penalty
17. **palmers'.** Of pilgrims
18. **withal.** With
19. **chinks.** Money
20. **my foe's debt.** Owed to my enemy; in that enemy's power
21. **sport . . . best.** Benvolio cautions Romeo to quit while he is ahead.

CAPULET.   Nay, gentlemen, prepare not to be gone,

135   We have a trifling foolish banquet towards.[22]

They whisper in his ear.

Is it e'en so? Why then I thank you all.

I thank you, honest gentlemen, good night.

More torches here! Come on, then let's to bed.

140   [*To Second Capulet.*] Ah, sirrah, by my fay,[23] it waxes late,

I'll to my rest.   *Exeunt all but* JULIET *and* NURSE.

JULIET.   Come hither, nurse. What is yond gentleman?

NURSE.   The son and heir of old Tiberio.

JULIET.   What's he that now is going out of door?

NURSE.   Marry, that, I think, be young Petruchio.

145   **JULIET.**   What's he that follows here, that would not

dance?

NURSE.   I know not.

JULIET.   Go ask his name.—If he be married,

My grave is like to be my wedding-bed.

150   **NURSE.**   His name is Romeo, and a Montague,

The only son of your great enemy.

JULIET.   My only love sprung from my only hate!

Too early seen unknown, and known too late!

Prodigious[24] birth of love it is to me

155   That I must love a loathed enemy.

NURSE.   What's tis? what's tis!

JULIET.   A rhyme I learnt even now

Of one I danc'd withal.   *One calls within,* "Juliet!"

NURSE.   Anon, anon!

160   Come let's away, the strangers all are gone.

Exeunt.

---

22. **towards.** Coming
23. **fay.** Faith
24. **Prodigious.** Ominous

READ ALOUD

With another person, read the highlighted dialogue of Juliet and the Nurse. How does Juliet learn Romeo's identity without letting the Nurse know of her interest? What is her response when she finds that Romeo is a Montague?

_____

_____

_____

_____

_____

Use THE STRATEGY

WRITE THINGS DOWN. Take time now to summarize the events in act 1 in your Summarize Sections Chart.

After Reading ➤ SUMMARIZE PARTS OF THE PLOT

Take time to finish your chart, summarizing each of the five scenes in act 1. Work with your group to clear up any confusion. Read aloud sections you are unsure about and answer the questions in the margins. Then work in your group to answer the Investigate, Inquire, and Imagine and Literary Tools questions below.

Investigate, Inquire, and Imagine

RECALL: GATHER FACTS ➤ INTERPRET: FIND MEANING

1a. When Prince Escalus arrives at the beginning of the play, what does he break up? What does the prince say will happen if the peace of Verona is disturbed again in this way?

1b. What "ancient grudge" is referred to in line 3 of the prologue? Who has a grudge against whom? What have been the consequences of this grudge, or feud, for the city of Verona? Why is the prince so upset in scene 1?

ANALYZE: TAKE THINGS APART ➤ SYNTHESIZE: BRING THINGS TOGETHER

2a. What are Romeo's words and impressions when he sees Juliet for the first time? What is Juliet's first reaction to seeing Romeo? What mixed feelings do they have about each other at the end of act 1?

2b. What do the emotions Romeo and Juliet experience tell you about the two main characters? What struggle or conflict do you foresee for the two?

EVALUATE: MAKE JUDGMENTS ➤ EXTEND: CONNECT IDEAS

3a. Evaluate the effectiveness of Lady Capulet in convincing Juliet to love Paris. What factors are most important to Juliet in considering Paris as a husband? What is more important: for Juliet to be a dutiful daughter or to follow her heart?

3b. What do you think of the idea of arranged marriages? Why do you think this practice was used among noble families, and why might it still be used in some cultures today? What would you do if your parents told you whom to date or marry?

Literary Tools

FORESHADOWING. **Foreshadowing** is the act of presenting materials that hint at events to occur later in a story. What does Romeo see "hanging in the stars" in act 1, scene 4, lines 126–123? What does he think is fated to happen? Examine the dialogue between Capulet and Tybalt in act 1, scene 5, lines 96–99. What information from Tybalt adds to this foreshadowing? Consider that the Chorus refers to Romeo and Juliet as "star-cross'd lovers" in the prologue. What do you predict will happen later in the play?

ACT 2

Enter CHORUS.

Now old desire doth in his death-bed lie,
And young affection gapes[1] to be his heir;
That fair[2] for which love groan'd for and would die,
With tender Juliet match'd[3] is now not fair.

5 Now Romeo is belov'd and loves again,[4]
Alike[5] bewitched by the charm of looks;
But to his foe suppos'd he must complain,[6]
And she steal love's sweet bait from fearful[7] hooks.
Being held a foe, he may not have access

10 To breathe such vows as lovers use to[8] swear,
And she as much in love, her means much less
To meet her new-beloved any where.
But passion lends them power, time means, to meet,
Temp'ring[9] extremities[10] with extreme sweet.

Exit.

SCENE 1: CAPULET'S ORCHARD

Enter ROMEO *alone.*

ROMEO.   Can I go forward when my heart is here?
Turn back, dull earth,[11] and find thy center[12] out.
Enter BENVOLIO *with* MERCUTIO. ROMEO *withdraws.*
BENVOLIO.   Romeo! my cousin Romeo! Romeo!
MERCUTIO.   He is wise,

5 And, on my life, hath stol'n him home to bed.
BENVOLIO.   He ran this way and leapt this orchard[13] wall.
Call, good Mercutio.
MERCUTIO.   Nay, I'll conjure[14] too.

PROLOGUE / ACT 2, SCENE 1
1. **gapes.** Desires
2. **fair.** Beauty
3. **match'd.** Compared
4. **loves again.** Loves back
5. **Alike.** Both
6. **complain.** Speak (of his love)
7. **fearful.** Dangerous
8. **use to.** Usually
9. **Temp'ring.** Lessening or making bearable
10. **extremities.** Difficulties
11. **dull earth.** The body, made of earth
12. **center.** Romeo is saying that Juliet is the center of his life. He turns
back to her as things on Earth fall toward its center.
13. **orchard.** Garden
14. **conjure.** Cause a spirit to appear

NOTE THE FACTS

What has now happened for Romeo and Juliet?

_____

_____

_____

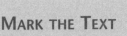

MARK THE TEXT

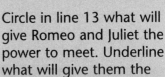

Circle in line 13 what will give Romeo and Juliet the power to meet. Underline what will give them the means.

Romeo! humors! madman! passion! lover!
10   Appear thou in the likeness of a sigh!
Speak but one rhyme, and I am satisfied;
Cry but "Ay me!", pronounce but "love" and "dove,"
Speak to my gossip[15] Venus one fair word,
One nickname for her purblind[16] son and heir,
15   Young Abraham[17] Cupid he that shot so trim,[18]
When King Cophetua lov'd the beggar-maid![19]
He heareth not, he stirreth not, he moveth not,
The ape is dead, and I must conjure him.
I conjure thee by Rosaline's bright eyes,
20   By her high forehead and her scarlet lip,
By her fine foot, straight leg, and quivering thigh,
And the demesnes[20] that there <u>adjacent</u> lie,
That in thy likeness thou appear to us!
BENVOLIO.   And if[21] he hear thee, thou wilt anger him.
25   **MERCUTIO.**   This cannot anger him; 'twould anger him
To raise a spirit in his mistress' circle,[22]
Of some strange nature, letting it there stand
Till she had laid it and conjur'd it down.
That were some spite.[23] My <u>invocation</u>
30   Is fair and honest; in his mistress' name
I conjure only but to raise up him.
BENVOLIO.   Come, he hath hid himself among these trees
To be consorted with the humorous[24] night.
Blind is his love and best befits the dark.
35   **MERCUTIO.**   If love be blind, love cannot hit the mark.
Now will he sit under a medlar[25] tree,

NOTE THE FACTS

Whom does Mercutio think Romeo still loves?

_____

_____

_____

---

15. **gossip.** Busybody or crone
16. **purblind.** Weak-sighted
17. **Abraham.** Beggar
18. **trim.** Precisely; accurately
19. **King . . . maid.** Love story from a popular ballad
20. **demesnes.** Regions
21. **And if.** If
22. **To raise . . . circle.** To call up a spirit as in a seance
23. **spite.** Vexation
24. **consorted . . . humorous.** In harmony with the wet or mood-provoking
25. **medlar.** Fruit

words for everyday use	
ad • ja • cent (ə jā´sənt) *adj.*, near or close to something. *The administrative office is <u>adjacent</u> to the guidance office.*
in • vo • ca • tion (in´və kā´shən) *n.*, act of calling on a god for blessing or inspiration. *After the <u>invocation</u>, the valedictorian gave her speech.*

And wish his mistress were that kind of fruit
As maids call medlars, when they laugh alone.
O, Romeo, that she were, O that she were
40 An open-arse,[26] thou a pop'rin pear![27]
Romeo, good night, I'll to my truckle-bed,[28]
This field-bed is too cold for me to sleep.
Come, shall we go?

BENVOLIO. Go then, for 'tis in vain
45 To seek him here that means not to be found.

Exit with MERCUTIO.

SCENE 2: CAPULET'S ORCHARD

ROMEO *advances.*

ROMEO. He jests at scars that never felt a wound.

Enter JULIET *above at her window.*

ROMEO. But soft, what light through yonder window
breaks?
It is the east, and Juliet is the sun.
5 Arise, fair sun, and kill the envious moon,
Who is already sick and pale with grief
That thou, her maid, art far more fair than she.
Be not her maid,[1] since she is envious;
Her vestal livery[2] is but sick and green,
10 And none but fools do wear it; cast it off.
It is my lady, O, it is my love!
O that she knew she were!
She speaks, yet she says nothing; what of that?
Her eye <u>discourses</u>, I will answer it.

---

26. **open-arse.** Another name for the medlar fruit
27. **pop'rin pear.** Kind of fruit
28. **truckle-bed.** Small bed that fits under a larger bed

ACT 2, SCENE 2
1. **maid.** Servant
2. **vestal livery.** Uniform belonging to a servant of Vestia, the virgin Roman goddess

words for everyday use

dis • course (dis kôrs´) *vi.*, express oneself. *The speaker <u>discoursed</u> on the problems of managed health care.*

Use THE STRATEGY

WRITE THINGS DOWN. Take time now to summarize the events in act 2, scene 1 in your Summarize Sections Chart.

Literary TOOLS

METAPHOR. A **metaphor** is a figure of speech in which one thing is spoken or written about as if it were another. Circle the object that Romeo calls Juliet in line 4.

THINK AND REFLECT

Read aloud the highlighted text on this page. What does Romeo wish that Juliet knew?

_____

_____

_____

Literary TOOLS

SOLILOQUY. A **soliloquy** is a speech delivered by a lone character that reveals the speaker's thoughts and feelings. The screened text on lines 2–26 marks the first long soliloquy in the play. What does this soliloquy reveal about Romeo's thoughts?

_____

_____

_____

SIMILE. A **simile** is a comparison using *like* or *as*. What does Romeo say Juliet is as glorious as in lines 31–39? To what does he compare her?

_____

_____

_____

NOTE THE FACTS

When Juliet speaks, the word "wherefrom" means "why." What is Juliet's dilemma? Does she know that she is not alone? How do you know this, considering what Romeo says in lines 40 and 41?

_____

_____

_____

_____

15 I am too bold, 'tis not to me she speaks.
    Two of the fairest stars in all the heaven,
    Having some business, do entreat her eyes
    To twinkle in their spheres[3] till they return.
    What if her eyes were there, they in her head?
20 The brightness of her cheek would shame those stars,
    As daylight doth a lamp; her eyes in heaven
    Would through the airy region stream[4] so bright
    That birds would sing and think it were not night.
    See how she leans her cheek upon her hand!
25 O that I were a glove upon that hand,
    That I might touch that cheek!

JULIET.   Ay me!

ROMEO.   She speaks!
    O, speak again, bright angel, for thou art
30 As glorious to this night, being o'er my head,
    As is a winged messenger of heaven
    Unto the white-upturned[5] wond'ring eyes
    Of mortals that fall back to gaze on him,
    When he bestrides the lazy puffing clouds,
35 And sails upon the bosom of the air.

JULIET. O Romeo, Romeo, wherefore art thou Romeo?
    Deny thy father and refuse thy name;
    Or, if thou wilt not, be but sworn my love,
    And I'll no longer be a Capulet.

40 **ROMEO.** [*Aside.*] Shall I hear more, or shall I speak at
        this?

    JULIET.   'Tis but thy name that is my enemy;
    Thou art thyself, though not a Montague.[6]
    What's Montague? It is nor hand nor foot,
45 Nor arm nor face, nor any other part
    Belonging to a man. O, be some other name!
    What's in a name? That which we call a rose
    By any other word would smell as sweet;
    So Romeo would, were he not Romeo call'd,
50 Retain that dear perfection which he owes[7]
    Without that title. Romeo, doff thy name,

---

3. **spheres.** Places in the heavens
4. **stream.** Shine
5. **white-upturned.** When the eyes look up, more of the whites of them show.
6. **Thou . . . Montague.** If you were to change your name, it would not change who you are.
7. **owes.** Owns; has

And for[8] thy name, which is no part of thee,
Take all myself.

ROMEO.   I take thee at thy word.
55   Call me but love, and I'll be new baptiz'd;
Henceforth I never will be Romeo.

JULIET.   What man art thou that thus bescreen'd in night
So stumblest on my counsel?[9]

ROMEO.   By a name
60   I know not how to tell thee who I am.
My name, dear saint, is hateful to myself,
Because it is an enemy to thee;
Had I it written, I would tear the word.

JULIET.   My ears have yet not drunk a hundred words
65   Of thy tongue's uttering, yet I know the sound.
Art thou not Romeo, and a Montague?

ROMEO.   Neither, fair maid, if either thee dislike.

JULIET.   How camest thou hither, tell me, and wherefore?
The orchard walls are high and hard to climb,
70   And the place death, considering who thou art,
If any of my kinsmen find thee here.

ROMEO.   With love's light wings did I o'erperch[10] these
walls,
For stony limits cannot hold love out,
75   And what love can do, that dares love attempt;
Therefore thy kinsmen are no stop to me.

JULIET.   If they do see thee, they will murther[11] thee.

ROMEO.   Alack, there lies more peril in thine eye
Than twenty of their swords! Look thou but sweet,
80   And I am proof[12] against their enmity.

JULIET.   I would not for the world they saw thee here.

ROMEO.   I have night's cloak to hide me from their eyes,
And but thou love me,[13] let them find me here;

NOTE THE FACTS

For what reward would Romeo reject his name?

_____

_____

_____

READ ALOUD

Assign the parts of Romeo and Juliet to yourself and a partner. Read aloud the highlighted text on this page. What holds more peril for Romeo than the hatred of Juliet's kinsman? What does he mean by this?

_____

_____

_____

_____

_____

---

8. **for.** In payment for
9. **counsel.** Meditations; private musings
10. **o'erperch.** Fly over
11. **murther.** Murder
12. **proof.** Protected
13. **And but thou love me.** If you do not love me

words for everyday use

en • mi • ty (en′mə tē) *n.,* hostility; antagonism. *The <u>enmity</u> between the Hatfields and McCoys resulted in endless feuds.*

Read in Shorter Chunks and Retell
If you have trouble understanding what Romeo means here, read aloud the highlighted text on this page. Then take the lines one sentence at a time and retell them in your own words. Use the footnote for help with the last three lines.

_____

_____

_____

_____

NOTE THE FACTS

What makes Juliet worry? What kinds of doubts does she have?

_____

_____

_____

My life were better ended by their hate,

85   Than death prorogued,[14] wanting of[15] thy love.

JULIET.   By whose direction foundst thou out this place?[16]

ROMEO.   By love, that first did prompt me to inquire;

He lent me counsel, and I lent him eyes.

I am no pilot, yet, wert thou as far

90   As that vast shore wash'd with the farthest sea,

I should adventure for such merchandise.[17]

JULIET.   Thou knowest the mask of night is on my face,

Else would a maiden blush bepaint my cheek

For that which thou hast heard me speak tonight.

95   Fain[18] would I dwell on form,[19] fain deny

What I have spoke, but farewell compliment![20]

Dost thou love me? I know thou wilt say, "Ay,"

And I will take thy word; yet, if thou swear'st,

Thou mayest prove false: at lovers' perjuries

100   They say Jove laughs. O gentle Romeo,

If thou dost love, pronounce it faithfully,

Or if thou thinkest I am too quickly won,

I'll frown and be perverse, and say thee nay,

So thou wilt[21] woo, but else not for the world.

105   In truth, fair Montague, I am too fond,[22]

And therefore thou mayest think my behavior light,

But trust me, gentleman, I'll prove more true

Than those that have more coying[23] to be strange.[24]

I should have been more strange, I must confess,

110   But that thou overheardst, ere I was ware,

My true-love passion; therefore pardon me,

And not <u>impute</u> this yielding to light love,

---

14. **prorogued.** Postponed
15. **wanting of.** Lacking
16. **By whose . . . place?** Who gave you directions to this place?
17. **I am . . . merchandise.** Romeo compares his willingness to work for her love to the willingness of sailors to risk dangerous voyages.
18. **Fain.** Gladly
19. **dwell on form.** Act formally
20. **compliment.** Etiquette, social graces
21. **So thou wilt.** So that you will
22. **fond.** Silly
23. **coying.** Coyness; skill at coquetry
24. **strange.** Distant; standoffish

words for everyday use

im • pute (im pyo͞ot´) vt., attribute. *I* _impute_ *the pains in my hands to the damp weather.*

Which the dark night hath so discovered.[25]

ROMEO.   Lady, by yonder blessed moon I vow,

115   That tips with silver all these fruit-tree tops—

JULIET.   O, swear not by the moon, th' <u>inconstant</u> moon,

That monthly changes in her circled orb,[26]

Lest that thy love prove likewise variable.[27]

ROMEO.   What shall I swear by?

120   **JULIET.**   Do not swear at all;

Or if thou wilt, swear by thy gracious self,

Which is the god of my <u>idolatry</u>,

And I'll believe thee.

ROMEO.   If my heart's dear love—

125   **JULIET.**   Well, do not swear. Although I joy in thee,

I have no joy of this contract tonight,

It is too rash, too unadvis'd, too sudden,

Too like the lightning, which doth cease to be

Ere one can say it lightens. Sweet, good night!

130   This bud of love, by summer's ripening breath,

May prove a beauteous flow'r when next we meet.

Good night, good night! as sweet <u>repose</u> and rest

Come to thy heart as that within my breast!

ROMEO.   O, wilt thou leave me so unsatisfied?

135   **JULIET.**   What satisfaction canst thou have tonight?

ROMEO.   Th' exchange of thy love's faithful vow for mine.

JULIET.   I gave thee mine before thou didst request it;

And yet I would it were to give again.

ROMEO.   Wouldst thou withdraw it? for what purpose,

140   love?

JULIET.   But to be frank[28] and give it thee again,

And yet I wish but for the thing I have.

---

25. **discovered.** Shown
26. **circled orb.** Orbit
27. **Lest . . . variable.** Because of its changes, the moon is a traditional symbol of
inconsistency, or fickleness.
28. **frank.** Generous

words for everyday use	**in • con • stant** (in kän´stənt) *adj.,* not remaining firm in mind or purpose. *Due to Emily's <u>inconstant</u> demands, Jeremiah did not know how to make her happy.*
	i • dol • a • try (ī däl´ə trē) *n.,* excessive devotion or reverence. *Jen's CD and poster collections demonstrate her <u>idolatry</u> of the rock star.*
	re • pose (ri pōz´) *n.,* rest; sleep. *Jeff's <u>repose</u> was interrupted by the doorbell, and he woke up.*

NOTE THE FACTS

What does Romeo swear by in line 114? What is Juliet's response?

_____

_____

_____

MARK THE TEXT

Underline or highlight the passage that tells how Juliet feels about their newly confessed love, which she calls "this contract tonight."

My <u>bounty</u> is as boundless as the sea,
My love as deep; the more I give to thee,
145 The more I have, for both are infinite.

NURSE calls within.

I hear some noise within; dear love, adieu!
Anon,[29] good nurse! Sweet Montague, be true.
Stay but a little, I will come again.   *Exit above.*
ROMEO. O blessed, blessed night! I am afeard,
150 Being in night, all this is but a dream,
Too flattering-sweet to be <u>substantial</u>.

Enter JULIET above.

JULIET. Three words, dear Romeo, and good night indeed.
If that thy bent of love[30] be honorable,
155 Thy purpose marriage, send me word tomorrow,
By one that I'll <u>procure</u> to come to thee,
Where and what time thou wilt perform the rite,
And all my fortunes at thy foot I'll lay,
And follow thee my lord throughout the world.

160 **NURSE.** [*Within.*] Madam!
JULIET. I come, anon.—But if thou meanest not well,
I do beseech thee—
NURSE. [*Within.*] Madam!
JULIET.   By and by,[31] I come—
165 To cease thy strife,[32] and leave me to my grief.
Tomorrow will I send.
ROMEO.   So thrive my soul—
JULIET. A thousand times good night!   *Exit above.*
ROMEO. A thousand times the worse, to want thy light.
170 Love goes toward love as schoolboys from their books,
But love from love, toward school with heavy looks.

Retiring.

---

29. **Anon.** Now, at once
30. **thy . . . love.** The purpose or inclination of your love
31. **By and by.** Now, at this moment
32. **strife.** Striving; endeavor. Other texts use the word "suit" here.

READ ALOUD

Read aloud the highlighted text on this page. What message does Juliet want Romeo to send her?

_____

_____

_____

WHAT DO YOU WONDER?

_____

_____

_____

words for everyday use

boun • ty (boun´tē) *n.*, something given freely; generous gift. *The Indians' <u>bounty</u> helped the Puritans to survive their first winter in America.*

sub • stan • tial (səb stan´shəl) *adj.*, real; actual; true. *The investigator found <u>substantial</u> verification of his client's claims.*

pro • cure (prō kyoor´) *vt.*, get or bring about by some effort. *Janet <u>procured</u> a backstage pass for the Rolling Stones concert.*

Enter JULIET *again above.*

JULIET. Hist,[33] Romeo, hist! O, for a falc'ner's voice,
To lure this tassel-gentle[34] back again!
Bondage is hoarse, and may not speak aloud,

175 Else would I tear the cave where Echo lies,
And make her airy tongue more hoarse than mine,
With repetition of my Romeo's name. Romeo!
ROMEO. It is my soul that calls upon my name.
How silver-sweet sound lovers' tongues by night,

180 Like softest music to attending ears!
JULIET. Romeo!
ROMEO. My niesse?[35]
JULIET. What a' clock tomorrow
Shall I send to thee?

185 **ROMEO.** By the hour of nine.
JULIET. I will not fail, 'tis twenty year till then.
I have forgot why I did call thee back.
ROMEO. Let me stand here till thou remember it.
JULIET. I shall forget, to have thee still[36] stand there,

190 Rememb'ring how I love thy company.
ROMEO. And I'll still stay, to have thee still forget,
Forgetting any other home but this.
JULIET. 'Tis almost morning, I would have thee gone—
And yet no farther than a wanton's bird,

195 That lets it hop a little from his hand,
Like a poor prisoner in his twisted gyves,[37]
And with a silken thread plucks it back again,
So loving-jealous of his liberty.
ROMEO. I would I were thy bird.

200 **JULIET.** Sweet, so would I,
Yet I should kill thee with much cherishing.
Good night, good night! Parting is such sweet sorrow
That I shall say good night till it be morrow.

Exit above.

---

33. **Hist.** Falconer's call
34. **tassel-gentle.** Male falcon of a type reserved for princes
35. **niesse.** Nestling hawk
36. **still.** Always
37. **gyves.** Chains around ankles

EXTENDED METAPHOR. An **extended metaphor** is a point-by-point presentation of one thing as if it were another. This page is filled with images related to falcons, birds of prey. Juliet begins using this metaphor by calling Romeo her "tassel-gentle," a type of male falcon. Underline the falcon imagery that you find on this page. What bird does Romeo wish he were (line 199)? What does Juliet say in line 201 that she would do if he were this bird?

_____

_____

_____

_____

_____

THINK AND REFLECT

How do Romeo and Juliet feel about one another, as revealed in the balcony scene? What does each hope? What does each fear? (**Summarize**)

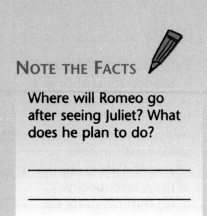

Where will Romeo go after seeing Juliet? What does he plan to do?

_____

_____

_____

ROMEO. Sleep dwell upon thine eyes, peace in thy breast!

205 Would I were sleep and peace, so sweet to rest!

Hence will I to my ghostly sire's close cell,[38]

His help to crave, and my dear hap[39] to tell.

Exit.

---

38. **ghostly sire's close cell.** Priest's (or confessor's) secluded room
39. **hap.** Fortune

Reflect ON YOUR READING

After you finish reading, complete your Summarize Sections Chart, including the first two scenes of act 2. What is the main conflict Romeo and Juliet will need to resolve? Discuss this, as well as what you predict will happen to them.

Reading Skills and Test Practice

IDENTIFY SEQUENCE OF EVENTS
Discuss with your group how best to answer the following questions about sequence of events.

1. Read the following list of events.
   a. Juliet tells Romeo their love is too rash and sudden.
   b. Juliet, wanting to please her mother, agrees to consider marrying Paris.
   c. Juliet asks Romeo to tell her the next day if and when he will marry her.
   d. Juliet worries that Romeo will think her too easily won.

   Which of the following reflects the correct sequence of events as Juliet experiences them?
   a. b, a, c, d
   b. a, b, d, c
   c. b, a, d, c
   d. b, c, a, d

What is the correct answer to the question above? How were you able to eliminate the other answers? How did your use of the reading strategy help you answer the question?

_____

_____

2. When does Romeo lose his interest in Rosaline?
   a. after Benvolio tells him to stay away from those who cannot love him in return
   b. when Rosaline tells him she wants to be like the goddess Diana
   c. as soon as he sees Juliet at Capulet's party
   d. when he hears Juliet on her balcony say that she loves Romeo and wishes he weren't a Montague

What is the correct answer to the question above? How were you able to eliminate the other answers? How did your use of the reading strategy help you answer the question?

_____

_____

THINK-ALOUD NOTES

_____

_____

_____

_____

_____

_____

_____

_____

_____

_____

_____

Investigate, Inquire, and Imagine

RECALL: GATHER FACTS
1a. What does Juliet say about the name Montague in the balcony scene? How does Romeo respond?

INTERPRET: FIND MEANING
1b. What problem lies in the path of the two lovers? What is Romeo ready to renounce in exchange for Juliet's love?

ANALYZE: TAKE THINGS APART
2a. Analyze Juliet's statements about marriage and love, starting from act 1, scene 3, in which Lady Capulet asks her how she feels about marriage, through act 2, scene 2, in which Juliet speaks to Romeo from her balcony. How do Juliet's feelings change? Who first mentions the subject of marriage, Romeo or Juliet?

SYNTHESIZE: BRING THINGS TOGETHER
2b. What conclusions about Juliet's character do you draw from her response?

EVALUATE: MAKE JUDGMENTS
3a. In what time of year and of day does the balcony scene take place? What do the two lovers both know at the end of the scene? Do you think their feelings will change once they have thought things over in the more rational light of day? Why, or why not?

EXTEND: CONNECT IDEAS
3b. After Romeo tells Juliet goodnight, he will go to Friar Lawrence to discuss marriage. What advice would you give to Romeo and Juliet? How much should they tell their parents about their newfound love? How carefully should they proceed in getting married?

Literary Tools

PLOT, EXPOSITION, CENTRAL CONFLICT, AND INCITING INCIDENT. A **plot** is a series of events related to a **central conflict**, or struggle, in a play or story. A typical plot involves the introduction of a conflict, its development, and its eventual resolution. The **exposition** sets the tone or mood, introduces the characters and the setting, and provides necessary background information. The **inciting incident** is the event that introduces the central conflict.

The opening acts of *Romeo and Juliet* establish the exposition, inciting incident, and central conflict. Review your Summarize Sections Chart and circle the key information and events. What important information and theme does the exposition provide? What inciting incident is introduced at the end of act 1? What is the central conflict of the play?

_____

_____

_____

WordWorkshop

OXYMORONS. In the act 1 Literary Tools on page 305, you were asked to list any oxymorons you found. An **oxymoron** is a statement that contradicts itself. Words and phrases like *cruel kindness, bittersweet* and *tragicomedy* are oxymorons that develop a complex meaning from two seemingly contradictory elements. Romeo uses several oxymorons in act 1, scene 1, including *brawling love* and *loving hate.* Add an adjective to each of the vocabulary words below to create an oxymoron. Then use the phrase in a sentence.

1. adversary _____

2. mutiny _____

3. transgression _____

4. fray _____

5. devout _____

Read-Write Connection

Do you think it is more important to respond to true love or to follow your parents' wishes? Why?

_____

_____

_____

_____

_____

_____

_____

Beyond the Reading

READ MORE OF THE PLAY. Get a copy of the complete play of *Romeo and Juliet* from your teacher or a library and finish reading it. Before you start, review the cast of characters at the beginning of act 1 and predict what will happen to each person. What will become of Romeo and Juliet? What will happen when their families find out about their secret love? When you are finished reading the play, go back and see if your predictions came true.

GO ONLINE. Visit the EMC Internet Resource Center at **emcp.com** to find links and additional activities for this selection.

Reader's resource

A screenplay is a drama written for television or film. **"The Monsters Are Due on Maple Street"** is a screenplay written for an episode of the *Twilight Zone*, one of the most watched series in the history of television. Most *Twilight Zone* teleplays combined science fiction or fantasy elements with biting social criticism and satire. In the teleplay you are about to read, dramatic events challenge the characters, causing them to reveal their true selves.

Word watch

PREVIEW VOCABULARY

all-pervading	intimidate
contorted	materialize
converge	metamor-
defiantly	phosis
idiosyncrasy	morass
incisive	reflective
incriminate	revelation
inexplicably	transfixed
instill	validity
intersperse	

Reader's journal

Have you ever wanted to participate in group behavior you knew to be wrong? What were your motivations for wanting to join in?

_____

_____

_____

"The Monsters Are Due on Maple Street"

by Rod Serling

Active READING STRATEGY

WRITE THINGS DOWN

Before Reading ➤ PREVIEW THE SELECTION

❑ Read the Reader's Resource and skim the selection, familiarizing yourself with the Words for Everyday Use and the footnoted words and phrases.
❑ Read over the list of characters, and notice where the screenplay is divided into two acts.
❑ As you read the play, fill in the Motivation Chart below.

Graphic Organizer

Character	Reason for Accusation
Les Goodman	
Steve Brand	
Charlie	
Tommy	
Bob Weaver	His house lights flicked off and on.
Don Martin	

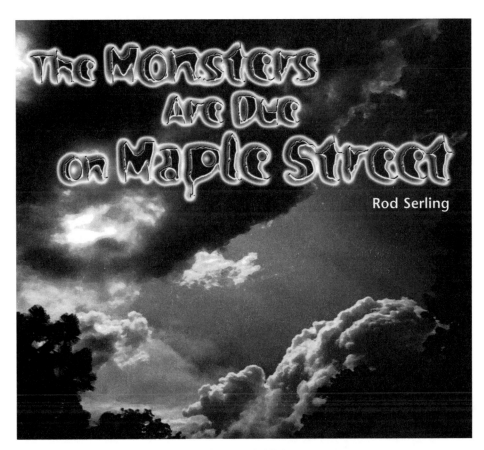

The Monsters Are Due on Maple Street

Rod Serling

ACT I

Fade in on a shot of the night sky. The various nebulae[1] and planet bodies stand out in sharp, sparkling relief, and the camera begins a slow pan across the Heavens.

NARRATOR'S VOICE. There is a fifth dimension[2] beyond that which is known to man. It is a dimension as vast as space, and as timeless as infinity. It is the middle ground between light and shadow—between science and superstition. And it lies between the pit of man's fears and the summit of his knowledge. This is the dimension of imagination. It is an area which we call The Twilight Zone.

10

The camera has begun to pan down until it passes the horizon and is on a sign which reads "Maple Street." Pan down until we are shooting down at an angle toward the street below. It's a tree-lined, quiet residential American street, very typical of the small town. The houses have front porches on which people sit and swing on gliders, conversing across from house to house. Steve Brand polishes his car parked in front of his house. His neighbor, Don Martin, leans against the fender watching him. A Good

---

1. **nebulae.** Groups of stars too far away to be seen distinctly; patches of misty light in the night sky
2. **fifth dimension.** Dimension beyond the three spatial dimensions: length, width, and depth—and also beyond the fourth dimension, which is time

During Reading

WRITE THINGS DOWN

- Screenplays, like drama, are written to be performed—in this case, for television. Work with the class to assign characters and read your parts aloud. Someone should take the part of reading stage directions. You can change characters at the end of acts.
- When you are not reading, follow along in the text. At the end of each page, stop reading and add details to your chart.
- When you reach the end of the first act, work with a small group to compare what you wrote in your chart and to discuss your thoughts on the selection so far.
- Continue reading the rest of the play aloud as a class, stopping to write things down at the end of each page.

Reading TIP

Stage directions in a teleplay are just as important as dialogue. They not only help actors speak their lines and move around the stage, they provide important information that can help you visualize the action.

MARK THE TEXT

Screenplays often have references to camera effects, such as *fading in* (slowing becoming distinct) and *panning* (moving across a field of view). Underline the camera references in the stage directions, set in italics, on this page.

READ ALOUD

Assign parts and work in a group to read the highlighted passage aloud. How do people treat each other?

_____

_____

_____

NOTE THE FACTS

Highlight or underline the sentence in the boxed area that tells how Maple Street is about to change. What is the event that will change life on Maple Street?

_____

_____

_____

20 *Humor man rides a bicycle and is just in the process of stopping to sell some ice cream to a couple of kids. Two women gossip on the front lawn. Another man waters his lawn.*

NARRATOR'S VOICE. Maple Street, U.S.A., late summer. A tree-lined little world of front porch gliders, hop scotch, the laughter of children, and the bell of an ice cream vendor.

There is a pause and the camera moves over to a shot of the Good Humor man and two small boys who are standing alongside, just buying ice cream.

30 **NARRATOR'S VOICE.** At the sound of the roar and the flash of light it will be precisely 6:43 P.M. on Maple Street.

At this moment one of the little boys, Tommy, looks up to listen to a sound of a tremendous screeching roar from overhead. A flash of light plays on both their faces and then it moves down the street past lawns and porches and rooftops and then disappears.

Various people leave their porches and stop what they're doing to stare up at the sky. Steve Brand, the man who's been polishing his car, now stands there <u>transfixed</u>, staring upwards. He looks at Don Martin, his neighbor from across the street.

40 **STEVE.** What was that? A meteor?

DON. (*Nods*) That's what it looked like. I didn't hear any crash though, did you?

STEVE. (*Shakes his head*) Nope. I didn't hear anything except a roar.

MRS. BRAND. (*From her porch*) Steve? What was that?

STEVE. (*Raising his voice and looking toward porch*) Guess it was a meteor, honey. Came awful close, didn't it?

MRS. BRAND. Too close for my money! Much too close.

The camera pans across the various porches to people who stand there watching and talking in low tones.

50 **NARRATOR'S VOICE.** Maple Street. Six-forty-four P.M. on a late September evening. (*A pause*) Maple Street in the last calm and <u>reflective</u> moment . . . before the monsters came!

The camera slowly pans across the porches again. We see a man screwing a light bulb on a front porch, then getting down off the stool to flick the switch and finding that nothing happens.

words for everyday use	**trans • fixed** (trans fikst´) *part.*, made motionless. *The raccoon robbing my shed was <u>transfixed</u> by the sudden light, his startled eyes glowing through his black mask.* **re • flec • tive** (ri flek´ tiv) *adj.*, meditative; thoughtful. *At sunrise he enjoyed a <u>reflective</u> pause over black coffee and the newspaper.*

Another man is working on an electric power mower. He plugs in the plug, flicks the switch of the power mower, off and on, with nothing happening.

60   *Through the window of a front porch, we see a woman pushing her finger back and forth on the dial hook. Her voice is indistinct and distant, but intelligible and repetitive.*

WOMAN.   Operator, operator, something's wrong on the phone, operator!

Mrs. Brand comes out on the porch and calls to Steve.

MRS. BRAND. (*Calling*)   Steve, the power's off. I had the soup on the stove and the stove just stopped working.

WOMAN.   Same thing over here. I can't get anybody on the phone either. The phone seems to be dead.

70   *We look down on the street as we hear the voices creep up from below, small, mildly disturbed voices highlighting these kinds of phrases:*

VOICES.   Electricity's off.

Phone won't work.

Can't get a thing on the radio.

My power mower won't move, won't work at all.

Radio's gone dead!

Pete Van Horn, a tall, thin man, is seen standing in front of his house.

80   **VAN HORN.**   I'll cut through the back yard . . . See if the power's still on on Floral Street. I'll be right back!

He walks past the side of his house and disappears into the back yard.

The camera pans down slowly until we're looking at ten or eleven people standing around the street and overflowing to the curb and sidewalk. In the background is Steve Brand's car.

STEVE.   Doesn't make sense. Why should the power go off all of a sudden, and the phone line?

DON.   Maybe some sort of an electrical storm or
90   something.

CHARLIE.   That don't seem likely. Sky's just as blue as anything. Not a cloud. No lightning. No thunder. No nothing. How could it be a storm?

WOMAN.   I can't get a thing on the radio. Not even the portable.

The people again murmur softly in wonderment and question.

FIX-UP IDEA

Ask a Question
If you have difficulty using the reading strategy, ask questions to help you focus on important events and characters. Before reading a page, review the questions on the page. Then, as the play is being read aloud, jot down your answers to the questions. Use these answers to help you fill in your chart.

NOTE THE FACTS

Why does Van Horn leave?

_____

_____

_____

_____

_____

CHARLIE.   Well, why don't you go downtown and check with the police, though they'll probably think we're crazy or something. A little power failure and right away we get all
100   flustered and everything.

STEVE.   It isn't just the power failure, Charlie. If it was, we'd still be able to get a broadcast on the portable.

There's a murmur of reaction to this. Steve looks from face to face and then over to his car.

STEVE.   I'll run downtown. We'll get this all straightened out.

He walks over to the car, gets in it, turns the key. Looking through the open car door, we see the crowd watching him from the other side. Steve starts the engine. It turns over sluggishly and then just stops dead. He tries it again and this time he can't get it
110   *to turn over. Then, very slowly and reflectively, he turns the key back to "off" and slowly gets out of the car.*

The people stare at Steve. He stands for a moment by the car, then walks toward the group.

STEVE.   I don't understand it. It was working fine before . . .

DON.   Out of gas?

STEVE. (*Shakes his head*)   I just had it filled up.

WOMAN.   What's it mean?

CHARLIE.   It's just as if . . . as if everything had stopped.
120   (*Then he turns toward Steve.*) We'd better walk downtown. (*Another murmur of assent at this.*)

STEVE.   The two of us can go, Charlie. (*He turns to look back at the car.*) It couldn't be the meteor. A meteor couldn't do *this.*

He and Charlie exchange a look, then they start to walk away from the group.

We see Tommy, a serious-faced fourteen-year-old in spectacles who stands a few feet away from the group. He is halfway between them and the two men, who start to walk down the
130   *sidewalk.*

TOMMY.   Mr. Brand . . . you better not!

STEVE.   Why not?

TOMMY.   They don't want you to.

Steve and Charlie exchange a grin, and Steve looks back toward the boy.

STEVE.   *Who* doesn't want us to?

TOMMY. (*Jerks his head in the general direction of the distant horizon*)   Them!

Use **THE STRATEGY**

WRITE THINGS DOWN.
Make sure to stop at the end of each page to add details to your graphic organizer.

STEVE. Them?

140   **CHARLIE.** Who are them?

TOMMY. (*Very intently*) Whoever was in that thing that came by overhead.

Steve knits his brows for a moment, cocking his head questioningly. His voice is intense.

STEVE. What?

TOMMY. Whoever was in that thing that came over. I don't think they want us to leave here.

Steve leaves Charlie and walks over to the boy. He kneels down in front of him. He forces his voice to remain gentle. He reaches

150   *out and holds the boy.*

STEVE. What do you mean? What are you talking about?

TOMMY. They don't want us to leave. That's why they shut everything off.

STEVE. What makes you say that? Whatever gave you that idea?

WOMAN. (*From the crowd*) Now isn't that the craziest thing you ever heard?

TOMMY. (*Persistently but a little <u>intimidated</u> by the crowd*) It's always that way, in every story I ever read about a ship

160   landing from outer space.

WOMAN. (*To the boy's mother, Sally, who stands on the fringe of the crowd*) From outer space, yet! Sally, you better get that boy of yours up to bed. He's been reading too many comic books or seeing too many movies or something.

SALLY. Tommy, come over here and stop that kind of talk.

STEVE. Go ahead, Tommy. We'll be right back. And you'll see. That wasn't any ship or anything like it. That was just a . . . a meteor or something. Likely as not—(*He turns to the group, now trying to weight his words with an optimism he*

170   *obviously doesn't feel but is desperately trying to <u>instill</u> in himself as well as the others.*) No doubt it did have something to do with all this power failure and the rest of it. Meteors can do some crazy things. Like sunspots.[3]

---

3. **sunspots.** Temporarily cooler places on the surface of the sun, which appear as dark spots and are sometimes associated with physical disturbances on Earth

words for everyday use

in • tim • i • date (in tim´ə dāt´) *vt.*, make timid or afraid. *Larry refused to be <u>intimidated</u> by the gruff manner of his football coach.*

in • still (in stil´) *vt.*, impart gradually. *Long experience with bug-ridden computer software had <u>instilled</u> in Colleen an unshakable distrust of technology.*

NOTE THE FACTS

Why does Tommy think that Steve shouldn't leave? What is his theory about the strange events on Maple Street?

_____

_____

_____

Reading STRATEGY
               REVIEW

TACKLE DIFFICULT VOCABULARY. If you have trouble understanding difficult words, use the definitions at the bottom of the page, as well as the context clues near the word. Tell yourself, "The lines near this word tell me this word means . . ." or "The Words for Everyday Use feature defines the underlined word as . . ." How can these questions help you with the underlined words *intimidated* and *instill* on this page?

_____

_____

_____

THINK AND REFLECT

Are Steve and Don convinced by their own explanations? Why do you think they are trying so hard to explain what is going on? **(Interpret)**

_____

_____

_____

_____

_____

Literary TOOLS

CHARACTERIZATION.
Characterization is the use of literary techniques to create a character. Writers use three major techniques to create characters: direct description, portrayal of characters' behavior, and representations of characters' internal states. Examine the way Tommy's character is developed on this page. Then highlight or underline text that reveals one example of a major characterization technique.

Reading TIP

Remember to use the footnotes at the bottom of the page to help with unclear references and obscure words you may not know.

DON. (*Picking up the cue*) Sure. That's the kind of thing—like sunspots. They raise Cain with[4] radio reception all over the world. And this thing being so close—why, there's no telling the sort of stuff it can do. (*He wets his lips, smiles nervously.*) Go ahead, Charlie. You and Steve go into town and see if that isn't what's causing it all.

180   *Steve and Charlie again walk away from the group down the sidewalk. The people watch silently.*
    Tommy stares at them, biting his lips, and finally calling out again.
TOMMY.   Mr. Brand!
The two men stop again. Tommy takes a step toward them.
TOMMY.   Mr. Brand . . . please don't leave here.
    Steve and Charlie stop once again and turn toward the boy. There's a murmur in the crowd, a murmur of irritation and concern as if the boy were bringing up fears that shouldn't be
190   *brought up: words which carried with them a strange kind of <u>validity</u> that came without logic but nonetheless registered and had meaning and effect. Again we hear a murmur of reaction from the crowd.*
    Tommy is partly frightened and partly defiant as well.
TOMMY.   You might not even be able to get to town. It was that way in the story. Nobody could leave. Nobody except—
STEVE.   Except who?
TOMMY.   Except the people they'd sent ahead of them. They looked just like humans. And it wasn't until the ship
200   landed that—
    The boy suddenly stops again, conscious of the parents staring at them and of the sudden hush of the crowd.
SALLY. (*In a whisper, sensing the antagonism of the crowd*) Tommy, please son . . . honey, don't talk that way—
MAN ONE.   That kid shouldn't talk that way . . . and we shouldn't stand here listening to him. Why this is the craziest thing I ever heard of. The kid tells us a comic book plot and here we stand listening—
    Steve walks toward the camera, stops by the boy.

---

4. **raise Cain with.** Create commotion with; biblical reference to Cain, the oldest son of Adam and Eve, who murdered his brother Abel

words for everyday use	**va · lid · i · ty** (və lid′ə tē) *n.*, quality of being firmly grounded on facts. *Although the findings of the doctor's study seemed unbelievable, the <u>validity</u> of his argument was proved later by many scientists.*

210 **STEVE.** Go ahead, Tommy. What kind of story was this? What about the people that they sent out ahead?

TOMMY. That was the way they prepared things for the landing. They sent four people. A mother and a father and two kids who looked just like humans . . . but they weren't.

There's another silence as Steve looks toward the crowd and then toward Tommy. He wears a tight grin.

STEVE. Well, I guess what we'd better do then is to run a check on the neighborhood and see which ones of us are really human.

220 *There's laughter at this, but it's a laughter that comes from a desperate attempt to lighten the atmosphere. It's a release kind of laugh. The people look at one another in the middle of their laughter.*

CHARLIE. There must be somethin' better to do than stand around makin' bum jokes about it. (*Rubs his jaw nervously*) I wonder if Floral Street's got the same deal we got. (*He looks past the houses.*) Where is Pete Van Horn anyway? Didn't he get back yet?

Suddenly there's the sound of a car's engine starting to turn
230 *over.*

We look across the street toward the driveway of Les Goodman's house. He's at the wheel trying to start the car.

SALLY. Can you get it started, Les? (*He gets out of the car, shaking his head.*)

GOODMAN. No dice.

He walks toward the group. He stops suddenly as behind him, <u>inexplicably</u> and with a noise that inserts itself into the silence, the car engine starts up all by itself. Goodman whirls around to stare toward it.

240 *The car idles roughly, smoke coming from the exhaust, the frame shaking gently.*

Goodman's eyes go wide, and he runs over to his car.

The people stare toward the car.

MAN ONE. He got the car started somehow. He got his car started!

words for everyday use

in • ex • pli • ca • bly (in eks´ pli kə blē) *adv.*, without explanation. *The train was <u>inexplicably</u> delayed just a few dozen feet from the station.*

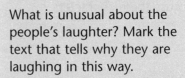

MARK THE TEXT

What is unusual about the people's laughter? Mark the text that tells why they are laughing in this way.

THINK AND REFLECT

When the car starts, do the people perceive this as a good thing? What is beginning to happen within the crowd? **(Interpret)**

_____

_____

_____

_____

MOTIVATION. A motivation is a force that moves a character to think, feel, or behave in a certain way. While reading the screenplay, think about what motivates the people on Maple Street to turn into a mob. Continue to fill in the graphic organizer on page 338, noting the reason(s) that others feel motivated to accuse these characters.

NOTE THE FACTS

About what is Steve worried? What does he want to stop?

The camera pans along the faces of the people as they stare, somehow caught up by this revelation and somehow, illogically, wildly, frightened.

WOMAN. How come his car just up and started like that?

250 **SALLY.** All by itself. He wasn't anywheres near it. It started all by itself.

Don approaches the group, stops a few feet away to look toward Goodman's car and then back toward the group.

DON. And he never did come out to look at that thing that flew overhead. He wasn't even interested. (_He turns to the faces in the group, his face taut and serious._) Why? Why didn't he come out with the rest of us to look?

CHARLIE. He always was an oddball. Him and his whole family. Real oddball.

260 **DON.** What do you say we ask him?

The group suddenly starts toward the house. In this brief fraction of a moment they take the first step toward performing a metamorphosis that changes people from a group into a mob. They begin to head purposefully across the street toward the house at the end. Steve stands in front of them. For a moment their fear almost turns their walk into a wild stampede, but Steve's voice, loud, incisive, and commanding, makes them stop.

STEVE. Wait a minute . . . wait a minute! Let's not be a mob!

270 _The people stop as a group, seem to pause for a moment, and then much more quietly and slowly start to walk across the street. Goodman stands alone facing the people._

GOODMAN. I just don't understand it. I tried to start it and it wouldn't start. You saw me. All of you saw me.

And now, just as suddenly as the engine started, it stops and there's a long silence that is gradually intruded upon by the frightened murmuring of the people.

GOODMAN. I don't understand. I swear . . . I don't understand. What's happening?

words for everyday use

rev • e • la • tion (rev´ə lā´shən) n., something disclosed. _The revelation that his "lost" glasses were perched on top of his head amused the man._

met • a • mor • pho • sis (met́ə môr´fə sis) n., transformation. _A novel by a German writer named Kafka describes the metamorphosis of a man into an immense cockroach._

in • ci • sive (in sī´siv) adj., penetrating. _The most incisive wit, political commentary, and general reflections on the state of the world are often heard in a taxicab._

280 **DON.**   Maybe you better tell us. Nothing's working on this street. Nothing. No lights, no power, no radio. (*And then meaningfully*) Nothing except one car—yours!

The people pick this up and now their murmuring becomes a loud chant filling the air with accusations and demands for action. Two of the men pass Don and head toward Goodman, who backs away, backing into his car and now at bay.

GOODMAN.   Wait a minute now. You keep your distance— all of you. So I've got a car that starts by itself—well, that's a freak thing. I admit it. But does that make me some kind of a criminal or something? I don't know why the car works— it just does!

This stops the crowd momentarily and now Goodman, still backing away, goes toward his front porch. He goes up the steps and then stops to stand facing the mob.

We see a long shot of Steve as he comes through the crowd.

STEVE. (*Quietly*)   We're all on a monster kick, Les. Seems that the general impression holds that maybe one family isn't what we think they are. Monsters from outer space or something. Different than us. Fifth columnists[5] from the

300 vast beyond. (*He chuckles.*) You know anybody that might fit that description around here on Maple Street?

GOODMAN.   What is this, a gag or something? This a practical joke or something?

We see a close-up of the porch light as it suddenly goes out. There's a murmur from the group.

GOODMAN.   Now I suppose that's supposed to <u>incriminate</u> me! The light goes on and off. That really does it, doesn't it?

(*He looks around at the faces of the people.*) I just don't
310 understand this—(*He wets his lips, looking from face to face.*) Look, you all know me. We've lived here five years. Right in this house. We're no different from any of the rest of you! We're no different at all. Really . . . this whole thing is just . . . just weird—

---

5. **Fifth columnists.** Citizens who help the invading enemies of their nation

words for everyday use   in • crim • i • nate (in krim´i nāt) *vt.*, charge with or show evidence of involvement in a crime. *The Fifth Amendment to the Constitution allows people to refuse to <u>incriminate</u> themselves in court.*

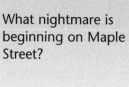
What is Steve's attitude toward the neighbors' growing fear of Goodman? How does he express this attitude? Why do you think he handles the situation as he does? **(Infer)**

_____

_____

_____

_____

Use THE STRATEGY

WRITE THINGS DOWN. When you reach the end of the first act, work with a small group to compare what you wrote in your chart. Discuss your thoughts on the selection so far.

WOMAN. Well, if that's the case, Les Goodman, explain why—(*She stops suddenly, clamping her mouth shut.*)

GOODMAN. (*Softly*) Explain what?

STEVE. (*Interjecting*) Look, let's forget this—

CHARLIE. (*Overlapping him*) Go ahead, let her talk. What
320 about it? Explain what?

WOMAN. (*A little reluctantly*) Well . . . sometimes I go to bed late at night. A couple of times . . . a couple of times I'd come out on the porch and I'd see Mr. Goodman here in the wee hours of the morning standing out in front of his house . . . looking up at the sky. (*She looks around the circle of faces.*) That's right, looking up at the sky as if . . . as if he were waiting for something. (*A pause*) As if he were looking for something.

There's a murmur of reaction from the crowd again.

330 *We cut suddenly to a group shot. As Goodman starts toward them, they back away frightened.*

GOODMAN. You know really . . . this is for laughs. You know what I'm guilty of? (*He laughs.*) I'm guilty of insomnia. Now what's the penalty for insomnia? (*At this point the laugh, the humor, leaves his voice.*) Did you hear what I said? I said it was insomnia. (*A pause as he looks around, then shouts.*) I said it was insomnia! You fools. You scared, frightened rabbits, you. You're sick people, do you know that? You're
340 sick people—all of you! And you don't even know what you're starting because let me tell you . . . let me tell you— this thing you're starting—that should frighten you. As God is my witness . . . you're letting something begin here that's a nightmare!

ACT II

We see a medium shot of the Goodman entry hall at night. On the side table rests an unlit candle. Mrs. Goodman walks into the scene, a glass of milk in hand. She sets the milk down on the table,
350 *lights the candle with a match from a box on the table, picks up the glass of milk, and starts out of scene.*

Mrs. Goodman comes through her porch door, glass of milk in hand. The entry hall, with table and lit candle, can be seen behind her.

Outside, the camera slowly pans down the sidewalk, taking in little knots of people who stand around talking in low voices. At the end of each conversation they look toward Les Goodman's *house. From the various houses we can see candlelight but no electricity, and there's an <u>all-pervading</u> quiet that blankets the*

360 *whole area, disturbed only by the almost whispered voices of the people as they stand around. The camera pans over to one group where Charlie stands. He stares across at Goodman's house.*

We see a long shot of the house. Two men stand across the street in almost sentry-like[6] poses. Then we see a medium shot of a group of people.

SALLY. (*A little timorously*)   It just doesn't seem right, though, keeping watch on them. Why . . . he was right when he said he was one of our neighbors. Why, I've known Ethel Goodman ever since they moved in. We've been

370 good friends—

CHARLIE.   That don't prove a thing. Any guy who'd spend his time lookin' up at the sky early in the morning—well, there's something wrong with that kind of person. There's something that ain't legitimate. Maybe under normal circumstances we could let it go by, but these aren't normal circumstances. Why, look at this street! Nothin' but candles. Why, it's like goin' back into the Dark Ages or somethin'!

Steve walks down the steps of his porch, walks down the street over to Les Goodman's house, and then stops at the foot of the

380 *steps. Goodman stands there, his wife behind him, very frightened.*

GOODMAN.   Just stay right where you are, Steve. We don't want any trouble, but this time if anybody sets foot on my porch, that's what they're going to get—trouble!

STEVE.   Look, Les—

GOODMAN.   I've already explained to you people. I don't sleep very well at night sometimes. I get up and I take a walk and I look up at the sky. I look at the stars!

MRS. GOODMAN.   That's exactly what he does. Why this

390 whole thing, it's . . . it's some kind of madness or something.

STEVE. (*Nods grimly*)   That's exactly what it is—some kind of madness.

***

6. **sentry-like.** Like a military guard

words for everyday use	**all-per • vad • ing** (ôl´ pər vād´ iŋ) *adj.*, prevalent throughout. *The trilling of the frogs in the local ponds created an <u>all-pervading</u> racket on spring nights.*

THINK AND REFLECT

What makes Charlie's comment ironic? In what way have the people on Maple Street gone "back into the Dark Ages"? Who has led them there? **(Infer)**

_____

_____

_____

_____

_____

_____

Use THE STRATEGY

WRITE THINGS DOWN. Continue to read the rest of the play aloud as a class, stopping to write things down at the end of each page.

CHARLIE'S VOICE. (*Shrill, from across the street*) You best watch who you're seen with, Steve! Until we get this all straightened out, you ain't exactly above suspicion yourself.

STEVE. (*Whirling around toward him*) Or you, Charlie. Or any of us, it seems. From age eight on up!

WOMAN. What I'd like to know is—what are we gonna do? Just stand around here all night?

400 **CHARLIE.** There's nothin' else we can do! (*He turns back looking toward Steve and Goodman again.*) One of 'em'll tip their hand. They got to.

STEVE. (*Raising his voice*) There's something you can do, Charlie. You could go home and keep your mouth shut. You could quit strutting around like a self-appointed hanging judge and just climb into bed and forget it.

CHARLIE. You sound real anxious to have that happen, Steve. I think we better keep our eye on you too!

DON. (*As if he were taking the bit from his teeth, takes a* 410 *hesitant step to the front*) I think everything might as well come out now. (*He turns toward Steve.*) Your wife's done plenty of talking, Steve, about how odd you are!

CHARLIE. (*Picking this up, his eyes widening*) Go ahead, tell us what she's said.

We see a long shot of Steve as he walks toward them from across the street.

STEVE. Go ahead, what's my wife said? Let's get it all out. Let's pick out every <u>idiosyncrasy</u> of every single man, woman, and child on the street. And then we might as well 420 set up some kind of kangaroo court.[7] How about a firing squad at dawn, Charlie, so we can get rid of all the suspects? Narrow them down. Make it easier for you.

DON. There's no need gettin' so upset, Steve. It's just that . . . well . . . Myra's talked about how there's been plenty of nights you spent hours down in your basement workin' on some kind of radio or something. Well, none of us have ever seen that radio—

---

7. **kangaroo court.** Unauthorized court that disregards regular legal procedure; named because its enforcement of justice occurs rapidly and unpredictably, in leaps and bounds

READ ALOUD

With your group, read aloud the parts marked in the highlighted box. How do Don's comments confirm Steve's fears? What is happening to the neighbors' tolerance for differences, or idiosyncrasies?

_____

_____

_____

_____

_____

_____

By this time Steve has reached the group. He stands there <u>defiantly</u> close to them.

430   **CHARLIE.**   Go ahead, Steve. What kind of "radio set" you workin' on? I never seen it. Neither has anyone else. Who you talk to on that radio set? And who talks to you?

STEVE.   I'm surprised at you, Charlie. How come you're so dense all of a sudden? (*A pause*) Who do I talk to? I talk to monsters from outer space. I talk to three-headed green men who fly over here in what look like meteors.

Steve's wife steps down from the porch, bites her lip, calls out.

MRS. BRAND.   Steve! Steve, please. (*Then looking around, frightened, she walks toward the group.*) It's just a ham radio

440   set,[8] that's all. I bought him a book on it myself. It's just a ham radio set. A lot of people have them. I can show it to you. It's right down in the basement.

STEVE. (*Whirls around toward her*) Show them nothing! If they want to look inside our house—let them get a search warrant.

CHARLIE.   Look, buddy, you can't afford to—

STEVE. (*Interrupting*)   Charlie, don't tell me what I can afford! And stop telling me who's dangerous and who isn't and who's safe and who's a menace. (*He turns to the group and*

450   *shouts.*) And you're with him, too—all of you! You're standing here all set to crucify—all set to find a scapegoat— all desperate to point some kind of a finger at a neighbor! Well now look, friends, the only thing that's gonna happen is that we'll eat each other up alive—

He stops abruptly as Charlie suddenly grabs his arm.

CHARLIE. (*In a hushed voice*)   That's not the only thing that can happen to us.

Cut to a long shot looking down the street. A figure has suddenly <u>materialized</u> in the gloom and in the silence we can hear

460   *the clickety-clack of slow, measured footsteps on concrete as the figure walks slowly toward them. One of the women lets out a stifled cry. The young mother grabs her boy as do a couple of others.*

---

8. **ham radio set.** Amateur radio operator's equipment

---

words for everyday use

de • fi • ant • ly (dē fī´ənt lē) *adv.*, openly resisting. *When she was a little girl, Myrtle had <u>defiantly</u> insisted on eating the frosting before the cake.*

ma • te • ri • al • ize (mə tir´ē əl īz´) *vt.*, appear in physical form. *Joe's impractical plan for acquiring wealth never made so much as a penny <u>materialize</u> in his bank account.*

Who is now being accused? Who is accusing this person?

_____

_____

_____

WHAT DO YOU WONDER?

_____

_____

_____

TOMMY. (*Shouting, frightened*)   It's the monster! It's the monster!

Another woman lets out a wail and the people fall back in a group, staring toward the darkness and the approaching figure.

We see a medium group shot of the people as they stand in the shadows watching. Don Martin joins them, carrying a shotgun.
470 *He holds it up.*

DON.   We may need this.

STEVE.   A shotgun? (*He pulls it out of Don's hand.*) Good Lord—will anybody think a thought around here? Will you people wise up? What good would a shotgun do against—
Now Charlie pulls the gun from Steve's hand.

CHARLIE.   No more talk, Steve. You're going to talk us into a grave! You'd let whatever's out there walk right over us, wouldn't yuh? Well, some of us won't!

He swings the gun around to point it toward the sidewalk.
480 *The dark figure continues to walk toward them.*

The group stands there, fearful, apprehensive, mothers clutching children, men standing in front of wives. Charlie slowly raises the gun. As the figure gets closer and closer he suddenly pulls the trigger. The sound of it explodes in the stillness. There is a long angle shot looking down at the figure, who suddenly lets out a small cry, stumbles forward onto his knees and then falls forward on his face. Don, Charlie, and Steve race forward over to him. Steve is there first and turns the man over. Now the crowd gathers around them.
490 **STEVE.** (*Slowly looks up*)   It's Pete Van Horn.

DON. (*In a hushed voice*)   Pete Van Horn! He was just gonna go over to the next block to see if the power was on—

WOMAN.   You killed him, Charlie. You shot him dead!

CHARLIE. (*Looks around at the circle of faces, his eyes frightened, his face <u>contorted</u>*)   But . . . but I didn't know who he was. I certainly didn't know who he was. He comes walkin' out of the darkness—how am I supposed to know

NOTE THE FACTS

Again, what is ironic about Charlie's statement? Who actually sends one of his neighbors into a grave?

_____

_____

_____

words for everyday use

con • tort • ed (kən tôrt´ əd) *part.*, twisted out of its usual form. *The gymnast's body was so flexible she could bend herself into the most <u>contorted</u> positions.*

who he was? (*He grabs Steve.*) Steve—you know why I shot!
How was I supposed to know he wasn't a monster or
something? (*He grabs Don now.*) We're all scared of the same
thing. I was just tryin' to . . . tryin' to protect my home,
that's all! Look, all of you, that's all I was tryin' to do. (*He
looks down wildly at the body.*) I didn't know it was somebody
we knew! I didn't know—

*There's a sudden hush and then an intake of breath. We see a
medium shot of the living room window of Charlie's house. The
window is not lit, but suddenly the house lights come on behind it.*

WOMAN. (*In a very hushed voice*) Charlie . . . Charlie . . . the
lights just went on in your house. Why did the lights just go
on?

DON. What about it, Charlie? How come you're the only
one with lights now?

GOODMAN. That's what I'd like to know.

A pause as they all stare toward Charlie.

GOODMAN. You were so quick to kill, Charlie, and you
were so quick to tell us who we had to be careful of. Well,
maybe you had to kill. Maybe Peter there was trying to tell
us something. Maybe he'd found out something and came
back to tell us who there was amongst us we should watch
out for—

Charlie backs away from the group, his eyes wide with fright.

CHARLIE. No . . . no . . . it's nothing of the sort! I don't
know why the lights are on. I swear I don't. Somebody's
pulling a gag or something.

*He bumps against Steve, who grabs him and whirls him
around.*

STEVE. A gag? A gag? Charlie, there's a dead man on the
sidewalk and you killed him! Does this thing look like a gag
to you?

Charlie breaks away and screams as he runs toward his house.

CHARLIE. No! No! Please!

A man breaks away from the crowd to chase Charlie.

*We see a long angle shot looking down as the man tackles
Charlie and lands on top of him. The other people start to run
toward them. Charlie is up on his feet, breaks away from the
other man's grasp, lands a couple of desperate punches that push
the man aside. Then he forces his way, fighting, through the
crowd to once again break free, jumps up on his front porch. A
rock thrown from the group smashes a window alongside of him,*

500

510

520

530

540

READ ALOUD

Read aloud the highlighted
section in your group,
using your graphic
organizer to fill in details
about the next person
accused in the play. With
what evidence is this
person accused? How does
he react?

_____

_____

_____

_____

_____

_____

the broken glass flying past him. A couple of pieces cut him. He stands there perspiring, rumpled, blood running down from a cut on the cheek. His wife breaks away from the group to throw herself into his arms. He buries his face against her. We can see the crowd <u>converging</u> on the porch now.

VOICES.   It must have been him.

He's the one.

We got to get Charlie.

Another rock lands on the porch. Now Charlie pushes his wife
550   *behind him, facing the group.*

CHARLIE.   Look, look I swear to you . . . it isn't me . . . but I do know who it is . . . I swear to you, I do know who it is. I know who the monster is here. I know who it is that doesn't belong. I swear to you I know.

GOODMAN. (*Shouting*)   What are you waiting for?

WOMAN. (*Shouting*)   Come on, Charlie, come on.

MAN ONE. (*Shouting*)   Who is it, Charlie, tell us!

DON. (*Pushing his way to the front of the crowd*)   All right, Charlie, let's hear it!

560   *Charlie's eyes dart around wildly.*

CHARLIE.   It's . . . it's . . .

MAN ONE. (*Screaming*)   Go ahead, Charlie, tell us.

CHARLIE.   It's . . . it's the kid. It's Tommy. He's the one!

There's a gasp from the crowd as we cut to a shot of Sally holding her son Tommy. The boy at first doesn't understand and then, realizing the eyes are all on him, buries his face against his mother.

SALLY. (*Backs away*)   That's crazy! That's crazy! He's a little boy.

570   **WOMAN.**   But he knew! He was the only one who knew! He told us all about it. Well, how did he know? How *could* he have known?

The various people take this up and repeat the question aloud.

VOICES.   How could he know?

Who told him?

Make the kid answer.

DON.   It was Charlie who killed old man Van Horn.

 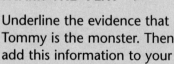
words for everyday use

con • verge (kən vʉrjʹ) *vi.,* come together. *The two superhighways <u>converged</u> in a black and grimy wasteland.*

WOMAN. But it was the kid here who knew what was going to happen all the time. He was the one who knew!

580 *We see a close-up of Steve.*

STEVE. Are you all gone crazy? (*Pause as he looks about*) Stop.

A fist crashes at Steve's face, staggering him back out of the frame of the picture.

There are several close camera shots suggesting the coming of violence. A hand fires a rifle. A fist clenches. A hand grabs the hammer from Van Horn's body, etc. Meanwhile, we hear the following lines.

DON. Charlie has to be the one—Where's my rifle—

590 **WOMAN.** Les Goodman's the one. His car started! Let's wreck it.

MRS. GOODMAN. What about Steve's radio—He's the one that called them—

MR. GOODMAN. Smash the radio. Get me a hammer. Get me something.

STEVE. Stop—Stop—

CHARLIE. Where's that kid—Let's get him.

MAN ONE. Get Steve—Get Charlie—They're working together.

600 *The crowd starts to converge around the mother, who grabs the child and starts to run with him. The crowd starts to follow, at first walking fast, and then running after him.*

We see a full shot of the street as suddenly Charlie's lights go off and the lights in another house go on. They stay on for a moment, then from across the street other lights go on and then off again.

MAN ONE. (*Shouting*) It isn't the kid . . . it's Bob Weaver's house.

WOMAN. It isn't Bob Weaver's house, it's Don Martin's place.

610 **CHARLIE.** I tell you it's the kid.

DON. It's Charlie. He's the one.

We move into a series of close-ups of various people as they shout, accuse, scream, <u>interspersing</u> these shots with shots of houses as the lights go on and off, and then slowly in the middle of this

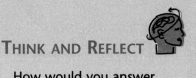

THINK AND REFLECT

How would you answer Steve's question? **(Respond)**

_____

_____

_____

DRAW A PICTURE

---

words for everyday use

in • ter • sperse (in´tər spʉrs´) *vt.*, scatter among other things. *Pressed flowers were <u>interspersed</u> among the pages of her grandmother's poetry book.*

READ ALOUD

With your group, read aloud the parts marked in the box. Whom, according to the aliens, is the most dangerous enemy that people can face? What qualities make this enemy dangerous?

_____

_____

_____

_____

_____

_____

nightmarish <u>morass</u> of sight and sound the camera starts to pull away, until once again we've reached the opening shot looking at the Maple Street sign from high above.

620   *The camera continues to move away until we dissolve to a shot looking toward the metal side of a space craft, which sits shrouded in darkness. An open door throws out a beam of light from the illuminated interior. Two figures silhouetted against the bright lights appear. We get only a vague feeling of form, but nothing more explicit than that.*

FIGURE ONE.   Understand the procedure now? Just stop a few of their machines and radios and telephones and lawn mowers . . . throw them into darkness for a few hours, and then you just sit back and watch the pattern.

FIGURE TWO.   And this pattern is always the same?

FIGURE ONE.   With few variations. They pick the most
630 dangerous enemy they can find . . . and it's themselves. And all we need do is sit back . . . and watch.

FIGURE TWO.   Then I take it this place . . . this Maple Street . . . is not unique.

FIGURE ONE. (*Shaking his head*)   By no means. Their world is full of Maple Streets. And we'll go from one to the other and let them destroy themselves. One to the other . . . one to the other . . . one to the other—

    Now the camera pans up for a shot of the starry sky and over
640 *this we hear the Narrator's voice.*

NARRATOR'S VOICE.   The tools of conquest do not necessarily come with bombs and explosions and fallout.[9] There are weapons that are simply thoughts, attitudes, prejudices—to be found only in the minds of men. For the record, prejudices can kill and suspicion can destroy and a thoughtless frightened search for a scapegoat has a fallout all its own for the children . . . and the children yet unborn. (*A pause*) And the pity of it is . . . that these things cannot be
650 confined to . . . The Twilight Zone! ■

---

9. **fallout.** Radioactive particles falling to Earth; for example, after a nuclear explosion

words for everyday use

mo • rass (mə ras´) *n.*, perplexing state of affairs. *When Godfrey attempted to register his antique car, he found himself caught in a <u>morass</u> of paperwork.*

Reflect ON YOUR READING

After you finish reading the play, complete your graphic organizer. Then compare with your group what you wrote during the second act. Review your answers to the questions and activities in the margins of the selection.

What do you learn about the people of Maple Street based on their reactions and accusations? Can you imagine something like this happening? Why, or why not?

_____

_____

_____

Reading Skills and Test Practice

IDENTIFY CAUSE AND EFFECT
Discuss with your partner how best to answer the following questions about cause and effect.

1. Why does Charlie accuse Tommy?
   a. He has seen Tommy contacting aliens.
   b. He knows he is guilty and wants to blame somebody else.
   c. He wants to get the crowd off his case.
   d. He holds a grudge against Tommy.

What is the correct answer to the question above? How were you able to eliminate the other answers? How did your use of the reading strategy help you answer the question?

_____

_____

2. What causes the neighbors to turn on each other?
   a. The aliens alter their brain chemistry and make them aggressive.
   b. They never did like their neighbors.
   c. They are jealous of each other.
   d. Human nature makes them turn on each other.

What is the correct answer to the question above? How were you able to eliminate the other answers? How did your use of the reading strategy help you answer the question?

_____

_____

THINK-ALOUD NOTES

_____

_____

_____

_____

_____

_____

_____

_____

_____

_____

_____

Investigate, Inquire, and Imagine

RECALL: GATHER FACTS
1a. What explanation does Tommy give of the peculiar events occurring on Maple Street? Where did he get his ideas?

INTERPRET: FIND MEANING
1b. What are the neighbors' first reactions to Tommy's story? How do their reactions change, and why?

ANALYZE: TAKE THINGS APART
2a. How do the people on Maple Street react to what happens to their machines at the beginning of the play? What emotion leads them to react this way?

SYNTHESIZE: BRING THINGS TOGETHER
2b. The play suggests that humans can quickly resort to mob violence because of fears and hatreds. Yet in reality, there are also other motivators of human action that form a powerful force to stop mob violence. What are some of these motivators?

EVALUATE: MAKE JUDGMENTS
3a. Who or what are the real monsters in this screenplay?

EXTEND: CONNECT IDEAS
3b. In the 1930s and 1940s the countries of Germany and Italy suffered severe economic hardships. Inflation and unemployment led people to look desperately for solutions and scapegoats. In both countries, brutal dictators came to power. What similarities can you find between these events in Germany and Italy and the events described in this play? What political point might the author be making?

Literary Tools

MOTIVATION. A **motivation** is a force that moves a character to think, feel, or behave in a certain way. Review your completed graphic organizer on page 338. What motivates the people on Maple Street to turn into a mob? What small differences between people become magnified in their minds? What is this play saying about how people are capable of reacting toward one another in times of stress or crisis?

_____

_____

_____

_____

_____

WordWorkshop

Using Vocabulary to Write a Story. Write a suspenseful story, using all the Words for Everyday Use from this selection. Use your own paper as necessary.

all-pervading	incriminate	metamorphosis
contorted	inexplicably	morass
converge	instill	reflective
defiantly	intersperse	revelation
idiosyncrasy	intimidate	transfixed
incisive	materialize	validity

Read-Write Connection

Which character or characters in this selection do you admire? What makes this person or these persons different from the rest of the inhabitants of Maple Street?

_____

_____

_____

_____

_____

_____

_____

_____

_____

Beyond the Reading

More from the *Twilight Zone*. Find out more about the television series whose name is now part of pop culture. Check out the *Twilight Zone,* which is still broadcast on television, available on video, and collected in anthologies by Rod Serling and other authors. View an episode and then read one of the stories. A good place to start might be with the stories collected in *The Twilight Zone, Journey to the Twilight Zone,* and *Return to the Twilight Zone.* What do you find more suspenseful—watching the shows or reading the stories? How would you turn one of the stories into a half-hour television episode? Stage a teleplay or report your ideas to the class.

Go Online. Visit the EMC Internet Resource Center at **emcp.com** to find links and additional activities for this selection.

Choose and Use Reading Strategies

Before reading the drama passage below, review with a partner how to use each of these reading strategies.

1. Read with a Purpose
2. Connect to Prior Knowledge
3. Write Things Down
4. Make Predictions
5. Visualize
6. Use Text Organization
7. Tackle Difficult Vocabulary
8. Monitor Your Reading Progress

Now apply at least two of these reading strategies as you read the following excerpt from *The Tragedy of Romeo and Juliet*, act 2, scene 3. Use the margins and mark up the text to show how you are using the reading strategies to read actively.

Friar Lawrence. God pardon sin! Wast thou with Rosaline?
Romeo. With Rosaline? my ghostly father, no;
I have forgot that name, and that name's woe.
Friar Lawrence. That's my good son, but where hast thou been then?
Romeo. I'll tell thee ere thou ask it me again.
I have been feasting with mine enemy,
Where on a sudden one hath wounded me
That's by me wounded; both our remedies
Within thy help and holy physic lies.
I bear no hatred, blessed man, for lo
My intercession likewise steads my foe.
Friar Lawrence. Be plain, good son, and homely in thy drift,
Riddling confession finds but riddling shrift.
Romeo. Then plainly know my heart's dear love is set
On the fair daughter of rich Capulet.
And mine on hers, so hers is set on mine,
And all combin'd, save what thou must combine
By holy marriage. When and where and how
We met, we woo'd, and made exchange of vow,
I'll tell thee as we pass, but this I pray,
That thou consent to marry us today.

WordWorkshop

Unit 6 Words for Everyday use

adjacent, 326
adversary, 302
all-pervading, 349
augment, 303
bounty, 332
brow, 312
contorted, 352
converge, 354
courtier, 317
defiantly, 351
devout, 310
discourse, 327
enmity, 329
flourish, 301
forfeit, 302
fray, 302
grievance, 304

idolatry, 331
idiosyncrasy, 350
impute, 330
incisive, 346
inconstant, 331
incriminate, 347
inexplicably, 345
instill, 343
intersperse, 355
intimidate, 343
invocation, 326
lineament, 313
materialize, 351
metamorphosis, 346
morass, 356
mutiny, 298
nuptial, 320

pernicious, 301
posterity, 306
procure, 332
propagate, 305
purge, 305
reflective, 340
revelation, 346
repose, 331
siege, 306
substantial, 332
transfixed, 340
transgression, 305
validity, 344
vex, 305
visage, 315

Mnemonic Devices. Work in groups of three to four people to play the Mnemonic Devices Game. Each person should choose ten words from the WordWatch list above. Working with index cards or small pieces of paper, use a mnemonic by writing a catchy phrase or drawing an illustration to help you remember each of your ten words. (For more information, see "Using Mnemonic Devices" in Unit 9, page 492–493.)

EXAMPLE

defiantly

When you have finished your words, read your phrase or show your illustration to your group. The first person to guess the word gets the card. The person with the most cards at the end of the game wins. (Note: For an extra challenge, try playing the game without looking at the Words for Everday Use list above for answers.)

Literary Tools

MATCHING. Select the best literary element on the right to complete each sentence on the left. Write the correct letter in the blank. You will not use every term.

_____1. In "The Monsters Are Due on Maple Street," this tells what kind of camera angle to use.

_____2. If an actor speaks alone onstage for a long time, he is giving a(n) ___.

_____3. In this part of the play, the Chorus tells the audience that the play about a "pair of star-cross'd lovers."

_____4. The ___ in a plot provides background information.

_____5. In "The Monsters Are Due on Maple Street," a tremendous screeching and flash of light is the ___ that introduces the central conflict.

_____6. A(n) ___ is the primary struggle dealt with in the plot of a story or drama.

_____7. When Romeo says that Juliet "is the sun," he is using a(n) ___.

_____8. A ___, such as the desire for everyone be like everyone else on Maple Street, moves characters to think, feel, or behave in a certain way.

_____9. A(n) ___ is a fourteen-line verse form written in iambic pentameter.

___10. Juliet's eagerness to please her mother, uncertainty around Romeo, and tendency to change her mind are all part of ___, which Shakespeare reveals through dialogue and other characters' reactions to her.

a. blank verse, 304, 313

b. central conflict, 336

c. characterization, 344

d. exposition, 336

e. foreshadowing, 324

f. iambic pentameter, 313

g. inciting incident, 336

h. metaphor, 327

i. motivation, 358

j. prologue, 298

k. simile, 328

l. soliloquy, 327

m. sonnet, 298

n. stage directions, 339, 347

o. tragedy, 296

On Your Own

FLUENTLY SPEAKING. Find a scene from a play that you like by going to the library and looking through drama anthologies, screenplays, and scripts. Then work with a small group or partner to do a dramatic reading of one scene. Introduce the scene with background information that will help your audience understand what the scene is about. Practice your lines until you and the other actors can present the play smoothly and with appropriate feeling.

PICTURE THIS. Draw a cartoon of one of the most memorable scenes from the selections you have read in this unit. Add cartoon bubbles that show the characters expressing thoughts that were not in the original selection.

Unit SEVEN

READING Nonfiction

Nonfiction is writing about real people, places, things, and events. It can also explore thoughts and ideas. Categories of nonfiction writing follow.

Forms of Nonfiction

ARTICLE. An **article** is a brief work of nonfiction on a specific topic. You can find articles in encyclopedias, newspapers, and magazines.

AUTOBIOGRAPHY. An **autobiography** is the story of a person's life told by that person. Consequently, autobiographies are told from the first-person point of view. *I Know Why the Caged Bird Sings* by Maya Angelou is an example of an autobiography.

BIOGRAPHY. A **biography** is the story of a person's life told by another person. Although biographies are told from a third-person point of view, autobiographical excerpts such as **letters**, **diaries**, and **journals** may be included.

DOCUMENTARY WRITING. **Documentary writing** records an event or subject in accurate detail. A profile of the Jazz Age or a report on human rights abuses in China would be examples of documentary writing.

ESSAY. An **essay**, originally meaning "a trial or attempt," is a short nonfiction work that explores a single subject and is typically a more lasting work than an article. Among the many types of essays are personal and expository essays. A **personal**, or **expressive, essay** deals with the life or interests of the writer. Personal essays are often, but not always, written in the first person. An **expository essay** features the developed ideas of the writer on a certain topic. "An Ethnic Trump" by Gish Jen and "It's Not Talent: It's Just Work" by Annie Dillard are both examples of essays.

Reading TIP

When you read nonfiction, you will often be reading to learn or reading for information. The purpose of this type of reading is to gain knowledge.

HISTORY. A **history** is an account of past events. To write their histories, writers may use **speeches, sermons, contracts, deeds, constitutions, laws, political tracts**, and other types of public records.

HOW-TO WRITING. **How-to writing** is writing that explains a procedure or strategy. A manual that explains how to operate a DVD player is an example of how-to writing.

MEMOIR. A **memoir** is a nonfiction narration that tells a story autobiographically or biographically. Memoirs are based on a person's experiences and reactions to events.

SPEECH. A **speech** is a public address that was originally delivered orally. "I Have a Dream" by Martin Luther King, Jr. is an example of a speech.

Purposes and Methods of Writing in Nonfiction

PURPOSE. A writer's **purpose**, or aim, is a writer's reason for writing. The following chart classifies modes, or categories, of prose writing by purpose.

Reading TIP

A nonfiction work can have more than one purpose. For example, in a memoir a writer could entertain with a story, then inform the reader about his or her reaction to a historical event. In a letter a writer could reflect on an anecdote, then persuade the reader to take action to help save the rainforest, for example.

Modes and Purposes of Writing

Mode	Purpose	Writing Forms
personal/ expressive writing	to reflect	diary entry, memoir, personal letter, autobiography, personal essay
imaginative/ descriptive writing	to entertain, to describe, to enrich, and to enlighten	poem, character sketch, play, short story
narrative writing	to tell a story, to narrate a series of events	short story, biography, legend, myth, history
informative/ expository writing	to inform, to explain	news article, research report, expository essay, book review
persuasive/ argumentative writing	to persuade	editorial, petition, political speech, persuasive essay

Types of Nonfiction Writing

In order to write effectively, a writer can choose to organize a piece of writing in different ways. The following chart describes types of writing that are commonly used in nonfiction, as well as tells how they are organized.

Type of Writing	Description
narration	Narrative writing tells a story or describes events. It may use chronological, or time, order.
dialogue	Dialogue reveals people's actual speech, which is set off with quotation marks.
description	Descriptive writing tells how things look, sound, smell, taste, or feel, often using spatial order.
exposition	Expository writing presents facts or opinions and is sometimes organized in one of these ways: ■ **Analysis** breaks something into its parts and shows how the parts are related. ■ **Classification** places subjects into categories according to what they have in common. ■ **Comparison and contrast order** presents similarities as it compares two things and differences as it contrasts them. ■ **How-to writing** presents the steps in a process or directions on how to do something.

Active Reading Strategy Checklists

When reading nonfiction, it is important to know that the author is telling you about true events. The following checklists offer things to consider when reading nonfiction selections.

1 **READ WITH A PURPOSE.** Before reading nonfiction, give yourself a purpose, or something to look for, as you read. Sometimes a purpose will be a directive from a teacher: "Find out what the author experienced on her trip to Arkansas." Other times you can set your own purpose by previewing the title, the opening lines, and instructional information. Say to yourself

- ❑ This selection will be about . . .
- ❑ I will keep track of . . .
- ❑ The author wants readers to know . . .
- ❑ The author wrote this to . . .

2 **CONNECT TO PRIOR KNOWLEDGE.** Being aware of what you already know and calling it to mind as you read can help you understand a writer's views. As you read, say to yourself

- ❑ I already know this about the author's ideas . . .
- ❑ These things in the selection are similar to something I have experienced . . .
- ❑ Something similar I've read is . . .
- ❑ I agree with this because . . .

3 **WRITE THINGS DOWN.** As you read nonfiction, write down or mark important points that the author makes. Possible ways to keep a written record include

- ❑ Underline the author's key ideas.
- ❑ Write down your thoughts about the author's ideas.
- ❑ Highlight the author's main points and supporting details.
- ❑ Create a graphic organizer to keep track of ideas.
- ❑ Use a code to respond to the author's ideas.

Reading TIP

To **connect to your prior knowledge**, compare what you are reading to
- things you've read before
- things you have experienced
- things you know about the topic

Reading TIP

Read nonfiction carefully the first time through. Take notes as you read. After you finish reading, reread your notes. Mark them up and make additions or corrections. Rereading your notes and clarifying them helps you remember what you've read.

4 MAKE PREDICTIONS. Before you read a nonfiction selection, use information about the author, the subject matter, and the title to guess what the selection will be about. As you read, confirm or deny your predictions, and make new ones based on what you learn. Make predictions like the following:

- ❑ What will come next is . . .
- ❑ The author will support ideas by . . .
- ❑ I think the selection will end with . . .
- ❑ The title tells me that the selection will be about . . .

5 VISUALIZE. Visualizing, or allowing the words on the page to create images in your mind, helps you understand the author's message. In order to visualize what a selection is about, imagine that you are the narrator. Read the words in your head with the type of expression that the author means to put behind them. Make statements such as

- ❑ This parts helps me envision how . . .
- ❑ My sketch of this part would include . . .
- ❑ This part helps me see how . . .
- ❑ This part changes my views on . . .
- ❑ The author connects ideas by . . .

6 USE TEXT ORGANIZATION. When you read nonfiction, pay attention to the main idea and supporting details. Learn to stop occasionally and retell what you have read. Say to yourself

- ❑ The writer's main point is . . .
- ❑ The writer supports the main point by . . .
- ❑ In this section, the writer is saying that . . .
- ❑ I can summarize this section by . . .
- ❑ I can follow the events because . . .

7 TACKLE DIFFICULT VOCABULARY. Difficult words can hinder your ability to understand a writer's message. Use context, consult a dictionary, or ask someone about words you do not understand. When you come across a difficult word in nonfiction, say to yourself

- ❑ The lines near this word tell me that this word means . . .
- ❑ A dictionary definition shows that the word means . . .
- ❑ My work with the word before reading helps me know that the word means . . .
- ❑ A classmate said that the word means . . .

Reading TIP

Skim a selection before you read it. Make a list of words that might slow you down, and write synonyms for each in the margins. As you read, use the synonyms in place of the words.

8 **MONITOR YOUR READING PROGRESS.** All readers encounter difficulty when they read, especially if the reading material is not self-selected. When you have to read something, note problems you are having and fix them. The key to reading success is knowing when you are having difficulty. To fix problems, say to yourself

- ❑ Because I don't understand this part, I will . . .
- ❑ Because I'm having trouble staying connected to the ideas in the selection, I will . . .
- ❑ Because the words in the selection are too hard, I will . . .
- ❑ Because the selection is long, I will . . .
- ❑ Because I can't retell what the selection was about, I will . . .

Become an Active Reader

The instruction with the nonfiction selections in this unit gives you an in-depth look at how to use one strategy. Brief margin notes guide your use of additional strategies. Questions and tips in the margins keep your attention focused on reading actively. White space in the margins allows you to add your own comments and strategy ideas. Using one active reading strategy at a time will greatly increase your reading success and enjoyment. Learn how to use several strategies in combination to ensure your complete understanding of what you are reading. When you have difficulty, use active reading solutions to fix a problem. For further information about the active reading strategies, see Unit 1, pages 4–15.

How to Use Reading Strategies with Nonfiction

The following excerpts illustrate how a reader might use active reading strategies with nonfiction.

Excerpt 1. Note how a reader uses reading strategies while reading this excerpt from *I Know Why the Caged Bird Sings* by Maya Angelou, page 371.

READ WITH A PURPOSE

I want to learn more about Angelou's life with her grandmother.

VISUALIZE

I am imagining two small, well-dressed children who look lost and have brown tags hanging from their wrists.

When I was three and Bailey four, we had arrived in the <u>musty</u> little town, wearing tags on our wrists which instructed—"To Whom It May Concern"—that we were Marguerite and Bailey Johnson Jr., from Long Beach, California, en route to Stamps, Arkansas, c/o Mrs. Annie Henderson.

Our parents had decided to put an end to their <u>calamitous</u> marriage, and Father shipped us home to his mother. A porter[1] had been charged with our welfare—he got off the train the next day in Arizona—and ourtickets were pinned to my brother's inside coat pocket.

I don't remember much of the trip, but after we reached the segregated southern part of the journey things must have looked up. Negro passengers, who always traveled with loaded lunch boxes, felt sorry for "the poor little mother-less darlings " and plied us with cold fried chicken and potato salad.

CONNECT TO PRIOR KNOWLEDGE

This reminds me of the lunch boxes my mother packs for long car trips.

MAKE PREDICTIONS

Because people in the "southern part of the journey" are so helpful, I think Marguerite and Bailey will like living in Stamps.

Excerpt 2. Note how a reader uses active reading strategies while reading this excerpt from Martin Luther King, Jr.'s "I Have a Dream" speech, page 386.

WRITE THINGS DOWN

I can use a chart to track repetition in the speech.

TACKLE DIFFICULT VOCABULARY

Heightening comes from *heighten*, or to grow taller, so "heightening Alleghenies of Pennsylvania" refers to tall mountains in Pennsylvania.

So let freedom ring from the prodigious hilltops of New Hampshire; let freedom ring from the mighty mountains of New York; let freedom ring from the heightening Alleghenies of Pennsylvania; let freedom ring from the snow-capped Rockies of Colorado; let freedom ring from the curvaceous slopes of California. But not only that. Let freedom ring from Stone Mountain of Georgia; let freedom ring from Lookout Mountain of Tennessee; let freedom ring from every hill and molehill of Mississippi. From every mountainside, let freedom ring.

And when this happens and when we allow freedom to ring, when we let it ring from every village and every hamlet, from every state and every city, we will be able to speed up that day when all God's children, black men and white men, Jews and gentiles, Protestants and Catholics, will be able to join hands and sing in the words of the old Negro spiritual: "Free at last. Free at last. Thank God Almighty, we are free at last."

MONITOR YOUR READING PROGRESS

To experience the power of King's words, I'm going to reread these paragraphs aloud with a partner.

USE TEXT ORGANIZATION

King's repetition of "let freedom ring" and use of semi-colons make it easier to understand the first paragraph.

Reader's resource

Maya Angelou's memoir, *I Know Why the Caged Bird Sings* (1970), recounts her life up to the age of sixteen. This excerpt tells about her and her brother Bailey's life in Stamps, Arkansas, where they live with their grandmother and uncle in the Wm. Johnson General Merchandise Store. Besides being a writer and poet, Angelou has also been a historian, actress, playwright, civil rights activist, producer, and director.

Word watch

PREVIEW VOCABULARY

calamitous	ply
exploit	prophesy
indeterminate	regale
inequity	renege
inordinate	resignation
intent	sparse
musty	staple
obscure	stereotyped

Reader's journal

What lesson(s) have you learned by watching someone you know?

_____

_____

_____

_____

from

I Know Why the Caged Bird Sings

by Maya Angelou

Active READING STRATEGY

VISUALIZE

Before Reading ▶ **PREVIEW THE SELECTION**

❑ Describe the setting of a popular movie to a classmate who keeps his or her eyes closed. Then have your partner tell you the title of the movie you have described.

❑ Discuss with the class how writers create setting.

❑ As you read the selection, try to visualize the setting, as well as the characters and their actions.

❑ On your own paper, draw a cluster chart like the one below with the circle in the middle labeled "Setting" and the connecting circles filled in with descriptions of Momma's general store.

Graphic Organizer

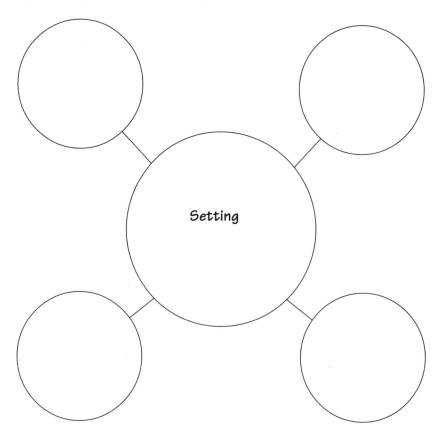

Setting

I Know Why the Caged Bird Sings

Maya Angelou

During Reading

VISUALIZE THE SETTING

- ❑ While your teacher reads aloud the first two pages, close your eyes and try to visualize the setting and characters.
- ❑ With a partner, take turns reading the rest of the story aloud, visualizing when it is your turn to listen and running a mind movie when you are speaking.
- ❑ As you proceed with the selection, add more descriptions of Momma's general store to the graphic organizer.

FROM CHAPTER 1

When I was three and Bailey four, we had arrived in the <u>musty</u> little town, wearing tags on our wrists which instructed—"To Whom It May Concern"—that we were Marguerite and Bailey Johnson Jr., from Long Beach, California, en route to Stamps, Arkansas, c/o Mrs. Annie Henderson.

Our parents had decided to put an end to their <u>calamitous</u> marriage, and Father shipped us home to his mother. A porter[1] had been charged with our welfare—he got off the train the next day in Arizona—and our tickets were pinned to my brother's inside coat pocket.

I don't remember much of the trip, but after we reached the segregated southern part of the journey,[2] things must have looked up. Negro passengers, who always traveled with

10

NOTE THE FACTS

Why are Bailey and Marguerite being sent away? To whom are they being sent?

_____

_____

_____

Reading STRATEGY
REVIEW

MAKE A PREDICTION.
After you hear your teacher read the first two paragraphs, jot down a prediction about what you think the selection will be about.

_____

_____

_____

---

1. **porter.** Carrier; in this case, a railroad employee who carries luggage
2. **segregated . . . journey.** Part of the trip took the children through states in which segregation was still practiced. Segregation is enforced separation of people based on race or ethnic origin.

| words for everyday use | **mus • ty** (mus´tē) *adj.*, dull; antiquated. *The library held many first editions.* |
| | **ca • lam • i • tous** (kə lam´ə təs) *adj.*, disastrous. *News of the <u>calamitous</u> living conditions prompted several aid organizations to visit the disaster area.* |

NOTE THE FACTS

Reread lines 18–22. Who else has made a journey similar to that of Marguerite and Bailey, and why?

_____

_____

_____

THINK AND REFLECT

What actions on the part of the grandmother show her business talents? (Infer)

_____

_____

_____

_____

Reading TIP

Review the footnotes before reading the selection in order to read uninterrupted.

loaded lunch boxes, felt sorry for "the poor little motherless darlings" and plied us with cold fried chicken and potato salad.

Years later I discovered that the United States had been crossed thousands of times by frightened Black children traveling alone to their newly affluent parents in Northern cities, or back to grandmothers in Southern towns when the urban North reneged on its economic promises.

The town reacted to us as its inhabitants had reacted to all things new before our coming. It regarded us a while without curiosity but with caution, and after we were seen to be harmless (and children) it closed in around us, as a real mother embraces a stranger's child. Warmly, but not too familiarly.

We lived with our grandmother and uncle in the rear of the Store (it was always spoken of with a capital s), which she had owned some twenty-five years.

Early in the century, Momma (we soon stopped calling her Grandmother) sold lunches to the sawmen in the lumberyard (east Stamps) and the seedmen at the cotton gin (west Stamps). Her crisp meat pies and cool lemonade, when joined to her miraculous ability to be in two places at the same time, assured her business success. From being a mobile lunch counter,[3] she set up a stand between the two points of fiscal interest[4] and supplied the workers' needs for a few years. Then she had the Store built in the heart of the Negro area. Over the years it became the lay center[5] of activities in town. On Saturdays, barbers sat their customers in the shade on the porch of the Store, and troubadours[6] on their ceaseless crawlings through the South leaned across its benches and sang their sad songs of The Brazos[7] while they played juice harps and cigar-box guitars.

The formal name of the Store was the Wm. Johnson

---

3. **mobile lunch counter.** Lunch stand that could be moved from place to place, for example, in a truck or on a cart
4. **points of . . . interest.** Businesses, here the lumberyard and cotton gin
5. **lay center.** Nonreligious civic center for all people to gather and talk
6. **troubadours.** Traveling folk singers and storytellers
7. **The Brazos.** River in southeastern and central Texas that flows into the Gulf of Mexico

words for everyday use	**ply** (plī) vt., keep supplying. *Grandmother plies me with cookies when I visit.*
	re • nege (ri nig´) vi., back out of an agreement. *If one side reneges on the agreement, the cease-fire will no longer be in effect.*

General Merchandise Store. Customers could find food
<u>staples</u>, a good variety of colored thread, mash for hogs,
corn for chickens, coal oil for lamps, light bulbs for the
50   wealthy, shoestrings, hair dressing, balloons, and flower
seeds. Anything not visible had only to be ordered.

Until we became familiar enough to belong to the Store
and it to us, we were locked up in a Fun House of Things
where the attendant had gone home for life.

Each year I watched the field across from the Store turn
caterpillar green, then gradually frosty white. I knew exactly
how long it would be before the big wagons would pull into
the front yard and load on the cotton pickers at daybreak to
carry them to the remains of slavery's plantations.

60   During the picking season my grandmother would get out
of bed at four o'clock (she never used an alarm clock) and
creak down to her knees and chant in a sleep-filled voice,
"Our Father, thank you for letting me see this New Day.
Thank you that you didn't allow the bed I lay on last night to
be my cooling board, nor my blanket my winding sheet.[8]
Guide my feet this day along the straight and narrow, and
help me to put a bridle on my tongue. Bless this house, and
everybody in it. Thank you, in the name of your Son, Jesus
Christ, Amen."

70   Before she had quite arisen, she called our names and
issued orders, and pushed her large feet into homemade
slippers and across the bare lye-washed[9] wooden floor to
light the coal-oil lamp.

The lamplight in the Store gave a soft make-believe feeling to our world which made me want to whisper and walk
about on tiptoe. The odors of onions and oranges and
kerosene had been mixing all night and wouldn't be disturbed until the wooden slat was removed from the door
and the early morning air forced its way in with the bodies
80   of people who had walked miles to reach the pickup place.

---

8. **cooling board . . . winding sheet.** *Cooling board*—place where a corpse
lies while being prepared for burial or cremation; *winding sheet*—sheet in which
a corpse is wrapped
9. **lye-washed.** Washed with a harsh, strongly alkaline soap

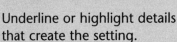

words for everyday use	**sta • ple** (stā′pəl) *n.*, item of trade, regularly stocked and in constant demand. *Rice is a <u>staple</u> of most Asian diets and is served with almost every meal.*

Literary TOOLS

SETTING. The **setting** of a
literary work is the time and
place in which it occurs
together with all the details
used to create a sense of a
particular time and place. As
you read, pay attention to the
details about Momma's
general store and its role in
the community.

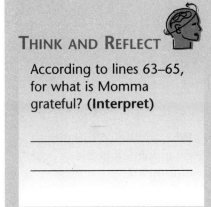

THINK AND REFLECT

According to lines 63–65,
for what is Momma
grateful? (**Interpret**)

_____

_____

MARK THE TEXT

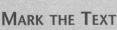

Underline or highlight details
that create the setting.

READ ALOUD

With a partner, take turns reading lines 81–85 aloud. What dialect are the characters speaking in?

_____

NOTE THE FACTS

Why are the cotton pickers disappointed in the afternoon?

_____

_____

_____

Use **THE STRATEGY**

VISUALIZE. Think about what new information you learn about the general store as you finish each page and how you would represent that information in a sketch.

"Sister, I'll have two cans of sardines."

"I'm gonna work so fast today I'm gonna make you look like you standing still."

"Lemme have a hunk uh cheese and some sody crackers."

"Just gimme a coupla them fat peanut paddies." That would be from a picker who was taking his lunch. The greasy brown paper sack was stuck behind the bib of his overalls. He'd use the candy as a snack before the noon sun called the workers to rest.

90   In those tender mornings the Store was full of laughing, joking, boasting and bragging. One man was going to pick two hundred pounds of cotton, and another three hundred. Even the children were promising to bring home fo' bits and six bits.[10]

The champion picker of the day before was the hero of the dawn. If he <u>prophesied</u> that the cotton in today's field was going to be <u>sparse</u> and stick to the bolls[11] like glue, every listener would grunt a hearty agreement.

The sound of the empty cotton sacks dragging over the

100   floor and the murmurs of waking people were sliced[12] by the cash register as we rang up the five-cent sales.

If the morning sounds and smells were touched with the supernatural, the late afternoon had all the features of the normal Arkansas life. In the dying sunlight the people dragged, rather than their empty cotton sacks.

Brought back to the Store, the pickers would step out of the backs of trucks and fold down, dirt-disappointed, to the ground. No matter how much they had picked, it wasn't enough. Their wages wouldn't even get them out of debt to

110   my grandmother, not to mention the staggering bill that waited on them at the white commissary[13] downtown.

The sounds of the new morning had been replaced with grumbles about cheating houses, weighted scales, snakes,

---

10. **fo' bits and six bits.** Fifty cents and seventy-five cents
11. **bolls.** Shell-like top parts of the cotton flower that hold the white seed pod, the cotton
12. **sliced.** Interrupted
13. **commissary.** Store

words for everyday use	proph • e • sy (präf´ə sī´) vt., predict. *Forecasters aren't always correct when they <u>prophesy</u> the weather.*
	sparse (spärs) adj., having few elements. *Kellie's first apartment had <u>sparse</u> furnishings.*

skimpy cotton and dusty rows. In later years I was to confront the <u>stereotyped</u> picture of gay song-singing cotton
pickers with such <u>inordinate</u> rage that I was told even by fellow Blacks that my paranoia was embarrassing. But I had
seen the fingers cut by the mean little cotton bolls, and I
had witnessed the backs and shoulders and arms and legs
120 resisting any further demands.

Some of the workers would leave their sacks at the Store to
be picked up the following morning, but a few had to take
them home for repairs. I winced to picture them sewing the
coarse material under a coal-oil lamp with fingers stiffening
from the day's work. In too few hours they would have to
walk back to Sister Henderson's Store, get vittles[14] and load,
again, onto the trucks. Then they would face another day of
trying to earn enough for the whole year with the heavy
knowledge that they were going to end the season as they
130 started it. Without the money or credit necessary to sustain a
family for three months. In cotton-picking time the late
afternoons revealed the harshness of Black Southern life,
which in the early morning had been softened by nature's
blessing of grogginess, forgetfulness and the soft lamplight.

FROM CHAPTER 14

The barrenness of Stamps was exactly what I wanted,
without will or consciousness. After St. Louis,[15] with its
noise and activity, its trucks and buses, and loud family
140 gatherings, I welcomed the <u>obscure</u> lanes and lonely
bungalows[16] set back deep in the dirt yards.

The <u>resignation</u> of its inhabitants encouraged me to relax.

---

14. **vittles.** Food
15. **St. Louis.** The children had been to St. Louis, Missouri, where they had
formerly lived, to visit their mother.
16. **bungalows.** One-story houses

words for everyday use

ster • e • o • typed (ster´ē ə tīpt) adj., conventional notion, not allowing for
individuality. Westerns of the 1940s and 1950s presented <u>stereotyped</u> images of
Native Americans.

in • or • di • nate (in ôr´də nit) adj., numerous. Because an <u>inordinate</u> number of
students had the same incorrect answer, the teacher concluded that many of them
had cheated.

ob • scure (əb skyoor´) adj., inconspicuous; hidden. The spare key to the front door
was kept in an <u>obscure</u> place in the garage.

res • ig • na • tion (rez´ig nā´shən) n., passive acceptance. Bill shrugged his shoulders in <u>resignation</u> when he was told he didn't get the job.

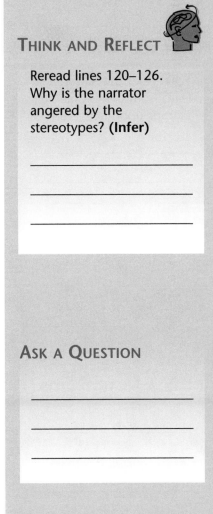

THINK AND REFLECT

Reread lines 120–126.
Why is the narrator
angered by the
stereotypes? **(Infer)**

_____

_____

_____

ASK A QUESTION

_____

_____

_____

FIX-UP IDEA

Write Things Down
Continue to fill in the
graphic organizer with
descriptive details about
Momma's general store.

NOTE THE FACTS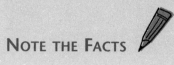

What does the narrator learn from the people of Stamps upon her return?

_____

_____

They showed me a contentment based on the belief that nothing more was coming to them, although a great deal more was due. Their decision to be satisfied with life's <u>inequities</u> was a lesson for me. Entering Stamps, I had the feeling that I was stepping over the border lines of the map and would fall, without fear, right off the end of the world. Nothing more could happen, for in Stamps nothing happened.

150   Into this cocoon I crept.

For an <u>indeterminate</u> time, nothing was demanded of me or of Bailey. We were, after all, Mrs. Henderson's California grandchildren, and had been away on a glamorous trip way up North to the fabulous St. Louis. Our father had come the year before driving a big, shiny automobile and speaking the King's English[17] with a big city accent, so all we had to do was lie quiet for months and rake in the profits of our adventures.

Farmers and maids, cooks and handymen, carpenters and
160   all the children in town, made regular pilgrimages to the Store. "Just to see the travelers."

They stood around like cutout cardboard figures and asked, "Well, how is it up North?"

"See any of them big buildings?"

"Ever ride in one of them elevators?"

"Was you scared?"

"Whitefolks any different, like they say?"

Bailey took it upon himself to answer every question, and from a corner of his lively imagination wove a tapestry of
170   entertainment for them that I was sure was as foreign to him as it was to me.

He, as usual, spoke precisely. "They have, in the North, buildings so high that for months, in the winter, you can't see the top floors."

"Tell the truth."

"They've got watermelons twice the size of a cow's head

---

17. **the King's English.** English as spoken by the king of England or well-educated people from England; very proper English

words for everyday use	
in • eq • ui • ty (in ek´wit ē) *n.*, lack of justice. *Many companies have adopted internal policies to address hiring <u>inequities</u>.*
in • de • ter • mi • nate (in´dē tʉr´mi nit) *adj.*, uncertain. *The elderly man's exact age is <u>indeterminate</u>, but his family believes he is at least one hundred years old.*

and sweeter than syrup." I distinctly remember his <u>intent</u>
face and the fascinated faces of his listeners. "And if you
can count the watermelon's seeds, before it's cut open, you
180   can win five zillion dollars and a new car."

Momma, knowing Bailey, warned, "Now Ju, be careful you
don't slip up on a not true." (Nice people didn't say "lie.")

"Everybody wears new clothes and have inside toilets. If
you fall down in one of them, you get flushed away into the
Mississippi River. Some people have iceboxes, only the
proper name is Cold Spot or Frigidaire. The snow is so
deep you can get buried right outside your door and people
won't find you for a year. We made ice cream out of the
snow." That was the only fact that I could have supported.
190   During the winter, we had collected a bowl of snow and
poured Pet[18] milk over it, and sprinkled it with sugar and
called it ice cream.

Momma beamed and Uncle Willie was proud when
Bailey <u>regaled</u> the customers with our <u>exploits</u>. We were
drawing cards[19] for the Store and objects of the town's ado-
ration. Our journey to magical places alone was a spot of
color on the town's drab canvas, and our return made us
even more the most enviable of people.

High spots in Stamps were usually negative: droughts,
200   foods, lynchings[20] and deaths.

Bailey played on the country folks' need for diversion. Just
after our return he had taken to sarcasm, picked it up as one
might pick up a stone, and put it snufflike under his lip. The
double entendres,[21] the two-pronged sentences, slid over his
tongue to dart rapier-like[22] into anything that happened to be

---

18. **Pet.** Brand of evaporated milk
19. **drawing cards.** Performers who attract an audience
20. **lynchings.** Illegal hangings
21. **double entendres.** Double meanings
22. **rapier-like.** Swordlike

<u>**words**
for
everyday
use</u>
    in • tent (in tent´) *adj.*, earnest, fixed. *The judge wore an <u>intent</u> expression as she listened to complicated testimony.*
    re • gale (ri gāl´) *vt.*, entertain. *During wartime, the U.S.O. <u>regaled</u> soldiers with choreographed shows.*
    ex • ploit (eks´ploit) *n.*, daring or bold deed. *The hero's reported <u>exploits</u> turned out to be fictionalized deeds.*

THINK AND REFLECT

From what you can infer in lines 186–187, is Momma really angry with Bailey's exaggerations? **(Infer)**

_____

_____

NOTE THE FACTS

What kinds of things usually catch the interest of the residents of Stamps? What interests them now?

_____

_____

_____

THINK AND REFLECT

Why would the statement that Bailey Junior is "just like his daddy" be a statement of pride? (Analyze)

_____

_____

_____

_____

in the way. Our customers, though, generally were so straight thinking and speaking that they were never hurt by his attacks. They didn't comprehend them.

"Bailey Junior sound just like Big Bailey. Got a silver tongue. Just like his daddy."

"I hear tell they don't pick cotton up there. How the people live then?"

Bailey said that the cotton up North was so tall, if ordinary people tried to pick it they'd have to get up on ladders, so the cotton farmers had their cotton picked by machines. ∎

210

Reflect ON YOUR READING

After Reading ➤ SKETCH THE SETTING

When you finish filling in the graphic organizer, review the descriptions you added. Draw a sketch with the details from your cluster chart that you want to emphasize. Then, tell a classmate why you included the details you did.

Reading Skills and Test Practice

ANALYZE SETTING

Discuss with your partner how best to answer the following comparison-and-contrast questions.

1. Which of the following best describes the store in the morning before it opens?
   a. bustling with preparation
   b. peaceful and almost enchanted
   c. tired and worn
   d. stuffy and eerie

What is the correct answer to the question above? How were you able to eliminate the other answers? How did your use of the reading strategy help you answer the question?

_____

_____

_____

2. Which of the following statements best contrasts St. Louis and Stamps?
   a. Stamps was full of nosy, gossipy people, and St. Louis was full of people who let you be yourself.
   b. St. Louis was fun, and Stamps was boring.
   c. Stamps was quiet and relaxing, and St. Louis was fast-paced and noisy.
   d. St. Louis was quiet and relaxing, and Stamps was fast-paced and noisy.

What is the correct answer to the question above? How were you able to eliminate the other answers? How did your use of the reading strategy help you answer the question?

_____

_____

_____

THINK-ALOUD NOTES

_____

_____

_____

_____

_____

_____

_____

_____

_____

_____

_____

Investigate, Inquire, and Imagine

RECALL: GATHER FACTS → INTERPRET: FIND MEANING

1a. What encourages the narrator to relax upon her return to Stamps from St. Louis?

1b. What is probably the reason that the inhabitants of Stamps come to the store "just to see the travelers"?

ANALYZE: TAKE THINGS APART → SYNTHESIZE: BRING THINGS TOGETHER

2a. Compare and contrast St. Louis and Stamps in the narrator's eyes.

2b. What do you think motivates Angelou to write about the residents of Stamps? Provide evidence from the text to support your response.

EVALUATE: MAKE JUDGMENTS → EXTEND: CONNECT IDEAS

3a. According to Angelou, living among the black people of Stamps taught her an important lesson: that it was best to be "satisfied with life's inequities," or in other words, to be content with things being unequal. Do you think this was a good lesson for young Marguerite to learn?

3b. If you were Marguerite, how would it have made you feel to see the people around you accepting the inequalities of life? Would you have taken the same attitude, or would you have wanted to fight?

Literary Tools

SETTING. The **setting** of a literary work is the time and place in which it occurs, together with all the details used to create a sense of a particular time and place. What details are used to create the setting of the store in the mornings, before "the wooden slat was removed from the door"? Compare the early morning setting in the store with the late afternoon setting. What role does the general store play in the community?

_____

_____

_____

_____

_____

_____

_____

_____

WordWorkshop

CONTEXTUAL SENTENCES. Review the Words for Everyday Use from this selection. Then use the pairs of words below together in contextual sentences. Contextual sentences give clues as to what vocabulary words mean. (See pages 13–14 of Unit 1.) Feel free to reverse the order of the paired words.

EXAMPLE
intent/calamitous
Juanita acted with good *intent* only to reap *calamitous* results.

1. staple/sparse

_____

2. prophesy/obscure

_____

3. stereotyped/resignation

_____

4. exploit/regale

_____

5. musty/indeterminate

Read-Write Connection

What kind of role model is Momma to Marguerite and Bailey?

_____

_____

_____

_____

Beyond the Reading

SHARECROPPER PROJECT. Some of the townspeople of Stamps were probably sharecroppers, poor tenant farmers in the South. Find out more about them by reading fiction or nonfiction excerpts. Then create a project that reveals something about the sharecroppers' lives, such as a skit, an oral interpretation, or a photography exhibit with commentary. Share your project with the class.

GO ONLINE. Visit the EMC Internet Resource Center at **emcp.com** to find links and additional activities for this selection.

"I Have a Dream"
by Martin Luther King, Jr.

Reader's resource

On August 28, 1963, Martin Luther King, Jr. joined other civil rights leaders in the March on Washington in support of civil rights legislation. To an interracial audience of more than 200,000 people, he delivered his famous **"I Have a Dream"** speech at the foot of the Lincoln Memorial. A leader of the nonviolent civil disobedience movement to combat racial discrimination, King was awarded the Nobel Peace Prize in 1964. In 1968, he was assassinated.

Word watch

PREVIEW VOCABULARY

brutality	manacle
creed	mobility
discord	redemptive
emerge	sear
exalt	tribulation
languish	wallow

Reader's journal

What changes would you like to make in this country?

_____

_____

_____

Active READING STRATEGY

USE TEXT ORGANIZATION

Before Reading ➤ PREVIEW THE SELECTION

❑ Brainstorm everything you know about Martin Luther King, Jr. and the civil rights movement.

❑ Read the Reader's Resource for additional background information about the speech and the speaker.

❑ Keep in mind that the selection that you are about to read was written to be delivered orally.

❑ Discuss as a class some of the common organizational techniques used to make an effective speech, and jot down these techniques.

❑ As you read, you will use the chart below to list the main idea for each paragraph.

Graphic Organizer

Introduction	Body	Conclusion
(Paragraph 1) King tells the crowd that this gathering will be remembered as the greatest demonstration for freedom in history.		

I Have a Dream

Martin Luther King, Jr.

August 28, 1963
Lincoln Memorial, Washington, D.C.

I'm happy to join with you today in what will go down in history as the greatest demonstration for freedom in the history of our nation.

Fivescore[1] years ago, a great American, in whose symbolic shadow we stand today, signed the Emancipation Proclamation.[2] This momentous decree came as a great beacon light of hope to millions of Negro slaves who had been <u>seared</u> in the flames of withering injustice. It came as a joyous daybreak to end the long night of their captivity.

10   But one hundred years later, the Negro still is not free; one hundred years later, the life of the Negro is still sadly crippled by the <u>manacles</u> of segregation[3] and the chains of discrimination; one hundred years later, the Negro lives on a lonely island of poverty in the midst of a vast ocean of material prosperity; one hundred years later, the Negro is

---

1. **Fivescore.** One hundred; one score equals twenty
2. **Emancipation Proclamation.** Document signed by Abraham Lincoln in 1863 that legally set free the slaves in the Confederate states
3. **segregation.** Enforced separation of people based on group characteristics

During Reading

IDENTIFY AND USE TEXT ORGANIZATION

- ❑ Follow along in the selection as your teacher reads the first paragraph aloud.
- ❑ Follow along again as your teacher reads the next three paragraphs.
- ❑ Discuss your answers with the class.
- ❑ Read the remainder of the speech on your own, pausing occasionally to identify how each paragraph fits into the speech's organization.
- ❑ Record the main idea for each paragraph in the graphic organizer.

READ ALOUD

Listen to an audio recording of King giving this speech; mark the words and phrases that King emphasizes and the passages where he raises his voice. Then read one of the marked passages aloud to a classmate. Tell your partner what King was trying to emphasize with the use of his voice.

MARK THE TEXT

Underline or highlight the lines that show how King believes this demonstration will be remembered.

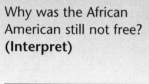

NOTE THE FACTS

According to lines 10–13, by what is "the life of the Negro" still crippled?

_____

_____

THINK AND REFLECT

Why was the African American still not free? **(Interpret)**

_____

_____

THINK AND REFLECT

Reread lines 27–32. Summarize how King answered the question, "When will you be satisfied?" **(Synthesize)**

_____

_____

_____

_____

Use THE STRATEGY

USE TEXT ORGANIZATION. Make sure to stop at the end of each paragraph to record the main idea of that paragraph in the appropriate column of the graphic organizer.

still <u>languished</u> in the corners of American society and finds himself in exile in his own land. . . .

Nineteen sixty-three is not an end, but a beginning. And those who hope that the Negro needed to blow off steam and will now be content, will have a rude awakening if the nation returns to business as usual. There will be neither rest nor tranquility in America until the Negro is granted his citizenship rights. The whirlwinds of the revolt will continue to shake the foundations of our nation until the bright day of Justice <u>emerges</u>. . . .

There are those who are asking the devotees of Civil Rights, "When will you be satisfied?" We can never be satisfied as long as the Negro is the victim of the unspeakable horrors of police <u>brutality</u>; we can never be satisfied as long as our bodies, heavy with the fatigue of travel, cannot gain lodging in the motels of the highways and the hotels of the cities; we cannot be satisfied as long as the Negro's basic <u>mobility</u> is from a smaller ghetto[4] to a larger one; we can never be satisfied as long as our children are stripped of their selfhood and robbed of their dignity by signs stating "For Whites Only"; we cannot be satisfied as long as the Negro in Mississippi cannot vote and a Negro in New York believes he has nothing for which to vote. No! No, we are not satisfied, and we will not be satisfied until "justice rolls down like waters and righteousness like a mighty stream."[5]

I am not unmindful that some of you have come here out of great trials and <u>tribulations</u>. Some of you have come fresh from narrow jail cells. Some of you have come from areas where your quest for freedom left you battered by the storms of persecution and staggered by the winds of police

---

4. **ghetto.** Section of a city in which many members of a minority group live, either by choice or because of economic or social pressure

5. **"justice rolls down . . . stream."** Biblical reference to Amos 5:24

---

words for everyday use

lan • guish (lan´gwish) _vi._, lose force or liveliness. _Children who don't receive love and affection <u>languish</u>._

e • merge (ē murj´) _vi._, become apparent or known; come forth into view. _The faint outlines of my surroundings began to <u>emerge</u> as my eyes adjusted to the dim lighting._

bru • tal • i • ty (broo tal´ə te) _n._, cruelty. _Protesters condemned the <u>brutality</u> of the police._

mo • bil • i • ty (mō´ bil´ə tē) _n._, ability to move from place to place. _A bicycle increases one's <u>mobility</u>._

trib • u • la • tion (trib´yoo lā shən) _n._, great misery or distress, as from oppression. _The <u>tribulations</u> of the refugees are detailed on the nightly news._

brutality. You have been the veterans of creative suffering. Continue to work with the faith that unearned suffering is <u>redemptive</u>. Go back to Mississippi. Go back to Alabama. Go back to South Carolina. Go back to Georgia. Go back to Louisiana. Go back to the slums and ghettos of our northern cities, knowing that somehow the situation can and will be changed. Let us not <u>wallow</u> in the valley of despair.

I say to you today, my friends, so even though we face the difficulties of today and tomorrow, I still have a dream. It is a dream deeply rooted in the American meaning of its <u>creed</u>, "We hold these truths to be self-evident, that all men are created equal."[6] I have a dream that one day on the red hills of Georgia, sons of former slaves and the sons of former slave owners will be able to sit down together at the table of brotherhood. I have a dream that one day even the state of Mississippi, a state sweltering with the heat of injustice, sweltering with the heat of oppression, will be transformed into an oasis of freedom and justice. I have a dream that my four little children will one day live in a nation where they will not be judged by the color of their skin, but the content of their character.

I have a dream today!

I have a dream that one day down in Alabama—with its vicious racists, with its governor having his lips dripping with the words of interposition and nullification[7]—one day right there in Alabama, little black boys and black girls will be able to join hands with little white boys and white girls as sisters and brothers.

I have a dream today!

I have a dream that one day "every valley shall be <u>exalted</u>

---

6. **"We hold these truths to be self-evident, that all men are created equal."** First line of the second paragraph of the Declaration of Independence

7. **interposition and nullification.** Dr. King was talking about the Alabama governor's refusal to obey a federal requirement to allow African-American children to attend public schools. *Interposition* is the disputed theory that a state can reject a federal mandate. *Nullification* refers to the refusal of a state to enforce any federal law.

words for everyday use

re • demp • tive (ri demp´tiv) *adj.*, serving to free from the consequences of sin. *The pastor's sermon discussed the <u>redemptive</u> promises of the New Testament.*

wal • low (wä´ lō) *vi.*, overly indulge oneself. *Jeremy <u>wallowed</u> in self-pity for a month after his girlfriend broke up with him.*

creed (krēd) *n.*, statement of principle or opinion. *The newly formed organization announced its <u>creed</u> in a statement of purpose.*

ex • alted (eg zôlt´) *vt.*, raised in status; elevated by praise. *The head of the relief organization <u>exalted</u> the group for its tireless efforts.*

FIX-UP IDEA

Read Aloud
If you have difficulty applying the reading strategy (identifying and using the text's organization), work with a partner to read the speech aloud. Notice how some techniques, such as repetition and parallelism, become more apparent while listening to the speech delivered orally. Continue applying the fix-up idea as you read.

NOTE THE FACTS

What was the dream King had for his four children?

_____

_____

_____

Reading STRATEGY REVIEW

VISUALIZE. Review the Reading Strategy for *I Know Why the Caged Bird Sings* on page 371. **Visualizing,** the act of making a conscious mental picture, can help you imagine the kind of society that King wants for all citizens of the United States. What does this society look like? Do you think that King's vision of equality exists today? If not, what problems still exist?

_____

_____

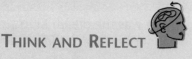

THINK AND REFLECT

Reread lines 106–108. What did King believe would happen if freedom were allowed to ring? (Interpret)

_____

_____

_____

_____

NOTE THE FACTS

What will African Americans sing when they are free?

_____

_____

and every hill and mountain shall be made low. The rough places will be made plain and the crooked places will be made straight, and the glory of the Lord shall be revealed, and all flesh shall see it together."[8]

This is our hope. This is the faith that I go back to the South with. With this faith we shall be able to transform the jangling <u>discords</u> of our nation into a beautiful symphony of brotherhood. With this faith we will be able to work together, to pray together, to struggle together, to go to jail together, to stand up for freedom together, knowing that we will be free one day. And this will be the day. This will be the day when all of God's children will be able to sing with new meaning, "My country 'tis of thee, sweet land of liberty, of thee I sing. Land where my fathers died, land of the pilgrim's pride, from every mountainside, let freedom ring."[9] And if America is to be a great nation this must become true. . . .

So let freedom ring from the prodigious hilltops of New Hampshire; let freedom ring from the mighty mountains of New York; let freedom ring from the heightening Alleghenies of Pennsylvania; let freedom ring from the snow-capped Rockies of Colorado; let freedom ring from the curvaceous slopes of California. But not only that. Let freedom ring from Stone Mountain of Georgia; let freedom ring from Lookout Mountain of Tennessee; let freedom ring from every hill and molehill of Mississippi. From every mountainside, let freedom ring.

And when this happens and when we allow freedom to ring, when we let it ring from every village and every hamlet, from every state and every city, we will be able to speed up that day when all God's children, black men and white men, Jews and gentiles, Protestants and Catholics, will be able to join hands and sing in the words of the old Negro spiritual: "Free at last. Free at last. Thank God Almighty, we are free at last." ■

---

8. **"every valley shall be . . . see it together."** Biblical reference to Isaiah 40:4–9
9. **"My country 'tis of thee, . . . let freedom ring."** Lines from a well-known American anthem

words for everyday use	**dis • cord** (dis´kôrd) *n.*, conflict. <u>Discord</u> among siblings is a natural part of family life.

Reflect ON YOUR READING

When you finish the graphic organizer, review the information you recorded. Write a short paragraph about whether the speech is more powerful when read or listened to. Give reasons for your answer.

_____

_____

_____

_____

_____

Reading Skills and Test Practice

ANALYZE DEVELOPMENT OF MAIN IDEAS

Discuss with your partner how best to answer the following questions about main ideas.

1. How does King emphasize the need for justice and equality?
   a. He alludes to Lincoln and the signing of the Emancipation Proclamation.
   b. He describes a nightmare that he had.
   c. He repeats the phrase "We can never be satisfied."
   d. He says, "We are free at last."

What is the correct answer to the question above? How were you able to eliminate the other answers? How did your use of the reading strategy help you answer the question?

_____

_____

2. What is the effect of King's repetition of the phrase "I have a dream"?
   a. It bores the listener.
   b. It angers the crowd.
   c. It gives hope.
   d. It helps the audience remember his point.

What is the correct answer to the question above? How were you able to eliminate the other answers? How did your use of the reading strategy help you answer the question?

_____

_____

THINK-ALOUD NOTES

_____

_____

_____

_____

_____

_____

_____

_____

_____

_____

_____

Investigate, Inquire, and Imagine

RECALL: GATHER FACTS
1a. In what kind of nation does King dream that his children will live?

→ INTERPRET: FIND MEANING
1b. What is the reason that "those who hope that the Negro . . . will now be content, will have a rude awakening"?

ANALYZE: TAKE THINGS APART
2a. Outline the main points King makes in his speech.

→ SYNTHESIZE: BRING THINGS TOGETHER
2b. Of what kind of relationship between African-American and white human beings does King dream in his speech? Does that kind of relationship exist today? Explain.

EVALUATE: MAKE JUDGMENTS
3a. Evaluate how well King's use of the Isaiah quote in paragraph 11 reinforces his message.

→ EXTEND: CONNECT IDEAS
3b. What religious foundation is there for King's new vision for America? In the Bible, read John 3:16 and Matthew 5:3–11.

Literary Tools

REPETITION. **Repetition** is a writer's conscious reuse of a sound, word, phrase, sentence, or other element. Complete the graphic organizer below, listing repeated phrases that King uses on the left. On the right explain what ideas are reinforced by the repetition. One example has been done for you. What is the effect of these examples of repetition on the style of King's speech?

Repeated Phrases	Ideas
"one hundred years later"	The idea is reinforced that African Americans are still not free a hundred years after the end of slavery

WordWorkshop

CONNOTATION. "I Have a Dream" is one of the most famous speeches ever delivered in the United States. In part, the speech resonates with listeners and readers because it uses such powerful language. Use the chart that follows to classify the words below according to connotation, the emotional association attached to a word.

brutality   creed   exalt   manacle   sear

Positive	Negative	Neutral

Next, using these same vocabulary words, create sentences that reinforce the connotation you decided on for each word.

1. brutality _____

2. creed _____

3. exalted _____

4. manacle _____

5. sear _____

Read-Write Connection

If Martin Luther King, Jr. were to give his speech today, how might he change paragraph 5? Use your own paper for your response.

Beyond the Reading

THE NOBEL PEACE PRIZE. Read about the accomplishments of another person who, like King, has won the Nobel Peace Prize. Write a short summary in your own words of why he or she was awarded this prestigious prize. If you want to do your research online, type in "Nobel Peace Prize" using your favorite search engine.

GO ONLINE. Visit the Internet Resource Center at **emcp.com** to find links and additional activities for this selection.

"Thinking Like a Mountain"

by Aldo Leopold

A Sand County Almanac (1949), from which **"Thinking Like a Mountain"** is taken, is a collection of essays by Aldo Leopold about nature and ecology. Leopold believed that all things in nature are interrelated and that human beings must be responsible to nature and its ecosystems, systems made up of an ecological community and its natural environment. In the selection, one of the main themes from the *Almanac* emerges—that nature was here first, long before human beings arrived on Earth; therefore, they have a responsibility to preserve nature.

Word watch

PREVIEW VOCABULARY

adversity	implicit
conviction	literally
decipher	mêlée
defiant	molder
defoliate	objectively
extirpate	requisite
ford	

Reader's journal

In what ways have you been respectful toward nature?

_____

_____

_____

Active READING STRATEGY

CONNECT TO PRIOR KNOWLEDGE

Before Reading ▶ ACTIVATE PRIOR KNOWLEDGE

❑ Read the Reader's Resource.
❑ Respond to the Reader's Journal question. Discuss your response with a small group of your classmates.
❑ With your class, brainstorm things you know or think about wolves and mountains.
❑ Then connect to your prior knowledge by filling out the before reading section of the Connections Chart below.

Graphic Organizer

Before Reading
Read the selection title. Then skim the selection and answer the following questions.
1. What kind of selection is this (poem, play, short story, essay, speech, etc.)?   _____
2. What do you think this selection will be about?   _____   _____
3. List three facts that you know, or experiences that you have had, that relate to the subject of this selection.   _____   _____   _____

thinking Like A Mountain

Aldo Leopold

A deep chesty bawl echoes from rimrock[1] to rimrock,
rolls down the mountain, and fades into the far
blackness of the night. It is an outburst of wild <u>defiant</u>
sorrow, and of contempt for all the <u>adversities</u> of the world.

Every living thing (and perhaps many a dead one as well)
pays heed to that call. To the deer it is a reminder of the way
of all flesh, to the pine a forecast of midnight scuffles and of
blood upon the snow, to the coyote a promise of gleanings[2]
to come, to the cowman a threat of red ink at the bank,[3] to
10 the hunter a challenge of fang against bullet. Yet behind
these obvious and immediate hopes and fears there lies a
deeper meaning, known only to the mountain itself. Only
the mountain has lived long enough to listen <u>objectively</u> to
the howl of a wolf.

Those unable to <u>decipher</u> the hidden meaning know

---

1. **rimrock.** Rock forming on the edge of a cliff
2. **gleanings.** Leftovers; remains
3. **red ink at the bank.** Debt; accountants sometimes use red ink to record losses.

words for everyday use	
	de • fi • ant (dē fī´ənt) *adj.*, openly resisting. *Jeremiah was <u>defiant</u> about going to bed early.*
	ad • ver • si • ty (ad vur´sə tē) *n.*, state of misery and misfortune. *Gwen lost her job, but even in her <u>adversity</u> she maintained a positive outlook.*
	ob • jec • tive • ly (əb jək´tiv lē) *adv.*, without bias or prejudice. *A judge is supposed to consider each case <u>objectively</u>.*
	de • ci • pher (dē sī´fər) *vt.*, make out the meaning of. *Language experts are trying to <u>decipher</u> the ancient writing found in the tomb.*

During Reading

CONNECT TO PRIOR KNOWLEDGE

❑ Follow along in the selection as your teacher reads the first three paragraphs aloud.

❑ With the class, discuss how Leopold's observations compare to your prior understanding of wolves and mountains.

❑ Jot down the connections you can make between your prior knowledge and the selection.

❑ Read the remainder of the selection on your own. Record how the new things you're learning about wolves and mountains relate to your prior knowledge.

NOTE THE FACTS

Reread lines 6–10. What different meanings does the "deep chesty bawl" have?

_____

_____

_____

_____

MAKE A NOTE

_____

_____

_____

_____

What kind of "small events" distinguish wolf country from" all other land"?

_____

_____

THINK AND REFLECT

Reread lines 24–25. What does Leopold personify, or speak of, as though it had human characteristics? What question is Leopold raising in the mind of the reader? **(Infer)**

_____

_____

_____

NOTE THE FACTS

In lines 37–38, why did they shoot the wolves?

_____

_____

Literary TOOLS

PERSONIFICATION.
Personification is a figure of speech in which an idea, animal, or thing is described as if it were a person. As you read, pay attention to what elements of nature are being personified and in what ways they are perceived as being human.

nevertheless that it is there, for it is felt in all wolf country, and distinguishes that country from all other land. It tingles in the spine of all who hear wolves by night, or who scan their tracks by day. Even without sight or sound of wolf, it

20 is <u>implicit</u> in a hundred small events: the midnight whinny of a pack horse, the rattle of rolling rocks, the bound of a fleeing deer, the way shadows lie under the spruces. Only the ineducable tyro[4] can fail to sense the presence or absence of wolves, or the fact that mountains have a secret opinion about them.

My own <u>conviction</u> on this score dates from the day I saw a wolf die. We were eating lunch on a high rimrock, at the foot of which a turbulent river elbowed its way. We saw what we thought was a doe <u>fording</u> the torrent, her breast

30 awash in white water. When she climbed the bank toward us and shook out her tail, we realized our error: it was a wolf. A half-dozen others, evidently grown pups, sprang from the willows and all joined in a welcoming <u>mêlée</u> of wagging tails and playful maulings. What was <u>literally</u> a pile of wolves writhed and tumbled in the center of an open flat at the foot of our rimrock.

In those days we had never heard of passing up a chance to kill a wolf. In a second we were pumping lead into the pack, but with more excitement than accuracy: how to aim a

40 steep downhill shot is always confusing. When our rifles were empty, the old wolf was down, and a pup was dragging a leg into impassable slide-rocks.

We reached the old wolf in time to watch a fierce green fire dying in her eyes. I realized then, and have known ever since, that there was something new to me in those eyes— something known only to her and to the mountain. I was

---

4. **tyro.** Beginner; novice

young then, and full of trigger-itch; I thought that because fewer wolves meant more deer, that no wolves would mean hunters' paradise. But after seeing the green fire die, I

50 sensed that neither the wolf nor the mountain agreed with such a view.

Since then I have lived to see state after state <u>extirpate</u> its wolves. I have watched the face of many a newly wolfless mountain, and seen the south-facing slopes wrinkle with a maze of new deer trails. I have seen every edible bush and seedling browsed, first to anaemic desuetude,[5] and then to death. I have seen every edible tree <u>defoliated</u> to the height of a saddlehorn.[6] Such a mountain looks as if someone had given God a new pruning shears, and forbidden Him all other

60 exercise. In the end the starved bones of the hoped-for deer herd, dead of its own too-much, bleach with the bones of the dead sage, or <u>molder</u> under the high-lined junipers.

I now suspect that just as a deer herd lives in mortal fear of its wolves, so does a mountain live in mortal fear of its deer. And perhaps with better cause, for while a buck pulled down by wolves can be replaced in two or three years, a range pulled down by too many deer may fail of replacement in as many decades.

So also with cows. The cowman who cleans his range of

70 wolves does not realize that he is taking over the wolf's job of trimming the herd to fit the range. He has not learned to think like a mountain. Hence we have dustbowls,[7] and rivers washing the future into the sea.

We all strive for safety, prosperity, comfort, long life, and dullness. The deer strives with his supple legs, the cowman with trap and poison, the statesman with pen, the most of us with machines, votes, and dollars, but it all comes to the

words for everyday use

ex • tir • pate (ek´stər pāt´) *vt.*, destroy or remove completely. *White hunters extirpated buffalo from most of North America.*

de • fo • li • ate (dē fō´lē āt´ ed) *vt.*, strip of leaves. *The harmful chemicals can defoliate acres of trees.*

mold • er (mōl´dər) *vi.*, crumble into dust. *Mummified human remains do not molder.*

READ ALOUD

Read the highlighted passage aloud (lines 43–51). Then discuss these questions with a classmate. What was Leopold's prior knowledge of wolves before the incident in which he saw a wolf die? Was the lesson he learned acquired through rational thought or emotional response?

NOTE THE FACTS

What idea did the narrator have about killing off all wolves? How did watching the wolf die change this view?

_____

_____

_____

MARK THE TEXT

Underline or highlight
Thoreau's attitude toward
nature.

80

same thing: peace in our time. A measure of success in this is
all well enough, and perhaps is a <u>requisite</u> to objective
thinking, but too much safety seems to yield only danger in
the long run. Perhaps this is behind Thoreau's[8] dictum: In
wildness is the salvation of the world. Perhaps this is the
hidden meaning in the howl of the wolf, long known among
mountains, but seldom perceived among men. ■

---

8. **Thoreau's.** Henry David Thoreau (1817–1862) was a well-known American
naturalist and writer.

**words
for
everyday
use**

req • ui • site (rek´wə zit) *n.,* necessity. *It is a <u>requisite</u> that students study math
during their freshman and sophomore years.*

Reflect ON YOUR READING

After Reading ➤ SUMMARIZE WHAT YOU LEARNED

After you finish reading, review your notes about the connections you made to your prior knowledge. Complete the after-reading section of the Connections Chart below. Describe below how your ideas about wolves and mountains have changed. Then discuss your summary with the small group you met with when you did the before-reading activity.

After Reading
Complete this section after reading the selection.
1. Did you guess correctly what the selection was about? Explain.
_____
2. What did you learn from this selection that you did not know before reading it?
_____

Reading Skills and Test Practice

IDENTIFY LITERARY ELEMENTS

Discuss with your partner how best to answer the following questions about literary elements.

1. What is the main conflict in the essay?
   a. deer vs. wolves
   b. man vs. deer
   c. mountains vs. deer
   d. human vs. nature

What is the correct answer to the question above? How were you able to eliminate the other answers? How did your use of the reading strategy help you answer the question?

_____

2. Which of the following words best describes the author's tone toward his subject?
   a. hostile
   b. reverent
   c. sad
   d. detached

What is the correct answer to the question above? How were you able to eliminate the other answers? How did your use of the reading strategy help you answer the question?

THINK-ALOUD NOTES

_____

_____

_____

_____

_____

_____

_____

_____

_____

_____

_____

Investigate, Inquire, and Imagine

RECALL: GATHER FACTS
1a. What has the narrator seen "state after state" do to wolves?

INTERPRET: FIND MEANING
1b. What are the consequences of destroying wolves?

ANALYZE: TAKE THINGS APART
2a. What kind of relationship between animals and nature is described in the essay? How does that relationship change when humans attempt to tame or destroy the "wildness" of nature?

SYNTHESIZE: BRING THINGS TOGETHER
2b. Does the narrator remain "full of trigger itch"? Explain.

EVALUATE: MAKE JUDGMENTS
3a. Are Leopold's attitudes toward preserving a balanced ecosystem still important today? Explain.

EXTEND : CONNECT IDEAS
3b. Today some farmers are growing biologically engineered crops. The pollen from these crops mixes unintentionally with non-biologically engineered crops. What do you think Aldo Leopold's attitude would be toward this agricultural practice?

Literary Tools

PERSONIFICATION. **Personification** is a figure of speech in which an idea, animal, or thing is described as if it were a person. Complete the graphic organizer below, placing the elements of nature that are personified on the left and their human characteristics on the right. How does the use of personification help Leopold to achieve his aim?

Object of Personification	Human Characteristics
the wolf	defiant sorrow contempt for all the adversities of the world

WordWorkshop

PREFIXES. A prefix is a group of letters that comes at the beginning of a word and has its own meaning. For example, *de–* is a prefix meaning "do the opposite of," "remove (from)," or "reduce." Identify the prefix in the following Words for Everyday Use for this selection. Look up each prefix in the dictionary, and note all of its meanings. Then, identify three new words that contain each prefix.

1. decipher
   prefix: _____
   meanings(s): _____
   three new words:

   _____   _____   _____

2. implicit
   prefix: _____
   meaning(s): _____
   three new words:

   _____   _____   _____

3. objectively
   prefix: _____
   meaning(s): _____
   three new words:

   _____   _____   _____

4. adversity
   prefix: _____
   meaning(s): _____
   three new words:

   _____   _____   _____

5. defiant
   prefix: _____
   meaning(s): _____
   three new words:

   _____   _____   _____

Read-Write Connection

What does it mean to think like a mountain? Use your own paper to write your response.

Beyond the Reading

ENVIRONMENTAL PRESERVATION. Aldo Leopold was one of the founding members of the Wilderness Society, a group dedicated to the conservation of the natural environment. Research this organization or one of many others dedicated to preserving the environment to find out the group's mission and how they pursue it.

Go Online. Visit the EMC Internet Resource Center at **emcp.com** to find links and additional activities for this selection.

"An *Ethnic* Trump"

by Gish Jen

"An Ethnic Trump" is a personal essay about Gish Jen's experiences as the mother of a biracial child. Jen is Chinese American and her husband is of Irish descent. Yet somehow, people think of their son, Luke, as mainly Chinese. Jen ponders what it means to be multiracial in American society, and wonders how important it really is to hold on to one's ethnic heritage. Jen has also written about the Chinese-American experience in her novels.

Active READING STRATEGY

READ WITH A PURPOSE

Before Reading ➤ SET A PURPOSE FOR READING

❑ Read the Reader's Resource.
❑ Preview the graphic organizer below. Decide on a purpose for reading this essay. For example, you might read to learn about the author's life, learn about some challenges faced by multiethnic children, or explore how children view race and ethnicity.
❑ Write down your purpose for reading in the before-reading section of the Reader's Purpose Chart below.

Graphic Organizer

Before Reading Set a purpose for reading.
During Reading Take notes on what you learn.
After Reading Reflect on your purpose and what you learned.

Word watch

PREVIEW VOCABULARY

brazen	inevitable
derision	manifest
ethnicity	trump

Reader's journal

How do you define your ethnic heritage?

_____

_____

_____

An Ethnic Trump

Gish Jen

That my son, Luke, age four, goes to Chinese-culture school seems <u>inevitable</u> to most people, even though his father is of Irish descent. For certain <u>ethnicities</u> <u>trump</u> others; Chinese, for example, trumps Irish. This has something to do with the relative distance of certain cultures from mainstream American culture, but it also has to do with race. For as we all know, it is not only certain ethnicities that trump others but certain colors: black trumps white, for example, always and forever; a mulatto is not a kind of white person, but a kind of black person.

And so it is, too, that my son is considered a kind of Asian person whose <u>manifest</u> destiny is to embrace Asian things. The Chinese language. Chinese food. Chinese New Year. No one cares whether he speaks Gaelic[1] or wears green on Saint Patrick's Day. For though Luke's

10

---

1. **Gaelic.** The Irish language

words for everyday use

in • ev • i • ta • ble (i ne' və tə bəl) *adj.*, unavoidable. *The race-car driver swerved to avoid a crash, but it was useless: the collision was <u>inevitable</u>.*

eth • nic • i • ty (eth ni' sə tē) *n.*, quality such as one's country or tribe of origin, religion, language, or other culturally distinguishing features. *Musician Lenny Kravitz has a mixed <u>ethnicity</u>: he is part Jewish and part African American.*

trump (trəmp) *vt.*, override or outrank. *In most card games, an ace <u>trumps</u> a ten.*

man • i • fest (ma' ń fest) *adj.*, obvious. *Megan's path in life was <u>manifest</u> from the very beginning: since she was a toddler, she wanted to be a dancer.*

During Reading

READ WITH A PURPOSE

- [ ] Follow along in the text as your teacher reads aloud the first two paragraphs.
- [ ] With the class, discuss the ideas presented in these first two paragraphs.
- [ ] If needed, revise your purpose for reading based on what the essay seems to be about.
- [ ] Read the remainder of the selection on your own, keeping your purpose in mind.
- [ ] In the during-reading section of the graphic organizer, take notes on information that helps you fulfill your purpose for reading.

MARK THE TEXT

Underline or highlight Luke's two ethnicities.

Literary TOOLS

ANECDOTE. An **anecdote** is usually a short narrative of an interesting, amusing, or biographical incident. As you read, try to discover the purpose for each anecdote. What point does the author want to reinforce with the anecdote?

THINK AND REFLECT

Reread line 36. Why do the boys assume Luke is Chinese? Why does Luke respond as he does? **(Infer)**

_____

_____

THINK AND REFLECT

Reread lines 43–44. What does Luke's mother tell him about his ethnicity? Why does she say this? **(Perspective)**

_____

_____

_____

skin is fair, and his features mixed, people see his straight black hair and "know" who he is.

But is this how we should define ourselves, by other people's perceptions? My husband, Dave, and I had origi-
20 nally hoped for Luke to grow up embracing his whole complex ethnic heritage. We had hoped to pass on to him values and habits of mind that had actually survived in both of us.

Then one day, Luke combed his black hair and said he was turning it yellow. Another day, a fellow mother reported that her son had invited all blond-haired children like himself to his birthday party. And yet another day, Luke was happily scooting around the Cambridge Common playground when a pair of older boys, appar-
30 ently brothers, blocked his way. "You're Chinese!" they shouted, leaning on the hood of Luke's scooter car. "You are! You're Chinese!" So <u>brazen</u> were these kids that even when I, an adult, intervened, they continued to shout. Luke answered, "No, I'm not!"—to no avail; it was not clear if the boys even heard him. Then the boys' mother called to them from some distance away, outside the fence, and though her voice was no louder than Luke's, they left obediently.

Behind them opened a great, rippling quiet, like the
40 wash of a battleship.

Luke and I immediately went over things he could say if anything like that ever happened again. I told him that he was 100 percent American, even though I knew from my own childhood in Yonkers that these words would be met only with <u>derision</u>. It was a sorry chore. Since then, I have not asked him about the incident, hoping he has forgotten about it, and wishing that I could, too. For I wish I could forget the sight of those kids' fingers on the hood of Luke's little car. I wish I could forget their loud attack,
50 but also Luke's soft defense: No, I'm not.

Chinese-culture school. After dozens of phone calls, I was elated to discover the Greater Boston Chinese

| words for everyday use | **bra • zen** (brā zən) *adj.*, overly bold; disrespectful. *The most <u>brazen</u> of the reporters pursued the movie star relentlessly, sneaking pictures of her in her own backyard.* |
| | **de • ri • sion** (di ri′ zhən) *n.*, scorn. *The French director looked down on American movies and regarded Hollywood productions with <u>derision</u>.* |

Cultural Association nearby in West Newton. The school takes children at three, has a wonderful sense of community, and is housed in a center paid for, in part, by great karaoke[2] fund-raising events. (Never mind what the Japanese meant to the Chinese in the old world. In this world, people donate at least two hundred dollars each for a chance at the mike, and the singing goes on all night.) There are even vendors who bring home-style Chinese food to sell after class—stuff you can't get in a restaurant. Dave and I couldn't wait for the second class, and a chance to buy more bao[3] for our freezer.

But in the car on the way to the second class, Luke announced that he didn't want to go to Chinese school anymore. He said that the teacher talked mostly about ducks and bears and that he wasn't interested in ducks and bears. And I knew this was true. I knew that Luke was interested only in whales and ships. And what's more, I knew we wouldn't push him to take swimming lessons if he didn't want to, or music. Chinese school was a wonderful thing, but there was a way in which we were accepting it as somehow nonoptional. Was that right? Hadn't we always said that we didn't want our son to see himself as more essentially Chinese than Irish?

Yet we didn't want him to deny his Chinese heritage, either. And if there were going to be incidents on the playground, we wanted him to know what Chinese meant. So when Luke said again that he didn't really want to go to Chinese school, I said, "Oh, really?" Later on, we could try to teach him to define himself irrespective of race. For now, though, he was going to Chinese school. I exchanged glances with Dave. And then together, in a most carefully casual manner, we squinted at the road and kept going. ■

---

2. **karaoke.** Device that plays musical accompaniment while the user is recorded singing along with the music (from Japanese *kara*, meaning "empty" + *oke*, short for *okesutura*, meaning "orchestra")

3. **bao.** Chinese name for a type of dried fish

NOTE THE FACTS

What does Luke say about Chinese school? How do his parents react in lines 70–72?

_____

_____

_____

NOTE THE FACTS

What do the author and her husband not want Luke to do? What do they want him to know? What do they plan to teach him later?

_____

_____

_____

When you finish reading, fill in the after reading section of your Reader's Purpose Chart. Did you learn what you set out to learn? Did having a purpose in mind help you focus on what you read? Hold a class discussion in which you share the purposes you set for reading and what the outcome was.

Reading Skills and Test Practice

IDENTIFY THE AUTHOR'S PURPOSE

Discuss with your partner the best way to answer the following questions.

1. What do you think was the author's primary aim in writing this essay?
   a. She wanted to share her ideas about how to be a good parent.
   b. She wanted to reflect on how multiracial people are perceived.
   c. She wanted to inform readers about racism against Chinese people.
   d. She wanted to make the point that children can be cruel.

What is the correct answer to the question above? How were you able to eliminate the other answers? How did your use of the reading strategy help you answer the question?

_____

_____

2. With which of the following statements do you think the author of "An Ethnic Trump" would most likely agree?
   a. A Chinese-American person is actually more Chinese than American.
   b. We should define ourselves by other people's perceptions.
   c. Children should not be forced to learn about their ethnic heritage.
   d. People should not be defined according to their race or racial background.

What is the correct answer to the question above? How were you able to eliminate the other answers? How did your use of the reading strategy help you answer the question?

_____

_____

Investigate, Inquire, and Imagine

RECALL: GATHER FACTS
1a. Which ethnicities "trump" others, according to the author? Which of Luke's ethnicities trumps the other?

INTERPRET: FIND MEANING
1b. Why do people think it inevitable that Luke go to Chinese-culture school? Why don't they expect him to speak Gaelic?

ANALYZE: TAKE THINGS APART
2a. According to the author, for what reasons do certain ethnicities trump others? What evidence can you find that Luke is perceived as more ethnically Chinese than Irish?

SYNTHESIZE: BRING THINGS TOGETHER
2b. What do the author and her husband want to pass on to Luke? How have they always wanted him to view his ethnic heritage? In your opinion, should Luke define himself by other people's perceptions?

PERSPECTIVE: LOOK AT OTHER VIEWS
3a. Why do you think Luke's classmate invites only blond children to his party? Why do you think the other children in the park harass Luke? Do you think these children are mean-spirited? Do you think their behavior is different from that of the adults who assume Luke is Chinese? Explain.

EMPATHY: SEE FROM INSIDE
3b. If you were Luke, how would you react to being harassed on the playground? How do you think Luke's response affects his mother? Why do you think the author uses the simile of "the wash of a battleship" to describe the quiet after the boys leave the playground?

Literary Tools

ANECDOTE. **An anecdote** is usually a short narrative of an interesting, amusing, or biographical incident. Complete the chart below to understand the meaning of each anecdote in the essay. How does each anecdote in "An Ethnic Trump" contribute to the aim(s) of Jen's essay?

Anecdote	Meaning

WordWorkshop

SYNONYMS. Each word below is a synonym—a word with the same or similar meaning—for one of the Words for Everyday Use for this selection. Next to each word, note the Word for Everyday Use that is its synonym.

1. surpass _____

2. shameless _____

3. disrespect _____

4. inescapable _____

5. unhidden _____

Read-Write Connection

Do you think Luke's parents made the right decision in insisting that Luke go to Chinese-culture school? What would you have done in their position?

_____

_____

_____

_____

_____

_____

_____

_____

Beyond the Reading

RACE AND ETHNICITY. Research words defining race and ethnicity, such as *mulatto, quadroon, Creole, Eurasian,* and *Jewish.* Then create a project to show what you have learned. For example, you might make a list of words and tell whether each word defines race or ethnicity, evaluate the connotations of the words in published works, or write a rap song using at least one of these words and its connotations.

GO ONLINE. Visit the EMC Internet Resource Center at **emcp.com** to find links and additional activities for this selection.

"It's Not Talent;
It's Just Work"

by Annie Dillard

Active READING STRATEGY

READ WITH A PURPOSE

Before Reading ➤ READ WITH A PURPOSE

- ❏ Read the Reader's Resource and think about the author's purpose, or aim, for writing the essay. For example, does she want to reflect, entertain, inform, or persuade?
- ❏ With the class, brainstorm the aims of specific types of writing, such as speeches, novels, short stories, poems, and essays.
- ❏ Fill in the before-reading section of the Author's Purpose Chart below before you begin reading the selection.

Graphic Organizer

Before Reading
Identify the author's purpose, the type of writing he or she uses, and the ideas he or she wants to communicate.

During Reading
Gather ideas that the author communicates to readers.

After Reading
Summarize the ideas the author communicates. Explain how these ideas help fulfill the author's purpose.

CONNECT

Reader's *resource*

"It's Not Talent: It's Just Work" is an essay by Annie Dillard that challenges readers to reconsider the concept of "talent." Dillard's perspective on the topic is unique. Instead of discussing whether talent is the result of forces in nature or environment, she focuses on the way love motivates a person toward achievement and fulfillment. A writer of creative nonfiction, Dillard won the Pulitzer Prize for *Pilgrim at Tinker Creek* (1975).

Word *watch*

PREVIEW VOCABULARY

alienation	prose
masochism	queasy
perpetual	regimen

Reader's *journal*

Think of a famous person whom you consider talented, and explain why you think he or she has talent.

_____

_____

_____

NOTE THE FACTS

In the first two lines, how does the author feel about hard work?

_____

_____

Literary TOOLS

ANALOGY. An **analogy** is a comparison of two things that are alike in some respects. As you read, pay attention so that you can identify the analogies and decide what purpose they serve.

It's Not Talent, It's Just Work

Annie Dillard

It's hard work, doing something with your life. The very thought of hard work makes me <u>queasy</u>. I'd rather die in peace. Here we are, all equal and alike and none of us much to write home about—and some people choose to make themselves into physicists or thinkers or major-league pitchers, knowing perfectly well that it will be nothing but hard work. But I want to tell you that it's not as bad as it sounds. Doing something does not require discipline; it creates its own discipline—with a little help from caffeine.

10   People often ask me if I discipline myself to write, if I work a certain number of hours a day on a schedule. They ask this question with envy in their voices and awe on their faces and a sense of <u>alienation</u> all over them, as if they were addressing an armored tank or a talking giraffe or Niagara Falls. We want to believe that other people are natural wonders; it gets us off the hook.

words for everyday use	**quea • sy** (kwē′ ze) *adj.,* nauseated; uneasy. *Riding the ferry made Rochelle seasick and* <u>queasy</u>.
	a • li • e • na • tion (ā lē ə nā′ shən) *n.,* distance or separation because of great differences. *Because Larry was quiet and very different from the others in his class, he often experienced* <u>alienation</u> *in school.*

Now, it happens that when I wrote my first book of <u>prose</u>, I worked an hour or two a day for a while, and then in the last two months, I got excited and worked very hard, for

20   many hours a day. People can lift cars when they want to. People can recite the Koran,[1] too, and run in marathons. These things aren't ways of life; they are merely possibilities for everyone on certain occasions of life. You don't lift cars around the clock or write books every year. But when you do, it's not so hard. It's not superhuman. It's very human. You do it for love. You do it for love and respect for your own life; you do it for love and respect for the world; and you do it for love and respect for the task itself.

   If I had a little baby, it would be hard for me to rise up and

30   feed that little baby in the middle of the night. It would be hard but certainly wouldn't be a discipline. It wouldn't be a <u>regimen</u> I imposed on myself out of <u>masochism</u>, nor would it be the flowering of some extraordinary internal impulse. I would do it, grumbling, for love and because it has to be done.

   Of course it has to be done. And something has to be done with your life too: something specific, something human. But don't wait around to be hit by love. Don't wait for anything. Learn something first. Then, when you are getting to know it,

40   you will get to love it, and that love will direct you in what to do. So many times when I was in college, I used to say of a course like seventeenth-century poetry or European history, "I didn't like it at first, but now I like it." All of life is like that—a sort of dreary course which gradually gets interesting if you work at it.

   I used to live in <u>perpetual</u> dread that I would one day read all the books that I would ever be interested in and have nothing more to read. I always figured that when that time came I would force myself to learn wildflowers, just to keep

---

1. **Koran**. Holy book of the Islamic faith

<table>
<tr><td rowspan="4">words
for
everyday
use</td><td>prose (prōz) n., broad term used to describe all writing that is not poetry, including fiction and nonfiction. The novelist writes wonderful <u>prose</u>.</td></tr>
<tr><td>reg • i • men (re′ jə mən) n., regular course of action, especially strenuous training. The boxer's daily <u>regimen</u> was to jump rope, lift weights, and spar with a partner.</td></tr>
<tr><td>mas • och • ism (ma′ sə ki zəm) n., pleasure in suffering. Mike considered tackle football a form of <u>masochism</u>—he much preferred touch football.</td></tr>
<tr><td>per • pet • u • al (pər pe′ chə wəl) adj., continuing forever. Carmen joked that her two-year-old sister was in <u>perpetual</u> motion because she never seemed to run out of energy.</td></tr>
</table>

READ ALOUD

Read aloud the highlighted text. According to the author, what enables people to do extraordinary things?

Use THE STRATEGY

READ WITH A PURPOSE. Be sure to stop after each paragraph to add more of the ideas the author is communicating about talent to the graphic organizer.

MARK THE TEXT

Underline or highlight the advice the author gives the reader.

FIX-UP IDEA

Unlock Difficult Words If you have difficulty understanding the selection and determining the author's purpose, work to unlock difficult words as you read. Use context clues and word parts to help you identify word meaning. Review the Words for Everyday Use and the footnotes. If you are still unable to unlock a word's meaning, consult a dictionary.

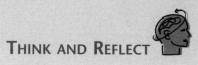
50 awake. I dreaded it, because I was not very interested in wildflowers but thought I should be. But things kept cropping up and one book has led to another and I haven't had to learn wildflowers yet. I don't think there's much danger of coming to the end of the line. The line is endless. I urge you to get in it, to get in line. It's a long line—but it's the only show in town. ∎

Reflect ON YOUR READING

When you are done reading, fill in the after-reading section of the Author's Purpose Chart. Then discuss the purpose or purposes Dillard had for writing the essay. Next, write an analysis of the author's purpose—first identifying the purpose(s) and then analyzing the information in the text that led you to the purpose(s). Also tell whether or not Dillard was effective in achieving her purpose(s). Finally, share your essay with a classmate.

Reading Skills and Test Practice

IDENTIFY THE AUTHOR'S PURPOSE
Discuss with your partner the best way to answer the following questions about an author's purpose.

THINK-ALOUD NOTES

1. Which of the following statements best describes Dillard's perspective on talent?
   a. Some people have talent, and others don't.
   b. Being a success requires talent and hard work.
   c. Exceptional achievements are the result of hard work and love of the task, not talent.
   d. Hard work is futile if a person doesn't have talent.

What is the correct answer to the question above? How were you able to eliminate the other answers? How did your use of the reading strategy help you answer the question?

_____

_____

2. What do you think was Dillard's primary aim, or purpose, for writing this essay?
   a. to inform readers about her life, especially the success she has achieved
   b. to entertain readers with stories about her success
   c. to persuade readers to change their views on talent and to take action in their lives
   d. to reflect on her experiences as a writer

What is the correct answer to the question above? How were you able to eliminate the other answers? How did your use of the reading strategy help you answer the question?

_____

_____

Investigate, Inquire, and Imagine

RECALL: GATHER FACTS
1a. According to the author, why do people like to think of those who are talented as "natural wonders"?

INTERPRET: FIND MEANING
1b. How does this belief relieve people of responsibility?

ANALYZE: TAKE THINGS APART
2a. In this essay, Dillard presents arguments contradicting some commonly held beliefs about talent and success. Identify these common beliefs.

SYNTHESIZE: BRING THINGS TOGETHER
2b. How does Dillard contradict these beliefs? What does she believe about talent? Does she regard certain people as "superhuman"? Does she think only a talented few can run marathons or recite the Koran? Explain.

PERSPECTIVE: LOOK AT OTHER VIEWS
3a. Knowing the author is a well-known writer and Pulitzer Prize winner, are you surprised by her opinions about talent? Why, or why not? Thomas Edison once said that genius is 1 percent inspiration and 99 percent perspiration. Explain whether Dillard would agree with that statement.

EMPATHY: SEE FROM INSIDE
3b. How does the author describe the attitude some people have about her talent? Why do you think their attitude bothers her? Why do you think it is important for the author to let people know that writing is hard work?

Literary Tools

ANALOGY. An **analogy** is a comparison of two things that are alike in some respects. Complete the chart below to record the examples of analogy in the selection. One example has been done for you. What purpose does each analogy serve?

Analogy	Thing described
as if they were addressing an armored tank	envious people asking about writing

WordWorkshop

WORDS WITH MULTIPLE MEANINGS. Each of the words below from "It's Not Talent; It's Just Work" has multiple meanings. Locate each word in the selection and identify its meaning as it is used in the selection. Then consult a dictionary and list an alternate meaning for the word. Finally, use the word in a sentence that illustrates the alternate meaning.

Word	Meaning in Selection	Alternate Meaning	Sentence Showing Alternate Meaning
1. discipline			
2. work			
3. course			
4. crop			
5. address			

Read-Write Connection

What things do you love to do? Do you consider yourself talented at these things?

_____

_____

_____

_____

_____

_____

Beyond the Reading

QUOTES ABOUT TALENT. Research another famous person's views on talent and then discuss or write about them. You might compare two similar or dissimilar quotes about talent, explain how a quote applies to one of your talents, or tie a quote to the life of its author.

GO ONLINE. Visit the EMC Internet Resource Center at **emcp.com** to find links and additional activities for this selection.

CONNECT

Reader's resource

Ian Frazier's book *Great Plains* (1989), from which this selection is taken, grew out of his experiences traveling through that part of the country. The Great Plains dazzled and challenged Frazier's imagination when he moved from New York to Montana in 1982. In the United States, the Great Plains include parts of North Dakota, South Dakota, Minnesota, Iowa, Nebraska, Kansas, Oklahoma, Montana, Wyoming, Colorado, New Mexico, and Texas.

Word watch

PREVIEW VOCABULARY

presumptuous

Reader's journal

How would you describe a landscape that you like?

____

____

____

from GREAT PLAINS

by Ian Frazier

Active READING STRATEGY

VISUALIZE

Before Reading PREVIEW THE SELECTION

- ❑ Read the Reader's Resource.
- ❑ With the class, hold a discussion about how you'd describe the landscape of any of the states that are part of the Great Plains.
- ❑ Preview the Sensory Details Chart below. Prepare to fill in sensory details in the graphic organizer as you read.

Graphic Organizer

Sight	Sound	Touch	Taste	Smell

Great PLAINS

Ian Frazier

During Reading

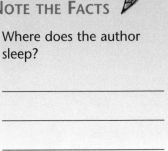

VISUALIZE

❑ Close your eyes and visualize while your teacher reads the first two paragraphs of the selection aloud.

❑ Jot down a description of or sketch your visualization.

❑ Share it with a few classmates, discussing the details that stand out.

❑ Read the remainder of the text on your own, continuing to visualize.

❑ Pause occasionally to add sensory details to the graphic organizer.

W hen I went for long drives on the plains, I might be on the road for weeks at a time. I could afford to stay in motels only every third or fourth night, so the others I spent in my van. I slept beneath the mercury lights of highway rest areas where my lone car was visible for six miles in any direction and the inside of the men's room looked as if it had been sandblasted with tiny insects, and on the streets of small towns where the lawn sprinklers ran all night, and next to dammed-up waters of the Missouri River

10 where the white top branches of drowned trees rose above the waves. My van had so many pinholes from rust that it created a planetarium effect on the ground when I turned on the interior light. After a day of driving there was usually a lot of dust on the bed, and maybe a stunned grasshopper that had come through the open window.

One night I tried to sleep at a picnic area at the Double Mountain Fork of the Brazos River in Texas, on U.S. Highway 83. Highway 83 runs from Mexico to Canada and is like the Main Street of the Great Plains. Cars went by

20 only occasionally, which somehow made them scarier. The moon was full, and the wind was blowing harder than during the day. I got up and walked around. By moonlight I

NOTE THE FACTS

Where does the author sleep?

_____

_____

_____

Literary TOOLS

SIMILE. A **simile** is a comparison using *like* or *as*. As you read, note Frazier's use of similes.

Reading TIP

Note that the author's method of organization is not chronological. Rather, he describes his experiences and impressions collectively.

Use THE STRATEGY

VISUALIZE. Make a mental picture of the places where Frazier stops to sleep.

FIX-UP IDEA

Read Aloud
If you have difficulty applying the reading strategy, try reading the text aloud with a partner. Take turns reading the text paragraph by paragraph. Close your eyes and visualize the descriptions as your partner reads aloud. Then tell your partner what you saw. Work with your partner to identify the details in the text that helped you visualize.

read a historic marker in the picnic area which said that in 1871 hunters brought more than a million buffalo hides to a trading post near this spot. When I lay down again, the unquiet spirits of a million buffalo were abroad in the windy night. My head kept falling through the pillow. The moon shone, the stars blinked, the trees tossed back and forth, the shadows waited under the picnic kiosks. I got up again and

30   drove until dawn.

  In New Mexico I slept well in front of a shuttered vegetable stand on the outskirts of a town. I woke in the morning to blue sky and the sound of small animals playing under my car and scurrying across the roof. On the vegetable stand I saw a sign posted. I went over to see what it said. It said:

PLAGUE
is passed to man by
WILD RODENTS, Rabbits,
and by their FLEAS
. . . DO NOT
Pitch tents or lay
Bedrolls on or near
nests or burrows.
Plague is CURABLE
WHEN TREATED IN TIME.

40

  The best places to sleep were truck stops. At two-thirty in the morning a truck-stop parking lot full of trucks is the capital of sleep. The trucks park in close rows, as if for

50   warmth. The drivers sleep with purposeful intent. The big engines idle; together, the trucks snore. Hinged moisture caps on top of the diesel stacks bounce in the exhaust with a pinging noise. I tried to park as close as I could without being <u>presumptuous</u>. Unlike tourists in rest stops, truck drivers seem careful about slamming doors and gunning engines late at night. Sometimes the truck I had gone to sleep next to would quietly leave and another would quietly pull in. One morning when I woke up a semi-trailer full of

words for everyday use

pre • sump • tu • ous (pri zəm(p)′ chə wəs) *adj.*, overstepping bounds of propriety or courtesy; taking liberties. *Anne thought it was <u>presumptuous</u> of Lance to assume she would go to the dance with him.*

pickup-truck camper tops had been replaced by a stock
truck. On the truck's door, in big letters, a poem:

Buck Hummer
Hog Hauler

In Colorado, Highways 71 and 36 make a big cross on the
map when they intersect at the town of Last Chance. Sixty
miles to the west, the prairie ends and greater Denver
begins, and the uplands are barnacled with houses for a
hundred miles along the Rocky Mountain front. Fewer than
seventy people live in Last Chance. The wheat fields are
eroding, the oil wells are running dry, the only store in town
burned down. "However, hope springs eternally in the
breasts of our decreasing high school enrollment," a citizen
of Last Chance wrote recently. On a night of many
thunderstorms, I pulled over to sleep at that intersection.
The wind made the streetlight sway, and made its shadows
sway inside my van. A full cattle truck came sighing down
the road and then squeaked to a stop at the blinking red
light. I could hear the animals shifting and bumping inside.
They were very likely on their way to one of the largest
feedlots[1] in the world, sixty miles north of Denver, where
they would stand around with a hundred thousand other
cows and eat until they were fat enough to slaughter. The
truck sat for a moment. Then the driver revved the engine
and found first gear, and the full load of cattle braced
themselves for the start. In step, they set their many feet all
at once, like a dance revue.

Now, when I have trouble getting to sleep, I sometimes
imagine that my bed is on the back of a flatbed pickup truck
driving across the Great Plains. I ignore the shouts on the
sidewalk and the bass vibrations from the reggae club across
the street. The back of this truck has sides but no top. I can
see the stars. The air is cool. The truck will go nonstop for
nine hours through the night. At first the road is as straight
as a laser—State Highway 8, in North Dakota say—where
nothing seems to move except the wheels under me and the
smell of run-over skunks fading in and out in my nose.
Then the road twists to follow a river valley, and
cottonwood leaves pass above, and someone has been

---

1. **feedlots.** Plots of land on which livestock are fattened for market

Reading STRATEGY
REVIEW

READ WITH A PURPOSE.
Identifying the author's
purpose for writing can
help you know what to
look for when you are
reading. Review the
reading strategy for "It's
Not Talent; It's Just Work"
on page 405. What do
you think is Frazier's
purpose for writing about
the Great Plains?

_____

_____

_____

READ ALOUD

Read aloud Frazier's description of the Great Plains, paying particular attention to his use of *metaphoric language,* or expressions that have more than a literal meaning. Try to capture his respectful tone with your voice.

cutting hay, and the air is like the inside of a spice cabinet. Then suddenly the wheels rumble on the wooden planks of 100 a one-lane bridge across the River That Scolds at All the Others. Ever since the Great Plains were first called a desert, people have gone a long way toward turning them into one. The Great Plains which I cross in my sleep are bigger than any name people give them. They are enormous, bountiful, unfenced, empty of buildings, full of names and stories. They extend beyond the frame of the photograph. Their hills are hipped, like a woman asleep under a sheet. Their rivers rhyme. Their rows of grain strum past. Their draws² hold springwater and wood and 110 game and grass like sugar in the hollow of a hand. They are the place where Crazy Horse will always remain uncaptured. They are the lodge of Crazy Horse. ■

---

2. **draw.** Gully shallower than a ravine

Reflect ON YOUR READING

After you finish reading, work with your group from the during-reading activity to evaluate the imagery the author uses. With your filled-in graphic organizer in front of you, consider the following questions: Were the settings easy to visualize? Which sensory details were the most effective? Why? When you finish your discussion, write a brief evaluation of the imagery in the selection, addressing these questions.

_____

_____

_____

Reading Skills and Test Practice

ANALYZE LITERARY ELEMENTS

Discuss with your group how to best answer the following questions about literary elements.

THINK-ALOUD NOTES

1. Read this sentence from Frazier's account of his trip.

   When I lay down again, the unquiet spirits of a million buffalo were abroad in the windy night.

   This line creates a mood of
   a. relaxation.
   b. stillness.
   c. wonder.
   d. anxiety.

What is the correct answer to the question above? How were you able to eliminate the other answers? How did your use of the reading strategy help you answer the question?

_____

2. Frazier says, "The Great Plains which I cross in my sleep are bigger than any name people give them." Which word best describes his tone?
   a. fearful
   b. reverent
   c. wistful
   d. annoyed

What is the correct answer to the question above? How were you able to eliminate the other answers? How did your use of the reading strategy help you answer the question?

_____

Investigate, Inquire, and Imagine

RECALL: GATHER FACTS
1a. In what places did Frazier stay overnight when driving through the Great Plains?

INTERPRET: FIND MEANING
1b. Does Frazier prefer the inhabited areas around Denver or the uninhabited plains?

ANALYZE: TAKE THINGS APART
2a. Why does Frazier say "[The Great Plains] are the place where Crazy Horse will always remain uncaptured"?

SYNTHESIZE: BRING THINGS TOGETHER
2b. What is the effect of ending the essay with a reference to Crazy Horse?

PERSPECTIVE: LOOK AT OTHER VIEWS
3a. If you were Frazier, what would you say you like the most about traveling through the Great Plains?

EMPATHY: SEE FROM INSIDE
3b. If you took a trip across the Great Plains, whom would you like to interview? Why? What would you ask him or her?

Literary Tools

SIMILE. A **simile** is a comparison using *like* or *as*. The figure of speech invites the reader to make a comparison between two things. The two things are the writer's actual subject, the *tenor* of the metaphor, and the thing to which the subject is likened, the *vehicle* of the metaphor. Complete the graphic organizer below to identify the tenor and vehicle for each of three similes found in the final paragraph of the selection. What do they reflect about the landscape of the Great Plains?

Tenor	Vehicle
straight road	laser

WordWorkshop

COMPOUND WORDS. Compound words are formed by combining two words to create a new word. The first word in the combination modifies, or describes, the second word. For example, *steamboat* is the combination of two words, *steam* and *boat*. The word *boat* by itself is the more general term. By combining *steam* with *boat*, a new word was created to describe a specific type of boat, one that is powered by steam and that goes on inland waterways.

Divide the compound words from the selection into the two base words from which they are formed. Then, use each word in a new sentence. Follow the example.

EXAMPLE
moonlight   moon + light
The <u>moonlight</u> guided Max to a gas station when his headlights went out.

1. sandblast _____

2. pinhole _____

3. feedlot _____

4. upland _____

5. flatbed _____

Read-Write Connection

If you were Frazier, what would you hope readers would glean from reading *Great Plains?* Use your own paper to write your response.

Beyond the Reading

TRAVEL WRITING. Other travel books include *On the Road* by Jack Kerouac (1957), *Travels with Charley* by John Steinbeck (1962), and *Blue Highways* (1983) by William Least Heat Moon. After doing some research, create a project that reflects one of these works or another travel book of your choice. For example, you could make a map that charts the writer's route, write a postcard the writer might have penned, or write an introduction to the author as a guest speaker at a bookstore.

GO ONLINE. Visit the EMC Internet Resource Center at **emcp.com** to find links and additional activities for this selection.

Unit 7 READING Review

Choose and Use Reading Strategies

Before reading the excerpt that follows, review with a partner how to use each reading strategy below with nonfiction.

1. Read with a Purpose
2. Connect to Prior Knowledge
3. Write Things Down
4. Make Predictions
5. Visualize
6. Use Text Organization
7. Tackle Difficult Vocabulary
8. Monitor Your Reading Progress

Next, apply at least two of these reading strategies as you read the following excerpt from *Black Elk Speaks* by Black Elk and John G. Neihardt. Use the margins and mark up the text to read actively.

> A long time ago my father told me what his father told him, that there was once a Lakota holy man, called Drinks Water, who dreamed what was to be; and this was long before the coming of the Wasichus. He dreamed that the four-leggeds were going back into the earth and that a strange race had woven a spider's web all around the Lakotas. And he said: "When this happens, you shall live in square gray houses, in a barren land, and beside those square gray houses you shall starve." They say he went back to Mother Earth soon after he saw this vision, and it was sorrow that killed him. You can look about you now and see that he meant these dirt-roofed houses we are living in, and that all the rest was true. Sometimes dreams are wiser than waking.

WordWorkshop

Unit 7 Words for Everyday Use

adversity, 391	exalted, 385	masochism, 407	regale, 377
alienation, 405	exploit, 377	mêlée, 392	regimen, 407
brazen, 400	extirpate, 393	mobility, 384	renege, 372
brutality, 384	ford, 392	molder, 393	requisite, 394
calamitous, 371	implicit, 392	musty, 371	resignation, 375
conviction, 392	indeterminate, 376	objectively, 391	sear, 383
creed, 385	inequity, 376	obscure, 375	sparse, 374
decipher, 391	inevitable, 399	perpetual, 407	staple, 373
defiant, 391	inordinate, 375	ply, 372	stereotyped, 375
defoliate, 393	intent, 377	presumptuous, 414	tribulation, 384
derision, 400	languish, 384	prophesy, 374	trump, 399
discord, 386	literally, 392	prose, 407	wallow, 385
emerge, 384	manacle, 383	queasy, 406	
ethnicity, 399	manifest, 399	redemptive, 385	

Using Context Clues. Complete the crossword puzzle using words you learned in the selections in Unit 7. Use context clues to figure out which word to use. The words to choose from are listed below.

adversity   exploit   literally   prose
discord   inequity   mobility   regimen
ethnicity   inevitable   presumptuous   staple

Across

1. Due to her lack of _____, Ms. Simmons didn't even own a car; I, on the other hand, need to be able to get around quickly.

4. Krista's daily _____ was to run before school and play soccer in the afternoon.

6. Shakespeare used both _____ and poetry in his plays.

7. Because his dad plays for the AFC and his uncle for the NFC, it was _____ that Brad would play football; there was no doubt about it.

8. Flour is a _____, or necessary ingredient, in the kitchen of every cook.

9. The _____ between the different interest groups has caused much environmental damage.

10. Marshall's ancestors had come from so many countries that when he was asked about his _____, he always said he was American.

11. The soldier was interviewed about his _____ that saved a civilian's life.

Down

2. The _____ of pay between male and female teachers in the 1950s was justified as necessary because men had families to support.

3. Taken _____, metaphors don't make much sense because they are intended to be figurative expressions.

5. The TV movie portrayed the _____ of a homeless girl who nevertheless ended up at Harvard.

6. Anne's friends thought that Jason was _____, or overstepping his bounds, when he sent her flowers without ever having gone on a date with her.

Literary Tools

Select the best literary element on the right to complete each sentence on the left. Write the correct letter in the blank.

_____ 1. If you talk about an animal as having regrets, you are using ___.

_____ 2. In the selection from *Great Plains*, when Ian Frazier talks about a night spent at a picnic area, he is telling a(n) ___.

_____ 3. If a political candidate giving a speech says, "When I am elected" six times, he is using ___.

_____ 4. When Ian Frazier says that Highway 83 is like the Main Street of the Great Plains, he is using a(n) ___.

_____ 5. If you make it clear where and when a(n) short story you are writing takes place, you are establishing the ___.

_____ 6. When Annie Dillard compares dreary college courses with life, she is using a(n) ___ to show how interests or hobbies can become more interesting with increased involvement.

a. analogy

b. personification

c. simile

d. anecdote

e. repetition

f. setting

On Your Own

FLUENTLY SPEAKING. With several classmates, read the three columns of words from the selections in Unit 7. The first person says the first word in Column A. The second person repeats the first word and then adds the second word, and so on, until all the words have been pronounced. Then go on to Columns B and C and repeat the activity. Try to go faster with eac h column. Appoint one person in your group to time your readings.

A	B	C
calamitous	alienation	commissary
prophesy	derision	ethnicity
redemptive	perpetual	inevitable
tribulation	regimen	masochism
troubadour	renege	presumptuous

PICTURE THIS. Choose one of the selections from this unit and draw a picture of the setting or one of the characters. Share your drawing and explain why you illustrated it the way you did.

PUT IT IN WRITING. Both Bailey in *I Know Why the Caged Bird Sings* and Ian Frazier, who wrote *Great Plains*, took a trip. Compare or contrast their experiences. You might discuss what impressed them, how they related their trips to others, or what they saw.

Unit EIGHT

READING
Informational
and Visual Media

Learning how to read online and print reference works, graphic aids, and other visuals will help you access, process, and think about the vast amount of information available to you.

INFORMATIONAL MEDIA

Media are channels or systems of communication, information, or entertainment. *Mass media*, designed to reach the mass of the people, refers specifically to means of communication, such as newspapers, radio, or television. *Journalism* is the gathering, evaluating, and disseminating, through various media, of news and facts of current interest. Journalism has expanded from printed matter (newspapers and periodicals) to include radio, television, documentary films, the Internet, and computer news services.

Newspapers, issued on a daily or weekly basis, report the news, provide commentary on the news, support various public policies, and furnish special information and advice to readers.

Periodicals, released at regular intervals, are publications that include journals, magazines, or newsletters. They feature material of special interest to particular audiences. "Ghost of Everest" and "Where Stars Are Born" are examples in this unit of periodical articles. "For the Future of Florida: Repair the Everglades!" is an example of a newsletter article.

Technical writing refers to scientific or process-oriented instructional writing that is of a technical or mechanical nature, such as **instruction manuals**, **how-to instructional guides**, and **procedural memos**. In this unit, "Research Strategies for the Learning Highway" provides a step-by-step procedure for using the Internet.

Reading TIP

The word *media* comes from a Latin word meaning "middle." The media are literally "in the middle." They pass information from its source to you. As you read texts from the media, consider whether they have altered or slanted the truth before passing information along to you.

Reading STRATEGY
REVIEW

CONNECT TO PRIOR KNOWLEDGE. What kinds of multimedia software have you used?

_____

_____

_____

Elements of Informational Media

NEWS ARTICLES. **News articles** are informational pieces of writing about a particular topic, issue, event, or series of events. They can be found in newspapers and periodicals and on Internet sites such as news groups or information services.

EDITORIALS AND COMMENTARIES. An **editorial** is an article in a newspaper or periodical that gives the opinions of the editors or publishers. A **commentary** expresses the opinion of a participant or observer of an event.

ESSAYS. An **essay** is a brief work of nonfiction that need not be a complete treatment of a subject.

INTERVIEWS. An **interview** is a question-and-answer exchange between a reporter who wants information and the person who has that information.

REVIEWS. A **review**, or *critique*, is a critical evaluation of a work, such as a book, play, movie, or musical performance or recording.

ELECTRONIC MEDIA

Electronic media includes online magazines and journals, known as **webzines** or **e-zines**, **computer news services**, and many **web-based newspapers** that are available on the **Internet**. In addition to handling web documents, the Internet also allows people to send e-mail, access archives of files, and participate in discussion groups. **Multimedia** means presenting information using a combination of text, sound, pictures, animation, and video. Common multimedia computer applications include **games, learning software, presentation software, reference materials**, and **web pages**. Using multimedia can provide a varied and informative interactive experience.

Elements of Electronic Media

ELECTRONIC MAIL. **Electronic mail**, or **e-mail**, is used to send written messages between individuals or groups on the Internet. E-mail messages tend to be more informal and conversational in style than letters.

WEB PAGES. A **web page** is an electronic "page" on the World Wide Web or Internet that may contain text, pictures, and sometimes animations related to a particular topic. A *website* is a collection of pages grouped together to organize the information offered by the person, company, or group that owns it.

NEWSGROUPS. Another use of e-mail is **listservs,** in which discussions on a particular subject are grouped together into **newsgroups** on a wide range of subjects. Messages to a newsgroup are accessible in the form of a list on a local news server that has a worldwide reach. Users can choose which messages they want to read and reply by posting messages to the newsgroup.

INFORMATION SERVICES. Information services, or *news services*, are providers of electronic news, information, and e-mail services.

BULLETIN BOARD SYSTEMS. A **bulletin board system**, or BBS, is an online service that allows users to post and read messages on a particular topic, converse in a *chat room*, play games with another person, and copy, or download, programs to their personal computers.

WEBZINES OR E-ZINES. Webzines or **e-zines** are periodicals that are available online. They may be available only online, or they may also be available in a magazine distributed by traditional methods.

ONLINE NEWSPAPERS. Major newspapers are now available online. Past editions of the paper are usually accessible through an online archive.

VISUAL MEDIA

Many books and news media rely on **visual arts**, such as **fine art**, **illustrations**, and **photographs**, to convey ideas. Critically viewing a painting or photograph can add meaning to your understanding of a text.

Elements of Visual Media

GRAPHIC AIDS. Graphic aids are visual materials with information such as **drawings**, **illustrations**, **diagrams**, **charts**, **graphs**, **maps**, and **spreadsheets**.

PHOTOGRAPHS. Photographs display news, historical documents, scientific evidence, works of art, and records of family life. New photographic technology allows for digital formats to be stored on disk and downloaded to computers.

DIGITAL PHOTOGRAPHY. With **digital photography**, images are converted into a code of ones and zeroes that a computer can read. Digital photographs can be manipulated into new images.

PHOTOJOURNALISM. Photojournalism is documentary photography that tells a particular story in visual terms. Photojournalists, who usually work for newspapers and periodicals, cover cultural and news events in areas such as politics, war, business, sports, and the arts.

NOTE THE FACTS

What is the purpose of a newsgroup?

_____

_____

THINK AND REFLECT

Why might someone doubt the accuracy of a digital photograph? **(Evaluate)**

_____

_____

VISUAL ARTS. The **visual arts** include painting, sculpture, drawing, printmaking, collage, photography, video, and computer-assisted art. With art, the artist tries to communicate with viewers, who may have different ideas about how to interpret the work. Learning about the location and time period of an artwork can contribute to a better understanding of it.

USING READING STRATEGIES WITH INFORMATIONAL AND VISUAL MEDIA

Active Reading Strategy Checklists

When reading informational and visual media, you will need to identify how the text is structured. Scan the material first. Headings, pictures, and directions will reveal what the selection wants to communicate. Use the following checklists when you read informational and visual media.

1 READ WITH A PURPOSE. Before reading informational and visual media, give yourself a purpose, or something to look for, as you read. Know why you are reading and what information you seek. Sometimes a purpose will be a directive from a teacher: "Keep track of sky sights that will occur in the 21st century." Other times you can set your own purpose by previewing the title, the opening and closing paragraphs, and instructional information. Say to yourself

- ❏ I need to look for . . .
- ❏ I must keep track of . . .
- ❏ I need to understand the writer's views on . . .
- ❏ It is essential that I figure out how . . .
- ❏ I want to learn what happened when . . .

2 CONNECT TO PRIOR KNOWLEDGE. Connect to information you already know about the writer's topic. As you read, build on what you know. Say to yourself

- ❏ I know this about the topic already . . .
- ❏ Other information I've read about this topic said . . .
- ❏ I've used similar visual aids by . . .
- ❏ I did something similar when . . .
- ❏ This information is like . . .

Reading—TIP

Use titles, heads, charts, and pictures to preview the selection before you read it.

3 WRITE THINGS DOWN. As you read informational and visual media, write down or mark ideas that help you understand the writer's views. Possible ways to keep a written record include

- ❑ Underline information that answers a specific question.
- ❑ Write down steps in a process.
- ❑ Highlight conclusions the writer draws.
- ❑ Create a graphic organizer that shows how to do something.
- ❑ Use a code to respond to the writer's ideas.

4 MAKE PREDICTIONS. Before you read informational and visual media, use the title and subject matter to guess what the selection will be about. As you read, confirm or deny your predictions, and make new ones based on what you learn. Make predictions like the following:

- ❑ The title tells me that the selection will be about . . .
- ❑ Graphic aids show me that . . .
- ❑ I predict that the writer will want me to . . .
- ❑ This selection will help me . . .
- ❑ This writer will conclude by . . .

5 VISUALIZE. Visualizing, or allowing the words on the page to create images in your mind, helps you understand what informational and visual media is trying to communicate. In order to visualize what an informational and visual media selection is communicating, you need to picture the people, events, or procedure that a writer describes. Make statements such as:

- ❑ I imagine these people will . . .
- ❑ A drawing of this part would include . . .
- ❑ I picture that this happening in this section . . .
- ❑ I envision the situation as . . .

6 USE TEXT ORGANIZATION. When you read informational and visual media, pay attention to the text's structure. Learn to stop occasionally and retell what you have read. Say to yourself

- ❑ The title, headings, and pictures tell me this selection will be about . . .
- ❑ The writer's directions tell me . . .
- ❑ There is a pattern to how the writer presents . . .
- ❑ The writer presents the information by . . .
- ❑ The writer includes helpful sections that . . .

Reading TIP

As you read, mark any "opinion words" you find. Opinion words express judgment (*good, wise, mistake,* and so on) or suggest policy (*should, ought to,* and so on).

Reading TIP

Drawing a diagram or creating a flow chart as you read can help you understand technical writing.

7 **TACKLE DIFFICULT VOCABULARY.** Difficult words can hinder your ability to understand informational and visual media. Use context, consult a dictionary, or ask someone about words you do not understand. When you come across a difficult word in the selection, say to yourself

❏ The writer defines this word by . . .
❏ A dictionary definition shows that the word means . . .
❏ My work with the word before reading helps me know that the word means . . .
❏ A classmate said that the word means . . .

8 **MONITOR YOUR READING PROGRESS.** All readers encounter difficulty when they read, especially if they haven't chosen the reading material. When you have to read something, note problems you are having and fix them. The key to reading success is knowing when you are having difficulty. To fix problems, say to yourself

❏ Because I don't understand this part, I will . . .
❏ Because I'm having trouble staying connected to the ideas in the selection, I will . . .
❏ Because the words in the selection are too hard, I will . . .
❏ Because the selection is long, I will . . .
❏ Because I can't retell what the selection was about, I will . . .

Become an Active Reader

Active reading strategy instruction in this unit gives you an in-depth look at how to use one active reading strategy with each selection. Margin notes guide your use of this strategy and show you how to combine it with other strategies. Using just one reading strategy increase your chance of reading success. Learning how to use several strategies in combination increases your chances of success even more. Use the questions and tips in the margins to keep your attention focused on reading actively. Use the white space in the margins to jot down responses to what you are reading.

FIX-UP IDEA

- Reread
- Ask a question
- Read in shorter chunks
- Read aloud
- Retell
- Work with a partner
- Unlock difficult words
- Vary your reading rate
- Choose a new reading strategy
- Create a mnemonic device

How to Use Reading Strategies with Informational and Visual Media

Read the following excerpts to discover ways to use reading strategies as you read informational and visual media.

Excerpt 1. Note how a reader uses active reading strategies while reading this excerpt from "The Ghost of Everest" by Jerry Adler, page 441.

READ WITH A PURPOSE

I want to discover if Mallory's remains are found.

PREDICT

Since this story was published, I predict they find something interesting.

. . . Thus, on the morning of May 1, five American climbers fanned out on a steep and rocky slope at about 27,000 feet. They were part of an eight-member team of some of the world's top mountaineers (and a PBS documentary crew), hoping both to find the remains of Mallory and Irvine and to determine if they had reached the summit before dying—29 years before Sir Edmund Hillary and Tenzing Norgay made the first recognized ascent, in 1953.

VISUALIZE

I can use this picture of the mountain to visualize where the climbers are.

MONITOR YOUR READING PROGRESS

I can retell this paragraph in my own words to make sure I understand.

Excerpt 2. Note how a reader uses active reading strategies while reading this excerpt from "Research Strategies for the Learning Highway" by Trevor Owen and Ron Owston, pages 457–458.

USE TEXT ORGANIZATION

I can use the headings in this article to follow the steps for finding facts on the Internet.

CONNECT TO PRIOR KNOWLEDGE

I have used search words to look for books in the library catalog.

Four Steps to Finding Facts

Often you'll want to find specific facts, statistics, definitions, and other data. For instance, we might want to know the answer to questions such as:

- How high is Mount Everest?
- What is the GNP of France?
- What countries belong to the British Commonwealth?
- Who wrote the novel *The Sun Also Rises?*

Here are the steps we suggest you take to find answers to questions such as these.

Step 1

Think of the most obvious search words, paying particular attention to key nouns: for example, *height, elevation, Mount Everest* would be good for the first question above. Enter these words into a comprehensive search index, such as AltaVista, and connect the keywords with appropriate search operators. For AltaVista these might be +(*height or elevation*) + "*Mount Everest.*" Then do the search. If you don't find what you want, go to the next step.

TACKLE DIFFICULT VOCABULARY

I'm not sure what AltaVista is. I will mark this word and discuss it with a classmate or my teacher.

WRITE THINGS DOWN

I can create a cluster chart to keep track of information in the article.

Reader's resource

"For the Future of Florida: Repair the Everglades!" is an article by Joette Lorion from the *Everglades Reporter*, a newsletter published by the organization Friends of the Everglades. After a century of being ditched, diked, and drained, only half of the Everglades remains. The article describes a plan to restore the Everglades and actions taken by Friends and other organizations to enact the plan. Lorion, former president of Friends of the Everglades, is an active environmentalist.

Word watch

PREVIEW VOCABULARY

accrued	enhancement
admonition	feasibility
array	integrity
coalition	levee
comprehensive	meandering
conservationist	sentiment
degraded	sustainable
ecosystem	wetland

Reader's journal

Select a plant or animal that you appreciate. How does it bring beauty into your life? On what in nature does it depend for survival?

_____

_____

_____

"For the Future of Florida: Repair the Everglades!"

by Joette Lorion

Active READING STRATEGY

WRITE THINGS DOWN

Before Reading ➤ PREVIEW THE SELECTION

❑ Read the Reader's Resource.
❑ Then read the opening quotation and the subheadings of the article.
❑ Skim the selection.
❑ On your own paper, make a chart like the one below. On the left, write the title of each section. On the right, you will fill in a summary of the main ideas of each section.

Graphic Organizer

Selection Title	Main Ideas
The Marshall Plan	1. Friends of the Everglades supports the Marshall Plan, which states that the sheetflow must be restored from the Kissimmee River down through Lake Okeechobee, south through the central Everglades and into Florida Bay.

For the Future of Florida: Repair the Everglades!

Joette Lorion

"If the people will it, if they enforce their will on the water managers of Florida's future, the Everglades can be restored to nature's design."
Marjory Stoneman Douglas.

SUMMARIZE

❑ Follow along in your text as your teacher reads the section "The Marshall Plan." Work with the class to identify the main ideas in this section. Fill in the first row of the graphic organizer with a short summary of the section.

❑ Read the remainder of the selection on your own. Stop at the end of each section to fill in the appropriate section of the graphic organizer.

Literary TOOLS

EXPOSITION. Exposition is a type of writing that presents facts or opinions in an organized manner. As you read, identify points that Lorion makes as either facts or opinions.

THINK AND REFLECT

How is the "Marshall Plan" related to "nature's design" in the opening quotation of the selection? **(Infer)**

_____

_____

_____

The Marshall Plan

Marjory Stoneman Douglas recently turned 108 years old, but the above words from her book *The Everglades: River of Grass* are as true today as when she wrote them. Equally true is the headline of this newsletter. This same headline appeared in the *Everglades Reporter* in 1981 when Friends announced a plan to restore the Everglades. The repair plan was developed by ecologist Art Marshall. The message of the "Marshall Plan" was simple: To repair the Everglades Ecosystem, sheetflow[1] must be restored, to the greatest extent possible, from the Kissimmee River down through Lake Okeechobee, south through the central Everglades and into Florida Bay.

10

---

1. **sheetflow.** Broad, shallow, relatively unconfined flow of water across sloping terrain (as opposed to controlled, resticted flow as in a channel or river)

Which natural resources were quickly being degraded?

_____

_____

_____

NOTE THE FACTS

What has happened to wading birds as a result of ditching, diking, and draining?

_____

_____

Use THE STRATEGY

WRITE THINGS DOWN. What is the main idea of the paragraph that includes lines 32–42? In other words, what general statement can you make about Art Marshall's most basic contribution to saving the Everglades?

_____

_____

_____

_____

The purpose of the Plan was to protect and recover a vast <u>array</u> of natural resources which were quickly being <u>degraded</u>—drinking water, freshwater fisheries, marine fisheries and Everglades National Park. Restoration of the <u>ecosystem</u> called for, among other things, resolving the pollution problems of Lake Okeechobee and the vast Everglades Agricultural Area, as well as dechannelizing the
20   lower Kissimmee River, which would provide the start of the long sheetflow of water which would pass through Lake Okeechobee and into the Everglades and the Park.

    Art Marshall's plan was necessary because the Central and Southern Florida Project, started in 1948, had created an 1800 mile canal and <u>levee</u> system to provide flood control for cities and farms. This ditching, diking, and draining of the Everglades reduced this four million acre <u>wetland</u> by half and resulted in a reduction of nesting wading birds by 94%. The Marshall Plan forms the basis of the plan for
30   restoration being supported by most <u>conservationists</u> today and guides the efforts of Friends of the Everglades.

    Marjory spoke of Art Marshall's role in her autobiography *Voice of the River:* "Although my phrase 'River of Grass' first awakened people to the notion of the Everglades as a river, it was Art Marshall who filled in the blanks. . . . More than any other person, he stretched our idea of the Everglades and how the system interacts with everything else, which created the most powerful arguments for preserving the water. Self-interest is a more reliable motivation than
40   environmental pity or noblesse oblige,[2] and Marshall

_____

2. **noblesse oblige.** Obligation of honorable, generous, and responsible behavior associated with high rank or birth

words for everyday use

ar • ray (ə rā') *n.,* large group, number, or quantity of people or things. *An impressive <u>array</u> of scholars sat with heads bent over their books in the library.*

de • grad • ed (di grā' əd) *part.,* reduced in quality or value. *Language purists believe that English is being <u>degraded</u> in much modern advertising.*

e • co • sys • tem (ē' kō sis' təm) *n.,* complex of a community of organisms and its environment functioning as an ecological unit in nature. *The <u>ecosystem</u> along the riverbank was threatened by a new housing development.*

lev • ee (le' vē) *n.,* embankment for preventing flooding. *<u>Levees</u> in Louisiana protect cities and farmland from flooding.*

wet • land (wet' land) *n.,* land or area (as tidal flats or swamps) containing much soil moisture. *Herons build their nests in <u>wetlands</u>.*

con • ser • va • tion • ist (kän sər vā' shə nist) *n.,* person who advocates conservation of natural resources. *Because John Muir was an important American <u>conservationist</u>, Muir Woods National Monument was named for him.*

accomplished the extraordinary magic of taking the Everglades out of the bleeding hearts category forever."

Taking It to the Streets

Art Marshall took it out of the bleeding hearts category and worked with Marjory Stoneman Douglas of Friends of the Everglades and Johnny Jones of the Florida Wildlife Federation to take the plan to the streets. Friends newsletters printed a petition and asked everyone to sign on. They described the environmental and human benefits that would be <u>accrued</u> from the repair of the Everglades system. They told Garden Clubs, Rotary Clubs, political organizations and County Commissions how fixing the Everglades would improve water quality and water quantity, and that restored sheetflow would remove pollutants and restore the health of the system.

Support for Restoration Grows

These Everglades ambassadors were so effective that soon plans to restore the Kissimmee from a canal back to a <u>meandering</u> river began to take form, and today that restoration is underway. By 1992, the movement to restore the Everglades had mushroomed and Congress authorized the Central and South Florida Project Comprehensive Review Study that directed the Secretary of the Army to study the <u>feasibility</u> of modifying the existing flood control project with particular reference to "modifying the project or its operation for improving the quality of the environment, improving protection of the aquifer,[3] and improving the <u>integrity</u>, capability, and conservation of urban water supplies affected by the project or its operation." In 1996,

---

3. **aquifer.** Stratum or zone below the surface of the earth capable of producing water as from a well

words for everyday use

ac • crued (ə krüd′) *part.*, accumulated after a period of time. *When I learned that interest could be <u>accrued</u>, I lent my sister money.*

me • an • der • ing (mē an′ der iŋ) *adj.*, wandering aimlessly or casually without urgent destination. *The <u>meandering</u> tourists found the cobblestone streets and canals of Amsterdam delightful.*

fea • si • bil • i • ty (fē zə bi′ lə tē) *n.*, suitability. *The <u>feasibility</u> of the plan to build a large cineplex in the small town was brought into question.*

in • teg • ri • ty (in te′ grə tē) *n.*, unimpaired condition; soundness. *The <u>integrity</u> of the ship's hull was compromised when it struck an iceberg.*

NOTE THE FACTS

Reread lines 79–83. What did the 1996 Water Resources and Development Act (WRDA) accomplish?

_____

_____

_____

NOTE THE FACTS

According to lines 91–93, what is the Everglades like today?

_____

_____

WHAT DO YOU WONDER?

_____

_____

_____

80 with public <u>sentiment</u> for restoration still growing, Congress passed the Water Resources and Development Act of 1996 (WRDA). This Act requires the Secretary of the Army to develop a "proposed <u>comprehensive</u> plan for the purpose of restoring, preserving and protecting the South Florida ecosystem." The plan is to provide for the "protection of water quality in, and reduction of fresh water from, the Everglades." It must also include "such features as are necessary to provide for the water-related needs of the region, including flood control, the <u>enhancement</u> of water supplies and other objectives served by the Central and Southern Florida Project." The Army Corps of Engineers 90 must present the Plan to Congress by July 1, 1999.

Currently the Corps is in the process of studying alternative plans to restore the system, now reduced by half and surrounded by cities and farmland. The Restudy plan must consider the Conceptual Plan that was developed by a variety of interests under the Governor's Commission for a <u>Sustainable</u> South Florida. It is a complicated process and the game is currently being played by interest groups and agencies. The environmental groups have scientists studying the alternatives, and Friends serves on the Everglades 100 <u>Coalition's</u> Restudy team. We continue to participate on behalf of the Everglades —calling for the right amount of clean water at the right time and in the right place.

Marjory's <u>admonition</u> in her 1947 book that the whole thing may depend on our ability to learn to work together is becoming painfully clear. Although restoration of the natural Everglades system is essential to the health of South Florida, it is often difficult for urban, agricultural, and

words for everyday use

sen • ti • ment (sen′ tə mənt) *n.*, opinion. *The <u>sentiment</u> of the governor was that more money should be spent on education.*

com • pre • hen • sive (cäm pri hen′ siv) *adj.*, covering completely or broadly; inclusive. *Because the notes he borrowed from Jerry were so <u>comprehensive</u>, Jon felt he wouldn't get behind in biology.*

en • hance • ment (in hant′ smənt) *n.*, improvement in value, quality, desirability, or attractiveness. *The <u>enhancement</u> of the ballet costumes was achieved by adding satin waistbands.*

sus • tain • a • ble (səs stā′ nə bəl) *adj.*, using a resource so that the resource is not depleted or permanently damaged. *<u>Sustainable</u> agriculture is realizable with crop rotation.*

co • a • li • tion (kō ə li′ shən) *n.*, temporary union of distinct parties for joint action. *The goal of the <u>coalition</u> is to achieve equal rights for minorities.*

ad • mo • ni • tion (ad mə ni′ shən) *n.*, warning or cautioning. *The teacher's <u>admonition</u> was enough warning to quiet the class.*

development interests to understand the ecological concept that is critical to a healthy South Florida. The health of South Florida—our people, wildlife, cities, farms, economy and drinking water—depends on a healthy Everglades. ■

110

MARK THE TEXT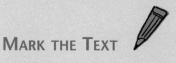

Underline or highlight who and what depend on a healthy Everglades.

Reading STRATEGY
REVIEW

VISUALIZE. Draw a sketch of what you think the Everglades looks like up close. Look back at the passage as necessary. Try to include both plants and wildlife.

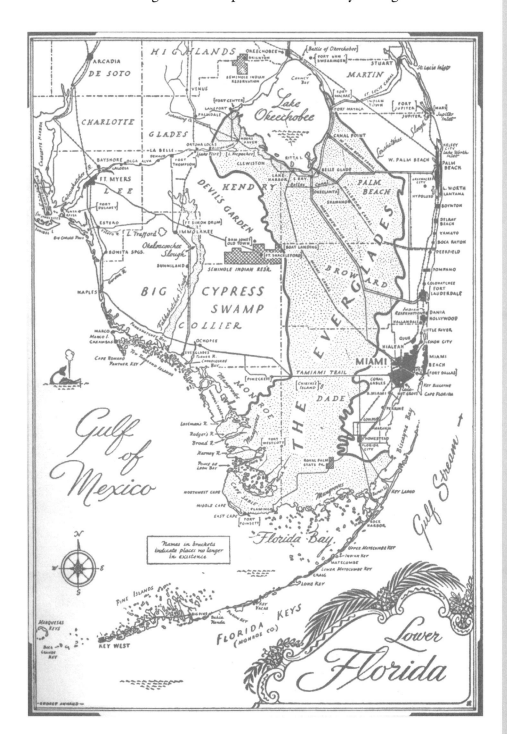

Reflect ON YOUR READING

When you finish reading, review the summaries you recorded in your chart. Then write a summary of the entire article based on your completed graphic organizer. When you finish, share your summary with that of a classmate.

Reading Skills and Test Practice

SUMMARIZE MAIN IDEAS

Discuss with a partner how best to answer questions that ask you to summarize main ideas.

1. Read this passage from the article:

> "Self-interest is a more reliable motivation than environmental pity or noblesse oblige, and Marshall accomplished the extraordinary magic of taking the Everglades out of the bleeding hearts category forever."

   How would you summarize the main idea of this passage?
   a. Environmental pity didn't work to motivate people to save the Everglades.
   b. People saw how important it was to save the Everglades even before Marshall came along.
   c. Marshall made people see that the state of the Everglades affected them personally.
   d. Marshall's plan was adopted only by important, influential people.

   What is the correct answer to the question above? How were you able to eliminate the other answers? How did your use of the reading strategy help you answer the question?

   _____

   _____

2. What is the effect of referring to the work of Marjory Stoneman Douglas and her book *The Everglades: River of Grass*?
   a. It shows how long the state of the Everglades has been a problem in Florida.
   b. It reinforces Lorion's points and lends credibility to them.
   c. It appeals to "bleeding heart" environmentalists.
   d. It attacks the Marshall Plan.

   What is the correct answer to the question above? How were you able to eliminate the other answers? How did your use of the reading strategy help you answer the question?

   _____

   _____

THINK-ALOUD NOTES

Investigate, Inquire, and Imagine

RECALL: GATHER FACTS
1a. Look at the map on page 435. What main body of water feeds into the Everglades?

→ ## INTERPRET: FIND MEANING
1b. What would happen if water from Lake Kissimmee, the Kissimmee River, and Lake Okeechobee were diverted from the Everglades?

ANALYZE: TAKE THINGS APART
2a. Identify the different groups that are working together to restore the Everglades.

→ ## SYNTHESIZE: BRING THINGS TOGETHER
2b. *Prescient* means knowing something before it happens. Explain why Marjory Stoneman Douglas's admonition in 1947 was prescient.

EVALUATE: MAKE JUDGMENTS
3a. After reading the newsletter, do you agree or disagree that action should be taken to restore the Everglades? Support your answer.

→ ## EXTEND: CONNECT IDEAS
3b. Read this excerpt from Douglas's book about the Everglades: "[The greatest mass of the saw grass] stretches as it always has stretched, in one thick enormous curving river of grass, to the very end. . . . Where the grass and the water are there is the heart, the current, the meaning of the Everglades." What characterizes the Everglades, according to Douglas? How does she write about the Everglades, scientifically or poetically?

Literary Tools

EXPOSITION. **Exposition** is a type of writing that presents facts or opinions in an organized manner. Complete the graphic organizer below with examples of facts and opinions from the article. Does Lorion use facts or opinions to make her points? If you had to summarize the main idea that all the facts and opinions support, how would you express it?

Points	Fact or Opinion
Marjory Stoneman Douglas's words are as true today as when she wrote them.	opinion

WordWorkshop

WORD FAMILIES. Knowing the meaning of one word can sometimes open a window to other related words whose meanings are then easy to figure out. For each word below, list another word in the same word family and use it in a sentence.

EXAMPLE
imagine   *imaginative*

Satya's <u>imaginative</u> drawings got the attention of the art teacher.

1. degraded

_____

2. conservationist

_____

3. admonition

_____

4. sustainable

_____

5. comprehensive

_____

Read-Write Connection

Do you think Lorion would support a letter-writing campaign to state and federal legislators in support of restoration of the Everglades? Why, or why not? Use your own paper for your response.

Beyond the Reading

READING ABOUT ENVIRONMENTAL PROBLEMS. What other environmental problems do you know about? Choose one in your region or elsewhere in the country to research. Then create a project to show what you have learned. You might make a cluster chart that illustrates possible solutions to the problem, role-play an interview with an environmental activist, or make a booklet illustrating the problem.

GO ONLINE. Visit the EMC Internet Resource Center at **emcp.com** to find links and additional activities for this selection.

"GHOST OF EVEREST"

by Jerry Adler

Active READING STRATEGY

TACKLE DIFFICULT VOCABULARY

Before Reading ➤ **PREVIEW VOCABULARY**

- ❏ Read each of the words in Words for Everyday Use, as well as its definition and accompanying sentence.
- ❏ Choose a word, and have your partner use it in an original sentence. Then have your partner choose a word and have you use it in an original sentence. Continue taking turns until you have covered all of the words.
- ❏ Make a Word Sort like the one below to be filled in as you read.

Graphic Organizer

Word: Definition: Part of Speech:	Word: Definition: Part of Speech:	Word: Definition: Part of Speech:
Word: Definition: Part of Speech:	Word: Definition: Part of Speech:	Word: Definition: Part of Speech:
Word: Definition: Part of Speech:	Word: Definition: Part of Speech:	Word: Definition: Part of Speech:
Word: Definition: Part of Speech:	Word: Definition: Part of Speech:	Word: Definition: Part of Speech:

CONNECT

Reader's resource

"Ghost of Everest" is a magazine article written by *Newsweek* reporter Jerry Adler. It appeared in 1999, two weeks after mountain climber George Mallory's body was found on Mount Everest, and 75 years after he disappeared. The article focuses on unraveling the mystery surrounding Mallory and asks the question: Did he make it to the top? If he did, then history will need to be rewritten. The news of finding Mallory's body broke on the Internet, one of the many modern tools that Mallory did not have at his disposal during his expedition.

Word watch

PREVIEW VOCABULARY

akin	formidable
ascent	lure
charismatic	novice
competent	practical
dispatch	sponsor
exasperation	summit
expedition	unnervingly
flayed	

Reader's journal

How do you feel toward someone who has already succeeded at something you have been working toward?

_____

_____

☐ Follow along in your text as your teacher reads the first three paragraphs aloud.

☐ Continue reading the selection on your own. Try to define the new words by using context clues or analyzing word parts—prefixes, roots, and suffixes. Each time you come to a new word you don't understand, jot it down in your graphic organizer.

Use THE STRATEGY

TACKLE DIFFICULT VOCABULARY. What do the prefix *un–* and the suffix *–ly* inform you about the word *unnervingly*? Try to figure out the meaning of each new word by looking at prefixes, root words, and suffixes before reading the definition.

———————————————

———————————————

Literary TOOLS

BACKGROUND INFORMATION. Background information is information provided to the reader, often at the beginning, to explain the situation. As you read, pay attention to the background information about Mallory and the other climbers.

Ghost of Everest

Jerry Adler

1999 Mallory & Irvine
Research Expedition Route

After 75 years, the mountain yields the body of the legendary George Mallory. But the mystery endures: did he reach the top?

H e must have died near, or even after, sunset, because he had taken off his goggles and stowed them in a pocket. The <u>unnervingly</u> white skin of his back was bare to the sky where the wind had <u>flayed</u> off his clothing, seven layers of cotton and wool. From the evidence, George Mallory, the first man to attempt the <u>summit</u> of Mount

10 Everest, had fallen to his death, landing several hundred feet below the ridge that leads to the peak. The astounding discovery of Mallory's body answers one question about what happened after he and Andrew Irvine disappeared into the clouds one day in June 1924. If it was near dark, he almost

---

**words
for
everyday
use**

un • nerv • ing • ly (ən nər′ viŋ lē) *adv.*, deprived of courage and physical strength; caused to become weak and ineffective, especially from fear. *The blizzard blew into town rapidly and unnervingly.*

flayed (flād′) *vi.*, strip off the skin or surface of. *His face was flayed by the sharp winds.*

sum • mit (sə′ mət) *n.*, highest point, ridge, or level of a mountain; peak. *His goal was to climb to the summit of the mountain.*

certainly fell on his way back down. But that only raises a second question, still unanswered: before turning around, did Mallory reach the summit?

Among the mountaineers, solving this puzzle would be <u>akin</u> to finding a manuscript of "Othello" in an envelope with Shakespeare's return address. Thus, on the morning of May 1, five American climbers fanned out on a steep and rocky slope at about 27,000 feet. They were part of an eight-member team of some of the world's top mountaineers (and a PBS documentary crew), hoping both to find the remains of Mallory and Irvine and to determine if they had reached the summit before dying—29 years before Sir Edmund Hillary and Tenzing Norgay made the first recognized <u>ascent</u>, in 1953. A similar expedition looked for Mallory in 1986, without success. But luck was with the searchers this time. As expedition leader Eric Simonson told Newsweek from base camp "there was very little winter snow, and the temperatures have been moderate by Everest standards," exposing areas usually covered. By Everest standards, "moderate" meant temperatures well below zero with winds of 30 miles an hour or more.

This was on the north, or Tibetan, face of Everest, not Hillary's route up the Southeast Ridge, where five climbers died in the famous 1996 storm. Compared with the southeast approach from Nepal, Simonson said, the north face avoids the dangerous passage under the teetering ice blocks of the Hkumbu Iceface but it requires a little more climbing expertise and involves more time spent above 25,000 feet. Yet Mallory himself was in the opinion of the definitive Everest historian Walt Unsworth, "a <u>competent</u>, rather than great, climber." He was experienced, to be sure, a veteran of two earlier British Everest expeditions, as well as handsome, <u>charismatic</u> and athletic. But he was pushing 38, a married man with three young children and a minor appointment at Cambridge. When the British Alpine Club

NOTE THE FACTS

What question remains unanswered?

_____

_____

NOTE THE FACTS

What was the goal of the 1999 expedition?

_____

_____

FIX-UP IDEA

Reread
Sometimes looking for word meanings as you read distracts you from what the article is all about. If you are having trouble, take your time to unlock the meanings of words first. Then reread the entire article focusing on understanding the events described.

words for everyday use

a • kin (ə kin′) *adj.*, showing the same nature; similar. *Her first roller coaster ride gave her a feeling <u>akin</u> to terror.*

as • cent (ə sent′) *n.*, act of going, traveling, or climbing up. *After the picnic they began their <u>ascent</u> of the mountain.*

com • pe • tent (käm′ pə tənt) *adj.*, having the neccessary abilities. *Before he was hired, Mr. Brown took a test to prove he was <u>competent</u> in math.*

char • is • mat • ic (kar əz ma′ tik) *adj.*, special or magnetic charm or appeal. *The boy's humor made him <u>charismatic</u>.*

Reading TIP

If you are having trouble
keeping the 1924 and 1999
expeditions straight, try
identifying each paragraph as
present (1999 expedition),
past (1924 expedition), or
both.

50 called him to be second in command of its eight-man team,
he almost turned it down. "This is going to be more like
war than mountaineering," he told a friend. He and
Mallory had seen combat in the war. "I don't expect to
come back." Yet he felt the inescapable <u>lure</u> of Everest. He
climbed it, he famously told an American reporter, "because
it is there"—a remark that either captured his deeply spiritual approach to mountaineering or (as friends claimed)
reflected his <u>exasperation</u> with being asked the same point-
less question time after time.

60 His chosen companion, Irvine, was only 22, a <u>novice</u>
climber but exceptionally strong and fit. He was also an
expert with the new technologies of bottled oxygen and
zippers. Mallory, of the old school, preferred to fasten his
anorak with tried-and-true buttons. The expedition (like
most of those today) relied on the indispensable Sherpa
porters,[1] but Mallory had no doubt which race made the
best mountaineers. When conditions turn bad, he wrote in
a <u>dispatch</u> quoted in *The New York Times*, "the splendid fellow who bore his load so proudly has become a veritable
70 child—a child for whom the British officer is at every turn
responsible."

On the morning of June 8, the two set out from a camp at
27,000 feet, where they had spent the night alone. Shortly
before 1 P.M., another member of their <u>expedition</u>, Noel
Odell, spotted from far below two distant figures climbing
a rocky ledge. If this was the Second Step, a sheer wall of
rock and ice very near the summit, then they almost certainly reached the peak that day. But Odell wasn't certain of
what he saw; the climbers may have been at the much lower
80 First Step, with the <u>formidable</u> Second still to come. As

---

1. **Sherpa porters.** Tibetan people skilled in mountain climbing who often
accompany climbers as guides

words for everyday use

lure (loor') *n.*, temptation. *The <u>lure</u> of the outdoors is recorded in many poems.*

ex • as • per • a • tion (ig zas pə rā' shən) *n.*, extreme annoyance. *His <u>exasperation</u> over the complicated instructions caused a delay in his work.*

nov • ice (nä' vəs) *adj.*, beginner; inexperienced person. *He was a <u>novice</u> horse-back rider.*

dis • patch (di spach') *n.*, report, news brief. *They waited for the latest <u>dispatch</u> on the storm.*

ex • pe • di • tion (ek spə di' shən) *n.*, journey, voyage, or excursion undertaken for a specific purpose. *As an archeologist, he had gone on many such <u>expeditions</u>.*

for • mi • da • ble (for' mə də bəl) *adj,.* fearful, dreadful, or intimidating. *The <u>formidable</u> size of the project worried the students.*

Odell watched, the figures disappeared into a cloud. When the weather cleared, hours later, Mallory and Irvine were nowhere to be seen. Nine years later another English expedition recovered an ice ax below the First Step, believed to be Irvine's. But there was no sign of their bodies until 1975, when a Chinese climber spotted what he described as "old English dead" near his expedition's Camp VI. Unfortunately, he kept the news to himself for three years, before confiding in a Japanese climber—and died himself
90 the very next day in an avalanche, taking with him the exact location of the bodies.

Still, that was enough information for Simonson and his team to go on, once they figured out where the Chinese climbers' camp had been. In a posting on the Mountain Zone website (www.mountainzone.com), an expedition sponsor, climber Conrad Anker described "looking to the west [and then] I saw a patch of white, that was whiter than the rock . . . and also whiter than the snow." "George was lying on his stomach," Simonson reported, "head uphill, arms out-
100 stretched, like a frozen statue." Anker put out a coded call on his radio—there were scores of climbers on the mountain, and he didn't want to attract a stampede—and his teammates gathered and began carefully digging in the icy gravel.

All along, the climbers had expected to find Irvine, whose ice ax had been recovered nearby. When a tag with Mallory's name turned up, they wondered why Irvine was wearing Mallory's shirt. "Then it hit us," climber Dave Hahn reported on Mountain Zone, ". . . we were in the presence of George Leigh Mallory himself. THE man of
110 the mountain." The body had evidently fallen some distance; a leg was fractured at the boot top, and he was tied to a broken rope—at the other end of which, presumably, had been Irvine. The climbers recovered a few personal objects, including letters, and collected a tissue sample for DNA analysis.[2] Then, with rocks laboriously gathered from

---

2. **DNA analysis.** Deoxyribonucleic acid analysis, a study of cell tissues to determine facts about the body

words for everyday use
spon • sor (spän[t]' sər) n., one who assumes responsibility for some other person or thing. *Acting as my sponsor, my uncle paid for my study abroad assignment.*

NOTE THE FACTS

What happened to Mallory and Irvine?

_____

_____

Reading STRATEGY REVIEW

WRITE THINGS DOWN. Writing things down helps you to remember the main points of a text. What two expeditions is this article talking about?

_____

_____

_____

NOTE THE FACTS

How do they know they found Mallory's body?

_____

_____

THINK AND REFLECT

Reread lines 115–117.
What did the members of
Simonson's expedition do
with Mallory's body? How
did the climbers feel
toward Mallory? **(Infer)**

_____

_____

_____

THINK AND REFLECT

What purpose for the 1999
expedition is identified in
lines 133–136? How is this
purpose related to the
purpose in lines 22–28?
(Analyze)

_____

_____

_____

READ ALOUD

Read aloud the
highlighted text on this
page. How would you
answer this question?
Why?

_____

_____

_____

_____

the steep slope, they buried Mallory where he lay on his
beloved Everest.

What they didn't find, though, was evidence that Mallory
had reached the top, such as a notebook or even his camera,
120 which might have contained recoverable images from a
summit picture snapped 75 years ago. Such a discovery
could be politically sensitive, since China claims as a matter
of national honor the first recorded ascent of Everest from
the north, in 1960. If Mallory did it in 1924, the *Beijing
Youth Daily*[3] noted last week, "history may be rewritten."

It may yet be. In 1960 the Second Step was conquered by
a climber who found footholds in the rock with his bare
feet, sacrificing his toes to frostbite. Modern climbers use a
ladder, fixed there in 1975. But sometime this week, Anker
130 hopes to climb the Second Step as Mallory would have
done it, without a ladder or ropes, just to see if it can be
done. His fellow climbers will search at 27,000 feet again
for Irvine. "This expedition," Simonson said, "is not just
about going out looking for bodies. We want it to be a cel-
ebration of what those guys accomplished 75 years ago in
leather boots and tweed jackets." Their achievement, of
course, had no <u>practical</u> significance even then. Hillary
himself, with a lifetime of honors behind him, said last
week he hoped Mallory did make the summit ("but I think
140 it's unlikely"). But who among us, imagining Mallory dying
as he hugged the mountain, can help but wonder: at the
moment he fell, was he looking down in disappointment—
or up at the darkening sky in triumph? ∎

---

3. *Beijing Youth Daily.* Newspaper published in China

words for everyday use	**prac • ti • cal** (prak′ ti kəl) *adj.,* capable of being put to use or account. *Nigel found carrying an umbrella to be <u>practical</u> in rainy London.*

Reflect ON YOUR READING

After reading, review your list of difficult words and their definitions. Then, work with a partner to create a fill-in-the-blank paragraph with at least eight of the words. You might provide definitions, synonyms, antonyms, or other hints for filling in the blanks. When you and your partner finish the paragraph, exchange your paragraph with another pair of students.

Reading Skills and Test Practice

USE CONTEXT CLUES

Discuss with your partner how to best answer questions about words used in context.

1. Read the following sentences from the article.

   From the evidence, George Mallory, the first man to attempt the summit of Mount Everest, had fallen to his death, landing several hundred feet below the ridge that leads to the peak.

   Based on the context clues, which is the best synonym for *summit*?
   a. ridge
   b. mountain
   c. peak
   d. climb

What is the correct answer to the question above? How were you able to eliminate the other answers? How did your use of the reading strategy help you answer the question?

_____

2. Read the following sentences from the article.

   Yet Mallory himself was in the opinion of the definitive Everest historian Walt Unsworth, "a competent, rather than a great, climber." He was experienced, to be sure . . . But he was pushing 38 . . .

   Based on the context clues, what does *competent* mean?
   a. excellent
   b. experienced
   c. capable
   d. incapable

What is the correct answer to the question above? How were you able to eliminate the other answers? How did your use of the reading strategy help you answer the question?

_____

THINK-ALOUD NOTES

_____
_____
_____
_____
_____
_____
_____
_____
_____
_____
_____
_____
_____
_____
_____
_____
_____

Investigate, Inquire, and Imagine

RECALL: GATHER FACTS
1a. Identify the nationalities of each of the climbers who led the expeditions mentioned in the article.

INTERPRET: FIND MEANING
1b. How would you describe the relationship among the climbers? How is mountain climbing also a competition between nations?

ANALYZE: TAKE THINGS APART
2a. What evidence is needed that would prove whether or not Mallory reached the peak?

SYNTHESIZE: BRING THINGS TOGETHER
2b. What would discovering the answer to this question mean? Do you think we will ever know the answer? Explain.

EVALUATE: MAKE JUDGMENTS
3a. Simonson called conditions "moderate" by Everest standards. How would you describe the weather conditions?

EXTEND: CONNECT IDEAS
3b. What hardships would have to be endured to climb Mount Everest?

Literary Tools

BACKGROUND INFORMATION. **Background information** is information provided to the reader, often at the beginning, to explain the situation to the reader. Complete the graphic organizer below with facts about the climbers mentioned in the article.

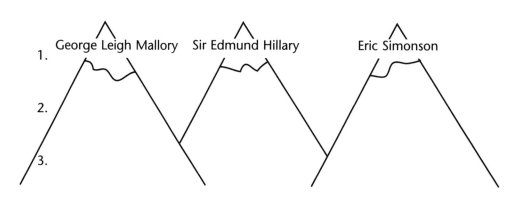

What is the role of the background information as it relates to the discovery of Mallory's corpse? What difficulties might you have had understanding this article if the background information was not provided?

_____

_____

_____

WordWorkshop

SUFFIXES. Preview the Common Suffixes chart in Unit 9, pages 483–484. Then make each of the Words for Everyday Use from this selection into a new, related word by adding or removing a suffix. The definition of the new word is given to help you identify it. Then, use the new word in a sentence.

1. ascent
   capable of being ascended: _____

2. competent
   state of being competent: _____

3. dispatch
   one who sends dispatches: _____

4. charismatic
   magnetic charm or appeal: _____

5. formidable
   state or condition of being formidable: _____

Read-Write Connection

If you had been a member of Simonson's expedition, what would be the most significant aspects of the discovery of Mallory's body for you?

_____

_____

_____

_____

_____

_____

_____

_____

Beyond the Reading

RESEARCHING AN EXPLORER. Read a book about an explorer or exploration. Some possibilities are James Cook, Amerigo Vespucci, Robert Falcon Scott, Robert Edwin Peary, Matthew Henson, Roald Amundson, and Anne Bancroft. Then create an assignment to show what you have learned. For example, you might make a time line of the important events in the explorer's life, write a personality profile, or write a banquet speech in which you honor his or her contributions to exploration.

GO ONLINE. Visit the EMC Internet Resource Center at **emcp.com** to find links and additional activities for this selection.

Reader's resource

"Best Sky Sights of the Next Century" appeared in *The Old Farmer's Almanac*. An almanac is a publication that provides weather and astronomical data, such as sunrises and sunsets, arranged according to the days, weeks, and months of a given year. In this article, Bob Berman tells about total solar eclipses, comets, meteor showers, and planetary conjunctions that will occur in the next 100 years. Berman directs two observatories and writes regularly about astronomy.

Word watch

PREVIEW VOCABULARY

celestial	predict
geyser	prominence
ineffable	spectacle
orbit	

Reader's journal

Think of a time you have seen something magnificent in the sky—a falling star, northern lights, a planet, or a space satellite. How did it feel to see it from Earth?

_____

_____

_____

_____

_____

"Best Sky Sights of the Next Century"

from *The Old Farmer's Almanac*

by Bob Berman

Active READING STRATEGY

CONNECT TO PRIOR KNOWLEDGE

Before Reading ➤ **ACTIVATE PRIOR KNOWLEDGE**

❑ Read the Reader's Resource.
❑ Discuss with your classmates any previous experiences you have had with witnessing "sky sights," visiting a planetarium, or viewing documentaries about astronomy.
❑ Fill in the first two columns of the K-W-L Chart below before you begin reading.

Graphic Organizer

What I Know	What I Want to Learn	What I Have Learned

Best Sky Sights of the Next Century

Bob Berman

The Magnificent Seven Total Solar Eclipses
(Four for Canada)

Totality causes humans and animals alike to moan and babble, as normally invisible deep-pink <u>prominences</u> leap from the Sun's edge like nuclear <u>geysers</u>. Alas, this <u>ineffable</u> experience of totality happens just once every 360 years, on average, from any given site on Earth.

August 21, 2017, will bring the first American totality: the 185-mile-wide shadow will slash the country from coast
10   to coast—west to east—like a calligraphy[1] brushstroke. Another mainland American totality will occur on **April 8, 2024,** followed by the longest eclipse in U.S. history (a six-

---

1. **calligraphy.** The art of ornamental, elegant writing

words for everyday use	**prom • i • nence** (prä′ mə nən[t]s) *n.,* object that stands out, or projects beyond a surface or line. *The skyscraper was an unusual <u>prominence</u> in the rural landscape.* **gey • ser** (gī′ zər) *n.,* spring that throws forth jets of heated water and steam. *Many visitors go to Yellowstone National Park to see its famous <u>geyser</u>, Old Faithful.* **in • ef • fa • ble** (i ne′ fə bəl) *adj.,* incapable of being expressed in words. *She watched the <u>ineffable</u> beauty of the sunset.*

During Reading

CONNECT TO PRIOR KNOWLEDGE

- ❑ Follow along in the text as your teacher reads aloud the first section. Put a check mark next to any information you already knew. Put an exclamation point next to any information that surprises or intrigues you.
- ❑ Record new information in the third column of your graphic organizer.
- ❑ Read the rest of the selection in a small group. Stop at the end of each section to discuss what you already knew about each section and what was new.
- ❑ Continue to record things you learn in your graphic organizer.

Reading TIP

Read the headings of the four sections. Then predict what you will be reading about in this article.

NOTE THE FACTS

Reread lines 1–5. What is "totality"? How often does one occur?

_____

_____

Literary TOOLS

ALLITERATION. Alliteration is the repetition of initial consonant sounds, or repeated initial vowel sounds. As you read, look for examples of alliteration.

FIX-UP IDEA

Refocus
If you have trouble, try refocusing. First, read a section of the text and record the future dates and events listed. Then, next to each event and date, write down how old you will be when it occurs. Doing so will help you make connections to your own life.

NOTE THE FACTS

Why are we not informed about most comets?

_____

_____

minute totality) on **August 12, 2045,** that again will cross the country from the Pacific to the Atlantic—an inspiration, perhaps, for today's observers to stay healthy.

20 After a shorter totality over Georgia in **2052,** the continental United States will then receive a rare present: two total solar eclipses within a single year, on **May 11, 2078,** and **May 1, 2079.** Finally, the century will close with a totality for the north-central and mid-Atlantic states in September of **2099.** And that's it—seven opportunities in the next 100 years for stay-at-home Americans to stand fully in the Moon's shadow (we should note, however, that brief totalities occur in northern Alaska in **2033** and **2097**).

For Canadian eclipse addicts, the **April 8, 2024,** event will also be seen from the Maritime provinces.[2] The next one, on **August 22, 2044,** will actually begin at sunrise on the border with Montana, then will hightail it northward 30 through the western Prairies toward the North Pole. After that, it's a long wait until the eclipse of **May 1, 2079,** visible from the Maritimes, and the totality of **September 14, 2099,** seen in southwestern Canada.

Great Comets

In terms of sheer <u>spectacle</u>, the closest runner-up to solar totality is probably Earth's encounter with a Great Comet. While 1996's Hyakutake and 1997's Hale-Bopp did indeed break a 22-year Great Comet drought, neither was as spectacular—that is, bright, with a long tail—as some of the 40 finest historical visitors. The most-demanding comet-lovers desire a comet with both qualities, like Halley's memorable 1910 visit, or the "Great January comet" of that same extraordinary year. Although most spectacular comets have initially uncharted <u>orbits</u> of thousands of years and therefore visit us with no advance notice, the one trusty short-period

---

2. **Maritime provinces.** Territory bordering on the sea

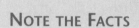

| words for everyday use | **spec • ta • cle** (spek' ti kəl) *n.,* remarkable or noteworthy site. *He was quite a <u>spectacle</u> in his clown costume.* |
| | **or • bit** (or' bət) *n.,* path of a celestial body, artificial satellite, or spacecraft around another body. *He studied the earth's <u>orbit</u> around the sun.* |

comet that *can* be <u>predicted</u> is also the most famous of all—
Halley's comet.

Unfortunately, during Halley's most recent visit, in 1985
and '86, Earth was in nearly the worst possible position, the
equivalent of the outfield bleacher seats. But the
Earth/Halley geometry will be wonderful for its return in
2061. Then, it should span half the sky. Moreover, it will
float in front of the stars of the Big Dipper, making it
prominent for observers in the United States and Canada.

Meteor Showers

The finest reliable showers will continue to be summer's
Perseids, from **August 11 to 13,** which will slowly creep to
August 12 to 14 as the century advances, and the rich
Germinid display on the night of **December 13–14,** which
will also migrate ahead one night toward century's end.
Anyone can predict which years these will appear at their
best by looking up the phases of the Moon for those dates.
Meteors are greatly diminished from view by a Moon that
falls between the first and last quarter phases.

Of course, for true spectacle, observers will be looking for
a meteor "storm," the 50-to-100-shooting-stars-per-second
display that happened in **1799, 1833,** and **1966.** Right
now, it appears that the on-again, off-again $33^1/_3$ -year
periodicity of the Leonids should continue, giving us good
opportunities in **2033, 2066,** and **2099.**

Planetary Conjunctions[3]

Truly awesome close encounters require a meeting of at
least two of the three planets that can attain dazzling bril-
liance (Venus, Jupiter, and, rarely, Mars), or the Moon with
one or more of these. We'll throw in bright but not brilliant Saturn and Mercury only when a meeting involving
them is ultraclose. To qualify, the <u>celestial</u> targets must pass
extremely close to each other in the night sky—perhaps

---

3. **Planetary Conjunctions.** When planets appear very close together in
the sky or on a map

---

words for everyday use	
pre • dict (pri dikt') *vt.,* declare in advance, to forecast or prophecy. *Amy accurately <u>predicted</u> which dessert Irving would choose from the menu.*   **ce • les • tial** (sə les' chəl) *adj.,* of or relating to the sky: specifically, representing the visible bodies in the sky. *Marvin got a <u>celestial</u> map so he could identify the planets.*

**TACKLE DIFFICULT
VOCABULARY.** Tackling
difficult vocabulary will
help you understand what
you are reading. Apply
your knowledge of
prefixes, root words, and
suffixes to help you
decode new words. If *pre–*
means "before" and *dict*
means "tell," what do you
think predict means?

_____

NOTE THE FACTS

What conditions are
perfect for viewing a
meteor shower? How
can conditions be
predicted?

_____

_____

Use THE STRATEGY

CONNECT TO PRIOR KNOWLEDGE.
Add any previous knowledge
you have remembered to the
graphic organizer, as well as
anything else you want to
learn while reading this article.

80

even merge into a single, ultra-bright, alien-looking sky object. (Although events involving Venus usually occur in twilight, the sky sightings below remain visible long enough to stand out against a satisfyingly dark backdrop.)

The following table presents a comprehensive list of the *best* planetary events of the twenty-first century that can be seen during the nightfall-to-10 P.M. period, when most people are willing to venture out.

Best Planetary Encounters

Date	Objects	Date	Objects
April 5, 2000	Ma, J	June 21, 2074	V, J
May 10, 2002	V, Ma	June 27, 2074	V, Mn, J
June 30, 2007	V, S	June 28, 2076	Ma, J
December 1, 2008	V, Mn, J	October 31, 2076	Mn, Ma, S
February 20, 2015	V, Mn, Ma	February 27, 2079	V, Ma
June 30–July 1, 2015	V, J	November 7, 2080	Ma, J, S
July 18, 2015	V, Mn, J	November 15, 2080	Ma, J, S
December 20, 2020	J, S	November 17, 2080	Mn, Ma, J, S
March 1, 2023	V, J	December 24, 2080	V, J
December 1–2, 2033	Ma, J	March 6, 2082	V, J
February 23, 2047	V, Ma	April 28, 2085	Mn, Ma, J
March 7, 2047	V, J	June 13, 2085	Me, V, J
May 13, 2066	V, Ma	May 15, 2098	V, Ma
July 1, 2066	V, S	June 29, 2098	V, J
March 14, 2071	V, J		

Attach this article to a refrigerator you plan to keep for ten decades. But there's no substitute for keeping your eye-wide open after nightfall—for many of the best celestial spectacles, such as awesome long-period comets, northern lights, and bolides (exploding meteors), arrive with little or no warning, brilliant bombshells in the heavens. ■

90

THINK AND REFLECT

Reread lines 81–84. What does Berman mean by the "best" planetary events?

_____

_____

_____

_____

READ ALOUD

Read aloud the highlighted text on this page. What is Berman's advice for those interested in sky sights? What tone is he using in the first sentence?

_____

_____

_____

_____

Reflect ON YOUR READING

With your during-reading group, discuss your reaction to the selection. Talk about the following questions: Which "sky sights" do you find most interesting? Which would you like to see? How did your previous knowledge affect your interest in the selection? How did the selection confirm what you knew? What did you learn that you did not know before?

As you discuss these questions, refer to the graphic organizer you completed.

Reading Skills and Test Practice

INTERPRET CHARTS

Discuss with your group how best to answer the following questions about the chart on the previous page.

1. Which two celestial bodies will have an encounter on June 30, 2007?
   a. Moon and Mars
   b. Venus and Mars
   c. Jupiter and Saturn
   d. Venus and Saturn

What is the correct answer to the question above? How were you able to eliminate the other answers? How did your use of the reading strategy help you answer the question?

_____

_____

2. How many times in this century will Mars and Jupiter have an encounter, according to the chart?
   a. 0
   b. 3
   c. 5
   d. 7

What is the correct answer to the question above? How were you able to eliminate the other answers? How did your use of the reading strategy help you answer the question?

_____

_____

THINK-ALOUD NOTES

_____

_____

_____

_____

_____

_____

_____

_____

_____

_____

_____

Investigate, Inquire, and Imagine

RECALL: GATHER FACTS
1a. When will the next sky event take place?

INTERPRET: FIND MEANING
1b. How old will you be on that date? What do you imagine your life will be like?

ANALYZE: TAKE THINGS APART
2a. Identify the main celestial events Berman discusses in his article.

SYNTHESIZE: BRING THINGS TOGETHER
2b. What is their relationship to each other?

EVALUATE: MAKE JUDGMENTS
3a. Why does Berman cover events that will be happening over a span of one hundred years?

EXTEND: CONNECT IDEAS
3b. Why does he tell us to take our vitamins and stick around, and to hang the article on a refrigerator for ten decades? What sense do you have of your own life span in relation to the life span of, for example, a comet?

Literary Tools

ALLITERATION. **Alliteration** is the repetition of initial consonant sounds, or repeated initial vowel sounds. Complete the graphic organizer below to show examples of alliteration from the selection.

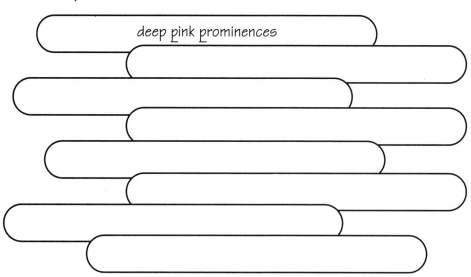

deep pink prominences

What is the effect of the alliteration in this selection?

_____

_____

WordWorkshop

Test Your Knowledge. Review the list of vocabulary from the selection. Use those words to complete the sentences below.

1. _____ comes from the Latin word *caelum,* meaning "sky."

2. *Forecast* is a synonym for _____.

3. _____ comes from the Icelandic word *geysa,* meaning "to rush forth."

4. Give an example of something that is *ineffable.* Tell why it is *ineffable.*

   _____

   _____

5. In whose *orbit* do you travel, and why? Does this mean that person has *prominence* in your life? Why, or why not?

   _____

   _____

Read-Write Connection

How does the information provided in the article change how you perceive the sky and time?

_____

_____

_____

_____

Beyond the Reading

Researching Constellations. The Babylonians are credited with being the first to identify constellations, in as early as 3000 BC While you are waiting for the big sky sights outlined by Bob Berman in the selection, you can look for constellations in the night sky. Research something about constellations. Then create a project to show what you have learned. For example, you might write the history of constellations, tell a mythological story related to a specific constellation, or make a star map to show your classmates how to find a certain constellation in the night sky.

Go Online. Visit the EMC Internet Resource Center at **emcp.com** to find links and additional activities for this selection.

Reader's resource

"Research Strategies for the Learning Highway" is a chapter from *The Learning Highway: Smart Students and the Net*, a book intended to help students use the Internet effectively. In this selection, university educators Trevor Owen and Ron Owston point out to students how to find facts, websites, and reading material on the Internet, as well as how to evaluate Internet sites. This selection is an example of *technical writing*, which is scientific or process-oriented instructional writing of a technical or mechanical nature.

Word watch

PREVIEW VOCABULARY

bias	erroneous
caveat	relevant
conversely	reputable
corroborating	scrutinized
credible	

Reader's journal

What are your goals when you use the Internet?

_____

_____

_____

"Research Strategies for the Learning Highway"

from *The Learning Highway: Smart Students and the Net*

by Trevor Owen and Ron Owston

Active READING STRATEGY

USE TEXT ORGANIZATION

Before Reading ➤ **PREVIEW THE SELECTION**

❏ Read the Reader's Resource.
❏ Read the organization subheads for the selection in order to predict what the selection will be about.
❏ For each section of the text, use your own paper to make an outline like the one below.

Graphic Organizer

1. Text subhead: Four Steps to Finding Facts
A. Step 1:
B. Step 2:
C. Step 3:
D. Step 4:

Trevor Owen and
Ron Owston

Research Strategies for the Learning Highway

During Reading

USE TEXT ORGANIZATION

❑ Follow along in the text as your teacher reads aloud the first section, "Four Steps to Finding Facts."

❑ Read the remainder of the selection with a partner. Stop at the end of each section to record in your outline the key steps.

Four Steps to Finding Facts

Often you'll want to find specific facts, statistics, definitions, and other data. For instance, we might want to know the answer to questions such as:

- How high is Mount Everest?
- What is the GNP of France?
- What countries belong to the British Commonwealth?
- Who wrote the novel *The Sun Also Rises?*

Here are the steps we suggest you take to find answers to
10 questions such as these.

Step 1

Think of the most obvi-
ous search words, pay-
ing particular attention
to key nouns: for exam-
ple, *height, elevation,
Mount Everest* would be
good for the first ques-
tion above. Enter these words into a comprehensive search
20 index, such as Altavista, and connect the keywords with

Reading TIP

The authors list sample questions that could be answered following the steps they give you. To make a personal link to the text, think of questions of your own that you want to answer.

Literary TOOLS

EXPOSITION. **Exposition** is a type of writing that presents facts or opinions in an organized manner. As you read, try to determine the organizational method used by the authors in this selection.

THINK AND REFLECT

Reread lines 25–27. What is step 2 for fact searches? Why is this step necessary? (Infer)

_____

_____

_____

appropriate search operators. For Altavista these might be +*(height or elevation)* + *"Mount Everest."* Then do the search. If you don't find what you want, go to the next step.

Step 2

Rather than refining your search with Altavista, try one or two Web search indexes because they typically produce remarkably different results with the same search words. You might even try MetaCrawler because it searches all of the major search engines in one step. Go to Step 3 if you
30   still have no luck.

Step 3

Your search skills will now be put to the test because you are going to have to go back and revise your search key-words and operators with the indexes and retry the search-es. For example, we might try *(elevation OR height OR high) NEAR "Mount Everest"* in an advanced Altavista search.

Step 4

If you're not successful in Step 3, then you should try searching the newsgroups with DejaNews. Given the vast
40   amount of discussion that takes place in newsgroups, per-haps someone has previously talked about your topic. If you still draw a blank after searching DejaNews, then try post-ing a message in an appropriate group to see if anyone knows the answer to your question.

Four Steps to Finding Websites

This is a more open-ended kind of search than looking for facts, because if you're trying to locate websites that deal with a certain topic, you may never be satisfied that you've found them all. But more important than finding all the sites on a
50   topic is locating good-quality sites that meet your needs. The steps we outline below will answer some of the following sample questions:

- What websites deal with modern English literature?
- Are there any sites dedicated to tornadoes—how they are formed and what safety precautions you can take if you see one?

WHAT DO YOU WONDER?

_____

_____

_____

Use THE STRATEGY

USE TEXT ORGANIZATION.
Think about how each question relates to the subheading. What is one type of website you would like to find on the Internet?

_____

_____

- Are there any sites that have tutorials to help me improve my Spanish?
60 - Where can I go to find information on and see pictures of the Mir space station?

To answer questions like this, we suggest you follow the four steps described below.

Step 1

Yahoo! is a good starting point. Begin by either browsing your topic or doing a keyword search. For the last example about the Mir space station, browsing the path *Science: Space: Missions* would take you to a list of sites, as would searching on *Mir*. Since Yahoo! is an excellent resource for locating websites you may not need to look any farther, but if you do, try the next step.

Step 2

70 Follow the path in Yahoo! to a subcategory that takes you closest to your topic and browse some of the links to sites that you find there. There's a good chance that a few of these sites will have links to your topic. But if you don't dis-
80 cover anything relevant, or <u>conversely</u>, if you find too many sites, go to Step 3.

Step 3

Browse another directory. Magellan is a good one to try—pay particular attention to their evaluated sites. It's possible to browse only sites that are highly rated, for example. You may also want to browse the Top 5% sites at Lycos.

NOTE THE FACTS

What is step 1 for finding websites? What should you do if searching Yahoo! provides no results (lines 65–82)?

_____

_____

_____

_____

FIX-UP IDEA

Connect to Prior Knowledge
If you have trouble, connect to what you already know by taking notes as you read. Place a check mark next to steps you already use. Place a long dash next to things that you would like to do the next time you conduct an Internet search.

words for everyday use

con • verse • ly (kən vers′ lē) *adv.*, in the opposite manner. *If you have trouble losing weight, try eating fewer carbohydrates and fatty foods; conversely, if you have trouble gaining weight, try eating more carbohydrates and fatty foods.*

Step 4

Try searching Altavista or any of the other major Web indexes if you still can't find what you want. We suggest using the indexes as a last resort for locating websites, because they often turn up too many links in their results list, especially when you are searching for a relatively broad topic.

Four Steps to Finding Reading Material

These steps will help you find articles, abstracts, essays, book excerpts, research papers, stories, poetry, and other kinds of original reading material. They are designed to help you locate suitable background reading for your courses or special interests, and to find material for assignments or papers. By following these steps, you should be able to answer questions like:

- What has been written recently about the treatment of dyslexia in young children?
- Is there any research that suggests a connection between movie stars smoking on screen and teenage use of tobacco?
- Why was the U.S. involved in the Vietnam War?
- Why do some economists say that high unemployment can be "good" for the economy?

Following are the four steps we suggest you try.

Step 1

Try doing a search on your topic using Altavista. As a first step you may even want to enter a natural language question like any of the above and see how Altavista handles it. If that doesn't work, try entering keywords connected by appropriate operators. At this point don't spend too much time attempting to formulate a "perfect" search.

90

100

110

120

Step 2

If Altavista doesn't locate what you want after a few tries, search a few other Web indexes or use MetaCrawler. Generally speaking, Yahoo! and the other Web directories are not as useful as the indexes for locating articles about specific topics, but there's no harm in giving them a go too.

130 **Step 3**

Try some of the other specialized search tools if you still are not satisfied with what you've found so far. For example, search the catalog of your local library or that of a highly regarded university for your topic. Also try searching Amazon.com. The libraries and bookstores will likely point the way to <u>relevant</u> print materials you might be able to borrow or purchase; they may also suggest authors and keywords you can use for Steps 1 and 2.

Step 4

140 Turn to DejaNews and search the newsgroups for your topic, if the first three steps prove unproductive. You won't find actual reading material about your topic there, but you may come across someone who has discussed the topic and has referred to resources on the topic. If a website is mentioned in the body of a newsgroup article, DejaNews turns it into a clickable link that you could pursue with your browser. As a last resort, you could post a newsgroup message for help in an appropriate group.

Evaluating What You Find

150 With the traditional publishing of articles, books, magazines, and newspapers there is a built-in editorial process. Publishing houses employ editors to review manuscripts for content and style before they go to press. This process gives the reader some assurance that, at a minimum, someone else has read the material and deemed it worthy of publication. However, as we said earlier, on the Internet

NOTE THE FACTS

Reread lines 140–148. Why does a person select DejaNews?

_____

_____

_____

MARK THE TEXT

Underline or highlight why published materials are sometimes superior to those found on the Internet.

words for everyday use

rel • e • vant (re′ lə vənt) *adj.,* having something to do with the matter being considered. *At the meeting about the prom, Stephen brought up fundraising for new football uniforms, which the chairperson said was not <u>relevant</u>.*

anyone can publish anything about any topic he or she wishes and can do so without having it <u>scrutinized</u> by an editor. Therefore, the <u>caveat</u> on the Internet is "Reader
160   Beware!"

Besides looking out for <u>erroneous</u> information and reading critically, there are some other criteria you can use to evaluate what you read on the Internet. Here are some we recommend.

- *Look at the resource's domain name.* Domain names can provide some clues to the credibility of a resource. Generally speaking, we tend to trust documents that have domain names ending in *edu* or *gov*, because those names tell you that the documents come from a
170   U.S. university or government site. If the site is outside the U.S., look for a university or government name as part of the domain name (e.g., *yorku.ca*). Commercial sites (*com*) of well-known, <u>reputable</u> companies are <u>credible</u>, too, but you must watch for <u>biases</u> that may relate to a company's product. For example, would you trust documents at a cigarette manufacturer's site about research linking smoking and cancer? Would these be as objective as a government report? Sites ending in *org* or *net* can be trusted if they are
180   operated by a reputable organization too (e.g., the Public Broadcasting System, whose domain name is <u>http://www.pbs.org</u>), but watch for advocacy and special interest group sites because they may be presenting a specific slant on a topic to further their organization's goals.
- *Look for a document's author.* Never accept or quote from a document that is anonymous. We believe that anyone

---

NOTE THE FACTS

What domain names do the authors trust? Why?

_____

_____

_____

_____

MAKE A NOTE

_____

_____

_____

---

words for everyday use

scru • ti • nized (skrü′ tən īzd) *part.*, closely examined. *The convenience store's videotape was <u>scrutinized</u> in an effort to identify the robber.*

ca • ve • at (ka′ vē ät) *n.*, warning or caution. *The laundromat's <u>caveat</u> was to start your last load of laundry by 9:30 P.M. unless you didn't mind picking it up the next morning.*

er • ro • ne • ous (i rō′ nē əs) *adj.*, containing or characterized by error. *Ron's <u>erroneous</u> assumptions about the weather in England in January led him to pack all the wrong clothes for his trip.*

rep • u • ta • ble (re′ pyə tə bəl) *adj.*, held in esteem. *Because she had a <u>reputable</u> lawyer, Mrs. White Eagle thought she would get a fair settlement.*

cred • i • ble (kre′ də bəl) *adj.*, believable. *Because his student's story sounded <u>credible</u>, Mr. Connell let him hand in his assignment late.*

bi • as (bī′ əs) *n.*, an attitude that favors one position. *My grandfather has a <u>bias</u> against foreign-made cars.*

---

who publishes a document on the Internet would sign it
if they think it's worthwhile. Once you identify the
author, try to find out about his or her background.
This may be as simple as clicking on a link on the document to the author's home page, or as bothersome as
searching for an author's name with a Web index to see
what you can unearth.

- *Try to determine a document's context if you have doubts
  about it.* There may be a good reason why a document
  appears anonymous. For instance, it may be a subdocu-
  ment of a large publication at a website. Therefore, see
  if you can find the document's context. Often you need
  only look higher up the directory in the site's URL.[1]
  For example, if you find a document with the URL
  http://www.anyu.edu/faculty/research/report2.html
  remove report2.html from the URL and enter it into
  your browser. At that point you may see a menu, with
  links to documents, that describes what the document is
  about and who wrote it. Failing that, there may be
  other clues or links that will help you identify it.

- *Find corroborating documents.* Always look for other documents or sites about the same topic that provide supporting evidence to the point of view or facts presented
  in a document you want to use for your research. News
  reporters routinely look for corroborating evidence
  before running an investigative story. Even though
  there's no guarantee that if several people say the same
  thing, it's true, there's a better chance that it is. The
  search engines that have the option "find more documents like this one" will help you find corroborating
  information.

If you still have doubts about a document's validity, don't
hesitate to show it to your teacher or professor. If she
welcomes email from students, you may want to use the
"mail document" function of your Web browser to send it
directly to her.

---

1. **URL.** Uniform Resource Locator, or Internet address

---

words for everyday use

cor • rob • o • rat • ing (kə rä′ bə rāt iŋ) *adj.,* supporting with evidence; confirm-
ing. *Because of the* corroborating *witness, the lawyer won the case with the evidence
she presented.*

NOTE THE FACTS

According to lines
208–211, what can a
person do to evaluate
what he or she reads on
the Internet?

_____

_____

Read aloud the highlighted text on this page. What are the rules about electronic media in regard to plagiarism?

_____

_____

_____

230

Finally, make sure to cite the source of material from the Internet that you use in a project or research paper. Your school's or university's policies about academic honesty apply to electronic material as well as printed material. Unless you are told otherwise, use the same reference format you would use for print publications, and add the document's URL and the date you viewed it in parentheses at the end of the reference. ■

Reflect ON YOUR READING

EVALUATE THE TEXT'S ORGANIZATION

After you finish reading, review your outline and evaluate the selection with your reading partner. Did the authors omit any important information? Did they place any information out of order? Was the text organization effective? Was any of the information wrong or outdated? Would you recommend this text to someone just learning to use the Internet? Include answers to these questions in a written evaluation. Use your own paper as needed.

_____

_____

_____

Reading Skills and Test Practice

IDENTIFY SEQUENCE OF EVENTS
Discuss with your partner how best to answer the following questions about sequence.

1. Which of the following is the first step in finding facts?
   a. Search newsgroups or post messages.
   b. Try a different web search index.
   c. Refine and enter your key nouns into a search index.
   d. Revise your keywords and retry the searches.

What is the correct answer to the question above? How were you able to eliminate the other answers? How did your use of the reading strategy help you answer the question?

_____

_____

2. Which of the following is the last step in finding websites?
   a. Enter a keyword into a search engine, such as Yahoo!
   b. Search AltaVista or another web index.
   c. Use another directory, such as Magellan.
   d. Follow the path in Yahoo! to a subcategory that takes you closest to your topic.

What is the correct answer to the question above? How were you able to eliminate the other answers? How did your use of the reading strategy help you answer the question?

_____

_____

THINK-ALOUD NOTES

_____

_____

_____

_____

_____

_____

_____

_____

_____

_____

_____

_____

Investigate, Inquire, and Imagine

RECALL: GATHER FACTS
1a. What is the authors' opinion about anonymous documents on the Internet?

→ INTERPRET: FIND MEANING
1b. Why do the authors say "Reader Beware!" when locating information on the Internet?

ANALYZE: TAKE THINGS APART
2a. Identify the three research strategies described in the selection.

→ SYNTHESIZE: BRING THINGS TOGETHER
2b. Why do the steps for these three research strategies differ?

EVALUATE: MAKE JUDGMENTS
3a. Evaluate which Internet site would probably provide more reliable information on Edgar Allan Poe.
http://www.poedecoder.com/
    PreciselyPoe
http://raven.ubalt.edu/features/poe

→ EXTEND: CONNECT IDEAS
3b. Write five questions, ranging in difficulty from factual to interpretive, about Edgar Allan Poe for which you would like to know the answer. Then, after each question, write down which research strategy you should follow: 1) finding facts; 2) finding websites; or 3) finding reading material.

Literary Tools

EXPOSITION. **Exposition** is a type of writing that presents facts or opinions in an organized manner. Among the most common ways to organize exposition are the following: *chronological, spatial, order of importance, comparison-and-contrast, cause-and-effect,* and *classification*. Review the methods of text organization in Unit 2, pages 22–23. Complete the graphic organizer below to show what the majority of the exposition in this article is about.

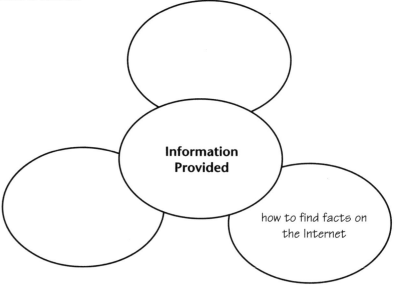

Information Provided

how to find facts on the Internet

Which method of organization do the authors use? _____

WordWorkshop

Jargon and Acronyms. Jargon is the specialized vocabulary that members of a profession or group use. The list that follows contains computer jargon. Sometimes jargon may be in the form of an **acronym**, or group of letters formed from the beginning letters of a compound expression; for example, *URL* comes from *Uniform Resource Locator*. Match each example of jargon on the left with its definition on the right. Then write an original sentence using each word that clearly shows you understand the word's meaning.

_____1. search engine

_____2. newsgroup

_____3. domain

_____4. URL

_____5. search word

a. a word keyed in that allows a search engine to find documents on a specified topic

b. computer software used to search data for specified information

c. the address of a document on the Internet

d. a group of computers administered as a unit and defined by their IP address

e. an electronic bulletin board on the Internet devoted to a particular topic

6. _____

7. _____

8. _____

9. _____

10. _____

Read-Write Connection

In what ways can you use the Internet to help you to become a better student? Use your own paper as needed.

_____

_____

Beyond the Reading

Documenting Internet Sites. Internet surveillance is a controversial topic. For example, some people think the government should wiretap all Internet traffic in order to find criminal activity. Others feel that wiretapping invades their privacy. Internet surveillance at the workplace is yet another issue. Locate five reliable Internet sites about Internet surveillance and write bibliography entries for them, following the model below.

Bromford, James. The Society for Civil Liberties. 15 Sept. 2003, updated 28 Feb. 2004. <http://www.scl.org/cybersnooping/ >

Go Online. Visit the EMC Internet Resource Center at **emcp.com** to find links and additional activities for this selection.

Reader's resource

In "**Where Stars Are Born**," *Sports Illustrated* writer Michael Farber reveals baseball's links with San Pedro de Macorís in the Dominican Republic, the hometown of Sammy Sosa. He also points out Sammy Sosa's achievements during the "Summer of 62," when he competed with Mark McGwire to see who could hit the most home runs during the 1998 season. The story of Sammy Sosa and others like him makes baseball the great equalizer, bringing fame and fortune to talented Dominican nationals.

Word watch

PREVIEW VOCABULARY

binge
crossover
flamboyant
outstrip
per capita
redoubt

Reader's journal

Do you have a particular sports star that you admire? If so, what do you admire about him or her?

_____

_____

_____

"Where Stars Are Born"

from *Sports Illustrated*

by Michael Farber

Active READING STRATEGY

CONNECT TO PRIOR KNOWLEDGE

Before Reading ➤ **ACTIVATE PRIOR KNOWLEDGE**

❑ Read the Reader's Resource.
❑ Discuss with your class what you know about baseball, its players, and the Dominican Republic.
❑ On your own paper make a Connections Chart like the one below, and fill in the before-reading section.

Graphic Organizer

Before Reading
Read the selection title. Then skim the selection and answer the following questions.
1. What kind of selection is this (poem, play, short story, essay, speech, etc.)?
2. What do you think this selection will be about?
3. List three facts that you know, or experiences that you have had, that relate to the subject of this selection.

After Reading
Complete this section after reading the selection.
1. Did you guess correctly what the selection was about? Explain.
2. What did you learn from this selection that you did not know before reading it?

WHERE Stars ARE BORN

Michael Farber

Sosa's season affirmed for all that the Dominican Republic is the real cradle of the game.

In this summer of statistics, when a nation counted down with more urgency than Casey Kasem,[1] you are asked once again to do the math. From Sammy Sosa's hometown of San Pedro de Macorís (pop. 125,000), there are currently 13 major league baseball players. If, say, New York City produced as many big leaguers per capita, the 30 dugouts would be crammed with 763 men with George Costanza[2] accents. If they played in Peoria[3] the way they do in San Pedro de Macorís, there would be 12 focus-group Americans in the bigs.[4]

In the greatest baseball city on earth they play in the alleys, in the streets, in the sprawling sugarcane fields that

10

---

1. **Casey Kasem.** Radio deejay who hosts countdowns of popular music hits
2. **George Costanza.** Television sitcom character from New York City
3. **Peoria.** One of the largest cities in Illinois; 1996 population 112,306
4. **bigs.** Baseball's big leagues

words for everyday use

per • cap • i • ta (pər ka' p´ tə) *adv. or adj.,* by or for each person. *The per capita income in Rhode Island was high, with each person earning an average of $75,000 a year.*

During Reading

CONNECT TO PRIOR KNOWLEDGE

❑ Look at the photo on this page. What information does it reveal?

❑ Follow along in the text as your teacher reads the first two paragraphs of the article aloud. Discuss with your classmates how this new information connects with your prior knowledge about baseball.

❑ Read the remainder of the article on your own, stopping periodically to reflect on any connections you can make to the content of the selection.

NOTE THE FACTS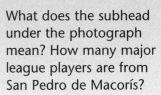

What does the subhead under the photograph mean? How many major league players are from San Pedro de Macorís?

_____

_____

_____

Literary TOOLS

ARTICLE. An **article** is a brief work of nonfiction on a specific topic. As you read, try to identify the main ideas and supporting details of the article.

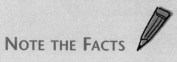

NOTE THE FACTS

According to lines 18–22, what gives the shortstops of San Pedro de Macorís such quick reflexes?

_____

_____

Use **THE STRATEGY**

CONNECT TO PRIOR KNOWLEDGE.
Think about the way children in the U.S. play baseball. Reflect on the similarities and differences with how it is played in the Dominican Republic.

FIX-UP IDEA

Read Aloud/Think Aloud
If you have trouble, read the selection aloud, stopping after each paragraph to think aloud about what you learn from each paragraph. Is any of this information surprising? How does it compare to other information you know? Take turns reading and thinking aloud with your partner.

line the city's outskirts—with bats made of branches from guava trees, crude gloves crafted from milk cartons, and stuffed socks that stand in for real balls. The fields are often rocky, which has tested not only the occasional protective cup but also the reflexes of the glovemen[5] who have forged San Pedro de Macorís's reputation as a <u>redoubt</u> of short-
20 stops. In the 1980s the city delivered, among others, Tony Fernandez, Julio Franco, Mariano Duncan and Rafael Ramirez to the majors. Frequently overlooked, however, are the boppers, men like Rico Carty, George Bell and Pedro Guerrero, all of them Macorisanos. Whereas Sosa spent the summer rewriting the record books, some of us are going to have to spend the winter rewriting the game's mythology.

This was Sosa's glorious role in the home run race: He changed everything. It was supposed to be the summer Ken
30 Griffey Jr. played long-ball cat and mouse with Mark McGwire. Instead, Sosa went on his 20-homer <u>binge</u> in June and established himself as Big Mac's most formidable challenger. He was the perfect mystery guest, whose humility and joyful, carefree approach to the game leavened[6] the most self-conscious record chase in history. Content to joyride in McGwire's wake, Sosa squeezed every last drop of pleasure from the race and even helped McGwire realize that Chasing Roger should be a kick, not a solemn duty. It was all great fun.
40 The Summer of 62 will ultimately be recalled as a time when baseball regained its health. Fans should also remember it as the year of the Dominican Republic, the nation where baseball never took ill. If not for Roger Clemens's remarkable late-season run, Boston Red Sox pitcher Pedro Martinez, of Santo Domingo, would most likely have become the first player to win consecutive Cy Young awards in different leagues. Moises Alou, who also grew up

---

5. **glovemen.** Slang term for fielders in baseball
6. **leavened.** Made lighter by mingling or mixing with some lightening agent

words for everyday use	**re • doubt** (ri daut´) *n.,* secure retreat or stronghold. *The animal shelter was a <u>redoubt</u> for lost animals.*
	binge (binj) *n.,* unrestrained and sometimes excessive indulgence. *Hal and I went on a fast-food <u>binge</u>, eating five hamburgers and milkshakes that day.*

in Santo Domingo, went from Florida to Houston, where
he led the Astros to the National League Central title and
emerged, along with Sosa, as a leading MVP candidate.
And 22-year-old Montreal Expos outfielder Vladimir
Guerrero, from Nizao Bani, quietly morphed into[7] Griffey
Jr., putting up numbers that might have challenged for a
Triple Crown in another year. Not one of these men, inci-
dentally, is a shortstop.

But it was Sosa who finally made the game a block party
that everyone could enjoy. Although baseball has been
international for decades and roughly one fifth of today's
major leaguers are from Latin America, the Cubs outfielder
is the sport's first true <u>crossover</u> Latin hero, <u>outstripping</u>
even his own idol, Roberto Clemente. When Sosa leaped
out of the batter's box, skipping two strides as he watched
his swats soar toward the bleachers, we skipped along with
him. If he didn't shatter any windows along Chicago's
Waveland Avenue, he did open plenty of others across the
country, letting in some much-needed fresh air. He challenged the assumption that North Americans could never
truly embrace Latin players, that they were too "<u>flamboyant</u>"
or, in the case of Clemente, too "moody" for gringo tastes.
McGwire might have been the first to get to 62, but Sosa's
home run quest was richer. It flattered America's vision of
itself as a land of acceptance, as a meritocracy[8] in which
color and language and origins don't matter.

In the Summer of 62, National League fences were not
the only things Sosa broke down. ■

---

7. **morphed into**. Became, turned into
8. **meritocracy**. System in which the talented are chosen and moved ahead
on the basis of their achievement

50

60

70

THINK AND REFLECT

According to lines 58–59,
what did Sammy Sosa do
for baseball? How might
the attitudes he brought
to the game reflect the
feelings about baseball in
his hometown?
(Synthesize)

_____

_____

_____

_____

READ ALOUD

Read aloud the
highlighted text on this
page. What did Sammy
Sosa's home run quest do
for America?

_____

_____

_____

**words
for
everyday
use**

cross • o • ver (krôs′ ō vər) *adj.,* breaking into another category. *After Jackson left
his heavy metal band, he decided he wanted to be a <u>crossover</u> rock/rap artist.*

out • strip (aut strip′) *vt.,* go faster or farther than; get ahead of, leave behind.
Star Wars <u>outstrips</u> any other science fiction movie in terms of its immense popularity.

flam • boy • ant (flam boi′ ənt) *adj.,* marked by or given to a strikingly elaborate
or colorful display or behavior. *Many running backs and wide receivers have a
<u>flamboyant</u> dance that they break into whenever they score a touchdown.*

Reflect ON YOUR READING

After you finish reading, complete the after-reading section of the graphic organizer. Then discuss with a few of your classmates the connections you made to the selection. For example, maybe you have seen one or more of the players mentioned in the article play, or you might compare your ideas about baseball with the author's. Then, on your own paper, write a paragraph expanding on one of the connections you made.

Reading Skills and Test Practice

IDENTIFY MAIN IDEAS

Discuss with your partner how best to answer the following questions about main ideas.

1. What is the main idea of paragraph 1?

   a. There are currently thirteen major league baseball players from San Pedro de Macorís.
   b. The number of major league baseball players from the Dominican Republic is astounding.
   c. It is important to consider the contributions of baseball players from the Dominican Republic.
   d. This was an interesting baseball season.

What is the correct answer to the question above? How were you able to eliminate the other answers? How did your use of the reading strategy help you answer the question?

_____

_____

2. What is the main idea of paragraph 4?
   a. Baseball regained its health in the summer of 1998.
   b. Sosa is the best player from the Dominican Republic.
   c. If it weren't for some bad luck, some of the players of the Dominican Republic would have received more recognition.
   d. Players from the Dominican Republic helped revive baseball in the "Summer of 62."

What is the correct answer to the question above? How were you able to eliminate the other answers? How did your use of the reading strategy help you answer the question?

_____

_____

Investigate, Inquire, and Imagine

RECALL: GATHER FACTS
1a. What are the playing conditions and equipment like for many baseball players in San Pedro de Macorís?

INTERPRET: FIND MEANING
1b. Why do you think the author chose to include this information?

ANALYZE: TAKE THINGS APART
2a. Compare and contrast the conditions in which the people of San Pedro de Macorís play baseball with those enjoyed by professional American players. Why do you think Macorisanos continue to play even in such poor conditions? How is their motivation different from the motivation of pros?

SYNTHESIZE: BRING THINGS TOGETHER
2b. Predict what would happen if all American players were asked to give up their salaries and expensive playing fields and play in conditions like the Macorisanos do.

EVALUATE: MAKE JUDGMENTS
3a. Evaluate who is the better baseball player, Mark McGwire or Sammy Sosa.

EXTEND: CONNECT IDEAS
3b. In 1947, Jackie Robinson became the first black baseball player in the major leagues. How is Sammy Sosa's experience like

Literary Tools

ARTICLE. An **article** is a brief work of nonfiction on a specific topic. List the two main topics of this article

_____

_____

How are the two main topics that the author discusses related?

_____

_____

In the article, what does the author do besides discuss these two topics?

_____

_____

WordWorkshop

USING CONTEXT CLUES IN YOUR WRITING. Use each of the new vocabulary words in an original sentence. Make sure to convey the meaning of each word by providing context clues in your sentences. Use *restatement, cause-and-effect, comparison,* and *contrast.* To learn about these types of clues, review Unit 1, pages 20–21.

1. binge

_____

2. crossover

_____

3. flamboyant

_____

4. outstrip

_____

5. per capita

_____

Read-Write Connection

What makes Sammy Sosa a good role model for young people?

_____

_____

_____

_____

_____

_____

Beyond the Reading

HALL OF FAME. Read an article or book about your favorite athlete. Write a letter of nomination for your favorite athlete to enter a Hall of Fame for his or her sport. Discuss the athlete's professional accomplishments and character traits that make him or her a good candidate.

GO ONLINE. Visit the EMC Internet Resource Center at **emcp.com** to find links and additional activities for this selection.

Unit 8 READING Review

Choose and Use Reading Strategies

Before reading the excerpt that follows, review with a partner how to use each reading strategy below.

1. Read with a Purpose
2. Connect to Prior Knowledge
3. Write Things Down
4. Make Predictions
5. Visualize
6. Use Text Organization
7. Tackle Difficult Vocabulary
8. Monitor Your Reading Progress

Next, apply at least two of these reading strategies as you read the following excerpt. You may want to use the margins in order to write down how you are incorporating the reading strategies. Feel free to mark up the text in any way that helps you read more effectively.

> When researching an author, keep in mind that it takes time to find a quality, informative site among the clutter and gigantic mass of the Internet. Web browsers are a great place to start; most of the sites you will find there will be well organized and in-depth. The best sites are often those that the authors put together themselves. When a writer creates a home page, you can often find personal messages and anecdotes that allow you to get a real sense of who he or she is. Good secondary sites include those authorized by the author or his or her agent, literary societies, publishers, and fans of the author. Literary societies and publishers often have author websites that are easy to use and fun to view. However, you may find that publisher sites often provide only a short author biography and a list of the author's published works. Fan sites, while of greatly varying quality and depth, can be rich sources of offbeat information and quirky stories. The main drawback to using a fan sponsored site as a resource is that the accuracy of the information may be unreliable.

Two sites, one fan-created and one maintained by the literary society of the University of California, Berkeley, serve as excellent examples of quality author websites. They both feature writer Jack London, best known for his novels The Call of the Wild, White Fang, and The Sea Wolf. The Berkeley Digital Library SunSITE "The Jack London Collection" is more scholarly, meant for use as a study tool. The fan site, "Jack London's Ranch Album," is a "get-to-know" site, with many interesting anecdotes about London's life but with fewer specific details and research aids.

Literary Tools

Select the best literary element on the right to complete each sentence on the left. Write the correct letter in the blank.

_____ 1. In "Where Stars Are Born," the author uses ___ when giving facts and his opinions about the contributions of Dominican baseball players.

_____ 2. Writing about Marjory Stoneman Douglas's book about the Everglades provides the reader of "For the Future of Florida: Repair the Everglades!" with ___ about how long the Everglades has been in trouble.

_____ 3. If you say you ate a "mediocre meatloaf" for dinner, you are using ___.

_____ 4. Jack read a(n) ___ about the World Series in *Sports Illustrated*.

a. background information, 446

b. article, 473

c. exposition, 437

d. alliteration, 454

WordWorkshop

Unit 8 Words for Everyday Use

accrued, 432
admonition, 434
akin, 441
array, 432
ascent, 441
bias, 462
binge, 469
caveat, 462
celestial, 451
charismatic, 441
coalition. 434
competent, 441
comprehensive, 434
conservationist, 432
conversely, 459
corroborating, 463
credible, 462
crossover, 471

degraded, 432
dispatch, 442
ecosystem, 432
enhancement, 434
erroneous, 462
exasperation, 442
expedition, 442
feasibility, 433
flamboyant, 471
flayed, 440
formidable, 442
geyser, 449
ineffable, 449
integrity, 433
levee, 432
lure, 442
meandering, 433
novice, 442

orbit, 450
outstrip, 471
per capita, 469
practical, 444
predict, 451
prominence, 449
redoubt, 469
relevant, 461
reputable, 462
scrutinized, 462
sentiment, 434
spectacle, 450
sponsor, 443
summit, 440
sustainable, 434
unnervingly, 440
wetland, 432

Synonyms. Use the synonyms below to identify nine vocabulary words from this unit. Fill in the blanks with the letters of the word that is being suggested. When you are done, you should be able to identify another vocabulary word vertically.

1. the state of being unexcitable _ _ _ _ | _ | _ _ _ _ _ _ _

2. correct, without fault _ _ _ _ _ | _ | _ _ _

3. not held in esteem | _ | _ _ _ _ _ _ _

4. unbelievable | _ | _ _ _ _ _ _

5. not wandering aimlessly _ _ | _ | _ _ _ _ _ _

6. incapable _ _ _ | _ | _ _ _ _

7. not showing the same nature _ _ _ _ | _ | _

8. irrelevant _ _ _ _ _ _ | _ |

9. heavenly _ _ _ _ _ _ _ | _ | _

On Your Own

FLUENTLY SPEAKING. Select a paragraph that interests you from one of the selections in this unit. Then read it to a classmate using the speed and volume that makes the most sense. Ask your partner for feedback. He or she should be able to tell you how clear and understandable your reading was, and whether or not your choices of speed and volume were appropriate.

PICTURE THIS. Choose one of the selections in this unit and draw a visual aid to help illustrate an idea in the text. You might decide to create a diagram, chart, graph, or map to convey information, or you might draw a picture visualizing what the author is writing about.

PUT IT IN WRITING. In a sense, each selection in this unit is about exploration. For example, "Research Strategies for the Learning Highway" explores new computer technology and "Best Sky Sights of the Next Century" explores the sky. What was your favorite domain to explore in this unit? What prior knowledge did you bring to your exploration? What did you learn in your exploration? What further exploration would you like to make about this topic? Include answers to these questions in a short essay.

Unit NINE

Developing VOCABULARY Skills

TACKLING DIFFICULT VOCABULARY AS YOU READ

To understand what you read, you need a set of tools for dealing with words you don't know. Glossaries and footnotes, context clues, prior knowledge of word parts and word families, and dictionaries are tools that can help you unlock the meaning of unfamiliar words.

Using Definitions, Footnotes, Endnotes, and Glossaries

Some textbooks, like this one, provide **definitions** of selected words on the page on which the word is used. **Footnotes**, like definitions, also appear on the same page as the words to which they refer. Specifically, footnotes appear at the foot, or bottom, of a page and are numbered to correspond to the words or phrases they explain. Sometimes footnotes cite a source of information. Other times they define uncommon words and phrases. If you see a superscripted number next to a word in the text you are reading (pertinacity[12]), but can't find the footnote at the foot of the page, check the end of the article, chapter, or book. A footnote that comes at the end of a document is called an **endnote**. A **glossary** is an alphabetized list of important words and their definitions. Glossaries usually appear at the end of an article, a chapter, or a book.

To use definitions, footnotes, endnotes, and glossaries, follow these steps:

❶ Read the paragraph or short section containing the unfamiliar word to get a sense of the meaning.

❷ Check the definition, footnote, endnote, or glossary entry for the word.

❸ Reread the paragraph or section, this time keeping in mind the definition of the new word.

NOTE THE FACTS

What is the most effective way to use definitions given on the page or in a glossary?

_____

_____

_____

_____

Using Context Clues

You can often figure out the meaning of an unfamiliar word by using context clues. **Context clues**, or hints you gather from the words and sentences around the unfamiliar word, prevent you from having to look up every unknown word in the dictionary. The chart below defines the types of context clues and gives you an example of each. It also lists words that signal each type of clue.

THINK AND REFLECT

If someone says, "The principal's decision is as catastrophic for the marching band as the destruction of the football stadium would be for the football team," what do you think *catastrophic* means? **(Apply)**

_____

_____

_____

Context Clues

comparison clue	shows a comparison, or how the unfamiliar word is like something that might be familiar to you
signal words	*and, like, as, just as, as if, as though*

EXAMPLE

Joan was as nimble as a mountain goat as she hiked along the steep, rocky trail. (A mountain goat is extremely agile and sure on its feet. *Nimble* must mean "agile.")

contrast clue	shows that something contrasts, or differs in meaning, from something else
signal words	*but, nevertheless, on the other hand, however, although, though, in spite of*

EXAMPLE

Hsuan is very reflective, but his friend Ku Min is known for jumping into things without thinking about them. (The word *but* signals a contrast between Hsuan's and Ku Min's ways of doing things. If Ku Min jumps in without thinking, Hsuan must think things through more thoroughly. *Reflective* must mean "thoughtful, meditative.")

restatement clue	uses different words to express the same idea
signal words	*that is, in other words, or*

EXAMPLE

I know Kayesha will prevail in the student council election; I have no doubt that she's going to win! (As the information after the semicolon indicates, *prevail* means "win.")

examples clue	gives examples of other items to illustrate the meaning of something
signal words	*including, such as, for example, for instance, especially, particularly*

EXAMPLE

Trevor has always been interested in celestial bodies such as planets, stars, and moons. (If you know enough about the examples listed, you can tell that celestial bodies are visible bodies in the sky.)

cause-and-effect clue	tells you that something happened as a result of something else
signal words	*if/then, when/then, thus, therefore, because, so, as a result of, consequently*

EXAMPLE

I hadn't planned on going to the party, but the host invited me in such a cordial way that I felt welcome. (If the host's cordial invitation helped the speaker feel welcome, you can guess that *cordial* means "friendly.")

Using Your Prior Knowledge

You can often use your knowledge of word parts and other words to help you figure out the meaning of a new word.

BREAKING WORDS INTO BASE WORDS, WORD ROOTS, PREFIXES, AND SUFFIXES

Many words are formed by adding prefixes and suffixes to main word parts called **base words** (if they can stand alone) or **word roots** (if they can't). A **prefix** is a letter or group of letters added to the beginning of a word to change its meaning. A **suffix** is a letter or group of letters added to the end of a word to change its meaning.

Word Part	Definition	Example
base word	main word part that can stand alone	form
word root	main word part that can't stand alone	struc
prefix	letter or group of letters added to the beginning of the word	pre–
suffix	letter or group of letters added to the end of the word	–tion

When you encounter an unfamiliar word, check to see if you recognize the meaning of the prefix, suffix, base word, or word root. In combination with context clues, these meanings can help you unlock the meaning of the entire word. On the following pages are charts listing the meanings of the most common prefixes, suffixes, and word roots.

Reading STRATEGY
REVIEW

READ WITH A PURPOSE. Rather than read the charts on the following pages all the way through from beginning to end, set a purpose for reading, and then let that purpose guide how you read the charts. For example, if you just want to become familiar with what prefixes, suffixes, and word roots are, read only a few lines from each chart, but read them carefully, studying how each word part contributes to the meaning of the words in the "Examples" column. Your teacher might set a purpose for you, too. If so, approach the charts as your teacher directs.

Common Prefixes

Prefix	Meaning	Examples
ambi–/amphi–	both	ambidextrous, amphibian
anti–/ant–	against; opposite	antibody, antacid
bi–	two	bicycle, biped
circum–	around; about	circumnavigate, circumstance
co–/col–/com–/con–/cor–	together	cooperate, collaborate, commingle, concentrate, correlate
counter–	contrary; complementary	counteract, counterpart
de–	opposite; remove; reduce	decipher, defrost, devalue
dia–	through; apart	dialogue, diaphanous
dis–	not; opposite of	dislike, disguise
dys–	abnormal; difficult; bad	dysfunctional, dystopia
em–/en–	into or onto; cover with; cause to be; provide with	embark, empower, enslave, enfeeble
ex–	out of; from	explode, export, extend
extra–/extro–	outward; outside; beyond	extraordinary, extrovert
hyper–	too much, too many, or extreme	hyperbole, hyperactive
hypo–	under	hypodermic
il–, im–, in–, ir–	not	illogical, impossible, inoperable, irrational
	in; within; toward; on	illuminate, imperil, infiltrate, irrigate
inter–	among or between	international, intersect
intra–/intro–	into; within; inward	introvert, intramural
meta–	after; changed	metamorphosis, metaphor
mis–	wrongly	mistake, misfire
non–	not	nonsense, nonsmoker
out–	in a manner that goes beyond	outrun, outmuscle
over–	excessive	overdone, overkill
per–	through, throughout	permeate, permanent
peri–	all around	perimeter, periscope
post–	after; later	postgame, postpone
pre–	before	prefix, premature *CONTINUED*

Common Prefixes (continued)

Prefix	Meaning	Examples
pro–	before; forward	proceed, prologue
re–	again; back	redo, recall
retro–	back	retrospect, retroactive
semi–	half; partly	semicircle, semidry
sub–/sup–	under	substandard, subfloor, support
super–	above; over; exceeding	superstar, superfluous
sym–/syn–	with; together	sympathy, synonym, synergy
trans–	across; beyond	transatlantic, transfer, transcend
ultra–	too much, too many, extreme	ultraviolet, ultrasound
un–	not	unethical, unhappy
under–	below or short of a quantity or limit	underestimate, understaffed
uni–	one	unicorn, universe

Common Suffixes

Noun Suffixes	Meaning	Examples
–ance/–ancy/–ence/–ency	quality or state	defiance, independence, emergency
–age	action or process	marriage, voyage
–ant/–ent	one who	defendant, assistant, resident
–ar/–er/–or	one who	lawyer, survivor, liar
–dom	state or quality of	freedom, boredom
–es/–s	plural form of noun	siblings, trees
–ion/–tion	action or process	revolution, occasion
–ism	act; state; or system of belief	plagiarism, barbarism, Buddhism
–ist	one who does or believes something	ventriloquist, idealist
–itude, –tude	quality of, state of	multitude, magnitude
–ity/–ty	state of	longevity, infinity
–ment	action or process; state or quality; product or thing	development, government, amusement, amazement, ointment, fragment
–ness	state of	kindness, happiness

CONTINUED

Common Suffixes (continued)

Adjective Suffixes	Meaning	Examples
–able/–ible	capable of	attainable, possible
–al	having characteristics of	personal, governmental
–er	more	higher, calmer, shorter
–est	most	lowest, craziest, tallest
–ful	full of	helpful, gleeful, woeful
–ic	having characteristics of	scientific, chronic
–ish	like	childish, reddish
–ive	performs or tends toward	creative, pensive
–less	without	hapless, careless
–ous	possessing the qualities of	generous, joyous
–y	indicates description	happy, dirty, flowery

Adverb Suffixes	Meaning	Examples
–ly	in such a way	quickly, studiously, invisibly
–ward, –ways, –wise	in such a direction	toward, sideways, crosswise

Verb Suffixes	Meaning	Examples
–ate	make or cause to be	fixate, activate
–ed	past tense of verb	walked, acted, fixed
–ify/–fy	make or cause to be	vilify, magnify, glorify
–ing	indicates action in progress (present participle); can also be a noun (gerund)	running, thinking, being
–ize	bring about; cause to be	colonize, legalize

Common Word Roots

Word Root	Meaning	Examples
acr	highest point	acrobat
act	do	actor, reaction
ann/annu/enni	year	annual, bicentennial
aqu	water	aquarium, aquatic
aster, astr	star	asteroid, disastrous
aud	hear	audition, auditorium

CONTINUED

Common Word Roots (continued)

Word Root	Meaning	Examples
bene	good	beneficial, benefactor
bibl, bibli	book	Bible
chron	time	chronic
cosm	universe; order	cosmic, cosmos
cred	believe; trust	credit, credible
cycl	circle	bicycle, cyclone
dem/demo	people	democracy
derm	skin	dermatologist
dic/dict	say	dictate, dictionary
duc/duct	lead; pull	conduct, reproduction
dyn	force, power	dynamic, dynamite
equ/equi/iqui	equal	equidistant, equitable, iniquity
fer	carry	transfer, refer
fin	end	finish, infinite
firm	firm, strong	confirm, reaffirm
flect/flex	bend	deflect, reflex, flexible
fort	strong	fortify, comfort
ge	earth	geode, geography
gress	go	progress, regress
hydr	water	hydrate
ign	fire	ignite, ignition, igneous
ject	throw	projector, eject
judic	judgment	prejudice, judicial
lect/leg	read; choose	lecture, election, collect
liber	free	liberate, liberal
loc	place	location, relocate
locut/loqu	speak	elocution, loquacious, colloquial
log/logue	word, speech, discourse	logic, dialogue
luc/lumin	shine; light	translucent, illuminate
mal	bad	malevolent
man/manu	hand	manufacture, manual

CONTINUED

Word Root	Meaning	Examples
metr	measure	metric
morph	form	morpheme, metamorphosis
mot	move	motor, emotion
mut	change	mutation, transmutable
nov	new	novelty, renovate
onym	name	synonym, antonym
path	feel; suffer; disease	sympathy, pathology
ped	foot, child	pedal, pediatrics
phon/phony	sound; voice; speech	symphony
phot	light	photography
physi	nature	physical, physics
pop	people	popular, populate
port	carry	transport, portable
psych	mind; soul	psychology, psychic
reg	rule	register, regulate
rupt	break	disrupt, interruption, rupture
scrib/script	write	describe, prescription
son	sound	sonic
spec/spect/spic	look	speculate, inspect, despicable
spir	breathe	spirit, inspiration
ter/terr	earth	inter, extraterrestrial, terrain
therm	heat	thermal
top	place	topography, topical
tract	draw; drag	retract, tractor, contract
typ	stamp; model	typical, type
ver	truth	veracity, verifiable
vert	turn	divert, introvert, extrovert
vid/vis	see	video, visual
viv	alive	vivacious, vivid
vol/volv	turn	evolution, revolve

The more meanings of prefixes, suffixes, and word roots you know, the better equipped you are to tackle difficult vocabulary words.

Even if you don't know the meaning of a word part, however, you can often figure out the meaning of a word using word parts. To do this, think of as many familiar words as you can that contain each part of the word.

For example, if you were tackling the word *biped*, you might first think of words beginning with the prefix *bi–*: *bicycle*, *biannual*, and *bisect*. You know that a bicycle is different than a tricycle because it has two wheels rather than three. You're pretty sure that the other two words also have something to do with the number two. (You could check out this hunch by looking in a dictionary.) Then you might think of words that contain *ped*: *pedal*, *pedestrian*, and *pedestal*. A pedal and a pedestal are both things you step on with your foot. A pedestrian is someone who is walking. From this information, you might guess (correctly) that *ped* means foot. A biped is something with two feet!

This process is even easier when you work with a partner. Think aloud with your partner about how to break apart a word. Then discuss the meanings of each part and a possible meaning for the entire word.

RECOGNIZING COMBINING FORMS

Some word roots have become very common in English and are used all the time in combination with each other and with base words to create new scientific, medical, and technical terms. These combining forms can look like prefixes and suffixes, but contain more core meaning. The chart on the next page defines and gives examples of some common combining forms that will help you tackle new words.

NOTE THE FACTS

How can you use word parts to figure out the meaning of a new word?

_____

_____

_____

_____

_____

THINK AND REFLECT

Think aloud about how you would use word parts to figure out the meaning of the word *introspection*. Record notes from your think aloud here. **(Apply)**

_____

_____

_____

_____

_____

Combining Forms

Word Part	Meaning	Examples
acro–	heights	acrophobia
anthropo–	human being	anthropologist
archaeo–/arche–	old	archeology
astr–/astro–	star	astronaut, astrology
audio–	hear	audiovisual
auto–	self	autobiography, automatic
bi–/bio–	life	biography, biosphere
bibli–/biblio–	book	bibliography
–centric	having such a center	egocentric
chron–/chrono–	time	chronology
–cracy	form of government; social or political class	aristocracy, democracy
ethno–	race; people; cultural group	ethnography
ge–/geo–	earth; soil	geography, geology
–graph/–graphy	something written, drawn, or represented by graphics	telegraph, photography
hydr–/hydro–	water	hydroelectric, hydrometer
–logy/–ology	study of	geology, biology
mal–	bad	malfunction, malnutrition
–mania	madness	kleptomania, megalomania
–metry	having to do with measure	geometry, symmetry
micro–	small; minute	microscope, microcosm
omni–	all	omnipresent, omnibus
–onym	name	synonym, antonym
–phile	one who loves	bibliophile
–phobe	one who has an irrational fear	arachnophobe, acrophobe
–phobia	exaggerated fear of	claustrophobia, photophobia
phon–/–phone/phono–	sound; voice; speech	telephone, phonograph
phot–/–photo–	light	photograph, telephoto
physi–/physio–	nature; physical	physiological
pseud–/pseudo–	false	pseudonym, pseudointellectual
psych–/psycho–	mind	psychiatrist, psychology
–scope/–scopy	view	telescope, microscopy
–ster	one who does or is	mobster, spinster
therm–/thermo–	heat	thermometer, thermodynamics
tel–/tele–	distant	telegram, telephone

EXPLORING WORD ORIGINS AND WORD FAMILIES

The English language expands constantly and gathers new words from many different sources. Understanding the source of a word can help you unlock its meaning.

One source of new words is the names of people and places associated with the thing being named. Words named for people and places are called **eponyms**.

> **EXAMPLES**
>
> **hamburger** Originally known as "Hamburg steak," the hamburger takes its name from the German city Hamburg.
>
> **spoonerism** The slip of the tongue whereby the beginning sounds of words are switched is named after the Rev. William A. Spooner, who was known for such slips. For example, after a wedding, he told the groom, "It is kisstomary to cuss the bride."

Another source for new words is **acronyms**. Acronyms are words formed from the first letter or letters of the major parts of terms.

> **EXAMPLES**
>
> **sonar,** from *sound navigation ranging*
>
> **NATO,** from *North American Treaty Organization*

Some words in the English language are borrowed from other languages.

> **EXAMPLES**
>
> **deluxe** (French), **Gesundheit** (German), **kayak** (Eskimo)

Many words are formed by shortening longer words.

> **EXAMPLES**
>
> **ad,** from *advertisement*
>
> **lab,** from *laboratory*
>
> **stereo,** from *stereophonic*

Brand names are often taken into the English language. People begin to use these words as common nouns, even though most of them are still brand names.

> **EXAMPLES**
>
> Scotch tape   Xerox   Rollerblade

THINK AND REFLECT

How might understanding word origins help you unlock word meanings? **(Extend)**

_____

_____

_____

_____

Using a Dictionary

When you can't figure out a word using the strategies already described, or when the word is important to the meaning of the text, and you want to make sure you have it right, use a dictionary.

There are many parts to a dictionary entry. Study the following sample. Then read the explanations of each part of an entry below.

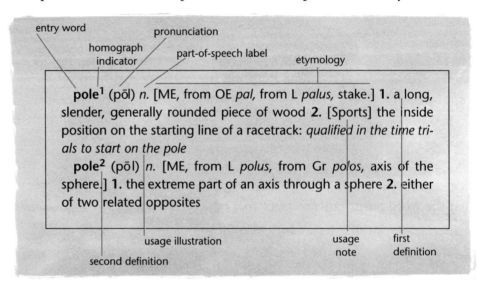

entry word
pronunciation
homograph indicator
part-of-speech label
etymology

pole¹ (pōl) *n.* [ME, from OE *pal,* from L *palus,* stake.] **1.** a long, slender, generally rounded piece of wood **2.** [Sports] the inside position on the starting line of a racetrack: *qualified in the time trials to start on the pole*
   pole² (pōl) *n.* [ME, from L *polus,* from Gr *polos,* axis of the sphere.] **1.** the extreme part of an axis through a sphere **2.** either of two related opposites

usage illustration
usage note
first definition
second definition

The **pronunciation** is given immediately after the entry word. The dictionary's table of contents will tell you where you can find a complete key to pronunciation symbols. In some dictionaries, a simplified pronunciation key is provided at the bottom of each page.

An abbreviation of the **part of speech** usually follows the pronunciation. This label tells how the word can be used. If a word can be used as more than one part of speech, a separate entry is provided for each part of speech.

An **etymology** is the history of the word. In the first entry, the word *pole* can be traced back through Middle English (ME) and Old English (OE) to the Latin (L) word *palus,* which means "stake." In the second entry, the word *pole* can be traced back through Middle English to the Latin word *polus,* which comes from the Greek (Gr) word *polos,* meaning "axis of the sphere."

Sometimes the entry will include a list of **synonyms**, or words that have the same or very similar meanings. The entry may also include an **usage illustration,** which is an example of how the word is used in context.

Understanding Multiple Meanings

Each definition in the entry gives a different meaning of the word. When a word has more than one meaning, the different definitions are numbered. The first definition in an entry is the most common meaning of the word, but you will have to choose the meaning that fits the context in which you have found the word. Try substituting each definition for the word until you find the one that makes the most sense.

If you come across a word that doesn't seem to make sense in context, consider whether that word might have another, lesser known meaning. Can the word be used as more than one part of speech, for example, as either a noun or a verb? Does it have a broader meaning than the one that comes to your mind? For example, a line from the *Odyssey* (Unit 4, page 211) reads "he gave me seven shining talents." The most common meaning of *talent* is "special skill or ability," but that doesn't fit here. Consulting the footnote at the bottom of the page, you would discover that the word *talent* can also refer to a type of old coin.

Keep in mind that some words not only have multiple meanings but also different pronunciations. Words that are spelled the same but are pronounced differently are called **homographs**.

Understanding Denotation and Connotation

The **denotation** of a word is its dictionary definition. Sometimes, in order to understand a passage fully, it is helpful to know the connotations of the words as well. A **connotation** of a word is an association the word has in addition to its literal meaning. For example, the words *cheap* and *thrifty* both denote "tending to spend less money," but *cheap* has a negative connotation similar to "stingy," whereas *thrifty* has a positive connotation involving being responsible with money. The best way to learn the connotation of a word is to pay attention to the context in which the word appears or to ask someone more familiar with the word.

IMPROVING YOUR ACTIVE VOCABULARY

Keeping a Word Study Notebook

Keeping a **word study notebook** is a convenient way to log new words, their meanings, and their spellings, as well as prefixes, suffixes, word roots, and other concepts. In addition, you can use your word study notebook to write down words that you have trouble remembering how to spell. You may even want to set aside a section of your notebook for word play. You can use this area to create jokes, silly rhymes, jingles, skits, acrostics, and games using the words you have logged.

NOTE THE FACTS

What is the difference between a *denotation* and a *connotation*?

_____

_____

THINK AND REFLECT

How would it be different if one character called the other *cheap* rather than *thrifty?* What would that tell you about the relationship between the two characters? **(Apply)**

_____

_____

_____

_____

_____

Reading TIP

In your word study notebook, record for each word:

- definition
- pronunciation
- etymology
- sample sentence or illustration

When you record a new word in your notebook, include its definition, pronunciation, and origins, along with an example sentence or drawing to help you remember it.

Here is a sample page from a word study notebook.

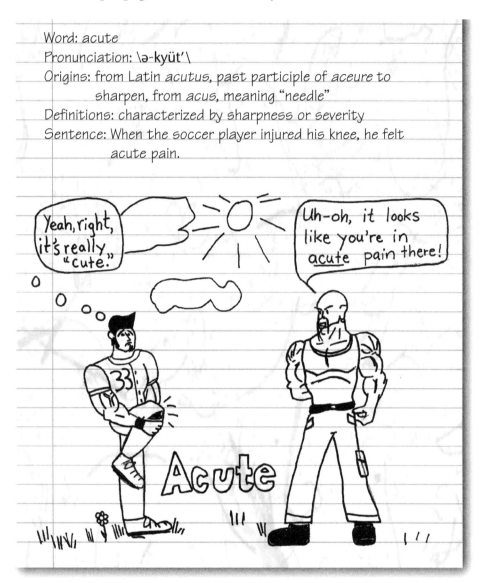

Review the words in your word study notebook and practice using the words in your speech and writing. Also, look for the words from your notebook as you read and listen. The more associations you develop and the more encounters you have with a word, the more likely you are to remember it.

Using Mnemonic Devices

A **mnemonic** (ni mä′ nik) **device** is a catchy phrase or striking image that helps you remember information. For example, you might have heard the phrase "the princiPAL is your PAL" as a trick for remembering the difference between *principal*, the person, and *principle*, the idea. The rhyme "*I* before *E* except after *C*" is a mnemonic for a spelling pattern.

Mnemonic devices are effective in learning new vocabulary words because you learn new information by linking it to words, images, and concepts that are already familiar to you. Vocabulary mnemonics can be sayings, drawings, jingles, or whatever works for you. To remember the definition of *neophyte*, you could say, "A neophyte fighter is new to fighting." To remember how to spell *museum*, you could associate the word with others like it; we are a<u>mused</u> at the <u>museum</u>. A mental picture can also help you remember meaning and spelling.

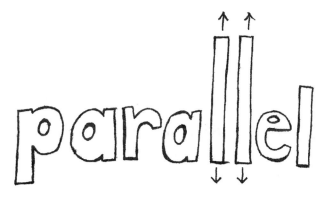

Categorizing and Classifying Words

Another technique for learning vocabulary words is categorizing and classifying the words. To categorize or classify a list of vocabulary words, sort them into groups that share a theme, topic, or characteristic. Then label each group. Like mnemonic devices, this technique works because it helps you create associations with and among new words.

For example, imagine that you need to learn the meanings of the following vocabulary words from the story "The Monkey's Paw," Unit 3, page 42.

amiably	frivolous	presumptuous
apathy	furtively	proffer
attribute	inaudible	prosaic
avaricious	intercept	provoke
burly	keenly	reverberate
compensation	liability	simian
condole	maligned	subdue
credulity	oppressive	torrent
dubiously	persist	
enthralled	poise	

Here is how one student classified these words.

"Monkey's Paw" Vocabulary	
words about belief	attribute, credulity, dubiously, enthralled, furtively
insult words	avaricious, frivolous, maligned, oppressive, presumptuous, prosaic, provoke, simian
words about movement	intercept, persist, poise, proffer, reverberate, subdue, torrent
money words	compensation, liability
words about caring or not	apathy, condole, keenly, enthralled, subdue

THINK AND REFLECT

In what other ways can these words be classified? (Apply)

_____

_____

_____

Learning Synonyms, Antonyms, and Homonyms

A good way to expand your vocabulary is to learn synonyms, antonyms, and homonyms. As with using mnemonic devices and classifying or categorizing words, working with synonyms, antonyms, and homonyms will help you build associations for new words.

synonym	same (or nearly the same) meaning	discover, find
antonym	opposite meaning	discover, conceal
homonym	same pronunciation but different meaning	bite, byte, bight

One way of using synonyms and antonyms to make many connections to a new word is to create a **concept map**. In a concept map, you list synonyms, antonyms, examples, nonexamples, and a contextual sentence for the word you are studying. The best way to use a concept map is to fill it out with a small group or as a whole class. That way, you get to hear everyone else's associations with the word, too. Look at the concept map for *caustic* on the next page.

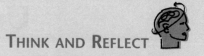
Add one more synonym, antonym, example, and nonexample to the boxes in the chart (**Apply**)

_____

_____

_____

_____

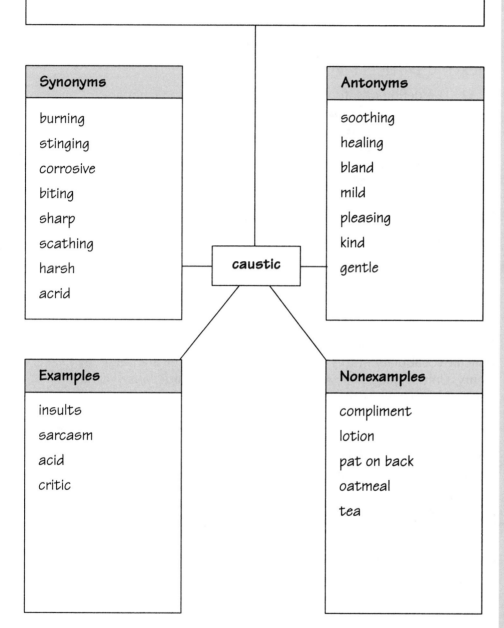

Real-Life Contexts

Danger! <u>Caustic</u> chemicals may burn skin.

Mark Twain had a <u>caustic</u> wit.

Synonyms

burning
stinging
corrosive
biting
sharp
scathing
harsh
acrid

Antonyms

soothing
healing
bland
mild
pleasing
kind
gentle

caustic

Examples

insults
sarcasm
acid
critic

Nonexamples

compliment
lotion
pat on back
oatmeal
tea

Unit 9 VOCABULARY Review

Choose and Use Vocabulary Strategies

Before completing the vocabulary activities below, review with a partner how to use each of these vocabulary strategies.

TACKLING DIFFICULT VOCABULARY

- ❏ Use definitions, footnotes, endnotes, and glossaries
- ❏ Use context clues
- ❏ Use prior knowledge of word parts, word origins, and word families
- ❏ Use a dictionary
- ❏ Understand multiple meanings
- ❏ Understand connotation and denotation

IMPROVING YOUR ACTIVE VOCABULARY

- ❏ Keep a word study notebook
- ❏ Use mnemonic devices
- ❏ Categorize and classify words
- ❏ Learn synonyms, antonyms, and homonyms
- ❏ Avoid clichés and euphemisms

Now read the passage below using the strategies from this unit to tackle difficult vocabulary in this excerpt from "The Gift of the Magi" by O. Henry, Unit 3, page 109. After you finish the passage, answer the vocabulary questions that follow.

One dollar and eighty-seven cents. That was all. And sixty cents of it was in pennies. Pennies saved one and two at a time by bulldozing the grocer and the vegetable man and the butcher until one's cheeks burned with the silent imputation[1] of parsimony that such close dealing implied. Three times Della counted it. One dollar and eighty-seven cents. And the next day would be Christmas.

There was clearly nothing to do but flop down on the shabby little couch and howl. So Della did it. Which instigates[2] the moral reflection that life is made up of sobs, sniffles, and smiles, with sniffles predominating.

While the mistress of the home is gradually subsiding from the first stage to the second, take a look at the home. A furnished flat at $8 per week. It did not exactly beggar description, but it certainly had that word on the lookout for the mendicancy[3] squad.

In the vestibule below was a letter box into which no letter would go, and an electric button from which no mortal finger could coax a ring. Also appertaining thereunto was a card bearing the name "Mr. James Dillingham Young."

The "Dillingham" had been flung to the breeze during a former period of prosperity when its possessor was being paid $30 per week. Now, when the income was shrunk to $20, the letters of "Dillingham" looked blurred, as though they were thinking seriously of contracting to a modest and unassuming D. But whenever Mr. James Dillingham Young came home and reached his flat above he was called "Jim" and greatly hugged by Mrs. James Dillingham Young, already introduced to you as Della. Which is all very good.

Della finished her cry and attended to her cheeks with the powder rag. She stood by the window and looked out dully at a gray cat walking a gray fence in a gray backyard. Tomorrow would be Christmas Day, and she had only $1.87 with which to buy Jim a present. She had been saving every penny she could for months, with this result. Twenty dollars a week doesn't go far. Expenses had been greater than she had calculated. They always are. Only $1.87 to buy a present for Jim. Her Jim. Many a happy hour she had spent planning for something nice for him. Something fine and rare and sterling—something just a little bit near to being worthy of the honor of being owned by Jim.

---

1. **imputation.** Charge; accusation
2. **instigates.** Prompts
3. **mendicancy.** Begging

1. In this passage, *parsimony* means _____.
   a. rudeness
   b. stinginess
   c. wastefulness
   d. timidity

2. By saying that sniffles *predominate,* the narrator suggests that _____.
   a. sadness is always followed by happiness
   b. the common cold is on the rise
   c. smiles and sobs are more common than sniffles
   d. sniffles are more common than either smiles or sobs

3. The word *appertaining* most likely means _____.
   a. opening onto
   b. being a part of
   c. recognizing
   d. getting in the way of

4. A *vestibule* is most likely _____.
    a. a room or space
    b. a food or drink
    c. a means of transportation
    d. a kind of person

5. Imagine that your teacher has given you the following list of vocabulary words.

adornment	imputation	parsimony
agile	inconsequential	predominate
appertain	laboriously	prudence
duplication	meretricious	scrutiny
falter	nimble	subside

Use a dictionary and your knowledge of word parts to determine the meaning of each of these words. Then, on your own paper, do the following activities.

    a. Create a word study notebook entry for one of the words.
    b. Create a mnemonic device for one of the words.
    c. Categorize the words.

On Your Own

FLUENTLY SPEAKING. Learn the pronunciations of each of the vocabulary words from the previous activity. Then practice reading the words aloud until you can read the entire list without stumbling. Record your personal best time.

PICTURE THIS. Choose a story, article, or poem that contains at least three words that are new to you. For each word, create a drawing that will help you remember its meaning. Then create a drawing that illustrates some aspect of the story, poem, or article and shows that you understand it.

PUT IT IN WRITING. Find and read a book, story, article, or poem that interests you. Identify a list of vocabulary words from the text you have chosen. If the text doesn't have many difficult words in it, pick easy words and use a thesaurus to learn more difficult synonyms for those words. Then use these words to create a crossword puzzle, an acrostic, or some other word game. Look at the Word Workshop activities in the Unit Reading Reviews in this book for ideas. Write instructions for your puzzle or game. Then have a partner study the list of vocabulary words and complete your activity.

Unit TEN

TEST-TAKING Strategies

Tests are a common part of school life. You take tests in your classes to show what you have learned in each class. In addition, you might have to take one or more standardized tests each year. Standardized tests measure your skills against local, state, or national standards and may determine whether you graduate, what kind of job you can get, or which college you can attend. Learning test-taking strategies will help you succeed on the tests you are required to take.

PREPARING FOR TESTS IN YOUR CLASSES

These guidelines will help you to prepare for and take tests on the material you have covered in class.

Preparing for a Test

❑ **Know exactly what will be on the test**. If you have questions about what will be covered, ask your teacher.

❑ **Make a study plan** to allow yourself time to go over the material. Avoid last-minute cramming.

❑ **Review the subject matter.** Use the graphic organizers and notes you made as you read as well as notes you took in class. Review any study questions given by your teacher.

❑ **Make lists** of important names, dates, definitions, or events. Ask a friend or family member to quiz you on them.

❑ **Try to predict questions** that may be on the test. Make sure you can answer them.

❑ **Get plenty of sleep** the night before the test. Eat a nutritious breakfast on the morning of the test.

Reading STRATEGY REVIEW

CONNECT TO PRIOR KNOWLEDGE. Which of these test strategies do you already use? Which might help you on your next test?

_____

_____

_____

_____

_____

_____

_____

_____

_____

_____

❑ **Survey the test** to see how long it is and what types of questions are included.

❑ **Read all directions and questions carefully.** Make sure you know exactly what to do.

❑ **Plan your time.** Answer easy questions first. Allow extra time for complicated questions. If a question seems too difficult, skip it and go back to it later. Work quickly, but do not rush.

❑ **Save time for review.** Once you have finished, look back over the test. Double-check your answers, but do not change answers too readily. Your first ideas are often correct.

Answering Objective Questions

An **objective question** has a single correct answer. This chart describes the kinds of questions you may see on objective tests. It also gives you strategies for tackling each kind of question.

MARK THE TEXT

Underline or highlight the guidelines in the chart that you want to try next time you take a test.

Questions Found on Objective Tests

Description	Guidelines
True/False. You are given a statement and asked to tell whether the statement is true or false.	■ If any part of a statement is false, then the statement is false. ■ Words like *all, always, never,* and *every* often appear in false statements. ■ Words like *some, usually, often,* and *most* often appear in true statements. ■ If you do not know the answer, guess. You have a 50/50 chance of being right.
Matching. You are asked to match items in one column with items in another column.	■ Check the directions. See if each item is used only once. Also check to see if some are not used at all. ■ Read all items before starting. ■ Match those items you know first. ■ Cross out items as you match them.
Multiple Choice. You are asked to choose the best answer from a group of answers given.	■ Read *all* choices first. ■ Rule out incorrect answers. ■ Choose the answer that is most complete or accurate. ■ Pay particular attention to choices such as *none of the above* or *all of the above.*

Short Answer. You are asked to answer the question with a word, phrase, or sentence.	▪ Read the directions to find out if you are required to answer in complete sentences. ▪ Use correct spelling, grammar, punctuation, and capitalization. ▪ If you cannot think of the answer, move on. Something in another question might remind you of the answer.

Answering Essay Questions

An essay question asks you to write an answer that shows what you know about a particular subject. Read the following essay question on *The Tragedy of Romeo and Juliet*, Unit 6, page 296.

> Compare and contrast the personalities of Romeo and Juliet as they are revealed in the balcony scene.

A simplified writing process will help you tackle questions like this. Follow these steps:

1 **ANALYZE THE QUESTION.** Essay questions contain clues about what is expected of you. Sometimes you will find key words that will help you determine exactly what is being asked. See the list below for some typical key words and their meanings.

Key Words for Essay Questions

analyze; identify	break into parts, and describe the parts and how they are related
compare	tell how two or more subjects are similar; in some cases, also mention how they are different
contrast	tell how two or more subjects are different from each other
describe	give enough facts about or qualities of a subject to make it clear to someone who is unfamiliar with it
discuss	provide an overview and analysis; use details for support
evaluate; argue	judge an idea or concept, telling whether you think it is good or bad, or whether you agree or disagree with it
explain	make a subject clearer, providing supporting details and examples
interpret	tell the meaning and importance of an event or concept
justify	explain or give reasons for decisions; be persuasive
prove	provide supporting reasons for a statement
summarize	state only the main points of an event, concept, or debate

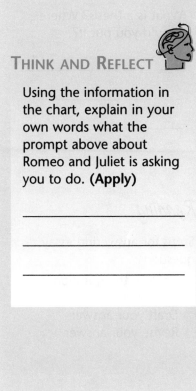

THINK AND REFLECT

Using the information in the chart, explain in your own words what the prompt above about Romeo and Juliet is asking you to do. **(Apply)**

_____

_____

_____

2 **PLAN YOUR ANSWER.** As soon as the essay prompt is clear to you, collect and organize your thoughts about it. First, gather ideas using whatever method is most comfortable for you. If you don't immediately have ideas, try freewriting for five minutes. When you **freewrite**, you write whatever comes into your head without letting your hand stop moving. You might also gather ideas in a **cluster chart**. (See Appendix B, page B-7, for an example of this kind of chart.) Then, organize the ideas you came up with. A simple outline or chart can help. For example, the following graphic organizer might help you organize the compare and contrast essay on *Romeo and Juliet* described above.

	Romeo	**Juliet**
Similarity or Difference #1	talkative; gives long speeches	less talkative; gives shorter speeches
Similarity or Difference #2		
Similarity or Difference #3		

Get to know other graphic organizers that might help you by reviewing those on the before-reading pages and in Appendix B of this book.

3 **WRITE YOUR ANSWER.** Start with a clear thesis statement in your opening paragraph. Your **thesis statement** is a single sentence that sums up your answer to the essay question. Then follow your organizational plan to provide support for your thesis. Devote one paragraph to each major point of support for your thesis. Use plenty of details as evidence for each point. Write quickly and keep moving. Don't spend too much time on any single paragraph, but try to make your answer as complete as possible. End your essay with a concluding sentence that sums up your major points.

4 **REVISE YOUR ANSWER.** Make sure you have answered all parts of the question and included everything you were asked to include. Check to see that you have supplied enough detail to support your thesis. Check for errors in grammar, spelling, punctuation, and paragraph breaks. Make corrections to your answer.

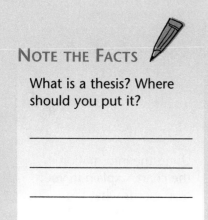

NOTE THE FACTS

What is a thesis? Where should you put it?

_____

_____

_____

Reading TIP

Steps for answering essay questions:
1. Analyze the question
2. Plan your answer
3. Draft your answer
4. Revise your answer

TAKING STANDARDIZED TESTS

Standardized tests are given to large groups of students in a school district, a state, or a country. Statewide tests measure how well students are meeting the learning standards the state has set. Other tests, such as the Scholastic Aptitude Test, or SAT, are used to help determine admission to colleges and universities. Others must be taken to enter certain careers. These tests are designed to measure overall ability or skills acquired so far. Learning how to take standardized tests will help you to achieve your goals.

You can get better at answering standardized test questions by practicing the types of questions that will be on the test. Use the Reading Skills and Test Practice questions in this book and other sample questions your teacher gives you to practice. Think aloud with a partner or small group about how you would answer each question. Notice how other students tackle the questions and learn from what they do.

In addition, remember these points:

- ❑ **Rule out some choices** when you are not sure of the answer. Then guess from the remaining possibilities.
- ❑ **Skip questions that seem too difficult** and go back to them later. Be aware, however, that most tests allow you to go back only within a section.
- ❑ **Follow instructions exactly.** The test monitor will read instructions to you, and instructions may also be printed in your test booklet. Make sure you know what to do.

Answering Multiple-Choice Questions

On many standardized tests, questions are multiple choice and have a single correct answer. The guidelines below will help you answer these kinds of questions effectively.

- ❑ **Read each question carefully.** Pay special attention to any words that are bolded, italicized, written in all capital letters, or otherwise emphasized.
- ❑ **Read all choices** before selecting an answer.
- ❑ **Eliminate** any answers that do not make sense, that disagree with what you remember from reading a passage, or that seem too extreme. Also, if two answers have exactly the same meaning, you can eliminate both.

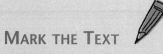

MARK THE TEXT

Underline or highlight the suggestions in this list that are new to you.

There are several types of multiple-choice questions that often appear on standardized tests. The guidelines below will help you to answer each type correctly.

Answering Reading Comprehension Questions

Reading comprehension questions ask you to read a passage and answer questions about it. These questions measure how well you perform the essential reading skills covered in Unit 2 of this book.

The Reading Skills and Test Practice questions that follow each literature selection in this book are reading comprehension questions. Use them to help you learn how to answer these types of questions correctly. Work through each question with a partner using a **think aloud**. Say out loud how you are figuring out the answer. Talk about how you can eliminate incorrect answers and determine the correct choice. You may want to make notes as you eliminate answers. By practicing this thinking process with a partner, you will be more prepared to use it when you have to take a standardized test.

The following steps will help you answer the reading comprehension questions on standardized tests.

❑ **Preview the passage and questions** and predict what the text will be about.

❑ **Use the reading strategies** you have learned to read the passage. Mark the text and make notes in the margins.

❑ **Reread the first question carefully.** Make sure you know exactly what it is asking.

❑ **Read the answers.** If you are sure of the answer, select it and move on. If not, go on to the next step.

❑ **Scan the passage** to look for key words related to the question. When you find a key word, slow down and read carefully.

❑ **Answer the question** and go on to the next one. Answer each question in this way.

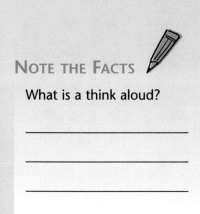

NOTE THE FACTS

What is a think aloud?

_____

_____

_____

Answering Analogy Questions

Analogy questions ask you to find the relationship between two words and then to recognize a similar relationship in another pair of words. Look at the example below.

MASK : FACE ::
a. rings : fingers
b. Halloween : costume
c. face : make-up
d. costume : body

In an analogy question, the symbols : and :: mean "is to" and "as." The example above would be read aloud as "*Mask* is to *face* as…." Follow these guidelines for answering analogy questions:

❑ Think of a sentence that relates the two words. For the example above, you might think "A mask is something that covers or disguises a face."

❑ Try substituting the words from each answer pair in the sentence.

"Rings are something that cover or disguise fingers."
"Halloween is something that covers or disguises costumes."
"A face is something that covers or disguises make-up."
"A costume is something that covers or disguises a body."

❑ Decide which sentence makes the most sense.

❑ If none of the options makes sense, try to think of a different sentence that relates the words, and work through the same process with the new sentence.

The following chart lists some common relationships used in analogy questions.

THINK AND REFLECT

Using the process described here, how would you answer the analogy question above? (Apply)

_____

_____

_____

Common Analogy Relationships

Relationship	Example
synonyms	busy : occupied
antonyms	arduous : easy
cause and effect	fatigue : carelessness
effect and cause	earthquake : fault line
general and specific	pasta : spaghetti
less intense and more intense	busy : frantic
part to whole	petal : flower
whole to part	flower : petal
age	horse : foal CONTINUED

gender	actor : actress
worker and tool	teacher : textbook
worker and product created	bricklayer : retaining wall
tool and associated action	scissors : cut
scientist and object of study	neurologist : nerve
raw material and end product	bricks : wall
person and associated quality	mother : nurturing
symbol and what it stands for	flag : patriotism

Answering Synonym and Antonym Questions

Synonym or antonym questions give you a word and ask you to select the word that has the same meaning (for a **synonym**) or the opposite meaning (for an **antonym**). You must select the best answer even if none is exactly correct. For this type of question, you should consider all the choices to see which is best. Always notice whether you are looking for a synonym or an antonym. You will usually find both among the answers. Think aloud with a partner about how to answer the following question:

Mark the letter of the word that is most nearly the OPPOSITE in meaning to the word in capital letters.

1. SAGE
    a. wise
    b. sweet
    c. sly
    d. foolish

Answering Sentence Completion Questions

Sentence completion questions present you with a sentence that has two words missing. You must select the pair of words that best completes the sentence. The key to this kind of question is to make sure that both parts of the answer you have selected work well in the sentence. Think aloud with a partner about how to complete the following sentence.

The newly remodeled main library was _____ to open in May, but it was postponed until the mayor was available for the _____.
    a. delayed. . .ceremony
    b. slated. . . dedication
    c. scheduled. . . taxes
    d. organized. . . reception

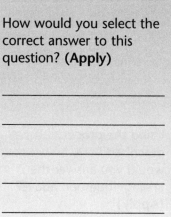

THINK AND REFLECT

How would you select the correct answer to this question? (**Apply**)

_____

_____

_____

_____

_____

_____

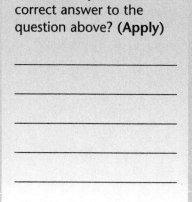

THINK AND REFLECT

How would you select the correct answer to the question above? (**Apply**)

_____

_____

_____

_____

_____

_____

Answering Constructed-Response Questions

In addition to multiple-choice questions, many standardized tests include **constructed-response questions** that require you to write essay answers in the test booklet. Constructed-response questions might ask you to identify key ideas or examples from the text by writing a sentence about each. In other cases, you will be asked to write a paragraph in response to a question about the selection and to use specific details from the passage to support your answer. For example, the following prompt might occur after Richard Connell's story "The Most Dangerous Game," Unit 3, page 81.

> **Essay Prompt:** Explain the conflict in the story. How does the opening dialogue between Whitney and Rainsford establish the conflict?
>
> **Short Response:** Person versus person conflict is established in "The Most Dangerous Game." This conflict is between General Zaroff and Rainsford. At the beginning of the story, Whitney and Rainsford discuss hunting. Rainsford describes the two opposing forces as "the hunter and the hunted." While this description would usually refer to a person and an animal, in this story, it refers to two people. General Zaroff is the hunter, and Rainsford becomes the hunted.

Other constructed-response questions ask you to apply information or ideas from a text in a new way. For example, imagine that you have just read "Ghost of Everest," Unit 8, page 440, on a standardized test. This article is about the team of explorers who found the body of a famous climber who died climbing Mount Everest. The question might ask you to write a letter home from the point of view of one of the members of the team who found the body. Another question might ask you to use information from the text in a particular imaginary situation. For example, you might be asked to write the first paragraph of a newspaper article reporting the discovery of the body. As you answer these questions, remember that you are being evaluated based on your understanding of the text. Although these questions offer opportunities to be creative, you should still include ideas, details, and examples from the passage you have just read.

THINK AND REFLECT

How do constructed-response questions differ from multiple-choice questions? **(Infer)**

_____

_____

_____

_____

NOTE THE FACTS

How are constructed-response questions evaluated? What should you be sure to include?

_____

_____

_____

The following tips will help you answer constructed-response questions effectively.

Tips for Answering Constructed-Response Questions

❑ **Skim the questions first.** Predict what the passage will be about.

❑ **Use reading strategies** as you read. Underline information that relates to the questions and make notes. After you have finished reading, you can decide which of the details you have gathered to use in your answers.

❑ **List the most important points** to include in each answer. Use the margins of your test booklet or a piece of scrap paper.

❑ **Number the points** you have listed to show the order in which they should be included.

❑ **Draft your answer to fit** in the space provided. Include as much detail as possible in the space you have.

❑ **Revise and proofread** your answers as you have time.

Unit 10 TEST-TAKING Review

Choose and Use Test-Taking Strategies

Before answering the sample test questions below, review with a partner how to use each of these test-taking strategies.

GENERAL STRATEGIES

- ❑ Know what will be on the test
- ❑ Make a study plan
- ❑ Review the subject matter
- ❑ Make lists
- ❑ Try to predict questions
- ❑ Preview the passage and questions
- ❑ Plan your time
- ❑ Use reading strategies to read the passage
- ❑ Come back later to questions that seem too difficult
- ❑ Save time for review

STRATEGIES FOR OBJECTIVE TESTS

- ❑ Read each question carefully
- ❑ Read all answer choices before selecting one
- ❑ Scan the passage again if you are uncertain of the answer
- ❑ Rule out some choices
- ❑ Beware of distractors
- ❑ Understand how to answer analogy questions
- ❑ Understand how to answer synonym and antonym questions
- ❑ Understand how to answer sentence completion questions
- ❑ Fill in circles completely

STRATEGIES FOR ESSAY TESTS

- ❑ Understand how to answer constructed-response questions
- ❑ Analyze the question
- ❑ Plan your answer
- ❑ Write your answer
- ❑ Revise your answer

Now read the passage below and answer the questions that follow. Use the strategies from this unit to complete this practice test.

Jane Kenyon and Donald Hall were husband and wife and lived together in an old New Hampshire farmhouse that had been Hall's grandparents' home.

Jane Kenyon was born in Ann Arbor, Michigan, in 1947 and graduated from the University of Michigan. She published four volumes of poetry in her lifetime. Kenyon found in the rural landscape a subject that allowed her to express her own inner world. She wrote about rural life, the complex currents of human relationships, and her husband's struggle with cancer. Her own lifelong struggle with depression was also a frequent subject of her poetry. Kenyon received a Creative Writing Fellowship from the National Endowment for the Arts and was awarded a Guggenheim Fellowship. In 1995 she was appointed New Hampshire's poet laureate.

Donald Hall was born in 1928 in Hamden, Connecticut. He gave up a long career teaching at the University of Michigan for the quiet life of a full-time poet and writer on Eagle Pond Farm in Wilmot, New Hampshire. Hall, who had spent childhood summers and had written his first poetry there, described his move to the farm as a "coming home to the place of language." In 1975, he moved to the farm with Kenyon, his second wife, and still lives and writes there. A <u>prolific</u> writer, he has published a number of volumes of poetry and essays as well as children's books, textbooks, and literary criticism. Hall was awarded the National Book Critics Circle Award for his collection *The One Day* and was nominated for the National Book Award for *The Museum of Clear Ideas*. From 1984 to 1989 he was poet laureate of New Hampshire.

In 1993, Hall confronted and survived a recurrence of cancer, which spread from his colon to his liver, a threat that made him acutely aware of the fragile nature of life and the importance of treasuring each day. In 1994, Kenyon was diagnosed with leukemia and died just over a year later at the age of 47.

In the final stages of her illness, Kenyon made the poem "Otherwise," which had been published prior to her diagnosis, the centerpiece of her final book. In retrospect, the poem seems prophetic. It celebrates the simple joys of an ordinary day and ends with the words "But one day, I know / it will be otherwise." The final poetry collection, *Otherwise: New and Selected Poems*, was published posthumously. In one of his own poems, "Last Days," Donald Hall recalls working with Kenyon to select poems for the book and to choose hymns for her funeral.

1. When summarizing this selection, which of the following details would be MOST important to include?
   a. Donald Hall and Jane Kenyon were both named poet laureate of New Hampshire.
   b. Donald Hall and Jane Kenyon were married.
   c. Donald Hall and Jane Kenyon lived on the farm where Hall spent much of his childhood.
   d. Jane Kenyon suffered from depression.

2. _____ used imagery from the natural landscape to write about _____.
   a. Donald Hall . . . living in the country.
   b. Jane Kenyon . . . her inner life.
   c. Donald Hall . . . his inner life.
   d. Jane Kenyon . . . life in the city.

3. Which of the following words is most clearly OPPOSITE in meaning to the word *prolific?*
   a. productive
   b. professional
   c. procrastinating
   d. promising

4. Based on the information provided in the text, how do you know that Hall and Kenyon championed each other's writing? What can you infer about their relationship based on this information?

   _____

   _____

   _____

   _____

   _____

   _____

   _____

   _____

5. FLOUR : CAKE MIX ::
   a. eggs : chickens
   b. plants : animals
   c. pizza : cheese
   d. tomatoes : spaghetti sauce

On Your Own

FLUENTLY SPEAKING. Review this unit and make a list of thirty key words about test taking. Use a word processor to key your words so that they are easy to read. Then exchange lists with a partner. While your partner listens and times you with a stopwatch, read the list of words your partner gave you as quickly as you can without making errors. Then have your partner read the list of words you made while you time him or her. Practice reading the words until you can do it with no errors, and try to beat your partner's time.

PICTURE THIS. Find an informational article on a topic that interests you. Read the article, using reading strategies to mark up the text as you would if it appeared on a standardized test. Use the margins to make notes, and underline key details and important ideas. Then create an illustration, graphic, or other visual element to go with the article.

PUT IT IN WRITING. Find and read an informational article on any topic that interests you. After you have read the article, write three multiple-choice and two constructed-response questions that test reading comprehension. As models, use the sample questions in this unit as well as those in the Reading Skills and Test Practice section that follows every literature selection in this book. Finally, exchange your passage and questions with a partner, and take one another's tests.

Appendix A:
Building Reading Fluency

WORD RECOGNITION SKILLS: INCREASE YOUR AUTOMATICITY

WHAT ARE WORD RECOGNITION SKILLS? **Word recognition skills** are skills that help you recognize and decipher words. Learning how to read increasingly more words with faster recognition leads to **automaticity,** the ability to recognize words quickly and automatically. The activities below develop word recognition skills.

1 CREATE A CROSSWORD PUZZLE. Put together a crossword puzzle that includes clues for words you are studying and clues for facts everyone should know. Look at puzzles in the newspaper or a puzzle book to learn how to number your clues and add blank spaces. Here is how you might set up a puzzle.

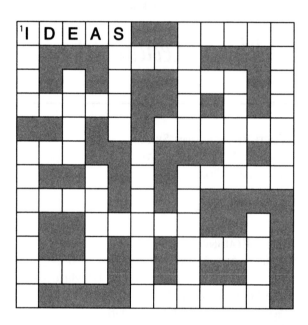

2 CREATE A WORD RACE. Make a list of 20 words you have studied. Practice reading the words aloud. Have a classmate keep track of how many seconds it takes you to read the entire list. Have another person keep track of the words you mispronounce. Have teams compete to see which team pronounces the same list of words the fastest with the fewest errors.

3 CREATE A WORD MATRIX. Choose vocabulary words that you find difficult to pronounce and place them in a chart. Add the same words to each row of your chart, but add the words to each row in a different order. Practice reading the words until you are comfortable pronouncing them. Have a partner time how many words in your chart you can read in 1 minute.

WORD RECOGNITION SKILLS: CROSSWORD PUZZLE

In a small group, list words to include in a crossword puzzle. You list should contain 10 vocabulary words and 10 words that refer to facts that everyone knows. For instance, if the word *Washington* is on your "facts" list, add a CLUE ACROSS that says, *Our nation's first president.* Your first word down can come from one of the letters in *Washington.* For instance, the vocabulary word *wallow* can use the *w* in *Washington* with a CLUE DOWN that says, *Indulge oneself immoderately.* Use as many of the words on your list as you can (you may not be able to use all of them). Use your own paper for the CLUES ACROSS and CLUES DOWN. After you fill in your puzzle and finish your clues, make another blank, numbered puzzle. Exchange blank puzzles and clues with another group. See which group can solve the their puzzle the fastest.

1. | w | a | s | h | i | n | g | t | o | n |
   | a |
   | l |
   | l |
   | o |
   | w |

WORD RECOGNITION SKILLS: WORD RACE

Create a list of 20 vocabulary words you have studied. Practice reading the list aloud. Have someone keep track of how many seconds it takes you to read the entire list. Have another person keep track of the words you mispronounce. After you have practiced the list, create teams. Have the team compete to see which team can pronounce the list the fastest with the fewest errors.

1.	11.
2.	12.
3.	13.
4.	14.
5.	15.
6.	16.
7.	17.
8.	18.
9.	19.
10.	20.

Keep track of the following data for each team member.

Number of seconds it took to read the list:

Number of words mispronounced:

WORD RECOGNITION SKILLS: WORD MATRIX

Choose 5 words that you find difficult to pronounce, and place them in the matrix below. Add the same words to each row, but use the words in a different order in each row. After a brief practice run-through, have a classmate use a clock or timer to see how many times you can make it through the chart in 1 minute. Have another classmate circle or check words you pronounce correctly. Use the second matrix below to run through your words a second time. Try to increase the number of words spoken correctly on your second reading.

Number of words correct in 1 minute: _____

Number of words correct in 1 minute: _____

SILENT READING SKILLS: INCREASE THE AMOUNT YOU READ

WHAT ARE SILENT READING SKILLS? Silent reading skills are skills you use as you read a text to yourself. Fluent silent readers can read a text quickly, easily, and smoothly. To build **silent reading fluency**, set aside time each day to read parts of a long selection or book. Most often, choose selections you consider easy and interesting. Vary the subject matter of selections you choose, and, over time, include selections from several different genres—fiction, nonfiction, drama, short stories, poems, and informational and visual media. Use the charts below to keep track of your silent reading activity.

1 FILL IN A FREE READING LOG. Read silently for a sustained period several times a week. Write down what you read, the number of minutes you read, the number of pages you read, and your thoughts and reactions. Selections you read may be easy, moderate, or challenging.

2 USE A PAGES-PER-MINUTE GRAPH. Chart the number of pages you read in a 30-minute reading session. Try to increase the number of pages you read in each session. Be sure the selections you use for this activity are easy to read.

3 USE A MINUTES-PER-SECTION GRAPH. Each reading session, chart the time it takes you to read 5 pages of a selection. Try to decrease the number of minutes it takes to read 5 pages. Be sure the selections you use for this activity are easy to read.

SILENT READING SKILLS: HOW MUCH CAN YOU LEARN IN 10 MINUTES?

READING RATE. Pay attention to your silent reading rate. Do you vary your rate as you read? Do you slow down for difficult vocabulary and long sentences? Do you speed up when the ideas are easy to understand? Learn to use different reading rates with different tasks. Here are three methods to try.

Scan	Skim	Read closely
To locate particular information (to find a quotation, verify a statement, locate a word, or answer a question)	To get the overall picture (to preview or to review)	To absorb the meaning of a book you're reading for fun or a textbook on which you'll be tested (to read with understanding the first time)

Practice using different reading rates as you read silently for 10 minutes. How much can you learn in 10 minutes? Write what you learn below.

SILENT READING SKILLS: FREE READING LOG

Develop your silent reading fluency by reading silently for a sustained period several times a week. Keep track of what you read each day. List your reactions and thoughts about what you read.

Week of _____

Date/ Minutes Read	Title/Author	Pages Read From/To	Reactions/Thoughts

Total number of pages read this week:
Total number of minutes read this week:

Genres read this week: (circle)
Fiction   Nonfiction   Poetry   Drama   Informational or Visual Media   Other _____

SILENT READING SKILLS: PAGES-PER-MINUTE GRAPH

Choose an easy and interesting book. Read for 30 minutes, and count the number of pages you read. Record the number in the chart below. Try to read more pages in each practice session.

Over 10 pages										
9 pages										
8 pages										
7 pages										
6 pages										
5 pages										
4 pages										
3 pages										
2 pages										
1 page										
Practice Number	1	2	3	4	5	6	7	8	9	10
Number of Pages Read										

SILENT READING SKILLS: MINUTES-PER-SECTION GRAPH

Choose an easy and interesting book. Record the time it takes you to read 5 pages of the book in the chart below. Try to decrease the time it takes you to read 5 pages each time you read. You can time several 5-page sections in one reading by placing paper clips at 5-page intervals. Each time you reach a paper-clipped page, stop to record the time it took you to reach that page.

10 minutes										
9 minutes										
8 minutes										
7 minutes										
6 minutes										
5 minutes										
4 minutes										
3 minutes										
2 minutes										
1 minutes										
Practice Number	1	2	3	4	5	6	7	8	9	10
Number of Minutes Read										

Oral Reading Skills: Perform Rereading Activities

WHAT ARE ORAL READING SKILLS? **Oral reading skills** are skills you use when you read aloud. Have you ever noticed how radio and television reporters read a news report? They do not read every word at the same speed and volume. They emphasize important points by putting more stress on some words. They use facial expressions and the tone of their voice to convey what words mean. They add pauses to give listeners time to think about what is being said. These news reporters exhibit **oral reading fluency**, the ability to read aloud smoothly and easily.

HOW CAN YOU BUILD ORAL READING SKILLS? To demonstrate that you are a fluent oral reader, you do not have to read fast without mistakes. Even the best news reporters mispronounce words or stumble over unfamiliar phrases. Good news reporters, however, use strategies that make the oral reading task easier. They read and reread material before they go on the air, and they vary their speed and vocal expression. The rereading activities below build oral reading skills.

1 PREPARE A REPEATED READING EXERCISE. Choose a 100–150-word passage that you consider difficult to read. With a partner, use the passage to prepare a repeated reading exercise. Read the passage aloud to your partner. Have your partner record the time it takes you to read the passage and the number of errors you make. Then have your partner read the passage to you while you record the time and number of errors. On your second reading see if you both can improve your initial time and error rate, and include more vocal expression. Reread the passage a third time, working to decrease your time and error rate and trying to increase your vocal expression.

2 PERFORM A CHORAL READING. Find a poem, song, or part of a story that would be fun for a group to read aloud. Practice reading the piece aloud. Everyone in the group should use the same phrasing and speed. Have group members add notes to the text that help them pronounce the words and pause at appropriate times. Poems such as "Mirror" on page 169, "Nikki-Rosa" on page 174, and "Hanging Fire" on page 179 work well as choral readings.

3 THINK ALOUD. Read a selection aloud with a partner. As you read, discuss thoughts you have about what you are reading. Ask questions, make connections and predictions, and respond to the ideas in the selection. When you are finished with your oral reading, reread the selection again, either orally or silently.

4 PERFORM A PLAY. Read aloud a play you have previously read silently. Assign parts. In small groups, have each speaker rehearse his/her part several times. Present the play to an audience. Use props and costumes, if possible.

5 WRITE YOUR OWN PLAY. Rewrite a prose selection, or a part of a prose selection, as a play. Assign parts. In small groups, have each speaker rehearse his/her part several times. Present the play to an audience. Use props and costumes, if possible.

6 MAKE A RECORDING. Read a 100–150-word passage into a tape recorder or DVD player. Listen to your recording. Keep track of errors you make: mispronouncing a word, leaving a word out, or adding a word that is not there. Rerecord the passage. Try to decrease the number of errors you make, and increase the smoothness with which you read the passage. Rerecord the passage until you can read it smoothly without error.

7 **MEMORIZE A PASSAGE.** Memorize a 100–150-word passage from a selection you have read. Have a partner help you memorize the passage by chunking it. Memorize short sections at a time, and work up to repeating the entire passage from memory. Possible passages to memorize include lines from a speech or poem, such Martin Luther King, Jr.'s "I Have a Dream" speech, or scenes from a short story or play such as one of Romeo's soliloquies from *The Tragedy of Romeo and Juliet*.

8 **MAKE A VIDEO.** Reread a selection with a partner. Prepare a video script that retells the selection. Record the retelling. Show the video retelling to an audience.

9 **EXPERIMENT WITH SPEED AND EXPRESSION.** Read a section of a selection silently. Reread the section aloud to a partner. Experiment with your speed and expression by rereading the section aloud in several different ways. Discuss which speed and means of expression work best.

10 **READ WITH A MASK.** Read silently, pretending that you are a character or the speaker in a selection. Reread aloud using a character or speaker mask that you hold in front of your face or wearing a costume that the character or speaker might wear.

11 **VIEW AND REENACT.** Watch a dramatic version of a selection on video. Read the print version, and reenact part of the selection.

ORAL READING SKILLS: REPEATED READING EXERCISE

❑ Choose a 100–150-word passage that you consider difficult to read. With a partner, use the passage to prepare a repeated reading exercise.

❑ Use a computer or a copier to make 6 copies of the passage: 3 for yourself and 3 for your partner.

❑ Read the passage aloud to your partner. Have your partner record the time you start reading, errors you make while reading, and the time you stop reading. Add this information to your Repeated Reading Record on page A-12.

❑ Have your partner read the passage to you. As your partner reads, record the time he/she starts reading, errors he/she makes, and the time he/she stops reading. See if your partner can improve your time and error rate. Record this information in your partner's Repeated Reading Record.

❑ Read the passage again. This time, work on varying your speed and vocal expression. Record the start/stop times and the number of errors you make, but this time your partner should listen for the meaning your words communicate. Have your partner comment on your speed and expression. For instance, your partner might note that "you read the first line too slow," "you had excellent pauses in the 2nd paragraph," or "show more anger in the last line."

❑ Have your partner read the passage again. Record your partner's start/stop times and errors. Write down ways that your partner can vary his/her speed and vocal expression.

❑ You and your partner should reread the passage one more time. Continue to work on varying your speed and expression, and try to decrease your time and your number of errors. Record the information in your Repeated Reading Record.

ORAL READING SKILLS: REPEATED READING RECORD

Name:_____

Text Read:_____

Date	Evaluator	Errors	Time	Speed/Expression

ORAL READING SKILLS: REPEATED READING RECORD

Name:_____

Text Read:_____

Date	Evaluator	Errors	Time	Speed/Expression

ORAL READING SKILLS: PASSAGE FOR FLUENCY PRACTICE

from *I Know Why the Caged Bird Sings* by Maya Angelou

When I was three and Bailey four, we had arrived in the musty little town, wearing tags on our wrists which instructed—"To Whom It May Concern"—that we were Marguerite and Bailey Johnson Jr., from Long Beach, California, en route to Stamps, Arkansas, c/o Mrs. Annie Henderson.

Our parents had decided to put an end to their calamitous marriage, and Father shipped us home to his mother. A porter had been charged with our welfare—he got off the train the next day in Arizona—and our tickets were pinned to my brother's inside coat pocket.

I don't remember much of the trip, but after we reached the segregated southern part of the journey, things must have looked up. Negro passengers, who always traveled with loaded lunch boxes, felt sorry for "the poor little motherless darlings" and plied us with cold fried chicken and potato salad.

Time started:_____   Number of errors:_____   Time stopped:_____
Comments about speed and expression:

When I was three and Bailey four, we had arrived in the musty little town, wearing tags on our wrists which instructed—"To Whom It May Concern"—that we were Marguerite and Bailey Johnson Jr., from Long Beach, California, en route to Stamps, Arkansas, c/o Mrs. Annie Henderson.

Our parents had decided to put an end to their calamitous marriage, and Father shipped us home to his mother. A porter had been charged with our welfare—he got off the train the next day in Arizona—and our tickets were pinned to my brother's inside coat pocket.

I don't remember much of the trip, but after we reached the segregated southern part of the journey, things must have looked up. Negro passengers, who always traveled with loaded lunch boxes, felt sorry for "the poor little motherless darlings" and plied us with cold fried chicken and potato salad.

Time started:_____   Number of errors:_____   Time stopped:_____
Comments about speed and expression:

from *To Kill a Mockingbird* by Harper Lee

We lived on the main residential street in town—Atticus, Jem and I, plus Calpurnia our cook. Jem and I found our father satisfactory: he played with us, read to us, and treated us with courteous detachment.

Calpurnia was something else again. She was all angles and bones; she was nearsighted; she squinted; her hand was wide as a bed slat and twice as hard. She was always ordering me out of the kitchen, asking me why I couldn't behave as well as Jem when she knew he was older, and calling me home when I wasn't ready to come. Our battles were epic and one-sided. Calpurnia always won, mainly because Atticus always took her side. She had been with us ever since Jem was born, and I had felt her tyrannical presence as long as I could remember.

Time started:_____ Number of errors:_____ Time stopped:_____
Comments about speed and expression:

We lived on the main residential street in town—Atticus, Jem and I, plus Calpurnia our cook. Jem and I found our father satisfactory: he played with us, read to us, and treated us with courteous detachment.

Calpurnia was something else again. She was all angles and bones; she was nearsighted; she squinted; her hand was wide as a bed slat and twice as hard. She was always ordering me out of the kitchen, asking me why I couldn't behave as well as Jem when she knew he was older, and calling me home when I wasn't ready to come. Our battles were epic and one-sided. Calpurnia always won, mainly because Atticus always took her side. She had been with us ever since Jem was born, and I had felt her tyrannical presence as long as I could remember.

Time started:_____ Number of errors:_____ Time stopped:_____
Comments about speed and expression:

Appendix B:
Graphic Organizers for Reading Strategies

READING STRATEGIES CHECKLIST

Use at least one before-, during-, or after-reading strategy listed below.

Reading Strategy	Before Reading	During Reading	After Reading
READ WITH A PURPOSE	___ I write down my reason for reading. ___ I write down the author's purpose for writing.	___ I read with a purpose in mind.	___ I reflect upon my purpose for reading.
CONNECT TO PRIOR KNOWLEDGE	___ I write down what I know about a topic.	___ I use what I know. ___ I add to what I know.	___ I think about what I learned.
WRITE THINGS DOWN	___ I have the materials I need for writing things down.	___ I mark key points. ___ I use sticky notes. ___ I take notes. ___ I highlight. ___ I react to text.	___ I summarize.
MAKE PREDICTIONS	___ I preview. ___ I guess.	___ I gather more information. ___ I guess again.	___ I analyze my predictions.
VISUALIZE	___ I picture the topic.	___ I make a mind movie. ___ I continue my mind movie.	___ I sketch or summarize my mind movie.
USE TEXT ORGANIZATION	___ I skim the text.	___ I read sections or stanzas. ___ I pay attention to introductions and conclusions. ___ I use headings and signal words. ___ I read charts and graphic aids. ___ I study the pictures. ___ I follow familiar plot, themes, and hidden outlines.	___ I use the organization to review the text.
TACKLE DIFFICULT WORDS	___ I study words beforehand.	___ I use context clues. ___ I look at prefixes and suffixes. ___ I consult a dictionary. ___ I ask a teacher or friend for help.	___ I use the words and add them to my working vocabulary.
MONITOR YOUR READING PROCESS		**Fix-Up Ideas** ___ I reread. ___ I ask questions. ___ I read in shorter chunks. ___ I read aloud. ___ I take time to refocus. ___ I unlock difficult words. ___ I change my reading rate. ___ I create a mnemonic device.	

READ WITH A PURPOSE: AUTHOR'S PURPOSE CHART

An author may write with the following purposes in mind:

- ❏ to inform (expository/informational writing)
- ❏ to entertain, enrich, enlighten, and/or use an artistic medium such as fiction or poetry to share a perspective (imaginative writing)
- ❏ to make a point by sharing a story about an event (narrative writing)
- ❏ to reflect (personal/expressive writing)
- ❏ to persuade readers or listeners to respond in some way, such as to agree with a position, change a view on an issue, reach an agreement, or perform an action (persuasive/argumentative writing)

The following types of writing reflect these purposes:

- ❏ Expository/informational: news article, research report
- ❏ Imaginative: poem, short story
- ❏ Narrative: biography, family history
- ❏ Personal/expressive: diary entry, personal letter
- ❏ Persuasive, argumentative: editorial, petition

Before Reading
Identify the author's purpose, the type of writing he or she uses, and the ideas he or she wants to communicate.

During Reading
Gather ideas that the author communicates to readers.

After Reading
Summarize the ideas the author communicates. Explain how these ideas help fulfill the author's purpose.

READ WITH A PURPOSE: READER'S PURPOSE CHART

Fill in the Reader's Purpose Chart at each stage of reading to set a purpose for reading and to help you attain it.

Before Reading

Set a purpose for reading.
(Example: I am going to determine the overall mood of this poem.)

During Reading

Take notes on what you learn.
(Example: mournful owl—sounds sad)

After Reading

Reflect on your purpose and what you learned.
(Example: I wanted to find the overall mood of this poem. From the notes that I took, I believe the mood is melancholy and sad.)

CONNECT TO PRIOR KNOWLEDGE: K-W-L CHART

Connect to what you know and what you want to know by filling in the first two columns before you read. Fill in the last column after you read.

What I *Know*	What I *Want* to Learn	What I Have *Learned*

CONNECT TO PRIOR KNOWLEDGE: REACTIONS CHART

Since you cannot write in, mark up, or highlight text in a textbook or library book, use this chart to record your thoughts and reactions. As you read, ask yourself questions, make predictions, react to ideas, identify key points, and/or write down unfamiliar words.

Page #	Questions, Predictions, Reactions, Key Points, and Unfamiliar Words

WRITE THINGS DOWN: NOTE TAKING CHART

Take notes in the chart below as you read nonfiction or informational selections.

Section or Page	Main Ideas	My Reactions

Summary of My Notes

WRITE THINGS DOWN: PRO AND CON CHART

As you read a persuasive or argumentative selection, take notes on both sides of each argument.

Arguments in Favor (PRO)	Arguments Against (CON)
Argument 1: Support:	Argument 1: Support:
Argument 2: Support:	Argument 2: Support:

WRITE THINGS DOWN: VENN DIAGRAM

Use a Venn diagram to compare and contrast ideas in one selection or to compare two selections.

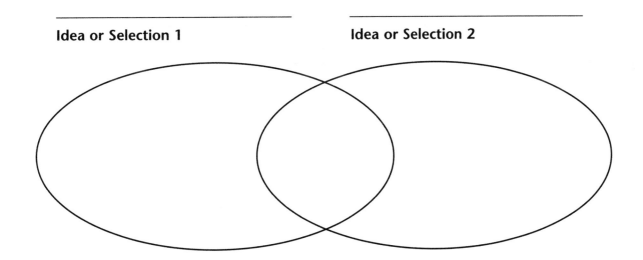

Idea or Selection 1   **Idea or Selection 2**

WRITE THINGS DOWN: CLUSTER CHART

Fill in the cluster chart below to keep track of character traits or main ideas. In the center circle, write the name of the character or topic. In the circles branching out from the center, write details about the character or topic.

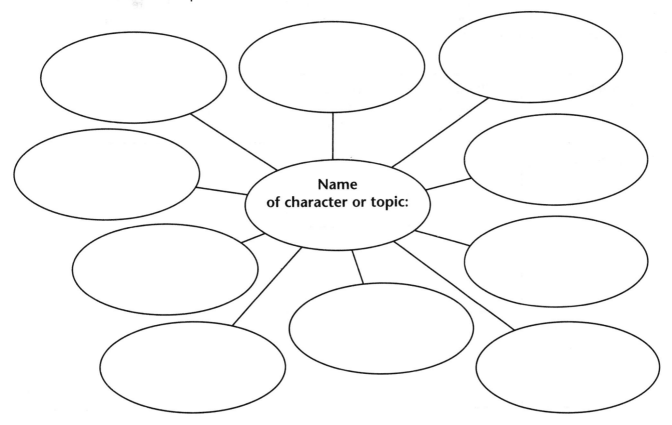

MAKE PREDICTIONS: PREDICTION CHART

Gather information before and during reading that helps you make predictions about a literature selection. Write your predictions in the "Guesses" column. Write reasons for your guesses in the "Reasons" column. As you read, gather evidence that either supports or disproves your predictions. Change your predictions and add new ones as you learn more about the selection.

Guesses	Reasons	Evidence

MAKE PREDICTIONS: CHARACTER CHART

A character is a person (or sometimes an animal) who figures in the action of a literary work. Choose one character from the selection and fill in the chart below based on what you learn about the character as you read.

Character's Name:	Physical Appearance	Habits/ Mannerisms/ Behaviors	Relationships with Other People	Other Characteristics
Your description of the character at the beginning of the story				
Your predictions for this character				
Your analysis of the character at the end of the story				

VISUALIZE: SENSORY DETAILS CHART

As you read, identify images or words and phrases that contain sensory details. Write each sensory detail beneath the sense to which it appeals.

Sensory Details				
Sight	**Sound**	**Touch**	**Taste**	**Smell**

VISUALIZE: FIGURATIVE LANGUAGE CHART

As you read, identify examples of figurative language. Write down examples of figurative language in the first column below. In the second column, write down the comparison being made by the figurative language, and in the third column, describe what the figurative language makes you envision.

Example of Figurative Language	What is Compared?	What You Envision
"The black canopy of nighttime sky was painted with dazzling jewels."	The night sky is described as a black canopy or painting. The stars are described as dazzling jewels.	A dark, cloudless night sky filled with bright, twinkling stars

USE TEXT ORGANIZATION: STORY STRIP

Story Strip. Draw pictures that represent key events in a selection. Then write a caption under each box that explains each event. Draw the events in the order in which they occurred.

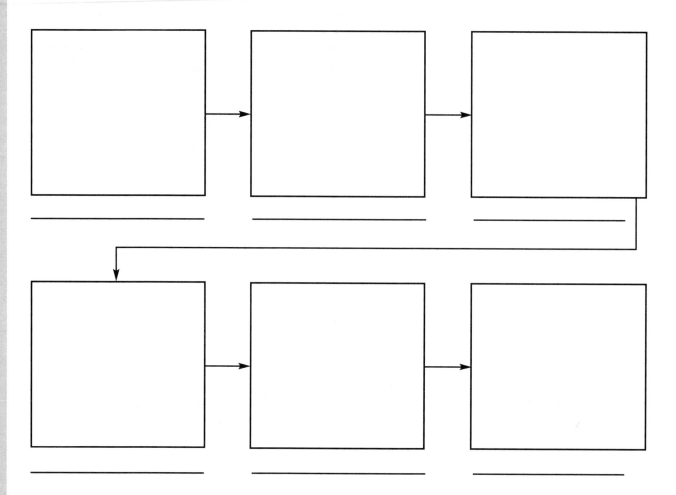

USE TEXT ORGANIZATION: TIME LINE

Use a time line to keep track of important events in a literature selection.

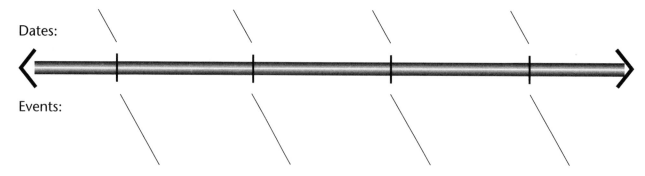

Using Text Organization: Plot Diagram

Use the plot diagram below to chart the plot of a literature selection. In the spaces provided, describe the exposition, inciting incident, rising and falling action, climax, resolution, and dénouement. Be sure to include in the rising action the key events that build toward the climax of the selection.

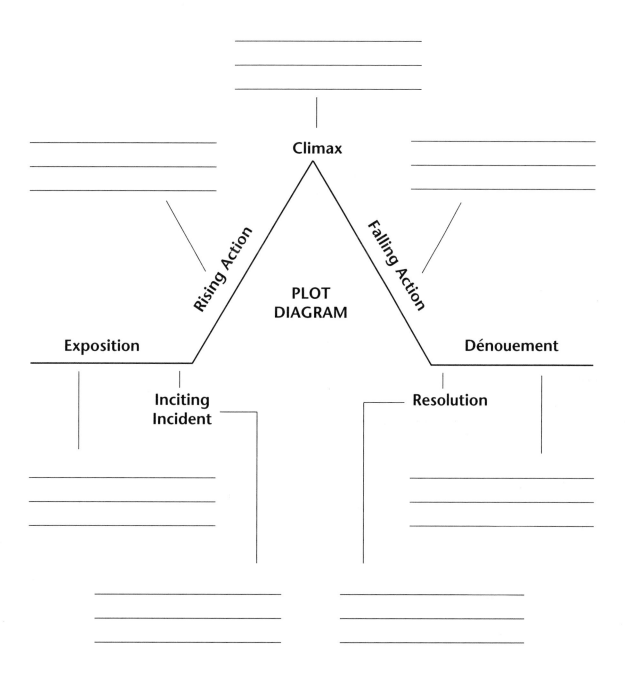

Use Text Organization: Cause-and-Effect Chart

Keep track of what happens in a story and why in the chart below. Use cause-and-effect signal words to help you identify causes and their effects. (Examples of cause-and-effect words: *as a result, because, if/then, since, therefore, this led to.*)

Cause ➤ ➤ ➤ ➤ ➤ ➤ ➤ ➤ ➤ ➤ ➤ Effect

_____   _____

_____   _____

↓
↓

**Summary statement of what happened
in the selection and why:**

_____

_____

Use Text Organization: Summary Chart

Read and summarize short sections of a selection at a time. Then write a summary of the entire work.

Summary of Section 1:
Summary of Section 2:
Summary of Section 3:
Summary of the Selection:

Use Text Organization: Drawing Conclusions Log

Draw conclusions about a selection by gathering supporting points for key ideas. Reread the supporting points and key ideas and draw a conclusion about the main or overall message of the selection.

Key Idea:	Key Idea:	Key Idea:
Supporting Points:	Supporting Points:	Supporting Points:

Conclusion about Overall Message:

Main Idea Map

To find the main or overall message of a whole selection or a part of the selection, gather important details into a Main Idea Map. Use the details to determine the main or overall message. Note: In fiction, the main idea is also known as the theme.

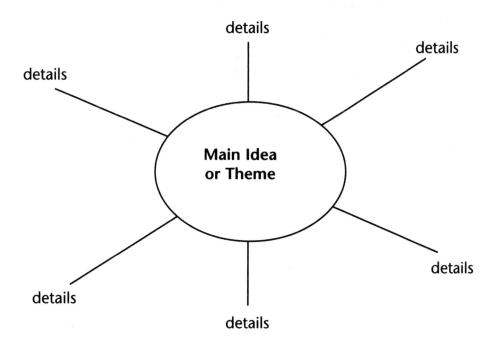

details

details

details

details

details

details

Main Idea or Theme

TACKLE DIFFICULT VOCABULARY: WORD SORT

Write one challenging word or phrase in each of the boxes below, along with its definition and part of speech. Cut the boxes apart. Then sort the words using one of the following methods.

- Same parts of speech
- Words with similar or opposite meanings
- Words with prefixes and suffixes
- Words that relate to each other or that can be used together
- My own sorting method: _____

Word: **Definition:** **Part of Speech:**	**Word:** **Definition:** **Part of Speech:**	**Word:** **Definition:** **Part of Speech:**
Word: **Definition:** **Part of Speech:**	**Word:** **Definition:** **Part of Speech:**	**Word:** **Definition:** **Part of Speech:**

TACKLE DIFFICULT VOCABULARY: WORD STUDY NOTEBOOK

Keeping a word study notebook is a convenient way to log new words, their meanings and their spelling, as well as prefixes, suffixes, word roots, and other concepts. When you record a new word, include its definition, pronunciation, and origins, along with an example sentence and a drawing to help you remember it.

Word: _____

Pronunciation: _____

Origins: _____

_____

Definition: _____

Sentence: _____

Drawing:

TACKLE DIFFICULT VOCABULARY: WORD MAP

Write a challenging word or phrase in the first box below. Beneath the word or phrase, include its definition, word parts you recognize, and several synonyms. In the two boxes at the bottom, write a sentence that uses the word or phrase and create a drawing that helps you remember it.

A Challenging Word or Phrase

Definition

Word Parts I Recognize

Synonyms

A Sentence That Contains the Word or Phrase

A Picture That Ilustrates the Word or Phrase

MONITOR YOUR READING PROCESS: FIX-UP IDEAS LOG

Recognizing that you don't understand something is as important as knowing that you do understand it. Sometimes you may find yourself just reading the words but not actually comprehending or getting the meaning of what you are reading. If you are having trouble comprehending something you are reading, try using some of the fix-up ideas listed below to get back on track.

- Reread
- Ask a question
- Read in shorter chunks
- Read aloud
- Retell

- Work with a partner
- Unlock difficult words
- Change your reading rate
- Choose a new strategy
- Create a mnemonic device

Problems I Encountered While Reading	Fix-Up-Ideas I Used

MONITOR YOUR READING PROGRESS: YOUR OWN GRAPHIC ORGANIZER

Graphic organizers help you understand and remember information. Use your imagination to modify a graphic organizer in this appendix, or invent a new one. Use your graphic organizer to arrange ideas as you read and to guide your discussion and writing actions after you read. Graphic organizer possibilities are endless!

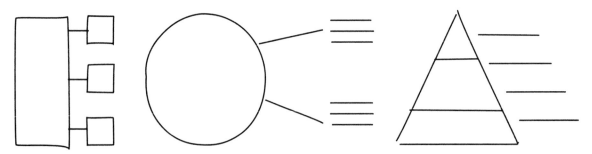

LITERARY ACKNOWLEDGMENTS

ART ACKNOWLEDGMENTS